THE LIFE AND TIMES OF
ERNEST BEVIN

VOLUME ONE

BOOKS BY
ALAN BULLOCK

Hitler: A Study in Tyranny
The Liberal Tradition (with Maurice Shock)
The Life and Times of Ernest Bevin

ERNEST BEVIN IN 1936.

ALAN BULLOCK

THE LIFE AND TIMES OF
ERNEST BEVIN

VOLUME ONE

Trade Union Leader
1881 – 1940

HEINEMANN

LONDON MELBOURNE TORONTO

William Heinemann Ltd

LONDON MELBOURNE TORONTO

JOHANNESBURG AUCKLAND

First published 1960

Reprinted 1969

434 09451 X

Printed and bound in Great Britain by

Bookprint Limited, Crawley, Sussex

Contents

Contents

Illustrations

Illustrations

SOURCES

* *Radio Times* Hulton Picture Library
† Reece Winstone
‡ The Port of Bristol Authority
§ *Daily Herald*

List of Abbreviations

A.E.U., Amalgamated Engineering Union.
A.F.L., American Federation of Labour.
A.S.L.E.F., Amalgamated Society of Locomotive Engineers and Firemen.
B.S.P., British Socialist Party.
D.W.R. and G.W.U., Dock, Wharf, Riverside and General Workers' Union.
F.B.I., Federation of British Industries.
I.F.T.U., International Federation of Trade Unions.
I.L.O., International Labour Organisation.
I.L.P., Independent Labour Party.
I.T.F., International Transport Workers' Federation.
I.W.W., Industrial Workers of the World.
N.J.I.C., National Joint Industrial Council.
N.T.W.F., National Transport Workers' Federation.
N.U.G.M.W., National Union of General and Municipal Workers.
N.U.R., National Union of Railwaymen.
N.U.S., National Union of Seamen.
N.U.V.W., National Union of Vehicle Workers.
N.U.W.C.M., National Unemployed Workers' Committee Movement.
O.E.E.C., Organisation for European Economic Co-operation.
O.M.S., Organisation for the Maintenance of Supplies.
P.L.A., Port of London Authority.
S.D.F., Social Democratic Federation.
S.S.I.P., Society for Socialist Inquiry and Propaganda.
T.G.W.U., Transport and General Workers' Union.
T.U.C., Trades Union Congress.
U.V.W., United Vehicle Workers.
W.E.A., Workers' Educational Association.
W.T.A., Workers' Travel Association.

Acknowledgements

THE AUTHOR AND PUBLISHERS are indebted to the following for permission to reproduce copyright material: The Controller of Her Majesty's Stationery Office, the International Labour Organisation, the *Daily Telegraph and Morning Post*, the *Daily Herald*, *The Spectator*, the *Yorkshire Evening News*, Messrs. Longmans, Green & Co. (*Beatrice Webb's Diaries* 1912–24 and 1924–32), Messrs. Hutchinson & Co. (*My Political Life* by Leopold Amery and *Ernest Bevin* by Francis Williams), Messrs. Frederick Muller (*Call Back Yesterday* and *The Fateful Years* by Hugh Dalton), Messrs. Victor Gollancz (*Harold Laski* by Kingsley Martin), Messrs. Allen & Unwin (*The Miners, the Years of Struggle* by R. Page Arnot).

NOTE

The author has followed throughout the unmannerly but convenient usage of dropping all prefixes and titles. He offers his apologies to all those named who may be offended by this practice.

1956

Preface

BETWEEN 1940 and 1951, Ernest Bevin played a leading part in ten of the most critical years of this country's history. These years form the subject of the second volume of this work. The theme of this first volume is different: how Bevin acquired the authority and experience which enabled him, when not even a Member of Parliament, to step straight into the front rank of Ministers, to become the most powerful Labour member of Sir Winston Churchill's inner War Cabinet and after 1945 to continue as the most influential figure next to the Prime Minister in the Labour Administration which governed Great Britain down to 1951.

The foundation of Bevin's ministerial career was the position which he created for himself in the trade union movement between 1910 and 1940. But this was something more than a protracted apprenticeship to political office. It was a record of achievement in its own right as the outstanding trade-union leader yet produced by this, or perhaps by any other, country. Bevin in fact had two careers in each of which he rose to the front rank, and to each of which his biographer must attempt to do equal justice.

To do this means deserting the well-worn track of most political biographies—local or party politics; the back-benches of the House of Commons; minor office; alternate periods of government and opposition—and entering the much less familiar world of the trade unions. While Bevin came to play a big role in the Labour Party in the 1930s, he acquired his experience in politics and the exercise of power, not in the House of Commons or even local government, but in the National Transport Workers' Federation, the Transport and General Workers' Union, the T.U.C. and its General Council. (It was none the less politics because it was conducted outside Parliament and the party system.)

If the reader will bear with this unfamiliarity, he will find that

Bevin's career sheds light on a side of the Labour Movement and of British politics which has been less explored than it deserves to be. The history of the Labour movement has been largely written from the point of view of the Left, or at least of its political wing. The trade unions are continually referred to in such accounts, but not much effort is made to understand their point of view. No one ever put that point of view with more force than Ernest Bevin and a study of his role in politics up to 1940 may help to make it more intelligible.

But the political influence of the trade unions cannot be treated in isolation from their main activity in the industrial field and a biography of Ernest Bevin which devoted more space to his activities in the Labour Party or the National Council of Labour than to the part he played in the dock, the road transport, the milling and the shipping industries would be badly out of focus. The rise of the trade union movement is, in fact, one of the distinctive features of twentieth-century British society, and I have tried to take advantage of the opportunity which Bevin's career affords to relate this to the general history of the period up to 1940.

I was invited to write Mr. Bevin's biography by his executor, the late Arthur Deakin, with the approval of Dame Florence Bevin. Although I met Mr. Bevin and heard him speak, this work makes no pretence to be a personal memoir. This was clearly understood by Mr. Deakin in inviting me. What he asked me to provide was an independent record of Bevin's career written by an historian sympathetic to, but not a member of, the Labour Movement, or of any political party. Mr. Deakin placed at my disposal the papers which Ernest Bevin had left behind and helped me to obtain access to the other sources on which I have drawn. I gladly accepted his invitation, on one condition, that there should be no question of a commission to write an 'official' life and that I should be under no obligation to submit the manuscript to anyone for approval.

In undertaking this task, I have received great kindness and much help from a large number of people who knew and admired Ernest Bevin. I wish to express my particular indebtedness to Dame Florence Bevin and Mrs. Wynne, Mr. Bevin's daughter; Mr. Albert Bevin, his elder brother; Miss Ivy Saunders, his secretary at Transport House, without whose invaluable aid this volume could never have been written at all; Lord Attlee; Mr. Omer Bécu; Mr. A. J. Chandler; Mr. Harold Clay; Mr. A. Creech Jones; Mr. Frank Cousins; Mr. W. Coysh; Miss Alison David; the Vicar of Winsford, the Reverend P. D. Fox; Captain L. H. Green; Mrs. M. A. Hamilton; Mr. Archie Henderson; Mr. Kenneth Hudson; Sir Godfrey Ince; Mr. A. P. Kinna; Sir Frederick Leggett; Sir Alexander McCall; Miss McCullough; Mr. Christopher Mayhew; Mr. F. J. Maynard; Mr. Morgan Phillips; Mr. H. R. Priday; Miss Sheppard; Mr. Frank Stillwell; Mr. W. Surrey Dane; Mr. J. J. Taylor; Sir Vincent Tewson; Mr. Harry Tomkins; Lord Uvedale; Sir Norman Vernon; and Mr. George Woodcock. I am much indebted for their assistance to the Librarian and staff of the Bristol Public Library, of Nuffield College Oxford, and of the T.U.C.

The preface to the second volume will afford me the opportunity to express my thanks to those who have already been of assistance in collecting material for Mr. Bevin's later career. I must, however, make it clear that in expressing my appreciation, I do not wish to involve any of those named in the responsibility for what I have said, which remains mine alone. The manuscript was completed well before the election of 1959 and nothing in it was written with the post-election situation of the Labour Party in mind.

The Leverhulme Trust was good enough to provide me with a grant towards the expenses of my research, for which I am very grateful. I should also like to thank those who have helped to reduce the chaos of my manuscript to a well-typed order, Mrs. Lawson, Mrs. Websper, Miss S. Buttar and Mrs. M. Faulkner. My friend, Mr. W. F. Knapp, greatly helped me by undertaking to read the proofs.

This volume has been written very largely from original sources. I believe it to be important for an historian to carry out his own researches and I have not employed a research assistant to read through any of the material for me. I hope that this, together with the claims of a full-time job at Oxford, will explain and excuse the length of the time I have taken to carry out a task which is still far from complete. This preoccupation has borne hard upon my family at times and hardest upon my wife, to whom I owe my greatest debt of all and to whom I dedicate this book in affection as well as gratitude.

St. Catherine's Society, Oxford, 1955–1959   ALAN BULLOCK

TO MY WIFE

CHAPTER I

Winsford to Bristol
1881 — 1910

I

THE ANCIENT FOREST of Exmoor lies in the extreme west of Somerset. Bounded on the north by the Bristol Channel, it is separated from the Brendon Hills to the east by the valley of the River Exe. In the second half of the nineteenth century it was still an undisturbed, remote part of the West Country. The main road and the railway to Exeter and Plymouth ran far to the south; only a single-track branch-line with an occasional train to Barnstaple skirted the moor. The traveller coming from the east might follow the high road up the wooded and winding valley of the Exe as far as Exton, but there the high road bore off north towards Dunster and the coast, leaving him to cross the bridge and push on up the Exe to Winsford, a village of not more than five hundred souls under the eastern edge of the moor. The surrounding hills and the close-set woods along the river valley combined to shut Winsford off from the outer world; its only link was the carrier from Dulverton calling once a week.

It was here that Ernest Bevin was born on 7th March 1881. He himself always gave the date of his birth as 9th March, but the date which his mother registered at Dulverton a month later was the 7th.

Forty years before, his mother had been baptised in Winsford Church. The entry in the church register reads: "1841, March 21st. Diana, daughter of Thomas and Mary Tidboald, Winsford, Labourer". By 1864, when she married William Bevin in the same church, the spelling of the name had been changed to Tudball. The family into which she married, like her own, was a Winsford family. William Bevin was eleven years older than his bride; he worked as an agricultural labourer on the Acland estate and they set up home in a tied cottage in the near-by hamlet of Howetown. Here their first child, Mary Jane, was born the following year.

At some date during the 1870s William Bevin took his wife and growing family across the Bristol Channel to South Wales in search of work. His wife later returned to Winsford but without her husband and from 1877 she described herself in various documents she signed as a widow. After her only daughter, Mary Jane, Diana Bevin had six sons of whom Ernest Bevin was the last. Who his father was remains unknown: when she registered the child's birth, his mother left the space for the father's name blank and this is confirmed by the baptismal register in Winsford Church.

Mercy Bevin, as she was commonly known, needed all her courage to face the task of bringing up a large family by herself. Shortly after the birth of her youngest child, Ernest, she moved from the house where she had been lodging to a cottage on the edge of the village. The older boys were sent out to earn their own living and Mary Jane married a railwayman, George Pope, leaving Winsford for Morchard Bishop in Devon. "I'm sure," says one witness who grew up with Ernest Bevin, "there's no one in this wide world was ever poorer than he and his mother." To keep herself and her children, she went out to work as a domestic help in neighbouring houses and farms. On occasion she acted as a midwife or helped in the kitchen at 'The Royal Oak'. At other times she drew a few shillings from the parish relief. Somehow or other she contrived to hold on to her cottage and provide enough to feed her children, but poverty and need coloured her youngest child's experience from his earliest days.

2

He was born twenty years before the end of the Victorian age, at a time when Britain was still the wealthiest and most powerful nation in the world. He grew up in the heyday of imperialism. The British occupied Egypt in 1882, the year after he was born; Burma was annexed in 1885, and the partition of Africa completed in the course of the next few years. Although it is tempting to draw the contrast between Britain's position in Bevin's childhood and sixty years later when he became Foreign Secretary, it would be idle to suppose that

Britain's imperial expansion, or the controversial issues of contemporary politics, Gladstone and Ireland, Gordon and the Sudan, produced more than a faint echo in the closed world of village life in which he was reared.

Far more important was the slow undramatic course of social change. In the late 1870s began the decline in British agriculture which soon expressed itself for the labouring class in a sharp increase of rural unemployment. (The word 'unemployed' was first used as a noun in 1882.) Between the censuses of 1871 and 1901, the number of agricultural labourers in England and Wales fell by over a third at a time when the general population increased by close on a half. The drift to the towns was accelerated, carrying with it every one of Diana Bevin's six sons, all of whom in early life went to find jobs in Bristol.

The old self-sufficient life of the English countryside as it was described by Thomas Hardy in his Wessex novels, was beginning to break up. Yet the lines of class division were still firmly drawn; the gentry and the clergy belonged to one world, the labourer to another. This line of division was reinforced by a second with which it partly coincided, that between church and chapel, which John Morley described as the most profound cleavage in English social life. Born into the labouring class, from the age of three to close on the age of thirty Ernest Bevin was bred in the Nonconformist tradition as a Sunday-school scholar, teacher and local preacher. His mother took care to see that her children got such schooling as was available in Winsford. This meant the Church School. But on Sundays, he and his two elder brothers were sent to the Wesleyan Sunday School, and the earliest known photograph of Ernest Bevin shows him as a round-faced little boy of three with a wide-brimmed straw hat and sailor suit at the Sunday-school treat of 1884.

Until the boy's eighth birthday his mother succeeded in keeping a home together, although it was increasingly difficult to make ends meet and she no longer enjoyed good health. At the beginning of 1889 she was forced to take to her bed. The spring brought no relief (she was suffering from a fibrous growth), and on 1st May 1889, at the age of forty-eight, she died, with her mother, Mary Tudball, and her children by her bedside.

The blow was bitterest to the youngest child. He never forgot his mother, the one human being who was close to him in childhood; he never forgot the affection she showed him and which he fully returned. Unhappy and lost, he came back from the funeral to his mother's cottage where for the last time Diana Bevin's seven children met as a family. The home was broken up, the furniture sold and the remaining boys, Albert and Fred, were sent out to service on farms. Ernest was too young to earn his own living yet. His half-sister, Mary, and her husband George Pope, the railwayman, offered to take him into their home at Morchard Bishop, and thither he set out with them in that early summer of 1889.

3

Thirty miles away from Winsford, Morchard Bishop lay in the rolling uplands north of Exeter with their fertile red soil and substantial farms. For a few months in the summer of 1889, Ernest went to Morchard Bishop Church School. Then in October of that year George Pope and his wife moved to the neighbouring village of Copplestone. The house, known by the incongruous name of Tiddly-Winks (since re-named Lee Mount), is a yellow-washed thatched cottage built above the cutting through which runs the railway line from Exeter to Barnstaple. Long afterwards the local postman remembered "on my rounds early on a winter's morning seeing that young boy getting water for the house or cleaning potatoes in the shute. There were two little streams which came down across a steep field opposite the house and broke through the hedge to the roadside. They didn't have pumps then. The water was always icy-cold and I'd see the boy getting the water and his hands all covered with broken chilblains".[1]

Half a mile away, on the other side of the cutting, stands the Ebenezer Chapel, opened the year before, the Methodist Chapel to which Ernest went every Sunday. On weekday mornings the boy walked the two miles down the valley through the deep Devonshire lanes to school at Colebrook, a handful of houses built on the hillside under the grey stone tower of its church. Its Board School, which had to serve the surrounding district, was opened in 1874, and consisted of two lofty classrooms divided by a partition. Ernest spent less than a year there and an old log-book records briefly: "August 8, 1890, E. Bevin has left".

1 W. C. Milton, quoted in *Picture Post*, 30th Nov. 1946.

His sister had found him a place at the Hayward Boys' School in Crediton, an old, placid Devonshire market town with a long main street running up the hill past its fine red-sandstone church. Crediton is just over five miles from Copplestone and Ernest made the journey by train with a pass which his brother-in-law and guardian, George Pope, was able to secure as a railway-worker. He entered the school on 2nd September 1890. By the end of his first school year, July 1891, he had reached Standard IV and was entitled to claim his Labour Certificate. In fact, he stayed on at the school for the best part of another year and did not leave until 25th March 1892.[1] By then he had a job as a farm-boy at Chaffcombe, a farm close to Copplestone, where he lived in for a wage of sixpence a week (paid in a lump sum of six shillings and sixpence on quarter-days) and learned to carry out a variety of chores from stone-picking to driving cattle and cutting up the mangels and turnips for their fodder. In the evenings he was pressed into service to read out items of news and leading articles from the Bristol papers while the family sat round the fire in the farm-kitchen.

During the winter of 1892–3, he moved to another farm, Beers, on the Okehampton Road. He had a room in an outbuilding overlooking the farmyard, reached by narrow winding stairs from the yard itself. According to local tradition, he left a little over a year later after a quarrel with his employer, William May. Whatever the truth in this, there is no doubt that farm work had no attractions for Ernest. When a letter arrived from his brother Jack urging him to come to Bristol, he jumped at the chance and in the spring of 1894 (the year Gladstone resigned for the last time) he set out to seek his fortune in the city.

4

Bevin was always reticent about his childhood and irritated by attempts to trick it out as the first stage in a sensational rise from labourer's cottage to Foreign Office. It was one of his most strongly-held beliefs that there was nothing odd in a man who began life as a labourer possessing the ability to run a department of State and sit in

[1] I am indebted for this information about Bevin's schooldays to Mr. D. Cook, of the Devon Education Authority.

the Cabinet. He had too much sense of his own dignity and of the dignity of the class from which he sprang to be either flattered or amused by a patronising curiosity about his 'humble' origins.

In fact, despite a crop of anecdotes assiduously collected when he became a Minister of the Crown, there is nothing in his early years to distinguish him from those with whom he grew up. It is highly unlikely that anyone who knew him as a boy in Winsford or even as a youth in Bristol believed that he would ever become anything more than a manual labourer or at most a shop assistant.

None the less, it is a serious mistake to underestimate the influence of these formative years on any man, particularly a man whose character and career show as much consistency as Ernest Bevin's. Despite the affection of his mother, which he remembered with gratitude all his life, it had been a hard childhood, with no father, with his mother dying and his home broken up when he was eight. From his earliest years he had known need and insecurity; from the age of eleven he was pushed out into the world to earn his own living. Neither the boy then nor the man later regarded this as exceptional: it was the common lot of the labouring class into which he had been born. Forced to look after himself, he learned to rely on himself; he was laying the foundation of that massive confidence and self-sufficiency which never failed him.

His formal education was limited to the rudiments of reading, writing and arithmetic. Apprenticed to no trade, his only prospect was to keep himself by manual labour, his only resource the native intelligence and strength of character with which he had been endowed. These qualities matured slowly. As a child he did not go through the forcing-house of town life; he was born and bred not in the slums of an industrial city but in the country, and he retained throughout his life many of a countryman's characteristics.

5

It is not difficult to imagine the mixed feelings of bewilderment and excitement with which this country lad of thirteen climbed out of the train at Temple Meads station one day in 1894 and was plunged for the first time into the crowded streets of a big town. The second city and port of the kingdom in the eighteenth century, when it sent

Burke to Parliament and dominated the West Indian and North American trade, Bristol was still the undisputed capital of the West Country. Around the city docks, with their outliers at Avonmouth and Portishead, had grown up a busy industrial and commercial town with a population of 300,000 and a variety of trades from wines and tobacco to the manufacture of paper and soap.

His eldest brother Jack who had brought him to Bristol was then working in a butcher's shop in Clifton and offered him a home out on the northern side of the city in Bishopston. The Priory Restaurant, where another brother, Albert Bevin, was learning the trade of pastrycook and where Ernest now began work in the bakehouse, stood on St. Augustine's Parade, in the centre of the city. For a wage of six shillings a week and his meals, he worked twelve hours a day six days a week. They were long hours but not exceptional and he was not treated at all unkindly.

One of his first jobs was to push a barrow loaded with pies and pastries to the refreshment rooms at Temple Meads station. This gave him time to stare and absorb the bustle of activity in the streets and around the docks: the heavily-laden drays rattling over the cobblestones, the carters shouting to their horses, the endless loading and unloading at the warehouses.

When he tired of the long hours in the bakehouse, he found a better job for himself out of doors at ten shillings a week as a van boy on one of the mineral-water wagons of Brooke and Prudencio's. The sequence of his employment is difficult to follow, but at some time in this period he worked at Jackson's butter shop in High Street, later returning to the Priory Restaurant where, dressed in a page-boy's uniform, he helped to wait at table.

From the Priory at the end of 1897 he went to a job as conductor on the horse trams, a useful apprenticeship for the man who was later to bring the bus and tramwaymen into the biggest of all transport unions. Here we are on firm ground. The Bristol Tramways Company's records show him to have left the Priory just before Christmas 1897. After three days' training he began work clipping tickets (twelve passengers outside and eighteen in) on the Horfield route which ran up past his home in Bishopston. His wages were now twelve shillings a week and he kept the job until March 1900 when he left of his own accord just before his nineteenth birthday.

In 1900 Jack Bevin gave up his house and Ernest had to find

7

lodgings for himself. He had also to find a new job. His brother Albert remembers him being unemployed for eight weeks before the relief of Mafeking (May 1900), but he then picked up a job with another firm of mineral-water manufacturers, G. C. King, of York Street, St. Paul's, where a third brother, Fred, was working. A year later he was made one of the firm's permanent drivers.

Chance has preserved the agreement signed between G. C. King and "Ernest Bevin of 9, Gloster Terrace, St. Michael's, hereinafter called the Servant", on 7th May 1901. Amongst other conditions, Ernest bound himself not to leave the service of his employer for twelve months "or to enter the employment of any other person or either alone or in partnership carry on or be concerned with the manufacture of mineral waters, cordials, syrups or hop bitters" within a radius of five miles from York Street. He was paid a weekly wage of eighteen shillings and commission at the rate of a penny a gross on empty bottles. His hours were six in the morning till six at night. After that he had to groom his horse. But once he had loaded up at the York Street yard in the morning he was his own master. The job, in fact, gave him the independence and out-of-doors life which he wanted and, with a sympathetic master who soon came to appreciate some of his unusual qualities, he was content to go on working for King's until 1906.

6

The young man had not lost the habit of chapel-going to which he had been bred as a boy. Bristol was a stronghold of Nonconformity and Ernest Bevin attended a number of chapels before identifying himself with the Manor Hall Baptist Mission in St. Mark's Road, Easton, a heavily built-up area of working-class houses. The origins of this Mission, which eventually became St. Mark's Church, are worth recording as a fragment of social history. In January 1897, forty members of the Kensington Baptist Tabernacle in Stapleton Road decided to break away and form a community of their own. They had neither funds nor wealthy members and for a few weeks they could do no more than meet for worship in each others' houses. Then, under the leadership of seven lay deacons, they succeeded in renting the Old Manor Hall which held a hundred and fifty people, with a gymnasium and house adjoining it. Here they began to hold services and to build up a Sunday school which in three years numbered three hundred and fifty and eventually close on six hundred. In 1904 they purchased a site for a church, which they built and opened in 1911 at a total cost of nearly £3,000, almost all of which was raised by the small community itself.

Bevin joined the Mission as a Sunday-school teacher, but soon became active in other ways as well. His first address to the Christian Endeavour Society (appropriately enough, on the history of Israel) is still remembered. Besides taking his share in sick-visiting and distributing tracts, he frequently spoke with evangelical fervour at the open-air meetings held in the district on Saturday evenings.

Towards the end of 1901, he applied for membership of the church, was visited by two of the deacons and on 5th January 1902 was admitted. He was baptised by immersion with eleven other members of the Mission at the Bethesda Chapel in Great George Street and remained an active member of the church until 1905, frequently attending church meetings, acting as sidesman and becoming (like his predecessor as Labour Foreign Secretary, Arthur Henderson) a local preacher on the Baptist itinerary for Bristol and the surrounding villages.

The contribution of Nonconformity to the British Labour movement is a commonplace: a chapel upbringing has been as characteristic of British trade-union leadership, for instance, as a public-school education of the leaders of the ruling class. It fostered in men with little or no education, pushed out into a rough world at an early age like Ernest Bevin and Arthur Henderson, a strong sense of duty and conscience, self-respect, a passion for justice and a conviction of righteousness. Nonconformity has indeed been the great seed-bed of radicalism in this country. Although Ernest Bevin was later to turn away from what he regarded as the narrowness of chapel folk on social questions, he carried over much that Nonconformity had taught him into his socialism and trade unionism.

The chapel not only gave him a religious faith and moral principles, it quickened in him the sense of latent intellectual powers. He was slowly beginning to discover his capacity to think, to argue and to speak. He began to read and to study—hard work for a man who worked all day in the open air, had left school at eleven and knew nothing of books. There was talk of his taking a theological course and qualifying as a Baptist minister or even as a missionary.

At this time a remarkable discussion class met on Sunday afternoons in the Old King Street Baptist Church and was attended by hundreds of working men every week. Its leader was the Rev. James Moffat Logan, the son of a Glasgow artisan who had begun work at ten and only entered the Baptist ministry in his late twenties. His ministry at Old King Street lasted from 1891 to 1903, and his readiness for debate on any subject under the sun, moral, social or theological, attracted men of different beliefs and many with no religious faith at all—agnostics, free-thinkers, radicals and socialists.

The class, with the church packed to the roof, opened with a hymn sung with the full power of several hundred men's voices, then a prayer. An open forum followed in which Moffat Logan submitted himself to questions and debate. His class was at the height of its fame at the turn of the century, when he took a courageous stand against the Boer War, and his personality, representative of the finest tradition of Nonconformist radicalism, made a lasting impression on the young Bevin. This was the atmosphere in which Ernest Bevin, like so many other radical and Labour leaders, first learned to speak and hold his own in debate.

He found another outlet for his love of discussion in the Adult School Movement which flourished in Bristol at this time. Alderman Milton gives this description of the adult school which he and Ernest Bevin used to attend:

"We met at seven o'clock on a Sunday morning, before breakfast, three hundred men or so. We began with a hymn and an accordion solo; then hymn practice with a conductor who taught us how to sing. After that we broke up into groups and discussed our theme for the day, which we got from the Adult School Handbook, with readings, an outline of the subject and suggestions for debate. There was one subject fixed for each Sunday in the year; it was the same for every Adult School in the country. Our theme might be, say, women in industry, or Christianity and poverty. Then we'd come back to the hall for a general discussion, sometimes with a talk by an outside speaker."[1]

Another contemporary, George Wallis, writes:

"My impression is that it was in the Adult School that Ernest Bevin learned
  1 Interview with the author, 19th Dec. 1956.

how to stand on his hind legs and express himself in public. You know how very free discussion could be in schools in those days and Ernest Bevin got the name for being extravagant in voicing social and industrial injustice. I remember a Citizen Sunday gathering at the Colston Hall (2–3,000 Adult School members with brass bands, etc.) which I think was addressed by Sir George Newman. When we were all coming out, Ernest Bevin was out quick and on a box, holding forth. I suppose something had provoked him. He did not want much provoking in those days."[1]

The same witness, George Wallis, remembers Bevin "as a member of a joint W.E.A.-trade union study class held in Broad Street, in some trade union rooms facing St. John's-on-the-Wall. Montague Fordham came a distance each Sunday morning (after Adult School) about 11 a.m. The subject was Agriculture—on which Fordham was an authority—and here again Ernest Bevin was vocal, sitting with papers and books bursting from his pockets".

7

Bevin had a passion for acquiring knowledge as well as for argument. He read whatever books he could lay hands on and attended evening classes run by the Y.M.C.A. in St. James's Square and by the City Education Committee. By day he continued to earn his living as a vanman, driving his mineral-water wagon and his two horses in all weather round the public houses, the little cafés and cottage shops of Bristol and the surrounding villages. He had the countryman's love of the open air and, most of all, he valued his independence; he could go his own pace, not the pace of a machine or a foreman. Driving out into the country, he had the leisure to turn over in his mind what he had seen and heard and read.

There are men and women still alive who remember him as he then was.

"During my schooldays at Patchway Church School around 1904," one of them writes, "I saw him every Monday when he called to deliver mineral waters at my grandmother's cottage shop. I used to take my lunch with him and afterwards race out to the lorry driver's seat and take possession of the reins in order to drive to the next stop, Almondbury Hill.

1 On 4th July 1954, Bevin's own career was the theme set in the Adult School Movement Handbook—after three weeks devoted to the history of Israel.

"A feature of this weekly episode was a book that he studied. During the meal his eyes were glued to its pages, even the knife and fork were ignored as his fingers wandered from plate to mouth. The journey to Almondbury was also taken for further study, but I could never discover the title of the book which was always carefully concealed."[1]

He was growing into a well-built figure of a man with broad shoulders and a deep chest. His personality too was beginning to expand as he became more sure of himself. Forthright in the expression of his opinions, he gave the impression of a man well able to look after himself either in an argument or in a fight. On fine evenings as he drove back into Bristol, in his carter's cap and green baize apron, he would sing hymns and music-hall songs in his rolling baritone voice, a habit to which he sometimes recurred years later during his wartime journeys as Minister of Labour.

8

The more Bevin read and thought, the more puzzled and angry he became with the conditions which he saw every day as he drove his horses and cart through the streets of Bristol.

In the early years of this century roughly a third of the population of Great Britain had insufficient means to provide themselves with more than the bare necessities needed to maintain life. Many had less, and Bristol, like every other industrial town, housed in its slums thousands of men, women and children who dragged out a degraded existence in conditions unfit for any human being. Bevin did not live in such conditions himself: he was a respectable working man with a reasonable wage by the standards of the time. But what he saw in the daily course of his work roused in him compassion and indignation. Like every working man, he knew how narrow was the dividing line between his own existence so long as he had a job and good health and what he might be reduced to if, through no fault of his own, he lost his job or fell ill. What happened to a man and his family then? What happened to the woman whose husband died and who was left with a family to bring up? There was no unemployment insurance, no old age or widow's pensions, no free medical service: only the pawnshop or the hated poor relief stood between a

1 Letter to the author from Leonard Kingsworth, 16th Jan. 1956.

family and destitution if misfortune befell them.

But this was not the lot of everyone, an inescapable part of the human condition. He had only to drive his cart up the hill to Clifton with its tall eighteenth-century terraces and well turned-out carriages to see the crude contrast not only with the slums but with the whole of working-class Bristol, the Bristol he knew with its row upon row of meanly-built houses, its shabby Board schools, its railway sidings and noisy, dirty back-streets.

In 1905 figures were published by an economist, Leo Chiozza Money, to demonstrate the unequal division of the national income. His book, *Riches and Poverty*, which Bevin and many other working men read, showed that just under half of the national income (£830 million) was divided between the five millions of the population whom he described as rich or 'comfortable'; the remainder (£880 million) had to be shared between the other 38 millions.

Why was there this gross inequality between the comfortable middle class (leave alone the rich) and the poor? What justice was there in such a system, what justification for the glaring disparity between the ease and comfort of one class and the long hours of work, low wages and insecurity of the majority? For the inequality was not one of wealth only, but of health, physique, security, education and every sort of opportunity.

The only answer Bevin could get was that such inequality was a part of the natural order, that it was inevitable (as not only the beneficiaries but many of the victims of the system believed), to be endured but not changed. This was not an answer to satisfy a man of his energetic temperament. In his eyes an economic and social system which produced such results stood self-condemned; it could and should be changed. Finding such radical opinions looked at askance in chapel circles, he became more and more critical of the timidity of organised religion on social questions. He began to look elsewhere, to listen to those who not only attacked the evils they saw in society as outspokenly as himself, but claimed to have found in the teachings of socialism an alternative method of social organisation which would get rid of them.

9

Bristol socialism had an independent history dating back to the 1880s. In February 1884 a Bristol branch of Hyndman's Democratic Federation was set up and two months later openly adopted a socialist programme. Withdrawing from the Social Democratic Federation in December 1885, after Hyndman and Champion had accepted Tory funds to promote S.D.F. candidates in London, the Bristol group formed the Bristol Socialist Society. They converted the young Ramsay MacDonald to socialism when he spent a few months in the city in 1885 and they began open-air propaganda meetings in Bristol the same year.

Although few in numbers, the pioneers of socialism in Bristol were men of courage who unselfishly devoted all their spare time to working for much-needed social reforms and to preaching their socialist faith in face of indifference or open hostility.

The roots of their socialism were as much moral as economic, and they were more influenced by the generous love of humanity preached by William Morris, Edward Carpenter and Bruce Glasier than by Marxist doctrines of class hatred and economic determinism. Men like the Sharland brothers, Bob Gilliard, Robert Weare, James Treasure, Frank Sheppard, Jack Milton, Watts Treasure, W. R. Oxley, expressed in their socialism that native genius for practical morality which Nonconformity was rapidly losing. For twenty years, denounced as cranks, Utopians, agitators and worse, they fought a series of local battles for freedom of speech and the right to combine, took up the unpopular causes of unemployment, sweated labour, bad housing and education, and strove to convert the working classes to the idea of direct Labour representation as a means of improving their conditions. By the end of the 1890s they had secured four seats on the city council and a small but invaluable representation on the Board of Guardians. These they used as a platform from which to draw the reluctant attention of the more prosperous classes to the social evils of the city's poorer districts.

By the 1900s, when Bevin began to attend socialist meetings, the Bristol Socialist Society (once again affiliated to the Social Democratic Federation) had been joined by two branches of the Independent Labour Party. Relations between the two bodies were sometimes strained and, although combining on occasion for common efforts, each conducted separate propagandist meetings. These were held every Sunday and sometimes on weekday evenings, out of doors, at the top of Old Market Street (the Batch), on the Horsefair, at St. George's Park Gates and Clifton Down or of an evening at the Shepherd's Hall (S.D.F.) and the Kingsley Hall (I.L.P.). The speakers were local men, with an occasional visitor— Ramsay MacDonald, Keir Hardie, George Lansbury, Philip Snowden—for larger meetings. Bevin became a frequent attender, often asking questions and engaging in discussion. He left the impression of a serious-minded young man, not easily swayed by emotion, thinking for himself about what he heard and about what he said. Sympathetic but critical, he was in no hurry to commit himself. When he did, it was the Bristol Socialist Society which he joined. In a letter to the author, Alderman Milton writes:

"I think the first time Ernest Bevin spoke was at St. George's Park Gates (an I.L.P. pitch), but he did not like the I.L.P. too well. He thought they were social reformers and preferred the Bristol Socialist Society who had now become affiliated to the S.D.F. and who, Ernest thought, had more of the revolutionist spirit."

Endowed with a powerful voice, fluency of speech and a vehemence which startled his audience, he was a valuable recruit to the panel of local speakers. The experience he had gained in local preaching and adult schools he now began to deepen in the more combative atmosphere of open-air discussion. Sunday after Sunday he got up on the Batch, the Horsefair or the Downs to attack the inequality and injustice of capitalism, to argue the case for working-class action to secure a socialist society. In the process his own convictions hardened, his command of argument grew more sure.

10

Bevin's conversion to socialism was accompanied by the transfer of his interests from the chapel to politics, and was completed between the beginning of 1905, when he left the Manor Hall Mission, and the beginning of 1908, when he became secretary of the Right-to-Work Committee.

These years marked a turning-point in his life for other reasons too. In March 1906 he gave up his job as a driver and for a year or more took over the Cabin Café, refreshment rooms which G. C. King had opened next door to his mineral-water factory at 7, York Street in the working-class district of St. Paul's. The *Bristol Directory* of 1907 contains the same entry for 7, York Street—"E. Bevin, refreshment rooms"—and records in addition a coffee stall kept by Ernest Bevin in Avon Street under the main-line railway running into Temple Meads station. By 1908, however, the York Street café had changed hands and Bevin was back at work as a mineral-water roundsman, this time for the firm of John Macey, of Old Market Street. He remained with Macey's until he joined the Dockers' Union as an organiser in the spring of 1911.

Most important of all, it was at this time that Ernest Bevin met and began his life-long partnership with his wife, Florence Townley, the daughter of a wine-taster at a Bristol wine-merchant's. She gave him the affection he needed, new confidence and, for the first time, a home of his own. He still went on living in East Bristol, but his new interests brought new friends who shared his political sympathies; he saw less of old friends (some of whom were shocked by his political activities) and less of his brothers, who gradually lost touch with him.

I I

By the time Bevin began to drive a horse and cart again, he was not only active as a socialist propagandist, but had been offered and had accepted the unpaid office of secretary to the newly-formed Bristol Right-to-Work Committee, an indication of the place he was beginning to make for himself in the local Labour movement.

1908 and 1909 were the two worst years for unemployment between 1886 and the post-war slump.[1] No State provision of any kind, either an insurance scheme or the dole, existed to aid men

1 Throughout the 1890s the average figure for unemployment had been 5.2% of trade union membership. In 1906 and 1907 it was 4%, but in 1908 and 1909 it rose to nearly 8%. This, of course, was an average which concealed much higher figures in certain trades and took no account of the widespread unemployment in the country outside the trade unions, especially amongst unskilled and casual labour.

Ernest Bevin at the age of fourteen.

Above. Early days in Bristol. Sitting next to Bevin in the front row is Ben Tillett and standing in the back row (with light waistcoat) is Frank Sheppard. *Below*. St. Augustine's Bridge, Bristol, at the time Bevin was a young man.

out of work. The Unemployed Persons Act of 1905 authorised the local authorities to set up distress committees and initiate schemes of work. The extent to which these provisions were taken advantage of, however, depended on local circumstances, and one of the objects of Bevin's campaign was to bring pressure to bear on the Bristol Distress Committee. The other was to rouse support for the Bill which the Labour group was to introduce in the House of Commons in March 1908 and which, instead of empowering, would have obliged local authorities to find employment for men out of work, or, if that were impossible, to provide relief for the men and their families.

The Right-to-Work Committee called its first meeting in the Haymarket on Sunday morning, 26th January. Hot coffee and bread and butter were provided for more than six hundred men. Then Ernest Bevin got up to propose:

"That this mass meeting of workers and would-be workers emphatically condemns the inaction of the Government with regard to the unemployed and demands immediate legislation for the purpose of settling the question on national lines which shall have justice as a basis and not inadequate almsgiving."

After a number of other speeches, the resolution was put to the meeting and carried with acclamation.[1]

Three days later, the Liberal Member for Bristol North, the urbane and witty Chief Secretary for Ireland, Augustine Birrell, came down to address his constituents. Bevin led a deputation from the Committee which Birrell agreed to see.

"Mr. Birrell was asked if something could not be done on national lines to solve the unemployed question: home colonisation, land cultivation, dairy farming being suggested by Mr. Bevin; taxing unearned increment and the interest on foreign investment by Mr. W. S. Parnall, and the issue of paper pound notes by Mr. C. Walker. Mr. Birrell shook his head and said: 'They must think of the Opposition and whether they would agree with it; that it might mean the disruption of the Liberal Party and they would then again have the Conservative Party in power'. The paper-money suggestion, the Rt. Hon. Gentleman thought, 'was sensible, very sensible, but would the other party agree to it?' At the conclusion of the interview Mr. Birrell was

1 Report of the Bristol Right-to-Work Committee, 1908, pp. 1–2; *The Bristol Observer*, 1st Feb. 1908.

B

fain to admit that the remedy for unemployment could only be brought about by the upset of the present commercial system. The deputation, after thanking Mr. Birrell, withdrew, having formed the opinion that it seemed plainly evident the Government had not seriously considered the question."[1]

The next week Bevin tried another line of approach. A. E. Ellery, one of the Labour city councillors who had taken part in the Committee's work, was walking along Old Market Street when he heard a loud shout of "Alf!" Turning round he saw Bevin pulling in his wagon to the side of the road for a word with him. "Alf," he said, "we need more publicity for our Right-to-Work Committee. You're a city councillor; you get the Mayor to see us."[2] So, on 4th February 1908, a deputation of twenty unemployed men led by the young carter (who had left his horse and cart outside) was ushered into the Council Chamber to meet the Lord Mayor of Bristol, the chairman of the Distress Committee and the Town Clerk.

"Mr. Bevin, who was the first speaker, pointed out that there was in the city a good deal of public work which could be put in hand without delay. By doing this work, a good deal of labour would be absorbed by men who were now unemployed. He laid before the Lord Mayor a list of the works suggested."[3]

Some of the items suggested, notably the construction of a lake in Eastville Park, were eventually put in hand, but the Committee, after holding a number of other propaganda meetings, suspended its activities for the summer with little of practical value accomplished.

Bevin's growing interest in municipal politics is shown by another newspaper report, this time of a meeting held at St. Simon's School on 2nd April 1908, to adopt Mr. Featherstone Witty as Liberal candidate for St. Philip's North ward. It was a noisy meeting with good many interruptions and some disorder. Finally, the burly figure of Ernest Bevin rose to his feet and moved an amendment to the resolution proposing the adoption of Mr. Featherstone Witty:

"That this meeting, after hearing Mr. Featherstone Witty and his denunciation of municipal trading, believes that the ownership of the three great municipal concerns, tramways, gas and water with their £290,000

1 Report of the Bristol Right-to-Work Committee, 1908, p. 2.
2 Recounted by A. E. Ellery to the author.
3 *Western Daily Press*, 5th Feb. 1908.

annual profit, should in the best interests of the city and the ratepayers be owned by the community as a whole, and pledges itself to do all in its power to return Mr. Jones (the rival candidate) at the end of the poll on Monday next."

Amid uproar, the amendment was put to the vote and lost. Nor was Mr. Jones successful when Monday came.

12

In the autumn, the Bristol Right-to-Work Committee, now affiliated to the National Right-to-Work Committee, opened its campaign with a crowded meeting at the Empire Palace of Varieties on 11th October. The resolution put to the meeting called for legislation laying upon local authorities the obligation to provide work at a living wage for all those willing and able to work. The following day Councillor Ellery introduced a second deputation from the Committee to the Lord Mayor, and a list of thirteen detailed proposals, including the improvement of roads and parks, an afforestation scheme and the construction of public baths, was left with the Distress Committee.

The Mayor was sympathetic, but finance was a great difficulty. Accordingly, on 11th November, Ernest Bevin appeared at a Local Government Board Inquiry in Bristol to support the City Council's application to borrow money for public works, including the East-ville Park Lake. He reported 3,000 men out of work without any form of relief; by the end of December 1908 the Committee put the total at over 6,000 with another 20,000 dependents who had no means of support. In many houses children were found with no more than rags to clothe them, no fire and only a handful of food.

The Committee's object was to rouse the public conscience and with this in view it circulated every minister of religion in the city, asking for support. Bevin appealed to the Dean and Chapter of the Cathedral and, with their agreement, led a procession of 400 unemployed men into Bristol Cathedral at the morning service on Sunday, 9th November. They were, says Alderman Sheppard, who took part, "a ragged lot led by a ragged band playing 'True to Death'," but their appearance made a considerable impression on the well-to-do congregation, not least their orderly behaviour in which Bevin had carefully coached them beforehand.

At the beginning of December the National Right-to-Work Committee held a conference in London and Ernest Bevin took two days off from work to attend as the Bristol representative. It was his first visit to London. At the annual meeting of the Bristol Committee which followed soon afterwards, George Lansbury and Ben Tillett both spoke and Bevin presented the Committee's report.

"Hunger has come" (he told his audience) "not because we are incapable of producing wealth, but because in the last few years we have produced too much. One criticism of the Committee is that its work is purely a palliative measure. The tremendous loadstone (*sic*) to progress, capitalism, will become greater and greater year by year and nothing but a complete social and economic revolution is going to solve the problem. We must feed the people in order that men may be strong enough physically and mentally to carry out that revolution which will come at no distant date."

Short of such fundamental change, relief work organised by the local authority was still the most practical form of help and in the following autumn of 1909 Bevin decided to stand for the City Council. In the third week of October a crowded meeting in the St. Clement's Parish Hall, with the vicar of St. Agnes among his supporters, adopted him as Socialist candidate for St. Paul's ward. At that time there were still only eight Labour councillors in a Council of ninety-two, and Bevin's opponent, a Liberal councillor, J. H. Gibbs, had been returned unopposed at the previous election. Rival posters exhorted the electors: "Vote for Bevin—Down with poverty and slums", and "Vote for Gibbs, the progressive candidate, and save the ward from Socialism".

Bevin fought the election on a fund of seven pounds. The contest attracted a lot of attention in the city and brought out a much larger percentage of voters than usual. It was still rare for a candidate to stand openly as a socialist, but Bevin made no bones about his beliefs. He called for the nationalisation of the docks, of the water supply and other public services. "Under the head of Education" (the *Western Daily Press* reported on 2nd November) "Mr. Bevin advocated the fullest use of the Acts for the feeding and medical inspection of school children. He strongly opposed the efforts being made locally to institute such impertinent inquiries as savour of the Poor Law system". On housing he advocated the erection of "artisans' cottages (not barracks) to be let at rents covering the cost of building and repairs only" and he ended his election address:

"Think! last winter in Bristol there were 5,000 heads of families out of work, 20,000 human beings suffering want and 10,000 paupers, and you will realise the chaos, misery and degradation brought upon us by the private ownership of the means of life. I claim that Socialism, which is the common ownership of those means, is the ONLY SOLUTION OF SUCH EVILS."[1]

At the poll Gibbs retained his seat by 1,052 votes to 663. Bevin was not only disappointed but angry. He demanded the impounding of the registers and claimed that the Liberal agent had broken the law by the way in which he marked off the names of voters. The charge was rebutted and, adds the local paper, "there were vigorous demonstrations by partisans of each candidate outside the school where a large crowd had assembled."

13

The months that followed his defeat were a difficult time for Ernest Bevin. He had drawn a good deal of attention to himself in the past two years and had been marked down, especially by the local Liberal politicians, as a dangerous agitator with outspoken views. The word was passed round and for several weeks he found that his sales to publicans and other customers dropped sharply. His commission fell in proportion and out of a sense of fairness to his employer he offered to give up his round. To his credit, John Macey, although a Liberal himself, refused to listen and stood by his employee. In the course of the winter the boycott was dropped, Bevin kept his job and gradually restored his earnings.

The setback also unsettled him personally. For a time he dropped his political activities and was not seen in his usual haunts. In the course of 1910 he gave up the secretaryship of the Right-to-Work Committee, and one of his friends remembers talk again of his taking a theological course, possibly with a view to becoming a missionary, an old plan he had discussed before.

During the summer, however, he resumed his part in the Labour Movement, this time in a new direction. His work for the un-

1 S. Bryher (S. Bale): *An Account of the Labour and Socialist Movement in Bristol* (1929) Part III, pp. 2–3.

employed had brought him into touch with the dockers, casual labourers taken on by the hour and frequently left without work for weeks on end. A strike at Avonmouth in June 1910 rapidly spread to the Bristol docks and held up the whole trade of the port for most of July. A small local relief fund was set up of which Bevin, as a result of his experience with the Right-to-Work Committee, was asked to take charge, although neither a docker himself nor a member of a union.

At the same time attempts by the employers to use carters in loading and unloading ships in the port brought home to Bevin and other carters the advantage of linking up more closely with the dockers. Up to that time the Bristol carters, of whom there were several hundreds employed in and about the docks, had not been organised in any union. They worked long hours, were frequently called on to carry excessive loads and had no organisation to form a common front against their employers. Harry Orbell, an organiser of the Dockers' Union, urged Bevin to take the initiative in bringing the carters together.

The same idea had occurred to Alf Ellery, a member of the I.L.P. and a city councillor, who had recently taken on a part-time job as organiser for the Workers' Union in Bristol. After two or three weeks of getting up early to talk to the carters at their depots and distributing handbills, he called a meeting at the Caxton Rooms by Bristol Bridge. Ellery's plan was to set up a carters' branch of the Workers' Union and he had piles of application forms at hand on a trestle table.

Prominent among the carters who attended was Ernest Bevin, sitting with arms folded in the second row. After Ellery's introductory talk, questions were invited. Bevin got up to ask whether the Workers' Union was affiliated to the Bristol Trades Council. This was an awkward question, for, as both Ellery and Bevin knew, the rival unions, Tillett's Dockers and Thorne's Gasworkers, annoyed by the Workers' Union invasion of Bristol, had succeeded in getting Ellery's application for recognition turned down by the Trades Council. To his chagrin, Ellery had to admit that the Workers' Union was not affiliated. Clearly then, Bevin concluded, this was not the appropriate body for the carters to join and he got up to push his way out, taking the rest of Ellery's meeting with him.[1]

1 Recounted to the author by A. E. Ellery.

The 1910 strike had shown the common interest between the dockers and the carters, most of whom were employed in or near the port. In Bevin's view, the proper step for the carters to take was to join the Dockers' Union, already well-established in Bristol, and not the Workers' Union which was trying to gain a foothold in the city—this would only produce further divisions in the local trade union movement.

A few days after Ellery's attempt Bevin took the initiative in calling another meeting under the auspices of the Dockers' Union, or to give it its full title, the Dock, Wharf, Riverside and General Workers' Union. This time there was no mistake: the meeting resolved, on Bevin's proposal, to set up a carmen's branch of the Dockers' Union forthwith, and elected Ernest Bevin as its first chairman. At the age of twenty-nine he became a trade unionist for the first time: to the end of his life his framed certificate of membership, dated 27th August 1910, with its old-fashioned Victorian illuminations and scrolls, held pride of place over the fireplace in his home.

CHAPTER 2

Apprenticeship
1910 — 1914

I

T HIS YOUNG WORKING MAN of twenty-nine, with his frank, serious
look attracted attention in any crowd by the firmness of his views
and the force of his personality. He was still content to earn his
living driving a cart. He did not see himself as a leader, but as an
ordinary working man driven to protest. What moved him was
neither ambition nor personal resentment, but anger at poverty,
injustice and the way in which his class was treated. His roots in
working-class life were deep and this remained his strength all his
life. Indifferent to the fruits of success, wealth or honours, disliking
publicity, he never sought to raise himself out of the class to which he
belonged, but to lift it up with him.

Still largely unconscious of the powers he possessed, he had so far
discovered no clear sense of purpose. His entry into the Dockers'
Union released and canalised his energies. Once he had an objective
in view, all his strength of character was engaged to secure it. The
results were soon evident. By the end of September 1911, Brother
Bevin could tell the annual general meeting of the branch he had
started no more than a year before that it now numbered 2,050
members (close on a third of the Dockers' membership in Bristol).
In future there would have to be two branches, one for the carters
and one for the warehousemen.

Not only had the new recruit built up a remarkable branch
membership; within six months of joining the union as a lay member
he had persuaded the Bristol employers to recognise it and negotiate
the first agreement they had ever signed with their men. In March
1911 he succeeded in bringing seven representatives of the em-

24

ployers and seven representatives of the union round a table to set up a joint Arbitration Board. By the end of the month he had got them to draw up and sign a comprehensive agreement covering the hours, wages and conditions of the Bristol carters which, with periodical revision, thenceforward governed the carting trade in Bristol. Later in the same year he secured a similar agreement for the warehouse-men.

At a time when trade unions were still treated with contempt by employers and their organisers frequently ordered off the premises, the new carters' branch had won a double victory in securing both recognition and a written agreement. Before this a carter had been obliged to work the hours fixed by his employer and to take what his employer was prepared to give him. Now rates and hours were fixed for the whole port, and a carter, with two horses to look after and a 67-hour week, was guaranteed a wage of twenty-six shillings with overtime at the rate of sixpence an hour.

A man with the ability to organise both men and employers and bring them to agreement in a few months was too valuable to be left on a mineral-water round. In the spring of 1911 Bevin was taken on to the staff of the Bristol office of the Dockers' Union as a district investigator at a weekly salary of £2.

2

The trade union movement in 1910–11 was very different, both in power and status, from what it was to become by the middle of the century. In 1910 there were altogether two million trade unionists in the country. This figure, however, gives a misleading impression of strength. In the first place, it represented a minority—no more than one in five—even of the men engaged in manual labour, without taking into account the women. In certain areas—the industrial North or South Wales—the proportion was much higher than the national average, but in others (London, for example, and all the agricultural areas) it was still lower. The same held true of different industries: some, like mining, printing, engineering and ship-building, had a relatively high percentage of trade-union member-ship; others, like transport, agriculture, shop-workers, the casually employed, were hardly touched by trade-union organisation.

In the second place, these two million members were divided between 669 unions. Only eighteen of these numbered more than 20,000 members and even this figure of eighteen includes a number of federations like the Miners' Federation of Great Britain which was composed of 38 individual unions. The great majority were small, often entirely local societies numbering a few hundred or at most a few thousand members with little organisation, few funds and limited interest. Many of them were not even affiliated to the T.U.C., which, despite its grandiloquent title, had little authority. Between its annual congresses the defence of trade-union interests was left to a Parliamentary Committee which was content to send occasional deputations to ministers and to consult with the small group of Labour Members of Parliament. Not only was the membership divided among a large number of unions, but their power was further diminished by bitter rivalries. Many claimed an exclusive right to organise a particular trade or district without the ability to enforce the claim, or defended the privileged position of one group of workers (such as the stevedores or the locomotive engineers) against other groups in the same industry.

As a consequence of this weakness and disunity, the status of the trade unions was still only half-accepted either by the employers or by the State. In a number of industries, amongst them railways and shipping, the employers flatly refused to negotiate with union representatives, and many managers would dismiss a man out of hand if they suspected him of belonging to a trade union. The engineers alone were sufficiently well-organised to secure national, as distinct from limited local, agreements. This was beyond the reach even of the Miners' Federation with its 600,000 members. The equality of bargaining power which the unions were to attain in the 1940s, leave alone the right to consultation, would have been dismissed as a visionary objective even by those sympathetic to the working-class movement.

Employers and public opinion in general looked upon the trade-union leader (not without some justification) as an agitator whose object was to disrupt industry and as likely as not society as well. The Government largely shared this point of view. It would never have occurred to the party leaders of 1910 that, by the mid-century, governments as well as management would consult the trade-union leaders as a matter of course and court their support. As late as 1903 the Government could set up a Royal Commission on Trade Disputes and Trade Combinations without inviting a single trade unionist to serve on it. In the world of Edwardian England an impassable gulf still separated the man in a cloth cap from the classes born and educated to conduct the affairs of State. In that world it would have been unthinkable to suppose that the Liberal Home Secretary of 1910 (who had just sent troops to suppress rioting in South Wales mining villages) would one day invite the Bristol carter (who in 1910 had just joined the Dockers' Union) to become Minister of Labour and National Service when he formed his Coalition Government in 1940, still more so that in 1945 the same trade unionist should become Secretary of State for Foreign Affairs.

3

Throughout the 1900s, the trade unions had been on the defensive. Between 1900 and 1905, their membership had actually fallen. Now, in 1910–11, at the moment that Ernest Bevin joined a union for the first time, the trade union movement was to erupt in a new explosion of industrial militancy.

The last time this had happened had been in 1889, the year in which the Dock, Wharf, Riverside and General Workers' Union was formed. The creation of the union Bevin joined was one of the achievements of that outburst of socialist and trade-union activity which marked the later 1880s and culminated in the great London dock strike of 1889. This, the most famous strike of the nineteenth century, brought huge processions of the worst-paid workers in London, the 'dock-rats', through the streets of the city of London and, with the mediation of Cardinal Manning and Sydney Buxton, won the 'dockers' tanner'.

Of the three men who led the dock strike of 1889, two were engineers, John Burns and Tom Mann. The third, physically insignificant but possessed of a defiant spirit, the cheek of the devil and a voice of silver, was Ben Tillett who, in the twenty-one years since he had been put to work at the age of seven, had tried his hand at everything from pit boy and circus hand to the navy, the merchant marine and docking. In 1887, Tillett formed a Tea Operatives' and General Labourers' Union, the membership of which fluctuated between two thousand and three hundred, and most of the time was closer to the lower figure. In 1889, it was almost the only union active among the London dockers, whose casual conditions of labour, attracting the poorest type of unskilled labourer, had led every other union to write them off as incapable of organisation. Overnight, Tillett saw the membership of his obscure union leap to a figure of 30,000. He proved equal to the occasion, not only playing a leading part in the dock strike itself, but converting his union into the Dock, Wharf, Riverside and General Workers' Union with branches as far afield as Bristol and the South Wales ports.

In the course of 1889, the total union membership affiliated to the T.U.C.[1] was almost trebled, rising from half a million to a million and a half. The greater part of this increase represented casual and unskilled workers—dockers, gasworkers, building and general labourers who had hitherto been left unorganised by the craft unions. Tillett's was one of a number of new unions set up within a few months of each other. Amongst the others was the National Union of Gasworkers and General Labourers (Will Thorne's union), the original of the other big general union of today, the National Union of Municipal and General Workers, as Tillett's was to be of the Transport and General Workers.

All of them had certain characteristics in common, distinguishing them as a group from older unions like the Engineers' or the Iron-founders'. Their weekly contributions were low (sixpence a week in the case of Tillett's union) and ruled out any friendly society benefits other than a few pounds to pay for a member's funeral. Their obligations were limited to strike and lock-out pay. But this, they claimed, rid them of the danger of conservatism inherent in unions with large funds and prevented the 'corruption' of their militant spirit.

Once the first rush of enthusiasm was over, the new unions did not find it easy to keep up their numbers. The unskilled, casually employed labourer, shifting from one trade to another, provided unreliable material with which to build up a permanent organisation. This had been the fatal weakness of other short-lived labourers' unions in the past. Tillett, Thorne and the other leaders of the new unions found an answer by concentrating on one or two industries and localities in which they were able to build up the nucleus of a

1 Up to 1892 there are no reliable statistics for the membership of trade unions apart from those affiliated to the T.U.C.

stable membership. In the case of Tillett's union this was provided by the dockside workers in one or two ports and by the tinplate industry of South Wales; in the case of Thorne's by the gas and municipal workers. They remained general unions, however, as distinct from the craft unions, in their readiness to pick up other members where they could, not confining themselves to any one group of workers or to these particular industries.[1]

Chance played a big part in their recruitment. An energetic organiser like Bevin in Bristol could bring in carters, warehousemen and tobacco workers who elsewhere belonged to other unions or were left unorganised. Each of the general unions thus became a rather haphazard collection of scattered groups of workers with certain geographical and industrial strongholds which they defended against invasion by rival organisations.

In the 1890s, the Dock, Wharf, Riverside and General Workers' Union[2] had seen its membership drop sharply, from 40,000 at the beginning of the decade to a quarter of this figure at its end. By 1910 it had crept back to a figure of 18,240.

The stronghold of Tillett's union was the Bristol Channel. Of the 119 branches listed in the annual report for 1910, 67 were in South Wales, 12 in Bristol and Gloucester.[3] The dockers in Liverpool, Glasgow, Newcastle, and to a large extent in London and Hull, were organised by other unions or belonged to none at all.[4] The strongest group in Tillett's union had no connection with the docks at all but was employed in the tinplate trade of South Wales. The twenty-nine branches in the Tinplate Section contributed close on one fifth of the Union's total income, more than four times as much as the ten branches in the London docks. This foothold in the metal trades was of great value to the Dockers' Union, for it provided a

1 Cf. E. J. Hobsbawm: 'General Labour Unions in Britain, 1889–1914.' *Economic History Review*, 2nd series, Vol. 1. (1949), pp. 123–42; Hugh Clegg: *General Union* (1954), pp. 2–4.

2 Henceforward referred to as the Dockers', or Tillett's, Union.

3 These details are taken from the Union's annual reports. Its remaining 40 branches were scattered up and down the country from Middlesbrough to Southampton and contributed no more than £1,620 of the total branch income of £11,400.

4 In his report to the National Transport Workers' Federation in 1914, the Secretary reported that there were 16 unions providing for the various grades and classes of dock work which might in some ports (like Bristol) all be included within the ranks of one union. Even this did not take account of purely local unions.

nucleus of men who were much more regular in their employment—and in their union contributions—than the casual docker employed by the day.

Apart from the metal trades, the Union attracted most of its members from port industries: dockers, coal and grain porters; bargemen and lightermen; carters and warehousemen; oil-cake and flour millers. In none, however, did it enjoy more than a local monopoly. Of the 235 branches listed in the 1914 report, 109 were still on either side of the Bristol Channel—Bristol, Cardiff, Swansea, Port Talbot, Barry, Gloucester—although by then the Union had revived its organisation in London, extended to the West of England and trebled its numbers in the Midlands.[1] It had still only a handful of branches in the industrial North or on the north-east coast and was excluded not only from Liverpool, the stronghold of Sexton's rival dockers' union, but from Scotland as well.

4

Ben Tillett had been born in Bristol, his home was there and he and his wife (whose habit of knitting at Socialist meetings once led Ernest Bevin to compare her to Madame Dufarge in Dickens' *A Tale of Two Cities*) were both members of the Bristol Socialist Society. It was natural therefore that the Dockers' Union should have strong roots in Bristol. The district headquarters were in a house at No. 36 Prince Street, not far from the docks. Beside the district secretary, Harry Geater, there were three full-time officials, each of whom (including Bevin) received £2 a week.[2]

There was little office work in Bevin's job. Most of his time in Bristol was spent in and out of the docks and warehouses, in and out of working-class homes, pubs and coffee houses, recruiting new members, looking up the backsliders, investigating complaints of broken agreements, settling disputes about overtime, extra payment for a dirty cargo or the case of someone wrongfully dismissed. To do his job properly, he had to acquire a detailed knowledge of the maze

1 In 1914 the Dockers' Union had 47 branches in London, 17 in the west of England, 39 in the Midlands and 10 round Salford.

2 In 1911 the total full-time staff of the Union, in addition to the General Secretary (Ben Tillett) and two national organisers, amounted to eleven district secretaries and eight district investigators.

of working conditions and customs in the docks and other waterside trades; even more, he had to know how to handle men—an overbearing employer, a bullying foreman, or a disgruntled gang of dockers. He learned not only how to negotiate with employers but how to go back afterwards and persuade the men he represented to accept the agreement he had concluded.

He learned when to call an employer's bluff and threaten a strike, when to make concessions and settle for less, how to gauge the mood of a branch or an angry meeting on the docks, how to hit on the argument that would convince the men.

Bevin played the leading part in making Bristol a stronghold of the Dockers' Union, and his views of what could be done by skilful and persistent organising were ever afterwards coloured by the success he had obtained in Bristol. Elected to the Trades Council by the Dockers, he put new life into the trade-union movement throughout the city. One of his most stubborn fights was with the Bristol tramways company, which threatened its men with instant dismissal if they joined a trade union. When Bevin held a meeting on a Sunday morning, inspectors were stationed in the doorways along Broad Street to take the names of those attending.[1] Where other unions had tried and failed, Bevin refused to give up and in the end forced the tramway company to sign an agreement.

Although he had now to concern himself with all sides of the Union's work, he kept a special interest in the carters and was much in demand to settle their problems. There is still in existence the battered exercise book in which the carters' branch minutes were kept from September 1911 to October 1913. The meetings, except on special occasions, appear to have been no better attended in 1911–13 than trade-union meetings are today, yet nobody who turns these pages can fail to be impressed by the instinctive democracy of the Bristol carters' branch.

Disputes with the employers, fines against members for overloading or failing to maintain their union contributions, appeals to attend branch meetings more regularly—these made up the routine business of the committee, but occasionally the proceedings were enlivened by a lecture or speech. A report of one such occasion (2nd December 1911) is worth quoting in the idiomatic original without amplification of the pencilled minutes:

1 Letter to the author from D. S. Morris, a former tram conductor in Bristol.

31

"The meeting was then honoured with a speech from our General Secretary [Ben Tillett]. We must have confidence in our leaders. Just think of our position. Hated by the employers. It was all right when on the winning side, but when we lost it was different. He said, 'Employers don't like Ben. I'm out to bleed them, with the men solid behind me. I can do it, you are the masters of the situation, realise your own strength in this great Labour movement. What can be done? Look what has been done. We are out for the full product of our labour, to fight Capital and Capitalists, they are out for cheap labour, let us realise this fight. Have a sense of our real strength. I am prepared to take my corner, you must take yours. Organisation will win. Don't tie our hands when we have them in employers' pockets, they don't like Trade Unions or Agitators. Be Brothers, love each other and work for our splendid movement'."

This was Tillett in characteristic vein, lighting up the crowded, smoke-filled room with his flamboyant personality, the Tillett who next year was to tell a mass meeting of dockers on Tower Hill to take off their hats and pray to God to strike the Chairman of the Port of London Authority, Lord Devonport, dead. Bevin, already distrustful of Tillett's volatility and flights of rhetoric, was more sombre and down-to-earth, but he was beginning to establish his authority. A dock strike in June 1912 put it to the test.

The carters, called out in support of the dockers, only partially responded to the Union's call and a branch meeting was summoned in the Kingsley Hall on 12th June to reach a decision—all out or all back. Bevin was not present but the men who had built up the branch with him, Dan Hillman, Arthur Dickenson and Jim Garmston, spoke out frankly.

"There was a time," Garmston told the meeting, "when you would carry Bro. Bevin on your shoulders and do almost anything for him, but now there seems to be a split in the camp. This meeting was called to do away with that split and get you men to show the same combination now as you did before. . . . If the constitution of the Union is wrong, it is up to you to put it right."

A resolution was carried in favour of an immediate and complete withdrawal of labour. But this did not settle the matter and ten days later another meeting was held in the Kingsley Hall at which the Secretary of the Master Carters' Association put the case for the carters forming a separate union and Bevin put the case for their remaining with the Dockers'. After questions had been put to both speakers, the independent chairman, a local city councillor, ordered ballot papers to be distributed and explained the question to be settled. The result was 391 in favour of remaining with the Dockers' Union, 16 against. "Councillor Burt then announced the result amidst terrific applause which was continued for many minutes and calls for Cheers for Bro. Bevin and the Dockers' Union were repeatedly asked for."

5

Bevin kept his home in Bristol and continued to play a principal part in the district affairs of the Dockers' Union until after the war. But, as early as 1911, Tillett and Harry Orbell, the Union's national organiser, began to use his gifts in a wider area. Throughout the years 1911–14, Bevin spent a great deal of time across the Bristol Channel in South Wales and travelling up and down the West Country as far west as Penzance, as far east as Southampton.

In 1911 he was sent to help organise the eastern district of South Wales—Cardiff, Newport, Barry and Penarth. South Wales was one of the black spots of industrial Britain. Not only were working-class conditions, especially in the mining villages, among the worst in the country, but the relations between masters and men were conducted with great bitterness on both sides. The Shipping Federation met the threat of strikes with the importation of blackleg labour and, when this led to trouble with the men, demanded police reinforcements and the despatch of troops. Violence and rioting were commonplace between 1910 and 1913 and troops were brought into the area on a number of occasions to hold down an industrial population which appeared to be on the edge of revolt.

For these were years in which labour unrest broke out on a scale which had not been seen in Britain before, certainly not since the 1830s and 1840s. The fundamental cause appears to have been the failure of wages to keep pace with the rise of prices and profits after 1900. Between 1900 and 1909 the average number of working days lost each year through strikes and lock-outs had averaged three and a half million. In 1910, however, the figure shot up to twelve million and in 1912 to over thirty-eight million. Miners, railwaymen, seamen, dockers and carters were all involved. At one time or another in 1911 and 1912, every port, every coalfield and every railway in the country was out on strike.

The trade unions, rapidly increasing their numbers, threw over the defensive attitude of the 1900s for militant and highly class-conscious policies. The parliamentary reformism of the Labour Party, collective bargaining and the cautious building up of trade-union reserves were abandoned for the slogans of syndicalism[1] and the class war—'Direct Action', the general strike, the use of industrial power for revolutionary purposes and the overthrow of the capitalist system. If the new ideas and the new slogans did not produce the unrest, they fitted well with the angry mood which was taking hold of large sections of the working class in these years.

The Dockers' Union was in the thick of the fight. During 1911 alone its membership trebled, rising from 18,000 to 55,000. In London, Tillett was one of the leaders in the dock strike which brought the trade of the world's biggest port to a standstill in 1911 and again in 1912. He took the initiative in setting up the National Transport Workers' Federation, an attempt to establish joint action between the different ports and different unions. After Tom Mann, the apostle of revolutionary syndicalism, Tillett was the best known mob orator in the country. He summed up his views in his annual report to the Union for 1912:

"The sequence of events in 1912 followed the usual course: claims for increases and recognition followed by refusal and consequent strikes; efforts of mediation, negotiations, conciliation; Board of Trade effort, police intimidation, coercion, brutality, riot, imprisonment; Home Secretary inter-

1 Syndicalism is the doctrine of revolution by industrial action. The object of trade unions, in the eyes of syndicalist leaders like the American Daniel De Leon, who founded the Industrial Workers of the World, was the organisation of a general strike as the means of seizing power in the State. With this in mind, the syndicalists advocated the organisation of the trade unions on the principle that all the workers in the same industry (e.g. the railways or the building industry) should be brought into a single union, or that there should be 'One Big Union' divided into industrial sections, one for each industry. This principle of organisation, known as 'industrial unionism', would, they believed, be the most effective for paralysing the State by strikes. Once the revolution had taken place the ownership and control of each industry were to be placed in the hands of the workers employed in it. The State itself was to be run by the 'One Big Union' or by a federation of industrial unions. Syndicalism had a considerable influence on the trade-union movement in Great Britain in the years immediately before and after the first World War. Its slogans; 'Direct Action', 'the general strike' and 'industrial unionism' were much in use and, if not always well understood by those who used them, carried revolutionary overtones.

venes with armed forces, attempts at suppression, Cossack methods of the Home Office forces, Parliament dumb and acquiescent, Labour Party impotent where not indifferent, struggle and end of same, in some cases with industrial gains.

"The class war is the most brutal of wars and the most pitiless. The lesson is that, in future strikes, the strikers must protect against the use of arms, with arms; protest against shooting, with shooting; protest against violence, with violence. . . . The other lesson is that Parliament is a farce and a sham, the rich man's Duma, the employer's Tammany, the Thieves' Kitchen and the working man's despot. . . In the 1912 strikes we had to fight Parliament, the forces of the Crown, the judges of the law. . . We had the press of both parties and the capitalists against us; the police were incensed by the employers and rewarded for every act of violence, the imported police as usual being the worst of the brutes. . . . Capitalism is capitalism as a tiger is a tiger; and both are savage and pitiless towards the weak."[1]

No part of the country was more stirred by the wave of unrest than South Wales, and both sides pursued their quarrel with a violence Bevin had not met before. There was no question of getting masters and men together round a table, as he had done in Bristol. He was up against employers who refused to recognise the unions, who were willing to pay high wages to strike-breakers and who made no bones about using the weapons of starvation and victimisation to enforce surrender. He saw police, troops and the courts flagrantly employed in the interests of one side and had to listen to threats to stop his mouth if he did not leave the district.

The threats did not come from one side only. There was suspicion towards a 'foreigner' from Bristol on the men's side as well. Three other unions competed in the organisation of labour in the South Wales ports, each claiming the exclusive right to represent this or that section of the dock workers. Bevin had to learn to hold his own against rival unions ready to use any trick to down him from charges of blacklegging to breaking up his meetings.

In 1911, the waterfront unions forced the employers to make substantial concessions in most of the major ports. In Cardiff the port was brought to a standstill in July. Several hundred police and detachments of the Royal Lancashire Fusiliers were brought in to keep order, and the Lord Mayor had to intervene to secure a settlement. In 1912, however, the Transport Workers' Federation failed to bring off a national strike in support of a second London stoppage

1 D.W.R. and G.W.U.: Annual Report, 1912, pp. 5–9.

and suffered a heavy defeat. There was much recrimination between the unions, and the employers began to hit back, blacklisting any man who had been active in the struggle. Victimisation was accompanied by a falling off in union membership. The sharp fluctuations in numbers, doubled one month, halved the next, showed up the weakness of the general labourers' unions.

It was slow work building up the local organisation again in the aftermath of the defeat but, by the end of 1913, Bevin had more than recovered the ground lost. In the report of the Dockers' Union for the year the three districts, Cardiff, Barry and Newport, returned an income of £5,500 against £3,500 two years before. He had overcome hostility as well as apathy, and at the end of 1913 the members of the Cardiff district "signified their appreciation of the services rendered by presenting Bro. Bevin with a gold watch and chain."

He was now, however, spending more time down in the southwest. In Somerset, Devon and Cornwall, a trade-union movement scarcely existed. There was no big industrial centre and only one big town, Plymouth, west of Bristol. Such industry as was to be found there was small-scale, local brickworks or quarries, small shipbuilding yards and decaying ports like Fowey or Falmouth. It was a new experience, very different from the conditions he had known in Bristol or South Wales, yet equally valuable training. Here he had to do the work of a pioneer, finding in each town a handful of men willing to run the risk of losing their jobs by joining a trade union and sufficiently resolute to carry on in isolation from the main movement.

Born and bred in the West Country, Bevin enjoyed advantages he had lacked in Wales, but he had an uphill struggle to establish any permanent organisation. In July 1913, the Plymouth district numbered only five branches, with no more than five hundred members in all. By the end of 1914, however, the number of branches in the Plymouth district had been doubled and another seven added in Somerset, seventeen altogether where there had been only three in 1911 and none in 1910.

His greatest success was at Bridgwater, where he enrolled a considerable membership from the brick, timber and coal yards. When George Lansbury spoke in Bridgwater Town Hall in March 1914, the local correspondent of the *Dockers' Record* wrote in a burst of enthusiasm: "To listen to a thousand men and women singing

Labour hymns in this antiquated town seems as though the revolution has already begun". That year membership of the
Bridgwater branch reached 2,500 and most of them turned out for
the May Day procession when the Town Hall was not big enough to
seat the audience gathered to hear Brother Bevin who, we are
assured by the same correspondent, was "in splendid form".

During the course of 1913, Bevin was transferred from the staff of
the Bristol district to work as an assistant organiser under the head
office. At the end of March 1914, on the death of Harry Orbell, he
took his place as one of the three national organisers. His principal
responsibility remained the South-west, but he had now, within
three years of his original appointment, become one of the half-
dozen men at the head of his union.

6

The fact that he served his apprenticeship in the trade-union movement between 1910 and 1914, when industrial conflict was suddenly
intensified, and that he served at least part of it in South Wales,
where the class war and inter-union rivalries were at their sharpest,
left its mark on Bevin. He had been set to learn in a rough school
and the experience toughened his character. It had also deepened
his hostility to the economic and social system under which he lived:
he hated its exploitation, its injustice and its inequality. But the cast
of his mind was practical rather than revolutionary or utopian.
Instinctively he turned to organisation rather than agitation: even
the Revolution would have to be organised.

He had no illusions about the employers: they would only listen to
working-class demands when they were backed by organised power.
But he had no illusions about his own side either: he had seen how
easily ignorance, envy and suspicion could obscure common
interests, how much energy the trade unions spent in fighting each
other. The working-class movement, for all its militant talk, would
only become powerful when it had overcome the conflicts of interest
within its own ranks.

The port strikes of 1911 had shown the strength the waterfront
workers could exercise when they acted together. But unity in 1911
had been due more to spontaneous action in a dozen different ports

than to organisation. The failure to bring about a national dock strike in 1912 showed equally clearly the incapacity of the movement for sustained action. Impressive as the strikes of these years were, they were bound to exhaust themselves in frustration unless the revolt which they represented could be canalised into more effective and permanent forms of organisation.

The first attempts to overcome this disunity coincided with Bevin's entry into the Dockers' Union. The initiative came from Tillett who, in July 1910, addressed a letter in the name of his executive committee to a number of other unions, inviting them to join in discussions designed to bring some order into the chaotic world of port labour. These discussions were the origin of the National Transport Workers' Federation,[1] hurriedly established in time to provide a strike committee for the conduct of the London dock strike of 1911.

The membership of the Federation alone is sufficient evidence of the divisions which it was designed to remove. In June 1913, when Ernest Bevin first attended its Annual General Council Meeting in Newport Town Hall, there were representatives of the following eighteen unions present:

Amalgamated General & Warehouse Workers' Union
Amalgamated Protective Union of Engine & Crane Drivers
Amalgamated Stevedores' Labour Protection League
Amalgamated Society of Watermen, Lightermen & Bargemen
Dock, Wharf, Riverside & General Workers' Union
Gasworkers' and General Labourers' Union
Hull Seamen & Marine Firemen's Association
Liverpool (South End) Coalbearers' Association
National Union of Vehicle Workers
Mersey Tug & Railway Carters' Union
National Amalgamated Labourers' Union
National Amalgamated Union of Enginemen & Firemen
National Amalgamated Union of Labour
National Sailors' and Firemens' Union
National Union of Dock, Riverside and General Workers
National Union of Ships' Stewards, Cooks, Butchers & Bakers
Scottish Union of Dock Labourers
United Carters' Association of England

Another eight unions belonged to the Federation but were too small to be represented at its annual conference. Altogether a

1 Referred to henceforward as the N.T.W.F. or the Federation.

membership of 150,000 men was affiliated and the N.T.W.F. was itself a member of the International Transport Workers' Federation with headquarters in Berlin. The Federation had been nominally responsible for the conduct of the London dock strikes of 1911 and 1912 and its secretary, Bob Williams, an ex-coal trimmer from Cardiff, whose left-wing views frequently embarrassed his committee, could claim to speak on behalf of the majority of transport workers (apart from the railwaymen) throughout the whole country. In practice, however, none of the unions surrendered any of their autonomy, some of them were bitter rivals and a great part of the committee's time was taken up with recriminations between the constituent members.

At the Newport meeting a resolution calling on the Executive Council to prepare a scheme for the complete amalgamation into a single union of all the separate unions affiliated to the Federation was carried with acclamation. The debate, however, revealed some of the difficulties that stood in the way. Representatives of the dockers and the seamen expressed their fear that, if all sections of the unions affiliated to the Federation were brought into the proposed amalgamation, without regard to the trades they followed, labourers out of a job who belonged to one of the general unions (Thorne's Gasworkers were the obvious example) would then be able to come down to the docks and use their Federation 'ticket' to get work, putting genuine dockers and seamen out of employment. This was long a source of dissension in the N.T.W.F.

The logical conclusion, of course, was an amalgamation of dockers only. This however was opposed by Tillett and Will Thorne, who organised other trades as well as the docks and feared that a transport amalgamation by itself would break off their transport sections and split their unions. In fact, one of the strongest arguments for amalgamation, as opposed to federation, was that only when the different unions merged their separate identities and formed a single union would the sectionalism represented by the dispute over the Federation 'ticket' disappear.

7

One suggestion made at Newport was joint action with the General Labourers' National Council, a body similar to the N.T.W.F. which had been set up in 1908 and to which the more important unions, like Tillett's Dockers and Thorne's Gasworkers, were affiliated as well as to the N.T.W.F. Bevin, as the representative of the Dockers' Union on the General Labourers' Council, attended a conference of the two bodies held at the Compositors' Hall, St. Bride Street, London, in December 1913. He spoke strongly in favour of "all in" amalgamation and used the example of Bristol to argue that the difficulties feared were more imaginary than real.

In fact, by 1st July 1914, a scheme for amalgamation had been drafted and was presented to a second conference called by the Federation and the General Labourers' Council at Caxton Hall on 8th July. Thirty unions were represented, including six not affiliated to either body. The conference was enlivened by the appearance of the two redoubtable leaders of the Irish Transport Workers' Union in the bitter Dublin strike of 1913, Jim Larkin and James Connolly.

When Clause 1 of the scheme was read out—"That the whole of the members contained in all the unions affiliated to both bodies, together with any other unions of a similar kind, be merged into one consolidated Union of Labour"—twenty-six unions voted for it, only two opposed and two remained undecided. Clause 7 provided for the establishment of "district and departmental sections, allowing full free play of initiative and autonomy, consistent with the powers of financial control exercised by the Central Executive", foreshadowing the structure Bevin was to provide for the eventual amalgamation into the Transport and General Workers' Union after the first World War.

There was all the difference in the world, as Bevin pointed out, between a single union articulated into different sections, and a federation in which there were separate unions for dockers, for carters, for seamen, for coal trimmers and all the other trades.

"I happen to be where the dockers and carters are in one union (in Bristol) and there the carters have been more successful than in any other town in the country in relation to the conditions they were under before. . . . I say it is the consciousness on the part of the employer, the whole time that he is negotiating with the coal trimmer, the docker, the carter or the seaman, that they have a central executive behind them representing the co-operation of their fellows in the same organisation, that gives the power to negotiate. It is not so much that it means a power to attack, as a power to negotiate, and that power to negotiate is the most valuable thing that we can have. Where there is practically one union covering all transport and the bulk of the general labourers' unions in one town, what is the first thing the employers ask? It is 'Will you all strike together?'[1]

This speech is worth noticing for two reasons. It demonstrates the continuity in Bevin's mind between his experience in Bristol, where the Dockers' Union was in the fortunate but unusual position of organising dockers, carters and general workers alike in a single society, and the arguments he was to employ in 1921–2 in favour of an amalgamated union covering the same groups on a national basis. At the same time, it underlines his preoccupation with the practical problem of organisation—unity to give "not so much a power to attack, as a power to negotiate . . . the most valuable thing that we can have"—as distinct from those who put in the forefront the syndicalist argument in favour of trade-union unity, the general strike as a means to the revolutionary seizure of power.

The result of the conference was an overwhelming majority in favour of the amalgamation scheme, and a committee of six was appointed to draw up the rules and call a further conference in a month's time. Within the month, however, war had broken out and the scheme was shelved.

The outbreak of war also postponed the most ambitious proposal to come out of the industrial unrest of these years, the Triple Industrial Alliance. The initiative in this case came from the miners during the strike of 1912, the first coal strike on a national scale in the history of the country. Its aim was neither amalgamation nor even federation but agreement on common action and mutual support between the Miners' Federation, the newly founded National Union of Railwaymen and the Transport Workers' Federation, representing between them over a million men.

The later history of the Triple Alliance was to show fatal weaknesses in its structure, but potentially it was the most serious threat

1 General Labourers' National Council and N.T.W.F.: Special Conference on Amalgamation, Caxton Hall, Westminster, 8th July 1914, pp. 22–23.

projected by the militant section of the trade unions before the General Strike of 1926. Ernest Bevin took no part in the preliminary discussions, which were still incomplete when the war broke out, but he was later to play a leading role in the Alliance and he joined with the other members of the N.T.W.F. in endorsing the acceptance of the miners' invitation in 1914.

8

The Federation's annual meeting at Hull had been immediately preceded by the Triennial Delegate Conference of the Dockers' Union, held in the newly opened Dockers' Hall at Swansea at the beginning of June 1914.

In his report, Tillett was able to point to a considerable expansion of the Union's strength, which now numbered 43,000. He was highly critical of the Labour Party and attacked its timidity in the House of Commons. The lesson of the last three years, Tillett argued, was the continued need for industrial mass action, whether called by syndicalism or any other name. "New names have an attraction, but so far we have depended upon mass action for most of the success we have wrought. Anything which condemns sectionalism should be welcomed by us." For this reason, he put great hopes in the scheme for amalgamation and strongly commended it to the delegates.[1]

Bevin himself had little to say at the conference. This was his first appearance as national organiser: when the previous conference had been held in 1911, he had not even been a delegate. After five days' work, much of it devoted to revision of the Union's rules, visits to the Mumbles and lunch with the mayor and corporation, the conference broke up with that odd combination of traditional sentimentality and revolutionary sentiment which, even then, was characteristic of the British Labour Movement:

"The delegates clasped hands and joined in singing 'Auld Lang Syne', after which were given three ringing cheers for the Social Revolution. The chairman then declared the meeting closed."

1 D.W.R. and G.W.U.: Minutes of the Triennial Delegate Meeting, Swansea, 2nd–6th June 1914, pp. 10–16

Neither at the Union's delegate conference nor at the Federation's meeting in Hull, was a word said about the international situation or the possibility of war. At Hull, Hermann Jochade was present as a fraternal delegate from the German Transport Workers' Union and was warmly welcomed. Even the denunciation of secret diplomacy and militarism which was to become so familiar a feature of Labour and trade-union conferences was missing. Like the rest of the British people, the trade unions were absorbed in their own affairs when the war came suddenly upon them in the summer of 1914. Far more than any of the schemes they were then discussing, however, it was to prove a decisive chapter in their development.

CHAPTER 3

War and the Transport
Workers' Federation
1914 — 1917

I

THE GREATEST AGENT of social change in twentieth-century
Britain has been war. It was the impact of the two wars with
Germany which did more than anything else to transform Edwardian England into the very different society of the late 1940s.
The chief beneficiaries of that change have been the working classes
and it was upon the impulse of this double tide that Ernest Bevin
rose to the most powerful position ever occupied by a working-class
leader in this country.

The effect of the second World War upon his career is too obvious
to need arguing. His appointment as Minister of Labour in the
Churchill coalition and the power which he exercised in that office
are among the most striking proofs of the changed status of the trade-
union movement. But the first World War marks no less decisive a
stage in trade-union history. For the first time, the unions were
taken into partnership by the State; their leaders (a short time before
denounced as agitators) were invited to join the Cabinet and
brought on to one committee after another. This was far from being
pure gain at the time, for it subjected the trade-union movement to
severe strain, especially in the relations between leaders and rank
and file. But what counted in the long run was the new position
which the unions acquired in the economy and politics of the
country, a position which the subsequent setbacks of the 1920s and
the Depression weakened, but could not destroy.

Thus, at the time when Bevin's abilities were beginning to win recognition, the scope of activity open to him was transformed, the scale of opportunity enlarged to proportions which promised to draw out, not frustrate, the powers he possessed.

2

The threat of war, suddenly blowing up in July 1914, took the Labour movement by surprise. The first reaction was one of angry protest and many Labour supporters joined the Radical wing of the Liberal Party in demanding that Britain should stay out and follow a policy of neutrality. On that first week-end of August, while the question was still undecided, there were demonstrations against war in Trafalgar Square and up and down the country. Among the speakers on the Bristol Downs was the young Ernest Bevin, calling for action by the workers in all countries to prevent war. Some months before he had spoken in support of a resolution urging all members of the International Federation of Trade Unions to proclaim an international general strike if hostilities appeared likely to break out. But any hopes of international action soon faded and in Britain, as in the case of the other belligerents, once the country was at war the overwhelming majority of the working class, whether politically conscious or not, rallied to the national cause. Ramsay MacDonald resigned the leadership of the Labour Party rather than support a war for which he believed the British Government to bear as much responsibility as any other, but his view was accepted by only a small minority in the Party, most of them members of the I.L.P., and indignantly repudiated by the majority.

The trade-union movement met the outbreak of war in an impulsive mood of patriotism. Hundreds of thousands of working men enlisted and the Joint Board (representing the T.U.C., the Labour Party and the General Federation of Trade Unions) renounced the use of the unions' bargaining power by proclaiming an industrial as well as a political truce. Considering the bitterness of the industrial conflict in the years before the war and the plans for combined strike action by the Triple Alliance in the autumn of 1914, this was an impressive gesture of solidarity.

At the Treasury Conferences of March 1915, Lloyd George proposed and most of the trade-union leaders accepted drastic innovations in the interest of greater production. For the duration of the war, the unions agreed that there should be no strikes; that where a dispute could not be settled by negotiation it should be referred to compulsory arbitration and that the network of trade practice built up by the unions to protect conditions of work should be relaxed to permit longer hours and overtime as well as the introduction of un-skilled and women workers. In return, the union leaders accepted the assurance of the Government that these concessions on their part would not impair their position after the war and that conditions would be fully restored at its end.

A few months after the Treasury Agreement had been concluded, the Government went a step further and introduced a system of compulsory arbitration (Munitions of War Act) which was rapidly extended to cover all essential industries and four-fifths of the working class. This too was accepted by the trade-union leaders despite their misgivings. At the same time, the Labour Party agreed to take its place in the coalition formed by Asquith (June 1915) and, even after Arthur Henderson's resignation in 1917, remained officially a partner in the wartime government down to November 1918.

Government, trade unions and employers alike, however, entered the war with no conception of the demands which it would make on manpower and industrial production. The Government was reluctant to accept the responsibility for organising the national economy, especially where this meant interfering with the 'rights' of private enterprise. Only slowly and painfully did it acquire the experience to enable it to do so effectively. It was many months before anything like the full industrial resources of the country were mobilised, months in which profiteering flourished, prices rose, confusion and waste were widespread.

This state of affairs put a considerable strain on working-class loyalty. Union officials used their influence for the greater part of the war to prevent or at least to limit stoppages of work. Strikes were fewer than might have been expected, and the majority of them unofficial. Compulsory arbitration, though disliked, was made to work and the wage awards of the Committee on Production generally accepted. Opposition to the speeding-up of work was overcome and large numbers of unskilled men and women workers allowed to take the place of skilled men. Even conscription, to which both unions and Labour Party showed strong opposition, was finally accepted. But the cumulative effect began to tell as the war dragged on. Distrust of the Government spread and with it the belief that the working class was being asked to make sacrifices not equally borne by the employers and other classes of the community. From the summer of 1917, labour unrest mounted sharply, though still pent up, and there was a marked shift in the weight of Labour opinion after Arthur Henderson's resignation from the Cabinet in August 1917.

3

Ernest Bevin's own attitude to the war did not fit into this general pattern. He was never a 'Jingo' as many of the other trade-union leaders became. He remained sceptical about the origins and the justification of the war. At the Bristol Trade Union Congress of 1915 when the vote showed a big majority in support of Labour's participation in the recruiting drive as well as in the wartime coalition, the first speech which he ever made at a trade union congress cut across the lines of the debate. Unlike the two other dockers' leaders, Ben Tillett and James Sexton, who vied with each other in patriotic outbursts against 'the Hun', Bevin said:

"What I want to get from the representatives of the Labour Party is some indication of the exact position they found themselves in at the outbreak of war. During the discussion of this war business we have heard a lot about atrocities, Prussian militarism and all the rest of it but those facts did not help the Labour Party to its decision when the war broke out, because they had not then taken place. I can quite understand my colleague Tillett, sensitive to suffering as he is, coming back from France obsessed with the sights he saw there, but if he had gone to Silesia or other places on the Eastern Front he might have been making the same speeches against Russia.

"From the Pacifists' point of view, I want to know what reply was given to the Pacifists in the conference room of the Labour Party. I do not take any notice of what Mr. Ramsay MacDonald on the one hand, or Mr. John Hodge on the other, may say. I want to know what happened when the Labour Party was called upon to make its decision. What, for instance, was the alternative to recruiting which Mr. MacDonald advanced? Was it conscription?

"Personally I decline to cast another vote in this business until I know what really happened. I want to know why they supported the foreign policy of the Government. Was it because they thought that Sir Edward Grey had done all that was possible that they agreed to join hands with the Government in this way, or was it because they felt that, if they did not take their share in the national defence, they would be handing the people over to the capitalist class of this country? I hope the representatives of the Labour Party will not indulge in mere rhetoric but will give us the actual facts in answering these questions."[1]

Bevin's doubts were deepened, not removed, during the course of the war. If he had been critical of Henderson's acceptance of Asquith's invitation to join the Government in 1915, he was openly opposed to Labour joining the coalition which Lloyd George formed in December 1916. His distrust of Lloyd George was intense. He believed none of his promises and was convinced that he would go back on them all once the war was over. On the other hand, Bevin would have nothing to do with the I.L.P. and pacifist minority in the Labour Party which opposed the war. He never concealed his contempt for Ramsay MacDonald and Philip Snowden, and he took no part in any of the left-wing protests.

A speech which he made at the Annual general Council of the Transport Workers' Federation in June 1917 sheds some light on the reasons for this attitude. Bob Williams, the secretary of the Federation, was under censure for his political activity in opposing the war. Bevin urged Williams' critics not to press their motion:

"I largely agree with Williams. He knows that. I objected to the foreign policy of this country for many years before the war. I regarded the Russian alliance as likely to lead to war. I did not change that view when it did lead to war. It came to this: when the psychology of two forms of organisation clashed I had to ask myself the question, what was to be my attitude. Tillett and I had some discussion and I came to the conclusion that I would do my best to preserve the economic unity of the men I represent and accept passively the opinions of the majority of men."[2]

In other words, given the attitude of the majority of trade unionists, Bevin believed it more important to concentrate on the defence of working-class interests than to risk splitting the movement by political action in opposition to the war.

If it was objected that this was to fall into what Lenin called the

[1] T.U.C. Report, 1915, p. 337.
[2] N.T.W.F.: Report of the 7th Annual General Council Meeting, 14th–15th June 1917, pp. 25–44

Unloading ships at the Avonmouth Docks (1910).

Strike-leaders of 1911: Ben Tillett on Tower Hill, *right*, and J. H. Thomas, *below*.

fallacy of 'Economism' and see the needs of the working-class movement in narrow terms of wages and hours, Bevin would have retorted that the only chance the working class had of making its political views effective was through the exercise of its industrial power. As he told the conference called by the Triple Alliance a week after the Federation Council meeting:

"There is only one language the present governing class understand. It is only power they will yield to, and that is the power of organised labour in its economic capacity. It is said I blow hot and cold on the war. I do not. What I am after all the time is that the only safe organisation, the only safe weapon for the workers—slow as it is at times—is that trade union form of organisation which has stood the test every time."[1]

In the long run, as these remarks show, Bevin was fully alive to the need to use the economic power of the unions for political ends, but he did not believe in acting prematurely. He had no use for the left-wing shop-stewards' movement, which captured the Labour leadership on Clydeside and organised a number of unofficial strikes. Such a movement, directed as much against the official leadership of the trade unions as against the Government and the employers, only weakened the organisation of working-class power by splitting it. It was sounder tactics, in Bevin's view, to hold back until you could carry the majority with you and build up for the decisive trial of strength which, he was convinced, would come at the end of the war.

4

In the meantime there was a host of practical problems to be dealt with in his work as a union organiser. The concessions agreed to in the interests of greater production were all very well, but they were far from easy to put into operation in the varying circumstances of a hundred different trades and localities. Travelling to and fro between South Wales, Bristol and the West of England, Bevin spent a great deal of his time settling disputes over wages, piece rates, hours and conditions of work, the introduction of new machinery and the recruitment of unskilled labour to take the place of the

1 Proceedings of the Special Conference of the Triple Industrial Alliance, 21st June 1917.

C

dockers, carters and other workers who had joined the Forces. He was in and out of meetings all the week, arguing the men's case for a war-bonus before an arbitration tribunal, arguing with the men to persuade them to accept the tribunal's award. He was highly critical of the Government's failure to organise transport effectively, but this did not prevent him, in face of the difficulties created by stubborn employers and suspicious, ignorant men, from working hard to prevent disputes turning into strikes, to keep the flow of goods and munitions moving through the ports. All the time, he had to see that the Union's branch organisation was kept up in his area, that the Union recruited new workers brought in by the war and broke fresh ground in unorganised industries.

Most of his work still lay in the west, with occasional visits to the Dockers' head office in London, to the quarterly meetings of the Executive or to argue a case for higher wages before the Committee on Production. During 1916, these visits became more frequent, as he began to play a part in the national affairs of the trade-union movement. But, even when he spent the week from Monday to Friday in London, his home was still in Bristol and he put a great deal of energy into making this the strongest district in the Dockers' Union.

Early in September 1915, the Trades Union Congress met in Bristol, its first meeting for two years. Six hundred delegates crowded into the Association Hall, amongst them for the first time Ernest Bevin, as one of the Dockers' delegates. Apart from Tillett, who was a national figure, the Dockers' Union carried no great weight and was relegated to the gallery, leaving the floor to the miners, the railwaymen and the older craft unions like the engineers.

Sitting up in the public gallery was Beatrice Webb, the disdainful, sharp-eyed and even sharper-tongued historian of the trade-union movement. Under the date 9th September, she wrote in her diary:

"The leading men have grown fatter in body and even more dully complacent in mind than they were twenty years ago; the delegates have lost their keenness, the rebels of today don't get elected to Congress and the 'old hands' know, from long experience, that it is more of an 'outing' than a gathering for the transaction of working-class affairs. What the delegates enjoy is a joke. . . . Indignation, righteous or unrighteous, is felt to be out of place. There is no anti-Government feeling, no determination to get evils righted. . . . The absence of intellectual leadership or consciousness of a common policy is really deplorable. The same old hackneyed sectional resolutions are languidly discussed and mechanically passed; and, in so far as there is any feeling, it is reserved for jealousy between leaders or for the disputes between rival unions."[1]

Ernest Bevin would hardly have disagreed with this disillusioned picture of his first T.U.C. He felt little respect for the older union leaders who composed the Parliamentary Committee (the forerunner of the General Council) and his maiden speech (quoted above) was sharply out of key with the conventional patriotism of the platform's contribution to the debates on the war.

The highlight of the conference was the visit of Lloyd George, now Minister of Munitions and the driving force behind the increased war effort. It was the first time a leading Cabinet Minister had ever thought it worth while to come down and appeal to the T.U.C. Beatrice Webb was sitting close behind Lloyd George:

"The floor, the galleries and the platform were packed and the heat was suffocating. . . . We could watch every gesture and every expression of his mobile face. He looked exactly like a conjuror and one expected him to say: 'No deception, gentlemen, there is nothing up my sleeve, you can see for yourself.' The audience, after giving him a great reception, settled down to be amused and flattered. But his speech left a bad impression: it lacked sincerity. He told obvious little lies and his tale of working-class slackness and drink was much resented. There was a curious strain of contempt underlying his pleasant banter and specious statement."[2]

Bevin, always suspicious of Lloyd George, was on his feet as soon as the applause had subsided, to ask whether he did not think that the workmen in the skilled trades would alter their regulations with more confidence if they were given a share in management. Lloyd George returned an evasive answer and after two or three more questions the session ended.

It was not until the Saturday morning, with half the delegates already leaving and Congress going through the rest of the agenda at a jog-trot, that Ernest Bevin was able to move his first resolution at a Trades Union Congress. The motion was to prove oddly appropriate: the man who was to make his reputation as a great Minister of Labour in the second World War stood up to move that

1 Beatrice Webb: *Diaries* 1912–1924 (1952), pp. 43–44.
2 Ibid., p. 44.

the Government should be called upon to appoint a Minister of Labour for the first time, with full Cabinet rank. He set out the main functions such a minister should discharge. "Many of the resolutions passed at this Congress," he declared to a rapidly emptying hall, "cannot be dealt with until after the war, but I suggest that the new conditions forced upon Labour make it imperative that this Ministry of Labour should be set up immediately." The later history of the war was fully to vindicate this view.

But the most exciting news for Bevin was his election as one of the T.U.C's two fraternal delegates to the annual convention of the American Federation of Labour. Normally this was much sought after, and a young, little-known delegate would have had no chance of being chosen. But the U-boat attacks (the sinking of the *Lusitania* had taken place in May) robbed most delegates of their enthusiasm for a visit to the U.S.A. and a hasty search had to be made for nominations for the second place. Bevin jumped at the chance and received double the votes of the next man. A month later, on 12th October, he left Liverpool in the company of Charlie Amman, of the Post Office Workers, on the S.S. *Orduna*: it was his first journey abroad.

5

The crossing was uneventful and ten days after leaving Liverpool they arrived in New York. Taken in hand by the American Federation of Labour, they were shown the sights (including Grant's tomb and Grand Central Station) before being hurried down to Washington for the ceremony to mark a start on the A.F.L.'s new eight-storey headquarters. This made a deep impression on Bevin. "In all Britain," he wrote home, "even in London itself, there is no building worthy of so great a movement as that of the organised workers." His imagination was kindled: within ten years he had begun the building of Transport House, designed to house under one roof not only his own transport union but the T.U.C. and the Labour Party as well.

From Washington, at the end of October, they set out on the five-day rail journey to San Francisco. They broke the journey at Denver, high up on the eastern flank of the Rockies, and again at

Salt Lake City. A brief visit to the Garden of the Gods and the Cave of the Winds in Colorado left Bevin amazed at their beauty (he sent off a folding picture postcard to his friends in Bristol) and he marvelled at the toughness of the pioneers.

"These must have been," he wrote, "the rebels and the dreamers of the old countries who went out into the wilderness to express what they were unable to do in their own countries. . . . These men who weathered the storms, planned those cities, tracked through the Rockies to the Pacific Coast and laid the foundations of civilisation, present themselves to me greater than those whose names are inscribed on the roll of fame."[1]

San Francisco and the Golden Gate swept him away as they have so many other visitors. An international exhibition to celebrate the opening of the Panama Canal was being held and, with something of the country lad still about him, he wandered fascinated through its grounds and pavilions.

The A.F.L. convention was opened by the Governor of California on 8th November. Bevin was keenly interested in its procedure and attended many of the standing committees to which the detailed work of the convention was remitted. The A.F.L., he soon discovered, showed striking differences from the British trade-union movement. Its president, the stumpy, flamboyant yet shrewd cigar-maker from London, Samuel Gompers, exerted a personal power unknown in the T.U.C. or its constituent unions. Gompers had first been elected president of the A.F.L. in 1882; from 1895 until his death in 1924, he was re-elected each year without a break. From this unassailable position he fought with much skill and few scruples to keep the conservative craft unions of the A.F.L. uncontaminated by the political radicalism of socialism or the industrial radicalism of syndicalism.

Bevin liked Gompers and was impressed by the power he exercised. He disagreed, however, with Gompers' view that "wherever the political movement is predominant, as against the industrial movement, there the Labour movement is weakest, wages lowest and general conditions the worst to be found". For all his rooted distrust of politicians and intellectuals, Ernest Bevin never doubted the need

1 A Visit to America: six articles by Ernest Bevin in the *Dockers' Record.* Feb.–July 1916. The quotations dealing with his visit to the U.S.A. are taken from these articles.

for political as well as industrial action. He was a socialist as well as a trade unionist and what he saw of American labour relations only confirmed his hostility to capitalism.

He listened with interest to Gompers' bitter attacks on the Industrial Workers of the World, who had attempted to make industrial unionism,[1] as opposed to the craft unionism of the A.F.L., the basis for a class-conscious, revolutionary working-class movement. The views of the I.W.W. exercised considerable influence on the left-wing syndicalist movement in Britain before 1914 and the issue of industrial versus craft unionism was to play a big role in trade-union politics in Britain after the war. As a member of a general union and the later architect of a trade-union amalgamation which cut clean across the principles of both craft and industrial unionism, Bevin had still not made up his mind. But, after spending two days listening to the A.F.L. committee on inter-union disputes, he wrote:

"I came to the conclusion that many of our own general workers' unions, chaotic as they may appear, yet adaptable to all conditions of industry, would be more effective in grappling with a combination of employers than the intense craft position developed here."

He added the shrewd observation that the American unions, in their attempt to develop along the lines of organisation by industry, had often only reproduced the sectionalism of the craft unions on an extended scale.

1 As these terms will recur, it may be convenient to define them now. *Industrial unions* aim at bringing all the workers in an industry, whatever their craft, into a single union, e.g. the N.U.R. aimed at bringing all railway workers (including van drivers, cleaners, engineers, carpenters etc.) into a single railway union. *Craft unions* seek to organise all members of a craft (e.g. carpentry) in whatever industry they may be employed. *General unions* (like the Dockers' Union Bevin belonged to) seek to organise any workers—usually unskilled or semi-skilled—wherever they are unorganised. *Industrial unionism* was usually associated with the revolutionary tactics of *syndicalism* aiming at the conquest of power, not by political, but by industrial means, i.e. by a general strike. It was argued that if each of the major industries were organised by a single union, instead of being criss-crossed by the ramifications of the craft unions, it would prove far easier to carry out a general strike effectively. When the revolution had been achieved by industrial action, the advocates of industrial unionism favoured the ownership of each industry, not by the State, but by the workers themselves organised through their unions. A British variation of this syndicalist view was *guild socialism*: the State would own the means of production but their operation would be entrusted to national guilds, combinations of all the producers in each industry.

6

His visit to America brought Bevin for the first time up against the fact that there were a lot of other people in the world beside the British. The discovery stimulated him. He took trouble to learn the views on the war of the different immigrant groups, the Russian-Americans, the Polish-Americans, the Germans and the Irish. He was deeply impressed by the strength of American neutralism and rightly concluded that any attempt to challenge Wilson's policy would meet with defeat in the 1916 election. He showed the same good judgement in concluding that the much more centralised structure of the A.F.L., though unlikely to suit the British trade-union movement, was well fitted to the organisation of labour in a country where a mixture of immigrant races, with great differences of language, customs and standards of life, had to be welded into a single movement.

At the end of the fortnight's convention, during which the fraternal delegates from the T.U.C. explained the British position in relation to the war, they were presented with the customary gifts. Gompers attempted to place a heavy gold ring, decorated with the figure of a naked woman, on Bevin's massive hand. When the ring proved to be too small, Gompers remarked disgustedly, "What's that you got —a bunch of bananas?" and sent it away to be enlarged. Bevin wore the ring to the end of his life and used it with delight to seal the North Atlantic Treaty between Great Britain, the United States and the other Western powers in 1949.

He was naturally interested in the American transport unions. The union which impressed him most was the dockers', the International Longshoremen's Association. He spoke at the Longshoremen's convention in San Francisco and visited their headquarters at Buffalo. He was struck by their efforts to organise all the North American ports, Canadian as well as American, and wrote on his return: "To me the organisation of men in one union, irrespective of the flag under which they live, is the most hopeful sign of the development of real working-class unity."

Another impression which bore fruit later was the improved working conditions provided under the Seamen's Law of 1915, the benefits of which were extended to foreign seamen entering American ports. Years later, at the I.L.O. conference in Geneva, Bevin was to put all his force behind the effort to secure better conditions of service for seamen on an international basis. Nothing was more permanent among the benefits he derived from his American visit than the deep interest it gave him in international action.

After nearly three weeks in San Francisco, the T.U.C. delegates set out for home by way of Los Angeles (where they visited the infant film industry housed in the 'Universal City'), the Grand Canyon, Kansas City and Chicago. Chicago, with its stockyards reminding him of Upton Sinclair's *The Jungle*, made a poor impression on Bevin. He much preferred Milwaukee, where a few years before Victor Berger and the local Socialists had captured the city council and briefly inaugurated a policy of municipal socialism. A big meeting in New York rounded off the trip and after another uneventful crossing they reached England early in the New Year of 1916.

Reviewing his three months' journey after his return, Ernest Bevin wrote:

"To me it was a source of education. It broadened my views in conception of the great world problems; it indicated, as we met representatives of the various races and creeds, how akin we were in human desires, weaknesses and ideas; it emphasised that the need of the workers was a common one, that the struggle was a common one, that the enemy was a common one; and it made one long for the time when the world to the workers will be as small as it is to the capitalists; when the common intelligence of the workers will develop to the same degree as the capitalists' intelligence to exploit it."

Six months before he would not have written in those terms. The journey had enlarged his imagination and added to that accumulation of experience out of which he fashioned his own education.

7

He returned to find the Labour movement in an uproar over conscription. The majority in the Party and the trade unions was still prepared to support the Government over the war, but opposed to compulsory military service. This was an issue which united both the patriotic and the pacifist wings of the movement. The Government's clumsy handling of the question laid them open to the charge of breaking their promises, and the quarters from which the demand for conscription came most insistently—the Northcliffe Press and the right wing of the Conservative Party—roused all Labour's suspicions. This, they argued, was exactly the sort of militarism they were supposed to be fighting. Once imposed, it would be continued after the war and extended to industry, denying a man's right to choose his own job and make his own terms of service. Two Labour conferences in January 1916 turned down compulsory military service by sweeping majorities, despite Arthur Henderson's appeal, and it was only by heavy political manœuvring that this clear expression of opinion was evaded and conscription introduced without the withdrawal of the Labour Ministers from the coalition.

Bevin was strongly opposed to conscription and angered by the less than plain dealing on the part of the Government. The debate produced a split in the local Bristol Labour Party and he found himself on opposite sides to a man for whom he had the highest regard, Frank Sheppard.

Perhaps it was the curious similarity of their early careers which drew Bevin and Frank Sheppard together. Both had been orphaned before the age of ten, both had left school soon afterwards and both came to Bristol from the country in their early 'teens. Apprenticed to the boot and shoe trade, Sheppard became a national organiser for his union. Twenty years before Bevin, he joined the Bristol Socialist Society and became its secretary. In 1893 he was elected to the City Council and by the time Bevin met him at Moffat Logan's class around the turn of the century, Frank Sheppard was one of the leaders of the working-class movement in Bristol, a man of singularly unselfish character and level-headed judgment. Bevin felt both respect and affection for the older man, whom he frequently referred to as his 'political father', and it saddened him to find himself opposed to Sheppard. He sat down and wrote a letter which is so characteristic of him at this time that it is worth quoting in full, exactly as he wrote it.

36, Prince Street,
Bristol.
January 23, 1916.

Dear Frank,

It is with regret that I have heard of the Charges and Counter Charges with reference to yourself.

And as I have not seen you since my return I have been wondering whether on account of my attitude to the Governments Compulsion bill, you were inferentially associating me with being agreed with what has happened.

I profoundly disagree with the government scheme and their policy which will I think enslave labour. And I am not satisfied with the conduct of foreign affairs Prior to the War, and while such an attitude may cause an intense division of opinion for the time being, yet I want to assure you that it has not affected my Personal regard and friendship for yourself, who I believe is following from highest motives of conscience and judgement just as I am.

Though I may find myself in company with some with whom on other grounds I differ and some whose characteristics you and I have discussed and I think are agreed, and my opinions of them on general grounds have not changed. Still convictions when they are deep rooted if we have any courage have to be fought for.

I have written thus because apart from the war, we have so much in common upon which we can unite that I am deeply desirous of retaining a valued friendship. I shall exchange opinion upon the world position and I hope by such an exchange we may mutually benefit.

I must say there are some with their tongue in their Cheek supporting the government whose only concern is the increasing of their bank balances in consequence of that to them I have a different feeling. It is because I am satisfied that in all things you are the last man to do things from petty personal aggrandisement or monetary benefit, that I am desirous of retaining a friendship that I think we can both say have been of benefit to the class we try to serve.

If you are down the office any day except Wednesday, or Saturday give a look in to say 'Hello'.

Regards to wife and family and best wishes for continued good health.

Yours sincerely,
E. Bevin.[1]

1 Frank Sheppard kept this letter to the end of his life and it is pleasant to record that their friendship was unaffected by their sharp political disagreements during the war. Bevin never visited Bristol without seeing Frank Sheppard. In January 1938, when Sheppard was unwell, he wrote, again in his own hand: ". . . Rest content, old friend, whatever I or any of the present generation may do is trifling compared to what you and others of your generation did for us. I never forget what the help, advice, encouragement you personally so willingly gave me in my younger days meant to me, but what I always admired the most of all, was the wonderful example you set, always striving for our people, ever ready to help and from glorious unselfishness." Alderman Sheppard, in fact, outlived his younger

Bevin was to give sharp expression to his views later in the year at the T.U.C. and at the conference of the Labour Party in January 1917. Meanwhile, he resumed work as an organiser in South Wales and the West of England and was soon in demand to present the workers' case for wage increases in local negotiations or before the Committee on Production in London. He was already showing evidence of that skill as an advocate which won him a national reputation at the Shaw Inquiry in 1920[1], and he argued the case for wage increases with conviction. The continued rise in prices, especially food prices, was due, he believed, to the half-heartedness of the Government in imposing economic controls and limiting profits. If the Government would not intervene effectively, they must accept the consequence of a periodical rise in wages to keep within sight of the rise in prices.

In November 1915 the Government set up the Port and Transit Executive Committee to deal with the serious congestion at the ports, where the docks were choked with accumulated goods. The Transport Workers' Federation had long been urging the Government to deal with this problem. When at last it acted, however, the Government failed to invite any representative of the unions concerned to join the Committee on which the shipowners and other commercial interests were strongly represented. The implication that working men and their trade-union leaders could have nothing to contribute to the solution of such a problem was fully in keeping with the attitude of employers and Government departments. The Transport Workers' Federation protested strongly, with the result that in February 1916 the Committee grudgingly invited Harry Gosling, the President of the Federation, to join it as the representative of Labour.

The Port and Transit Committee survived the many administrative reorganisations of the war (including the creation of a Ministry of Shipping) and accomplished a great deal of practical work before it was disbanded and its functions taken over by the Ministry of Transport in 1920. It organised the diversion of shipping from one port to another, instituted measures to secure a quicker turn-round of ships, the pooling of railway waggons and the clearing of over-

---

friend and died in 1956 at the age of 93, after more than sixty years of public service, preserving to the end those qualities which had first attracted Bevin to him.
1 See c. 6.

crowded warehouses. At the same time it was made responsible for the reservation of port workers and the employment of Transport Workers' Battalions eventually numbering 15,000 men. After their initial reluctance, the Committee co-operated more and more closely with the N.T.W.F. and Bevin was drawn into its work as a member of one of the local sub-committees set up in Bristol.

It was his first experience of working directly with Government departments. If he proved an awkward customer to deal with when the men's interests were involved, he soon impressed the other members of the Committee with his ability as an organiser. One reform which he was able to start at Cardiff, despite the objections of the dock manager, was the registration of dock-workers, a first step in the campaign he was to wage for thirty years to secure the re-organisation of the dock industry.

The transport workers' grievances and criticisms were given full vent in the annual General Council meeting of the N.T.W.F. in Glasgow in June. The Federation had gained in importance during the war. It was one of the partners in the Triple Industrial Alliance with the miners and the railwaymen and the one body which the Government could consult in all matters affecting labour in the transport industry. Twenty-three of its thirty member unions were represented at the 1916 council meeting. The Dockers' delegation consisted of Ben Tillett, Ernie Bevin and Bill Devenay, the grain porter who had become the Union's London organiser, an alderman of West Ham and a member of the Port of London Authority.

In his opening address, the President, Harry Gosling, declared:

"Had we, on behalf of the transport workers of the country, taken advantage of the monopoly of our labour power as the ship-owners have taken advantage of the monopoly of their ships, we could have doubled, trebled or increased more than tenfold the wages of our labour, as the ship-owners have multiplied by more than twenty times the freight rates for the use of their ships."[1]

The profits made by the ship-owners out of the national emergency were brought up again and again in wartime trade-union conferences and a special report, rich in figures and percentages, was given to this Glasgow Council meeting of the Federation. Nothing

1 N.T.W.F.: Report of the 7th Annual General Council Meeting, 14th–15th June 1917, pp. 11-13.

angered these working men more than the contrast between the shipping companies' inflated profits and the wages paid to the sailors (also members of the Federation) who risked their lives in face of U-boat attacks.

Bevin spoke six times in all and clearly impressed his small but highly critical audience, entirely composed as it was of full-time union officials. At the end of the meeting, although the youngest delegate present, he secured the second highest vote for election to the Executive Council and took the place of Tillett who did not stand for re-election.

Three months later, when the T.U.C. met at Birmingham (September 1916), the two fraternal delegates to the A.F.L., Charles Amman and Ernest Bevin, attempted unsuccessfully to defend Gompers' proposal of an international Labour peace congress to be held at the same time and place as the general peace conference at the end of the war. This suggestion, although supported by the Parliamentary Committee, came under heavy fire from those who angrily refused to sit in the same room with any German delegate. Bevin tried to reason with the opposition:

"You have got to take the Germans into consultation after this war. You have got to reckon with the Germans as an economic factor . . . and there will not be many scruples about the settlement when the diplomats are in conference together. . . .

"In sending out this circular from the A.F.L., I believe it was done with the sole idea that the impress of Labour might be placed upon the future peace of the world, or at any rate that an effort should be made in that direction. I think everybody in this Congress will agree that the present war has largely arisen as the result of the settlements of every other war in Europe over the last three hundred years. It has not come about through the touch of a spring, as it were, because a certain monarch's son was killed by a Serbian revolutionist. I stand here for a republic of Europe absolutely, for the complete democracy ruling throughout Europe; but that seems impossible for the moment. However, let me say this . . . such a subject as the attitude of organised Labour towards the peace is worthy of a special Congress . . ."[1]

Such arguments were drowned in the storm of anti-German feeling and the proposal, twisted into a suggestion of a negotiated peace, was voted down by three quarters of a million majority on a card vote. Apart from this, a series of technical amendments to the Workmen's Compensation Act and a short speech breathing

[1] T.U.C. Report, 1916.

suspicion of every action of Lloyd George, Bevin sat silent. He was still a minor figure, one of the 670 delegates in a T.U.C. which was dominated by the older leaders or by the men with the voting strength of the big unions behind them, the six hundred thousand of the Miners or the three hundred thousand of the N.U.R.—a card vote with which the Dockers' membership of 40,000 could not compare.

9

It was through the Transport Workers' Federation, with its combined strength of thirty unions and its central position in negotiations with the Government and employers, that his way to the front lay, and from the day that he was elected to its Executive Council in the summer of 1916 Bevin took every chance the Federation offered for the exercise of his abilities.

Harry Gosling, the president of the Federation, came of an old family of Thames Watermen. His great-grandfather (apprenticed in the 1780s), his grandfather and father had all been master-lightermen on the Thames; he himself was secretary of the small but proud London Society of Watermen, Lightermen and Bargemen. Now in his fifties, Gosling was widely respected in the trade-union movement for his fair-mindedness and integrity. A gentle and kindly man, born to be a chairman, he later became the first (and only) president of the Transport and General Workers' Union.

Bob Williams, the secretary of the Federation and a man of Bevin's own age, had begun life as a coal-trimmer in South Wales. He was an able speaker and negotiator, Bevin's one serious rival for the leadership of the transport workers, but politics proved a dangerous distraction to him. He had strong left-wing views which he did not bother to conceal[1] and his position was too closely bound up with the fortunes of the Federation to escape eclipse when Bevin drew the principal unions forming the Federation into amalgamation.

Tillett, the man who had brought the Federation into being in

[1] A conscientious objector during the war, Williams later joined the Communist Party and was presented by Trotsky with the Soviet Military Medal for his services to Communism. This did not prevent him being expelled from the Communist Party in 1921. See c. 7.

1911, possessed greater natural gifts than either Gosling or Jimmy Sexton, the other dockers' leader. He had an expansive personality, a quick imagination and plenty of ideas. But he lacked application and he was beginning to live on the reputation of past triumphs. His relations with Bevin were already equivocal: closely associated in the work of the union, neither trusted the other. At heart, Tillett was bored with union and committee work. He was in poor health, had political ambitions (he became M.P. for Salford in 1917), and liked to travel and cut a figure in the public eye. He was very willing to surrender his seat on the Federation Executive to Bevin, retaining the ill-defined position of vice-president.

The Federation was still called upon to settle disputes between its member unions, most of them arising out of accusations of bad faith, blacklegging and the invasion by a rival of another union's territory. But its most important function had become the representation of the transport workers' interests to Government departments like the Board of Trade or the Admiralty, to the Port and Transit Committee and on occasion to the Prime Minister or the Minister of Munitions when the Federation would join its partners in the Triple Alliance to present a combined protest.

Many of the issues discussed by the Federation Executive in 1916–17 reappear again and again on the agenda of the committees Ernest Bevin was now beginning to attend. Some were of general application: protests against rising prices and profits, the demand that greater attention should be paid to Labour's views, especially in appointments to committees; criticism of the much disliked employment exchanges. Others were of particular concern to the Federation's own members. The Seamen's Union kept up a persistent fight against the employment of Chinese and Lascar crews on British ships at cut-rates. The Dockers' Union sought to limit the employment of the Transport Workers' Battalions in the docks and insisted that, where they were employed, they must be paid civilian rates. Bevin accused the port authorities of deliberately creating labour shortages in order to have an excuse for bringing in this non-union labour which was under military discipline and could be used for strike-breaking if need arose. Memories were still fresh of the strike-breaking force organised by the Shipping Federation, and Bevin had no doubt that the same tactics would be tried again once the war was over. He never forgot the remark made to him by an employer: "All right, our day will come," and he was convinced that the Government would take the employers' side when it did.

Once he had found his feet, Bevin showed a flexibility of mind and a grasp of policy which no one else on the Executive could approach. Indeed, it soon became common practice to form a sub-committee of Bevin, Gosling, Williams and either Sexton or Tillett, to deal with any difficult problem. Bevin and Williams were often sent off together to settle a dispute in one of the ports, a tough and able pair, well-matched round a negotiating table or on a platform in the local dockers' hall.

10

The two biggest steps taken by the Federation in 1917 owed much to Bevin's initiative. At the July meeting of the Executive held in the Old Ship Hotel, Brighton,[1] it was decided that the President should resign his seat on the Port and Transit Committee and that the Federation representatives on all local port consultative committees should be instructed to withdraw. The aim was to secure the reconstitution of both the national and the local committees with increased representation for Labour and full executive powers over the administration of the ports. It was a proof of the growing power of the Federation that this manœuvre succeeded. After discussion by the Cabinet in October, the central and local Port and Transit Committees were re-modelled and Gosling was joined on the main committee by four other representatives including Bevin.

At the March meeting of the Federation Executive, Bevin had secured the appointment of a sub-committee to consider his proposal of a national programme for transport workers. He was after a programme agreed upon and launched in advance, even if it could not be put into effect until the end of the war. The Executive accepted his recommendations, the most important of which were the abolition of overtime and a systematic reduction in the hours of work (both with a view to absorbing demobilised men); and

---

1 It is remarkable how much trade-union history has been made in hotels, especially those of the big conference resorts, Brighton, Blackpool, Margate, not to mention Anderton's Hotel, Fleet Street, now pulled down, but once a favourite venue of trade-union conferences and committees.

national joint action by the Federation to maintain the wage increases secured during the war and abstention by individual unions from any isolated negotiations.

"We want you to have confidence in the Federation," Bevin told the annual council meeting in June. "Range yourselves so that the employers shall not be able to use one port against another, shall not be able to make one port the cockpit of the fight. . . . When the employers know that if they attack Bristol, the local officials will say, 'You must approach the Federation,' there will be less likelihood of any of the ports being tackled singly. There must be co-ordination and a national policy."[1]

Once he had got the programme accepted by the Federation, Bevin put up a further plan to divide the country into six districts for the purpose of explaining the campaign to the men during the coming autumn.

This scheme, simple as it appears, illustrates two characteristics which already distinguished Ernest Bevin from the ordinary run of trade unionists. First, he thought in terms, not of his own union, nor even of the dockers, but of the transport industry as a whole, with each union subordinating its particular interests to an overriding common interest and each section ready to support the others. When the Federation proved an inadequate instrument for this purpose, he created his own in the amalgamation which established the Transport and General Workers' Union.

Secondly, unbeguiled by promises, by the high wages earned by certain sections of the working class or by the place accorded to the unions during the war, he stubbornly persisted in looking ahead and asking what would happen when it was over. It was in this perspective that he viewed every decision called for by the needs of the moment. If this made him appear unduly suspicious at the time, events were later to justify his foresight. Nor was his attitude purely negative. He did not attempt to obstruct the effort required to win the war; on the contrary, unlike the leaders of the Shop Stewards' Movement, he spent a great deal of energy in eliminating congestion at the ports and preventing strikes. He refused to be drawn into exploiting temporary advantages for the pursuit of short-term objectives or the fantasy of revolutionary action. Instead he con-

1 N.T.W.F.: Report of 7th Annual General Council Meeting, 14th–15th June 1917, p. 98.

centrated on building up positions of strength which, when those advantages had disappeared, might prevent the working class being driven to accept a lower standard of living than that of 1914.

What Bevin and the more far-sighted union leaders feared was the prospect that, with demobilisation flooding the labour market and those who had taken the places of men in the Forces clinging to their jobs, wages would be forced down and the trade unions' attempt to restore conditions of work defeated. In the scramble for employment and in the economic dislocation caused by the end of hostilities, the precarious unity of the trade-union movement might well be destroyed and the employers left a free hand to impose their own terms on isolated and disorganised groups of workers.

Bevin urged these views on all four of the trade-union executive committees or councils to which he now belonged: his own Dockers' Union, the National Federation of General Workers,[1] the National Transport Workers' Federation and the Triple Industrial Alliance. It was in these small meetings, at close quarters, where oratory had no place and he had to argue his case with other union leaders, that Bevin made his reputation with the professionals long before he learned to get a crowded T.U.C. or Labour Party conference to listen to him.

The Triple Alliance of miners, railwaymen and transport workers formed in 1914 had not had time to hold its inaugural conference when the war broke out. Between June 1914 and December 1916, its council only met twice and ventured on nothing more striking than a deputation to the Prime Minister to express its anxieties about demobilisation. Bevin first attended a meeting of its council just before Christmas 1916 and soon became one of the spokesmen of the Transport Workers who was listened to with interest by such experienced critics as Bob Smillie, the Miners' President, the shrewd Jimmy Thomas and Herbert Smith, that Yorkshireman of Yorkshiremen.

The original aggressive purpose of the Triple Alliance could not be pursued during the war, but Bevin urged the council to make clear the Alliance's opposition to such highly suspect expedients as the introduction of coloured labour and the extension of industrial

1 The National Federation of General Workers was established in July 1917 and replaced the National Council of General Labourers on which Bevin had represented the Dockers' Union.

conscription. No Government in time of war could ignore the views of three out of the four most important groups of workers in the country and Bevin saw in the Triple Alliance an organisation which, if it could be held together, might well play a decisive part in the renewal of industrial conflict which he anticipated when the war was over.

"There is nobody in the world," he told his colleagues in the Triple Alliance council, "who submits to anything but force. Force is the logic of reason after all and the only reason they will respond to is that which is backed up by power."[1]

What the trade-union movement needed, he concluded, was the effective organisation of its power: it was up to the Triple Alliance to supply it.

1 Bevin's speech to the Joint Conference of the three executives composing the Triple Alliance, held at the Imperial Hotel, London, 21st December 1916.

CHAPTER 4

The Prospect of Change
1917 – 1918

I

BEVIN habitually spoke of industrial relations at this time in terms of conflict with the employers and with the State. But the impact of war, the feeling that nothing would ever be the same again, the belief that great social changes were already taking place led those who were dissatisfied with this state of affairs to ask whether such conflict was inevitable. Towards the end of July 1916, Beatrice Webb noted in her diary:

"It is interesting to watch the ferment of ideas and proposals going on in Government departments and social reform circles, and even among employers, with regard to the Conduct of Industry."[1]

The Government set up a Reconstruction Committee, one of whose sub-committees produced the Whitley Report on the relations of capital and labour. The Webbs themselves were active in trying to create a Labour Research Society, while Seebohm and Arnold Rowntree (the former a member of the Reconstruction Committee), directed their energies to bringing employers and trade unionists together to discuss the future of industrial relations.

Arnold Rowntree was in touch with a group in Bristol and on 5th November 1916, met Ernest Bevin, Frank Sheppard and a number of other local trade-union officials at 'Penscot', a house up on the Mendips in the Somerset village of Shipham. They spent the day in the discussion of Labour's claims and grievances. Bevin and the other trade unionists were not optimistic about the prospects of

1 *Diaries* 1912–1924, p. 68.

closer co-operation with the employers, especially after the war, nor were they convinced of the value of such co-operation from their point of view. The typescript notes of the discussion, corrected in Bevin's hand begin:

"Grave doubts about co-operative spirit, now being preached, between employers and workmen. Revolt may be injurious to the country momentarily, but the final result would undoubtedly win the objects the working class had in view."

None the less, Bevin agreed to join in the discussions with employers which Arnold Rowntree was anxious to promote, and he acted as the spokesman of the trade-union side at a meeting held in the Bristol Council Chamber under the chairmanship of the Lord Mayor on 12th January 1917. "You have had one set of education for yourselves and another for us," he told the employers.

"I had to work at ten years of age while my employer's son went to the university until he was twenty. You have set out for me a different set of conditions. I was taught to bow to the squire and touch my hat to the parson; my employer's son was not. All these things have produced within me an intense hatred, a hatred which has caused me to organise for my fellows and direct my mind to a policy to give to my class a power to control their own destiny and labour.
"What is capital prepared to concede? Will it concede, if labour-saving machinery is introduced, that it is to lighten the burden of the working classes? And then, after the War, will employers restore trade union conditions without question and not merely restore conditions so far as production is concerned, but accept the principle of real wages instead of mere money wages? If these points are not conceded, then peace can never be."[1]

Bevin was giving nothing away. He had no use for vague formulas of goodwill. Better to break off the discussions than allow the well-meaning advocates of industrial reconciliation to be under any illusions about the conditions of success.

2

It was precisely because he put the workers' point of view forcefully that Bevin was of so much value in these discussions. It is not sur-

1 *Western Daily Press*, 13th Jan. 1917.

prising then to find him invited to attend a conference of Leeds trade unionists at Ilkley, presided over by Arnold Rowntree, a week after his speech in Bristol. This was followed by a two-day meeting of Bristol employers and trade unionists at Penscot in the following month. Both were devoted to the same theme, the industrial outlook, and, under the guidance of Arnold Rowntree, covered much the same ground. Neither conference produced any concrete result (they were not intended to), yet it was through such discussions that Bevin began to feel his way towards a number of the characteristic conceptions which were to mark the later period of his career as a trade-union leader and as Minister of Labour.

The Penscot conference set out to answer the question: What are the causes of the distrust and suspicion which bedevil industrial relations? Powerfully prompted by Bevin on the trade-union side, it put at the head of its answer the question of status:

"The primary demand of labour today is not only an economic but a human demand. The operatives demand recognition by employers and managers that they are intelligent human beings—men and women, and not merely cogs in the wheels of the industrial machine. . . . At present employers and employed are, too often, separated by something akin to a barrier of 'caste' . . . The operatives are frequently regarded by employers as being of a different and inferior order. . . . So long as these views continue to exist they inevitably produce an intense class bitterness."

From this barrier there naturally followed complete ignorance of each other's point of view. But its removal would not produce a major improvement unless it was accompanied by other changes aimed at ending the dissociation of the workmen from responsibility.

The workers not only claimed to have some voice in the control of the industry in which they worked and on which they were dependent; they also claimed a larger share in the products of industry.

"It is conceded by all taking part in this conference that, speaking generally, the operatives in the past have not had the share to which they were fairly entitled. . . . The right of the operatives to seek to advance their interests and standard of life by means of combination is frankly recognised. . . . The Trade Union movement has done much to create in the country the deep sense of social responsibility already noticed. . . . The Unions are not only of advantage to the operatives but to the employers as well."

Making the same proposal as the Whitley Committee report (published three weeks later) the Penscot conference urged that each industry should set up local and national joint councils, with equal representation of employers and trade unions, to regulate wages, hours and conditions of work for the trade as a whole. When a majority of employers and operatives in an industry were parties to any agreement reached, then, they argued, the national joint council should have the right to apply to the Government for an Order to make its provisions obligatory on all engaged in the industry.[1]

An immediate result of this meeting of employers and trade unionists was the foundation in June 1917 of the Bristol Association for Industrial Reconstruction, with Ernest Bevin as one of its vice-presidents. Amongst its objects was to give effect to the recommendations of the Penscot conference and, in particular, "to encourage the organisation of industry so as to secure (a) joint control by associations of employers and employees; and (b) economic security and an equitable share in the wealth produced to all engaged in the industry".

In November 1917, the Association launched a series of lectures in the Bristol Museum. The subject of the first was "Finance in relation to Industry". At the end of the lecture, Ernest Bevin rose to propose a vote of thanks and to move "That this meeting calls upon the Ministry of Reconstruction to institute a close examination of the banking system, especially into the effects of the private control of banking, the gold standard, bank rates and credit in relation to industry, social reconstruction and poverty". The resolution had to wait twelve years before it was put into effect, but when the Macmillan Committee was set up by the Government in 1929 to report on precisely this question of finance and industry, among its distinguished members—Reginald McKenna, Keynes, R. H. Brand, Lord Bradbury—was the former vice-president of the Bristol Association for Industrial Reconstruction, Ernest Bevin.

The bitter period of industrial conflict between the end of the war and the General Strike of 1926, the disillusionment which overtook the hopes raised by the Ministry of Reconstruction and the National Industrial Conference of 1919 have led historians to treat the wide-

1 *Report of a conference of Bristol Employers and Trade Unionists on the industrial outlook, 'Penscot', Shipham, Somerset, 17th–18th February* 1917. This report was handed to Arthur Greenwood and came into the hands of Lloyd George.

spread discussion of social and industrial problems in 1916–18 with undeserved scorn.

It was the first time in British history that there had been such a searching examination of the social problems of industry, contributed to by all the parties most concerned: employers, trade unionists, civil servants, social reformers, economists and social scientists. Even three or four years before it would have been inconceivable for a representative group of employers to sit down and discuss with trade unionists the issues raised at the Penscot conference or to serve together on the many Government committees set up to deal with reconstruction after the war. Nor are the angry strikes of the early 1920s the whole story of the sequel. After the General Strike the conception of a joint effort by employers and unions to reach agreement on economic policy and the reform of industry was revived in the Mond-Turner talks, in which Ernest Bevin played a leading part,[1] and the development of industrial relations over the past forty years, although it has been a chequered history continually falling short of expectations, has shown the persistent influence of ideas first given currency in these wartime discussions.

3

So long as he was thinking or talking about trade unions and industrial affairs, Bevin's grasp was sure. When he ventured into politics (where he had no experience on which to draw) he was far less effective.

The turning point in the politics of the first World War came in December 1916 when Asquith was forced out of office. Lloyd George was prepared to promise anything in his eagerness to secure Labour support for his new coalition. Arthur Henderson was offered a seat in the inner War Cabinet of five; a Ministry of Labour was set up and a trade-union leader appointed to this as well as to the Ministry of Pensions. Amongst other measures long demanded by the Labour movement which Lloyd George undertook to put into effect were the control of the mines and shipping by the State during the war, the appointment of a Food Controller and the introduction of rationing.

1 See c. 15.

When the Labour Party conference met at Manchester towards the end of January 1917, Henderson's action in taking office under Lloyd George was the main item of debate. Bevin, making his first appearance as a delegate of the Dockers' Union, was one of his sharpest critics.

The debate, opened by Henderson, led to an attack on the official policy of the Party by Philip Snowden and other members of the I.L.P., from which Bevin took pains to dissociate himself. "He was not concerned with the dialectics of a clever man like Mr. Snowden," he said, and he rebuked Snowden for his sneer at Labour Ministers who could not resist the temptations of office. His own fears sprang from the character of the men with whom the Labour members would have to serve and once again demonstrated his distrust of Lloyd George. But his laboured invective had no more effect than the I.L.P. attack, and Arthur Henderson's action in joining the coalition was endorsed by a big majority.

It was hardly a successful conference from Bevin's point of view. When he and Bob Williams attacked the Government's interference with the Committee on Production in order to hold back wage advances, his own colleague as national organiser of the Dockers' Union, James Wignall, told him that he had got his facts wrong and that the Government instruction of which he complained had been withdrawn. When he moved that the debate on manpower should be brought forward, he was voted down, nor was he much more successful when he launched a second attack on Arthur Henderson for the lukewarmness of his opposition to the use of coloured labour. On the other hand, his criticisms of the Party's official line did not draw him any closer either to the I.L.P. or to other opposition groups such as that which gathered round George Lansbury and the *Daily Herald*.[1] He made this perfectly clear when, in June 1917, he attended the once famous, now long-forgotten, Leeds Convention called to welcome the Russian Revolution.

---

[1] The *Daily Herald* first appeared in January 1911 as a London printers' strike sheet. Re-founded in April 1912 (with the support of Ben Tillett), it maintained a precarious but lively existence with Lansbury as editor and a brilliant if erratic list of contributors. Far from being the official Labour daily at that time, it was heretical by instinct as well as conviction. See Raymond Postgate: *The Life of George Lansbury* (1951) cc. 11–12.

73

4

The March Revolution which overthrew the Tsarist state was not, of course, a Socialist, still less a Communist revolution. The Bolsheviks did not seize power until November. But the events of March 1917 had already made a deep impression upon the Labour movement in Great Britain.

Socialists were delighted with the spectacle of a successful and spontaneous rising of 'the people' against 'Reaction' in which the working classes had played the leading part. Overnight, revolution was transformed from a dream into something that might actually take place, something that actually had taken place, and this in the most police-ridden State in Europe. In the Petrograd Soviet of Workers' and Soldiers' Deputies, which acted with contemptuous independence towards the Provisional Government, enthusiasts saw the prototype of a new form of revolutionary power closer than any Parliament or Cabinet to the democratic ideal.

But the most immediate effect of the Russian Revolution in Britain was the crystallisation of the hopes, and fears, of an early end to the war without a clear-cut military decision. By May 1917 the popular demand for peace had grown so strong in Russia that a new Government, hastily formed, had to adopt as its own the demand of the Petrograd Soviet for a negotiated peace with no annexations and no indemnities. Here was an issue on which the pacifist and anti-war minority in the Labour movement could hope to exploit the prestige of a successful revolution.

On 3rd June, twelve hundred delegates met in the Leeds Coliseum at the invitation of a small unofficial group calling itself the United Social Council. The organising secretaries were Francis Johnson of the I.L.P. and Albert Inkpin of the small Marxist British Socialist Party. George Lansbury, whose *Herald* gave the meeting strong support, was prevented from attending by illness, but among the heterogeneous assembly drawn from Trades Councils, local Labour Parties, the I.L.P., and other socialist societies were Ramsay Mac-Donald; Philip Snowden; Bob Williams; Bob Smillie (the Miners' President and a member of the I.L.P., who took the chair); Sylvia Pankhurst; Tom Mann; Bertrand Russell; Pethick-Lawrence; Willie Gallacher and Jimmy Maxton. It was a preview of the

British Left between the wars, anarchical, Utopian, already fascinated by and profoundly ignorant of Russian experience. Neither of the two delegates from the Dockers' Union, Ben Tillett and Ernest Bevin, felt at home in this assembly. Tillett, identified as one of the leaders of the 'patriotic' wing of the Labour movement, said little, but Bevin, unimpressed by either the views or the hostility of the other delegates, meant to speak his mind.

Four resolutions were moved, two of which, hailing the Russian Revolution and demanding the removal of all restrictions on civil liberties, touched no controversial issue. The interest lay in the other two. The first, moved by Philip Snowden of the I.L.P., called on the British Government to announce its agreement with the declared war aims of Russia—"a peace without annexations or idemnities and based upon the rights of nations to decide their own affairs." An attempt by the discredited Captain Tupper of the Seamen's Union to ask who would support the widows and children of dead seamen if there were no indemnity was silenced by shouts of "the ship-owners".

Then Ernest Bevin rose. Knowing his man, Smillie appealed for a fair hearing.

"Supposing (Bevin asked) this resolution becomes the policy, we will say, of a large majority of the Labour movement of this country and that it is then forced upon the Government. Where do our fatuous friends of the I.L.P. stand? When we have arrived at this policy and have associated ourselves with our Russian friends, and there is no response from Germany, will they join us in a vigorous prosecution of the war until Germany *does* respond? Our experience of the German Social Democrats in the past was not altogether a happy one. Has any evidence come to this country that the German Social Democrats are prepared to reverse their policy? . . . .
"We all know that in the industrial world the capitalists would give us peace tomorrow if we would surrender. But I am not going to surrender. I am not going to be a pacifist in the industrial movement. I believe that even in our own country there will have to be the shedding of blood to attain the freedom we require. . . . The platform says that the tide is on the rise for us. For whom? The professional politicians of the Labour Party. . . ."[1]

This gratuitous insult led to immediate disorder during which the Chairman told Bevin that his time was up and he returned to his

[1] Report in the *Daily Herald*, 9th June 1917. Reprinted in *What Happened at Leeds* (2nd ed.), 1917, pp. 10–11.

seat. None the less it had been a shrewd attack on the I.L.P., and the *Herald*, recognising it as such, devoted the greater part of its leading article to what it described as his "critical but extremely able speech . . . the only able speech in opposition."

The last resolution, moved by William Anderson, M.P., called upon the bodies represented at the conference "at once to establish in every town, urban and rural district councils of workers' and soldiers' delegates for initiating and co-ordinating working-class activity . . . for the complete political and economic emancipation of international labour". Anderson, after declaring that "the sooner we have a revolution in this country, the better", added that the organisation envisaged would only be subversive or unconstitutional if the authorities made it so. This was much too cautious for Bob Williams, Bevin's colleague in the N.T.W.F. The resolution, he insisted, meant the dictatorship of the proletariat and those with cold feet had better leave. Attacking the industrial and political organisation of Labour as decrepit, he told his enthusaistic audience that, if the Russians had respected their constitution, they would still be slaves of the Romanovs. After carrying the resolution with acclamation, the Convention ended by standing to sing 'The Red Flag'.

5

The Leeds Convention had no sequel. No British Soviets or Councils of Workers' and Soldiers' Deputies were founded and even the Provisional Committee elected by the conference soon broke up. In the meantime, however, the proposal, strongly urged by the Russians, of an international socialist conference at Stockholm (to which representatives of the German and Austrian as well as the Allied Socialist parties should be invited) had an unexpected effect upon the British Labour movement.

For reasons which are still far from clear, Lloyd George sent Arthur Henderson to Russia in the summer of 1917 to report on the situation to the War Cabinet. Henderson returned convinced that the British Government should put no obstacles in the way of the proposed conference and that the Labour Party should send a strong delegation to Stockholm. He was at once involved in a sharp conflict with Lloyd George and resigned from the Government. This was a turning-point in the history of the Labour Party. Although Labour continued to support the war effort and to be represented in the coalition until the Armistice, Henderson resumed his freedom of action as secretary of the Party and launched it on an independent course.

In the year which followed his resignation he persuaded the Party to take three major steps.

First, after the breakdown of the plans for the Stockholm conference, he took the lead in drawing up a declaration of Labour's views on the peace settlement which was adopted not only by the Labour Party and T.U.C. at the end of December 1917, but by the Allied Labour and Socialist Conference in February 1918. This declaration of war aims preceded by several days Lloyd George's statement on the same subject in January 1918 (which it undoubtedly influenced) as well as President Wilson's enunciation of his Fourteen Points. It represented the starting-point of the alternative foreign policy which Labour attempted to develop in the course of the 1920s.

Second, Henderson persuaded the Labour Party conference in February 1918 to accept a new constitution transforming it from a federation of trade unions and socialist societies into a nationally organised party with local parties and individual membership in every constituency. Throughout the rest of 1918 he worked with great energy to create the organisation which would turn this paper scheme into fact.

Finally, in June 1918, he got a second Party Conference to adopt a detailed statement of policy drafted by Sidney Webb under the title of *Labour and the New Social Order.* For the first time this committed the Party explicitly to the socialist objective of "the common ownership of the means of production and the . . . popular administration and control of each industry and service".

Taken together, these three steps mark the creation of the modern Labour Party and the charting of the course which it was to follow, in domestic affairs at least, until the fall of the Attlee Government in 1951. They are Arthur Henderson's decisive contribution to the Party's development.

Bevin's part in all this was a minor one. He was not a member of any of the committees in which these decisions were shaped and, although he attended all the conferences at which they were ratified, he contributed little to the debates.

At the special conference which decided in favour of Henderson's proposal to send a delegation to Stockholm (10th August 1917), Bevin seconded the Miners' amendment excluding the I.L.P. or any other socialist society from being represented. This was fully in keeping with trade-union opinion, which was prepared to accept a change of policy recommended by one of its own leaders, but had not altered its opinion of those pacifist groups which first advocated this step for reasons of their own. At the two conferences held to adopt the new constitution and programme[1] he limited himself to two brief speeches, one criticising the Party's policy on education as too timid, the other expressing disagreement with proposals for the devolution of government, including separate assemblies for Scotland, Wales and even England, as well as for Ireland.

He was certainly not in disagreement with the direction in which Henderson was turning the Labour Party. On the contrary, his criticism of Henderson (by origin, a manual worker and a trade unionist like himself) had always been that he had compromised Labour's independence by joining the coalition Government. Henderson's new course between the 'patriots', support of Lloyd George and the I.L.P.—Left Wing's opposition to the war was much closer to Bevin's own views and he no longer felt politically isolated. Between the summer of 1917 and the Armistice, however, he was so hard at work on Government committees, the Transport Workers' Federation, the Federation of General Workers and the Dockers' Union that he had little time to spare for politics. So heavy were the demands Bevin made on himself in this period that even his energy was exhausted and he suffered a nervous breakdown in the summer of 1918.

6

In the course of 1917 Bevin was offered a paid post as labour adviser by the Government. He took only a week-end's reflection to

---

1 Nottingham, 23rd–25th Jan. 1918, adjourned to the Central Hall, Westminster, 26th Feb.; Central Hall, 26th–28th June 1918. The first adopted the new constitution, the second twenty-six resolutions based on *Labour and the New Social Order*.

refuse the sort of offer which tempted more than one poorly-paid trade-union leader to surrender his independence. This Bevin would never give up and at the Blackpool conference of the T.U.C. (September 1917) he criticised the Parliamentary Committee of the T.U.C. for accepting the Whitley Report's recommendation of joint industrial councils without a sufficiently critical examination of what was involved. He argued that, if necessary, the Committee should call a special conference to discuss it. "We always wait until legislation has been passed before taking action and the Labour movement spends most of its time protesting against what it could have avoided if it had used imagination enough beforehand." He secured the appointment of a special sub-committee to consult the unions and arrive at an agreed view in advance of any legislation.[1]

This was constructive criticism springing from his attempt to foresee and provide for the social and economic problems which would come with the end of the war. At the Blackpool conference he moved a resolution on preparations for demobilisation which still aroused little general interest in the trade-union movement and was carried without debate. The same interest led him to accept an invitation from the Ministry of Reconstruction (which replaced the Reconstruction Committee in 1917) to serve on its advisory council[2] and on two of its most important committees. The Committee on Trusts, appointed in February 1918, had the economist J. A. Hobson and Sidney Webb among its numbers as well as Ernest Bevin. It did not present its report until April 1919. The Committee on Adult Education produced a final report which is a classic statement of the case for adult education. Bevin, who showed great interest in education at this time, had to resign from the committee before the final report was drafted, but signed two earlier reports, one dealing with the industrial and social conditions affecting adult education, the other with education in the Army.

He was by now fully involved in the operations of the Port and Transit Executive Committee, the responsibilities of which were increased by the intensified U-boat campaign and the introduction of the convoy system. In February 1918, a sub-committee, known as

1 T.U.C. Report, 1917, pp. 226–235.
2 He was vice-chairman of Section II of the Council (Production and Commercial Organisation) and a member of Section III (Labour and Industrial Organisation).

the West of England and Bristol Channel Committee, was set up with headquarters at Bristol. Its task was to relieve the strain on the railways by using the sea communications across the Bristol Channel with the South Wales ports. It was the sort of practical problem which brought out Bevin's great gifts as an organiser and much of the credit for the Committee's success was due to his initiative.

7

His membership of these committees gave Bevin an insight for the first time into the methods and problems of government, but this did not for one moment shake his loyalty to the working class or his conviction that it was only the organised strength of the working class which would force the Government to pay attention to their demands.

He flung himself with great energy into the organisation of the national campaign which he had persuaded the Transport Workers' Federation to adopt. Together with Bob Williams and Harry Gosling, he visited one centre after another to speak to crowded meetings of dockers, carters and tram-drivers packed into ill-lighted halls or picture palaces in the mean and dirty back-streets of industrial Britain. The original programme put forward by Bevin had now been reduced to one immediate claim, but the significance of a *national* movement had not been lost. Bevin's object was to overcome the petty rivalries and divisions of more than thirty unions sufficiently to present a united demand to the employers and the State for a uniform increase which would bring the wartime wage up to twenty shillings over pre-war rates of pay.

In August, the ex-carter from Bristol presided over a conference at Salford representing seventeen unions with members among carters, lorrymen and motormen. A sub-committee appointed by the conference, with Bevin as chairman, organised local applications for the same increase by each of the unions at the same time. Faced with the possibility of simultaneous disputes in fifty different places, the Government naturally preferred to deal with the Federation, and Bevin, Gosling and Williams were invited to meet Sir George Askwith, the Chief Industrial Commissioner, with a view to a national conference of employers and workmen and a national

Above. Arrests during the London dock strike of 1912. *Below*. Transport workers marching across Tower Bridge to a strike meeting in July 1912.

Above. The Executive Committee of the International Transport Workers' Federation elected at Amsterdam in 1919. Bevin is seated between Charles Lindley (Sweden) and J. Döring (Germany) on the right. Edo Fimmen is third from the left in the back row. *Below*. The International Transport Workers' Federation Conference in Amsterdam, 1919. Seated on the other side of the table to Bevin is Bob Williams. Harry Gosling is between the two, turning round to face the camera.

settlement. Both sides agreed to ask Sir George to act as arbitrator and his award, when it was published on 8th January, gave the carters everything they asked for.

The next move was to secure the extension of the carters' award to tram and bus workers as well. The employers resisted the idea of a national award to the point where the unions threatened to strike, but then capitulated and accepted the Federation's claim. Finally, at the end of January, Bevin and Williams travelled to Manchester a second time to persuade a conference of dockers to agree on a national claim which would bring them up to 8d. an hour above pre-war rates. This time the Federation's negotiators secured an award, not of 8d. but of 7d. None the less Bevin could claim three striking successes for his policy of national action within a matter of weeks.

We have become so accustomed to national negotiations that it is easy to miss the importance of this innovation in industrial relations. Before 1914 all negotiations on wages and conditions in the transport industry, as in practically all other industries, had been conducted locally; the unions were local organisations dealing with local employers. The war, however, changed this. Under the system of compulsory arbitration, it was natural for the Committee on Production and the other tribunals to make national awards to meet increases in the cost of living. For similar reasons, the Government encouraged unions and employers to negotiate national agreements for the revision of wages. Bevin and other trade-union leaders were quick to see the advantage of such national negotiations. It would greatly strengthen the unions by creating a common interest among all workers in the same industry and enable them to operate on a national scale.

But to do this they had to create an organisation capable of representing the many local groups of transport workers on a national basis. This had always been the force of the argument in favour of amalgamation into a single transport workers' union such as the railwaymen had attempted to create in the N.U.R. That was out of the question during the war. What Bevin did was to bypass the difficulty and find a means of conducting national negotiations by making use of the Federation's machinery, cumbersome though it was.

It was an astute move, for not only did it secure substantial advantages for the men but it drove home the case for amalgamation with greater effect than any propaganda. Despite the handicap of having to consult the individual unions at every step and persuade them to look further than their local interests, Bevin and Williams convincingly demonstrated the advantages of national action.

The demand for amalgamation had been revived at the Salford carters' conference in August 1917. A joint standing committee, set up by the N.T.W.F. and the N.U.R. in December 1917 with Bevin as one of its members, was instructed to discuss common action and the possibility of amalgamation with the railwaymen. Another committee, set up to consider the future of the Federation, recommended that its success should be consolidated by amalgamation or at least a much more effective centralisation of powers. The same year, 1918, a carefully negotiated scheme[1] for amalgamation between the National Union of General Workers (the old Gasworkers) and the Dockers was completed, an amalgamation which might have had a big future. It broke down for lack of sufficient support when it came to a vote of the rank and file membership.[2] The time had not yet come, but the contrast between what could be accomplished by common action and the repeated frustration of every attempt to give it a permanent form created the atmosphere in which Bevin was able to carry through his own amalgamation scheme three years later.

8

Bevin complained at this time that he lived on the doorstep of the Committee on Production. Many of the individual unions belonging to the Transport Workers' Federation tried to get Bevin or Williams to act for them in arbitration cases and no sooner was one award given than Bevin had to master the details of another case.

---

1 The details are to be found in the *Dockers' Record*, July 1918, pp. 4–5.

2 The negotiations between the two Executives began in July 1916. A scheme was finally worked out which both Executives accepted in 1918. Had this amalgamation been carried out, it would certainly have altered the course of Bevin's career. As it was, instead of combining, the unions went on to a series of separate amalgamations out of which grew the two big general unions of today, the Transport and General Workers and the National Union of General and Municipal Workers.

Each claim involved detailed and often exhausting negotiations with the different unions and the employers leading up to the presentation of the case to the arbitration tribunal and then more meetings with the union leaders and men to persuade them to accept the award. Week after week that winter and spring Bevin spent his life in third-class railway carriages and committee rooms, snatching a meal or finding a bed where he could, away from home all the week and sometimes at week-ends as well.

He was not only involved in the transport industry, he was also active in the National Federation of General Workers which had been set up in July 1917 to replace the National Council of General Labourers. It was another move towards the concentration of trade-union strength, an attempt to provide for workers belonging to the general unions in a variety of industries—chemicals, cement, flour-milling, brick-making, building and engineering—a more effective form of organisation such as the N.T.W.F. provided for the transport workers. Bevin played a considerable part in creating the General Workers' Federation, and in September 1917 he produced to its Executive Council proposals for promoting national wage claims on the lines he was already following with the transport workers. At the end of its first year the new Federation, by now representing 740,000 trade-union members, was able to claim that it had secured or joined in securing national advances for workers in the chemical, aluminium and aircraft industries, gas undertakings, brick-making and flour-milling. Bevin, with an eye to Bristol and the Dockers' Union membership, took a particular interest in flour-milling and the confectionery, chocolate and cocoa trades, all of which were well established in the city. His objective was not only advances in wages but the establishment of joint industrial councils on the lines of the Whitley Report and of the Penscot discussions. He served on the sub-committee which negotiated the constitution of another joint industrial council with the Paint, Colour and Varnish Manufacturers' Association and he played a leading part in setting up a joint conciliation board for the copper industry in which the Dockers' Union had a large number of members in South Wales.

Membership of the committees on which he served in the Ministry of Reconstruction had made Bevin aware of the big changes taking place in the organisation of industry. The concentration of economic power which he was anxious to see in the trade-union movement was.

already taking place on the other side of industry. To provide the General Workers' Federation with accurate information of these changes he urged and carried the appointment of an additional assistant. It would have been a fully equipped statistical department, if he had had his way. For immersed though he was in the detailed negotiations of a score of different trades, spending so much of his time in argument over an additional ½d. an hour for this or that specialised process, his interest in the broad developing pattern of industry and society was never submerged. It was this breadth of mind which already marked him out amongst trade-union leaders.

9

All this work on committees and for the two Federations was unpaid apart from his expenses and an occasional honorarium. He was still a working man who had to earn his salary of £6 10s. a week as an official of the Dockers' Union. At the end of every committee meeting or arbitration case, every time his journeys brought him back to Euston, King's Cross or Paddington, he made his way to the Union's head office off the Strand, at Effingham House in Arundel Street, to see what had come in by post or telephone. Often it meant turning round and going off to another meeting out in the East End, or taking the night train down to Plymouth or Wales.

After setbacks in the first year of the war, the Dockers, like most other unions, steadily increased their membership. In 1914 this stood at 38,000, by 1918 it had risen to 85,000. In the same year the Union's income topped £81,000; in 1914 it had been just under £30,000.

When the Triennial Delegate Conference was held at Anderton's Hotel, Fleet Street, the union which had been damned for holding up the trade of the Port of London in 1911–12 was entertained to dinner by the Lord Mayor in the Mansion House, to the unabashed delight of the delegates. The following day, the Minister of Education, H. A. L. Fisher, came down to address the conference. The idea of inviting him had been suggested by Bevin at the end of a debate in which the delegates endorsed an educational programme ranging from the establishment of nursery schools and the raising of the school-leaving age to fifteen, to free secondary and university education. In thanking Fisher for his address, Bevin said with feeling:

"The desire that the children shall have a better chance than their parents is inherent in the working class. The bolder the Minister of Education is in his proposals, the bigger the response he will get from the people. The working class will only be able to emancipate itself when it has the power of knowledge."[1]

Tillett's report to the Triennial Conference showed that the Union's biggest expansion had come in the two districts with which Bevin was personally associated, Bristol and the South-west. This was no coincidence. He still kept in close touch with the district offices at Bristol and Plymouth, took a hand in all their major negotiations and was always looking for fresh ground to break. Between 1914 and 1918 the number of branches in the Bristol district rose from fourteen to thirty-eight and the district's income from £3,700 to £17,400. The only other district in the Union which could rival these figures was Plymouth where the number of branches increased from ten to forty-one and income from £850 in 1914 to £7,550 in 1918.

Among the new branches started at Bristol were three in the confectionery and chocolate trade. Bevin was active on the workers' side of the Trade Board set up in 1916 for the sugar, confectionery and food preserving industries; fought a strong battle with the old Bristol firm of J. S. Fry for recognition of the Union,[2] and became vice-chairman of the Interim Industrial Reconstruction Committee for these industries when it was established in 1919. This is an interesting example of Bevin's ability to work outwards from his base

1 In October Fisher spent a week-end at Bristol at Bevin's invitation, was entertained to dinner by the Union (together with the Lord Mayor, the Vice-Chancellor of the University and the President of the National Union of Teachers) and addressed a meeting of 3–4,000 at the People's Palace on the Sunday morning. Bevin got the N.T.W.F. to back the Dockers' protest at the inadequacy of the Government's provision for the Minister of Education's plans, and at the Labour Party conference in January 1918 he attacked the Party's resolution on education for not going far enough.

2 When Fry's celebrated their bicentenary in 1928, Bevin was invited to contribute to the souvenir publication and presented with a gold medal by the firm in recognition of his services—a striking instance of his success in converting employers to the value of trade unionism.

in Bristol to national agreements. Two other examples of the same tactics are to be found in the tobacco industry (from the Wills' branch of the Imperial Tobacco Company in Bristol) and flour-milling. The contribution he made to the organisation of the milling industry in Great Britain was a source of pride to Ernest Bevin all his life, and justifiably so.[1] It began with the agreement which he negotiated with the South-western Millers in May 1918 and which he promptly turned into the basis of a national award from the Committee on Production the following month. The flour-milling industry was one of the first to set up a Joint Industrial Council and from 1918 until he became Minister of Labour in 1940, Bevin served as chairman and vice-chairman of the Council in alternate years.

In the South-west he took up the cause of the fishermen, helped to establish branches for them at Plymouth, Brixham and a number of other places, led a deputation to the Minister of Food to secure a modification of the Government order controlling fish prices and in October 1918 submitted proposals for a fish-distribution scheme to a conference of fishermen in Plymouth.

Another sally into new territory was a visit to Ireland in the summer of 1917 to visit the Union's newly-established branch at Cork. He was depressed by what he saw in Ireland, not least by a poverty which, even by the standard of English slums, was startling. In Bristol itself he joined with Frank Sheppard in promoting a scheme for a new housing estate—a garden suburb, in the jargon of the time—at Kingsweston. A public utility society was set up and the Dockers, the Engineers and Bristol University were among those represented on its Board of Management. Bevin was insistent that they must plan and build this experiment in working-class housing in such a way as to break with the tradition of terrace houses which would turn into slums in a few years' time. The end of the war came too soon for much to be done, but the scheme was taken over by Bristol Corporation as the nucleus of a remarkable housing pro-gramme which, between 1918 and 1939, saw 36,000 houses built within the City boundaries.[2]

A plan for the better distribution of fish supplies, the Avonmouth housing project, the employment of short sea communications to ease the burden on the South Wales railways—these were exactly

1 See pp. 94-5; 380-1; 604-5.
2 R. Jevons and John Madge, *Housing Estates* (1946). pp. 13–14.

the sort of schemes which Bevin, with his intensely practical and fertile imagination, was always ready to take up and lend a hand with. We shall come across many other examples in the course of his life, from the Workers' Travel Association and holidays with pay to the support he gave to plans for building road bridges over the Severn, the Tay and the Humber. He had an inexhaustible fund of ideas and energy, the imagination to see a need, the resource to know how to meet it.

Towards the end of 1917 Frank Sheppard became the first Labour Lord Mayor of Bristol. His friend, Ernie Bevin, was delighted and promptly organised the presentation of a cheque from the Dockers' Union to pay for the new mayor's official robes and a tea and coffee service for Mrs. Sheppard. He secured Bristol's famous Colston Hall for the ceremony and did it in style, taking immense pleasure in the opportunity of honouring—and helping—a man for whom he had an affectionate regard, a working trade-union organiser and an orphan like himself.

10

The strain of overwork in the next few months proved too much even for Bevin's strength. By July 1918 he was suffering from a nervous breakdown, had to be given sick-leave and for two or three months was too unwell to undertake anything like his full duties. There was one thing his friends could do to help. They organised a mass meeting in Bristol to express the gratitude of the ordinary members for the gains he had secured in his national campaign. Tillett and Bob Williams came down for the occasion and after an evening of speeches in his praise, Brother Bevin was presented with an illuminated address and a wallet of Treasury notes.

By October he had sufficiently recovered to play the leading role in another ceremony which expressed in characteristic vein the native genius of the English Labour movement. The People's Palace was packed to the doors on Sunday, 20th October, when the Lord Mayor of Bristol, Frank Sheppard, took the chair. With the end of the war in sight, there was a fervour of emotion in the air as the men and women of the Dockers' Union sang Lowell's opening hymn:

"Once to every man and nation
Comes the moment to decide."

Songs ('Roses of Picardy', 'Nirvana', 'When the ebb tide flows'), a
collection and a pianoforte solo followed. Then Ernest Bevin
advanced to the front of the platform to unfurl the Carters' Banner
which had cost £100 to make and had been paid for by the members
of the branch he had founded eight years before. As he did so, the
audience rose to its feet:

"Lift up the people's banner
Now trailing in the dust
A million hands are ready
To guard the sacred trust . . ."

This was the faith, drawn from the Nonconformist and Chartist
traditions of the working class, which made the Labour movement
what it was in the first half of the twentieth century; in this lay both
its weakness and its strength. It was a scene which would have
baffled and exasperated the foreign observer, yet in its own way it
was a scene as unmistakeably English as the man who stood there,
feet firmly planted, holding the banner erect, to join wholeheartedly in the final chorus:

"Soon we march to battle,
With souls that shall not rest
Until the world God gave us
Is by the world possessed."

Three weeks later the Armistice was signed. The war was over:
the unquiet years of peace had begun.

CHAPTER 5

Labour's Offensive
1918 – 1919

I

THREE DAYS after the Armistice, on 14th November 1918, a specially-summoned conference of the Labour Party voted to withdraw from the coalition and to resume unfettered opposition to the Government. The minority had prudence on their side. The coalition was popular; Lloyd George would exploit the prestige of victory to win a general election and Labour would exclude itself from any share in the making of the Peace. The Party organisation was not yet prepared for an election and might well suffer a crushing defeat. But the majority demanded the independence for which they had long been hankering and, although the pessimists proved right and they lost the election, in the long run independence was worth the price they had to pay for it.

There was never any doubt which way Ernest Bevin would vote. He was confirmed in his views by the speed with which Lloyd George rushed on the election and by the campaign to brand opposition to the coalition as unpatriotic.

To his regret he found himself once again on the opposite side to Frank Sheppard. A few weeks before, while the Labour Party was still a member of the coalition, Sheppard had been adopted as Parliamentary candidate for Central Bristol, with every prospect of being returned unopposed. Now, however, his union (the Boot and Shoe Operatives) accepted the majority vote of the Labour Party conference and withdrew their financial support. Sheppard had no option but to stand down.[1] The next day the local Conservatives

---

1 He did not add that, in keeping with his personal integrity, he had refused an offer from Lloyd George which would have given him financial independence but compromised him politically.

adopted T. W. H. Inskip, son of a former Bristol Alderman as the official coalition candidate and the Bristol Central Labour Party put up Ernest Bevin to oppose him.

The local Labour Party was determined to fight all four seats in Bristol and, with little time before polling day, had to select a strong candidate if it was to make any showing at all in the Central division. Bevin was the outstanding Labour leader in the city (Tillett was contesting his own seat in Salford) and the one man who might overcome the effect of the split produced by Sheppard's withdrawal. Even the *Morning Post* correspondent admitted that of the four Labour candidates in Bristol Bevin was much the most likely "to get within measurable distance of Parliament".

Frank Sheppard, then and later, acquitted him of any suggestion of dishonourable behaviour and wrote a letter which Bevin read out at one of his meetings:

"I don't accuse you of any act of treachery towards myself in any way. All that I say is, I do not agree with the majority vote of the Congress. My union having decided that they must be guided by its decision left me no option but to state that I was not a candidate."[1]

The *Morning Post*'s comment was: "How Jacob jockeyed Esau."

With only twelve days between his adoption and election day, Bevin had to improvise his campaign. It was a lively contest, with Bevin speaking half a dozen times a day and the members of the Dockers' Union campaigning vigorously in his support. Although he was sincere in his disavowal of political ambition, his anger was roused by Lloyd George's attempt to steam-roller the democratic expression of opposition.

"I cannot see the need of returning members to Parliament at all," he told a critical audience in the Bristol Corn Exchange, "if they are going to be gramophones in the constituencies and voting machines in the House of Commons. The position created by the Coalition is one of political slavery (Cries of 'no' and cheers) . . .
"One reason why I complain of the election being forced upon the country is that it deprives so many of the men who have been serving their country of the opportunity of seeing the problems calling for solution in their right perspective. The election is an attempt to snatch power before democracy is properly organised."[2]

1 *Western Daily Press*, 7th December 1918.
2 Ibid.

"Making Germany pay" was the most popular of the coalition's slogans and Bevin found himself attacked, not only as a Bolshevik, but as a pacifist and a pro-German. With a common sense which history was to vindicate, he retorted by asking *how* Germany was going to pay. If she paid in goods, it would certainly not be to the advantage of Great Britain.[1]

"Germany must make good all damage and reparation to the fullest extent, but I am opposed to a penal indemnity: that is quite a separate thing. . . . I am not going to imitate the Bismarckian policy of 1871, recreating any festering sores in Europe which will lead to a future war."[2]

When the *Morning Post* correspondent asked him if the Labour Party was not preaching revolution, Bevin retorted:

"If my principles are accepted, it *is* Revolution. I stand for a social re-volution brought about by a freely elected Parliament. . . . You cannot have the schoolmaster ahead for fifty years and still keep the working classes at only a living wage. It is like calculating the cost of keeping a horse simply on a fodder basis."[3]

Polling took place on 14th December and Inskip secured 12,232 votes to Bevin's 7,137.[4] The results followed the same pattern in the rest of the country. Out of 363 candidates endorsed by the Labour Party, only 57 were returned. The independent Liberal Party, led by Asquith, fared even worse with 26 members, and the coalition of Lloyd George Liberals, Conservatives and Coalition Labour (the National Democratic Party) won 484 seats. It was the 'patriotic' wing of the trade-union movement which was returned to Parliament: Tillett, Sexton, Jimmy Thomas, J. R. Clynes, Will Thorne, Havelock Wilson. In a fervour of nationalism, the country turned out anyone suspected of opposition to the war, and few paid

1 Ibid. 14th December 1918.
2 Ibid. 13th December. His election address is reprinted in full in the *Dockers' Record* for December 1918, pp. 5–8.
3 *Morning Post*, 13th Dec. 1918.
4 One old Bristol docker, who served on the Executive Committee of the Dockers' Union, remarked to the author: "The dockers admired Ernie and turned up to cheer at his meetings, but they didn't vote for him. They had more sense. They knew what he was worth to them and didn't want to lose him. If he had gone into Parliament, they wouldn't have got the Shaw Award and the guaranteed day." I record this opinion without comment.

much attention to the fact that Labour's share of the total votes cast for the three main parties rose from 8 per cent in the two elections of 1910 to 24 per cent in 1918.

Bevin's defeat was decisive. While his opponent went on to become as Sir Thomas Inskip a not very successful Minister for the Co-ordination of Defence in the Chamberlain Government, and as Baron Caldecote a Lord Chief Justice, Bevin returned with relief to his trade-union work. It is tempting to speculate what his career might have been, if he had entered Parliament in 1918 when he was not yet forty, instead of in 1940 when he was in his sixtieth year. With his ability directed into Parliamentary channels, he might well have succeeded MacDonald in 1931, or Lansbury in 1935, as Leader of the Labour Party and become Prime Minister in 1945 instead of Attlee. But this is idle speculation, for Bevin's exclusion from Parliament after 1918 was self-imposed. Far from making any effort to secure a safe Labour seat—which he could have obtained at virtually any time in the later 1920s or 1930s—he refused a number of invitations and only stood at Gateshead in 1931 as a gesture of trade-union solidarity at the blackest moment in the Labour Party's history. Without ever wavering in his belief in the necessity of political action, he chose to identify himself with the trade-union and industrial side of the Labour movement. The decision, whether right or wrong, was deliberate and his own. It was made, as all his major decisions were made, not from ambition but from the conviction that he could best serve the class to which he belonged in this way.

2

Until the summer of 1920, Bevin remained a national organiser of the Dockers' Union. A great deal of the work of the Central Office fell to his share as Tillett's health was poor, he was often away from work and both he and James Wignall, the other national organiser, were Members of Parliament with political as well as industrial interests. In July 1919, Bevin told the recalled Delegate Conference of the Dockers' Union (a body which was in a position to check his claim):

"Many of the workpeople have now secured a 44- or 48-hour working week with enhanced rates of pay. In my own case I estimate my hours of labour average about eighty per week of six days and, in addition to this, I devoted, last year alone, thirty-eight Sundays to work away from home, for which I was paid nothing.

"As an instance, last week was fairly typical. On Monday morning I left home at 8.30 a.m., travelled from Bristol to London to attend to a week's accumulated work whilst I had been to the Labour Party conference. I put in a rush day and left for Bristol at 10 p.m., arriving home at 1.30 a.m. Left for Cardiff 7.30 a.m., attended five conferences there, left again soon after 10 p.m., arriving London 4 a.m., having sat all these hours wet through from a rainstorm in Cardiff. I was at the Central Office early Wednesday morning and attended three conferences, stopping work at 11 p.m. Thursday I was at Central Office before 9.30 a.m., attended three conferences and the Executive meeting, which closed about 10 p.m. and from there caught the mail for Penzance for special arbitrations and meetings and conferences Friday and Saturday. I travelled back all Sunday to be in time for this conference. In all, last week, I actually spent 115 hours working and travelling for the Union."[1]

No wonder that in April the Dockers' Executive received a warning from Bevin's doctor that he had "worked himself to a standstill" and must take more rest.

The Delegate Conference agreed to raise his salary to £10 a week. In May 1920, the next Conference created the post of Assistant General Secretary and fixed the salary at £650 a year. All the branches nominated Bevin, and his appointment was unanimous. In practice it made little difference, for he had been doing the job for a couple of years, but it was a welcome recognition of the position he now held in the Union.

Down to the beginning of 1920, the Bevins went on living in Bristol. In February of that year, however, Mrs. Bevin came up to London for the Shaw Inquiry and stayed on. She found a furnished flat in Adam Street, then one that was unfurnished in Gloucester Place, close to Regent's Park. Finally they bought a house out at Golders Green where they lived for the rest of the 1920s.

One of the disadvantages which forced Bevin to leave Bristol was the incessant travelling in which he was involved and for which London was a much better base. Wherever possible he sought to place negotiations for wages, hours and conditions of work on a national basis. In the opening months of 1919 he and Bob Williams

1 D.W.R. and G.W.U.: Minutes of the recalled Triennial Delegate Meeting, 7th–9th July, 1919, p. 16.

successfully negotiated agreements for a shorter working week (generally of 48 hours) and wage increases for all the principal industries represented in the Federation: road transport, tramway, bus and canal workers, dockers, coal tippers and trimmers.

An immense amount of work was required for the preparation and successful prosecution of each of these claims. All the unions concerned, some of them jealous rivals, others clinging to petty advantages in local negotiations, had to be persuaded to agree upon a single scheme of hours and wages applicable to the industry throughout the country. The employers, with equally diverse local interests, had to be persuaded to come together to discuss a national agreement. Only then could the main negotiations begin. Finally, when they were completed, Bevin and Williams had to spend more weary hours dealing with local variations and trying to persuade the unions they represented to accept the agreement as the best obtainable under the circumstances.

3

Similar applications for shorter hours and higher wages were made by the National Federation of General Workers, of whose Executive Council Bevin was an active member, to twenty-six employers' federations, again with considerable success. The variety of trades with which he was connected was, of course, a reflection of his position as organiser of a general union. His interest was never limited to one or even three or four industries, but spread over a wide sector of employment.

The chance of persuading, or forcing, the employers to enter into national negotiations pre-disposed Bevin and the other leaders in both Federations to accept the Whitley Committee's proposals for setting up national joint industrial councils.[1] Bevin played a big part in getting such councils into operation (under a variety of titles) for the road transport industry, tramways, the chemical industry, flour milling, the confectionery trades and eventually for the docks. At the beginning of 1920, he told Lord Shaw's Court of Inquiry that he was a member of fourteen, acting as the chairman of two and the

1 Cf. report of the N.T.W.F. Executive Committee, Annual General Council Meeting, 1918, pp. 48–51.

vice-chairman of three. Not all of these councils survived. The one for the road transport industry, for instance, broke down in 1920 when the employers refused to continue national negotiations and walked out. Others became an accepted part of the structure of industrial relations and one or two provided proof that the hopes entertained by the Whitley Committee and by meetings like those at Penscot were not chimerical.

No industry in the country offered a better illustration than flour-milling of what could be done, given the goodwill and the intelligence on both sides which were so notably lacking in the coal industry. Flour-milling, a small but highly important industry, had been virtually unorganised before the war. In the autumn of 1918, however, the employers formed a federation which in March of the following year met the unions concerned—thirteen of them, at this time—in order to set up a joint industrial council. A. E. (later Sir Albert) Humphries, one of the employers' representatives, was elected as chairman, Ernest Bevin as the vice-chairman. Thereafter, until Humphries' death in October 1935, the two men took it in turn to act as chairman and, after Humphries' death, Bevin was re-elected as chairman on the proposal of the employers.

Having reached a national agreement on hours before the Council was actually set up, their first task was to settle a national basis for wages. This they found by grading all flour-mills into three classes, according to the population and importance of the area in which they were situated. In the course of the next few years wages rose and fell on several occasions but the increase or reduction was agreed upon by the Council and the industry had the unique record of no strikes at all in the inter-war period. More than that, it soon began to develop that co-operation in other directions besides wages and hours to which the Whitley Report attached so much importance but which languished or was never attempted in the case of most industrial councils. Joint schemes were put into effect by the Council for technical education; for a national pension fund; for compensation to those put out of jobs by rationalisation and the concentration of mills; and for the protection of the workpeople's health.[1]

1 The details are to be found in the annual reports of the National Joint Industrial Council for the Flour-Milling Industry, 1919–1940. Cf. also the contribution by L. H. Green (secretary of the Council) to *Industrial Relations in Great Britain*, ed. F. E. Gannett and B.F. Catherwood (New York, 1939).

In 1920 the National Union of Millers amalgamated with the Dockers' and, after the larger amalgamation which followed, the Transport and General Workers' held a clear majority of the seats on the workers' side of the Council. Bevin was thus able to play a big part in these developments and most of the schemes owed much to his initiative. He regarded the record of joint consultation in the flour-milling industry as pointing the way to what could be made out of co-operation between employers and unions.

Very different was his attitude towards the National Industrial Conference which the Minister of Labour opened, with a flurry of Government publicity, at the end of February 1919. Bevin looked on this as another device of Lloyd George's to keep the trade unions talking and thereby gain a breathing-space until the country settled down and the demand for sweeping changes had exhausted itself.

Committees were set up representing both sides of industry, reports prepared, recommendations drafted and adopted—with little more result than had followed the equally admirable proposals framed by the Ministry of Reconstruction and its committees. In July 1921 the trade-union members resigned in disgust: by then, industrial depression had succeeded the post-war boom and Labour was on the defensive.

From the start, Bevin strongly urged the Executive of the Transport Workers' Federation to have nothing to do with the Industrial Conference and none of the partners in the Triple Alliance—transport workers, miners, railwaymen—took any part in its proceedings. The one asset the workers had was their bargaining power: in Bevin's view it was folly to put themselves in a position in which they would compromise the right to use it in return for promises which they could not trust the Government to carry out.

4

He was, indeed, suspicious of any invitation which might hamper his independence of action and, at a time when the Government was lavish in offering places on committees and advisory posts to trade-union leaders, agreed to serve on no more than four committees, two of which proved not to be important and the third of which had already been set up during the war.

The Committee on the Restoration of Trade Union Practices might have been important, but was not: the ability of trade unions to restore practices protecting the skilled worker depended on the bargaining power of each union within its own trade, not on legislation. Full employment in the year after the war was of more value to the unions than the Restoration of Pre-War Practices Act, of which little use was made. As for the Committee on Inland Waterways (1920–21), this proved as well-meaning and ineffectual as every other attempt to rescue the canal system of the country from neglect. Its chairman was Neville Chamberlain and Bevin was appointed as the representative of the Dockers' Union, which counted a number of canal workers among its members. He soon ceased to attend its meetings, however, and three box files of minutes and papers in the cellars of Transport House are the only surviving evidence of his interest.

The Committee on Trusts had been set up by the Ministry of Reconstruction in February 1918, with John Hilton as its secretary and J.A. Hobson and Sidney Webb among its other members. The Committee presented its report in April 1919. It found that there had been a great increase in the number of trade combinations during the war and recommended the establishment of machinery for their investigation similar to the commissions and tribunals already set up in the U.S.A., Canada and other overseas countries. A minority report signed by Bevin, Hobson and Sidney Webb criticised these proposals as inadequate guarantees of the public interest.

"The fact is that Free Competition no longer governs the business world. We do not suggest that any action should be taken to prevent combination or association in capitalist enterprise. . . . [They] are steps in the greater efficiency, the increased economy and the better organisation of industry. It is, however, plain that the change from competitive rivalry to combination calls for corresponding developments to secure for the community both safeguards against the evils of monopoly and at least a large share of the economic benefits of the better organisation of industry which it promotes."[1]

The only two safeguards to which Bevin and the other signatories of the minority report looked with any confidence were the control

[1] Ministry of Reconstruction: Report of Committee on Trusts (Cd. 9236. 1919), p. 13.

of prices and public ownership of monopolistic enterprises. War-time experience, they argued, proved the first to be practicable and effective. As for the second, "where the enterprise is national in scope . . . and its product enters into practically universal consumption, we see no alternative to State Ownership."[1]

The insight which the Committee on Trusts gave him into the workings of the capitalist system was extended by his appointment to the Central Committee set up by the Board of Trade under the Profiteering Act of 1919. The Central Committee itself split up into a large number of sub-committees to investigate complaints of price-rings, monopolies and profiteering in a wide range of trades. Altogether, they published fifty-seven detailed reports between 1919 and 1921.

It would be tedious to summarise the work of these different committees, but they continued Bevin's education in practical economics.[2] This was the way in which over the next twenty years he acquired the remarkable knowledge of industry and trade which he was to put to such good use as Minister of Labour in the second World War. He had an unusually retentive memory in which he stored away an extraordinary collection of information and on which he could draw, quite unexpectedly, to the surprise—and some-times discomfiture—of anyone with whom he was talking. The next year, for instance, he was to show to what good use he could put the evidence accumulated by the Committees on Trusts and on Pro-fiteering in preparing the dockers' case for the Shaw Inquiry.

All this was incidental, however, to Bevin's real interests at this stage of his career, the effective organisation of working-class strength to force the Government and the employers to pay attention to Labour's demands.

5

The three years after the war were more disturbed by open conflict between the trade unions and the employers, or between the unions and the Government, than any other period in modern British

1 Ibid. p. 14.

2 Apart from the Standing Committee on Trusts, Bevin served on four of the sub-committees dealing with road transport rates, fixed retail prices, the sale of fish and the farriery trade.

history, with the solitary exception of 1926, the year of the General Strike. From 1911 to 1913, another period of labour unrest, the average number of working days lost each year through strikes was a little over twenty million. During the war it fell to 5.3 million, then, from the beginning of 1919 to the end of 1921 the average shot up to 40 million days a year.

The force behind this sudden outburst of industrial conflict derived not so much from particular claims over hours and wages (most of these were soon met) as from a pent-up, passionately felt demand for drastic change, an angry refusal to return to pre-war conditions. Nationalisation of the mines, the railways and the land; workers' control of industry; a capital levy; work or maintenance; an end to the old class distinctions; the abolition of poverty and riches—these were the slogans which captured a considerable section of the working class.[1] Change was in the air. The Russian Revolution and the defeat of the Central Powers had been followed by a wave of revolutionary violence sweeping across Europe east of the Rhine. In Britain too, men felt that the war had left a gulf between them and the past. Inured to violence after four years of fighting, they were impatient of compromise and delay.

Bevin's gloomy view of what would happen at the end of the war proved to be wrong—or at least premature. The Armistice was followed, not by a slump, but by a boom. There was comparatively little unemployment to take the edge off Labour's demands, and the union leaders, no longer restrained by the patriotic argument of the nation in danger, and with a membership which doubled between 1913 and 1920, were in a militant mood.

But how were they to secure their demands? Lloyd George had forestalled Labour by his snap election at the end of 1918, while the nation was still under the influence of wartime emotions and before the angry mood of 1919 had time to crystallise. Less than sixty per cent of the electorate—only one man in four in the Forces—had voted and Labour angrily protested that the electorate had been tricked and the new House of Commons was unrepresentative of the nation. The fact remained, however, that the Labour Party could muster no more than 59 members against Lloyd George's coalition bloc of 484.

1 Cf. A. H. Gleason, *What the Workers Want: a Study of British Labour.* (New York, 1920.)

The contrast between the Parliamentary weakness of the Labour Party and the numerical strength of the trade unions outside Parliament[1] strengthened the case of those who argued that the trade unions should use their strength to force the Government, despite its majority in the House, to concede their demands. The Government still controlled the mines and the railways; it was through the extension of these and other powers which the State had assumed during the war that Labour sought to secure the changes it desired and prevent the restoration of private control over the nation's economic resources. At the same time, there was a strong radical element in the trade-union leadership, especially among the men of Ernie Bevin's and Bob Williams' generation, which was impatient of the cautious outlook of the older leaders and prepared to consider the use of the industrial power of the unions for political as well as economic ends. It was not indeed until after the failure of the General Strike of 1926 that the left-wing of the trade unions and the Labour movement finally abandoned the idea of a short cut to their objectives by the extra-Parliamentary methods of 'Direct Action'.

'Direct Action' was a fine slogan, but what did it mean? For all their talk of revolution, those who employed it, with few exceptions, were no Bolsheviks deliberately aiming like Lenin at the revolutionary seizure of power. Their object was not to overthrow the Government but to remedy what they regarded as the deficiencies of the democratic system by forcing the Government to concede specific demands, the nationalisation of the mines or the abandonment of intervention against Russia. The proof of this is the simple fact that, although a General Strike was constantly referred to and threatened between 1919 and 1926, no one on the trade-union side ever worked out the problems of organisation involved, leave alone prepared for armed insurrection.

This was all right so long as the General Strike was employed only as a threat and the Government found it expedient to compromise. But it was a dangerous game to play: when the Government made up its mind to call the unions' bluff, as it did in 1926, they had either to go forward—a course for which they were quite unprepared—or to retreat ignominiously.

Bevin himself looked on 'Direct Action' in the light of a demon-

1 Total trade-union membership reached the figure of 8,334,000 in 1920, of whom 6,418, 000 were affiliated to the T.U.C.

stration, a form of pressure on the Government rather than a prelude to revolution. Although he took his stand with the radical wing of the trade-union leadership he was never a Communist and his practical common sense stopped him from falling into the verbal extremism of the Left. For he was quick to see that if pressure was to be brought to bear on the Government, whether for industrial or political purposes, it had to be organised. Impatient of the rhetoric of 'Direct Action', he turned to the practical problem: how to create a more satisfactory instrument for mobilising working-class strength. His instinct was right: what defeated Labour was its inability to make its potential strength effective.

6

On paper the most powerful working-class organisation in the country was the Triple Industrial Alliance which was renewed during the course of February 1919. Bevin took part in its proceedings as a member of the Transport Workers' Federation Executive Committee. Acting in agreement, all three—the Miners' Federation, the National Union of Railwaymen and the National Transport Workers' Federation—refused to take part in the Government's National Industrial Council. The Miners had already tabled formidable demands: the reduction of the miners' working day from 8 to 6 hours; a 30% increase in earnings; the nationalisation of the mines. They voted by a six to one majority for a national strike to enforce them.

Stocks of coal were at a very low figure and London had no more than three days' supply. The miners were in a strong position and, with the prospect that the railwaymen and transport workers might support them, the Government adopted a conciliatory attitude. Lloyd George invited the miners' leaders to Downing Street and offered them a commission of inquiry into the coal industry with the widest terms of reference, strong representation of the workers' side and an obligation to report before the end of March 1919. The miners accepted the offer and the commission under the chairmanship of Sir John Sankey began its inquiry almost at once.

The transport workers and railwaymen as well as the miners were at this time engaged in 'national movements' and it was agreed that none of the three should make a separate settlement until the other two had reported how they stood. When the three executives met on 21st March 1919 they found that, although the Miners and the N.T.W.F. appeared to be in sight of a satisfactory settlement, the railwaymen had reached a deadlock. The Alliance therefore decided to send a deputation to the Government the next day. The result of this intervention, under threat of a combined strike, was to reopen negotiations for the N.U.R.

These were striking illustrations of the *potential* strength of the Triple Alliance, and so long as it limited itself to the threat of a strike its power was impressive. For the moment this was sufficient. Despite the big majority it commanded in the Commons, the Government in the first half of 1919 was very much on the defensive. It was unsure how far Labour would press its demands for nationalisation; unsure how far it could rely on its own forces (there were police strikes in 1918–19); unsure, in fact, of the mood of the nation now that the war was over.

This situation brought out all Lloyd George's skill and resource. He avoided any head-on clash with Labour until demobilisation had taken place and the country had settled down. At the same time, he took every possible step to reduce the pressure of discontent behind Labour's demands.

The demobilisation scheme was drastically revised to release four million men from the Forces within the year. An "out of work donation" (the forerunner of the dole) provided assistance for ex-servicemen and civilians displaced by the ending of the war. The unions' demand for a shorter working week was conceded with little resistance. The post-war boom made it possible for employers to meet most of the unions' wage claims, enabled the demobilised servicemen to be easily absorbed into industry and smoothed the transition from war to peace.

In the meantime, Lloyd George beguiled the union leaders by such devices as the Sankey Commission on the coal industry and the National Industrial Conference, spinning out time in a series of inconclusive negotiations. In the end he was able to evade any major decisions until the psychological moment for Labour to act had passed.

7

During the spring of 1919, the Triple Alliance extended its claims to the political as well as the industrial sphere. The question of British intervention in Russia was rapidly becoming (as intervention in Spain became in 1936-8) the political, even more perhaps the emotional, touchstone of the Left. Lansbury's *Herald*, the I.L.P. and the more radical union leaders were agreed in denouncing the Government's 'conspiracy' to keep British troops in Russia and use them to overthrow the Soviet régime. They had little sympathy with Communism in practice—certainly not Ernest Bevin nor a man like Philip Snowden—but they were not prepared to see the Russian Revolution suppressed by capitalist governments. Soviet Russia had become for both Left and Right a symbolic issue, the right of any working-class movement to work out its own destiny free from outside intervention. It was this symbolic quality, often bearing little relation to the real state of affairs in the Soviet Union, which helped to make the Russian Revolution, like the French Revolution of 1789, an event of such international importance in the next thirty years.

At a meeting in Southport on 16th April 1919, the three Executives composing the council of the Triple Alliance called on the Parliamentary Committee of the T.U.C. to summon a special conference and there decide what action should be taken to secure the withdrawal of British troops from Russia. To this they added three more political demands—the withdrawal of the conscription bill before Parliament, the release of all conscientious objectors and the raising of the blockade against Germany—and in the course of May a fourth: the repudiation of the War Office circular inquiring into the reliability of the troops in the event of civil and industrial troubles. The Parliamentary Committee, with a right-wing majority, contented itself with a deputation to Bonar Law, the Conservative Leader of the House of Commons, and refused to call a conference.

The procrastination of the Parliamentary Committee touched off a debate which divided every Labour and trade-union conference that summer and autumn. At the Transport Workers' Federation annual council meeting at Swansea in June, the action of the Triple Alliance in taking a *political* initiative was attacked by Will Thorne, the founder of the Gasworkers' Union in 1889, and by Havelock Wilson, the seamen's leader, who boasted that he was a 'reactionary'. It was defended by Bob Williams and Bevin, although the latter supported Tillett's amendment that the Executive should not have power to commit the Federation to strike action in support of the Triple Alliance, without first taking a ballot vote of its own constituent unions.

The debate was resumed at the Labour Party conference at Southport on 25th and 26th June. In his opening speech, the chairman, John McGurk, told the delegates:

"A movement is already afoot to employ the strike weapon for political purposes. . . . It is both unwise and undemocratic, because we fail to get a majority at the polls, to turn round and demand that we should substitute industrial action."[1]

The Party Executive put up Arthur Henderson to sound a warning:

"If the British Labour Movement is to institute a new precedent in our industrial history by initiating a general strike for the purpose of achieving not industrial but political objects, it is imperative that the Trade Unions, whose members are to fulfil the obligations implied in the new policy and whose finances are to be involved, should realise the responsibilities such a strike movement would entail and should themselves determine the plan of any such new campaign."[2]

The 'Old Guard', Sexton, Tillett, J. R. Clynes—the elders of the T.U.C. Parliamentary Committee—urged the conference to adhere to constitutional methods of action.

"Were they going" (Clynes asked them) "to concede to every other class the right they were claiming to exercise? . . . The blow which they were threatening would not be a blow at a Government, but a blow at democracy."[3]

The opposition to the official view came, not from the 'intellectuals' but from the leaders of the Triple Alliance, from Bob Smillie, the upright and inflexible Scot who was the Miners' Pre-

1 Labour Party Conference Report, 1919, p. 113.
2 Ibid, p. 116.
3 Ibid, pp. 160–1.

sident, Frank Hodges (Secretary of the Miners' Federation), Bob
Williams and John Bromley, of the Locomotive Engineers and
Firemen. What was more, they carried the conference in protesting
against Allied intervention in Russia and calling on the National
Executive to consult the T.U.C. "with a view to effective action
being taken to enforce these demands by the unreserved use of their
political and industrial power".[1]

Bevin did not speak in the debate. He was not opposed to the use
of industrial power for the objects set out by the Triple Alliance, but
as he told the Dockers at their conference in July, "the question has
been taken too lightly. It is of no use to keep on threatening. We
know what it means, we know what is involved." An authoritative
decision had to be taken, and this could only be done by the T.U.C.,
not by the Labour Party conference. If the Trades' Union Congress
decided in favour of industrial action, the question ought then to be
submitted to a ballot of the individual unions:

"We say, if we are going to call upon the Trade Union movement to strike,
then the people who have to take the strike action and be responsible for it
should decide; it should not be foisted on us by irresponsible people. . . .
In asking the Parliamentary Committee to call a conference, that step was
taken because we agree that the Triple Alliance must not usurp the functions
of the Trade Union movement."[2]

8

But what was to happen if the Parliamentary Committee declined to
act? In face of their refusal, a full delegate conference of the Triple
Alliance, summoned to meet at Caxton Hall on 23rd July, decided
by 217 votes to 11 to act on its own initiative. A ballot paper to be
circulated to all the members asked whether they were in favour of
withdrawing their labour to secure the abolition of conscription,
of military intervention in Russia, and of military intervention in
trade-union disputes.[3]

1 Ibid, pp. 116–23; pp. 156–61.
2 D.W.R. and G.W.U.: Minutes of the re-called Triennial Delegate Meeting,
7th–9th July 1919, pp. 37–38.
3 This is a reference to a War Office circular which asked commanding officers
to report, *inter alia*, whether their troops could be relied on in the case of civil
disturbance, for strike breaking or for service in Russia.

Not all the leaders of the Triple Alliance agreed. J. H. Thomas wrote in the *Daily Herald*:

"I cannot understand and do not subscribe to the policy that asks men to strike today for what they refused to put a cross on the ballot paper yesterday. At the General Election, Labour made its appeal, declaring our policy both with regard to Russia, conscription and the nationalisation of monopolies. The other parties made their appeal—and our people believed them and not us. We ought clearly to recognise that, if Labour is going to govern, we can't have some outside body attempting to rebel against Parliamentary institutions without it recoiling on our own heads."[1]

It was not, however, the logic of these doubts which persuaded the Triple Alliance to call off the strike ballot, but the fact that within a week of its announcement Churchill told the House of Commons that all British troops would be withdrawn from Russia by the end of the summer and compulsory military service ended by the close of the financial year.

At the Glasgow T.U.C. (8th-13th September 1919), Smillie, Williams and Frank Hodges renewed their attack on the Parliamentary Committee and secured the reference back of that section of the annual report which excused its refusal to call a conference. This was tantamount to a vote of censure on the platform and was repeated when Tom Shaw, of the Weavers, introduced a motion disclaiming the use of industrial weapons for purely political ends. The 'previous question' was moved and carried by the radicals over the protests of the moderates. The two votes together showed the extent of the disillusionment with Parliamentary action.

Yet, when it came to something more than protests and threats, 'Direct Action' no longer commanded the same enthusiasm.

With a shrewd eye to the political weather, Lloyd George felt strong enough in August to announce that the Government would not accept the recommendation of the majority of the Sankey Commission to nationalise the coal mines. In September the T.U.C. gave virtually unanimous support to the miners' demands and spoke of 'compelling' the Government to adopt national ownership. But when the Prime Minister repeated his refusal to act, the most that a special T.U.C. conference in December was prepared to do, was to launch a publicity campaign, "The Mines for the Nation". At a

1 *Daily Herald*, 29th July 1919.

second conference held in March 1920, the delegates decided by nearly four to one against a general strike in support of the miners and restricted themselves to intensive propaganda in preparation for the General Election.

The truth was that the trade-union movement, as Bevin saw, possessed neither the organisation nor the solidarity required to force through even an issue on which it was agreed. The miners would have done better to have relied on their own strength rather than let themselves be put off from striking, first by the Government, then by the T.U.C. In the end they found they had lost a battle they never succeeded in joining.

9

While the miners were hesitating, in the autumn of 1919 the Government suddenly brought its negotiations with the railway-men, the second partner in the Triple Alliance, to a head. These negotiations had been going on for months in an effort to draw up a new wage agreement with the Government, which still controlled the railways. The Government was strongly suspected of spinning out the negotiations deliberately as part of its tactics of delay. Having tested the strength of the unions' reaction over the refusal to nationalise the mines, Lloyd George was ready to go a step further and force the issue with the railwaymen. He took steps to divide them in advance. In August the Government reached agreement with the Locomotive Engineers and Firemen (A.S.L.E.F.) and then felt free to present the N.U.R. with a 'definitive' offer, the main feature of which was a sharp and unexpected reduction in wages.

The N.U.R., led by J. H. Thomas, one of the critics of 'Direct Action' for political purposes, retorted by calling a national railway strike for midnight on 26th September. The engine-drivers and firemen, loyally refusing to be bought off by the Government's bribe, joined the N.U.R. and within a matter of hours the whole railway system of the country had been brought to a standstill.

The N.U.R. Executive had neither consulted nor appealed to its partners in the Triple Alliance. (It did not even consult the other railway unions.) Yet the impact of the strike could not be isolated and there were obvious reasons why the other unions could not remain indifferent. The Government had made preparations for a show-down and had organised emergency food supplies as well as a system of road transport. The railwaymen might well be defeated and this was bound to lead to wage reductions in other industries. This was one danger. The other was that the rest of the trade-union movement might be drawn into a half-organised, half-spontaneous general strike for which it had made no preparation and in which it might well be defeated along with the railwaymen.

The strike started on a Friday night. Bevin spent the week-end in Bristol and South Wales and learned enough of the temper of his members to see the danger of the strike spreading sporadically. On Monday, when he got back to London, he found busmen and dockers demanding that the Transport Workers' Federation should call a strike in support of the railwaymen. On Tuesday, when the Federation Executive met, he urged them not to stand by and let events take their course. Bevin was far from wanting to extend the strike, which had been launched without consultation and (in his opinion) without foresight; but he realised the consequences of stumbling into an ineffectual challenge to the power of the State. Someone had to take the initiative in setting up a mediatory body which could bring the weight of organised Labour to bear in favour of a settlement which the railway unions could accept.

He proposed that the Federation, without waiting to be asked, should call a meeting of all the other unions it could reach, invite the railwaymen to state their case and see how they could best help them. At a time when Thomas and the other railwaymen's leaders had no idea what to do next, this proved a fruitful suggestion. The conference duly met at the Caxton Hall on 1st October, listened to the arguments put forward by Thomas and Bromley and set up a committee (with Bevin as a member) which acted as mediator between No. 10 Downing Street, where Lloyd George had taken over the conduct of the dispute, and Unity House, Euston Road, where the N.U.R. Executive was in permanent session. Bevin complained privately that he did not know which was the more unreliable to deal with, Jimmy Thomas or Lloyd George, both Welshmen and both extremely hard to pin down.

Neither side was at first willing to make any concessions, yet Bevin, as he told the Dockers' Executive on 4th October, saw nothing but danger in an extension of the strike. "I think it must be civil war, for I cannot see how it is possible, once all the trade unions are brought in, for the Government to avoid fighting for supremacy and power and I do not believe that our people, if they knew what it meant, would be prepared to plunge into it."[1] He was suspicious of Thomas, whom he believed to be looking for a way of shifting the blame for failure on to the other unions, and baffled by Lloyd George's lightning changes of mood and tactics. It was only after days and nights of anxious discussion that a compromise was found which enabled the wage negotiations to be resumed and the strike called off on 5th October.

Bevin's part in the settlement won him widespread praise. Although Harry Gosling, Clynes and Arthur Henderson played an equal part in the negotiations, the initiative had been his. The railwaymen were satisfied with a settlement which avoided any wage reduction. On the other hand, the *Daily Express*, later to become one of his most hostile critics, printed Bevin's photograph alongside those of the Prime Minister and Bonar Law and wrote:

"Hitherto he has been regarded as an extremist, but he has played a great part in bringing about the settlement of one of the most threatening industrial disputes the country has ever experienced. He is a broad-shouldered, full-figured man of middle stature, black-haired and keen-eyed and he bids fair to become one of the leading men of the Labour movement. A big-voiced orator of the passionate type, he can handle a crowd as few men have been able to do since Ben Tillett was in the hey-day of his fame. Many have been inclined to regard him as a crowd-handler only but his statesmanship has been brought out by the needs of the crisis."[2]

IO

Such praise was no doubt gratifying, but what worried Bevin was the situation which had called for his improvised action. Earlier in the summer he had written an article for the *Daily Herald* under the title of "Labour's Urgent Need". Pointing out that the opportunity to secure public ownership of the means of production (for instance,

1 This account is based on the minutes of the Executive Councils of the N.T.W.F. and the Dockers' Union which met several times between 29th Sept. and 6th October 1919.

2 *Daily Express*, 6th Oct. 1919.

in the coal mines) had come much earlier than expected, he under-lined the inability of the Labour movement to make the most of its opportunities:

"It is a great shapeless mass, all the time struggling to co-ordinate its efforts, but finding itself without a head to direct. . . . There is no national body representing the whole of the trade unions of the country with any real directive authority—co-ordinating claims and policy; marshalling all the forces of Labour; adopting methods to educate its membership . . .; ready to inaugurate a campaign which would rally all its political and industrial forces in order to fight the vested interests."[1]

The success of the railway strike in forcing the Government to withdraw its 'definitive' offer and resume negotiations could not disguise the justice of this criticism. Neither the T.U.C. nor the Triple Alliance had been brought into the picture at all; the strike, begun without consultation, had been ended by the self-invited intervention of an unofficial body. The idea of simultaneous con-certed action by all the partners in the Triple Alliance broke down in face of the fact that the crisis in the mining and the railway in-dustries had come to a head at different times while the major claim on behalf of the transport workers, the dockers' national programme, had not yet been put forward.

If the unions' jealous regard for their own autonomy made it im-possible to create a unified command, was it possible to make more effective arrangements for acting together through the T.U.C.? In the autumn of 1919 a Co-ordination Sub-committee, representing the *ad hoc* committee which had settled the railway strike, the Parliamentary Committee of the T.U.C. and the trade-union side of the National Industrial Conference, sat down to consider the problem. Bevin was one of its most active members and helped to draw up the preliminary report which was adopted by a special Trades Union Congress convened in London on the 9th and 10th of December.

The report recommended the creation of a General Council for the T.U.C. in place of the Parliamentary Committee, a proposal which aroused considerable opposition. Amongst those who moved the reference back of the report were Frank Hodges, the Miners' Secretary, and John Bromley (of A.S.L.E.F.), as well as the con-

1 *Daily Herald*, 17th July 1919.

servative members of the Parliamentary Committee. It was Ernest
Bevin, making a passionate appeal to the older leaders to give the
young men a chance, who got the report carried and backed it up by
securing the adoption by the Sub-committee of a draft scheme for the
constitution of the General Council which formed the basis of the
proposals finally accepted by the T.U.C. in September 1920.

Bevin's draft, set out in a memorandum dated 19th November
1919, had already been seen by the Sub-committee and, as a comparison of the texts shows, strongly influenced the ideas and language
of its report. He began without beating about the bush:

"I hold the view that Congress should develop the industrial side of the
Movement as against the 'deputizing' or 'political' conception, and to this
end I suggest the abolition of the Parliamentary Committee and the substitution of a General Council which shall be representative of the various
groups of economic interests affiliated to Congress."[1]

He then went on to sketch the division into groups (nine in place
of the seventeen eventually adopted) and the method of election—
nomination by unions within their group but election by the whole
congress—which characterise the General Council to this day.
Some of his phrases survived the revision of the next year and appear
in the final proposals; so did his suggestion that the General Council
should have at its disposal the product of a penny levy on the
membership of the affiliated unions. His original scheme also contained provision for the establishment of the later research, international and legal departments, each under the charge of a sub-
committee, and for the setting up of advisory committees from the
different trade-union groups to assist the General Council. It was
therefore, with considerable justification that he later claimed
to have been one of the architects of the General Council.

II

At the same Trades Union Congress of December 1919, Ernest
Bevin got up to make an appeal on behalf of another project to

---

1 "Suggested Re-organisation of the Trades Union Congress", by Ernest Bevin.
This is a mimeographed memorandum dated 19th November and submitted to the
T.U. Co-ordination Sub-committee.

which he was to devote many years of unpaid and, in some ways, unrewarding labour. On the morning of 25th November he came to the Union office early and before beginning his day's work started to dictate three articles which the *Daily Herald* published under the title "The Written Word".[1] It was the first of many pleas which he was to make for the development and support of a Labour Press, and it contains a number of characteristic ideas which he was to try to implement for twenty years.

"The first and most important thing is to stir, enlighten, organise the minds of the people. *Physical poverty will remain as long as there exists mental poverty.* There is, at this moment, in the world less apathy than bewilderment; and therefore the whole of the people's position needs clarifying.

"The spoken word has been a mighty factor in the past. But it is not enough. We must have the written word daily. It is as essential as a political instrument or the strike weapon. It is needed to make either of these effective."[1]

The *Herald* had resumed publication as a daily in March 1919, under the editorship of George Lansbury and Gerald Gould. For the next three years it was at the height of its reputation as a brilliant, anarchical, independent daily without an equal in Fleet Street.[2] Unrestrained by any respect for 'official' policy, the *Herald* fought hard to break down the parochialism and enlarge the horizons of the Labour movement. Even when he disagreed with it, Bevin saw its value and threw himself with enthusiasm into the campaign to raise money for its support.

In November 1919, a *Daily Herald* Trade Union Committee was set up, with Bevin as secretary. Largely thanks to his efforts, £100,000 was raised, sufficient to keep the paper going for a few more months, although not enough to launch the Northern edition for which Lansbury and Bevin had hoped. At the same time, the Board of Directors was enlarged to bring on three representatives of trade unions besides the existing directors, Lansbury, Bob Williams and Francis Meynell. This was the beginning of the connection with the trade-union movement (not with the Labour Party) which was

1 *Daily Herald*, 28th Nov., 1st and 5th Dec. 1919.
2 Among its contributors were Bernard Shaw, Siegfried Sassoon, E. M. Forster, H. M. Tomlinson, H. W. Nevinson, and less frequently Rebecca West, Rose Macaulay, Aldous Huxley and Robert Graves.

Above. Bevin arriving for a meeting of the Triple Alliance in the coal crisis of April 1921. *Below*. The 'Dockers' K.C.' and his colleagues at the Shaw Inquiry. Sexton and Tillett are on the left of Bevin.

Above. End of the 1923 dock strike: strikers returning to work in the Surrey Docks.
Below. Bevin at the court of inquiry into the 1924 London bus and tram strike.

to keep the *Herald* afloat through its successive crises. Bevin was one of the original trade-union directors, a position he continued to hold until he became a Minister in 1940 and to which he devoted more time and energy than any other member of the trade-union movement.

12

Ever since his visit to the U.S.A. in 1915, Bevin had been impressed by the need to overcome national frontiers in trade-union organisation. Shortly after the end of the war the Dutch and Swedish Transport Workers' Unions took the initiative in proposing the reconstitution of the International Transport Workers' Federation. Started in the 1890s by the founder of the Swedish dockers' union, Charles Lindley, the Federation had reached a membership of one million by 1914. Its main strength lay in the affiliation of the German trade unions, its headquarters were in Berlin and the proposal to revive it after the war roused bitter opposition from Havelock Wilson and the strongly anti-German Seamen's Union in Britain.

None the less towards the end of April 1919, Ernie Bevin, Bob Williams and Harry Gosling set out for Amsterdam to represent the British Transport Workers' Federation at a preliminary meeting attended by no more than two Germans, two Belgians and five Dutchmen. The British and German delegations met by chance while crossing a bridge in the centre of Amsterdam and after a moment's hesitation advanced, shook hands and greeted each other as friends. It was a curiously dramatic meeting which Bevin never forgot and to which he often referred afterwards.

The next day one of the Belgian delegates, Chapelle, raised the question which aroused more passion than any other, the failure of the former Central Council of the Federation to protest against the unrestricted German U-boat warfare and the responsibility of the German Transport and Railway Workers' Unions for this silence. By contrast with the Belgians, who introduced a resolution protesting at the murder of 20,000 seamen by the Germans, Bevin was firm but moderate. He expressed without rancour the anger which the German U-boat attacks had created in Britain:

"We realise the difficult position in which the Germans found themselves, but all the same we are of the opinion that they should have protested. Had anything of the nature of the torpedoing of the *Lusitania* occurred on the British side, the English Transport Workers would not have failed to do all that was in their power, even by means of a strike, to cause the downfall of their government. . . . The German workers are not to be blamed for this method of warfare, but the Central Council has not done its duty because it did not protest."[1]

Despite Belgian protests a moderate resolution in keeping with Bevin's views was passed and Bob Williams proposed the re-establishment of the Federation, with Amsterdam as its temporary headquarters. With that settled, Bevin presented and carried a draft scheme for the constitution of the revived Federation.

This same interest in international economic problems and his inclination to take more than an insular view of them comes out in a number of speeches Bevin made during 1919[2], most clearly perhaps in the address which he delivered to the Bristol Rotary Club on 16th June.

Taking as his subject "Over-Production and the Inevitable Revolution", Bevin surprised his audience of Bristol business men by never mentioning trade unions but discussing the future of international trade. Arguing that the development of industry in Asia, especially Japan, and the over-production of European and American manufacturers were bound to lead to an intensified trade rivalry, he derided the belief that it would be possible to reach international agreements to limit production and divide markets. Over-production, he declared, would lead to war ("The great war between Germany and Great Britain was a trade war"), unless there was a revolution which was bound to come in the end. Bevin was

1 Proceedings of the International Conference of Transport Workers' Organisations, Concertgebouw, Amsterdam, 29th–30th April 1919.

2 Cf. for instance his support for the International Labour Charter at the Annual General Council meeting of the National Federation of General Workers, Manchester, 14th–15th August 1919 (Proceedings, pp. 94–6); his support for the financial appeal on behalf of the Indian trade unions at the T.U.C., 12th Sept. 1919; his speech at the Dockers' Union dinner, 5th May 1920 (*Dockers' Record*, May 1920, pp. 11–12); and his advocacy of the boycott which the International Transport Workers' Federation organised against Hungary as a protest at the persecution of the Hungarian trade unions by the 'Whites' after the suppression of Bela Kun's régime (Report of the N.T.W.F. Annual General Council Meeting, June 1920, pp. 70–90).

not thinking now of the exchange of goods for commercial profit in a world in which only a restricted minority enjoyed a tolerable standard of life. He was reaching out towards the vision, which never ceased to attract him, of the exchange of goods for the supply of each others' needs in a world for which unlimited prospects could be opened up by ending the poverty and exploitation of the submerged masses.

"It is assumed that because the war has been won Britain is going to capture the trade of the world, but you cannot determine the world's production by armies and navies. You cannot limit ideas, ingenuity or developments by any form of external force. The whole world will first attempt to repair what has been lost. It will go from that to the struggle for supremacy. In that struggle for supremacy I am quite satisfied that the present capitalist system will inevitably go under. . . ."[1]

The belief that the world and Britain were on the verge of great changes was still strong in him; only reluctantly did he come to realise that, at least as far as his own country was concerned, it was stagnation rather than change which was to characterise Britain's social and economic situation after the war.

1 Reprinted in the *Western Daily Press* and in the *Dockers' Record*, June 1919, pp. 3–5.

CHAPTER 6

The Shaw Inquiry and the
Council of Action
1920

I

BY THE END of 1919, Bevin had established himself in the trade-
union movement as one of the most promising of the younger
generation of leaders. In 1920 he acquired a national reputation
almost overnight—thanks to his part in two episodes, the Shaw
Inquiry and the Council of Action.

The Shaw Court of Inquiry into dock labour was a turning-point
in Bevin's career, perhaps the most important of all. The position
which he won as the 'Dockers' K.C.' opened the way for him to carry
through the amalgamation which set up the Transport and General
Workers' Union. For this reason and because of his life-long concern
with the problems of dock labour, it is important to understand what
those problems were.

All dock work was governed by the constant fluctuation in the
flow of trade and the arrival of ships in the ports. This fluctuation
was due to a variety of causes. Some were remote: the impact of a
trade boom or a depression; the rise and fall of prices. Others were
more immediate like the vagaries of weather, storms, fog and the
tides. Some were predictable: the seasonal character of a particular
trade, in grain, cotton, wool or fruit. Others were a matter of
chance: a severe winter or an early thaw could alter the date of
arrival of the timber boats from Canada and the Baltic Ports by a
matter of weeks. One week a dozen boats might arrive together, the
next week none at all. One week there would be work for hundreds,
day and night; the next for no more than a handful.

The demand for labour at the docks, therefore, varied widely from day to day, and still does. But the method of recruiting labour up to the first World War left the difficulties arising from this fact to be borne wholly by the men. The employers, apart from a comparatively small staff of permanent men, took on labour for each day as they required it and dismissed the men again the moment they had finished loading or unloading a particular vessel. Such a system of casual employment, paid by the day, could only work so long as there existed in every port a pool of surplus labour available to meet the demands of the port on its busiest day. The employers took full advantage of this, but refused to accept any responsibility for the fact that during most of the year a large number of the men forming the pool were either unemployed or at best under-employed, living on one or two days' work a fortnight.

The work itself was hard and often dangerous. When work was plentiful, a docker might carry seventy or even a hundred tons of grain a day on his shoulders, exacting labour on a poor diet. Safety regulations were inadequate and frequently ignored: the accident rate in dock work was exceeded only by that in the mines.

The hardness of the work and its irregularity did not deter the genuine docker, the man who never looked for work elsewhere than at the docks. Dockers in all countries are a race apart, very much like miners. The best of them took a pride in their strength and skill and bred their sons to the same calling. They looked upon their freedom to work hard for two or three days, then to 'play', as a superior state to the monotony and discipline of work in a factory.

What the docker wanted was more security. The steady man with a family and a home to keep wanted to be sure that he could take home a living wage at the end of the week, that he would not be left "on the stones" for weeks at a time by a system of recruiting labour which maximised, instead of reducing, the hazards of casual employment. It was a source of bitter complaint that work at the docks was open to anyone, the last refuge of the shiftless and the unemployed who turned up at the dock gates on the chance of earning a few shillings whenever a factory or a building site closed down or went on short time.

The degrading scenes at the daily 'calling-on' when the men fought each other for a place at the front and for the tallies distributed by the foremen have been described by many witnesses.

One, an experienced and dispassionate observer, wrote in 1916:

"The foreman stood on the edge of a warehouse and eyed the crowd all over as if it were a herd of cattle. Then very deliberately he beckoned a man with his finger and after a considerable interval a second and a third until he had taken ten in all. There was an evident enjoyment of a sense of power . . . and the whole proceedings were horribly suggestive of the methods of a slave market."[1]

The Royal Commission on the Poor Law (1909) pointed to casual labour, and particularly casual labour at the docks, as one of the principal causes of pauperism and of that demoralisation which produced the mentality of the slums. Every inquiry into the poverty and social evils of the industrial towns condemned the system of recruiting dock labour. Even from the employers' own point of view it was inefficient and they were loud in complaints of time-wasting, low output and unreliability. The merit of the system in their eyes was that it supplied them with a sure supply of cheap labour whenever they wanted it, that it kept their labour costs down and enabled them to maintain the whip-hand over the men if there was a dispute.

2

The men themselves were divided by the clash of interest between the regular docker and the man who came to pick up a few shillings, as well as by the petty rivalries of local unions, especially when (as in the case of the London stevedores or the South Wales coal trimmers) a privileged group was determined to preserve its superiority to the mass of general cargo workers, the 'dock rats'. To organise a dockers' union at all was an achievement and nothing so much surprised contemporaries as the unexpected solidarity of the dockers in the strikes of 1889 and 1911.

The more intelligent of the dockers and their leaders realised that only fundamental reforms aimed at the decasualisation of dock labour could permanently improve their lot. They also realised, however, that they would encounter resistance to such reforms, not only from the employers but from the men as well. Suspicion,

1 H. A. Mess: *Casual Labour at the Docks* (1916), quoted by E.C.P. Lascelles and S. S. Bullock: *Dock Labour and Decasualisation* (1924), p. 19, n. 1.

ignorance, dislike of being 'regimented', fear of losing their 'freedom', all these would have to be overcome. When Sexton's union in Liverpool joined with the employers in 1912 to carry out a scheme for registering regular dock workers and organising the transfer of labour from one dock to another, they met with strong opposition. In Birkenhead, the men went on strike against their own union. At another port, Glasgow, the men's insistence on regarding schemes for registration and decasualisation as infringements of their freedom was to be demonstrated again and again.

The war, however, forced both masters and men to accept changes. Large numbers of dockers joined the colours and, in order to keep a sufficient labour force in the ports, dock work was added to the list of reserved occupations. Several port committees adopted schemes for the registration of regular dockers as a way of deciding who could legitimately be given exemption. At the end of the war these were continued and extended to all the larger ports except London, Glasgow and Newcastle as a means of protecting the genuine dock labourer returning from the army. This experience broke down a good deal of prejudice on both sides and proved that registration at least was practicable.

Bevin played a big part in working out the scheme for Bristol and Avonmouth. It drew a ring round the docks and provided some protection against the influx of the unemployed during the trade depression which set in shortly afterwards. But Bristol, thanks to men like Bevin and the local strength of the Dockers' Union, offered more favourable conditions than most ports. The limitations of registration were clearly shown in London, where Bevin spent a long time in the summer of 1919 trying to devise a scheme to cover the world's biggest port.

A committee was appointed under Mr. Justice Roche to examine the situation in the London docks. After producing an interim report in March 1919, the committee invited Ernest Bevin to join it and it was he and Will Devenay, the Dockers' Union district secretary, who did most of the work on the trade-union side. One of the problems, of course, was to discover the facts about dock work in a port which employed up to 34,000 men on a normal day. The Committee's final report, presented in July 1919, cautiously recommended a voluntary registration scheme. It took a year to get even this adopted and when registration was complete, it was found

that 61,000 men had registered, a total far above any estimate ever
made of the number seeking work in the port. Far too many casual
labourers had secured a place on the register as a form of re-insurance
for it to be of any value as a protection to the genuine docker.

Bevin never viewed registration as anything more than a first step
which would be ineffectual unless it were accompanied by two other
measures: a reduction of the numbers registered to a figure approaching the actual needs of the port and much more efficient
arrangements for the transfer of labour from one dock to another
within the port. Even then there was bound to be unemployment
during slack periods, and Bevin argued that this could only be dealt
with by the decasualisation of the industry and the provision of a
guaranteed minimum wage. He pursued these further reforms
persistently for over twenty years, and twenty-one years after he first
demanded them at the Shaw Inquiry he had the satisfaction of
introducing them as Minister of Labour in 1941 and seeing them
given statutory force in the Dock Workers (Regulation of Employment) Act, 1946, an achievement which was recognised by everyone
to be peculiarly Bevin's own.

3

In the last year of the war Bevin drafted a scheme providing for
maintenance (i.e. a guaranteed minimum weekly wage) as well as
registration. After seeing it turned down by the Ministry of Labour
in April 1918, the Transport Workers' Federation put the scheme up
to the Central Joint Committee on Port Labour. No progress was
made, however, partly because everyone concerned was waiting for
the Government's unemployment insurance bill. Growing impatient at the delay, the N.T.W.F. decided to take the initiative and
to put forward a national wage claim on behalf of the 125,000
dockers employed throughout the kingdom. The Federation asked
for a national minimum for all dock-workers of 16/- a day, with
complicated provisions for overtime and shift-work. If the claim
were granted, it was certain that the Federation would press for the
reorganisation of the industry and the adoption of both registration
and maintenance.

The application was sent to every employer and port authority in

October 1919. Instead of rejecting the claim out of hand, the employers put up the suggestion of a public court of inquiry to be appointed by the Minister of Labour under the new Industrial Courts Act of 1919. The Federation Executive was taken by surprise and hesitated. If they went before a court, they would have to submit their claim and the supporting evidence to cross-examination by the ablest lawyers the employers could brief. Was their case strong enough to run such a risk? Bevin urged them to go forward and at a special General Council meeting held on 30th December the decision to accept the offer and ask for an inquiry was taken by a large majority. Harry Gosling, Robert Williams and Ben Tillett were nominated as the Federation's representatives on the court, but one man and one man alone, the Council felt, had the ability to present their case. It was handed to Ernest Bevin, with James Sexton as his 'junior'.

Bevin had very little time in which to prepare. The first sitting of the Court was fixed for 3rd February and before that he had to master the detailed methods of recruitment, work and pay, varying from dock to dock and cargo to cargo, for a substantial proportion of the three hundred ports of the country. Since so much turned upon the ability of the industry to pay higher wages, he had also to discover and familiarise himself with the financial arrangements of the dock undertakings and shipping firms and to have the detailed trade returns for several years at his finger-tips. At the same time, he had to organise and rehearse witnesses who could testify to the conditions of the docker's life, his family budget and earnings, what he paid for rent, food and clothing. It was a formidable task, the more so as the employers promptly briefed Sir Lynden Macassey, K.C., who was acknowledged to be the most experienced counsel then practising in industrial cases, and prepared to bring up expert witnesses to overawe their working-class opponents.

Every man the meagre staff of the Dockers' Union and the Federation could spare was turned on to dig up information and witnesses. Without this help Bevin could never have gone into the court and he owed a particular debt to his secretary Mae Forcey, who revealed unsuspected gifts for research. A Bristol docker, Harry Tomkins, hurriedly summoned overnight to London to give Bevin detailed local information, remembers lights still burning in Effingham House in the early hours of the morning and Bevin and his secretary hard at work preparing for the next day in court. If Miss Forcey and others helped him to prepare his brief, however, it was Bevin alone who framed and marshalled his arguments, and produced the intellectual power and force of personality needed to drive the case home.

The Court of Inquiry held its first sitting on the morning of 3rd February at the Law Courts in the Strand. The chairman was Lord Shaw of Dunfermline, a Law Lord who had formerly served for several years as a Radical member of Parliament, a shrewd Scots lawyer and a fair-minded judge. One of the Court's two secretaries, G. H. Ince, was later (as Sir Godfrey Ince) to become Bevin's Permanent Secretary in the Ministry of Labour of the second World War.

The inquiry attracted widespread attention; the public gallery was full (frequently with dockers waiting to hear Bevin put their case) and the Press devoted a lot of space to the proceedings. With the success of the miners' representatives at the Sankey Commission in his mind, Bevin meant to put the employers in the dock and shock the public conscience with the revelation of the conditions in which the dockers and their families were obliged to live. Before he finished, the inquiry had become an indictment of the industrial system which allowed such conditions to continue and he himself the spokesman of the whole working class. It was his, and his audience's, sense of this role that gave his advocacy its curiously dramatic quality.

4

Bevin's opening speech occupied the whole of the first and second days and part of the third. He spoke for eleven hours in all without ever losing the thread of his argument or repeating himself, an astonishing feat for a man with little education and no forensic training.

His argument was directed to the support of two major propositions. The docker's wages, inadequate when they were fixed in 1889, had steadily fallen behind the rising cost of living until they had become insufficient to maintain life and health, especially when the casual nature of his employment was taken into account. On the other hand, the dock employers, the shipowners and the principal industries using the docks could fully afford to pay the wages asked and to finance a system of maintenance for the men out of the large profits they had made during and since the war, without adding a penny to the price of their goods or services.

What impressed the Court and the public most was the wealth of evidence Bevin adduced to support his argument and the challenging manner in which he attacked the employers for their selfishness, their indifference to the claims of humanity and their inefficient organisation of the industry.

He began by recalling the history of wage negotiations in the docks since 1872 and went on to describe the degrading conditions in which the docker was expected to work and live.

"It is true and we say it with pride that, by sheer weight of organisation we have effected improvements, but never yet can I remember a single concession ever handed out to the workmen willingly. . . .
"The dockers have had one of the highest death rates in this country, due to their irregular life and the horrible slum conditions. Men were injured and it was a common thing for the bullying foreman to say: 'Throw him in the wing and get on with the work . . .' If the men dared to protest . . . it was 'To the office and get your money and clear out.' And then they might stand on the stones for weeks . . . as an example to other people for obedience."[1]

During the war the dockers' wages had steadily fallen behind the rising cost of living. The working man had been told he must not exploit the economic difficulties of the country. The State, however, in fixing the rates which the *employers* were to get referred the case to the employers themselves. "I find that the Admiralty Arbitration Board to fix the rates for requisitioning ships were all shipowners with one exception. . . . They were trusted to fix the rates which they still charge the State . . . and their rates were accepted, with the result that at the end of the war, while they have added millions to their profits, our men are worse off than they were in 1914."[2] As one illustration Bevin quoted Bonar Law's admission in the House of Commons that in the last year he had made a profit on his

1 Industrial Courts Act, 1919: *Proceedings of a Court of Inquiry into wages, rates and conditions of men engaged in dock and waterside labour.* First day, pp. 7–9.
2 Ibid, p. 11.

shipping shares of 47 per cent, after the excess profits tax had been paid.

When the Court resumed its sitting on the second day, Bevin set out in detail the effects of the claim for 16/– a day and explained how it would apply to the different categories of workmen. In support of the claim, he went through the items of working-class expenditure and produced a budget of £6 a week as a moderate estimate of what it cost a family of five to live.

Bevin then took up his contention that those who used the ports could afford to meet the dockers' claim without placing a further charge on the consumer. In passing he noted the answer given by the Chairman of the Port of London Authority, Lord Devonport, an old enemy of the dockers, when he was questioned by the Coal Commission on the question of labour representation on the P.L.A. "While labour representation has not been detrimental to us," Lord Devonport had said, "yet on the whole they appear to be looking out for themselves and the interests they represent."

"This, to me," Bevin remarked, "is a serious matter. I am glad to have found a super-man who can abstract himself from his 280,000 shares in Kearley & Tonge and the Independent Tea Stores and all that that means in money and goods going to these firms through these ports—who can abstract himself from any of these influences and look after the interests of the great public, while we who have not a penny invested in the world, nothing but an investment in the well-being of the great human element which we represent, are described as looking out in the main for ourselves and for our interests. I leave it at that."[1]

5

One after another Bevin went through the large profits made by the shipowners, the textile manufacturers and other interests using the ports. There had been gross profiteering during and immediately after the war, especially by the shipping interests, and 1919 had been a year of excessive speculation. 'Profiteering' and 'speculation' had become ugly words and Bevin exploited them to the full. These, he told the Court, were the people, not the dockers, who took out of the common pool without making any return.

1 Second day, pp. 17–18.

On the third day, Bevin set out his proposals for the decasualisation of the dock industry. He made use of the experience he had gained in the Roche Committee's inquiry into conditions in the Port of London to support his demand not simply for registration (for which the unions should be made responsible), but for maintenance as well.

"I am in favour of the industry maintaining its own unemployed. I urge that if it is right to levy dock dues or charges upon the handling of goods to keep the dock in a proper state of repair and maintenance and efficiency, surely it is just as moral to levy a charge upon all shipping entering a dock to form a pool to maintain the worker when there is no employment."

The casual system of labour recruitment was bound to be in-efficient; why then was it continued?

"The easiest thing to get rid of has been the human. He has not been sufficient trouble. If he had only been more audacious and more aggressive, then possibly they would have found other means, but the reason why casual labour has been perpetuated is because it has been the easiest method of dealing with shipping up to this point. . . . But there was another motive behind it too. I am convinced that the employers have always had at the back of their heads that economic poverty producing economic fear was their best weapon for controlling labour. I do not think civilisation built upon that is worth having. We believe in developing self-discipline as against maintaining control by economic poverty and economic fear."

It was the same point to which Bevin returned again and again: the assertion of the working man's dignity as a human being, his right to self-respect. He came back to it once more at the conclusion of his speech, in a passage which held the courtroom silent by the passion and eloquence with which he spoke.

"I suggest that your Court cannot refuse our claim either on grounds of equity or of reason. If the captains of industry who have claimed monopoly control for themselves, who have argued that we are not capable of taking part in control, say that they are unable to organise their concerns so as to give us work for a decent standard of life, then I say that they ought to lose their place. . . . By whatever means they have got control, there comes with it responsibility; and if they cannot improve the organisation of industry then I say they ought to make way.

"If your Court refuse our claim, I suggest you must adopt an alternative. You must go to the Prime Minister, you must go to the Minister of Education and tell him to close our schools, tell him that industry can only be run by artisan labour on the pure fodder or animal basis, teach us nothing, let us learn nothing, because to create aspirations in our minds, to create the love of the beautiful and then at the same time to deny us the wherewithal to obtain it, is a false policy and a wrong method to adopt. Better keep us in dark ignorance, never to know anything, if you are going to refuse us the wherewithal to give expression to those aspirations which have thus been created."[1]

6

When Bevin sat down there was spontaneous applause from all parts of the courtroom. Lord Shaw complimented him on the "care and cogency" with which he had presented his case and Sir Lynden Macassey expressed his admiration, adding: "I think we may predict for Mr. Bevin in the cause which he has so much at heart a very great future." This was a view echoed by the Press which fastened on the phrase invented by the *Daily Herald*, the 'Dockers' K.C.'.

Bevin had now, however, to meet the counter-attack by the employers' counsel. Sir Lynden Macassey chose his ground with care. The employers, he assured the Court, were sympathetic but the plain fact was that the proposal for a *national* minimum wage was wholly impracticable. So great were the differences between one port and another in conditions of work, trade practices, cost of living and actual rates of pay (leave alone the differentials between different sorts of work in the same port) that it simply could not be put into effect and would certainly meet determined resistance from the men. Like the mineowners, the dock employers offered district negotiations and a rise in district wages where necessary, but strongly resisted any national claim. To grant it for the docks, Sir Lynden argued, was bound to have immediate repercussions and disturb the wage structure of the whole country. In any case, Mr. Bevin had exaggerated the degree of want among the dockers and the rise in the cost of living: his budget of £6 for a family of five was far too high, a more reasonable figure would be £3. 13. 6. a week.

As for the high profits made during the war and capital appreciation, this was irrelevant. What mattered were the present costs and returns: the dockers' claim could certainly not be met

[1] Third day, p. 9.

without passing on the increase to the consumer, the more so as there was strong opposition on the part of the men to changes designed to increase productivity. The same opposition to change made schemes of registration unworkable.

Both sides then proceeded to bring up witnesses whose examination and cross-examination occupied fifteen days spread over a month. Macassey's star witnesses were Sir Alfred Booth, a leading Liverpool shipowner and chairman of the Cunard Line, Lord Devonport, Chairman of the Port of London Authority, and Professor A. L. Bowley, who held the chair of Statistics at London University. Bevin pressed all three fiercely in cross-examination.

He asked Sir Alfred Booth what was the wage a docker could earn in Liverpool at the existing rate.

"£3. 4. 2.
"Do you seriously suggest that is a living wage?—I do.
"I put it to you very straight. Could you maintain your family on it?—No, I could not.
"Then are you any more to the community than the docker who handles your ship?—That is a matter of opinion. As an individual, certainly not.
"Do you think it right to ask a man to live and maintain himself on what you would not dream of asking your own family to live upon?—It is not a question of what I ask him to live upon; it is what the economic conditions render possible."[1]

He failed to shake Booth or Lord Devonport, who was as blunt in his replies as Bevin in his questioning. But he had more success with Professor Bowley, the expert witness responsible for the figure of £3. 12. 6 which the employers put forward as an alternative to Bevin's suggested budget of £6 a week for a family of five.

After a long-drawn-out dispute about the cost of living, Bevin and his secretary, Mae Forcey, went down to a street market in Canning Town and spent exactly the amount on vegetables and cheese allowed in Bowley's budget. Next morning he produced it in court divided equally into small portions on five plates. Turning to his witness, a docker from Birkenhead, he asked him what would happen, "if you went home from the dock to a meal like that and you were told by your wife that Counsel said there was sufficient calorific value in it to sustain you? What would be the result?"

[1] Fifth day, p. 16.

"I think the dockers would emigrate in a body."

"You think the employers' request that you should give bigger output and their desire that there shall be happiness and contentment cannot be achieved on a budget of this character?"

"Certainly it cannot."[1]

When Professor Bowley went into the witness-box, Bevin's anger was aroused by the dry academic manner of the expert witness calculating precisely the lowest number of calories on which it was possible for a man to live and work. Again he resorted to the device of producing in court the exact amount of bacon, of fish and bread prescribed. Pushing the scraps of food in front of him, he asked Bowley whether this was what a Cambridge professor thought a sufficient breakfast for a man who had to go out and carry heavy bags of grain on his back all day. When the witness protested, Bevin pulled out the menu of the Savoy Hotel restaurant:

"This is a menu which an ordinary shipowner, whom we are asking for a living wage, would go to the Savoy to have today at 7/–. You allow for five persons 40/– a week for food, and that is 7/– for one person for one lunch. What is the calorific value of that when he has eaten it?

"As a scientist have you entered into a careful diagnosis of what the rich live on compared with the poor; have you worked out a budget for them? Do you live on 40/– worth of food?

"You have never carried 5 cwt. bags on your back for eight hours continuously?—No."[2]

This was rough treatment but Bevin was determined not to let the scientific terms of the expert evidence cover up what was to him a flesh and blood question. Sir Lynden Macassey protested at his opponent's misrepresentation, but Bevin cared nothing for such protests. Photographs of the meagre portions of food appeared in half a dozen newspapers over the caption, "A Docker's Breakfast". They were worth volumes of statistics in their effect on public opinion.

1 Seventh day, p. 2.
2 Eighth day, pp. 21–24.

7

The brush with Professor Bowley, however, can easily give a false impression of the Inquiry. Most of the time was devoted to eliciting the facts about dock work, with Macassey bringing out the wide variations between ports and the poor performance of the men, and Bevin exposing the bad conditions under which the docker was expected to work and the evil consequences of casual employment. His technical knowledge of detail was tested to the full, for he was up against men who knew quite as much about dock work as he did and were unimpressed by appeals to sentiment. Yet his mastery of the case was such that he was never at a loss for a fact, whether it was the rates paid for the discharge of iron ore at Ardrossan, the profits of master stevedores at Plymouth, the precise hours of shift working at Liverpool, or the extra money paid for 'dirty' cargoes at Avonmouth. For twenty days in all he kept up the pressure on the other side with a natural skill in pleading his case which was equal to every move made by opposing counsel.

When he came to make his closing speech, Bevin put the claim for a national scheme of registration and maintenance in the forefront of his submission. To those who declared such a scheme to be impracticable at the present stage, he gave this reply:

"I want the Court to declare for the principle of maintenance. The reason is this. . . . Take education. The State did not build all the schools and then say all children should be educated. Parliament declared that it was essential that children should be educated and then proceeded to build the structure. I want the same principle adopted here.
"The method I have indicated may not be the correct method, after further examination. . . . You, with your experience in Parliament, know that in shaping Bills you have never been able to see, My Lord, the exact structure and organisation that was going to develop. . . . You agree to the principle; you place it in a Bill and your structure begins to grow and you change it with experience until you finally get the right method to solve your problems."[1]

Dropping the aggressive manner he had frequently adopted in cross-examination, he reviewed the whole proceedings in a closely argued speech, all the more persuasive because of the reasonable

[1] Twentieth day, pp. 7–8.

tone in which it was presented. One of his most telling points was the failure of the employers to put forward any alternative suggestion for reducing the evils of the casual system of recruiting labour. Only at the end did he allow emotion to colour his argument, and used it then, with great effect, to shift the case he was pleading on to the grounds of humanity and justice.

"The discharged soldier and sailor has come back to the same old grind of casual conditions, the same old uncertainty, the same negative attitude of the employers, the same old wearisome negotiations to get improvement; the twenty days' Court of Inquiry to get just an ordinary standard of life that ought to have been able to be arranged across the table in a week. They come back and I assure you they are resentful.
"I appeal to you, whatever the economic consequences may be—surely, my Lord, justice cannot be dependent upon consequences. If the claim I have made is just, then the consequences of its granting must follow and be met."[1]

When Bevin sat down, the chairman, Lord Shaw, leaned forward:

"Mr. Bevin, at the close of your opening speech I felt authorised by the feeling of the Court to express our satisfaction with it. That satisfaction has not lessened during the course of these proceedings. . . . Be assured that, whatever the result be, the Court will be unanimous in this: that you shall get justice, nothing more nor less than justice, in this case. We congratulate you on the cogent and impressive address which you have now delivered."[2]

8

The dockers did not wait for the result of the Inquiry to express their admiration of the way in which Bevin had put their case. On 7th March, a long procession, complete with banners, costers and band, marched from the Temple Station to the Albert Hall where a mass meeting gave the 'Dockers' K.C.' a great ovation. What especially roused their enthusiasm was the feeling that a working man, a man of their own class, had forced the employers and the nation to listen for once to things they and millions of other working-class men and women had wanted to hear said, had expressed their anger at the conditions in which they were forced to live, their resentment at

1 Twentieth day, p. 19.
2 Ibid.

being treated as an inferior race, their claims to be men of flesh and blood with human feelings.

Harry Gosling, a member of Lord Shaw's Court, took the chair.

"I want to say," he told the crowded audience, "that I have sat on the bench all through the Inquiry and there has never been a case put in the whole history of our movement more clearly and with greater ability than your case has been put by Ernest Bevin."

Bevin himself summed up the universal feeling when he said that this had been "something bigger than merely an inquiry into 16/- a day. It has been a platform on which it has been possible . . . to unfold the great human tragedy of men and women fighting year in and year out against the terrible economic conditions with which they have been surrounded. . . . When the time comes, if it ever does, for a great struggle between Capital and Labour, I want it to be for something bigger than a penny an hour . . . I want it to have a very definite object—that of achieving for those who toil the mastery of their own lives." [1]

When the Court reassembled three weeks later, the majority judgment which it delivered was a triumph for Bevin's advocacy. Although two of the employers dissented and a third expressed reservations, the chairman and five of the members emphatically condemned the system of casual labour; declared for registration and the principle of maintenance, as Bevin had urged them to do, and awarded a *national* minimum of 16s. a day for a 44-hour week. [2]

All this was gratifying, but what effect was the report going to have in practice? Bevin was well aware of the need to act quickly and press hard. A delegate meeting of the Federation was called the same evening that the report was published, and accepted it at once. This move placed the onus of refusal on the employers, who had been forced by the national claim and its acceptance by the Court to set up a provisional national organisation of their own, as Bevin had foreseen. After three weeks' delay, they finally announced that they were prepared to adopt the majority report and appointed nine representatives to sit on a joint negotiating committee. Ironically,

1 Report in the *Daily Herald*, 8th March, 1920.
2 Industrial Courts Act, 1919: *Report of a Court of Inquiry concerning Transport Workers*, 1920, pp. 6–7.

the nine representatives included the two employer members of the Court who had signed the minority report and four of Sir Lynden Macassey's witnesses, amongst them Lord Devonport.

The negotiating committee sat continuously from 19th April until 5th May and in that time reached agreement on the way in which the national award was to be implemented in each port, taking account of all the local differentials, customs and grades which had to be fitted in. The employers had protested that this was an impossible task, but under the impulse of the Court's report and Bevin's persistence, it was accomplished with their co-operation in a fortnight's hard work. On 10th May the new rates came into operation in every port in the country.

In fact, the minimum of 16s. a day did not last long. The trade depression which set in soon afterward and the weakening of the men's position to which it led forced wages down from 16s. to 10s. a day by July 1923. The same adverse circumstances destroyed whatever hope there was of getting a scheme for maintenance adopted. Yet the fact that a tribunal of uncontested authority, after hearing the case on both sides, had come out with an unqualified public condemnation of the casual system and proposals for its reform was to prove of great importance. Circumstances might be unfavourable, but the Report itself remained—and with it one man at least who was determined never to give up until he saw its principles implemented.

When the seventy delegates of the Dockers' Union, representing a membership of 200,000, assembled at Plymouth for their triennial conference on 18th May, they could congratulate themselves on the biggest advance in the dockers' wages since the original dock strike of 1889. Addressing a crowded public meeting in the Guild Hall, Bevin told his working-class audience:

"Before our movement developed, you responded to the whip of the master. You obeyed him in your work because you feared him. You were afraid of the sack and you swallowed your convictions. You used to tell him off, but it was only in your mind. . . . You responded to the whip; I want you to respond to the call of liberty. I want self-discipline, self-sacrifice, self-control, to take the place of the whip. . . . There are ninety-nine per cent of the men and women in this audience tonight who believe they are of a lower order than the other class. You accept it, and I want to get rid of it.

"I have been praised for the case in the court and now they are beginning to say I have been to the university. . . . The great struggle of my own people has been my university. I do not decry education. I lament the lack of it and I curse the other class for monopolising it."[1]

9

The greater part of Bevin's speech at Plymouth, however, was devoted to international affairs.

"There is too common a misconception," he remarked, "that the Labour Movement's particular function is to regulate wages. That is not my view. If my work were confined only to Courts of Inquiry to win awards, it would be a limited sphere because the Biblical maxim that no man can live unto himself is even more true in these days when means of communication make the whole world smaller than was England one hundred and fifty years ago. Ten thousand times more true is it that no nation can live alone."

Bevin went on to give forceful expression to the disillusionment, the sense of having been tricked, which Labour felt over the terms of the peace settlement. Now, he pointed out, a new war had broken out, between Poland and Soviet Russia, and despite the withdrawal of British troops from Russia, there was a strong suspicion that some members of the British Government, in particular the Minister for War, Winston Churchill, were eager not only to see but to assist the defeat of the Red Army at the hands of the Poles or the Whites.

This suspicion was not removed by Lloyd George's assurance that the Government would neither encourage nor support a Polish attack on Russia,[2] and it flared up at the end of April when the Polish armies launched a major offensive deep into Russian territory. The *Daily Herald* voiced a general Labour view when it wrote: "The marionettes are in Warsaw, but the strings are pulled from London and Paris."[3]

Rumours soon spread that the British Government was dispatching arms to Poland. Cases with the label: "O.H.M.S. Munitions for Poland" were reported to have been seen in the East India Docks, where one of the Watford Line boats, the *Jolly George*,

1 D.W.R. and G.W.U. Minutes of the Triennial Delegate Conference, Plymouth, 18th–22nd May, pp. 129–36.
2 House of Commons, 19th February 1920.
3 *Daily Herald*, 30th April 1920.

was waiting to load them. Angered by what they regarded as the duplicity of the Government, a deputation of London dockers went to see Bevin. Without hesitating, he told them they could count on the Union's backing if they refused to load or coal the ship. As a result, the *Jolly George* was unable to sail and the suspect cases had to be disembarked.

This example of spontaneous 'direct action' had attracted much attention and when the Dockers met at Plymouth a few days later, the first item on the agenda was an emergency resolution, moved by Ernest Bevin, congratulating the London dockers on their initiative and calling on the whole Labour movement to follow the same tactics.

Bevin had no sympathy with Communists but, with a grasp of the classic principles of British foreign policy which neither Canning nor Cobden could have bettered, he declared:

"Whatever may be the merits or demerits of the theory of government of Russia, that is a matter for Russia, and we have no right to determine their form of government, any more than we would tolerate Russia determining our form of government."

Praising the action of the London dockers in refusing to load the *Jolly George*, he added:

"When the shipowner got on the telephone to me and said 'What about my ship?', I told him to ask Bonar Law or Lloyd George, as I was not going to ask the dockers to put a gun in a ship or to carry on these further wicked ventures and wars among people in the East. . . . I think the working people—I have not talked about direct action or general strikes—have a right to say where their labour and how their labour should be used, and if we are being called upon either to make munitions or transport munitions for purposes which outrage our sense of justice, then I think we have a right to refuse to have our labour prostituted to carry on wars of this character."[1]

For the moment the Government was content not to force the issue. The Polish armes were still advancing and on 12th June captured Kiev. Lord Curzon, the Foreign Secretary, refused to bring the dispute before the League of Nations and expressed himself satisfied with the reaffirmation of Britain's neutrality.

---

1 Triennial Delegate Conference, Plymouth, 18th–22nd May 1920, pp. 34–6.

10

A new situation, however, was created when in the course of the summer the Red Army, to the surprise and alarm of the Allies, not only chased the Poles out of Russia, but pushed on into Poland and was soon menacing Warsaw. Armistice talks between the Russians and the Poles broke down at the beginning of August and when Curzon warned the Russian Government that, if they advanced further Britain would have to come to Poland's aid, *The Times* spoke of war as imminent and called for national unity. "We must face it with the same unanimity and the same courage with which we faced the crisis of 1914."[1]

For once, every shade of opinion in the Labour movement was united in its determination not to be jockeyed into war, as Bevin for one believed they had been in August 1914, only six years before. A manifesto signed by the leaders of the trade unions (including Bevin) as well as by the leaders of the Parliamentary Labour Party warned the country against an unnecessary war; demonstrations were organised and the *Daily Herald* produced a special Sunday edition with the banner headline: "Not a Man, Not a Gun, Not a Sou!" Not satisfied with demonstrations, Bevin got hold of Arthur Henderson and Bowerman, the General Secretary of the T.U.C., and persuaded them to call a joint conference of the T.U.C. Parliamentary Committee, the Labour Party Executive and the Parliamentary Labour Party on Monday 9th August. The conference adopted Bevin's proposal for a Council of Action, appointing Bevin himself as one of the members and coming out with the blunt statement that "the whole industrial power of the organised workers will be used to defeat this war".[2]

While local Councils of Action, eventually numbering three hundred and fifty, were set up throughout the country, the central Council asked the Prime Minister to see them and were promptly given an appointment on the following day, 10th August, an indication of the sensitiveness of the Government to any serious threat

1 *The Times*, 6th August 1920.

2 Bevin's papers include a file of working papers and correspondence relating to the Council of Action on which this account is based. Cf. Labour Party Report, 1921: pp. 11–18, and S. R. Graubard: *British Labour and the Russian Revolution, 1917–24* (1956), c. 5.

of direct action. Bevin, although one of the youngest members of the Council, was chosen to present the case to the Prime Minister.

Lloyd George was then at the height of his reputation, the most experienced and the most brilliant statesman of the Western world. Accompanied by Bonar Law, he received the deputation at No. 10, Downing Street immediately after his return from a meeting with the French President at Lympne. He warned them that he had only a short time to spare before he must leave to address the House of Commons. Bevin, however, was unimpressed by the occasion, the historic setting or by the aura of success and power which surrounded the Prime Minister.

"At the outset," he told Lloyd George, "I want to make it perfectly clear that the resolution is not merely one in opposition to direct military action, but it is a declaration in opposition to what I would describe as an indirect war, either by blockade or by the supply of munitions or by assisting the forces that are now at war with Russia."[1]

Poland had let herself be used as the cat's-paw of those forces, especially strong in Paris, which were opposed to peace with Soviet Russia and intent on keeping the war going at any cost.

"Another vital principle is at stake, which we want you to note especially— we feel we cannot admit the right, in the event of a revolution in a country, of every other nation using . . . their armed forces to crush out or stem a change that is being made."

So long as Russia was ruled by the Tsars, its Government had been free to commit outrages and murders as it liked and Britain's policy had been not to interfere with the internal affairs of another state. But the moment Russia came under the control of a workers' government, non-intervention was abandoned.

"The majority opinion in this country is that we have not played straight over this Russian business. We feel very strongly that, while France has been our ally, we have on too many occasions allowed her to be the master of our policy.

"We are satisfied of this and have no hesitation in putting our cards on the

---

1 With a foresight born of suspicion, the deputation took along its own shorthand writer and a verbatim record of the interview was published in the *Daily Herald* for 11th August 1920.

table—that, if war with Russia is carried on directly in support of Poland or indirectly in support of General Wrangel, there will be a match set to an explosive material the result of which none of us can foresee today. . . . We are ready and determined to resist the triumph of reaction and war. . . . It is not merely a political action, but an action representing the full force of Labour and we believe it represents the desire of the great majority of the British people."

Lloyd George tried to pin the deputation down on what they would do if Poland's independence were menaced.

ERNEST BEVIN: "Our answer is this—that the hypothesis does not hold good, that the independence of Poland is not at stake."

PRIME MINISTER: "How do you know?"

ERNEST BEVIN: "This Council proposes if you have no objection—to see Kameneff and Krassin (the Russian representatives in London) as well as making our declaration to you, and also to see the Poles, if you have no objection. The public declarations of Russia up to now are that they are not challenging the independence of Poland."

Labour, Bevin added, had always stood for an independent Poland, but they believed that external influences had prevented a Russo-Polish settlement and encouraged the Polish Government to attack Russia.

PRIME MINISTER: "Let us assume everything you are putting and let us assume that the French have interfered and we have interfered and the Poles have interfered—I ask you again: If Soviet Russia does what Tsarist Russia did and says 'We mean to destroy your independence' (they will not put it like that but it will substantially mean the destruction of Poland's independence), do you mean to say that then Labour will not permit the Government to send a single pair of boots to people who are fighting for their liberty?"

ERNEST BEVIN: "Labour will consider the position when that occasion arises."

PRIME MINISTER: "Very well. That is quite good enough for me."

ERNEST BEVIN: "But I want to make this perfectly clear—that that condition has not arisen."

PRIME MINISTER: "No. You need not make that clear to me, because I agree with you . . ."

ERNEST BEVIN: "But, suppose the Polish people themselves agreed upon a constitution which did not suit the Allied Powers?"

PRIME MINISTER: "What have we to do with that? That is their business, not ours."

ERNEST BEVIN: "It is their business?"

PRIME MINISTER: "Certainly. What have we to say to that? I do not care what the Constitution is. If they like to have a Mikado there, that is their business."

ERNEST BEVIN: "That is what we wanted to know."

PRIME MINISTER: "Not if it is done by force, you understand; only if it is done by their choice."

ERNEST BEVIN: "I quite understand."

II

The same evening while the debate was continuing in the House of Commons, the *Daily Herald* secured a 'scoop' on the Russian peace terms offered to Poland and published these in a special edition. The Russian proposal, on paper at least, was generous: it offered a guarantee of Polish independence and a frontier more favourable than that proposed by the Allies in the Curzon Line. Meeting the next morning (11th August), the Council of Action sent a letter to the Prime Minister, reminding him that he had made Polish independence the main issue in his discussion with them and asking him, now that this issue had been dealt with by the Russian declaration, to state the terms on which he was prepared to make a peace settlement between Great Britain and Soviet Russia. Lloyd George waited a day and then asked Bevin to go and see him in Downing Street. He evaded the Council's question about Anglo-Russian peace terms, declaring that he was not at all satisfied with the Russian offer to Poland and suspected trickery.

To meet this objection Bevin and his colleagues saw Kamenev and Krassin several times during the week and sent messages to the Soviet Government urging them to adhere at all costs to the published terms they had offered to Poland and to their earlier declarations on respect for Polish independence. These representations appear to have had some effect. Further negotiations between the Council of Action and the Prime Minister, however, only led to Lloyd George's statement that everything would depend upon the character of the settlement arrived at between Russia and Poland and that until the negotiations at Minsk bore fruit it would be premature to discuss terms for an Anglo-Russian settlement.

While the Council was continuing its arguments with the Prime Minister, more than a thousand delegates were assembling for a special conference, representative of the whole Labour movement, to discuss what action should be taken in support of its protests. The conference opened at the Central Hall, Westminster, on the morning of 13th August and Bevin was again the principal speaker for the Council of Action. Most of his speech was devoted to an account of the negotiations with the Prime Minister, but he roused his audience by the emphatic way in which he declared:

"In the name of the British Labour Party, I say that no one man or set of men has the right to say that the honour of a country is at stake when the country does not know the facts. I hope Labour is going to fight this to the bitter end. . . . Our great work in life until now has been mainly wages, but I say in all sincerity that this question you are called upon to decide today—the willingness to take any action to win world peace—transcends any claim in connection with wages or hours of labour. (Cheers)"[1]

When Bevin sat down, it was left to two men who had hitherto strongly opposed direct action, J. R. Clynes and J. H. Thomas, to introduce a resolution approving the formation of the Council of Action. A second resolution was passed at the same time instructing the Council of Action to remain in being until it had secured guarantees that British forces would not be used in support of Poland or against Russia, that the Soviet Government would be recognised and trade relations with Russia restored. To this end they were authorised "to call for any and every form of withdrawal of labour which circumstances may require". The presence of close on seven hundred trade-union representatives and the unprecedented unanimity of all sections of the movement made this an impressive threat.

In fact, the threat did not need to be implemented. The Council of Action remained in being until the end of the year, firing off an occasional manifesto or protest.[2] A file of telegrams and letters

1 The Council of Action: *Report of the Special Conference on Labour and the Russo-Polish War.*

2 Bevin's papers contain a number of fly-sheets issued by the Council and a report dated 18th Oct. 1920 covering the Council's activities from August to October.

among Bevin's papers testifies to the enthusiasm with which the local Councils picked up every rumour of munitions being moved, only to see them proved unfounded. For whatever intentions the British Government may originally have had—and Lloyd George insisted that Labour was kicking at an open door—no further British intervention in the Russo-Polish conflict was attempted. The Poles saved themselves largely by their own exertions, with some aid from the French. Under the leadership of General Weygand, they reorganised their armies, successfully defended Warsaw and drove the Russians back out of Poland. An armistice was signed between the two countries at Riga on 12th October and the crisis ended.

12

The *Daily Herald* had been an outspoken critic of the Government's policy towards Russia and a strong advocate of direct action. A clumsy effort by the Government to discredit the *Herald* led to a spirited exchange of letters between Bevin and Lloyd George. On 19th August, the Admiralty published eight intercepted telegrams which had passed between Litvinov (in London) and Chicherin, the Soviet Foreign Minister, the earlier of which dealt with Lansbury's attempts to buy paper from the Russians, and in the later of which there was mention of a gift of money to help the *Herald*. The charge of being bought by 'Russian gold' was a damaging one, but only if it could be shown that Lansbury and the directors of the paper (of whom four, including Ernest Bevin, were now trade-union officials) had accepted the offer. The following day, the *Herald*—the only paper to which the Government statement had not been sent— issued a categorical denial: "Not a bond, not a franc, not a rouble." Lansbury published a full list of subscriptions to the paper, not one of which had come from outside the country.

The Government said no more at the time, but in September, Francis Meynell, a director of the *Herald* who had been buying paper in Copenhagen, arrived back in London with a mysterious package of jewels valued at £75,000 which the Russians offered as a free gift to keep the *Daily Herald* going. The jewels were sold with the help of Edgar, George Lansbury's son, and on 10th September the *Herald* published on its front page the naïve question: "Shall we accept £75,000 of Russian money?" A storm of controversy broke over Lansbury's head and Downing Street kept the controversy alive by issuing an official statement on the 16th:

"The Government permits itself to doubt whether the *Daily Herald* would have taken the public into its confidence but for the fact that it had been apprised that the secret could no longer be kept."

This accusation of dishonesty got under Bevin's skin and he wrote an angry letter of protest to Lloyd George. The Prime Minister was on strong ground and made the most of it. After setting out the facts at length—and the facts alone must have made Bevin curse the unwise way in which Lansbury and Meynell had acted—he ended his reply:

"It appears to me to be inconceivable that directors who are *really* exercising business control over the concern of which they are trustees for the Trade Unions should not have been acquainted with what was going on. If they were ignorant, such ignorance on matters of vital moment is a sinister comment on the amount of control exercised by the Trade Union representatives on this organ."

Bevin retorted by accusing Lloyd George, "with your usual ability to sidetrack the issue," of merely re-hashing what had already been published in the Press, ending his letter with a not very effective jibe at Asquith's failure to exercise control over his Cabinet (including Lloyd George) in the case of the Marconi shares. He had scarcely had the better of the exchange, but he insisted on the refusal of the Russian offer, Meynell resigned his directorship and in October the *Herald* raised its price to twopence.

The row over the *Herald* was a side-issue, badly mishandled but not substantiallly detracting from the impressive demonstration of Labour's strength in the Council of Action. How far, in fact, had that demonstration forced the Government to alter its policy? The Government, naturally enough, claimed that it had no effect at all; Labour, that its action alone saved the nation from war. Both claims were exaggerated. It is unlikely that Lloyd George would have been willing to go further than the threat of military intervention, but the unexpected strength of Labour's reaction clearly took him by surprise and robbed the Government of freedom of action. If they had wanted to go further, they could hardly have done so in face of the storm of protest which even the suggestion of armed intervention aroused.

For all the talk of 'direct action' in the early 1920s, the Council of Action was the sole occasion on which the threat of a general strike was used with effect to secure a political objective.[1] Why was it effective in the summer of 1920? Because two conditions essential for its success were realised then which were unfulfilled on every other occasion when direct action for political ends was proposed.

The first was the unanimity of the Labour movement, not the paper unity of formal resolutions passed without opposition at the annual conference, but readiness to commit themselves to taking action at once. The weakness of the Labour movement has always been its tendency to confuse verbal protests with action. This was one of the few occasions in its history when the trade-union leaders, the men who, Bevin so often insisted, had to assume the responsibility for calling out their members, took the initiative on a political issue instead of applying the brake and were sure of the support of the rank and file. Intervention in Russia, even for those who strongly disliked Bolshevik methods, had become, as we have seen, a symbol of the right of self-determination of any working-class régime on which moderate and conservative opinion in the movement was prepared to unite with the Left.

The second condition, which in part accounted for and in part overlapped with the first, was the state of public opinion in the country at large. Those who called for action to prevent war had majority opinion on their side. The Government's recognition of this fact was reluctant but decisive. The paradox of 'direct action' was that the conditions which alone made success possible—the unanimity of the Labour movement and widespread support outside it —made it also unnecessary, since no Government was likely to fly in the face of the opinion of the majority. It was because these conditions were not repeated that the Council of Action had no sequel and led nowhere.[2]

1 The General Strike of 1926 was launched for an industrial objective in support of the miners, and any political purpose was indignantly repudiated.
2 Beatrice Webb made the same comment in her diary at the time: "I very much doubt whether 'direct action', unless it proved to be a symptom of public opinion among all classes, would have been sufficiently universal to be effective." *Diaries* 1912–24, p. 187.

CHAPTER 7

The Triple Alliance and
Black Friday
1920 — 1921

I

BEVIN'S INITIATIVE in setting up the Council of Action and the leading part he played in it attracted a good deal of attention in the Labour movement, by no means all of it favourable. If some spoke of him enthusiastically as a future Labour Prime Minister, others resented his readiness to tell leaders who had been twenty or thirty years longer in the movement what ought to be done. Still under forty and a member of neither the Party Executive nor the T.U.C. Parliamentary Committee, he spoke his mind without deferring to anyone and did not trouble to conceal his contempt for many who were senior to him in the official hierarchy. He made no concessions to his critics, preferring independence to tact, even when it made him enemies. He did not fit easily into any of the accepted divisions of Labour opinion, left-wing, right-wing or middle of the road, any more than he had during the war. He was as much an individualist in his views as in his behaviour, owning allegiance to no group and making up his own mind.

The members of the Transport Workers' Federation were eager to exploit the skill as an advocate which Bevin had revealed at the Shaw Inquiry, and in the course of 1920 Bevin secured wage advances on a national basis for the carters (or as they were now coming to be known, lorry drivers); for tram and bus workers; for canal boatmen (one of the worst-paid trades with appalling living conditions); for coal-trimmers and coal-tippers, both specialised forms of dock work.

Economic conditions throughout most of 1920 were still sufficiently buoyant to make it possible for the employers to concede wage advances with small cost to themselves, but the employers' resistance was beginning to stiffen and Bevin failed to repeat the success of the Shaw Inquiry in securing the full amount for which the men asked. There was a more ominous setback in the autumn of 1920 when the campaign to secure a national minimum wage for lorry drivers of 87/– a week had to be abandoned. The Joint Industrial Council for the road-transport industry broke up in face of the refusal of the employers to continue national negotiations and, after an unsuccessful attempt to organise a strike, the Federation was forced to admit defeat and advise the individual unions to make the best settlement they could locally. This was the first major defeat in the "national movement" which Bevin had initiated towards the end of the war and the fact that two of the unions concerned in Lancashire and Yorkshire broke away from the national negotiations not only encouraged the employers but revealed all too clearly the shortcomings of a Federation of thirty-odd unions, jealous of their autonomy and jealous of each other.

At the annual Council meeting in June, Bevin put forward a plan for strengthening the Federation. Its main feature was to establish a standard weekly contribution of 1/– a week for all the affiliated unions. Half of this sum was to be handed over to the Federation. From the funds placed at its disposal the Federation would then be able to pay for a full-time staff to carry out all national and international negotiations and to provide additional strike pay to equalise the amount received by the members of the different unions involved in a dispute.

The scheme was roughly handled in discussion. Bevin had to meet objections both from those who felt that it went too far in undermining the autonomy of the unions, and from those who argued that it did not go far enough in stopping short of complete amalgamation into a single union. The proposals were finally referred to the Executive and there conveniently allowed to drop. By the time the next Council meeting came round Bevin had already launched his own amalgamation scheme—outside the Federation.

2

The incontestable achievement of the Federation remained the Shaw Award. Bevin was not content with framing the schedules for the application of the minimum wage in the different ports. He at once set to work to draft a scheme to carry out the principle of maintenance accepted by the Court. He took great care to make it as practicable as possible. Every man whose name was on the port register was to receive £4 a week guaranteed wage, whether work was available or not, provided he offered himself for employment. With a properly-kept register excluding casual labour, Bevin calculated that there would not be more than an average of ten per cent unemployment. The cost of providing a guaranteed wage for that ten per cent he put at £2,600,000 a year, to be borne by the industry and met by a levy of 4d. a ton on all goods passing through the ports. The scheme was adopted, without revision, by the Federation and presented by Bevin to the National Joint Council on Dock Labour for the establishment of which he had persistently pressed.

Even if his proposals were accepted by the employers, he knew that they would certainly meet with strong opposition from the men. He told the London dock officers of the Union whom he briefed as missionaries of the scheme that they could expect to hear complaints that it interfered with the men's liberty—"being interpreted, the expression mainly means liberty to go home with nothing"—and to find resistance rooted in conservatism and fear of every change suggested. He counselled patience: "it has been proven elsewhere that those who browbeat at first eventually are blessed."[1]

Bevin was right in believing that London would prove the most difficult port to organise. The other unions with members on the docks were jealous of the credit claimed by the Dockers' Union as a result of Bevin's part in the Shaw Inquiry and roundly accused Bevin of putting on additional organisers to 'poach' their members. The greater part of the two days' General Council meeting of the Federation in July 1920 was taken up with these accusations and counter-accusations of bad faith (in which Bevin gave back quite as

1 D. W. R. and G. W. U.: Minutes of the meeting of London District Officers, 13th Sept. 1920.

F

good as he got) and with a still more bitter quarrel between the two principal road-transport unions, the United Vehicle Workers and the National Union of Vehicle Workers. Even the long-suffering patience of Harry Gosling, the Federation's President, was strained by the quarrels between the delegates. Everyone present condemned the sectionalism and jealousy to which the existence of rival unions was bound to lead, yet, so long as they existed, no one could see a way of achieving the amalgamation into a single union which many of them genuinely wanted.

Bevin kept his own counsel, but the scenes he took part in at the Council meeting confirmed him in his determination to find a means, if it were humanly possible, to provide an alternative to the Federation, the value of which he regarded as exhausted.

He felt less dissatisfaction with the International Transport Workers' Federation, the second post-war conference of which he attended at Christiania (Oslo) in March 1920 as one of the five representatives of the British Federation. The I.T.F. was still in process of being re-established, but its value was proved that spring when a strike of dockers and seamen at Rotterdam and Amsterdam received invaluable help from the British. The Transport Workers' Federation subscribed £1,000 to the strike fund and instituted a boycott on Dutch-owned and Dutch-bound traffic in British ports. This was maintained, with the support of the N.U.R., for the eleven weeks the Dutchmen remained out, and helped them to secure an increase of 2/- a day. Without the boycott, the strike must have collapsed at an early stage.

Sceptical of the eloquent but ineffectual resolutions of exhortation launched by the Socialist International and the International Federation of Trade Unions, Bevin was much more attracted by the I.T.F.'s attempt to secure co-operation between the unions of different countries on practical questions arising from their common calling. He put a great deal of unspectacular effort into helping to build up the I.T.F., as he did later into the work of the I.L.O., and became familiar with the leaders of the continental trade-union movement and their problems. This was to prove an apprenticeship of value, unique among the experience of British Foreign Secretaries, when he went to the Foreign Office in 1945.

3

Since the special conference held in December 1919, the T.U.C. Co-ordination Committee had been working on its draft scheme for a General Council in order to have it ready for submission to the Trades Union Congress in September 1920. Bevin's original memorandum remained the basis of the scheme, although the detailed plan to form the different unions into groups for the nomination of members was drawn up by G.D.H. Cole, then a young political economist working in the Labour Research Department.

Bevin laid great stress on the need to provide the new General Council with economic and statistical information, a suggestion which sounded strange to the older generation of trade-union leaders, but the value of which he had proved in the preparation for the Shaw Inquiry. As management became professionalised, Bevin argued, the trade unions too had to abandon the old-style rough and ready methods of conducting negotiations and equip themselves with a trained staff and the economic information to meet the employers on an equal footing.

The reforms, as they were finally adopted by the T.U.C. at Portsmouth in September 1920, provided for a General Council of thirty to replace the old Parliamentary Committee which had acted as the executive committee of the T.U.C. since 1871. It was to be elected annually. Each of the unions affiliated to the T.U.C. was allocated to one of seventeen groups (mining; railways; engineering; building; transport, etc.) and each group had the right to nominate for the seats allotted to it on the Council, although the vote was taken by the Congress as a whole.

The unions remained autonomous. The General Council could plead, persuade, invite, cajole, but never give orders. It was to act as a 'general staff' (a favourite metaphor of the time) to an army which had no chain-of-command or commander-in-chief and whose divisions would decide for themselves whether to fight or not.

The Council's duties were modestly defined:

"1. The General Council shall keep a watch on all industrial movements and shall attempt, *where possible*, to co-ordinate industrial action;
"2. It shall promote common action by the Trade Union movement on general questions, such as wages and hours, and any matter of general

concern that may arise between trade unions and employers or between the trade union movement and the Government, and shall have power to assist any union which is attacked on any vital question of trade union principle.

"3. Where disputes arise, or threaten to arise, between trade unions, it shall use its influence to promote a settlement."[1]

To provide for the increased cost of staff, the committee proposed an affiliation fee of 1d. per member of the unions affiliated which, on a total membership of 6 million, would produce an annual income of £25,000. Each union, however, retained firm control over its own funds.

The scheme was presented to Congress and defended by the familiar Transport Workers' team, Harry Gosling, Bob Williams and Ernie Bevin. Clynes, an old hand on the Parliamentary Committee, made the most damaging criticism. For all the talk of a re- volutionary proposal, he told Congress, the committee had been so anxious to respect the autonomy of the individual unions that it had produced a scheme which added virtually nothing to the powers of the existing Parliamentary Committee. He moved the rejection of the scheme and instructions to the committee to draw up a new plan.

Bevin got up to reply. Clynes's real object, he claimed, was to stop anything being done and any argument would serve his purpose. Had the Committee made radical proposals along the lines Clynes now suggested, then he would have come down and made an equally effective speech against it on the grounds that it went too far in interfering with existing bodies.

Clynes protested, but Bevin brushed his protest aside:

"I know your dialectical ability, Mr. Clynes, which is a greater power than your consistency, but I am not in the least moved by that debating ability. . . . It is true that the Co-ordination Committee has not attempted to lay down an actual final, detailed plan as to how this new thing will work out. It would be a mistake if we did. There is no finality in our conception of organisation. But we realise that there is greater danger in trying, before we are allowed to create confidence by the existence of a body, to ride rough- shod over the natural conservatism of our movement."[2]

The Committee carried the day and the report was adopted.

1 T. U. C. Report, 1920, pp. 310–15.
2 Ibid. pp. 319–20.

Bevin's defence was justified by time. Given the refusal of the individual unions to surrender any substantial part of their independence, a central body must work by influence and could not proceed by the exercise of authority. Influence, unlike authority, is not susceptible of constitutional definition. The influence of the General Council would be what the General Council made it, and that no one could foresee in 1920. The General Council never became what the radicals hoped for, a unified command of the trade-union movement, except briefly during the General Strike of 1926. Such a conception was out of keeping with the highly individualistic history and character of the British unions. But within the limits of what was possible, its influence has been greater than might reasonably have been expected, particularly when it has had men of the calibre of Bevin and Citrine to provide it with leadership.

Bevin himself did not stand for election to the General Council until 1925, being content until then to let Harry Gosling and Ben Tillett hold the two seats allotted to the Transport Workers. No one, however, who compares the Trades Union Congress of 1920 with those of earlier years can fail to be struck by the much greater confidence with which he spoke and the attention with which he was listened to even before he took his seat on the platform and could use the big block vote of the T.G.W.U. to command a hearing.

Bevin again appealed to the unions to give financial support to the *Herald* which had now reached a circulation of 370,000, despite an advertisement boycott and the fact that it was losing £2,500–£3,000 a week. He did not succeed in getting sufficient support to avoid raising the price of the *Herald* to 2d., but he kept on pegging away and in November took George Lansbury and the other directors with him to Manchester where he made a special appeal to the North of England unions for funds to start a northern edition printed in Manchester. "It seems to have had not nine, but ninety lives, but it has now become an established proposition. The greatest tribute to it from my point of view is the fact that it gets into every Minister's speech, from Lloyd George to Churchill."[1] The unions, already beginning to feel the pinch of the depression, had no money to spare and Bevin had to wait another ten years for the *Herald*'s northern edition, but he secured it in the end.

1 Transcript of speeches delivered at a conference in the Downing Street Co-operative Hall, Manchester, 6th Nov. 1920.

4

The Portsmouth T.U.C. met under the shadow of yet another crisis in the long-drawn-out dispute in the mining industry. During the course of 1920 the miners were forced to realise that they had been defeated in their demand for nationalisation. The 'Mines for the Nation' campaign launched by the special Trades Union Congress of December 1919 proved a fiasco. The impression made by the Sankey Commission had faded; public opinion outside the mining areas was apathetic and, at another special conference called in March 1920, the T.U.C. turned down the proposal of a general strike by a huge majority. The miners remained in an angry mood. They felt they had been cheated by the evasive tactics of the Government and, with the continued rise in the price of coal and the cost of living to justify them, now decided to press for further advances in wages.

The Government was still in control of the mines and making large profits out of high prices for coal. The justice of the miners' claims, however, counted for less than the fact that the dispute had come to be regarded as a trial of strength between employers and Government on the one hand and Labour on the other. The Miners' Federation was the largest body of organised labour in the country: their victory or defeat was bound to have immediate consequences over the whole battlefield between Capital and Labour.

'Battlefield' is not an exaggerated metaphor. Nothing is more striking in reading through the speeches and newspaper comment of the early 1920s than the frank recognition by both sides that industrial relations had become a running class war and the concession or rejection of wage demands symbols of victory or defeat for one side or the other. The miners, more class-conscious than any other group of workers in the country, stubborn, proud, intensely loyal and convinced of the justice of their cause, were in the forefront of the battle.

After protracted negotiations with the Government which failed to satisfy the men's demands, a ballot in August gave a majority of over two-thirds of the miners in favour of a strike. The date was fixed for 25th September and the miners' leaders turned to their partners in the Triple Industrial Alliance for support.

Little had been heard of the Triple Alliance since the summer of 1919. Neither the railway strike of September 1919 nor the Council of Action had been organised under its auspices. The original proposal had been for all three partners to place their demands before the employers at the same time. Except for the accidental coincidence on the reduction of hours in 1919, however, this had never happened. It was not until 31st August, when the decision of their own members in favour of a strike was already known, that the miners approached their partners, leaving them—without regard to their circumstances—only the option of saying whether they would or would not come out on strike to support the miners in a dispute in which they themselves were not involved.

Neither the railwaymen nor the transport workers were blind to the consequences of a defeat for the miners. They believed, in the words of the Triple Alliance communique, "that the claims are both reasonable and just and should be conceded forthwith". But they were far from enthusiastic at the prospect of taking strike action if they were not conceded.

In the case of the transport workers, even a successful strike was unlikely to bring them direct advantage. On the contrary, any strike at this time, whether successful or not, was against their interests. They were pressing the dock employers to adopt a maintenance scheme and the road-transport employers to resume national negotiations. The employers would be delighted to use the excuse of a sympathetic strike to justify the rejection of both claims. Nor was it at all certain that the men would respond to a strike call. Williams reported to the Federation Executive on 30th September that only ten of the thirty-two unions affiliated to the Federation were prepared to give plenary powers to the Federation's Executive.[1]

Moreover, the miners' leaders were known to be divided. Bob Smillie, the president of the Miners' Federation, was in favour of accepting the Government's offer to place the dispute before an independent tribunal, a course rejected by the Secretary, Frank Hodges, and other members of the Miners' Executive in favour of 'fighting'. This meant, as Bevin said at a delegate conference of the Triple Alliance on 23rd September, flying in the face of the dockers' own experience with the Shaw Inquiry:

1 N.T.W.F.: Minutes of the Executive Council, 30th Sept. 1920.

"Why, seeing we had to use considerable influence to get our people to accept a Court of Inquiry, we have to use our influence now to get them to strike because you will not accept the Court of Inquiry."

If neither of the miners' partners was prepared to turn down a strike, they were clearly very reluctant to engage in one. The result was a postponement of the miners' own strike, further negotiations throughout September, and finally on 16th October a coal strike, called by the miners acting alone.

The Triple Alliance, it appeared, had failed, yet its potential strength was demonstrated almost at once when a delegate conference of the railwaymen on 21st October belatedly decided that, if negotiations with the miners were not resumed by Saturday, 23rd October, they would bring the railways to a standstill. As if by magic, Lloyd George suddenly found it practicable to invite the miners' leaders to new talks and four days later a compromise was reached which conceded the miners' claim for an immediate advance of 2/– a shift.

A month before, at the delegate conference of the Triple Alliance on 24th September, Bevin had voiced an opinion which many others shared:

"My charge is that the six men who are at the head of affairs have not constructed an organisation that is capable of working when the test comes. . . . I have said over and over: 'When the test comes, if you do not make a real organisation it will be found to be a paper alliance.' By God, it has revealed itself to be a paper alliance this week."

The fact that in the end the railwaymen's intervention helped the miners to secure a partial victory did not invalidate Bevin's argument. That winter both he and Bob Williams pressed for a meeting, in advance of the next industrial crisis, to overhaul the constitution of the Alliance. They got no response from the miners, however, and when the next crisis blew up in the spring of 1921, the weakness which had been so obvious the previous autumn was still unremedied and destroyed the Alliance for good.

The Government was not so slow to learn from events. Before the settlement with the miners was reached, they passed through both Houses of Parliament an Emergency Powers Act which was to be used with great effect in the General Strike of 1926. The unions had no cause to complain. For eighteen months they had been talking about 'direct action' and "challenging the power of the capitalist State". They had only themselves to blame if the Government took them at their word and made its preparations.

5

Although Bevin had made a number of striking contributions to the trade-union cause in the past three years, he had not yet found what he was looking for, a more adequate form for the organisation of trade-union strength. The Dockers' Union was too small for his purpose. The Transport Workers' Federation and its international counterpart, the I.T.F., the Triple Alliance or the T.U.C. (even with its reformed General Council) failed to produce the concentration of power for which he was seeking, since all were federal bodies which left the autonomy of the individual unions intact. During 1920, however, he took up again the idea of amalgamation into a single transport union which had been discussed ever since he had been a trade unionist, and in the course of the next two years fashioned his own answer to the problem of organisation.

The advantages of amalgamation were obvious. A single union would overcome all the weaknesses of disunity from which the Federation suffered, would provide greater strength in negotiations, greater economy and efficiency in administration. What stood in the way?

Many of the difficulties arose from that conservatism which has been one of the most strongly-marked characteristics of British trade unionism, from loyalty to old-established societies especially on the part of voluntary officers, from the vested interests of officials, personal jealousies and traditional rivalries. There were also difficulties of a practical nature. The smaller unions, especially, feared not only the loss of identity but the loss of representation and autonomy for their particular trades. Unions which had husbanded their funds looked askance at taking over the liabilities of those which had been improvident and felt they were being asked to make an unequal financial sacrifice. How to pool the financial assets of a number of unions was a thorny problem; so was the equalisation of different rates of contribution and different scales of benefit.[1] Some unions offered one but not another benefit; almost all differed in the amounts they were prepared to pay. Finally, the fact that amalgamation would mean greater economy in administration also meant that a number of the officials of the existing unions would lose their jobs.

These difficulties have again and again prevented amalgamation between unions and to this day the structure of the British trade-union movement presents a complicated, confused and overlapping pattern which can only be explained (it can hardly be defended) on historical grounds.

Before the first World War the legal obstacles in the way of amalgamation (set up by the Trade Union Act Amendment Act of 1876) had also been formidable: each union involved had to secure a majority in a ballot vote of two-thirds of its entire membership. Only one big amalgamation had been brought about under these conditions, the National Union of Railwaymen in 1913 and, as Professor Cole remarks, it may have been fortunate that no one was concerned to scrutinise closely the methods by which it was done.[2] In 1917 John Hodge, the first Minister of Labour, altered the requirements of the law by the Trade Union (Amalgamation) Act, making it sufficient to obtain a fifty per cent vote in the ballot, with a majority of twenty per cent in favour of amalgamation.

The new act produced a marked change immediately the war was over. Of the eighteen major trade unions affiliated to the T.U.C. today all but five are the product of amalgamations, the majority of which took place in the years, 1917–24. Even then it was by no means easy to get the percentage of votes required unless there was real determination on the part of the unions' leaders to push the amalgamation through and overcome the reluctance of their members to fill up the ballot paper at all.

This inertia wrecked the scheme for amalgamation between the Dockers and the National Union of General Workers which had been accepted by the two Executives at the end of the war. While the General Workers (whose officials strongly supported the scheme)

1 These might cover accident and death; unemployment, strikes, victimisation, legal aid and superannuation.
2 G. D. H. Cole: *An Introduction to Trade Unionism* (1953), p. 90.

polled a 73% vote of their total membership in favour, not more than 40% of the Dockers voted for it. Opposition was negligible but close on 60% of the Dockers' members did not take the trouble to vote. The fact that the rate of abstentions was unusually high in the Bristol Channel area inevitably led to the accusation that Bevin had not been in favour of the scheme and by refusing to put his energy and influence behind it had killed it.[1]

Bevin indignantly denied the accusation but there was almost certainly some truth in it. He had taken little part in the two years' negotiations leading up to the ballot and he was little attracted by an amalgamation which would give the new society the character of a general workers', rather than of a transport workers', union. Nor was he indifferent to the prospect that the National Union of General Workers, with three times the membership of the Dockers', would be bound to have the dominant voice and their officials to take the leading part in any such amalgamation.

The Shaw Inquiry did more than anything else to create the atmosphere in which the sort of amalgamation Bevin favoured became possible. Harry Gosling told the Amalgamation Conference at Leamington eighteen months later:

"At the Dockers' Inquiry, it was found that, whether we were amalgamated or not, we must appear to be, we must show a bold and strong front to the employers. I do not think it is giving away secrets to say now that we went to that Inquiry with a very thin camouflage. . . . All the time we were trembling in case we had to expose the weakness of the solidarity of those whom we represented. Bevin had to consult this body and that body which said he had not said enough for them, but had said too much for somebody else, because he had no Executive behind him that represented the whole thing. We scrambled through but it brought more clearly to our notice than ever before the necessity of not taking that risk again."[2]

Fortunately, the result of the Inquiry was not only to produce an unanswerable case for the advantages of combined action but to give Bevin a prestige with the rank and file dockers throughout the country, whatever their union, which made it very much easier for him to overcome the inevitable opposition.

1 N.T.W.F.: Report of the 10th Annual General Council Meeting, Southampton, 3rd–4th June 1920, p. 83.

2 T. and G. W. U.: Proceedings of the Special Rules Conference, Leamington 27th–29th Sept. 1921, at which Harry Gosling acted as chairman.

6

In March 1920, immediately after the Shaw Award, Bevin met the Executive and officers of the National Union of Docks, Wharves and Shipping Staffs (a new union of shipping clerks in the London docks of which Alf Short, M.P. was the secretary) and expounded his ideas on amalgamation. The reception he got encouraged him to go ahead and at a further meeting in Effingham House, off the Strand, on 7th May he put before four representatives of Short's Union and three members of the Dockers' Executive a sketch for amalgamation which is recognisable as a first draft of his later proposals.[1]

These were preliminaries. The first real step was taken on 14th July when a sub-committee of the Dockers' Executive met a delegation from the other principal dockers' union, Sexton's National Union of Dock Labourers, who agreed to join forces in creating a new union. The debate at the Transport Workers' Federation council meeting in June had fortified Bevin's purpose and he persuaded Harry Gosling, a member of neither union but President of the Federation, to take the chair. On the other hand, Bevin deliberately went outside the Federation and got both his own and Sexton's union to agree to set up an entirely new organisation.

Between them, Tillett's and Sexton's unions counted 120,000 and 70,000 members respectively; the next largest waterside union numbered less than 11,000. If these two were in agreement, therefore, there was a good chance of carrying the other unions with them. They agreed to appoint Bevin as the provisional secretary and Harry Gosling as the provisional chairman of an amalgamation committee, fixed a date for the next meeting and decided on the list of other unions, all connected with the dock industry, whom they would invite to attend.

There were fifty-nine delegates present, representing thirteen unions, when the 'Conference re amalgamation' opened at Anderton's Hotel in Fleet Street, on the morning of 18th August. Six of the unions (including Bevin's) could claim to represent London.[2] From

1 This account of the amalgamation is based upon the minutes and other records of a series of meetings carefully kept by Miss Forcey, who acted as Minute Secretary.

2 Besides the Dockers' Union, which, of course, had a strong membership in the Bristol Channel and the West of England as well, the London unions were: the

Cardiff came Clatworthy and four other delegates of the sixteen hundred Cardiff, Penarth and Barry Coal Trimmers; from Swansea, John Twomey and three delegates of the National Amalgamated Labourers' Union just under eleven thousand strong. Glasgow was represented by Houghton's Scottish Union of Dockers; Liverpool by Sexton's Union, the Liverpool Clerks and the Mersey Watermen (186 members in all and three delegates); Newcastle by the North of England Trimmers' and Teamers' Association. Together they could claim to speak for a membership of between two hundred and forty and two hundred and fifty thousand men, although it is unlikely that any of the delegates would have accepted the others' figures without scepticism.

They knew each other too well to indulge in speech-making and neither Bevin nor anyone else could have found anything fresh to say on the subject of amalgamation which had not been said already a score of times.

But Bevin had not come unprepared. He had gauged the situation exactly. It was no good going back to previous schemes or trying to bring about a fusion of existing unions. The only chance of succeeding where others had failed was to hit upon some new proposal which would break out of the dreary round of all too familiar arguments, objections and jealousies. He proved equal to the occasion. After the conference had appointed a drafting committee with one representative from each union, he produced a series of suggestions on the organisation of the new union which were not only to enable him to carry through the amalgamation of eighteen separate unions before the end of 1922, but proved so successful that they provided the framework within which the Transport and General Workers' Union grew by the year of his death, 1951, to a membership of 1,337,000, by far the largest trade union in this country. The promise of that achievement is already contained in the sheet and a half of typed notes which he persuaded the conference to accept as the drafting committee's terms of reference.

Turning over the problem in his mind, Bevin had come to see that

National Union of Dock, Wharves and Shipping Staffs (Short's) with a membership of 6,500; the Amalgamated Stevedores' Labour Protection League (Ruark's), 5,500; the South Side Labour Protection League, 2,500; the National Union of Ships' Clerks and Grain Weighers (known as the East Ham Union), 732; and Harry Gosling's Amalgamated Society of Watermen, Lightermen, and Bargemen, 7,000.

the structure of the new union had to meet a double need. It had to leave each industrial group—the dockers, road transport, the clerical staffs—the autonomy to deal with their own affairs. But, at the same time, it had to prevent this autonomy undermining the unity of the organisation and reducing it to the unsatisfactory status of another federation.

The first need had led the Webbs (in their *Industrial Democracy*) to the conclusion that it was virtually impossible to combine men of different occupations in a stable amalgamation. The dockers, for instance, were certain to insist that they alone, not a mixed committee containing carters and tramwaymen as well, should have the right to decide on matters affecting their own trade. Bevin recognised this. He met the difficulty by suggesting the creation of trade groups, in which each member of the union would be grouped with those following the same calling. The dockers, for instance, through regional and national trade group committees with their own officers would be responsible for negotiation and organisation in the dock industry. But, as a check on the particularism of the trade groups, Bevin also proposed to set up a second, territorial structure with area committees and area secretaries, grouping members of the union together, irrespective of their calling or membership of different trade groups, on a geographical basis.

It was this double structure which made the new union something more than a federation of trade groups. The trade group was an ingenious way of meeting the first of his problems, but without his answer to the second, the union could hardly have survived. The two have to be taken together to grasp the originality of his design and the documents leave little doubt that the design was his.

At the top, holding the whole together, there was to be a national executive representative of both the national trade groups and the territorial areas, with control over finance, strike action and the general policy of the union.

Thus, right at the beginning, Bevin provided what earlier attempts at amalgamation had lacked, a clear plan of a new type of organisation which survived unchanged the discussions of the next eighteen months and still stamps the Transport and General Workers' Union as his creation.

7

The framework had now to be filled in, a process which took over twelve months to complete, and brought out Bevin's gifts for guiding the work of a committee and persuading it to accept his suggestions.

When the drafting committee met on 3rd September, they were ready to approve his draft of the 'Objects, Constitution and Methods' of the new union and set up a small sub-committee of three to work out the details. This suited Bevin very well. Besides himself, the sub-committee consisted of Harry Gosling, the best chairman possible to handle the full committee and the recalled conference when the time came, and Alf Short, whose enthusiasm had encouraged Bevin from the beginning.

When the three of them met on 14th September, Bevin was able to report a big step forward. He had been eager to bring in the road transport as well as the waterfront unions, and unofficial talks with their leaders suggested that the time was ripe. Accordingly, it was decided to issue an invitation to an informal conference and meanwhile to make five trade groups, adding road transport to those already proposed for docks, waterways, clerical and supervisory staffs and general workers.

The accession of the road transport unions (the United Vehicle Workers and the National Union of Vehicle Workers) meant a major increase not only in the membership of the new union but in its strength as a negotiating body. The employers had just withdrawn from the National Joint Industrial Council for the Road Transport Industry and the whole principle of national negotiations was in question, facts of which Bevin as chairman of the workmen's side of the Council was very well aware. The union leaders were, therefore, in a mood to combine in order to acquire the support of the dockers,[1] and their representatives joined the full drafting

1 One of these unions, the United Vehicle Workers, was itself the product of a recent amalgamation between the London and Provincial Union of Licensed Vehicle Workers and the Amalgamated Association of Tramway and Vehicle Workers; the other, the National Union of Vehicle Workers, had a few months before turned down a scheme for amalgamation with the U.V.W., its chief rival, but was prepared to come into the larger amalgamation scheme proposed by Bevin. This was another powerful argument in its favour. Five other unions, all of local importance, were invited and accepted. They were the Amalgamated Association of Carters and Motormen (Leeds), the North of Scotland Horse and

committee when it met on 5th October to consider the report of its
sub-committee.

Bevin, in the meantime, had been hard at work elaborating the
draft scheme and putting it into form for submission to ballot by the
members of each of the unions. This is worth examining with some
care, for it shows how Bevin faced and found solutions for each of the
controversial issues, step by step.

Of the five trade groups now proposed, the general workers',
with a special sub-section for the metal and chemical trades, was
designed for the development of further trade groups as the union
expanded and extended its industrial interests. This proved a
valuable device providing sufficient flexibility to allow the separation
out of seven new trade groups and four trade sections in the course of
time.

Bevin next dealt with two issues either of which, if wrongly
handled, could have wrecked the amalgamation. The new union,
he proposed, should take over all the officers of the existing unions
and see that none of them suffered financially as a result of the
amalgamation. This was a far-sighted move. It would over-
burden the administration and finances of the new society, but at
one stroke it removed a formidable obstacle to its establishment and
it could be left to the retirement of officials with the passage of time
to reduce the establishment to its correct level.

In the same way Bevin proposed to bypass the problem of reducing
the different scales of contributions and benefits to a single uniform
scale. Every member of the existing unions, he suggested, should be
given a choice between retaining the benefits of his old society
(subject to a minimum contribution) and going on to the new scales
of benefits. Here again he showed a wise respect for vested interests,
leaving it to time to reduce the anomalies.

Choosing the average figure among the existing unions, he proposed 6d. a week as the minimum contribution (3d. for women)
with an additional quarterly payment of 6d. (quarterage) part of
which would be used to build up a political fund, part retained by

Motórmen's Association (Dundee), the Scottish Horse and Motormen's Association
(Glasgow), the United Carters' and Motormen's Association of England (Manchester) and the Liverpool and District Carters' and Motormen's Union. The
variety and length of the names assumed by the earlier trade unions prompts the
reflection, which it is tempting to state as a sociological 'law', that the splendour of
the title varies in inverse proportion to the size and importance of the union.

the areas to form benevolent funds for use at local discretion. The control of finance, he was careful to insist, should be in the hands of the central Executive Council which should pay all affiliation fees to national and international bodies (a subject of much controversy with Communist members in the later history of the union). He was equally clear in the division of responsibilities. Wage applications, working rules, the conduct of negotiations were to be left to the trade groups to settle, but the power to sanction strike action, to authorise lock-out pay and to decide the general policy of the union was vested securely in the central Executive.

The committee accepted his main proposals but they had changes of their own to propose. They altered the title from the Inland Transport Union to the Transport and General Workers' Union. They wrote the words 'aerial transport' into the list of occupations to be covered. Characteristically, they increased the limit of funeral benefit, that hall-mark of trade-union respectability, from £5 to £10 and they referred back to the sub-committee Bevin's proposals for transferring funds from the old unions to the new.

A further meeting of the sub-committee on 15th October was sufficient to clear up most of the outstanding points. It cut through the complications over the transfer of funds and proposed simply that "all the funds, assets and properties of the amalgamating unions shall become the property of the new union and be under the control of the Executive". It also remembered to add that the new union would take over the responsibility for all existing wage agreements and see that they were honoured. With this and a certain amount of redrafting before seeking legal advice, Bevin, Gosling and Short were content to put up the completed document for approval to the full amalgamation committee and to call a delegate conference for 1st December.

Once again the delegates assembled at Anderton's Hotel where nineteen unions answered the roll-call. Some were represented in strength, thirteen from the London Watermen, ten from the London Stevedores, thirteen from the Dockers' Union. In all there were eighty-three delegates besides the chairman and secretary.

The meeting did not open auspiciously. Sexton got up to complain that the Liverpool dockers had not had sufficient time to send in amendments and that there was some suggestion of personal ambition in the part played by the secretary. It soon became clear, however, that the meeting was in favour of the scheme. 11 of the amendments sent in were carried unanimously, another 17 withdrawn. Of the 11 which led to debate, 9 were defeated and only two carried.

These two, both moved by the Dockers' Union, touched on points of importance. The first, which Bevin fully approved, insisted that the Executive Council must be wholly composed of lay members,[1] a practice by no means universal in the trade-union movement. The other laid it down that, in the event of a demand for a general strike, the Executive should first call a national conference fully representative of all groups in the Union. Both changes were made without opposition.

At the end of the conference, Bevin moved and Sexton seconded a resolution endorsing the scheme: it was carried unanimously and the conference instructed a sub-committee to make the necessary preparations for the ballot to be taken.

When the sub-committee met just before Christmas, Bevin not only had the printed scheme and ballot-paper in proof ready for their final approval, but a very effective leaflet to go out at the same time, embellished with the facsimile signatures of each union's officers and a message in favour of amalgamation which ended with the words:

"NOTHING CAN PREVENT IT—only two things can delay it—namely—VESTED INTEREST AND APATHY.
"It is said, it is the duty of Leaders to lead—We now give you the lead—Don't fail to respond".

550,000 ballot papers were printed and sent out. The decision was now in the hands of the rank and file, especially of that active minority in every one of the eighteen hundred branches from which the voluntary officers, the local committee men and delegates have always been recruited. Nobody yet knew how they would vote. But Bevin could go home that Christmas with the satisfaction of knowing that at the end of months of hard work he had at last brought the issue of amalgamation to the point of a decision.

1 As distinguished from full-time paid officials.

8

During the course of that winter, while the ballot-papers were being returned, the economic situation turned sharply against the unions. The post-war boom had been a boom in prices, not production, a speculators' field-day which could not last once world production revived and British export prices were forced down by competition. Towards the end of 1920 an abrupt fall in prices began and was accompanied by a contraction in the volume of trade. The 1921 figure for British exports was little more than half the value of that for 1920.

Although few realised it at the time, Britain's old supremacy as a manufacturing and commercial power had gone for good. The temporary boom after the war concealed this, but now her staple export industries, coal, shipbuilding, iron and steel, engineering and textiles, slow to adjust themselves to new conditions and new techniques, entered on a long period of stagnation. Largely as a result of this, unemployment not only mounted rapidly but remained for years at a level considerably higher than had been known in the worst of the trade depressions before the war.

At the end of 1920, 691,000 or 5.8% of the total of insured work-people were out of work. By the end of March 1921 the figure shot up to 1,355,000 (11.3%); by the end of June, to 2,171,000 (17.8%). Thereafter, it fluctuated between 1.2 and 1.5 millions for the rest of the 1920s and rose to two and a half million in 1930. These figures did not include the many other thousands of workers involved in disputes and the average, of course, concealed very much higher percentages unemployed in certain trades and certain districts.[1]

No one yet grasped the scale or permanence of the change in Britain's economic position. Most people assumed that sooner or later there would be a return to normalcy (by which they meant the situation before 1914) and that the dislocation caused by the war and its aftermath would prove to be temporary. The limit of the employers', the bankers' and the Government's ideas on economic

1 In December 1921, 36.1% of the insured workers in shipbuilding were unemployed; 36.7% in iron and steel; 27.2% in engineering. The figure for Scotland was 21%, for Northern Ireland 25%. Among the towns worst hit in England were Barrow-in-Furness (49% of the insured population out of work in August 1922), Hartlepool (60%), Stockton (49%), Jarrow (43%).

policy was to force down wages and cut public expenditure.

Bevin made no claim to be an economist, but he could see further than that. In a report to the Dockers' Union Executive at the beginning of February 1921, he wrote:

"The Government and the capitalists are very hard to please. They shout 'Increase production' in one breath, and 'Reduce wages' in the next, and then close their works because they cannot sell the over-production immediately following.

"The economics of the Government have proved wrong. The greater output of coal, like the greater output of boots and clothing, *without a greater consuming power being developed simultaneously*, merely results in intensification of unemployment."[1]

In his own reading of the situation, he laid stress on three factors: the effect of the peace settlement in destroying the markets of Central and Eastern Europe; the collapse of the international credit and exchange system, and finally the banks' policy of restricting credit and so preventing industrial expansion. To deal with the immediate problem of unemployment he looked to the policy agreed upon by the joint conference of the Labour Party and T.U.C. in January 1921:

"The policy of the Government should be one of expansion, not of contraction, of rightful and economical public expenditure; the necessary public works and services which must certainly be executed within each decade ought to be, as far as possible, concentrated on the years of industrial depression, so as to avoid the waste of keeping workers in one year in idleness upon unemployment benefit, and in another year on excessive hours of labour at overtime rates."[2]

This anticipation of the 1944 White Paper on Employment Policy, however, proved to be far too advanced for the economic orthodoxy of the 1920s. Official policy clung to the classical remedies of deflation and economy: the high rate of unemployment was regrettable but inevitable.

1 Minutes of the Dockers' Union Executive Council, 4th–11th Feb. 1921.
2 Labour Party Conference Report, 1921, p. 28.

9

The fall in prices justified some reduction in wages, but Bevin and other trade-union leaders believed, not without reason, that this would be used as an excuse to drive wages down further than the cost of living had fallen.[1] Despite the fears of early 1919, the Government, the employers and the bankers had weathered the critical years of transition without having to make any major concession impairing the restoration of private enterprise as the dominant feature of the national economy. During the same period one after another of the wartime controls had been abolished,[2] the ambitious plans for the re-organisation of industry and the social services produced by the Ministry of Reconstruction and its committees quietly dropped and the crucial demand of the Miners' Federation for the nationalisation of the mines evaded.

Labour's hopes of changing the balance of power in British society had failed. Almost the only permanent gain the unions retained from the 'offensive' of 1919 was the shorter working week. Now they were to be forced on to the defensive in face of a mass unemployment which remained a permanent feature of the British economy down to the middle of the 1930s. The trade unions were convinced that the employers meant to take advantage of the situation in order to break their power, to end collective bargaining (at least on a national basis), to lengthen the working day and reassert their right as masters to pay the wages they saw fit. These fears were not exaggerated: they corresponded very closely to the intentions of many employers and of the Conservative majority in the House of Commons eager to end the 'insolence' of the trade-union leaders and put them in their place.

The unions were ill-prepared for a fight. The slump affected them in half a dozen adverse ways. Rising unemployment meant a heavy drain on union funds and a decline in membership. The total

1 Average wage rates reached a peak of 260 in 1920 and declined to 170 by 1922 (1913–100). Actual earnings, allowing for the number of workers unemployed, were 244 in 1920 and had fallen to 147 in 1922. The Ministry of Labour's cost of living index, for comparison, went down from 276 points in Nov. 1920 to 180 by Dec. 1922. These figures are taken from C. L. Mowat: *Britain between the Wars* (1955), p. 125.

2 Cf. R. H. Tawney: 'Abolition of Economic Controls, 1918–21', *Economic History Review*, XIII (1943).

number of trade-union members in the country fell from the peak figure of 8.3 millions in 1920 to 6.6 millions in 1921, and went on falling. With a million and a half men looking for jobs, union leaders were bound to hesitate before calling a strike: any man was going to think twice before coming out on strike if there were a score of unemployed ready to take his job. Working-class solidarity, precarious at the best of times, was undermined by 'blacklegging' or the fear of it. Individual unions, faced with demands for wage reductions, were inclined to settle for what they could get, thankful to keep their members at work.

The dockers were the worst hit of the trades with which Bevin was concerned. The falling off in overseas trade meant far less work in the ports, while unemployment in other trades, like building, swelled the number of men looking for a casual day's pay at the docks. It was hard enough to uphold the principle of registration for the regular dockers; Bevin's hopes of carrying it a stage further and persuading the employers to adopt his scheme for maintenance and a guaranteed weekly wage were swept away. The employers rejected his scheme at the beginning of March 1921 and followed this up by successive cuts in the 16/– a day award which reduced it to 12/– by March 1922. The most that Bevin and the Federation could do was to retreat in good order, preserving the machinery for national negotiations (the National Joint Council for Dock Labour) and using it to negotiate each reduction by agreement. This was at least an improvement on the situation in the road transport industry where national negotiations had to be abandoned with the break-up of the Joint Industrial Council and each union left to make the best settlement it could locally.

The changed circumstances were clearly shown by the result of the inquiry into the wages and conditions of tramwaymen in January–February 1921. The court which conducted the inquiry was set up under the same procedure (the Industrial Courts Act, 1919) as Lord Shaw's court and Bevin again appeared as the principal advocate on the men's side.[1] The findings of the court, however, were very different from the 16/– a day and the endorsement of the principle of maintenance which Bevin had been able to secure for the

---

[1] He was supported by John Cliff and Harold Clay, each of whom in turn was to serve as Assistant General Secretary of the future Transport and General Workers' Union.

dockers the year before. In place of the 12/– a week increase for which Bevin argued, the Court awarded no advance at all and even its recommendation that existing wages should be stabilised until the end of 1921 was successfully contested by the employers. Before the year was out the tramwaymen had to accept a sliding scale varying with the cost of living, a formula which Bevin had rejected with scorn at the Shaw Inquiry.

In one after another of the trades covered by the Federation— road transport, canals, coal tipping and trimming, seafaring—the first few months of 1921 saw the same pattern repeated. Alarmed at the proposal of further reductions and at the steadily mounting figures of unemployment, the Federation called a conference of all its affiliated unions for the first week in April.

10

By the time the conference met it had become clear that, as so often in the years from 1919 to 1926, the critical battle would be fought over the mines. The defeat of the Miners' Federation over nationalisation of the mines had settled the fate of the rest of the nationalisation programme adopted by the T.U.C. at the end of the war. Now the miners' refusal to accept drastic cuts in their pay was recognised by unions, employers and Government alike to be the decisive trial of strength on the issue of wage reductions and national negotiations.

Hitherto the Government had subsidised cheap coal at home, the miners' wages and the losses in operating unprofitable mines out of export prices three times as high as the price charged for domestic supplies. When the export price of coal tumbled with the recovery of the continental coalfields and the beginning of Germany's reparation payments, the Government found itself running the coal industry at a loss. It thereupon hastened to divest itself of its powers of control five months earlier than had been expected. On 31st March, it was announced, the Government would hand back full responsibility for the mines to the owners.

The owners at once gave notice that the new rates of pay would represent big cuts in wages[1] and that they could not agree to national

1 In the worst case, that of South Wales, the cuts ranged from 40 to 49 per cent.

negotiations but would resume the old pre-war practice of district scales which the miners had fought hard to abolish for good.

The Miners' Federation refused to accept these terms and on 1st April more than one million men employed in the collieries accepted their notices and withdrew their labour. The same day the Government declared a state of emergency under the Emergency Powers Act of 1920, and began to call up reservists, concentrate troops and mobilise motor transport.[1]

Not until 31st March had the miners approached their partners in the Triple Alliance and asked for their support. Neither the railwaymen nor the transport workers felt able to commit their members without consulting delegate conferences. The Federation had already summoned its own meeting of affiliated Executives for 5th–6th April, and the N.U.R. agreed to call its conference at the same time.

What appealed strongly to the transport workers was the argument Harry Gosling used: "We regard this as an attempt to get back to the old days of district negotiations rather than national negotiations, which would affect us in the same way as the Miners." The railwaymen took the same view: it was a "prelude to a general attempt to destroy national negotiations and to reduce wages."[2] There was strong support at both conferences for making a stand and the two executives were given a mandate to call for a strike, if necessary.

On the 7th Gosling, Sexton, Bevin and Bob Williams saw the Minister of Labour and Lloyd George at the House of Commons. They refused to be drawn into any discussion of the merits of the miners' claims, contenting themselves with making plain their own attitude as partners in the Triple Alliance. The following day the three Executives met and reached agreement that none of them

1 The account that follows is based upon the contemporary minutes of the Transport Workers' Federation Executive; the minutes of the Dockers' Union Executive Council and its emergency sub-committee; on the report presented to the General Council of the Transport Workers' Federation by Robert Williams in June 1921 (N.T.W.F.: Report of Annual General Council Meeting, June 1921, Appendix 1, pp. 189–223); on the Council's debate on the Report (pp. 21–58) in which Bevin, Williams, Sexton, Tillett and Havelock Wilson took part; and on the minutes of the Dockers' Union Executive Council Sub-committee meeting of 12th May at which Bevin made a full report on his part in the proceedings.

2 N.T.W.F.: National Conference of Affiliated Unions, 5th–6th April 1921, Report on Wages Crisis, p. 7.

would resume work, if a strike had to be called, until a complete return to work without victimisation was secured for the members of all three organisations. This was of great importance to transport workers like the dockers who were much more vulnerable to the introduction of blackleg labour than the miners. With this difficulty out of the way, the Executives of the N.U.R. and the Transport Workers' Federation were ready to commit themselves and issued a joint warning that unless negotiations were re-opened with the Miners "the full strike power of the Triple Alliance shall be put into operation as from Tuesday next midnight, 12th April".[1]

To put the matter to the test, while sending out instructions to prepare for strike action on the 12th, the railwaymen and transport workers (with the miners' approval) sent a deputation of twelve, including Bevin, to meet the Prime Minister and other members of the Cabinet at No. 10 Downing Street on Saturday, 9th April.

Lloyd George was entirely reasonable. He was prepared to summon a conference of both parties at once—if the miners would agree to the condition on which he had insisted all the week of sending the safety-men back to safeguard the pits against flooding. The charge that the miners were destroying "the property of the nation" had been used with great effect by the Government, although the crisis had been provoked by its own refusal of national responsibility for operating the mines. The miners' leaders were angered by the campaign which had been whipped up against them and were well aware that to order the safety-men back would remove half the urgency of the pressure they were exerting on the other side. Their allies, however, pressed them hard, arguing that it was still more important not to lose the support of public opinion. Very reluctantly the miners agreed and the way was then clear for a conference of miners and mine-owners which opened on Monday, the 11th, under the chairmanship of the Prime Minister.

I I

The transport workers and the railwaymen were not present at these negotiations, the miners' leaders insisting that until they actually came out on strike the other partners in the Triple Alliance had no

1 N.T.W.F.: Letter to affiliated unions, 9th April 1921.

standing in the dispute. In fact, the transport and rail strike had to be postponed when the discussions continued into the Tuesday. The Miners offered to accept a reduction of 2s. a shift, but they refused to compromise at all on their demand to continue a national pool of profits and a national settlement of wages.

On the afternoon of the 12th the Prime Minister stated the Government's views: a national pool for the equalisation of wages was impossible without the resumption of State control over the industry. The Government was not prepared to consider this. They supported the owners' proposal of standard district wages, offering a Government subsidy for a short period in order to mitigate the rapid reduction of wages in the districts most severely affected.

The miners turned down these proposals at once. Herbert Smith, the acting president of the Miners' Federation, dour and inflexible, told the Prime Minister to his face:

"The scheme that you have put before us, with the exception of Clause 8 (the offer of Government assistance) is absolutely the owners' scheme. If you had copied the words from their scheme it could not be put in more explicit language. . . .
"If the owners are determined that they are going to carry on nearly like they carried on before the war we will be starved to submission before we accept it. . . . It is a bad thing when a case has to be won through women's and children's stomachs."[1]

These were not idle words, as the miners proved again and again in these years. Their courage matched their bitterness and now they turned to their allies to implement their promise of support.

On Wednesday, 13th April, the three Executives of the Triple Alliance met and agreed to call out the railway and transport workers at 10.0 p.m. on Friday the 15th.

That Thursday, the 14th, there was every prospect of the nearest approach to a general strike the country had so far known. Everything had to be improvised and Bevin was in the thick of the preparations. Communications between headquarters and the local branches might well be cut. This had to be allowed for, local committees formed and some system devised for the distribution of food and milk. The Electrical Trades Union, responsible for the generating stations which supplied power to London's Under-

1 R. Page Arnot: *The Miners, Years of Struggle* (1953), p. 312.

ground and tramways, offered their support and, after Bob Williams had overcome the reluctance of the N.U.R., the other railwaymen's union, the Locomotive Engineers and Firemen, was brought in on equal terms with the other members of the Triple Alliance. On the afternoon of the 14th, the National Council of Labour, made up of the National Executive of the Labour Party, the Executive of the Parliamentary Labour Party and the General Council of the T.U.C., met in the Grand Committee Room of the House of Commons and after cross-examining the representatives of the Triple Alliance, called on all sections of the Labour movement to support the miners.

The Prime Minister received the leaders of the railwaymen and the Transport Workers' Federation but was unable to move them. Harry Gosling, moderate but resolute, denied that they were taking political action: he insisted that it was purely a question of wages.

"To support ourselves we must help the Miners and there is no other way of helping them that we can see now except to stand by them in this test of endurance."[1]

Gosling was followed by J. H. Thomas, who spoke in the same terms for the railwaymen. If the strike had been called for that night, Thursday the 14th, the trial of strength of 1926 would have been anticipated by five years.

12

The same evening two meetings of back-benchers were held in the House of Commons. The first was addressed by Evan Williams, the chairman of the Mining Association, speaking for the owners, the second by Frank Hodges, the secretary of the Miners' Federation. Hodges put his case well and afterwards answered questions, most of them directed to finding a way out of the deadlock by some form of temporary settlement. In answer to one questioner, Hodges was reported to have said:

"We are prepared to consider wages provided they are not to be regarded as permanently on a district basis, but only of a temporary character."[2]

1 Robert Williams' report to the N.T.W.F. Annual General Council, June 1921, Appendix I, p. 213.
2 This was the version issued by the Press Association at the time. Ibid. p. 216.

According to another version, in answer to a question whether the miners would accept a compromise which guaranteed that wages would not fall below the cost of living but which shelved the question of a national pool, Hodges replied: "Any such offer coming from an authoritative source would receive very serious consideration."[1]

Up to this time, the miners had refused to discuss anything but a national settlement, a point on which the Triple Alliance leaders had pressed them repeatedly and which they had accepted as the irreducible core of the miners' claim. That very afternoon Hodges had stated categorically at the meeting with the National Council of Labour that the Miners' Federation stood absolutely by this demand. His unexpected admission of the possibility of district negotiations, whatever his intention[2] and however much it may have been magnified in importance by his hearers, produced sensational results. There were a number of miners' M.P.s present when he made his statement and it was generally assumed that he spoke, if not after consultation with his full Executive, at least (as Sexton, who was present, told the Transport Workers' Federation later), "with a safe number of the Executive to justify it being made." Nor did any of the miners' representatives present repudiate what he said.

In a very short time, a self-appointed deputation of M.P.s was off round to Downing Street to see the Prime Minister and tell him that Hodges had suggested what appeared to be a new basis for a settlement. Lloyd George needed no prompting. In the early hours of the morning he sat down and wrote at once to Frank Hodges, inviting the miners to talks on the basis he had mentioned, "leaving aside the controversial issue of a national pool of profits and settling the immediate question of wages by a temporary agreement, without prejudice to further discussion of proposals for a National Pool when a permanent settlement comes to be dealt with."[3]

While all this was happening, Bevin and the other Triple Alliance leaders who were not members of the House of Commons had gone off home to bed. It was not until he opened his newspaper the next morning that Bevin, like most of the others, learned for the first time

1 Ibid.

2 Hodges' intentions have never been satisfactorily cleared up. His own explanation to the Miners' Federation Delegate Conference on 22nd April (Page Arnot, *op. cit.* pp. 319–20) only makes his statement more difficult to understand.

3 Page Arnot, *op. cit.*, p. 315.

of the invitation to Hodges to address the informal meeting at the House. Now they were confronted with banner headlines reporting that the miners' strike was approaching a settlement and that the Triple Alliance strike would be called off. The midday editions added the news (which was perfectly true) that Frank Hodges had resigned and that the Miners' Federation was sharply divided. Telegrams and telephone calls poured into Unity House, the N.U.R. headquarters in Euston Road, asking whether the news was true and whether the strike was off or not.

As quickly as he could, Bevin made his way to Unity House, only to find that nobody knew what was happening. As soon as the three Executives met, the Miners asked leave to retire to consider the Prime Minister's invitation by themselves. For the best part of two hours they argued heatedly behind closed doors while the transport workers' and railwaymen's representatives were left in ignorance of what was taking place. "When I went downstairs" (Bevin told the Dockers' Executive later) "I found Frank Hodges in a room by himself and his Executive arguing in the corridor and we learned that, by a majority of one, they had turned down the statement of Hodges."[1]

Not only was the majority a slender one, but three members of the Miners' Executive were absent. On learning of the decision, Hodges sat down and wrote out his resignation, but the Executive un-animously refused to accept it and he later agreed to withdraw it. When the miners came back to the conference room, Herbert Smith, angry and ruffled, told the members of the other two Executives bluntly, without offering any explanation, that they intended to turn down Lloyd George's invitation and were going back to their own headquarters in Russell Square to draft their reply. When he was asked to sit down and discuss the situation which this created, he made the famous reply: "Get on t' field. That's t' place." Until the other parties in the Alliance called their men out, he refused to admit their right to discuss the offer made by the Prime Minister or to question the conduct of the negotiations.

Throughout the day the confusion and uncertainty mounted, while the telephone bell never stopped ringing and more and more telegrams came in from all parts of the country demanding to know

1 Minutes of the Dockers' Union Executive Council Sub-committee, 12th May 1921.

what was happening. A message was sent round asking the miners not to despatch their reply until the other sections of the Alliance had had the chance to consider it. When this failed to elicit a response, Bevin moved that a sub-committee should go to Russell Square to meet the miners.

After being kept waiting in an ante-room, Harry Gosling, as the spokesman of the sub-committee, urged the miners to meet the owners and Government again and to make a break, if it had to be made, on the clear issue of the reduction in wages, leaving aside the question of national or district negotiations. Herbert Smith's answer was that the reply to the Prime Minister was already being typed, that they refused to enter into further negotiations and held to their original demands. He added, in his most uncompromising manner, that they expected their allies to stand by them as they had agreed and to call out their men that evening.

Back at Unity House, the railwaymen and the transport workers had to make up their minds for themselves. They were not allowed to see the miners' reply to the Prime Minister until they read it in the Press. After consulting Tillett, Bevin moved a resolution to invite the miners to come back and to put out an announcement that the Triple Alliance was meeting to complete arrangements for the strike. This, Bevin urged, was the only way to hold the situation. But the railwaymen, angered by the treatment they had received at the hands of the Miners' Executive, voted Bevin's motion down by 28 votes to 12. Instead, they put forward a resolution to call off the strike and Bevin, convinced that a partial stoppage in the prevalent confusion would be disastrous, voted for it. The resolution was carried with only three dissentients, all the members of the Transport Workers' Federation present supporting it. The strike was off.

13

The Triple Alliance decision produced a wave of anger and disillusionment throughout the trade unions. The all-important minority who hold local office and serve on committees had thrown themselves into rousing support for a fight in face of apathy on the part of many of the rank and file. They felt badly let down by their leaders, the more so since, from a wish not to start recriminations and weaken the miners' position, the other members of the Triple Alliance gave no explanation of their action.

Meanwhile the miners' determination to resist was only strengthened by what they regarded as their allies' desertion. Ten weeks after the lock-out had begun, when many miners' families had been reduced to destitution, a fresh ballot showed a majority of more than two to one for continuing the fight. Not until 1st July did they admit defeat and return to work on terms which meant the abandonment of their claim to a national wages settlement.

Their long-drawn-out struggle, with the sacrifices it involved for every mining family, stirred the conscience of the whole Labour movement. Frustration was vented in angry accusations against the leaders of the railwaymen and the transport workers who had 'betrayed' the miners. In the miners' eyes it was a straightforward issue of loyalty: their allies had not the guts to face a fight and keep their promises. There were many in the Labour movement who accepted the miners' view. 'Black Friday' became a taunt which Bevin and the other leaders of the Triple Alliance had to face for years to come. The issue, however, was not so simple as the miners made it appear.

After their experience with the miners in the previous October, both Bevin and Bob Williams had pressed hard for a drastic reform of the machinery of the Triple Alliance. The original intention in founding the Alliance had been to agree beforehand on the demands of all three partners, to present them simultaneously and enforce them by common action. In a long memorandum[1] addressed to his colleagues on the sub-committee of the Triple Alliance in February 1921, Williams had argued cogently that, unless they went back to this original procedure and agreed in advance on their plans, they were bound to run into trouble. Williams' warning and others from Bevin and the Dockers' Union to the same effect were ignored by the Miners for the simple reason, as they candidly admitted later, that they thought they would never want to make use of the Alliance again. They made no effort to consult their allies in fixing their demands or in conducting the negotiations which led up to the acceptance of the mine-owners' notices. Only when they had taken their stand and committed themselves to a trial of strength which

[1] Printed in N.T.W.F.: Report of Annual General Council Meeting, June 1921, Appendix 1.

must inevitably affect every other trade union in the country, did they turn round and ask for support.

Both the railwaymen's and the transport workers' leaders resented this. Bevin did not conceal the fact that his original re-action on 31st March was against striking in support of the miners "not because the justice of their case did not call for it but because we had not made adequate preparations for such a move."

The Transport Workers, in particular, had difficulties to face of which the Miners took no account. The Federation with more than thirty unions scattered over a variety of occupations (some of which such as road transport were very incompletely organised) had noth-ing like the cohesion or discipline of the Miners' Federation which was confined to one industry, with its members living in tight com-munities, and virtually proof against blacklegging. As Bob Williams pointed out in his report, "the use of strike-breaking labour is never contemplated in underground work. The miners are able sub-stantially to return to their work as one solid army, unbroken and unbreakable." By contrast, all the Government's preparations, the recruitment of volunteers, the use of the army and navy, were designed to break a transport strike and it was the dockers, the lorry-drivers, the busmen and tramway-drivers, by the nature of their occupations far more vulnerable to blacklegging than the miners, who would have to bear the brunt of the Government's counter-measures. With unemployment higher than ever before, the chances of blacklegging were correspondingly greater. In calling a strike at such a time, a sympathetic strike in which no vital issue for its own members was directly involved, the Federation ran the risk of in-flicting serious damage on the unions it represented and of destroy-ing its own organisation.

The original object of their intervention was not a general strike but the resumption of the negotiations with the full weight of the Triple Alliance brought to bear on the miners' side under the *threat* of an extension of the stoppage. This was far from satisfying the miners: they wanted, not the threat of a strike, but the men called out there and then. Until the railwaymen and transport workers were actually out, they refused to allow their allies any part in the negotiations.

1 Ibid., p. 30.

They were simply offered the alternative of striking or not. "Get on t' field; that's t' place." It was hardly surprising, as Bob Williams remarked later, that they began to ask themselves: "Is this an alliance in which we are all equally involved, or are we to be dragged along, at the tail, willy-nilly, of the Miners' Federation?"[1]

Having gone so far, however, they did not feel they could go back. Accordingly when the negotiations broke down again on the 12th, they agreed to re-issue the instructions to strike, even though, as Bevin admitted, they had grave doubts of getting anything like a full response, especially among the road transport workers.[2] Their feelings on learning from the newspapers that Frank Hodges had suggested a possible compromise at the last moment can easily be imagined: relief was mingled with exasperation. Bevin and most of the other experienced negotiators in the Triple Alliance believed that the miners were exaggerating their economic power (as, indeed, proved to be the case) and that they would be better advised to negotiate a compromise than to strike for their full demands.[3] While they admired the courage and solidarity of the miners, they also felt that their leaders were poor tacticians, constantly out-manœvured and throwing away the advantages of negotiation out of a stiff-necked inflexibility which led them to one defeat after another.

Whatever the importance to be attached to Hodges' remark the night before, it had elicited a new offer from the Prime Minister. At that stage on the Friday morning, if the miners wanted to carry their partners with them, they ought, as Bevin and Williams said, to have sat down and frankly discussed the advantages and disadvantages of accepting Lloyd George's offer, not only from their own but from the railwaymen's and transport workers' point of view. Instead, they behaved as they had done throughout the crisis, holding their partners at arms' length and refusing to take them into their confidence. (One reason for this may well have been the division of opinion inside their own Executive.) Ignoring the confusion caused by the action of their own secretary, Hodges, and the predicament of those responsible for calling the best part of a million men on strike,

1 Ibid., p. 24.
2 Ibid., p. 32.
3 According to G. D. H. Cole, Robert Smillie's abrupt resignation from the presidency of the Miners' Federation in March 1921 was caused by his disagreement with the policy of no compromise on which the Executive had decided (*A History of the Labour Party from* 1914 [1948], p. 115).

the Miners' Federation finally decided to turn down the chance of a settlement and left the others to make the best of it.

Bevin told the Council of the Transport Workers' Federation:

'They did not say, 'Well, brothers, this happened in the House, and before we take a final decision, we want a consultation.' I submit, if there is going to be unity in action there must be unity in counsel. . . . They went into a room by themselves; they were there two hours or more, and they came to the other constituent parties . . . and the President of the Miners' Federation read out to us about a three-line resolution which was their decision. . . .

"I have read the speeches of A. J. Cook and others, but I fail to find the lion-like conduct inside the Triple Alliance that is on the platform . . . There are a lot of men who shout that we ought to strike. . . . We knew that there were a number of men in the Transport Workers' Federation who had decided to come out that night, but we also knew that there were a number who had volunteered for the Government Volunteer Forces. . . . We are not worrying about the docks; the docks were not our trouble. . . . Road transport was our serious anxiety in the whole business. We knew that these things were going on and we said we must try to keep a united front. We appealed for a common consideration of our problems. We were told that it was not a matter for us. They—the miners—were going off to Russell Square. . . .

"We never saw the letter to the Prime Minister or knew what it contained until it was read in the House of Commons; and we were partners to the Alliance! I am not blaming the miners. I am only pointing out it is their method and it did not correspond with the difficult situation we had to handle with a million men . . .[1]

The fact that the Miners' Executive was sharply divided, that their decision had been taken by a chance majority of one and that their secretary was known to have resigned scarcely added to the confidence of those who had now to make up their minds whether to bring out the railwaymen, the dockers and the rest, when the confusion halved whatever chance there had been of success.

The easy course was to let the strike take place. None of those who made the decision had any illusions about the outcry there would be, even if many who later criticised were secretly relieved that their retrospective militancy was not put to the test. But the only responsible course, Bevin argued, was to act as they did and call the strike off, and the Transport Federation Executive, including as strong an advocate of direct action as Bob Williams (by now a

1 N.T.W.F.: Report of Annual General Council Meeting, June 1921, p. 32.

member of the Communist Party), was unanimous in recommending it.

'Black Friday' was a severe defeat for the trade-union movement and a bitter one to accept: it was not, however, a 'betrayal' and the responsibility for the defeat must rest at least as much with the miners' leaders as with the other members of the Triple Alliance. Unfortunately, the lesson of 1921 was not learned, with the result that five years later the trade-union movement was to suffer an even worse defeat for almost identical reasons.

CHAPTER 8

The Transport and General Workers' Union

1921 — 1923

I

IMMEDIATELY AFTER the strike had been called off, Bevin went abroad. The International Transport Workers' annual congress was about to open at Geneva on the 18th and he planned to stay on for a fortnight's holiday with his wife to restore his energies before the final round of the amalgamation negotiations. In the absence of Bob Williams and Thomas, Bevin was the leading British representative and was elected to form a small steering committee with Döring, the German transport workers' leader, and Bidegaray, a French railwayman.

The congress opened with a resolution calling on the members of the Federation to use all their efforts to fight imperialism, capitalism and militarism. This was introduced with the support of Edo Fimmen, the big voluble Dutchman who served as general secretary of the I.T.F. from 1919 to 1942. Resolutions of this sort were a familiar feature of most trade union and socialist conferences. After a spate of emotional oratory they were habitually carried with acclamation, and no practical consequences. To the surprise of the Geneva conference, this time there was opposition, from Charles Lindley, the Swedish transport workers' leader, and from Ernest Bevin.

Such criticism was coldly received: it outraged the proprieties of the occasion. But Bevin was not impressed by finding himself in the minority and voted down. He saw very clearly the effect of concrete issues like reparations and the breakdown of international trade on the working class, and the month before he had protested sharply to the Parliamentary Labour Party at their failure to oppose the second reading of the Government's Reparations Bill. But he was distrustful of the verbal internationalism of the Left; he believed that if co-operation between the trade unionists of different countries was to mean anything more than words it had to deal with the hard practical questions of wages, hours and conditions.

Bevin was most at home on the third day when the congress split up into three sections and he presided over the conference of dock and transport workers. During the year 1920, seventeen new organisations had joined the Federation, bringing the total number of transport and railway workers affiliated to two and three quarter millions. On paper this was an impressive total, but it was uphill work to turn this into agreement on practical programmes for the improvement of the dockers' or railwaymen's conditions of work. It meant overcoming differences in national psychology (leave alone in language), differences in working practices as well as in standards of living, conflicts of interest between unions as well as between nations. How much easier to ride away on splendid gaudy resolutions condemning capitalism, militarism and all the other evils of human society.

But Bevin was right. If the I.T.F. was to have any permanent value, it had to prove that organisation on an international scale could produce as solid benefits for the rank-and-file member of a trade union as organisation on a national scale had done. The opportunities in occupations so much affected by international conditions as the dockers' and the seamen's were obvious; was it possible to devise a method of organisation capable of meeting them? As a preliminary, Bevin persuaded this Geneva conference to send out a detailed list of questions asking for information about wages, hours, overtime and conditions of employment among dock-workers in each of the affiliated countries. The first need was to collect the facts. It was unexciting but practical advice and it was thanks to the work that it did along these lines, far more than to the now long-forgotten series of general resolutions it passed, that the I.T.F. built up an organisation strong enough to weather the storms of the next thirty years.

2

Bevin came home on 8th May to find the trade-union world still in turmoil after the fiasco of 'Black Friday'. The miners remained out and protest meetings were held up and down the country, at which, in the absence of any explanation, accusations of having 'sold' the miners were repeated and largely left unanswered.

The Communists had a field-day. Bob Williams, who had recently joined the newly-founded Communist Party, was publicly expelled for having 'betrayed' the miners. The Party weekly *The Communist* made violent personal attacks on Bevin as well as on J. H. Thomas, accusing Bevin of deliberately misleading the miners and of acting in co-operation with Lloyd George. The London officers of the Dockers' Union resigned in a body and a deputation from the London District Committee on which the Communists were strongly represented was received by the Dockers' Executive on 5th May. It accused the Union leadership of being out of touch with the rank and file and levelled all the other charges which were to be repeated a thousand times in the next thirty years.

Bevin's absence abroad clearly embarrassed his Executive. Not until the 12th did they get a full statement from him of what had happened in the Triple Alliance meetings. He made no attempt to disguise his dissatisfaction at the failure of the Alliance but he was firm in repeating that, given the circumstances, he believed no other decision to have been possible. Neither then, nor later, did he hesitate to say, "If I had to live through that Friday again in exactly the same circumstances, with exactly the same machine, I should take exactly the same action."

On 22nd April the Dockers' Union sent a deputation to urge on the Federation (and on the two railway unions) a boycott on the import of foreign coal and on any movement of coal stocks so long as the miners remained on strike. The Federation adopted the Dockers' proposal and sent out firm instructions to all its member unions. The result justified to the hilt the hesitations Bevin had felt in calling a transport strike in support of the miners: the Federation's organisation was simply not equal to the demands made upon it.

One union, Havelock Wilson's Seamen and Firemen, refused out of hand to carry out the Federation's instructions.[1] Another, Sexton's Dockers, with 70,000 members in Liverpool, Hull and Leith, declared them to be impracticable. Others, especially the road-service unions, while paying lip-service, took no effective action to prevent their members evading the ban on moving coal. Throughout May, Williams with Bevin's full support used every appeal he could to make the embargo effective but at the end of May, they had to admit defeat and call off the boycott, which had already collapsed.

When the General Council of the Federation assembled for its annual meeting in Edinburgh (June 1921) almost the whole of the two days was taken up in bitter recriminations between the members. Speaker after speaker declared that the Federation could not survive such quarrelling, and promptly proceeded to add to the bitterness by further accusations of 'scab' and 'blackleg'. Apart from defending his part in the Triple Alliance proceedings, another occasion for recrimination, Bevin took no part in these exchanges. He had already made up his mind not to stand again for the Executive, having withdrawn from the other Federation of General Workers the year before.

Like the Triple Alliance, the Transport Workers' Federation was destroyed by the shock of Black Friday. Although it lingered on for another six years, it never regained the authority it had enjoyed between 1916 and 1921. Bevin walked out of its Edinburgh Council meeting with relief. He had served the Federation well and made his reputation in doing so. But he was determined not to let the new amalgamation be dragged down by the quarrels which were destroying the Federation.

3

Between the end of December 1920 and March 1921 the amalgamation negotiations had been suspended while the ballot was taken by the individual unions. Bevin, however, did not relax his efforts. From November to April he allowed hardly a week to pass without

1 At a meeting held by the rival Ships Stewards in Liverpool Stadium to organise a breakaway from the Seamen and Firemen, the banners bore the legend: "Judas sold one man, but Havelock Wilson sold the lot".

making a journey out of London to speak on behalf of the scheme.

Taking at random the first fortnight in the New Year, we find him speaking at the People's Palace, Commercial Road, on the 2nd; at Plymouth on the 7th; at Barry and Cardiff on the 8th; at Barry Dock, Cardiff again and Newport on the 9th; at Canning Town on the 12th; Bermondsey on the 14th and then travelling by night train to Glasgow where he spent the whole of Saturday and Sunday, the 15th and 16th, addressing conferences on the amalgamation scheme. In between these meetings he prepared for the big Tramways Inquiry at which he was to lead for the men, spending two whole days examining officers and witnesses before they appeared in the court; took part in the proceedings of the joint industrial councils dealing with dock labour, the chocolate and cocoa trades, flour-milling and the chemical trade; dealt with an accumulation of district problems in Plymouth, South Wales and Bristol; super-intended the work of the Dockers' Union central office (where he was acting as general secretary in Tillett's absence), and attended meetings of the Transport Workers' Federation Executive, the Federation of General Workers and the directors of the *Daily Herald*.

Apart from the big meetings, at which he often spoke to two or three thousand men, he held a series of amalgamation conferences with the officers in every centre in which any of the unions involved had a substantial membership. These conferences brought together two or three hundred officers at a time, many of whom he had not met before. He took great pains to explain the scheme to them, using a set of coloured lantern slides to demonstrate the new organisation and answering every question put to him.

Bevin realised that the way the ballot went would be largely determined by the local officers—the branch secretary, the district committee member, the men who ran the sub-office (often no more than a room in their own houses), collected the weekly contributions and stamped the members' cards. It was all very well to get a unanimous vote at a delegate conference in London, but unless he could get at the active minority which turned up at branch meetings and gave a lead to the opinion of the rank and file, he could still fail to get the percentage of votes in the ballot which the law required. At this level, misunderstandings, suspicion and the prejudice created by local loyalties were strongest. He set about removing them at their source. He used few appeals to emotion, relying upon the force of argument and the impact of his personality to convey the impression that here at last was a scheme which would work and a man capable of carrying it through.

He could never have carried it through if there had not been men in each of the unions sufficiently convinced of the necessity of amalgamation to back him up. But it is equally true that this good-will could never have been mobilised if there had not been a man of Bevin's calibre to direct and hold it together. Nothing in his career more clearly bore the stamp of his own creation than the amalgamation. For ten years and more it had been talked of. Now at a time when circumstances had turned sharply against him, in the middle of a trade depression when every trade union was losing members and facing wage reductions, when the Triple Alliance had collapsed, the Transport Federation was breaking up and the miners had to admit defeat, he succeeded in founding his new union and in founding it to last.

By the middle of March, he knew that he was winning. Not only had his own union voted by 117,500 to 1,463 to come into the amalgamation, but seven others, including the United Vehicle Workers with its 130,000 members, had secured a sufficient number of votes and the necessary majority to satisfy the law's requirements. By the end of the month, when the Amalgamation Committee re-assembled at Anderton's Hotel, two more had come in. Only three unions, Bevin reported to the committee, had voted against the scheme or failed to get enough votes—the London Stevedores, the Cardiff Coal Trimmers and the Scottish Dockers. He urged the committee to go ahead, with a potential membership of 362,000 already guaranteed. They agreed to summon a delegate conference for May and, in the meantime, to invite nominations for the provisional officers and executive of the new union.

This third delegate conference opened in the improbable setting of the Venetian Room at the St. Pancras Station Hotel on 11th May. After hearing Bevin's report, the delegates agreed that the new union should come into existence on 1st January 1922 and proceeded to appoint the provisional officers and executive committee by a card vote.

Harry Gosling was elected as president without opposition, a tribute to the role he had played as chairman of the amalgamation committee. There were four candidates for the Treasurership, of whom H. W. Kay, the Dockers' Union treasurer, received the most votes. This left the general secretaryship, the key position. Bob Williams had been nominated, but withdrew his name; Stanley Hirst, the general secretary of the United Vehicle Workers, received his union's vote of 130,000; Bevin, nominated by nine of the amalgamating unions, received 225,000.

The provisional Secretary wasted no time. He held the first meeting of his provisional Executive the same afternoon and immediately got down to business. So far he had produced the amalgamation scheme and done more than any other man to get it accepted. Now he was to display to their full advantage his gifts as an organiser.

4

Until the New Year the new Union had no legal existence, no funds and no authority. Until then the old unions had to carry on. This awkward transition period might well have proved fatal to the scheme and was in fact accompanied by a considerable drop in membership. Every officer complained that he did not know what he was expected to do; the blame for anything that went wrong was laid at Bevin's door. With a new executive and new committees who had never worked together before, with two hundred and fifty full-time officials, many of whom had been fighting each other in rival unions for years, some of whom were jealous of Bevin and all of whom were anxious about their jobs, he had to try and create a new loyalty, the sense of all belonging to one not to a dozen different unions.

Bevin had no illusions about the number of well-wishers who would be delighted to see him fail. Boldness was the only policy which could succeed. He went straight ahead, taking every decision that came up without hesitation, trusting to his own impetus to carry the rest with him. At the first meeting of his still unknown Executive he asked for a detailed list of all the unions' branches and branch secretaries; a list of all the officers; a statement of their property and financial reserves, together with an explanation of how each union collected and distributed its funds. At the second meeting he submitted the draft constitution, secured the appointment of a Rules Committee to put it into legal form and advised the Executive to begin appointing provisional officers and committees in each of the eleven areas.

On 15th June, a hundred officers of the amalgamating unions in Area No. 1 (London and the South-east) met Bevin and the Executive, established the geographical limits of the area, and agreed to set up six trade group committees for the Area, as well as an Area Committee. Not to waste any time, the existing officers of Area No. 2 (Southern England) were present as observers and immediately afterwards held a conference of their own at which similar decisions were reached. Between mid-June and mid-July Bevin, Gosling and representatives of the Executive visited Bristol, Cardiff, Birmingham, Manchester, Leeds and Hull, met the officers and set up provisional organisations for seven more areas, covering the whole of England and Wales.

The commitments of the new Union were alarming. Owing to the large number of paid officials to be taken over, considerably in excess of an economical establishment, weekly salaries of £1,662 would have to be found, without counting the wages of the clerical staff. New offices had to be bought or rented in several towns and the head office alone (in Central Buildings, Westminster) cost £1,000 a year to rent. To establish a uniform system of collecting and auditing the hundreds of small sums paid in weekly by each branch was bound to take time, and in any case the new Union had no funds of its own to dispose of until January 1922. By September 1921 the levy raised from the unions was exhausted and Bevin had to turn to his own Dockers' Union and the United Vehicle Workers for advances to meet expenses.

While he was building up the shadow organisation of the new union, an attempt had to be made to establish some control over any decisions the eleven unions might make before the end of the year. Taking the bull by the horns, Bevin persuaded his provisional Executive to adopt his proposal that all general secretaries should act as assistant secretaries during the period of transition. On 11th August, he met the thirty-two general secretaries and national officers of the eleven unions and got them to accept this as a working arrangement.

To vote for amalgamation in principle had cost little, but now every decision which Bevin pressed home meant the surrender, step by step, of each union's deeply cherished autonomy. It says much for the men concerned that, despite the divided feelings this aroused, no one pulled back or contested the decisions of the provisional Executive and its General Secretary.

By 12th August the Rules Committee had finished its work and after a full day's examination by the Executive, copies of the rules were sent to every branch. The branches were invited to send in amendments to be considered by a final delegate conference summoned to meet at Leamington before the end of September.

5

The 140 delegates who pressed up the steps of Leamington Town Hall on the morning of 27th September were still representatives of the separate unions which had voted in favour of amalgamation. Most of those present were members of their unions' executive committees. Lay members alone had the right to vote, although a limited number of the officials of the individual unions were present with the right to address the conference but not to vote. The new Union was represented by its three principal (though still provisional) officers, Gosling, Bevin and Kay, by the provisional Executive Committee and the provisional area secretaries.

In opening the conference, Harry Gosling, the veteran chairman of so many transport workers' fights, appealed to the delegates:

"Do not be too finicky this next day or two: do not be too nice about these rules. They are a long way from perfect. Your amendments in some cases will make them better, and in some cases if they were passed I think they would make them worse; but whatever happens do not let us think we are going to leave this building with a complete and perfect set of rules, because we are not. The only way in which to get perfect rules is to base them on experience, and we cannot have the experience until we have had a year or two of actual work.

"Now one word about the older men. There are old men in this room who have nearly put in their time. Do not despise them; they have done some very good work—and I am speaking as one of them. You younger men can pick it up where we leave it. You need not kick us down because you are going to put up: we can help you. You have to go on and on, and if in ten or twenty years' time you are meeting somewhere and still talking about amalgamation, still trying to get it into a better form than it is in now, you will have all the difficulties that we have, although perhaps in another form."[1]

In fact the conference was business-like in character and free from those recriminations which had marred the unity of so many of the Federation's meetings. The delegates spent most of the three days in the discussion of a 70-page agenda containing the final draft of the new Union's rules together with the proposed amendments, not far short of two thousand in number, which had been sent in by the branches. Fortunately none of the amendments attempted to alter the structure Bevin had proposed for the new union. There were few, if any, long speeches and all of them were severely practical. Most of the time Bevin replied for the Executive and showed not only a complete mastery of the complicated agenda but patience and good temper. He was careful not to antagonise his opponents, ready to consider adjusting the draft to meet suggestions and improvements, and never once tried to browbeat the conference or claim undue credit.[2] On the other hand, he was always prepared to give a lead and express his own opinions without fear of being defeated. His intervention was decisive on all but a handful of occasions. The only major issue on which the conference disregarded his views was when it voted in favour of an annual, instead of a biennial, conference.

One of the most interesting debates took place on the procedure to be followed if the Union's Executive decided in favour of a general strike. Bevin had provided a double check in the draft rules: the Executive had first to summon a special delegate conference and then, if the conference agreed that such action was advisable, had also to take a vote by ballot of all the members of the Union. A number of branches thought that this was carrying caution too far. Bevin's defence of his proposal is worth quoting, not only for the interest of what he said, but as an illustration of the way in which he handled the conference:

1 Proceedings of the Special Rules Conference, Leamington, 27th–29th Sept. *1921* (a verbatim typescript record), pp. 15 seq.
2 In a reminiscent moment at the 1939 conference of the Union, Bevin told the delegates: "There are two contributing factors to amalgamations—one is sweet temper and the other is overdrafts. Both are helpful, but if you discuss with any-body with a big stick you create the wrong kind of atmosphere to begin with. You have got to begin persuasively and you would not be in this room today as you are, if I had not been congenial personally."

"Ordinarily I am opposed to the ballot vote, because I think that on many things recently ballots have become a coward's refuge. I have seen in the trades-union movement during the past two years men who are leaders not having the courage to say to their members: 'This is the right course to take.' As long as I am a leader I am going to say to the members what I think is the course they ought to take. If they vote against you, well and good, that is their decision, but I do not think you can evade your obligation by not pronouncing an opinion on the subject matter that you are submitting to them.

"Ballot votes become a question of education. Ballot votes can be made effective if continually through your journal the responsibility of the member is inculcated and taught, but that is the only way. This is a new Union: I have had five years of bitter experience. I have seen delegates go to a delegate conference in London and heard them shout, 'Strike', for all they were worth, and then met them outside the door and heard them express the hope that it would not come off. I have had enough of that. . . . I know that after a movement like that of the Triple Alliance there is resentment, and some of those who shouted the loudest were the people who were damned glad that they were not called out. I have never funked a fight, and I never will, but I do not want to be in a position to sacrifice the men or to victimise them before I am sure of their strength. . . . It is the experience of dealing with national movements, that has caused this to be put in. I have had Hell's own work to hold them together in an arbitration, to say nothing about a strike, on more than one occasion, and I know the difficulties that have to be overcome in building up these movements. . . .

"Friends, do not let us live in a fool's paradise. We have brought into the Union men and women, and we are proud of it, but they are not yet out of servility; confidence has not been established, and it has got to be established. I would plead for a trial of this. In 1923, a year and a half from now, we can see whether the new confidence has grown, and no one will welcome it more than I shall when we can stand upon the platform and say 'A ballot vote is entirely unnecessary.' "[1]

The number of unions likely to join the amalgamation besides the eleven represented at Leamington was still uncertain. Sexton's Liverpool Dockers had failed to secure the necessary majority but, before the conference was over, further talks between Gosling and Sexton in London gave hope that the hesitations which held them back would be removed, as in fact they were. In other cases, too, Bevin reported continued negotiations with some prospect of success —if necessary, after holding a second ballot. Only in one case, that of the London Stevedores, did the decision not to join appear to be final.

1 Proceedings, pp. 182, seq.

By the evening of the third day, the conference had finished its work and appointed a compilation committee to go through the final draft of the rules and see that all the amendments were incorporated. Bevin's original plan for the construction of the new Union had been accepted with remarkably few changes. As he caught the train to Wednesbury, tired but not dissatisfied, he reflected that all he had to do now was to make it work. Just how difficult that was going to prove the next two years were to show.

6

His work for the amalgamation left Bevin with little time for anything else outside his trade-union work in 1921. He attended the Labour Party conference at Brighton in June, the T.U.C. at Cardiff in September, but he did not speak at all at the first and only once at the second. Nor did he stand for election to the General Council.

An article in the new *Record*[1], however, shows the interest he kept in the wider questions of trade-union policy against the time when he would again be free to play a bigger part himself. A series of articles in the *Herald* on the functions of the General Council had incensed Bevin, in particular the suggestion that it should begin by 'sorting out' the trade unions and allocating members according to different categories. Not for the last time Bevin fulminated against "middle-class place seekers . . . who proceed to organise the movement for us". Allocation of members by craft or even by occupation, he argued, although satisfying to the tidy mind of the theorist, did not necessarily make for greater strength: what mattered were the natural economic links between different groups of workpeople. It was this community of economic interest between the different groups represented in the new Union which Bevin put forward as its justification, with a growl of warning to anyone who proposed to break it up along neater lines of demarcation.

Bevin was very much aware that the employers were pressing harder than ever for reductions in the trades represented by the new Union, hoping to take advantage of the strains produced by the

1 This took the place of the *Dockers' Record* and three other union journals. The first number appeared in August 1921 and Bevin's article 'Facts for Theorists' in September.

amalgamation to weaken the unions' resistance and, if possible, to compromise the new organisation in the men's eyes. Virtually every negotiation undertaken in 1921 resulted in a reduction in wages, an increase in hours or some other advantage conceded to the employers. It was not difficult for the disaffected to represent this and the drop in Union membership as due to the amalgamation. Although he fought hard in one set of negotiations after another to limit the concessions made, it took all his courage and energy to keep up his own and others' spirits in face of the difficulties which threatened to swamp the new Union before it was launched.

He was all the more anxious that the organisation of the new Union should be sufficiently complete by 1st January to take over its responsibilities. He wanted no break-down in the Union's defence of the men's interests of which the employers might take advantage. In the last three months of 1921 he worked as hard as he ever worked in his life to be ready in time for the transfer.

His biggest problem was London. Nowhere had the rivalry between the different dock unions been so bitter and it was asking much of human nature for men who had been fighting each other and each others' organisations for years to settle down amicably now as members of the same union. There was a lot of unregenerate human nature in the London docker and the old quarrelling went on inside the Union and its committees. The London District Committee of the Dockers' Union had already become a sounding-board for Communist resolutions, and Fred Thompson, the Dockers' District Secretary, who had been disappointed in his claim to be made provisional Area Secretary of the new Union, ran a fine line in honest-John, rank-and-file criticism of the bureaucracy. These discontents were to find expression in the unofficial dock strike of 1923. They dated from long before the foundation of the new Union and Bevin himself rarely referred to the situation in the London Docks without going back to the strikes of 1911–1912 and the legacy of bitterness left behind. The Port of London, he declared, was enough to break any trade-union organiser's heart.

Another herald of future storms was the decision of the Croydon No. 2 bus lodge of the United Vehicle Workers to secede from the amalgamation. Over the next twenty years the London busmen were to give Bevin more trouble than any other group in the Union. He met this initial revolt with a firm hand, but recommended the

Executive to accept the claim of the London busmen to be allowed to form a special section within the Passenger Transport Group, with their own Central London Bus Committee. A similar concession eased the entry of Sexton's Liverpool Dockers into the amalgamation, but Bevin realised only too well that if he gave way on too many occasions he would undermine the already precarious unity of the new Union.

With the area organisation roughed out, the next step was to set up the national trade group committees. Stanley Hirst, the Secretary of the U.V.W., suggested that until electoral machinery was established, these should be constituted from those members of the existing executive committees connected with particular trades. Bevin again agreed, foreseeing that this proposal would help to smooth the transition, but it did not prevent a good deal of jockeying and argument about the representation of the different unions on the six national committees. With some difficulty he persuaded his own Dockers' Union to be content with six out of the seventeen places on the Docks National Committee, and similar diplomatic adjustments had to be made on the other five.

These petty details are worth recalling in order to illustrate the suspicions, vested interests and jealousies with which Bevin had to reckon and which could still have wrecked the scheme. It was a curiously appropriate training in diplomacy: the man who was later to spend much time and patience in promoting co-operation between the sovereign partners of the North Atlantic alliance first demonstrated his ability to circumvent the intractable problem of sovereignty by persuading fourteen autonomous trade unions to amalgamate.

7

At every step the problem was aggravated by personalities, by the resentment of those dispossessed of independent office in the old unions or disappointed in their hopes of position in the new. The most notable case was that of Ben Tillett, and since Bevin's personal conduct was directly called in question, it is necessary to examine it with care.

Tillett's place in the history of trade unionism was already secure.

He had founded the Dockers' Union in 1889, taken the initiative in setting up the Transport Workers' Federation in 1910–11 and played a leading part in the big strikes of 1889 and 1911. For thirty years he had been the general secretary of the Dockers' Union, the one leader of national reputation the dockers had produced, a Member of the Parliamentary Committee of the T.U.C., a member of Parliament, one of the characters of the Labour movement. At a time when trade unionism needed missionary fervour and faith, Ben Tillett's dramatic power as an orator was a great asset. With his vivid personality and panache, he put life and spirit into the dockers when their greatest need was to find sufficient self-respect and solidarity to fight at all against the evils under which they suffered.

After the war the situation had changed, and so had Tillett. The need now was not to proselytise but to organise, to find the means to make effective the huge membership the trade unions had attracted. Tillett had little talent and less taste for the sort of work that Bevin put into the organisation of national movements on behalf of the Federation, the preparation of the case for the Shaw Inquiry or the negotiations leading up to the amalgamation. Nor was Tillett the leader he had been. During the war he became a patriotic orator, acquiring the status and the tastes of a public figure. Like an ageing actor, he had fallen into the habit of mechanically repeating his repertoire of roles and phrases. There were still flashes of the old Ben, but he was no longer an active leader in the trade-union movement, especially after he entered the House of Commons; he was content to rest on the laurels he had acquired, and made the most of his opportunities to appear at conferences and travel abroad. To be fair, one must add that his health was poor (he suffered much from chest trouble) and that he was frequently absent on sick-leave.

The older generation of dockers were still attached to him. They remembered what he had done for them and they were tolerant of his faults. The younger men, however, were more critical and were repelled by his obvious showmanship and emotionalism.

The legend, which Tillett himself did most to propagate, that he was the victim of Bevin's ingratitude and ambition does not stand up to critical examination. Bevin had more than repaid any debt of gratitude he owed by the hard work he put into building up the Dockers' Union. If Tillett gave him his original chance, the Union was in poor shape when Bevin joined it and Tillett did himself a good turn by recruiting a man of Bevin's ability. Bevin rose, not by Ben Tillett's patronage, but by his own exertions. Once he had discovered a means for their expression, his natural gifts were such that he was bound to rise to the top of any organisation in which he found himself. For years before the amalgamation he carried the responsibility and did the work of general secretary in the Dockers' Union while Tillett enjoyed the privileges and prestige. The evidence for this is to be found on page after page of the Union's Executive Council minutes.

For some time relations between the two men had been strained. Although appearances were kept up in public, Tillett was jealous of the independent reputation Bevin had created for himself, Bevin scornful of a nominal chief for whom he had long since ceased to feel any respect. Tillett took virtually no part in the negotiations leading up to the amalgamation. He was ill for long periods in 1920 and 1921 and attended very few of the meetings even of his own Union Executive. He had long been an advocate of amalgamation but the prospect in practice was a bitter one.

The Dockers' Union which he had created was to disappear and with it the independent position of general secretary which he had held for more than thirty years. The fact that Bevin, the young man he had picked out and brought on, should succeed where he and others had failed did not make it easier for Tillett to pocket his pride and step down. Yet, no more than Bob Williams (the secretary of the Federation) could Tillett oppose the amalgamation, ignore the advantage it would bring or deny that its realisation was largely due to the efforts of the man who, he felt, was pushing him out.

8

As a consolation, Tillett set his heart on becoming the first president of the new Union. He would not have made a good president but this was not what worried Bevin. If the amalgamation was to succeed, he believed it impossible for more than one of the three leading posts to go to any one of the old unions. The fact that Kay, the Dockers' treasurer, had been chosen as provisional financial secretary in addition to himself as provisional general secretary had already caused complaint. If he was to be confirmed as general secretary—and about this there could be no question, for without Ernest Bevin the amalgamation could neither have been brought to birth nor have survived six months—then the offices of president and of financial secretary must be filled by two of the other unions. Harry Gosling, the provisional president, not only came from another union (and a key one so far as London was concerned, the Watermen and Lightermen), he had performed valuable service as president of the Federation and chairman of all the amalgamation conferences. If he lacked Tillett's personality, he was more widely respected, had served as chairman of the T.U.C. and was leader of the Labour group on the L.C.C. Gosling had been a member of the Port of London Authority since its inauguration in 1909, had an unequalled experience of the problems involved and was likely to prove a far more reliable colleague.

When Bevin put the difficulties to Tillett, his answer was: Let the members decide, leave it to the ballot. But this was an answer Bevin could not accept, for Harry Gosling at once made it clear that, if Ben Tillett was nominated, he would not stand against him. Gosling's withdrawal at this stage threatened to unsettle the prospects of the amalgamation. It would almost certainly have led to the withdrawal of his union—with important repercussions on the other unions in London, where the Stevedores had already refused to come in—and it would have strengthened the impression which Bevin was anxious to avoid, that the amalgamation was only a façade for the aggrandisement of the Dockers' Union. This was not only Bevin's, but the provisional Executive's, opinion.

Convinced that much more than a personal question was now at stake, Bevin went back to Tillett and told him to his face that he would have to withdraw. The latent antipathy between the two men flashed out and Bevin did not hesitate to assert his mastery. Tillett withdrew his name and the Election Committee took the unusual step of selecting his withdrawal out of many others for a special explanation to the voters which Tillett drew up himself.

Tillett never forgave Bevin. Nor could he accept the situation with a good grace. While he declared that he was willing to sacrifice himself to the needs of the movement, the vehemence of his protest belied the magnanimity of his gesture. He told a conference of the Dockers' district secretaries in December: "If I were asked whether I had been jockeyed, I would answer 'Yes'. If I were asked if I had been elbowed out, I would answer 'Yes'."[1]

Bevin did not reply. He let Tillett go on repeating his version of what had happened, certain that he had taken the only possible course, not in his own interests (they were scarcely affected) but in the interests of the new Union. It was not ambition that moved Bevin. By 1921, Tillett was no longer a serious competitor. Bevin did not need to jockey or elbow him out. But he was determined that no man should endanger the chances of bringing about the amalgamation.

Once he had secured his withdrawal from the contest for the presidency, Bevin went out of his way to see that Tillett did not suffer materially under the amalgamation. He secured his appointment as International and Political Secretary at his former salary, a post which gave him every opportunity to travel and attend conferences without burdening him with administrative responsibility; he saw to it that his seat on the General Council was not challenged and Tillett in fact became president of the T.U.C. in 1929. By a special dispensation Tillett was allowed to continue in office in the Union until the age of seventy. Even then, he could not accept retirement and insisted on making an appeal to an embarrassed delegate conference which turned down his application. He lived on until well over the age of eighty, described by Francis Williams as "small, wizened, loquacious, with bright birdlike eyes, sitting in a corner of the Trade Union Club telling of triumphs long ago and of the way in which Bevin, the man he had 'found and made' had pushed him to one side."[2]

9

The other nominations presented fewer problems. The Communists, however, were already taking an interest in the affairs of the new Union and the Industrial Secretary of the Party, A. H. Hawkins, circularised members of the amalgamating unions thought to be sympathetic with the recommendation that they should vote for W. J. Sturrock as president and Fred Thompson as general secretary,

1 D.W.R. and G.W.U.: Minutes of the Conference of District Secretaries, 9th Dec. 1921.
2 Francis Williams: *Ernest Bevin* (1952), p. 109.

both of whom had been endorsed by the Party. Sturrock was not a serious candidate, but Thompson made a fight of it and remained as Bevin's only opponent in the ballot after the twenty-four other nominees had withdrawn. "My candidature," he told the voters, "is a challenge to autocracy and a protest against the building up of a new Union round individuals instead of policy." The ballot papers were distributed early in December. On the last day but one of the old year, the vans rolled up to Effingham House, the Dockers' headquarters off the Strand, and the other union offices to move the furniture and files to the new offices in Central Buildings, Westminster. On the 31st the Election Committee presented its report. Harry Gosling was declared elected as president, to Bevin's relief. His own vote of 96,842 gave him a convincing majority over Fred Thompson's 7,672.

In the midst of his anxieties the news of his election, however much a foregone conclusion, was reassuring. On 1st January 1922 the Transport and General Workers' Union came into legal existence. The next day, the new General Secretary walked up the stairs of Central Buildings and sat down at his desk. By trade-union standards his period of membership had been short. It was only eleven years since he had left his van round to found the Bristol carters' branch: now he had founded his own union.

IO

What was this institution which he had created and with which he henceforward identified himself?

In 1922, the Transport and General Workers' Union consisted of some 300,000 men and women, mostly men. Although many trades were represented in the new Union, from building and flour-milling to the tin-plate industry, the majority of the members made their living by working on the docks, on trams and buses or by driving lorries and carts. Every union at that time (and the great majority today, despite attempts to introduce a closed shop in certain industries) was a voluntary body, drawing men together on the basis not of common religious or political beliefs, like churches or political parties, but of common economic interests. Like the churches and political parties, they depended for their membership on their ability to satisfy the needs of their members, just as they depended for much of their work on their members' willingness to undertake voluntary service. There was nothing automatic about the growth of a union: in six of its first ten years the T.G.W.U. lost members, and even to hold the level of membership steady took hard work.

In return for a contribution of sixpence a week, which, with the standing levy of sixpence a quarter known as quarterage, brought in 28 shillings a year, the Union offered three main benefits. The first, and by far the most important, was action to maintain and improve the wages and working conditions of its members. The second was legal protection, of great value to transport workers who might be involved in court cases, and to dockers with a high accident rate. The third were the benefits properly so called: £1 a week for strike, lock-out and victimisation pay (and 2/– for each child under 14); £5 to £10 to pay for a member's funeral.

The basic unit of the Union's organisation was its local branch of which there were over fifteen hundred at the time of the amalgamation. Some, especially those in small towns where a scattered membership might be employed by half a dozen or more firms, were based on locality and brought together men working in a number of different occupations. More common was the branch based on a workplace: a garage, a dock or a factory, where all the members followed the same employment and worked for the same employer.

A branch might number several hundred members, or as few as fifty. Its officers—chairman, secretary, branch committee, collectors, auditors—were elected; almost without exception, they were working dockers or drivers, unpaid except for an occasional honorarium or commission. Indeed, apart from the churches, no organisations have made more use of voluntary effort than the trade unions, which to this day have a surprisingly small number of full-time paid officials.

The branch met at least once a month, but attendance then as now was sparse unless there was a strike or some other crisis to attract members. The majority took no part in branch business, any more than the majority do in other voluntary organisations. Most Union members paid their contributions, drew their benefits and left the running of the branch to the handful who formed the committee and served as officers. Their knowledge of the Union's constitution and policy was hazy, and even on a major issue, like the election of a general secretary or a strike ballot, a fifty per cent vote was only obtained with difficulty.

In certain sections, the dockers for instance and the London busmen, there was a strong sense of solidarity, the consciousness of belonging to a particular group which produced an active, critical and at times excitable interest in the Union's affairs. In general, however, it was left to an active minority to fill the branch offices, to serve as delegates to other bodies (e.g. the local trades council) and take part in local negotiations with employers, as well as to recruit new members and stir up backsliders who had fallen behind with their weekly contributions.

One of the perennial problems of trade unions, once they became more than local societies, has been how to maintain contact between the organisation and the rank-and-file members, especially the passive majority who not only express no views but have none to express. The problem was particularly acute in the case of a union like the T.G.W.U. which covered a growing number of different trades, without the homogeneity of a craft union like the printers. Casual or seasonal labour like the dockers or general labourers inevitably meant a large turnover in membership, men who frequently changed their jobs and were in and out of the Union several times in the course of a few years.

An important part of the answer to this problem of communication lay in the branch and in the effectiveness of its officers, for the branch was the point of direct contact between the members and the Union. At every other level of organisation—delegate conferences, area, trade-group and national committees—the democratic process worked by representation; the branch was the one place where the ordinary member could make his views heard directly, could cast a vote or move a resolution. Indeed, the branch was the only part of the Union with which nine out of ten members ever came into contact.

I I

This is one way of looking at the Union: more than 1,500 branches scattered up and down the country with a total membership of 300,000. Another way is to describe it as a network of interlocking committees, formally dependent upon the votes of the total member-ship, but in practice confined to a few hundred active members who were intimate with the details of Union business, shaped its policy and took its decisions.

At the bottom of the pyramid were the branch committees. The next level was that of the *area*, of which there were eleven covering the whole of the British Isles, each with its headquarters in a big town like Cardiff, Bristol, or the biggest of all, Area No. 1, in London. In each area there were elected *trade group committees*, dealing with the dockers' and the other sections' specific trade interests, wages, hours, etc. All the area trade group committees were represented on the *area committee* itself, which did not deal with trade matters at all (unless they affected more than one trade group) but represented the interests of the union as a whole. The area committee, for example, was responsible for the general administration of the union within its geographical limits, for organisation, recruitment and propaganda and particularly for financial administration, always a problem because of the large number of small sums to be handled.[1]

At the next step up came *the national trade group committees*, elected from the corresponding trade group committees in each area and reinforced at need—for instance, when variations in a national agreement were proposed—by a *national delegate conference* drawn from the trade group concerned.

The supreme authority in the Union was vested in the Annual (or as it soon became the Biennial) Delegate Conference, which alone had the power to make, amend or revoke the rules. The full *Biennial Delegate Conference*, bringing two or three hundred delegates together for the best part of a week, consisted of lay representatives elected by the area trade groups. It did not deal with trade matters, respecting the principle of trade autonomy, but discussed the report of the Executive, the general policy and administration of the Union and a series of resolutions submitted by the branch, area and trade group committees.

Between the meetings of the Biennial Conference, authority was exercised by the *General Executive Council*, elected partly by ballot vote

1 In Area 4 (South Wales) and Area 3 (the South-west—with the exception o. Bristol) the area trade group committees were abandoned soon after the amalga-mation and replaced by a number of district committees. In practice, the member-ship of a trade group (e.g. the docks) frequently coincided with a particular district.

of the general membership within each area and partly by the national trade group committees, thereby uniting the territorial and functional principles of representation. Meeting once a quarter (with a smaller Finance and Emergency Committee meeting monthly), its sixteen members received reports from all the area and trade group committees, from the national officers and from the General Secretary of the Union. The Executive's sanction was necessary for any major expenditure, any major decision of policy, national wage demands and strike action. To complete the picture, we must add the independent *Appeals Committee* elected by the full Delegate Conference to hear appeals lodged against decisions of the Executive, with the right to reverse them if the Committee saw fit. The Appeals Committee did not meet often, but its existence was an important safeguard of democratic procedure and of the rights of the officials.

The membership of all these committees was confined to lay members of the Union, working men who, even if they gave several days a month to Union business, were paid no salary but received payment for lost earnings together with their expenses and continued to earn their livelihood by working at their trades. This was by no means true of all British trade unions either then or now. Amongst important unions whose executive committees were either wholly or in part drawn from full-time officials were the Miners' Federation, the A.E.U., the General and Municipal Workers, the Woodworkers and the Boilermakers. Although there was a constant turnover in membership of the T.G.W.U. committees, at any one time they were recruited from a group of no more than a few hundred men who carried a great part of the responsibility for the Union's affairs and represented an impressive display of working-class experience and democracy.

12

There was still, however, a third element in the composition of the Union besides the rank-and-file membership, the representative committees and delegate conferences—the full-time, paid officials.

Trade-union constitutions, with their formal definition of responsibilities, give an inadequate idea of the great part which full-time officials, especially national officers, play in every union. The position of the trade-union official and his relationship to the lay members of his union have no parallel outside the working-class movement. Certainly at the time of the T.G.W.U. amalgamation, he was still looked upon, and looked upon himself, less as a professional administrator than a working man like the other members, paid enough to free him for full-time attention to the affairs of the Union. It was a natural extension of the system whereby members of committees and deputations were paid compensation for their loss of earnings while on union business. This was the way in which almost all union officials began their careers, graduating from part-time to full-time officers, remaining all the time members of the union, still addressed as 'Brother' and acting as the representatives rather than as the paid servants or employees of the other members.

The role of the trade-union officials has often been misunderstood. What the members of a union expect from their national officers and especially from their general secretary is not simply to run the day-to-day administration and advise its main committees, but to provide leadership, to display initiative in formulating policy and act as their representatives in meeting employers, the State and other unions. In terms of government, his role is closer to that of a minister (in the case of a general secretary, to that of a Prime Minister) than to the position of a civil servant.

British trade-union leadership in this century has formed an unusually homogeneous and distinctive group, quite clearly marked off from other professional groups. Almost invariably it has been drawn from the ranks of the particular union, with little if any outside recruitment. It has displayed a strong sense of social conscience and of identity with the members which has counted far more than the often meagre material rewards. Bevin's salary as General Secretary after the amalgamation, for example, was exactly the same (£650) as it had been as Assistant General Secretary of the Dockers' Union with one tenth of the membership. His expenses allowance while in London (£1 a day) was actually five shillings a day less. Most able trade-union officials, leave alone a man of the outstanding ability of Ernest Bevin, could have earned a better salary if they had left their Union's service and gone outside. Few of them did, at least before 1945. In most cases the two important reasons were loyalty to the organisation with which they had identified themselves and the desire to go on serving the working class from which they sprang.

The T.G.W.U. in its early days was over-staffed, especially in certain areas like London and Liverpool where there was more than a suspicion that one or two of the amalgamating unions had hastily increased the number of full-time officers in order to take advantage of the offer of no loss of salary or place when they were taken over. How to keep that promise and at the same time reduce the number of officials to economic proportions was a problem which gave Bevin a great deal of trouble in the first few years of the new Union. It was a burden not only on financial but also on administrative efficiency, for many of those taken over were passengers.

So far as national officers were concerned, Bevin made good use of the House of Commons (with a Union grant for constituency and election expenses) to find a place for those who could not be fitted easily into the new organisation. In recognition of their past services, Gosling (President of the new Union), Tillett and Sexton were allowed to combine Union work and an official salary with their Parliamentary duties. The others resigned their Union posts on election to the House.

In the early years of the Union, the relations between Bevin and the other officers, especially the other national officers, were far from easy. Neither he nor they could forget that a short time before there had been fourteen unions and fourteen general secretaries where now there was only one. A number of those who came from other unions, especially the other big union, the Vehicle Workers— not to mention Tillett—resented Bevin's assertion of authority, complained that he behaved dictatorially, could not work with a team and could not accept criticism. In the first two or three years, the possibility that the Union might break up was never out of Bevin's mind, and he tended to take too much on his own shoulders. The blame for this situation did not rest on Bevin alone: there was jealousy on the other side as well as suspicion on his.

From the first, the T.G.W.U. was fortunate in finding a number of able officers even if they did not find it easy at times to work with Bevin. Once the amalgamation receded into the past and its success was assured, confidence grew and at the end of the 1920s a new generation began to come into office to whom the amalgamation was ancient history and who took Bevin's position for granted more easily.

Amongst the officers, the President, the Financial Secretary and those responsible for the big trade groups formed one clearly defined group; the area secretaries a second. A third group, which played an important role behind the scenes, was the central office staff: Frank Stillwell, head of the very successful Legal Department; A. J. Chandler, the Minute Secretary of the General Executive; Bevin's secretary, Miss Forcey and her successor Miss Saunders, and J. J. Taylor who became secretary of the Political Department on Ben Tillett's retirement.

13

But far the most important office, and deliberately designed to be so, was that of General Secretary. All the other officers were appointed by the Executive. The General Secretary alone was elected by a ballot of all the members, for the office of president to which Gosling had been similarly elected, did not survive his retirement. Apart from the Financial Secretary whose duties concerned only the finances of the Union, the General Secretary was the only national official recognised by the constitution.

There were excellent reasons for this unique authority. The decentralised structure of the Union with the large measure of autonomy granted to the trade groups made it essential to create a strong counterpoise at the centre, if the Union was not to develop the weaknesses of a federation. The General Secretary represented the unity of the Union. He was the man who held it together and resisted the particularist tendencies of the trade groups. In its early years when old jealousies and habits of mind from the pre-amalgamation period were still strong, when the different sections had still to learn to work together, the survival of the amalgamation depended upon Bevin's judgment and strength of purpose.

It was to the General Secretary that the Executive looked for guidance in formulating policy and under his supervision that the officers carried out the Executive's decisions. In the first few years he took a leading part in all major negotiations, built up the administrative structure of the Union, represented it and spoke for it on all important occasions. Few, if any, British trade unions have enjoyed such positive and powerful leadership as the Transport and General Workers' Union during Bevin's tenure of office.

His critics called him a dictator, but the word is ill-chosen. Far from being incompatible with a democratic constitution, such leadership is essential to its successful functioning. Without leadership, democracy is an inert and feeble form of government, a truth still imperfectly comprehended by many who regard democracy and the exercise of power as mutually exclusive. The difference between autocracy and democracy is not that the first provides leadership, while the second eliminates it; the true distinction is in the character of the leadership, the conditions under which power is exercised, arbitrary in the first case, responsible and liable to account in the second.

The arbitrary exercise of power is not unknown in trade unions, especially in the United States where the presidents of certain unions (e.g. John L. Lewis, of the United Mineworkers) have acquired dictatorial powers. Perhaps the nearest approach to this state of affairs in Great Britain was the position Havelock Wilson created for himself as President of the Seamen's Union, but in general there is no parallel in British trade-union practice for the position of such 'tsars' of American labour as John Lewis and Sam Gompers. In the sense in which the term has been used in American politics, neither Ernest Bevin nor any other general secretary of a British union has been a trade union 'boss'.

Bevin's whole life was lived in an atmosphere of discussion and uninhibited argument. His power derived from his ability to carry his Executive, the Biennial Delegate Conference and ultimately the rank-and-file members of the Union with him, a fact which he never for one moment forgot. He had often to meet criticism, and at times bitter attacks, from disgruntled members of his Union, but he never hesitated to carry the issue to the floor and fight it out with his critics and on few important occasions did he fail to win his case, not by intrigue or jobbery, but in open debate. Nor were his opponents much more successful when, defeated within the Union, they attempted to organise a breakaway from it, further proof of the confidence Bevin commanded among the Union's members. Bevin's career as a trade-union leader, indeed his career from beginning to end, is a striking illustration of democratic leadership and what it can achieve.

The pages that follow can be left to supply the proof of this. It is important to make the point, however, that the power exercised by the General Secretary and in lesser degree by the other officials, far from being a usurpation of the members' rights or a perversion of the Union's constitution, was an essential complement to both. A true picture of the Union must hold all three elements in view: the rank-and-file membership, the hierarchy of constitutional committees, and the position of the full-time officials, especially of the Union's chief officer, its General Secretary. All three were essential to the effective working of the organisation.

14

What was the purpose of this elaborate organisation?

Trade unions were an expression of the anger and the impotence of working men in face of the gross exploitation practised upon them during the early industrial revolution. Trade unionism has a long history in this country, and it is a history of struggle against a hostile environment right up to the second World War. Born in revolt, the trade unions grew up in opposition. They had to fight for the right to exist and when they secured that (in 1824) they had to go on fighting to remove the legal restrictions with which Parliament and the courts sought to hamper them, a process not completed until the Trade Union Act of 1913.

Throughout the greater part of their history, they had to meet not only the opposition of the employers—that they expected—but the settled suspicion and hostility of the State, the propertied classes and every established institution, from the courts and the police to the Church and the Press. They have been accused of subverting society, usurping the coercive powers of the State, behaving tyrannically, holding the community to ransom, endangering the welfare of the nation, restricting the freedom of the individual, interfering with the rights of management and the operation of economic laws. Some of the charges levelled against the trade unions today might make more impression on them if they had not been heard so often before, at times when the unions had every justification for fighting in defence of their members' interests, and when their struggle to limit the arbitrary power of the employers and raise the status of the working class produced an expansion, not a restriction, of freedom.

The second World War brought a big change, and at the end of the war the unions found themselves in the position of having achieved some of the most important demands for which Bevin and the leaders of his generation had campaigned. The State, for example, assumed the obligation, accepted by all political parties, of maintaining a stable level of high employment and of extending the social services to form the framework of the Welfare State. At the same time full employment has given the working classes a prosperity, and the trade unions a bargaining power, which they have never enjoyed before. This change in circumstances has been accompanied by a marked change in attitude towards the trade unions. Ever since the end of the war the T.U.C. has been exhorted to accept a major share in the responsibility for the country's economic stability, even if in practice 'responsibility' has largely meant holding back wage demands, discouraging strikes and persuading the unions that to ask for a larger share of the profits of industry and trade is against the national interest.

The problem with which these post-war changes have confronted the trade-union movement lie outside the scope of the present volume. By the time they became acute, Ernest Bevin had become Foreign Secretary and it fell to his successor as General Secretary of the T.G.W.U., Arthur Deakin, to wrestle with them.[1] There is a very good reason, however, for taking a glance at the future at this stage. For it throws into relief the fact that the position of the trade unions up to a year or two before the war, was very different from that which they have occupied since 1940. They had neither the opportunity nor the responsibility of contributing in any positive way to the solution of the economic problems from which they suffered. With the exception of their brief and unsatisfactory experience under the two minority Labour Governments, the trade unions were excluded from any voice in economic policy and were neither consulted nor considered by the Conservative and 'National' governments before 1939.

1 The courageous effort which Deakin made to meet the new responsibilities thrust upon the trade-union movement is still too little appreciated. It is well presented in Dr. V. L. Allen's book, based on a study of Arthur Deakin's career: *Trade Union Leadership* (1957).

Bevin continually protested at the stupidity of excluding the workers from any share in the responsibility for the running of industry or for the economic policy of the country. In 1939, war brought a change of attitude on the part of the Chamberlain Government, which came to fruition in the emergency of 1940 when Churchill brought Labour into the coalition and invited Bevin to become Minister of Labour and National Service. But for most of the years in which Bevin was an active trade-union leader, the only role open to the trade unions was the negative one of opposition, of defending working-class interests against the consequences of economic policies and circumstances over which they were permitted no share in control. Nor can it be doubted, in view of the protracted depression, the persistent unemployment and the low standards of living of a large section of the working class, that those interests needed to be defended as vigorously as possible.

15

How was this to be done?

The basis of trade-union action has always been the same—combination. No individual working man could hope to bargain on equal terms with an employer; if he refused what was offered, his only alternative was to go without work and see someone else take his place. But a group of men, if they were ready to support each other and not to blackleg, was in a very different position. It was the realisation of this that led to the formation of the first trade unions and to the violent opposition which they encountered from the masters throughout the nineteenth century.

The first object of any trade union, therefore, was to build up sufficient power by organising the men to make the employers, the State and other trade unions take its claims seriously. This problem had occupied Bevin for years. The amalgamation was his answer to it. But it was not a problem to which an answer was found once and for all. The Union was a voluntary organisation which had constantly to justify its value to its members. With high unemployment and a big turnover in membership, every union had to keep up an unremitting effort to hold its own in numbers and finance. In six of the first ten years, the T.G.W.U. lost more members than it gained

and in 1932 had only 75,000 more members than in 1922, despite
the big accession of numbers from the amalgamation with the
Workers' Union in 1929. (This was still a better record than the
average for the trade-union movement which lost a million and
a quarter members between 1922 and 1932.) No trade-union leader
could afford to sit back complacently when for most of the years
between the wars not more than a quarter to a third of the
workers in the country belonged to any union. Down to the middle
of the 1930s Bevin's first preoccupation as General Secretary was
to look to the strength of his organisation.

To what use was this strength to be put?

Until 1926 both employers and trade unions looked upon the
natural state of industrial relations as a conflict of power in which
first one side, then the other, enjoyed a temporary advantage and
wages were forced up or down. The weapons on the one side were
the strike or the threat of a strike, on the other dismissal or the lock-
out. Each side took advantage of economic circumstances—the
state of trade, the level of unemployment, the rise and fall of wages in
other occupations—to wring the maximum concessions out of the
other.

Strikes were not a weapon which could be used indiscriminately.
In 1922, for instance, Bevin was prepared to go to almost any length
to avoid a major strike for which he judged the Union to be unprepared and circumstances unfavourable. On the other hand, in
1924, when he judged the advantage to be on the Union's side, he
was not deterred from following an aggressive policy by fear of em-
barrassing the Labour Government. Negotiations of some sort, of
course, usually followed a strike, unless the Union or the employers
capitulated; but they only registered gains or losses already settled
by the exercise of force.

The alternative, to which Bevin had long been attracted in
principle, was for both sides to recognise the common interest they
shared in industrial peace and to replace these periodical and wasteful conflicts by negotiations in which strikes and lock-outs were
treated as weapons of last resort.

The industrial truce during the first war led to a great increase in
the settlement of disputes by negotiation, conciliation and
arbitration. But the hopes expressed in the Whitley Report that this
might continue after the Armistice were soon dashed. The unions

took advantage of the immediate post-war situation, and the employers of its ending, to resume the old contest of power. Not until after the General Strike was there a change of heart, fortunately on both sides.

Between 1926 and 1940 the use of the strike weapon was largely abandoned in favour of negotiation, and the provision of regular machinery for negotiation was steadily extended from one industry to another. The strength of the union's organisation, the solidarity and discipline of the men in backing the case which the officials presented, were still decisive factors, but they were no longer employed crudely. They were confined within conventions which were as well understood and used to the same advantage by both sides as the rules in a game of chess.

Collective bargaining, with a great variety of procedures, thus became the principal method by which the unions defended and improved their members' wages and working conditions, with the strike pushed into the background. Bevin welcomed the change as a more intelligent way of settling disputes and worked persistently to create negotiating machinery in industries like road transport where it was lacking. In fact, the unions had little choice. It took them ten years to recover from the setback of 1926 and until the recovery of the later 1930s they were forced on to the defensive by economic circumstances.

Besides collective bargaining and the strike, the unions had two other courses open to them.

The first was self-help. From the contributions they collected, they paid strike or lock-out benefit, provided some insurance against sickness or unemployment and organised a legal service with which to help their members fight unjust treatment and secure compensation in the courts.

The second was political action, the original purpose of the Trades Union Congress with its Parliamentary Committee and of the Labour Representation Committee out of which grew the Labour Party. Political action meant, in the first place, legislation to protect the worker's interest—the Factory Acts, workmen's compensation, industrial health and safety regulations, the establishment of trade boards for selected industries, statutory provisions for negotiation and arbitration—and ultimately the Socialist programme for changing the distribution of power between the classes and modifying or replacing the capitalist system of production for private profit.

In every case, successful action by a class whose members possessed no individual resources depended upon combination, and this in turn upon effective organisation. Bevin had argued this for years. Now that he had created his organisation, how effective was it?

16

At the beginning of 1922, when the new union was born, just under two million insured workers (over 16 per cent of the total) were unemployed and three quarters of a million were on outdoor relief. Throughout 1922 and the greater part of 1923, trade remained depressed and the trade unions stood on the defensive. The most that Bevin and the new Executive could do was to limit the wage reductions which every union was forced to concede, to preserve the national agreements which they held against the day when they could press for restoring wage cuts, and to avoid being manœuvred into a hopeless fight with the odds against them. Neither the unity nor the finances of the new transport Union were sufficient in the first year or two after amalgamation to run risks in any of the trades in which it had the major membership.

The employers knew this as well as Bevin and less than a week after the new Union was inaugurated, on 5th January 1922, Bevin found on his desk what amounted to an ultimatum from the Port Labour Employers, calling for a meeting of the National Joint Council for Dock Labour within ten days and tabling a demand for a reduction of two shillings a day in the dockers' wages. The original Shaw award of 16/- a day (i.e. when work was available) had already been cut down to 12/-; the employers' demand, if conceded, would now reduce it to 10/-, and this at a time when a docker was lucky if he got two days' work a week.

Despite the recommendation of the Shaw Report, no scheme for maintenance had been introduced and under-employment as well as unemployment was common in every port. When Bevin met the employers to discuss decasualisation, Lord Devonport, the chairman of the P.L.A., laughed at him: "Maintenance is a hardy annual. You know very well that was put in to help your men swallow a reduction."[1] The employers, Bevin was convinced, meant to take advantage of the situation not only to drive down wages, but to undermine the Shaw Award, weaken the Union and recover their old position of being able to dictate terms to the men.

Bevin played for time. Taking the lead in the negotiations (he was acting as National Secretary of the Docks Trade Group as well as General Secretary of the Union) he succeeded in spinning them out until the autumn. He could not in the end avoid the reduction demanded, but he only conceded a shilling to begin with. This was not to take effect until the autumn of 1922; the reduction of a further shilling not until June 1923—and then, only if the cost of living index showed a fall of ten points from the level of September 1922. In return for these concessions, Bevin secured the employers' agreement not to seek any further cuts before 1st January 1924 and to drop any claim to extend the working week of forty-four hours or alter existing conditions of work. To the delegate conference of the Docks Group which he was careful to call at each stage of the negotiations, he argued that, if they could preserve the conditions of work and the 44-hour week, they could win back wage reductions when trade recovered. Most important of all was to maintain the machinery for a *national* settlement and, if they had to retreat, to do so in good order with their unity unbroken.

The delegate conference accepted Bevin's argument and endorsed the settlement, but the successive reductions placed a heavy strain on the loyalty of the rank and file towards the new Union and offered an easy opening for anyone who wanted to make mischief. In the London docks, in particular, there were plenty of enemies ready to say that Bevin had no guts for a fight, that he had sold out to the bosses and that the only benefit the men had got from the amalgamation was to see their wages reduced without the Union calling a man out in protest. When mass meetings were held in the East End to explain and defend the settlement to the men, the Union officers had difficulty in securing a hearing in face of organised rowdyism. Of the seventy-six London branches to whom the terms were submitted, only twenty-six returned a favourable majority. Twenty-one voted against and twenty-nine did not bother to reply.

1 Bevin repeated this remark, which he never forgave, at the Court of Inquiry into the dock dispute of February 1924 (*Daily Herald*, 21st February 1924).

This was in the autumn of 1922. There were rumblings of rebellion that winter and spring, but no action was taken until the summer of 1923 when the further reduction was put into effect. The trouble began in Hull at the beginning of July. Hull had always been a difficult port to organise, partly on account of quarrels between the unions, and it was an official of the rival Workers' Union who encouraged the men to down tools in protest. The unofficial strike spread rapidly to other ports, Grimsby, Cardiff, Manchester, Birkenhead and London.

When Bevin, Gosling, and other union officials went down to Bermondsey Town Hall to address a mass meeting, they were howled down and refused a hearing. The hall was packed by some two thousand dockers and neither Bevin nor Gosling could obtain a hearing. They were met with cries of 'Traitors and blacklegs'. Gosling later wrote: "I felt the only thing to do was to smile, but Bevin thrust out his underlip and let his face boldly say what his tongue was not allowed to express." The next day, the *Daily Express*, delighted at Bevin's discomfiture, described him as white to the lips with anger and rubbed in the point that at a signal from Coombes, chairman of the unofficial strike committee, the uproar stopped immediately, leaving him to move a vote of no confidence in Bevin and the Union's leadership. The vote was carried unanimously and at Coombes' suggestion the men then pushed their way out of the building, leaving Bevin and the officials to face an empty hall. The same tactics were used on other occasions and effectively prevented Bevin or anyone else putting the Union's case to the men.

17

Undoubtedly, there was widespread resentment among the dockers at the wage-cut, but it was something more than a spontaneous protest which Bevin had to meet in London. When the first Annual Delegate Conference of the Union, hastily transferred from Hull, met in Central Hall, Westminster on 9th July, he faced the issue squarely. Harry Gosling abandoned his Presidential address. In its place, the first item on the agenda was a full debate on the dock strike. "I am standing here this morning," Bevin told the hundred and seventy-five delegates, "with the whole existence of this Union at stake." He chose his ground shrewdly, refusing to be drawn into a discussion of the case for and against strike action which would only have inflamed the tempers of the men. In a debate on policy he would have conceded the initiative to his critics and been placed on the defensive. On procedure, the ground on which he chose to fight, Bevin was able to attack and put the strike leaders in the awkward position of defending themselves.

If the members had complaints to make or disagreed with policy, he argued, they had a perfectly clear course open to them through the constitutional machinery of the Union provided by the National Docks Group, but neither the Executive Council nor he himself were prepared to meet the unofficial strike committee. Bevin was determined to defend the constitution of the Union; had he gone outside it, he would have undermined the authority of its officers and of its elected committees. At the same time he insisted that agreements which had been endorsed by a delegate conference and submitted to all the branches concerned must be honoured if the process of collective bargaining was not to be annulled.

"There are between two and three hundred agreements—286 to be correct —held by this Union. If the policy to be adopted now is that agreements can be made one day and broken the next—well, do it with your eyes open, but trade unionism is finished as an organised body for dealing with wages and conditions."[1]

Bevin's argument for responsibility was challenged from the floor by two of the strike leaders, Fitzgerald and Maguire, who put the argument for militancy. 28,000 men were already out in London— and would stay out.

"I am going to say," Maguire told the conference, "that if this organisation is not going to back the members out on strike, you are going to lose forty to fifty thousand men. Things have not been done to support the men as they should be. They have been shouted at times out of number that they should build up this organisation to fight and when the time comes to fight we were told: 'March is not the time to fight. Fight in June or when the summer comes'."

Maguire admitted that he was a Communist, but claimed, not

1 Verbatim record (typescript) of the First Annual Delegate Conference of the T. G.W.U., 9th–14th July 1923.

very convincingly, that he did not allow this fact to influence him. Bevin retorted that the unofficial strike committee was deliberately trying to break up the Union. A confused and angry debate followed. At the end of the morning, Fitzgerald's amendment to support the men on strike was defeated by 136 votes to 18 and the original resolution urging them to return to work was carried with only five delegates in opposition.

Bevin had successfully avoided any open condemnation of the strikers and the appeal to solidarity began to tell. In the next few days most of the men in the other ports returned to work, leaving Hull and London to continue the strike. In Hull, most of them were back before the end of the month, but in London it was seven weeks in all before the strike finally ended.

18

The unofficial strike committee which had assumed the leadership in the London docks used every means, including breaking up meetings and physical violence, to prevent the Union's case from being put to the men. Handbills were circulated and meetings held to attack the Union and its leaders for their refusal to recognise the strike. The quarrel with the Union came to play a bigger part in the minds of the strike committee than their grievances against the employers. It is possible to identify at least two, and possibly a third group, who had an interest in promoting such a quarrel.

When the amalgamation took place, one small London union had remained outside, the Amalgamated Stevedores' Labour Protection League. Stevedores had always held aloof from dockers since the days of sail and the distinction between the stevedores who worked on shipboard and the dockers who were confined to the quayside. More important was the fact that the Stevedores' was a small union with a close personal relationship between officers and members and no wish at all to be swallowed up in the new large-scale organisation.

The Stevedores had been a party to the negotiations with the port employers. This did not prevent them, however, from fishing in troubled waters and encouraging several thousand London members of the new Union (many of them former members of Gosling's

Watermen) to break away and join in setting up the re-named National Amalgamated Stevedores, Lightermen, Watermen and Dockers Union. The feud between the two unions was not ended by the expulsion of the Stevedores from the T.U.C. for this act of disloyalty to trade-union solidarity; it flared up again in the dock strikes of 1954 and 1955.[1]

Another interested party was the Communists. Their instrument was the National Unemployed Workers' Committee Movement founded by Wal Hannington, a London toolmaker, and other Communists in 1921. Like the Minority Movement and the later Rank and File Movement, the N.U.W.C.M. kept up a steady attack on the official leadership of the unions as traitors to the working class and called monotonously, in season and out, for militant tactics. A copy of *New Charter* (incorporating *Out of Work*) which was published by the N.U.W.C.M. is preserved among Bevin's papers. The headlines read:

Strike One! Strike All!!

Dockers Out—Now for the Big Transport Fight.

Bevin and Gosling Must Go!

To Hell with Peace Talk![2]

Communist members of the T.G.W.U. were prominent on the unofficial strike committee and there was a strong suspicion, which Bevin shared, that Fred Thompson, who held the key post of Secretary of the Union's Dock Group in Area No. 1 (London), was playing a double game. Thompson had been London district secretary of the old Dockers' Union and had never made any bones about his membership of the Communist Party. Personal animosity against Bevin, as well as against Tom Scoulding who had been placed over him as Area Secretary for London, no doubt stiffened his political convictions. Ostensibly, he remained loyal to the Union

1 In 1927, the lightermen and watermen broke away from the Stevedores and formed the separate Watermen, Lightermen, Tugmen and Bargemen's Union. In 1938 the Stevedores had a membership of 7,000, the Watermen of 4,000 and the Docks Group of the T.G.W.U. 87,000. This stubborn survival of particularism has constantly disturbed the course of industrial relations in the London docks.

2 *New Charter* No. 2, 6th July 1923.

and no action was taken by the committee of inquiry which investigated the strike in November, but Bevin took the charges
against Thompson and another London official, Potter, sufficiently
seriously to place a memorandum detailing them before the committee.[1] Three years later the trouble with Thompson and Potter
came to a head, leading to an open breach and an unsuccessful
attempt by the two men to organise a breakaway union.

Once the strike had collapsed—as it was bound to do, if the Union
refused to pay strike benefit—Bevin was prepared to let the issue
drop. On his recommendation, the General Executive Council
wrote off seven weeks' contributions from London members who had
been involved in the strike and voted £2,000 for organising campaigns in Hull and London to repair the damage done.

Faced with a crisis which might well have broken up the Union,
Bevin kept his head and avoided both the traps into which he might
have fallen, either a fight with the employers for which the Union
was not yet ready, or a head-on clash with his own members.
Within a few months he showed that, when he judged the situation
to be ripe, he could act to protect the dockers' interests with as much
decision and far more success than his critics.

19

Bevin's problems were not confined to the dockers. Before the new
Union came into existence the tramway employers had already
tabled demands for the revision of the national agreement which
Bevin and Bob Williams had secured for the tramwaymen in 1919.
Bevin led the negotiating team which met the employers' representatives during the winter of 1921–22. Agreement was
difficult to reach, but Bevin was prepared to fight on the principle of
the guaranteed week of 48 hours and summoned a national delegate
conference to stand firm.

"You established in 1919," he told the delegates, "a principle which is, I
think, the greatest principle ever achieved in the industrial world. The great
thing in this fight is the guaranteed week. . . .

"To get the 8-hour week established it took thirty years of effort. You can
recover wages—the money side is not so difficult. When trade revives, then

1 Dated 9th November 1923.

is the chance to recover wages. But it is the conditions. Conditions take years to recover . . . and you must fight to keep them."[1]

With solid backing from the men, Bevin secured a revised agreement in April 1922 which left the guaranteed week intact. Then, in September, the employers returned to the attack, calling for the abandonment of the sliding-scale agreement on wages and a reduction of 12/– a week on an average wage of under 60/–. Again Bevin led the negotiations, preserved the sliding scale and reduced the proposed cut in wages from 12/– a week to 4/–. A ballot gave a 2—1 majority in favour of accepting the terms, which were hailed by the Labour Press as a signal victory for the new Union.

In January 1923 it was the London busmen he had to defend. The companies operating bus services in the capital proposed a modification of the sliding scale which governed wages, beginning with a 2/– reduction in the weekly wages of the bus drivers. The men twice rejected this on a ballot vote as well as a modified proposal for a shilling reduction. At midnight on 24th February a mass meeting of 10,000 busmen, conveyed by 200 special buses, crowded into the Albert Hall to hear Bevin report on the negotiations. It was a rowdy gathering, but Bevin completed his report and silenced his critics with the announcement that the bus companies had withdrawn their proposals for further consideration. No more was heard of them.

These were only the more important disputes in which the Union was involved. In addition there were half a dozen or a dozen different local strikes or lock-outs to report each month, from coal workers at Falmouth and Northampton to tramwaymen in Newcastle and Sunderland, from cold storage workers at Smithfield Market and flour-millers in Rotherhithe to galvanising workers at Connah's Quay.

The Union could hardly have been founded at a worse time. Bevin was still wrestling with problems of organisation from which he had continually to break off in order to conduct trade negotiations. The new amalgamation had no fund of loyalty on which to draw and plenty of enemies, inside as well as outside, who would have been delighted to see it fail. Bevin's most powerful argument had been the

1 *The Record*, March 1922, pp. 8–9, reporting Bevin's speech to the delegate conference on 20th February.

accession of strength which amalgamation would bring. But during the first two years of the new Union's existence there was scarcely a single advance in wages or conditions to which he could point. No doubt some reduction in wages was inevitable and could be justified by the fall in prices, but this was not an argument which made any appeal to the dockers or tramwaymen. They judged by results and so far the results were meagre. The most that Bevin could claim, for all his efforts, was a limit to the reductions which might otherwise have been forced upon the individual unions if there had been no amalgamation.

His energies and confidence taxed to the limit, Bevin refused to let himself be shaken. No other union was doing any better and the year 1922 saw the biggest proportional drop in trade-union members between the wars, over fifteen per cent in twelve months. The next year, while the total figures for all British trade unions fell by a further 3.5%, the T.G.W.U. figures rose by 3.3%, a net gain of 10,000, despite the unofficial dock strike and its losses. It was the first sign of progress and doubly welcome after so many setbacks.

CHAPTER 9

The Union and the First
Labour Government
1923 — 1924

I

ONE OF THE REASONS for the Union's growth was a continuation of the process of amalgamation. By the end of 1923, the original unions joining together to form the Transport and General Workers' Union had grown to twenty-two; by the end of 1926 to twenty-seven.[1] None of the new unions was individually large, but together they represented a considerable accession of strength.

Bevin would have liked to carry the process much further. Down to the time of the General Strike, he entered into negotiations (none of which in the end proved successful) with fifteen other unions, including the Electrical Trades Union and the General and Municipal Workers' Union, the other big amalgamation of general workers which had grown out of Thorne's Gasworkers. The executives of the two general unions actually endorsed an agreement on amalgamation in 1926, but the General Strike supervened and, although negotiations were resumed, they lapsed inconclusively in October 1926.

It is notable that the direction in which Bevin pursued amalgamation was now more towards the creation of a single union for

---

1 The most important were: the Scottish Union of Dock Labourers (Glasgow); the National Union of Enginemen, Firemen, Motormen and Mechanics (headquarters at Rotherham) which gave the amalgamation an interest in the mining industry and formed a new national trade group, the Power Workers, with a large degree of autonomy; the North Wales Quarrymen's Union which with another local union enabled Bevin to set up a new territorial area with the young Arthur Deakin as one of its officials; and the United Order of General Labourers (London).

general workers than of a union bringing together all sections of the transport industry. Although there was talk of amalgamation with the National Union of Railwaymen and even with the Seamen, there was never sufficient prospect of success to enable serious negotiations to begin. Apart from civil aviation, the T.G.W.U. has not extended its interests in transport outside the sphere marked out by the original amalgamation. While it has strengthened its position in the dock and road transport industries, its biggest expansion in membership has taken place in the general workers' group and in the metal, engineering and chemical trades. In the thirty-five years since its foundation, its development has made it steadily more of a general and less of a transport union.

For a time Bevin had great hopes that the National Transport Workers' Federation might provide a framework for closer co-operation with the railway unions. The prospects, at first, were promising and all three of the railway unions[1] agreed to take part in negotiations during 1922. An unexpectedly adverse ballot by the N.U.R., however, turned down the scheme by a narrow majority and this killed it.

At its first annual conference in July 1923, the Transport and General Workers' Union voted to withdraw from the Federation, a mortal blow since the T.G.W.U. represented over 75 per cent of the affiliated membership. The Federation, once an equal partner with the miners and the railwaymen in the Triple Alliance but now reduced to an affiliated membership of 75,000, survived for three more years, conducting a protracted controversy with the T.G.W.U. about arrears of fees. It finally faded away after the annual council meeting of 1927 at which no more than eleven delegates were present.

The chief casualty was the Federation's secretary, Bob Williams. For ten years he had played a leading part in the Labour movement as one of the most militant and able of trade-union leaders. The weakness of his position was his dependence on the Federation; unlike Bevin, who remained Assistant Secretary of the Dockers' Union even when he was spending the greater part of his time acting as a representative of the Federation, Bob Williams held no other post.

1 These were the National Union of Railwaymen; the Amalgamated Society of Locomotive Engineers and Firemen, and the Railway Clerks Association (now the Transport Salaried Staffs Association).

As the Federation was overshadowed by the amalgamation Bevin had created, Williams' influence rapidly dwindled. Although he was now disillusioned with Communism, his political activities had made him plenty of enemies; he failed to get into Parliament and his personal life was not without difficulties. After he resigned from the Federation in 1925, he acted for a time as general manager of the *Daily Herald,* but never again made the running and, increasingly depressed by failure and personal troubles, finally drowned himself.

2

The effective life of the Federation had been a little more than ten years, from the dock strike of 1911 to the creation of the amalgamation. With its decline and the disappearance of many of the individual unions which belonged to it, the names which have become familiar in earlier chapters are replaced by the new men who took the lead in the amalgamated union. Only one of the older leaders still held an important post—Harry Gosling, whose nomination as President had precipitated the breach between Bevin and Tillett. Bevin agreed to a permanent president as part of the price to be paid for bringing about the amalgamation. He owed a real debt to Gosling for his support in the difficult negotiations which preceded the establishment of the new Union. But a permanent president had no place in Bevin's conception of the Union. There was room for only one permanent official at the head of the union, the general secretary. Although he had little interference to complain of from Gosling, Bevin saw dangers not so much to his own position as to the unity of the Union, if there were any other office whose holder could claim to share the general secretary's responsibilities and, in case of disagreement, challenge his authority.

There was plenty of trade union experience to support Bevin's view and when Gosling finally gave up the presidency of the Union in 1930, there was little opposition to Bevin's move to have his duties discharged by a lay chairman of the Executive Council. Bevin made the mistake, however, of trying to force the issue and confusing the future of the presidency with the personal position of Harry Gosling. Bevin thought he saw his opportunity at the beginning of 1924 when MacDonald invited Gosling to become Minister of Transport in the first Labour Government. In congratulating him on the appointment and granting him leave of absence, the Executive assured him of a position in the Union if the Government fell, but added: "The Council proposes, however, to review the whole question of the presidency of the union with full liberty of action."[1]

When the Labour Government fell in October 1924, Gosling appeared at the next Executive Meeting and requested the restoration of his former office. The Council hesitated, then decided that it was unnecessary to continue the presidential position and appointed Gosling at his former salary as National Secretary of the small Waterways Trade Group, a post which he had held in conjunction with the presidency. Bevin failed to show his usual judgment. He was met by a virtually unanimous demand on the part of his officers that the General Executive Council should rescind its decision and restore Gosling as President. In face of the storm, the Executive climbed down and voted to reinstate Gosling. The incident was smoothed over, but it left resentment behind and was at once taken up by the Press as further proof of Bevin's dictatorial ambitions.

In the early years of the amalgamation, Bevin carried a far heavier burden of administration and negotiation than anyone else. This was one of the main grounds of complaint by the other officers: that he failed to make good use of his team, kept too much in his own hands and would not delegate power. Yet it is easy to understand why Bevin saw it differently. He was anxious about the future of the amalgamation and he knew perfectly well that no one else had his ability either as an organiser or a negotiator. It was quicker to do things himself and make sure they were done properly than to waste time arguing with others who could not—and would not—see what he was driving at.

There was another reason, too. The suspicion and particularism of the different sections had still to be overcome. This was the biggest job he had to do and it was one he alone could do, not only because of the personality and driving force which he exerted, but because he was identified with the new Union as no one else could be. To the dockers and the tramwaymen, to the tinplate workers and the millers, to the Cornish fishermen and the London bus-drivers, to

1 T.G.W.U. Minutes of the General Executive Council, 11th–18th February 1924.

the North Wales quarrymen and Belfast carters, the unity of the organisation to which they now belonged was embodied in the burly figure of the General Secretary, hands thrust into pockets, head down, listening to their complaints, or with clenched fists coming up to hammer home his point as he argued the case for accepting a wage reduction rather than risk defeat in an ill-timed strike. Few other men could have held so heterogeneous a membership together through two years of industrial retreat.

The strain, increased by continuous travelling, led to a breakdown of his health in December 1922. He collapsed while on a visit to Lancashire and was laid up for seven weeks suffering from nervous exhaustion. When he returned, it was to resume as heavy a schedule as before. Not until the end of 1924 did he feel the Union's financial position justified the appointment of an assistant general secretary, a post for which John Cliff, National Secretary of the Road Passenger Transport Group, was selected.

3

While he turned to the national trade groups and their officers for the detailed work of industrial negotiation, Bevin relied on the General Executive Council for support in enforcing the sense of a common interest which alone bound the different groups together. Each of the territorial areas and each of the national trade groups was represented, with a total membership of eighteen, all lay members. Its quarterly meetings in London lasted for five days at a time, and the full council was usually summoned to an emergency meeting when any major crisis developed.

The Executive held the responsibility not only of formulating the Union's policy—whether, for instance, to press for or restrain wage demands—but of deciding upon its application in particular cases. The constitution of the Union reserved to it the right to approve or reject any proposal for strike action: this was a power which had to be exercised with courage as well as judgment in the early years when the interests of the Union as a whole and its financial stability might well have been endangered by precipitate action on the part of a single group like the dockers. In any conflict between Union policy and the demands of a particular section, Bevin looked to the

Executive, and especially to those of its members connected with the trade or area concerned, for support. He insisted that there should always be Executive members present when he received deputations and that one or two should accompany him when he went down to justify the Union's policy to an angry meeting of strikers who had to be persuaded to resume work.

Apart from the General Secretary (who was always to be elected by ballot of the entire membership) the Executive had also to select and appoint all the officers of the Union, who were responsible to it for the discharge of their duties. This was a right which was frequently disputed at delegate conferences and led eventually to the secession of the Glasgow dockers. It was an issue on which Bevin refused to compromise, believing that if officers were to be chosen by election, popularity and vote-catching would count far more than ability and the Union's interests suffer in consequence.

Far from seeking to reduce the role of the Executive in order to increase his own power, Bevin went out of his way to build up its authority and to bring to it questions which its members would have been content to leave the General Secretary to settle. As part of this policy he took care to see that the Executive was kept well-informed, and most of the five days of each quarterly meeting were taken up with the presentation and discussion of reports by each of the national officers, including himself.[1]

There was nothing perfunctory about these discussions. The initiative in putting up proposals rested with Bevin (frequently acting, of course, on suggestions made by the other officers), but he did not expect the Executive to approve automatically of his proposals; discussion in the Council was the way in which he sought to discover the likely reactions of the rank and file to the course he had in mind. If he usually secured approval, it was not because he browbeat his committee, but because he was persuasive and could advance strong arguments in support of his case.

Ernest Bevin exercised an unusual authority as general secretary but he was wise enough to grasp that he added to, rather than detracted from, his authority by working as closely as possible with his Executive. Nobody who reads through the printed volumes of

[1] These quarterly reports by the General Secretary are a valuable source for Bevin's views on political as well as economic developments and have been much used in writing this volume.

the minutes over the whole period of eighteen years from 1922 to 1939 can fail to be impressed by Bevin's clear conception of the relationship between a general secretary and his executive, by his combination of initiative with a steady insistence on the responsibilities of the Council.

4

If the Executive was the effective organ of authority in the Union, sovereignty rested with the Biennial Delegate Conference which received its report and alone possessed the right to alter the Union's rules.

Critics of trade-union democracy have sometimes dismissed the delegate conference as a democratic sham incapable of exercising any real control over union policy in the interests of the rank and file. If the democratic character of the T.G.W.U. had depended upon a single conference meeting for a week every two years, this would be a valid criticism. But this was far from being the case. The representation of the interests and views of the membership was made effective by many other means besides the Biennial Delegate Conference: by the whole network of committees which met all the year round; by the constant contact between the officers and ordinary members of the Union; by deputations, area conferences and national delegate conferences of the different trade groups. To take only one example: during the tramway negotiations of 1923 a national delegate conference of tramwaymen was summoned six times and discussed every step proposed by their representatives before the agreement was finally signed. It was then submitted to the branches for a national ballot of all the members concerned and only ratified when the vote showed a decisive majority in favour.

Trade matters were deliberately excluded from the agenda of the Biennial Delegate Conference and dealt with by national delegate conferences of the different trade groups summoned whenever the need arose. That did not prevent any section with a grievance challenging action taken by the Executive Council when its report came up for discussion at the Biennial Conference. This happened at the first conference of all (1923) which met while the unofficial dock strike was still in progress and led to fierce criticism of

the Executive's attitude. Similar debates occurred at many subsequent conferences and during the 1930s the London busmen in
particular could usually be relied upon to attack the Executive's
report in the sharpest terms.

Most of the time of the Conference, however, was taken up with
the discussion of the general policy of the Union both in industrial
and political matters. It expressed in visible form the unity of the
Union, bringing together representatives of all the areas and all the
trade groups and impressing upon the delegates as well as upon the
outside world the growing strength and common purpose of an
organisation whose activities ranged over widely separated occupations. Like the Executive Council and the office of general
secretary, the Delegate Conference represented the common
interests of the Union against the sectional preoccupations of the
different groups which composed it. Most valuable of all was the
effect on the delegates themselves who returned to their branches
with an enhanced sense of the importance of the organisation to
which they belonged and an increased willingness to undertake the
often tiresome local duties upon which it depended.

As Bevin saw very clearly, if the working classes were ever to pull
themselves up by their own boot-straps, they had to overcome the
lack of confidence in themselves, the sense of inferiority which their
poverty, isolation and lack of education all too easily induced. He
never lost sight of the psychological as well as the economic function
of trade unionism or forgot that the basis of trade-union strength lay as
much in working-class self-confidence and solidarity as in common
economic interests. For these reasons, occasions like the Biennial
Delegate Conference, by virtue of their impact on those who took
part in them, had an importance not to be reckoned simply in terms
of the business transacted.

5

The first of the Union's delegate conferences, held in July 1923, was
only a qualified success. It was overshadowed by the unofficial dock
strike which led to a last-minute change of venue from Hull to
London and threatened to endanger the whole future of the
amalgamation. Quite apart from the dock strike, Bevin and the

Executive had to face opposition on half a dozen other issues. The conference refused to leave the question of officers' salaries in the hands of the Executive and appointed its own committee of investigation; referred back the Executive's scheme for Union representation at the T.U.C. and Labour Party conferences and turned down Bevin's recommendation of a triennial delegate conference in favour of meeting every two years. Bevin had to use all his powers of persuasion to get the conference to agree on the principles to be adopted in electing delegates and narrowly defeated a demand for the circulation of the Executive Council's minutes.

On the last day of the conference, Gosling paid a warm tribute to Bevin:

"This amalgamation is due a great deal to the work of the General Secretary. He is young and strong but he will kill himself if he is not careful. He really did the greatest part of the work in connection with the amalgamation, but he gives credit to those who were associated with him."

Bevin, however, was far from satisfied: the amalgamation, he felt, was not yet finally cemented, the Union's authority had been badly shaken by the unofficial dock strike and confidence was not yet established either between the officers or between the members and those who represented them.

At first sight, the second Conference for which two hundred and eighty delegates assembled in Scarborough towards the end of July 1925, was as troubled by storms as its predecessor. It began with another heated debate on an unsuccessful strike, this time in the Covent Garden market.[1] Criticism in the Executive's report of disruptive elements and the Communist-inspired Minority Movement was challenged by London delegates; the Liverpool dockers protested angrily at the reduction of their funeral benefit from £12 to £10, and widespread dissatisfaction was expressed at the lack of uniformity in the organisation of branches and the payment of branch secretaries. The London delegates, a number of them Communists, renewed the attack on officers' salaries, demanded the election of officers in place of appointment by the Executive and criticised wasteful expenditure. Several times Bevin was involved in angry exchanges and four of the leaders of the hostile group from London were elected to the Appeals Committee.

1 See below, p. 246.

Bevin, however, took this in his stride. The opposition he encountered did not worry him; he gave as good as he got, made no concessions to his critics and carried the conference with him without much difficulty. The note of anxiety which had been there in 1923 was replaced by one of confidence; he was much more sure of himself and of his audience. The two big debates on support for the miners and the Industrial Alliance[1] reached a high level of responsibility. By 1925, the new Union had substantial achievements to its credit and Bevin could afford to admit mistakes, as he did in the case of the Covent Garden dispute. What pleased him most was the new spirit he found amongst the delegates and he told the Executive Council when it met a week later: "I regard the Scarborough Conference as the consummation of the amalgamation, which I had never really felt before."

6

During these years, the need for Bevin to concentrate his energies on establishing the amalgamation imposed restrictions on the part he was able to take in anything outside the Union. This is noticeable even in relation to the T.U.C. Although he attended all the annual congresses and by 1923 was the leader of the third biggest union in the movement, he took little part in the big debates of the T.U.C. before the 1924 Congress, and did not make any move to secure the place on the General Council which would have been his for the asking. The same thing was true of Bevin and the Labour Party. He led the Union's delegation of thirty-nine to the Party's annual conference, but he hardly got to his feet on any issue before 1925 and stood for election to none of the Party's committees, letting Stanley Hirst, the Financial Secretary, be nominated by the Union for the Labour Party National Executive, a body of which he himself was never a member.

There was no contraction, however, in the range of his interests, even if for the present he deliberately kept in the background. He retained his connection with the *Herald*, for instance, and was one of the sponsors of the Workers' Travel Association, started in November 1921 to organise working-class travel abroad. He took a similar

1 See below, pp. 273-6.

practical interest in the Manor House Hospital at Golders Green which was supported by the trade-union movement. He persuaded his own union to affiliate to the Hospital and to make a succession of grants and loans over the years to meet its needs.

During the course of 1922, Bevin paid two visits to the Continent, both of which are of interest in the light of his later career at the Foreign Office. The first was as an observer to a preliminary conference held in Berlin in April to discuss the possibility of agreement between the three quarrelling groups into which the international Socialist movement was now divided.

The arguments for affiliation to the rival organisations deeply divided the Labour Party between 1919 and 1923. The I.L.P. in particular, unable to swallow the Third International's insistence on Bolshevik methods yet reluctant to abandon the claim to re-volutionary virtue for the reformism of the Second, long wandered in a no-man's-land of earnest illusion. While the Third Inter-national lavished abuse on the Labour Party and its leaders as "the lackeys of the bourgeoisie", the I.L.P. joined with a number of Continental Socialist parties,[1] to set up the Vienna Working Union of Socialist Parties, generally known as the 'Two-and-a-Half' International.

The dearest wish of the Vienna Union was to restore the unity of the international movement and create a comprehensive organisation. The sudden decision of the Third International in December 1921 to reverse its propaganda and adopt the tactics of the united front offered an opportunity on which the 'Two-and-a-Half' eagerly seized. As a first step towards restoring unity, each of the three groups (the Second International with unconcealed scepticism) agreed to attend a preliminary meeting in Berlin. Harry Gosling as well as Ramsay MacDonald, the Belgians Emile Vander-velde and Huysmans and the German Otto Wels were among the Second International's spokesmen. From Moscow came two of the Communists' ablest dialecticians, Bukharin and Radek, accom-panied by the veteran Clara Zetkin.

The unexpectedly conciliatory attitude of Radek and his fellow delegates allowed the conference to set up a committee of nine for future negotiation and to express its hopes of unity in a joint

1 These were the French, Austrian and Swiss Socialist Parties and the German U.S.P.D.

declaration. These hopes, however, proved short-lived. The Second International's suspicions of Communist sincerity were not removed by the change in Communist tactics. Lenin and Zinoviev were critical of the concessions Radek had made and the Communists soon resumed their attacks on the good faith of the Second International with such sharpness that the illusions of the Vienna Union were destroyed for good. A year after the Berlin Conference a meeting at Hamburg marked the unification of the Second International and the 'Two-and-a-Half' without the Third.

Bevin was not a delegate at the Berlin meeting but he was highly interested by what he observed of the leaders of European socialism, particularly by the attitude of the Communist delegates. A year later when the first delegate conference of the Union debated a Communist amendment in favour of affiliation to the Third International, Bevin told the delegates:

"Up to the time I attended the Berlin conference, I did not understand the Russian position as well as I did when I came away. . . . It is contrary absolutely to our conception of democracy and the curious thing is that the supporters of the Red International are ultra democrats one moment and ultra dictators the next. You can't reconcile the two. . . . You must carry democracy with you and change stage by stage by democratic consent."

Unlike some of his colleagues in the working-class movement Bevin never flirted with Communism and, although he defended the right of the Russians to work out their own destiny, from first to last he rejected Bolshevik methods as incompatible with the democratic traditions of the Labour movement.

7

His second visit abroad in 1922 took him to Vienna where the International Transport Workers' Federation held its annual congress at the beginning of October. Sixteen nationalities were represented at the conference, the proceedings of which were conducted in three languages. Bob Williams presided and there were strong delegations from the United Kingdom, from Germany, Austria, France, Belgium and Holland. Bevin took the lead in discussing working conditions in the docks and the possibility of securing uniform standards. He was far from optimistic but he joined with the other dockers' representatives in drawing up a common programme and presented it to the main conference.

On the afternoon of the second day, Ben Tillett started a debate on the peace treaties which lasted most of the third day as well, and elicited an impressive measure of agreement between the German and Austrian spokesmen on the one hand and the French and British on the other. The reconstruction of Europe after the war was a problem which much occupied Bevin's mind at this time. In his quarterly report to the Executive Council of his union in August 1922, he wrote:

"Europe is slowly dragging the world down into the abyss of bankruptcy and despair. Statesmen seem incapable of cutting the knot they tied at Versailles: neither trade can revive nor peace be established while the present lopsided position remains."

The following year, when the French occupied the Ruhr, the Union at Bevin's suggestion took the unusual step of sending its own delegation to find out what was happening in the occupied areas. Their report was published and was debated at the Union's conference in July 1923.

His preoccupation with industrial negotiations and union problems never led Bevin to lose sight of the importance of foreign affairs and the direct effect of unsettled conditions abroad on working-class fortunes at home. When he spoke at the Vienna I.T.F. conference he expressed the view that during the past three years trade unionists had left the revision of the peace treaties far too much to the political side of the movement. "Today we must give special attention to the economic side of these treaties and look at their devastating effects in the economic sphere."

Bevin singled out reparations and tariffs for his main attack:

"The Peace Treaties have completely destroyed the balance of power in Europe and we know that, so long as this haggling over payments continues, there can be no restoration of it. . . . On us, as transport workers, it is especially incumbent to combat with all the means at our disposal the placing of obstacles in the way of free traffic between country and country. This incitement to nationalist feeling in the various states is in reality a crime."[1]

[1] Proceedings of the I.T.F. Congress, Vienna, 2nd–6th October 1922.

Bevin had not far to look for illustrations in support of his argument. It was his first visit to Central Europe and he was impressed by the economic distress which followed the break-up of the Austro-Hungarian monarchy into national States. The young Austrian Republic had almost collapsed under its difficulties and nowhere were the economic consequences of the peace settlement more plainly to be seen.

But Vienna was not only the capital of Austria, it was also one of the strongholds of European socialism. His hosts were eager to show their plans for the development of the working-class quarters of the city, and Bevin came back with a lively impression of the strength and achievements of the Vienna working-class movement to offset the depressing picture of the price the Austrian people were paying for defeat, inflation and the political dismemberment of Central Europe.

8

He had barely returned from Vienna when the Lloyd George coalition which had governed Britain since the end of 1916 finally broke up (October 1922). At the General Election which followed, the Conservatives were returned with a clear majority to form a Government in which, first, Bonar Law, then Stanley Baldwin, held the office of Prime Minister. The Labour Party, however, very nearly doubled both its vote in the country and its representation in the House of Commons, replacing the Liberals as the chief opposition party. A year later (December 1923) when Baldwin unexpectedly appealed to the country for a mandate in favour of tariff protection, the Tories lost heavily and Labour again increased its numbers in the House from 144 to 191. The Liberals held the balance of power and used it to turn the Tories out and put the first Labour Government, under Ramsay MacDonald, into office.

In principle, Bevin was a firm believer in political action and trade-union support for the Labour Party. The Union contributed generously to Party funds even when its financial resources were slender. In 1923, for instance, Bevin placed a detailed scheme before the delegate conference which provided for the allocation of £6,250 a year to the Union's political fund and for the support of nine Parliamentary candidates. This was in addition to the affiliation fees which the Union paid to the Labour Party at the rate of £2,500 a year. At every election Bevin, as well as the other officers, campaigned vigorously and the T.G.W.U. had the largest trade-union group in the House after the Miners.

In 1925, the Biennial Conference of the Union accepted the Executive's recommendation to support eleven instead of nine candidates at the next election. Later the same year, the Executive agreed to make a loan of £5,000 to the Party and, when this proposal was dropped in favour of raising the affiliation fee, volunteered to pay the increased fee at once on a membership of 250,000. All this is evidence of solid support at a time when the Union was far from rich and had to watch expenditure closely.

In practice, however, Bevin's attitude to politics and the Labour Party then and for a long time to come was dominated by his trade-union experience. He looked upon the political activity of the Party as necessary, but subordinate to and dependent on the industrial strength of the Labour movement organised in the trade unions. His view was summed up in a sentence taken from one of his reports to the Union Executive:

'Whatever the defeats or gains on the political side may be, the immovable, defence of the workman is always the trade unions and, whilst at all times using our efforts to capture the Government of the country, we must not for one moment slacken our efforts to strengthen the industrial machine."[1]

The Labour Government was dependent upon the continued support of the Liberals. This meant that any programme of a socialist character was ruled out, but most people in the Party believed that Labour could not refuse the opportunity, if only to show that it was capable of taking responsibility and fit to govern. Bevin wholeheartedly accepted this view and even later argued that it was the right decision to take, given the situation at the time.[2] What no one foresaw, however, was the problem created for the trade unions in their industrial action when their own Party came into office and for the first time assumed the responsibility for the government of the country.

1 General Secretary's Quarterly Report, February 1925.
2 Cf. the editorial in *The Record* for December 1923: "Fit to Govern and Ready," and Bevin's speech at the Labour Party conference of 1925. (See below, p. 258.)

9

Towards the end of 1923 the trade returns showed the first signs of economic revival for many months. It proved to be no more than a limited recovery, but it encouraged Bevin and other union leaders to believe that the time had come to call a halt to the unbroken run of wage reductions and try to recover some of the ground lost. As the amalgamation approached the end of its second year, he was anxious to prove that it could achieve successes beyond the strength of the separate unions. Nor was he prepared to accept the argument that the unions should hold their hands for political reasons. When the Executive met for the first time in 1924, Bevin reported:

"A great deal has been said during the past few weeks regarding the taking of industrial action now that we have a Labour Government, but I am of the opinion that if we rest on the industrial side for one moment it will be fatal to our progress and even to the Labour Government. It would be too big a price to pay and we must therefore go on with the economic war, waging it the whole time and utilising every opportunity on behalf of the class we represent."[1]

On the very day that the Baldwin Government was overthrown by a vote of censure in the new House of Commons, the Locomotive Engineers and Firemen went on strike rather than accept a wage award to which their own representatives had agreed. The T.U.C. General Council intervened and the strike was ended before the newly formed Labour Government was called upon to take action. Three weeks later, however, on Bevin's advice the T.G.W.U. called out over a hundred thousand dockers and brought every port in the country to a standstill.

Ever since the unofficial dock strike in the summer of 1923 Bevin had been watching for the first favourable moment at which he could get back some of the cuts imposed since the Shaw Award. At the end of November 1923, i.e. before the election, a national dockers' conference held at York decided unanimously, in view of the improvement in trade, to press for an increase of two shillings a day. This claim was submitted to the employers on 15th December, together with a renewal of the demand for maintenance and the

1 General Secretary's Quarterly Report, February 1924.

guaranteed week recommended by Lord Shaw's Court of Inquiry in 1920. The employers took a month to consider the claim and then at a meeting of the National Joint Council for Dock Labour in January turned it down without discussion.

The employers were as well aware as the Union that a Labour Government was about to assume office. Their challenge was direct and Bevin knew that he must meet it equally directly. Had he compromised at this stage, all the resentment and suspicion aroused by the Union's refusal to recognise the unofficial strike of the preceding summer would have flared up again and might well have destroyed the Union for good. He did not hesitate. At a further delegate conference on 29th January the dockers decided to tender notice to strike in accordance with their agreement on 16th February, unless their claim was met before then.

In the intervening fortnight the employers twice met the Union's representatives and on the second occasion made an offer of a shilling a day increase. Bevin refused to accept it. On 12th February the Minister of Labour, Tom Shaw, a trade unionist himself, summoned both sides to a conference but failed to move either party. The Labour Government, alarmed at the prospect of a national dock strike, appointed Colonel Josiah Wedgwood, Chancellor of the Duchy of Lancaster, as Chief Civil Commissioner to operate any emergency scheme which might be necessary. Bevin was adamant. Too much was at stake for him to worry about the embarrassment he was causing to the Government. On 16th February every docker in the country came out on strike. A private warning from Wedgwood that, if the strike continued, troops would be used to move food supplies, had no effect. Within ten days the employers conceded the two shillings a day and agreed to a joint inquiry into the problem of decasualisation and maintenance.

10

A month later, Bevin called out London's tramway workers and secured the Executive's approval for the decision of the London busmen to withdraw their labour in support at the same time.

This, too, like the dock strike, was a dispute with a history. Since the Court of Inquiry held at the beginning of 1921, no progress had been made at all in carrying out the recommendation for the standardisation of rates of wages, any more than the port employers had taken steps to work out a scheme for maintenance. Instead, the tramwaymen (like the dockers) had seen their wages cut, by five shillings a week, for instance, between October 1922 and October 1923. In June 1923, the three private companies operating trams in London gave notice that they proposed to make further reductions, giving as their reason the financial losses they were suffering from the growing competition of the motor buses.

Bevin's scornful reply announced a change of attitude on the part of the Union. Rather than accept further reductions, they would fight. Bevin pointed out that, if the competition from the buses was increasing, most of these were operated by the combine of which the private tram companies formed a part. The solution was to set up a single traffic authority for London which would bring some order into the unregulated competition between the different companies and the various forms of transport. The Union had long been pressing for such a step.

"On our part, we regret that everybody else seems to refuse to move or act until there is a crisis with consequent inconvenience to the public; but we are resolved that the policy of inaction pursued by the Government [in relation to the traffic recommendations of the Royal Commission on London Government], together with the stupid policy of the competitive interests in London shall not be used for the purpose of depressing the standard of life of our members employed by your companies."[1]

Bevin's firm reply stopped any further proposal for wage reductions and in August 1923 the men took the initiative in asking the district Joint Industrial Council to take under consideration not only the level of wages but the long-drawn-out negotiations for the standardisation of rates and the need for legislation to regulate public transport in London. Negotiations continued spasmodically between the autumn of 1923 and the spring of 1924, by which time the Labour Government was in office. On 19th December the Union submitted a claim for a rise in wages of 8/– a week, pointing out that while a London bus-driver started at 80s. 6d. and rose to 86s. 6d. in six months, a London tram-driver began at 58s. and only reached the maximum of 67s. after two years' service.

1 Letter of 23rd June 1923, printed in *Report by a Court of Inquiry concerning the stoppage of the London tramway and omnibus services*, 1924, (Cmd. 2101), Appendix 3.

This claim was addressed not only to the private companies but to the L.C.C. and the municipalities which operated the majority of London's tram services. On 12th March 1924 the employers finally informed the Minister of Transport (by now, Harry Gosling, the President of the T.G.W.U.) that they were unable to meet the claim made.

The men were originally instructed by the Union to cease work on 15th March but at the request of the Minister the strike was deferred for six days. At a meeting of both sides at the Ministry of Labour on the 20th the employers offered to go to arbitration and the L.C.C. put up a figure of five shillings in place of the eight demanded. The employers' twelfth-hour conversion to arbitration, however, which they had repeatedly resisted in the past, failed to impress the men. At midnight on 21st March London's trams stopped running and the 22,000 employees of the London General Omnibus Company came out in support. Next morning most of London walked to work.

I I

The outcry in the Press and Parliament was immediate. Bevin was accused of inconveniencing the public, holding the community up to ransom, sabotaging the national economy and undermining the Labour Government. The popular Press described him as 'Boss Bevin' and the staid *Spectator* wrote:

"Whatever our opinions may be of the economic rights and wrongs of a strike, it is not tolerable that a series of sympathetic strikes, frequently directed for all practical purposes by a single man—in the present case, Mr. Bevin—should in effect place the public under a dictatorship."[1]

Bevin made no effort to placate or appeal to public opinion. He was brusque and hostile with journalists and appeared to go out of his way to adopt a truculent and defiant attitude.

In part, this was deliberate. Bevin was not interested in public opinion, but in strengthening his position with his own members. Pictures of Bevin with his chin stuck out, declaring roundly that he would not make a single concession in his demands, might anger the ordinary newspaper reader, but not the docker or the tramwayman

1 *The Spectator*, March 29th 1924.

whose interests he was representing. The Union was solidly behind
him. His reputation as a tough and successful leader shot up—and
so did the Union's recruiting figures.

But Bevin's attitude was only partly due to calculation. It also
expressed a genuine anger with the public's and the newspapers'
attitude to trade-union claims. Accepting the invitation of the Tory
Morning Post to put his point of view, he criticised the Press for never
paying any attention to the miners' or dockers' grievances until
there was a strike, then denouncing the men for acting to remedy the
evils from which they suffered.

"Just the same with the tramway industry. We accepted reduction after
reduction in wages, used the will and power of the Union in preventing an
industrial upheaval two years ago and prior to that went through a lengthy
court of inquiry. We resented the fact that the recommendations of that
court were not accepted by the employers, but I do not remember a single
section of the Press denouncing the employers for this stupid and un-
reasonable attitude.
"Can it be wondered at that the men have been developing discontent—
their employment has been seriously intensified by the traffic conditions of
London,—and we have appealed to the Government, held public meetings,
sought the aid of the Press and tried to stir the public to a consciousness of
the position—but the men continued in their work, so who cared? Then
one day, the resentment of the men reaches its limit and they will not work—
and we are told we are wilfully incommoding the 'public'."[1]

Meanwhile the Government had appointed a court of inquiry
which produced an interim report on 24th March. Bevin presented
the men's case and the first point made by the court in its report was
that no one seriously questioned the merits of the claim which he had
made for an increase of wages. The trouble was that the tramway
undertakings, saddled with the cost of maintaining a track from
which the bus companies were exempt, could not earn sufficient to
meet the claim in face of the competition they were now encountering from the buses. The only permanent solution, both sides
agreed, was the co-ordination by a single authority of London's
public transport services.

But what was to be done about the present wage claim? On this
the court had nothing to say beyond reproving both sides for the
protraction of the negotiations and the failure to submit the dispute to

[1] *Morning Post*, 24th March 1924.

Bevin speaking to strikers at Covent Garden, 1924.

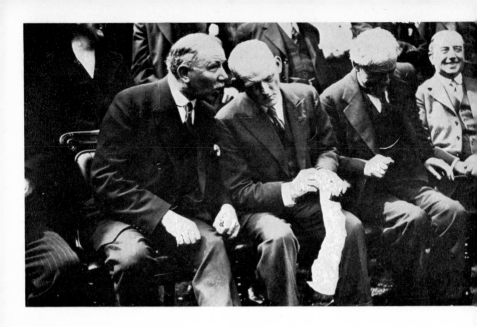

The first Labour Cabinet. *Above*. Left to right, J. H. Thomas, Philip Snowden, Ramsay MacDonald, Arthur Henderson. *Below*. MacDonald, Thomas, Henderson and J. R. Clynes.

arbitration long before the strike began. Ramsay MacDonald himself now intervened, writing a personal letter to Bevin to express his concern. He can hardly have been reassured by the reply he received in which the General Secretary of the T.G.W.U. addressed the Prime Minister as if he were negotiating with an equal power.

After telling the Prime Minister that he had been badly advised by his own Ministry of Labour, Bevin went on:

"Our demand was before the employers before we even knew there was a likelihood of a Labour Government coming in, so why should you accept the responsibility? I am making a statement to the Press today which I think will help the Government, but if you desire me to come round and see you first, I will do so. . . . It is merely a question now of a difference of £130,000 which gives you your chance."[1]

The same day Bevin announced that the three railway unions had agreed to bring the London Underground system to a standstill as well, at midnight on 28th March.

In face of this threat, MacDonald retorted that "the major services must be maintained and the Government must give protection to those engaged in legal occupations". The Emergency Powers Act which Labour had bitterly attacked Lloyd George for introducing in 1920, was now invoked by the Labour Government and a Cabinet committee set up under Wedgwood to prepare plans for emergency action. It was to this occasion that Bevin referred when he told the Labour Party conference in 1933:

"I know something about emergency powers. The first Labour Government rushed down to Windsor to get them signed in order to operate on me. . . . I do not like emergency powers even when they are operated by my friends."[2]

Bevin was not the only person who disliked the threat to use emergency powers. The T.U.C. General Council and the National Executive of the Labour Party issued a joint resolution deploring the Government's intention to invoke the Act and urged MacDonald instead to follow the Executive's proposal that the Government should take over London's transport and pay the men the new wage with the help of a subsidy.

1 Ernest Bevin to the Prime Minister, 26th March 1924.
2 Labour Party Conference Report, 1933, p. 161.

Fortunately, before a head-on collison occurred between the Labour Government and the trade unions, the hurried introduction of a London Transport Bill in the Commons allowed the employers and the Union to reach a compromise. In view of the promise to bring some order into the chaos of public transport in the capital, the employers agreed to an advance of six shillings a week, the Underground strike was called off and, after meetings of the tramwaymen on Sunday 30th March, a ballot produced a majority in favour of accepting the offer. At midnight on the 31st the strike ended after lasting ten days.

12

From the standpoint of the Union, Bevin had every reason to congratulate himself on the outcome of the dock and tram strikes. Both had been carried out with a remarkable degree of solidarity. The dockers, no longer divided between rival unions, acted together at the same time in all the ports of the country. The tramwaymen received the immediate support of the busmen, who were not involved directly in the dispute but were members of the same Union, and they had been assured of further support, if necessary, from the members of the railway unions employed on London's underground railways. For the first time the Union had convincingly proved the force of Bevin's argument that amalgamation, by ridding the men of the fatal handicap of disunity, would dramatically increase their strength. For the first time he had been able to demonstrate what he meant by the 'scientific organisation' (a favourite phrase) of trade-union strength. The value of such action —by contrast with the failure of the unofficial dock strike of 1923— was shown by the success of the Union in reversing a three-year-long trend and restoring at least part of the cuts imposed by the employers. For the time being, at least, the left-wing critics who accused Bevin of lacking a militant spirit were silenced by his success. Not only were wages improved, but a committee was promptly set up under Sir Donald MacLean to take up the Shaw Report's recommendations on registration and maintenance in the docks, while the Government rushed the London Traffic Bill through Parliament and gave effect to some at least of the traffic proposals of the Royal Commission on London Government which, like the recommendations of the Shaw Report, had been conveniently shelved.

This satisfaction was not shared by the Labour Government. MacDonald, in particular, out of sympathy with down-to-earth trade-union demands and increasingly inclined to take a high line about national responsibilities, was greatly angered by the strikes and never forgave Bevin for the embarrassment he caused the Government. This did not worry Bevin. But there were others in the Labour Party besides MacDonald who felt that Bevin had behaved irresponsibly and shown less than the loyalty the unions owed to the first Labour Government ever to take office. This impression was strengthened by the aggressive manner in which Bevin asserted his independence and expressed his contempt for politicians as a race.

13

Scarcely had the tramwaymen returned to work than J. A. Hobson started off a debate in the *New Leader* which soon spread to the columns of the *Daily Herald*. It was a muted controversy for, with Labour still in office, neither side was willing to say all that it thought. Bevin defended himself in the April number of the Union's journal, *The Record*.

"Mr. Hobson tells us that a separatist policy is hostile to Socialism. We cannot agree with that contention. What is described as separatist policy is the seizing of opportunity. The alternative to this so-called separatist policy is to await the development of machinery and a co-ordinated policy which we have no doubt will in time be reached; but while this is developing must we do nothing? . . . The bulk of the unions want something done in their own time and they are right in their demand. . . . Were we to sit and theorise as to the action we will take some day when our machinery is perfected we should never get the machinery, nor would there exist the spirit to utilise such machinery were it available.
"We are all too aware of the Government's difficulties and desire as much as anyone to assist in the success of Britain's first Labour Government. A policy of industrial truce would, in our view, even if it were possible, not be to the best interests of the Government. There is work to do on the industrial field as well as in the political arena. While it is true that the two are to some extent part of the same effort, we must not lose sight of the fact

that governments may come and governments may go, but the workers' fight for betterment of conditions must go on all the time . . ."[1]

The last sentence is revealing. Bevin was to repeat it to his Executive, not without a certain satisfaction, after the fall of the Labour Government in the autumn. And, indeed, there was more in Bevin's argument that his critics cared to admit. By the time the Labour Government fell, it had not succeeded in carrying into law a single socialist measure. Dependent as it was upon Liberal votes for its survival, its record of achievement (for example, Wheatley's Housing Act) was creditable, but nothing could disguise the fact that it was in office, not in power. In Bevin's view, the situation had not fundamentally changed. The capitalist system was intact, public control had not been established over a single industry, the status of the working class—and its wages—remained unaffected by the fact, however gratifying, that Ramsay MacDonald was occupying No. 10 Downing Street and the Cabinet contained seven former trade unionists out of a total of twenty. In Bevin's eyes it would have been political sentimentality to abandon, for reasons as insubstantial as this, disputes which had been begun before Labour came into office and which, if compromised now, would have produced great discontent in the Union without any corresponding advantage to the Government.

Nor did the rank-and-file members of the Union disagree with Bevin. They had waited a long time to recover the wage cuts they had suffered and to see some practical benefit from the Union they supported. They saw no reason why, the first time they gained the advantage in a dispute, they should not press it home simply because a Labour Government was in office. If that fact made the employers more reluctant to fight it out, so much the better: what did they pay the political levy and support the Labour Party for, if not to secure such advantages? No one could say the employers were reluctant to take advantage of the Tories being in office to force wages down and use the power of the State to defeat the miners. It was too high a price to pay for office if the only way the Labour Government could retain the Parliamentary support of the Liberal Party was to take sides against the unions in the legitimate defence of their members' industrial interests. If that was going to happen, then the Labour

1 *The Record*, April 1924, p. 12.

Party had better not accept office again without a majority in the House of Commons—the conclusion which Bevin drew when he moved a resolution to this effect at the 1925 Party conference.[1]

In the long run, however, the issue raised by the 1924 strikes could not be settled as simply as that. Historically, it was true, the Labour Party was the creation of the trade unions and still depended on them for financial support. But once it came to power, it was bound to assume national responsibilities which might conflict with the immediate sectional interests of the trade unions. Bevin was unwilling to face this issue in 1924. He argued that it was premature until a Labour Government was in power with a sufficient majority to carry through its programme. This argument was not without force in the circumstances of 1924. But the issue was only postponed. When the Labour Government came back after the election of 1945 with an absolute majority in the Commons, it had to insist in the national interest on a policy of wage restraint which placed a heavy strain on the loyalty and forbearance of the trade unions. By then Bevin had acquired a broader view of politics than he possessed in 1924. Influenced, no doubt, by the fact that he was a leading member of the 1945 Government and no longer a trade-union secretary, he held firmly to the belief that it was in the long-term interests of the trade unions to support the Government's policy. So, fortunately, did his successor, Arthur Deakin, who with real courage and at the cost of considerable unpopularity threw all the weight of the Transport and General Workers' Union on the side of political responsibility.

14

The Labour Government had other strikes to contend with before it ended its short term of office, notably in the building trades and the shipyards. Industrial unrest was on nothing like the scale that the years 1919–21 had seen, but Ministers were sensitive to the Tory taunt that they could not control their own supporters and inclined to exaggerate the damage which the strikers did to the Government's reputation.[2] A major coal strike was averted, largely thanks to the

1 See below pp. 258–60.
2 Cf. Arthur Henderson's remark to Sidney Webb, quoted by Beatrice Webb:

efforts of the Labour Secretary for Mines, Emmanuel Shinwell, and Bevin used all his influence to prevent the militant leaders of the London busmen from staging another hold-up of London's traffic.

The last big strike in which Bevin was involved was a fiasco. On 14th August, a dispute between the Covent Garden porters and the employers led to a stoppage of work which the Union recognised. It soon appeared, however, that Bevin and the Executive Council had been badly advised by the officers concerned. The men had a much weaker case than they had been led to believe and the report of the court of inquiry went in favour of the employers rather than of the men. Alternative arrangements for handling the fruit and vegetables worked only too well and the Union's organisation in the market broke down in face of the numbers of men resuming work. Bevin was left with a dispute which he could neither settle nor extend. On the one hand, the employers refused to meet him or to take back the men who had first walked out. On the other, a national strike involving the dockers and carters was out of the question on so ill-chosen an issue. After five weeks the Union had to call off the strike unconditionally, after spending £18,000 in paying dispute and victimisation benefits and without being able to get 400 of the men back to work.

His activities in 1924 had made Bevin the most hated and most abused man in the country. The Press and the public were delighted to see him taken down a peg. An unwise threat to extend the market strike and hold up all supplies was not forgotten. More than one paper wrote with satisfaction of his 'eclipse' and accused him of seeking to make trouble in order to magnify his own power. From the other side, he had to answer angry attacks on the officers responsible at the Biennial Delegate Conference of 1925 when the handling of the strike was debated. Bevin defended the officers and the Executive vigorously, insisting that the responsibility for any mistakes must be his, but he made no attempt to conceal the extent of the Union's failure.

"The Covent Garden dispute," he told the delegates, "is quite rightly debated at this conference. It was a failure. It is not the first and, possibly, it will not be the last. It has brought forth and taught its lessons."

"The epidemic of strikes reminds him of what was happening in Russia against the Kerensky Government". *Diaries, 1924–32* (1956), p. 18.

The first and most important of those lessons, Bevin argued, was never to let yourself be drawn into a strike except at a time of your own choosing and only then after the most careful preparation. The contrast between the highly organised and successful dock strike in February 1924 and the ill-prepared, unsuccessful Covent Garden strike in August could not have been plainer and Bevin, far from trying to blur the contrast, went out of his way to underline it.

By the time the Covent Garden strike collapsed, the Labour Government had more urgent cause for anxiety than its difficulties with the trade unions. Its clumsy handling of the Campbell case[1] aroused a political storm which led to its defeat on a vote of censure in the House. The Cabinet accepted the challenge, dissolved Parliament and appealed to the country. The election campaign was distinguished by the episode of the Zinoviev letter and the unscrupulous exploitation of a 'Red Scare' to whip up prejudice against the outgoing Government. Its result was a decisive victory for the Conservatives over both the other parties. Labour increased its popular vote by more than a million and had the satisfaction of seeing the Liberals suffer a far more crushing defeat. But nothing could alter the fact that the Tories were back in office with an absolute majority in the House of Commons and every prospect of remaining in power for the full term of five years.

---

1 J. R. Campbell, editor of the Communist *Workers' Weekly*, published an article urging soldiers, "neither in the class war nor in a military war", to turn their guns on their fellow workers. The Government first announced its intention of prosecuting Campbell under the Incitement to Mutiny Act of 1795, then abandoned the prosecution in face of a storm of protest from the Labour Party. Both the original intention and its abandonment were ill-judged.

CHAPTER 10

The Industrial Alliance and Red Friday

1924—1925

I

ANY ACCOUNT of Ernest Bevin's life which jumps from one head-line crisis to the next and ignores the nine out of ten negotiations which attracted no attention because they were settled without a strike is bound to be misleading. In a single quarter, for instance, selected at random (May–August 1924) we find Bevin reporting to his Executive that he has taken part in more than ninety different sets of negotiations with employers. Because it was continuous rather than dramatic in character, it is impossible to represent this large mass of detailed work except by occasional examples, although in fact it represented a much greater part of a General Secretary's day-to-day activity than leading strikes or intervening in politics. To correct a distortion of focus which it is easy to forget, it is worth while to halt the narrative for a moment before plunging into the events leading up to the General Strike and pick out two of the problems which occupied much of Bevin's attention in 1924–25.

Coal-mining apart, no British industry in the twentieth century has presented more intractable labour problems than the docks. By 1924 the registration of regular dock workers, started at Liver-pool in 1912, had been extended to all the big ports with the exception of Glasgow, Leith and Hull. A national agreement on wages and hours had been secured as a result of the Shaw Inquiry, and all but a small number of dock workers had been brought into a single organisation by the amalgamation.

Bevin was now bent upon two further reforms: the extension of registration to all the ports in the country (together with a more effective operation of the register where it already existed) and the provision of maintenance, a guaranteed minimum wage for every docker on the register.

By the agreement which ended the 1924 dock strike, both sides agreed to set up a joint committee with an independent chairman, Sir Donald Maclean, to strengthen registration and examine the proposal for a guaranteed week. Bevin was appointed a member of this committee: not only did he draft the schemes which the Maclean Committee discussed but his determination alone prevented it abandoning its task in face of the difficulties it encountered.

Few of the port employers liked a system of registration which imposed restrictions on their traditional right to engage casual labour as and when they liked. Even where a register was compiled, it was only too easy to place so many men on it that it soon ceased to be effective. The men themselves strongly resisted the need for periodical revision of the register on which Bevin equally strongly insisted. Bevin found himself faced with opposition or indifference from his own members, or with a tacit connivance on the part of employers and men in a particular port to ignore the system the Union was trying to establish.

The first business of the Maclean Committee was to make a survey of the extent to which registration had been adopted and made to work effectively. With the information brought to light by the Committee, Bevin (as chairman of the workmen's side of the National Joint Council for Dock Labour) and the Union's officials were able to keep up steady pressure in each port, without which most of the schemes would have broken down completely.

At the same time, Bevin drew up a plan for a guaranteed minimum wage, a first draft of which, based upon experiments at Bristol and Manchester, he placed before the Maclean Committee in February 1926. Arguing that the problem of the docks was under-employment, not un-employment, he proposed to divert the insurance contributions of the men, the employers and the State from the payment of unemployment benefit to the supplementation of a guaranteed wage equal to four days' work a week for every man on the port register. It was not until 1941 that Bevin as Minister of Labour was able to introduce the guaranteed wage on Clydeside and Merseyside, but in season and out of season he argued for it over more than twenty years and never allowed the dock industry to lose sight of it as the Union's ultimate objective.

2

The evils resulting from casual labour in the docks go back a long way. The 1956 Report of the Devlin Committee of Inquiry into the Port Transport Industry quotes the complaint of John Taylor, a London waterman in 1630: "Our hope is that we shall be as much reckoned of as horses, for horses have meat, drink and lodging, though they be but seldom ridden and many of them have a warm footcloth when thousands of serviceable men are likely to famish and starve through want and nakedness."[1] "Work or Maintenance" had been the slogan of the dockers' leaders as long ago as the great dock strike of 1889. The problems of the road transport industry, however, were new. Just as the motor-bus and the trolley-bus began to replace the trams in the towns, so the motor-lorry began to replace the horse-drawn van and cart at the end of the first World War.

To organise the drivers locally, as Bevin had done in the Bristol carters' branch of the Dockers' Union, was no longer sufficient. A new industry, long-distance road haulage, was springing up. But every sort of obstacle stood in the way of the national organisation which, Bevin believed, could alone be effective.

To begin with, road transport covered the widest variety of working conditions—the local delivery services maintained by shops and individual firms, from dairies to railways; the owner-driver prepared to work any hours at cut rates to make a living; the big road-haulage contractors like Pickford's or Carter Paterson's. There was no national organisation of employers and the industry was characterised by the large number of small firms who maintained a marginal existence by under-cutting each other. Any attempt to secure decent working conditions and wages for the men employed by such firms threatened their ability to go on operating, yet the bigger firms refused to make agreements which were ignored by contractors running one or two lorries and often driving themselves. In London alone the Union had to deal with three thousand employers. The men were as difficult to organise as the employers,

[1] Cmd. 9813 (1956), pp. 4-5.

constantly on the move and working alone, with little sense of solidarity, often on familiar terms with their employers (especially when employed by a small firm) and ready to ignore safety regulations and drive excessive hours for a few extra shillings or the chance of getting home for the night.

Public safety alone required the restriction of driving-hours, the regulation of speeds, limitation of loads (the number of trailers, for instance) and insistence on properly-maintained vehicles with adequate brakes. Not until 1930, however, and the Road Traffic Act of that year did the Union succeed in getting legislation carried to this effect, despite persistent representations to the Government.

Before the end of 1924 Bevin and the Union officers drafted a national programme for the industry, but in practice all that they were able to do was to negotiate agreements with the bigger firms or in particular areas. Even to secure so much required great efforts in organising the men. There was scarcely a meeting of the General Executive Council in the 1920s and 1930s when Bevin and the National Secretary of the Commercial Road Transport Group did not bring up some new proposal for extending membership among the lorry-drivers. The Union spent thousands of pounds on a series of such campaigns as the essential preliminary to fighting for the improvement of wages and hours of work.

Road transport long remained the weakest link in the trade-union organisation of the transport industries, far behind the dockers, the busmen or the railwaymen. It rarely got into the headlines, partly because the large number of employers and the lack of organised strength among the men made strike action impracticable. No industrial problem taxed Bevin's skill or patience more highly and none shows to better advantage the resources of both on which he could draw. For, in the end, he found a way round the worst difficulties and by the time he left the Union to become Minister of Labour had gone a long way towards enforcing organisation on both sides of the industry.

3

In 1924 Bevin bore the reputation of being the most aggressive trade-union leader in the country. Yet he had not forgotten the wartime discussions at Penscot and Bristol on a more fruitful co-operation between labour and management. Towards the end of September 1924, he went to Oxford where the Rowntrees had organised the nineteenth of a series of conferences for managers and foremen at Balliol.

Bevin argued that the old conception of management which excluded the workman from any voice in the direction of the industry on which he depended had to go and that, until it was abandoned, either appeals for co-operation or scolding the working man for indifference to the industrial situation of the country were so much waste of time. Why should he care, when any suggestion for the more efficient conduct of industry was rebuffed by management as intervention in a sphere in which no employee had any right to interest himself or any competence to express a view?

The extension of responsibility in management, however, could only succeed, if it was accompanied by a gradual change in the ownership of industry. Here Bevin had an interesting suggestion to make:

"Assuming that we recognise the right of profit, the royal road towards the democratisation of industry is to make accumulated reserves the property of the living industry itself. The conception that they are the property of the shareholders who have already been rewarded in the form of interest or profit must go, and such reserve capital must be regarded as the product and property of all who are contributing by hand and brain to the industry in question. The joint stock company was, after all, the logical development of industry from the old private owner and such a step would follow naturally upon the conception of a joint stock company.

"The struggle for economic possession is bound to come. How shall it come? Will public opinion welcome an expansion of possession and with it the extension of responsibility among the workers in industry? Or will public opinion, especially among the employing classes, be negative at best, at worst retrogressive and obstinate? That will mean revolt and probably violence and disaster."

Bevin made perfectly plain that his own preference was for a gradual and peaceful change, but he did not disguise his pessimism about the future.

"Experience has driven me," he told his audience at Oxford, "to the conclusion that we shall be drifting in the next five years towards a great upheaval. That is a hard statement to make, but I am on the inside. I see that, whatever we do, it will be almost impossible to satisfy the great masses of our people unless any forward step, whether we call it evolutionary or revolutionary, is based upon a real re-cast of values."[1]

4

Bevin's belief in the inevitability of a head-on clash grew stronger as the winter drew on. In an article which he contributed to *The Record* in December 1924, he picked up the phrase he had used at Oxford and wrote:

"Can a re-cast of values be accomplished without industrial conflict? I very much doubt it. . . . There must, I fear, be an assertion of power before the new values are recognised."

Bevin was right in speaking of 'values', for there was more at issue than the questions of wages and hours with which industrial relations were ostensibly concerned. What gave intensity to every dispute was the underlying moral conflict between two opposed attitudes. Employers and management still largely held to the view summed up in that phrase of the early industrial revolution 'masters and hands'. They were the masters, the men who took the decisions, who hired or fired the hands as they thought fit, without any need to give a reason or to consider how their decisions might affect the men they employed. In their eyes, their employees were 'hands' to whom they repudiated either obligation or relationship other than to pay a wage, and that at the lowest rate possible. For a hundred and fifty years working-men had hated and repudiated such a view. They too, they claimed, were human beings, not to be treated as if they were creatures of a lower order, without rights or status. From this sense of outrage, from rebellion against their inferior social and moral status, quite as much as from indignation at the actual poverty in which so many working-class families lived, sprang the bitterness of the class war. For the relations between the two sides of industry in the years up to 1926 can only be described as a class war in which neither side expected anything to be conceded except under threat. Bevin, like any other trade-union leader, had been brought up in a world in which either the masters or the men were on top and used

1 From Bevin's notes for his address.

their advantage to the full. Industrial relations were naturally conceived of in terms of a conflict in which whatever was good for the men must be bad for the masters and the other way round.

Long before the General Strike Bevin asked himself why this should be so, even without a socialist revolution, if both sides could be brought to take an intelligent view of their own interests. His experience of arguing with employers and management across the negotiating table, however, had taught him the futility of hoping that persuasion could effect a change. By the autumn of 1924 he had reached the conclusion that the industrial conflict which had so far marked the history of the 1920s with its record of strikes and lock-outs would have to work itself out, most probably in an open clash of force, before any change became practicable. In November 1924, he warned his Executive to prepare for trouble:

"It is obvious that the great body of reaction in the House of Commons will badger the Government to back them in an attack on Labour in the industrial field and it may indeed be the prelude of a real struggle."[1]

As part of the preparation, Bevin presented the Executive with a memorandum on the policy to be adopted by the Union in relation to all wage claims, negotiations and strikes. He looked upon strike action as a weapon to be employed sparingly, and his memorandum, which was approved by the Executive Council, embodied several of the lessons to be drawn from the Covent Garden affair. Its main purpose was to tighten the Executive's control and to make sure that, if the Union became involved in a strike, it should do so deliberately, with full knowledge of the facts and the consequences in the possession of the Executive first.

"Sectional stoppages," he wrote, "must be discouraged, especially those of a lightning character. The experience of the Union during the past three years is that lightning strikes are the reverse of successful; that their cost is very heavy and that, following upon their termination, they invariably result in loss of prestige to the Union and loss of membership."

Behind this was a desire on Bevin's part, not to avoid a fight, but to avoid being drawn or provoked into unnecessary strikes which would fritter away the Union's resources. The dock and tram strikes

1 General Secretary's Quarterly Report, November 1924.

had cost the Union £130,000 and the year 1924 was to show an excess of expenditure of more than £78,000 over a total income of less than half a million. Bevin was no longer so anxious about the amalgamation. Thanks in part to the successful strikes of the spring, 1924 saw an increase of 65,000 (over 21 per cent) in membership. But he wanted to husband his resources and hold his fire for the major battle which he thought it likely the Union might have to face.

5

Bevin, however, was interested in more than his own Union. At their previous meeting, in August 1924, he remarked to his Executive that he hoped one result of the appointment of an Assistant General Secretary would be "sufficient freedom to enable me to take my proper place in the various councils of the movement which I have found it necessary to forgo during the past two and a half years."

Of what was he thinking when he said this? Hardly of the Labour Party, to the National Executive of which he declined nomination by his own Executive.

Bevin's attitude to the Labour Government had not been accidental. It sprang naturally from his view of the Labour Party as a working-class party, concerned with the promotion of working-class interests in the political field as the trade unions were in the industrial. He had little sympathy for the Party's efforts to broaden its original role of political agent of the trade unions into that of an independent national party drawing members from any class on the basis of a common belief in socialist principles. This was the role of the Party as MacDonald saw it, but not at all as Bevin and many of the other trade-union leaders saw it.

Bevin had become a socialist by experience. He distrusted those who joined the Labour Party from intellectual conviction, from conscience or the characteristic mixture of frustration and rebellion, rather than by simple virtue of belonging to and sharing the experience of the working-class. He resented the patronising attitude of many Socialist intellectuals towards "ignorant trade unionists" like himself and viewed with the scorn of a man immediately involved in the industrial battle the discussion of Socialist principles unrelated to the realities of working-class life.

In an article printed in *The Record* in May 1924, Bevin commented on the call of G. D. H. Cole[1] for "a new workers' organisation" to remedy the 'failure' of the Labour movement and to make its definite purpose "intensive thinking and extensive propaganda of the results of thought".

"There is no need to retire from the movement, in order to think," Bevin wrote; "members can do all the thinking they want inside, and to much better purpose.
"New organisations are not wanted. If there is one thing that has retarded the progress of the Movement it is the continual popping up of new factions who imagine that the workers can be *led* from Capitalism to Socialism by the simple method of carrying out a set of rules based upon such knowledge of the working class as has been gleaned from the theoretical treatises in the University library. The workers will never be *led* out of the land of bondage; they will *get* out. . . .
"To understand the workers one must live with them and work with them. . . . The men and women who make up our Movement will go no further and no faster than *their* appreciation of economic facts will allow them. . . ."

There was another reason for Bevin's impatience with the politicians of the Labour Party. He lived in a world dominated by the industrial conflict, a world in which he had all the time to deal with hard, often unpalatable facts and to take real decisions. The politicians lived in a different world where Parliamentary manœuvres, Party resolutions and conference speeches were neither taken nor meant to be taken literally, a world in Bevin's eyes of make-believe, of shadow politics and sham decisions.

Bevin's view did less than justice to the lot of any party in opposition. Even when the Labour Party held office it was still in a minority. The first task of the Party was propaganda; it had to appeal to and win over the unconverted. After the defeat of 1931, Bevin saw this clearly enough, but in 1924–5 he was too close to the immediate industrial conflict to take a long view of the Labour Party's problems.

On the politicians' side there was less understanding than there might have been of the real difficulties with which trade-union leaders like Bevin had to contend. Of all the Labour politicians, MacDonald, with his upper-class tastes, his lack of industrial ex-

1 In an article in *New Standards*.

perience and air of aloofness, had least sympathy with the trade-union side of the movement. He and Bevin each embodied many of the characteristics which the other most disliked in the Labour movement and neither had much time for the other. MacDonald was furious with Bevin's independent attitude during the dock and tram strikes which he condemned as plain disloyalty. "Disloyalty?" Bevin retorted:

"There is one thing that the politicians in our Movement must remember, that on the Trade Union and industrial side they were given a loyalty unprecedented in the history of any Party. Even when certain factions in the I.L.P. particularly, and the late Prime Minister himself, set out to lecture us, we refrained from retaliation."[1]

For once, Bevin would have warmly agreed with Beatrice Webb if he had seen what she wrote in her journal on 15th March, 1924, only three months after the first Labour Government was formed:

"It was MacDonald who alone determined who should be in his Cabinet; it is MacDonald who alone is determining what the Parliamentary Labour Party shall stand for in this country. . . . And it is clear that the Prime Minister is playing-up—without any kind of consultation with the majority of his colleagues or scruple or squeamishness about first pronouncements—towards the formation of a Centre Party. . . . MacDonald wants 8 million voters behind him and means to get them . . .
"I do not accuse him of treachery," added Mrs. Webb, "for he was never a Socialist, either revolutionary like Lansbury or administrative like the Webbs; he was always a believer in individualist political democracy tempered in its expression by Utopian Socialism. Where he has lacked integrity is in *posing* as a Socialist and occasionally using revolutionary jargon."[2]

At the beginning of the next year, Bevin was writing in the Union journal:

"I have not much faith that the middle class politician will give us Socialism; the type of mind revealed in the last Government indicated a mid-Victorian outlook."[3]

1 *The Record,* January 1925, p. 122.
2 *Diaries* 1924–32, pp. 13–14.
3 *The Record,* January 1925, p. 122.

6

The fall of MacDonald's Government in October 1924 was followed by disillusionment and recrimination in the Labour Party. MacDonald had to face widespread criticism of his leadership. Many who had kept silent out of loyalty while the Party was in office felt that MacDonald had leaned over backwards in his anxiety to show that a Labour Government could be as official and 'responsible' as any other and to demonstrate that middle-class fears were groundless. Even his record in foreign affairs, where he had been at his best, was marred by his clumsy handling of the Zinoviev letter. Amongst those who wanted to see him replaced in the leadership of the Party were some strange allies—Philip Snowden, the I.L.P., Brailsford and Bevin. Any chance of forcing him out, however, broke down in face of the loyalty of Arthur Henderson, the obvious man to take his place, and of Henderson's conviction that MacDonald alone had the political gifts and prestige to lead the Party.

If MacDonald was to remain leader, Bevin wanted a pledge that at least the Party would never again accept office without a majority in the House of Commons. He had no chance to put his case until nearly a year after the end of the first Labour Government, at the Liverpool conference of the Labour Party in September 1925. By then the mood in the Party had changed but Bevin insisted on moving a resolution from the floor calling on the Party not to accept office again as a minority government.

Bevin did his best, in opening the debate, to avoid criticism of the decision to accept office in 1924 or of MacDonald's leadership, but his distrust and his inexperience of politics stood out in every sentence of his speech.

"I want to suggest, with a fairly good knowledge of trade unionists, that what they want is as straight a line in politics as they are compelled to take in industrial affairs, and if the great mass of working men in the country knew that if they wanted legislation as laid down by the Conference, they must give the Party a majority, it would be a very strong position. . . . I object to tactics and to manœuvring, and I think you will win quicker and get greater power if you are absolutely straight on that issue.

"Is there," he asked, "a single resolution that has been carried at this conference, that you could get through the House of Commons with Labour in a

minority? If you cannot do that, then you must be prepared to compromise, and if you compromise you will destroy the confidence of the
people in sending you to the House to represent them."

This statement was greeted with cries of "Question", but Bevin
retorted:

"I do not know whether you question it as trade unionists, but I do know the
standard set for me as a negotiator and why you should set up a different
standard for me as a negotiator for wages than you do for the politician who
has greater power in the House of Commons, I do not know . . .
"If I were in Parliament and called upon to take office and represent a great
movement like ours, I would not accept it unless, when I spoke to other
Nations or to our own people, I was able to speak with the power which
rested on the knowledge that I had a majority behind me both inside the
House and outside in the Nation."[1]

Bevin's views received little support. The conference was against
him. The miners moved the previous question in the hope of stopping further discussion and, when that failed, spoke and voted in
opposition. In the months since the fall of the Labour Ministry
(the last conference had been held on the eve of its resignation)
sufficient time had elapsed for the delegates to become dismayed at
the prospect of an indefinite prolongation of Tory government. The
miners in particular, faced with a major industrial struggle, were
anxious to see a Labour Government in office again on any terms.
With the support of a witty speech from J. H. Thomas who made fun
of Bevin's innocence of tactics, MacDonald had no difficulty in
persuading the conference that to vote in support of the resolution
would be to tie the Party's hands without knowing the circumstances
in which it might be urgent for it to take office even with minority
support. A declaration that they would never take office without a
majority, MacDonald added, would only lose the Party votes at an
election.

Bevin was angered by his failure to carry the conference with him
and let his true feelings appear in his reply to the debate. He spoke
with contempt of "the politician's clever art", of "the dictatorial
attitude" shown by MacDonald and roused a storm of interruption
by referring to the deal MacDonald had made with the Liberals to
secure his election at Leicester before the war.

1 Labour Party Conference Report, 1925, p. 244.

"We are spending our money in politics and trying to build up the Party, but when we have done it and are on the eve of victory we may find the Party coalescing with the Liberals or coalescing with the Tories."[1]

When the chairman restored order, Bevin let himself be side-tracked into defending his actions during the 1924 Government.

It was not an effective speech and Bevin threw away his case by losing his temper and trying to hector a hostile audience. When he insisted on a card vote he suffered a resounding defeat. Indeed the Liverpool conference was a triumph for the ex-Prime Minister who reasserted his hold over the Party after the divisions of the previous twelve months. Bevin took his defeat hard and made no effort to conceal his feeling against MacDonald. When W. J. Brown, the Secretary of the Civil Service Clerical Association, remarked to Bevin that he had been shocked by the hatred MacDonald showed in referring to him privately as "a swine", Bevin replied with equal intensity: "Ah, you've found him out, then? We all do sooner or later."[2]

7

In describing Bevin's attitude to the Labour Party we have been carried in advance of the narrative to which we must now return in the winter of 1924–5.

Long before his rebuff at the Liverpool conference, it was clear that Bevin did not look to the Labour Party to take a leading part in the 'show-down' which he had come to consider only a matter of time between the unions on the one side and the employers, with the support of the Tory Government, on the other. Nor had he any faith in the political Left represented by James Maxton, John Wheatley and the Clydeside group which was carrying the I.L.P. towards an open breach with MacDonald. His views on the I.L.P. with its doctrinaire, sectarian socialism, had always been caustic and he did not revise them when the I.L.P. moved to the left and began to proclaim revolutionary socialism in increasingly shrill tones.

The trade unions, in Bevin's view, would have to rely on their own strength which they should proceed to mobilise, without paying

1 Ibid., p. 251.
2 W. J. Brown: *So Far* (1934), p. 132.

much attention to what was happening in the Labour Party or accepting advice either from MacDonald and the Right or the I.L.P. and the Left. There were many in the trade-union movement who shared this view, which reflected the same mood of disillusionment with political action that had taken hold of the trade unions in 1911–12.

The presidential address at the Hull Congress of the T.U.C. early in September 1924, though diplomatic in its references to a Labour Government still in office, was couched in terms of which Bevin wholeheartedly approved. The president, Alf Purcell, told the conference:

"Even the Labour Party having a sufficient majority and in power leaves us still confronting capitalism on the field—capable of resistance and with the will to resist to the last ditch. A well-disciplined industrial organisation is the principal weapon of the workers—a weapon to strike with, if need be."[1]

These words form an apt introduction to the course followed by the trade-union movement between the Hull T.U.C. (September 1924) and the General Strike, a course to the left of the Labour Party and increasingly independent of it.

The new course had already begun to be charted before the Hull Congress, during Purcell's year of office as chairman of the General Council. Purcell, a french polisher by trade, an organiser of the Furnishing Trades Association and M.P. for Coventry from 1923 to 1924, was highly critical of the reformist tendencies of MacDonald's Government and attracted towards Communism. Several of the more moderate members of the General Council—J. H. Thomas, Gosling and Margaret Bondfield—had resigned on their inclusion in the Government, and a left-wing group composed of Purcell, George Hicks of the Bricklayers, and Alonzo Swales of the Engineers took the lead in the General Council during 1924 and 1925.

The early 1920s had already seen a considerable concentration of trade-union power by the process of amalgamation: close on half the affiliated membership of 4,300,000 at the 1924 T.U.C. was organised in six major amalgamations or federations, the miners, the railwaymen, the transport workers, the engineers, the iron and steel and the building workers. If the trade unions were going to act

1 T.U.C. Report, 1924, p. 68.

effectively, they must carry this process a stage further. So proposals for a fighting alliance which had lapsed after the failure of the Triple Alliance were revived, together with the demand to strengthen the powers of the T.U.C.

The General Council still fell far short of that general staff of the industrial movement which Bevin and many others had hoped to see it become. The changed mood of the unions at the Hull Congress, however, opened new possibilities.

First, George Hicks asked Congress on behalf of the General Council to give it the right to intervene in the event of a breakdown in industrial negotiations which affected other bodies of workpeople outside the industry, and, if necessary, to "organise all such moral and material support as the circumstances may appear to justify".

Second, the General Council presented a clear statement of trade-union aims (known as the Industrial Workers' Charter) which, at a time when the Labour Government had failed to introduce a single socialist measure, committed the T.U.C. unequivocally to the nationalisation of land, mines and railways.

Third, on the invitation of the miners, Congress instructed the General Council to draw up a scheme for the concentration of the workers in each industry into a single union.

All three proposals were carried, the first by an overwhelming majority, the second unanimously. The third resolution, in favour of industrial unionism, met with greater opposition from the craft as well as from the general workers' unions. It found little favour in Bevin's eyes, but he was otherwise well satisfied with the disposition which the General Council and Congress showed to follow an independent policy and, as a necessary preliminary, to concentrate the power of the industrial movement more effectively.

8

The second direction in which the General Council's move to the Left carried it was one with which Bevin had much less sympathy. No step taken by the first Labour Government roused more opposition amongst Tories and Liberals than the resumption of diplomatic relations with the Soviet Union and the negotiation of two draft Anglo-Soviet treaties designed to open the way for a

British loan to Russia. This opposition no doubt helped to strengthen the determination of many in the Labour movement who were far from being Communists to establish closer relations at other levels than the diplomatic. In the course of 1924, a Russian trade-union delegation was invited to Britain and for the first time a Russian fraternal delegate, Michael Tomsky, chairman of the All-Union Central Council of Trade Unions,[1] addressed the T.U.C. at Hull. He was given a warm reception and Congress endorsed the action of the General Council in attempting to bring about a joint meeting between the International Federation of Trade Unions, with its headquarters at Amsterdam, and the rival Red trade-union international, with its headquarters at Moscow.

The intensity of Tory and Liberal propaganda on the 'Red scare' at the 1924 election and the use made of the Zinoviev letter gave a further stimulus to the campaign for reunification between the two internationals to which the General Council, under the leadership of Purcell and Hicks, was now committed. In November and December 1924 a strong delegation from the Council visited the Soviet Union and later sponsored a proposal for a joint conference. When this proposal ran into violent opposition from the Continental trade unions, the General Council went ahead on its own and invited Russian representatives to attend a meeting in London in April 1925. An Anglo-Russian Joint Advisory Council was set up and the T.U.C. undertook to summon an international unity conference on its own initiative, if the I.F.T.U. persisted in its refusal. This proposal was again endorsed unanimously by the 1925 T.U.C. at Scarborough.

Bevin took no part in these transactions which failed, in the end, to produce any permanent result, but they are further evidence of the trend to the Left in the trade-union movement at this time.

In the meantime, the miners, facing a renewed battle with the coalowners, took up again the role of industrial pacemakers which they had played at the time of the Triple Alliance. Apart from their dour and unyielding president, Herbert Smith, they found a new leader in Arthur Cook, who became the secretary of the Miners' Federation during the course of 1924 in succession to the ambitious and pliable Frank Hodges. A. J. Cook, although no more than thirty-nine, had long been known as a fire-brand and the miners'

1 A member of the 'Right Opposition' of 1928–29, Tomsky committed suicide during the Stalinist purge of 1936.

choice of him as their secretary was symptomatic of their mood. He
had helped Noah Ablett to write the syndicalist pamphlet *The
Miners' Next Step* (1912) and had served his apprenticeship as a union
official in the militant South Wales Miners' Federation. Twice im-
prisoned for his strike activities and now a member of the Communist Party and the Minority Movement, Cook was the advocate
of uncompromising class-war and a policy of direct industrial action.
Beatrice Webb described him as the 'Billy Sunday' of the Labour
movement, "an inspired idiot, drunk with his own words, dominated
by his own slogans. I doubt whether he even knows what he is going
to say or what he has just said."[1]

Cook was a man of complete personal integrity, devoted to the
cause of the miners and possessed of great powers of revivalist
oratory. Caring little for the routine duties of administration, he set
out to visit each of the coalfields in turn and whip up the long-
smouldering anger of the miners. He succeeded to such an extent
that he was listened to and trusted more widely than any miners'
leader had ever been: not even Keir Hardie had been able to
express and arouse such passionate intensity of feeling among the
miners. He wasted no time on the niceties of policy or tactics, of
which, indeed, he understood little. He confined his agitation to two
points, the need for unity and the need to fight.

At the Hull Congress, Cook strongly supported the plan to increase
the powers of the T.U.C. and spoke eloquently of the need for unity.
At the same time, the miners took the lead in advocating the
formation of an industrial alliance to include, this time, the engineers
as well as the transport workers and the railwaymen. It was through
this proposal that Ernest Bevin was drawn into the new course of
trade-union policy.

9

The Tory-inspired attack upon the trade unions and their members'
wages which Bevin and many others expected after the defeat of the
Labour Government did not materialise. Although there were some
members of the Cabinet and many on the back-benches who were
not averse to a 'show-down' with the unions, the Prime Minister,

[1] *Diaries*, 1924–1932, p. 116.

Stanley Baldwin, did not share their views. With considerable courage, he refused to support a Conservative private member's Bill aimed at removing the unions' power to levy their members for a political fund and in the course of his speech made his famous plea for "peace in our time".

"We, at any rate," the Prime Minister declared, "are not going to fire the first shot. . . . We believe we know what the country wants, and we believe it is for us in our strength to do what no other Party can do, and to say that we at any rate stand for peace."[1]

The trade unions remained sceptical, but they too were not anxious to fire the first shot and for the first few months of 1925 an uneasy industrial truce prevailed.

It was shattered by the Government's decision at the end of April to return to the gold standard at the pre-war parity of the pound to dollar. This step, recommended by the Cunliffe Committee in 1918, had long been regarded by the Bank of England and the bankers as the essential condition of a return to 'economic reality' which at the same time would restore the prestige and power of the City as the principal money-market of the world. By the spring of 1925 the foreign exchange position was judged to be sufficiently favourable for the step to be taken and on 28th April the new Chancellor of the Exchequer, Winston Churchill, announced the necessary legislative changes in the course of his Budget speech.

J. M. Keynes was almost alone among economists in his criticism of the Government's policy. He composed three articles for the *Evening Standard* which were published as a pamphlet under the title, *The Economic Consequences of Mr. Churchill.* Keynes fastened on the effects of a restoration of the gold standard on British industry, particularly the export industries, the interests of which had been subordinated, he claimed, to the preoccupation of the bankers with London's position as a centre of international banking and exchange. By returning to the gold standard at the pre-war parity of the pound with the dollar, Keynes argued, the pound was over-valued by as much as ten per cent. This meant an immediate rise in the price at which British exports sold abroad. In order to avoid pricing themselves out of overseas markets, the export industries (the very industries worst hit by the trade depression and unemployment) would

1 6th March 1925.

have to drive their costs down by an equivalent amount. How was this to be done? It could only be done by reducing wages. "Mr. Churchill's policy of improving the exchange by 10 per cent is, sooner or later, a policy of reducing everyone's wages by 2s. in the £." If the workers resisted such reductions (thereby preventing the necessary fall in export prices), this in turn could only lead to greater unemployment through the loss of overseas markets to foreign competitors.

Keynes urged that at the very least the Government ought to meet the responsibilities it was creating by making sure that the sacrifices were equally borne. Amongst the measures he suggested were a 5 per cent levy on all wages as well as salaries, together with a shilling increase in the income tax. This advice was ignored. The workers in the export industries were left to bear the brunt of the adjustment and, apart from a temporary subsidy to the coal industry wrung from it by the determined resistance of the trade unions, the Government washed its hands of any responsibility for the consequences of its action.

The return to the gold standard did not create the difficulties from which Britain's staple industries were suffering in the 1920s. Those sprang from the fact that Britain was no longer the workshop of the world. With the rise of industrial competitors (in the United States, Germany, Japan) her share of international trade was bound to contract. Even the war and the unsettled conditions which followed afford only a partial explanation, for the problem would have had to be faced, whether there had been a war or not. But the restoration of the gold standard, especially at the pre-war parity, meant an over-valuation of the pound which handicapped the efforts of the export industries to adapt themselves to the changed situation and imposed a heavy additional burden upon them.

Even more to the point for a trade-union leader like Ernest Bevin, it left that burden to be borne almost entirely by the working class. It may be true that the worse consequences of a deflationary policy did not follow, that wages were not forced down to the extent Keynes feared,[1] but this was only thanks to the resistance of the unions and is, in any case, hardly an argument in favour of a policy which was thereby prevented from achieving its object. In the end, the national economy received few of the benefits which on abstract

1 As Sir Henry Clay argues in his life of Lord Norman (pp. 156–7).

economic grounds might be put forward as arguments for adopting such a policy, while the country found itself plunged into an inevitable series of industrial conflicts culminating in the General Strike of 1926.

The industrialists were far from enthusiastic about the change announced by Churchill. Had their views been given as much weight as those of the City, it is unlikely that the change would ever have been made. But, provided they could cut their prices abroad by reducing wages, they were prepared to accept it, or at least not to lead a protest against it, especially when it was presented as a reassertion of Britain's power and prestige by a Conservative Government. The trade unions, however, whose working members were expected to pay for this expensive gesture, could not be expected to accept its consequences so complacently.

10

Bevin commanded none of Keynes' subtle skill as an economist, but he was one of the first to grasp what the Government's announcement meant. Quite apart from the immediate effect on the wages of men employed in the export trades (and the docks) he saw no sense at all in a policy which artificially forced wages down when the obvious need, as he saw it, was an increase in purchasing power. In an article on the shipbuilding industry which he contributed to the *Herald* three weeks before Churchill's announcement, he wrote:

'The fact is that, with the tremendous development of productive capacity, in order to employ the whole of the unemployed and the employed, this country needs to consume or sell at least 60 per cent more goods. How can this be reconciled with the constant demand that the purchasing power of the largest consuming class shall be decreased?"[1]

The fact that the return to the gold standard had been made at the insistence of the bankers roused all his old suspicions of financial interests. Industry, by which the nation lived, was being sacrificed to the profit of financiers who were indifferent to what happened to those employed by industry, so long as they could make increased profits from their speculation and money-lending.

1 *Daily Herald*, 6th April 1925.

He went down to Swansea early in May for the annual conference of the tinplate workers. The Welsh tinplate industry was badly hit by foreign competition in its overseas markets and suffered heavily from 'slack time' and unemployment. Bevin used the occasion to give his views on trade conditions and ways in which they might be improved. He described the mistake the Government had made in restoring the gold standard as "one of the great disturbing factors of the normal development in this country to hold its place in the world's markets."

"The restoration of the gold standard will, in my judgment, only result in an intensification of the unemployment problem. . . . The bankers have too much power; the Cunliffe Committee paid too little regard to trade; and the Government adopted the view that finance must take first place."

Bevin told his audience that they had better give up any idea of eliminating foreign competition:

"The new world conditions cannot be met by trying to compete in the same manner as hitherto: namely, a race in lengthening hours of labour and reducing standards of living. That way will never bring prosperity. The nations have ruled largely according to the view that if you can only reduce the standard of living there will be some other public in the world that is going to consume enough to keep trade going, but you cannot get away from the fact that the public in the main with whom you have to exchange is composed of the workers themselves in other countries. And if every country is setting out to reduce the consuming power of its population, how on earth are you going to improve trade?"[1]

As Bevin went on to argue, if the employers persisted in reducing wages, productive capacity was bound to outstrip consumption.

I I

No industry was so certain to be affected by the return to the gold standard as coalmining. Two lean years in the coalfields had been followed by an artificial boom in 1923, thanks to the French

[1] His speech was subsequently printed as a pamphlet: *A Review of Trade Conditions and their Effect upon Unemployment*, published by the T.G.W.U. (July 1925).

occupation of the Ruhr and the sharp drop in German production. That year, British coal exports reached the record figure of 79 million tons. The Miners' Federation thereupon gave notice to end the 1921 agreement and negotiated a new settlement, more satisfactory to the men, to run from June 1924. The fact that a Labour Government was in office, no less than the increased profits earned in 1923–4, no doubt helped to make the owners more amenable to bargaining. Unfortunately, the new agreement was out of date almost as soon as it was concluded. With the French withdrawal from the Ruhr and the negotiation of a new reparations agreement under the Dawes Plan (1924), German coal exports shot up and the volume as well as the price of British exports slumped.

To meet this situation and to offset the increase in prices caused by the revaluation of sterling, the coalowners fell back on the one remedy they proposed for all difficulties: lower wages and longer hours. Keynes' prophecy that the miners would be the first "victims of the economic juggernaut" was proved to be only too true.

"They represent in the flesh the 'fundamental adjustments' engineered by the Treasury and the Bank of England to satisfy the impatience of the City fathers to bridge the 'moderate gap' between $4.40 and $4.86. They (and others to follow) are the 'moderate sacrifice' still necessary to ensure the stability of the gold standard."[1]

On 30th June 1925, just two months after the restoration of the gold standard, the owners gave a month's notice of the termination of the 1924 agreement. Their new proposals, published the following day, not only meant an immediate reduction in wages but abolished the complicated provisions contained in the 1924 agreement which amounted to a national minimum wage. The owners' standard profit was to remain the same, however low wages might fall.

It was too easy for the owners to evade the necessity for the drastic reorganisation of an inefficient industry still using nineteenth-century methods by letting the whole of the economic burden fall on the mine-workers, while still guaranteeing their own continued rate of profit. Why, the miners asked, should the owners' lack of enterprise and incapacity for managing the industry efficiently be paid for by driving those who earned their profits for them down to a starvation level of wages? For their sheer lack of imagination, leave

1 J. M. Keynes, *The Economic Consequences of Mr. Churchill* (1925) p.23.

alone of humanity, the coalowners must bear a great share of the responsibility for the troubles which beset the industry in the 1920s.

Not unnaturally, their proposals touched off the accumulation of anger in the coalfields which had already been stirred by A. J. Cook's activities as an agitator. At a special conference in the Kingsway Hall, London, on 3rd July 1925, the miners not only rejected the new terms proposed by the owners but deliberately refrained from putting forward counter-proposals. This time they meant to fight: they were not prepared to discuss any proposals, Cook told the Minister of Labour, to accept mediation or to appear before a court of inquiry "that has for its object the ascertainment of whether mineworkers' wages can be reduced or their hours extended". On this they were adamant. They would only negotiate if the owners' proposals were withdrawn: neither Cabinet efforts at mediation nor the setting up of a court of inquiry by the Minister of Labour persuaded them to change their minds.

If the miners refused to accept the terms offered and came out on strike, would they come out alone? Everything, as both sides knew, turned on the answer to this question. In 1925, the miners could argue with every justification that a defeat for them would be the signal for a general attempt to force down wages. But the obvious truth of this had not prevented the breakdown of the Triple Alliance in 1921: would the same argument prove more effective now?

12

There had been further talk of a revived alliance during the winter and in March 1925 the Miners' Federation made definite proposals to a number of the other principal unions. On 3rd April, the Executive Council of the T.G.W.U. met the Miners' Executive and agreed to take part in a joint conference to be held on 4th June. The other unions invited to attend included the three railway unions, the A.E.U. and the Federation of Shipbuilding and Engineering Trades.

The conference met on the day fixed at the Midland Hotel, St. Pancras Station. Neither the miners nor their former allies had forgotten Black Friday and the atmosphere was cool. Their experience since had convinced Bevin and his Executive that the only effective way to secure the unity the Miners argued for was by amalgamation.

None the less a committee was appointed to carry the discussion further and report back to the full conference in July. Bevin agreed to serve on this committee and took a leading part on the small sub-committee which set to work on drawing up the draft constitution of a new Industrial Alliance.

Bevin approached this new commitment in a wary and sceptical frame of mind. No one more resented the criticism to which he had been subjected after the failure of the Triple Alliance and he was determined, at all costs, not to be involved in another Black Friday. Nor was he much affected by the left-wing tendencies of the T.U.C. group led by Purcell, Hicks and Swales which were now finding un-orthodox expression in *Lansbury's Labour Weekly*, started by George Lansbury at the end of February 1925. Always inclined to take an individual line of his own, suspicious and often scornful of other trade-union leaders, he shared neither the intellectual nor the emotional assumptions of the Left. Intensely practical in his judg-ment, he had as little sympathy for the revolutionary revivalism of an A. J. Cook or a Lansbury as he had for the doctrinaire syllogisms of the Marxists.

What moved Bevin to join in taking common action was a concrete situation, a situation demanding the organisation of working-class strength in order to prevent a general attack on wages led, as it had been in 1921, by the coalowners. Taught by hard experience that it was useless to appeal to the employers' sense of justice, humanity or even long-run identity of interests with their workpeople, he turned to industrial action not as a prelude to revolution but as a necessary "counter-assertion of power" designed to force the employing class and the Government to pay attention to the interests of the class he represented.

It is true that he failed to grasp fully the political implications of industrial action on the scale of a general strike, but if he had been prepared to admit them he would have rejected them, not welcomed them as some on the Left as well as the Communists certainly did. Bevin had no patience with those who wanted to play with re-volution. He saw the action he took in 1925 and 1926 in a different light, not as a challenge to the constitution, a first step towards the seizure of power, but as a legitimate act of industrial self-defence forced on the trade unions by the threat of aggression on the part of the employers with the connivance of a Tory Government.

The constitution of the Industrial Alliance in the framing of which he had the biggest part, was as practical and precise a document as he could make it.[1]

Besides the unions already invited the Alliance was to bring in the iron and steel industries and all forms of power production and distribution, especially the Electrical Trades Union. Special care was taken to prevent the confusion of authority which had led to Black Friday from recurring. With this in mind, the Constitution insisted that any union, before committing itself to a national stoppage, must communicate the whole circumstances and facts to the Alliance Executive and through them to the other unions; that the Executive should not have power to take action without the authority of the General Conference; and that, once such action had been sanctioned, *the conduct of the dispute should pass into the control of the Executive* (Clause 6).

To make doubly sure, clause 7 required the Executive to state in their recommendation to the General Conference the form and extent of the assistance proposed; clause 8 safeguarded the right of the Conference to decide whether to ratify any settlement, to order or terminate assistance, while clause 9 said specifically:

"The conditions of membership of this Alliance shall involve other allied organisations in definitely undertaking, notwithstanding anything in their agreements or constitutions to the contrary, to act as directed by the General Conference."

Finally, clause 14 regulated the conditions of withdrawal from the Alliance, insisting that any union desiring to secede must give a year's notice in writing and, during the expiration of the notice, continue to observe its obligations.

13

While the joint committee was still at work on the draft for the new Alliance, the coalowners' notices, delivered on 30th June and due to expire on 31st July, made it clear that the crisis in the mining industry would come to a head before the Alliance could be brought

[1] The text, together with the accompanying memorandum, is to be found in *The Record*, August 1925, pp. 11–13.

A. J. Cook speaking in Trafalgar Square.

The General Strike: food convoy passing down East India Dock Road led by an armoured car.

into being. Foreseeing this, the Miners' Federation decided to take advantage of the wider powers conferred on the General Council by the T.U.C. at its 1924 Congress. On July 10th the General Council received the Miners' Executive and after hearing a statement of their case announced that they "completely endorse the refusal of the Miners' Federation to meet the owners until the proposals have been withdrawn". They added that they placed themselves "without qualification and unreservedly at the disposal of the Miners' Federation", appointing a Special Industrial Committee of nine members to keep in continuous contact with the negotiations.

Negotiations had not yet begun, despite the efforts of the Government to get the two sides together. A week later (17th July) the executives of the unions involved in the Industrial Alliance, reinforced by the Iron and Steel Trades Confederation, the E.T.U. and the foundry-workers, met in plenary conference at the Essex Hall. As secretary of the drafting committee, Bevin presented the proposed constitution. He told his audience, as he had told his own Executive earlier in the day, that if they were prepared to accept the full implications of the document before them, there was a possibility of creating an effective alliance, but he warned them that, if they tried to whittle down the safeguards of the constitution, they would do better to drop the proposal altogether.

His advocacy had its effect. The assembled executives unanimously accepted the draft for consideration by their unions and the tone of the meeting, as well as the clear provisions of the scheme now published, gave strong encouragement to the miners. "Through the Industrial Alliance," Herbert Smith told the miners' special conference a month later, "we got such an atmosphere created in the trade union world as we have not had before." Once again, Bevin demonstrated the influence which his ability as an organiser gave him in the movement.

He was to confirm it when, three days later, the Biennial Delegate Conference of the T.G.W.U. assembled at Scarborough. It so happened that his own union was the first to be called upon to express its opinion of the new Alliance. Knowing the importance of the transport workers in the case of any action to prevent the movement of coal, Bevin was determined to secure the strongest support he could for the scheme he had sponsored.

By way of preparation, *The Record* for July carried a special article by the General Secretary in which he argued forcefully in favour of surrendering sectional autonomy for a greater measure of unity in the trade-union movement.

"I can only hope," he wrote, "that we shall rise to the occasion; not waste time squabbling over small things—temporary failures, internecine strife and difficulties—but rise above it and try to focus our minds upon the great things in a manner which will force us to say to ourselves: What effect will this, which I do today, have upon the people living in half a century or a century ahead?"[1]

When the conference met, Bevin wisely determined to deal with the question of the miners' dispute first and so forestall the efforts of the Press to play off the Industrial Alliance against the Miners' appeal to the General Council of the T.U.C. Such a move by the Miners, he told the delegates, was entirely right; it did not prejudice the question of the Alliance and, in order to leave no doubt in any-one's mind, he moved a resolution pledging full support to the Miners and full co-operation with the General Council in carrying out any measures they might decide to take.

"We have been told that this virtually means a revolution. . . . A re-volution in industry is not a serious thing. It is revolutionising itself every day in some form or another. But they will try and introduce the State. I would say a word to my Labour friends who are always raising the con-stitutional issue. It won't be raised by those of us who have to lead the strike. The question of the form of Government in this country will not come within the purview at all. . . .
"If Parliament says it is involved, it ought to make a general strike un-necessary by opening up negotiations and securing justice for this great body of men. . . . If Parliament stands by and says, as Baldwin has said, that this dispute must be settled between the parties, then I suggest, Mr. President, the constitutional issue is out of the way, the Miners have the right to come to their fellows and say: This being an issue between the owners and our-selves, with Parliament as looker-on, we have the right to ask for your assistance—and we have the right to give that assistance."

Bevin concluded with a strong plea, if it came to a strike, for strict self-control, and no incidents:

"I want this to be a cold-blooded, well-thought out, calculated, disciplined struggle if it does come. . . . We shall not win national gains out of the

1 *The Record*, July 1925, pp. 276–277.

struggle immediately. Not for one moment do I believe that you will pull down the citadel of capitalism about your ears. I do not for one moment think that you will jump a century, but the demonstration of power will usher in an era of constructive effort to follow which will lay a sound basis for the generation to come."[1]

The debate which followed showed remarkable unanimity in support of the miners as well as a clear realisation that the Union was surrendering its right of decision to the General Council. The resolution, passed without dissent, was sent off to the Government, the T.U.C. and the Miners' Federation.

14

Two days later, having cleared the immediate issue of support for the Miners out of the way, Bevin got up to move that the Union should accept the constitution of the Industrial Alliance (subject to confirmation by a vote of the branches) and make the necessary amendments in its own constitution, waiving the right to hold a ballot vote of the members in the event of the Alliance ordering a general strike.

He made no claim to responsibility for the scheme which he now laid before the conference, and, far from trying to influence the delegates to adopt his own point of view, underlined the need to make their minds up as coolly as possible.

"In the Labour movement you can always get a conference to talk unity, but when you begin to practise it you always get up against the constitutional rule . . .

"You cannot have autonomy and unity at the same time. That is impossible. You can have a great measure of autonomy but when it comes to a critical movement, like the present Miners' movement, it is a different matter . . .

"If there is any attempt to whittle down the vital principles of this Alliance there can be no Alliance. I am not going to have any more Black Fridays. . . . If the movement wants unity, let it have it. It is no use to keep talking about it, but let every member of the Union know what he is accepting. . . . If they are not prepared to take the risk, let them say so quite definitely and we cannot have an Alliance."

1 Verbatim record of the First Biennial Delegate Conference, 1925. A full report of this and the debate on the Industrial Alliance is to be found in *The Record* (August 1925), pp. 4–18.

With that he left it to the Delegates to decide:

"It is the future of the Union at stake. If men in this delegate conference cannot see their way to support this, I want there to be no glamour. I appeal for a full debate, if a man is opposed to it. I want to hear the opposition today as much as the support. . . . I do not want them shouted down but I would rather they said it. I want it debated coolly, in order that both sides can be brought out, and the risks you will be asked to undertake carefully examined. Then either accept or reject the resolution with open eyes."

The debate that followed was sober and shrewd. At the end of the day, the delegates voted (with only two dissentients) in favour of joining the Alliance and accepting the necessary limitations on their autonomy.

15

These two votes of the Transport and General Workers came at the psychological moment. The Government and the Press, watching eagerly for any sign of the disunity which had led to Black Friday, were reluctantly impressed; the miners, perhaps equally suspicious at heart, were similarly encouraged.

Before the week was out, two further important developments took place. On Thursday, 23rd July, the Miners' Executive had a frank discussion with the General Council's Committee and left no doubt that they were prepared to place their case in the hands of the General Council without reserve. Reassured on this point, the General Council decided not only to see the Prime Minister but to call on the executives of the railway and transport unions to prepare for an embargo on the movement of coal. The Miners at the same time sought and received promises of support in preventing coal reaching Britain from the International Transport Workers' and the International Miners' Federation.

The unions which were now called upon for practical assistance set up a small transport committee (with Bevin as one of its members) to draft the instructions needed to enforce the embargo. The policy was solidly endorsed by a special trade-union conference, and, with the announcement of plans to halt the movement of coal, it was clear that the Government would have to intervene if it wanted to avoid a general stoppage of industry.

On Monday, 27th July, the Prime Minister met a deputation from the General Council which had now become a principal in the dispute. Neither then nor in his discussion with the coalowners the following day was Baldwin able to make any progress towards a compromise. On the 29th he told the miners' leaders categorically that the Government would give no subsidy to the coal industry, although, as the miners pointed out, Government policy (in restoring the gold standard, for instance) had materially contributed to its economic difficulties. He proved quite unable, however, to shift the miners in their resolution to strike rather than to accept or even discuss the owners' proposals. When he turned to Herbert Smith and asked him what the miners were prepared to give in return for the reluctant concession by the owners of a minimum wage he received the laconic reply, "Nowt. We have nowt to give."

By the 30th, there were no more than thirty-six hours to go before the trade-unions' embargo came into effect. The whole day was spent in meetings, amongst them a special conference of union executive committees to hear the report of the T.U.C. Special Industrial Committee which had now approved the embargo instructions.

The thousand delegates gathered in Central Hall, Westminster, listened with anger to the miners' report that the Prime Minister had twice repeated the remark, "All the workers of this country have got to take reductions in wages to help put industry on its feet."[1] This was enough to settle any doubts. The conference approved the General Council's report, authorised the issue of orders to strike and, on Bevin's motion, agreed that all unions, whether involved in the dispute or not, would accept a common financial liability for any measures necessary to support the miners.

That night, instructions drafted by Bevin and Cramp of the N.U.R. were sent out, providing for a complete embargo on the movement of coal by rail, road or sea from midnight on 31st July.

Like most of the documents in which Bevin had a hand, it was a plain matter-of-fact statement, almost ostentatious in its avoidance of a single word of revolutionary or moral appeal. Its practical character only heightened its effect. The Cabinet met again that

1 Cf. R. Page Arnot, *The Miners: Years of Struggle*, p. 377, footnote 1.

night and by the afternoon of 31st July, the Prime Minister announced a settlement which, in view of his own earlier statements, represented a direct reversal of Government policy—under the threat of strike action by the trade-union movement. The owners agreed to suspend their notices, a Royal Commission was to inquire into the coal industry (the fourth inquiry in six years) and the Government, within two days of Baldwin's refusal of a subsidy, agreed to provide financial assistance up to 1st May 1926.

At 4 o'clock on the last day of July, the Miners' Federation sent out telegrams with the five words: "Notices Suspended. Work as usual. Cook, Secretary". The *Daily Herald* found all it needed to say in two words: RED FRIDAY.

The Mining Dispute
1925 — 1926

I

BALDWIN'S SURRENDER to the trade unions brought a storm of criticism about his head. The *Daily Express* described the subsidy as Danegeld, the *Daily Mail* wrote angrily of a "Victory for Violence". Baldwin, although never inclined to anticipate trouble, found it necessary to supplement his defence in the House of Commons by a warning to those who might be playing with the idea of a general strike. It was clear that opinion in the Conservative Party would not allow him to climb down in face of the unions' demands a second time. It was equally clear that there were members of his own Cabinet who were not at all averse to a 'showdown' with Labour. Sir William Joynson-Hicks, the Home Secretary, who was ready to see revolutionary dangers behind every lamp-post, told an audience at Northampton, "coming straight," as he said, "from Cabinet councils":

"The thing is not finished. The danger is not over. Sooner or later this question has got to be fought out by the people of the land. Is England to be governed by Parliament and by the Cabinet or by a handful of trade union leaders? If a Soviet is established here . . . a grave position will arise."[1]

The Government had not been ready to face the threat of an extended strike in July 1925. It now set to work to prepare plans for such an emergency. These plans have sometimes been described in terms appropriate to the machinery of the police state erected by a Hitler or a Stalin. This is as exaggerated as the inability of a Joynson-Hicks to tell the difference between the Central Committee

1 *The Times*, 3rd August 1925.

of the Russian Communist Party led by Lenin and Trotsky and the General Council of the T.U.C. Yet these fears and exaggerations were part of the atmosphere of 1925-6, without taking account of which much that happened is not to be understood.

Just as angry Tories fastened on the irresponsible declarations of A. J. Cook—"Next May, we shall be faced with the greatest crisis and the greatest struggle we have ever known, and we are preparing for it . . . I don't care a hang for any Government or army or navy. . . . We have already beaten not only the employers but the strongest Government in modern times"[1]—so the militants of the Communist Party and the I.L.P. seized on the recruitment of the O.M.S., the Organisation for the Maintenance of Supplies. Established by private initiative with the blessing of the Government, the O.M.S. called for volunteers and claimed to have recruited 100,000 by May 1926. The Left saw in the O.M.S. a body of legalised Blackshirts, and a number of British Fascists certainly joined the organisation. Average trade-union opinion, however, was better represented by the comment of Charlie Cramp, the Industrial Secretary of the N.U.R.:

"Personally, I have not the slightest fear of these jokers. They are people who have never worked in their lives. If they started to do it in a strike they would make a very poor job of it."[2]

Cramp's scepticism was largely justified by the later history of the O.M.S. The Government's serious preparations, however, were made by one of the ablest organisers of his generation, Sir John Anderson, then Permanent Under-Secretary at the Home Office. The country was divided into ten areas, each under a civil commissioner with his own staff of civil servants and local committees appointed in advance. Anderson's plans paid particular attention to the organisation of road transport and were sufficiently advanced to be communicated to local authorities in November 1925.

The object of these plans and of those prepared by the Services was not to intimidate the strikers, still less to employ armed force against them, but to maintain essential supplies and services. The maintenance of public order was to be left to the police, and troops

1 A speech of August 1925, quoted in W. H. Crook: *The General Strike* (1931), p. 295.
2 Quoted in Julian Symons: *The General Strike* (1957), p. 22.

were only to be called out in the last resort. The army was to be used, not to shell working-class quarters (as happened in Vienna in 1934), but to convoy food supplies, and the navy to keep the power stations running. The Government, in fact, took care to avoid provocation, but by the spring of 1926 was well-prepared for any emergency. If it had shown anything like the same initiative in approaching the problems of the coal industry, the emergency need never have arisen.

2

The first reaction of the Labour movement to the news of 'Red Friday' was one of astonishment—an illuminating comment on the extent to which the brave talk of united action had concealed doubts (in Bevin's mind as much as anyone else's) of the capacity of the working-class movement to make its strength felt. The walls of Jericho had fallen, or so it seemed for a day or two until second thoughts showed the insubstantiality of the triumph. "We have no need to glorify about a victory," Herbert Smith told the miners at their delegate conference on 19th August. "It is only an armistice and it will depend largely how we stand between now and 1st May next year[1] . . . as to what will be the ultimate result." But even Herbert Smith's Yorkshire canniness could not prevent him adding that, so far as common action was concerned, "it has been a glorious victory for unity of purpose."

What conclusions were to be drawn from the events of July? The Left had no doubts. Beatrice Webb noted in her diary, on 16th September:

"A. J. Cook on behalf of the T.U. Left and Maxton and Wheatley on behalf of the Clyde talk about immediate revolution, whilst George Lansbury thunders threats of the immediate dissolution of Capitalist civilisation."[2]

The Left, however, represented only a small minority in the working-class movement, given disproportionate importance by the attention its windy assertions attracted. The majority on both the industrial and the political sides of the movement had no intention

---

1 The Government subsidy was to be paid for nine months, from 1st August 1925 to 30th April 1926.

2 *Diaries*, 1924–32, pp. 70–71.

of taking part in a revolution or in a general strike aimed at the seizure of power.

In an article which he wrote for the *Herald* in August 1925, Bevin condemned loose talk of taking up arms and forming a Labour defence corps to fight Fascism as irresponsible. Labour's weapon was passive resistance carried out through the strike: "it is useless to try and jump periods by any short cut in the way of physical warfare methods."[1]

Bevin discussed the situation with his Executive in the third week of August:

"I do not think," he told the Council, "that the time has arrived for any 'cock-a-hoop' attitude. The other side studied the recent movement and will organise against us; moreover, they have clearly learnt the value of waiting—and if we tried the same move a second time it is just as easy to be smashed.

"The one essential thing to concentrate upon at this stage is to discipline our movement. After all, much as we may criticise the other side and deny their competence, they have learnt the art of governing, with this advantage, that they draw their power from comparatively small numbers; whilst we have large masses, and, by too much shouting, may give a wrong idea of success and lead to extravagant assumptions.

"If the other side could once get us to take up arms, then we shall be playing their game and it will be the excuse they want to take up arms against the people in civil strife. . . . Resorting to physical force is the way to set the clock back a century . . . I have no doubt that if the best brains of the movement are brought to bear coolly upon the situation, we can utilise this demonstration of power in such a constructive way as to prove of immense benefit for generations to come."[2]

It was in this frame of mind, thinking of industrial action as a "demonstration of power", a form of passive resistance to force the other side to look to other means than a reduction of wages to solve the economic problem, that Bevin travelled up to Scarborough for the opening of the Trades Union Congress on 7th September.

1 *Daily Herald*, 24th August 1925: "Should the Workers take up arms?" Cf. Bevin's reply to John Wheatley in the same paper, 17th September 1925.
2 General Secretary's Quarterly Report, August 1925.

3

The 1925 T.U.C. has frequently been described as the high-water mark of the leftward trend in the trade-union movement. Swales, of the Engineers, who presided, called for a "militant and progressive policy" and the strengthening of the powers of the General Council in order to carry it out. In vague but impressive tones he spoke of the revolt against capitalism throughout the world, hailing the Soviet Union as "a workers' republic rising, Phoenix-like, from the ashes of the most despotic régime of History", and leaving no doubt of his own belief "that a new order of society is inevitable before we can remedy the existing evils".

In keeping with the President's address, a Communist motion called on the T.U.C. to organise for the overthrow of capitalism. Introduced by both mover and seconder as revolutionary in character—the deliberate use of industrial power for political ends—the motion went on to demand well-organised workshop committees to lead the struggle and was carried by a two to one majority.

Other 'Left' resolutions for which Congress voted by large majorities with little opposition condemned the Dawes Plan for German reparations (accepted by MacDonald and the Labour Government), denounced imperialism and expressed solidarity with the struggles of "our working-class Chinese comrades". Tomsky was again invited to speak at the conference and there was enthusiastic support for continued efforts to bring the Russians into a single trade union international.

But left-wing hopes that the Scarborough conference might become a turning-point in the history of the British working-class movement proved insubstantial. Scarborough marked the end rather than the beginning of a new mood in the trade unions; it was a high point from which the tide at once began to ebb. The place of Purcell and Swales as successive chairmen of the General Council was taken by the staid Arthur Pugh. Within a month, Fred Bramley, a sincere advocate of closer relations with the Russians, was dead and Walter Citrine became the T.U.C.'s acting secretary. J. H. Thomas and Margaret Bondfield came back on to the General Council after two years' absence, and with them for the first time came Ernest Bevin. Purcell, Hicks and Swales all remained members of the Council, but they played a minor role in the events of the next few months by comparison with that of Pugh, Thomas and Bevin.

Even before the eclipse of the Left on the General Council, the most important debate at the Scarborough conference had shown the underlying conservatism of the trade-union movement when it came to translating resolutions into action. In his presidential address, Swales fastened on the powers of the General Council as the key to militant industrial policy. On the following day a resolution was moved from the floor to confer on the General Council power to call for a levy, to order a stoppage of work and to arrange with the co-operative societies for the provision of supplies in the event of a strike. The motion was strongly supported by A. J. Cook who promised the 800,000 votes of the Miners' Federation, and in many ways it accorded with Bevin's own views on the need for greater unity. But neither Bevin nor the leaders of any other of the big unions was willing to be rushed. J. H. Thomas (N.U.R.), J. T. Brownlie (A.E.U.) and J. R. Clynes (General and Municipal Workers) all spoke against, and Bevin's speech was decisive. "Unity," he argued, "must come from the people . . . I do not want to see a forced unity." Refusing to vote for or against the motion, Bevin asked that it should be referred to the General Council for consideration. Swales tried to rule him out of order, but failed. Bevin's speech ended the debate. Congress accepted his view without protest and agreed to leave the matter to the General Council without a vote.

The next day Charlie Dukes, of the General and Municipal Workers, got up to move a resolution in favour of amalgamation directed towards the goal of One Big Union. He was immediately attacked both by the representatives of the craft unions and by the advocates of industrial unionism. After a sharp debate which roused the delegates in a way that none of the facile left-wing resolutions had done, the motion was defeated by 2,138,000 votes to 1,787,000. The vote fully vindicated Bevin's attitude the day before. "I do not want half a million or two million to drive the others out," he said, "because they cannot see eye to eye with you." Once 'unity' came to mean something more than a slogan, unanimity disappeared and an attempt to force the pace could split the T.U.C. in two.

4

If Bevin had little use for the revolutionary nostrums of the Left, however, it would be a mistake to regard him as belonging to the right wing. He showed his independence of both when he attended the Liverpool conference of the Labour Party at the end of September.[1]

Cramp, of the N.U.R., the retiring chairman, made a strong defence of the Labour Government's record in his opening address and flatly repudiated talk of revolution as foreign to the purpose of the Labour Party. The mood of this conference was very different from that at Scarborough a fortnight before.

The first business on the agenda was the recommendation of the Executive to deny membership of the Labour Party to any member of the Communist Party following the decision of the year before to refuse the affiliation of the Communist Party itself. William Gallacher and Harry Pollitt were at once on their feet to oppose the Executive but they met with little support.

When the conference re-assembled in the afternoon, the first speaker was Ernest Bevin.

"If I thought," he said, "for one moment that this resolution was put down by the Executive Committee merely because the Communists take an advanced line, I would be against the Executive. But having had experience of the agitation carried on within my own Union, I feel that the Communists cannot conscientiously reconcile the Communist basis with the basis of evolutionary democracy that the Labour Party represents. I am tired of tactics. Working-class men in this country want people to be straight with them."[2]

Pollitt's attempt to move the reference back of the Executive's proposal was defeated by 2,870,000 to 321,000. But Bevin's speech made it clear that if he was opposed to Communist methods, he was equally dissatisfied with the attitude of MacDonald and the right wing. For Bevin went on to rebut MacDonald's criticism of the sympathetic strike in support of another union. This, Bevin

---

1 See above, pp. 258–60. This was the conference at which Bevin unsuccessfully demanded that the Labour Party should never again accept office as a minority Government.

2 Labour Party Conference Report, 1925, pp. 183–84.

declared, was no Communist policy, as MacDonald had suggested, and he told the Leader of the Party in so many words to mind his own business and leave the conduct of industrial affairs to the trade unions.

Where then did Bevin stand? Neither on the Left, with Lansbury, Maxton, Pollitt and Cook nor on the Right with MacDonald, Snowden and Thomas. If he had no faith in revolution or the syndicalists' general strike, industrial action for political ends, he was not content with the Labour Party's programme of social reform secured by constitutional methods. The industrial wing of the movement was just as important as the political and not to be subordinated to it. So far as politics went, he accepted the limitations of democratic action, but politics did not fill the whole picture. Let the politicians get on with their job of winning a majority, a job in which they had a right to call on trade-union support. (It was Bevin who proposed and carried the doubling of affiliation fees to the Party at this same conference.) But, as a union leader, he claimed the right to take independent industrial action for industrial ends, and to organise such action on as wide a scale as was necessary to make it effective. The experience of the General Strike did not convert Bevin from a belief in industrial action for political ends, for this he steadily repudiated. What it did was to force him to recognise that, beyond a certain point, industrial action, if organised on a sufficiently wide scale, inevitably became a political and constitutional issue, however much the unions might disclaim such an intention.

5

The old question Bevin had still to answer was *how* the unions were to organise their power effectively, even for industrial purposes.

Ideally, the answer was, by amalgamation to form a single union, the One Big Union, articulated in trade groups like those of the Transport and General Workers' Union. There was not the slightest prospect of this taking place. The T.U.C. delegates at Scarborough were not even prepared to pay lip-service to the proposal, as they were to most motions which involved the blessed word 'Unity'.

Failing amalgamation, an alliance on the terms Bevin had designed for the Industrial Alliance promised to overcome the most obvious weaknessess in co-operation between autonomous unions, and in the autumn of 1925 the negotiations for setting up the Alliance were resumed. By 5th November, when a delegate conference was held at the Essex Hall, several of the unions had completed the ballot of their membership and were in a position to make the necessary alterations in their rules. Amongst them was the T.G.W.U. with a favourable vote of 45,934 to 3,495. The small number who took the trouble to vote out of a total membership of 350,000 was an illuminating comment on the degree of interest the proposal aroused. The N.U.R. withdrew from the scheme altogether.

A second delegate conference finally adopted the Alliance constitution on 25th November. But further delays and hesitations followed and, by the spring of 1926, the Alliance had lost its original impetus. When his own Executive met in February, Bevin warned them against committing the transport workers further until they knew what the other unions were prepared to do. Another conference was summoned for 1st July 1926, but the General Strike was over before it could meet and the best-prepared attempt to create an effective trade-union alliance lapsed before it could be put into effect.

Thus, the only machinery for mobilising the trade-union movement on the side of the miners—in 1926 as in 1925—was the T.U.C., in effect the General Council.

The day on which Ernest Bevin first attended a meeting of the General Council—1st October 1925, in St. George's Hall, Liverpool, during the Labour Party conference in that city—was an important date in his life and in the history of the T.U.C. After the T.G.W.U. amalgamation, Bevin's election to the General Council was the next decisive stage in his career. For fifteen years he was to find in it the main platform from which to exert his influence upon the development of the working-class movement. The General Council came to play a big part in his life and he, in return, did more to shape its policies than any other individual member. By an odd coincidence the man who was to share the chief role in the leadership of the T.U.C. with him, Walter Citrine, was appointed its Acting General Secretary the same month (October 1925) after the sudden death of Fred Bramley.

The General Council, of which Bevin had been one of the architects, was no more than four years old. The role it was to play in the trade-union movement and in the community at large was still unsettled. It was the events which we are now to describe which decided this role and provided the starting-point from which Bevin and Citrine developed the policy which has given it a unique place among the institutions of twentieth-century Britain.

By comparison with the constitution of the Industrial Alliance, the T.U.C. represented a slow-moving and cumbersome piece of machinery. The General Council had been designed not so much to provide effective leadership as to afford equal representation to all the different interests represented in the Congress—craft, industrial and general unions alike.

A fixed number of seats was allotted to each of the eighteen trade groups, the smaller and less important of which tended to be over-re-presented at the expense of the big unions. Thus the National Union of Gold, Silver and Allied Trades, with a membership of 5,080 had one representative (its secretary, W. Kean, was a member of the General Council uninterruptedly from 1921 to 1939), while the Miners' Federation, with over 800,000 members, had only two, the A.E.U. and the N.U.R. one each.

This was not simply a question of the under-representation of numbers. The unions which would have to bear the brunt of any industrial conflict—miners, railwaymen, transport, electricians, engineers—were in a minority on a Council designed to represent the widest possible span of organised trades.

The powers granted to the General Council showed the same respect for the autonomy of the independent unions. The only two Standing Orders which gave it power to act in an industrial dispute were Nos. 8 and 11. The first empowered it "to assist any union which is attacked on any vital question of Trade Union principle". The second, added in 1924, strengthened the Council's right to intervene when negotiations broke down and authorised it "to organise on behalf of the Union or unions concerned all such moral and material support as the circumstances of the dispute may appear to justify". The composition of the General Council, however, was a guarantee that these powers would be interpreted conservatively.

Thirty-two was in any case too large a number for an effective executive committee. The full Council was rather to be looked upon as a representative body, which its members attended as delegates between meetings of the full Congress. Most of its business was done by committees, the Council meeting once a month to receive their reports.

There were over fifty of these committees, many of them joint bodies with other organisations like the Labour Party. A number of them were standing committees, but none of them corresponded to an executive committee. To deal with the mining dispute in 1925-6, for instance, a Special Industrial Committee was set up *ad hoc*; not until the very eve of the General Strike was a small Ways and Means Committee established to consider how support for the miners was to be organised.

Bevin took his place as a member of the joint committee on the nationalisation of the mines, to which the Parliamentary Labour Party as well as the National Executive, the Miners' Federation and the General Council all sent representatives. Its immediate business was to prepare an agreed statement to be submitted to the Royal Commission on the Coal-mining Industry which, in accordance with Baldwin's promise, began its sittings in September 1925. Once that had been done, however, it took no further part in the mining dispute.

6

In the seven months between Bevin's first meeting and the crisis at the end of April 1926 which led straight into the General Strike, the full General Council did not once discuss what was to happen when the Government subsidy came to an end on 30th April nor concern itself with preparations for the support of the Miners—apart, of course, from receiving the reports of the Special Industrial Committee in the normal course of its monthly meetings. Everything was left in the hands of this Committee which met under the Chairman of the General Council (Arthur Pugh) and included among its seven other members the general secretaries of the three railway unions; Ben Tillett and Arthur Hayday, M.P. (representing the two big general unions), together with two members of the left wing, Swales (who had made the leading speech at the Scarborough T.U.C.) and George Hicks of the Bricklayers.

But the Industrial Committee took no more active steps than the General Council itself. It met twice between 1st October 1925 and

1st January 1926, resolving on the first occasion (25th October) to watch the course of events and meet again in 1926 "if circumstances warrant it", and on the second occasion (18th December) *not* to seek additional powers as suggested at Scarborough. "This Committee," reads the minute, "is of the opinion that the powers already vested in the General Council in regard to intervention in industrial disputes are as exhaustive as can reasonably be exercised at the present time." When this decision was taken, four members were present besides the Secretary: they were Arthur Pugh, A. G. Walkden (of the Railway Clerks), and the two left-wingers, Swales and Hicks.

In the course of January, Walter Citrine drew up a characteristically clear-headed memorandum in which he asked a number of pointed questions on policy and preparation. The Special Industrial Committee, however, decided it could not answer these until it had talked to the Miners' Executive, and the miners, despite Cook's provocative speeches, were in no more of a hurry than the Industrial Committee. When a meeting eventually took place between the Committee and the miners, on 19th February, Herbert Smith and A. J. Cook agreed to leave any decisions to be taken until after the Royal Commission had issued its report.[1] In the meantime, the Special Industrial Committee issued a joint statement with the Miners reaffirming the T.U.C.'s support for the Miners' position: "no reduction in wages, no increase in hours, no interference with the principle of national agreements."

If we ask why there was this reluctance on the trade-union side to make preparations, the answer is plain enough. The Industrial Committee knew enough of official preparations and of feeling on the Tory side of the House to be sure that the Government would not surrender so easily a second time. It was anxious to avoid a clash if it could and waited for the Commission's report in the hope that, when published, it would afford a solution which the Miners could accept. It also knew enough of feeling in the trade-union movement to be sure that most trade unionists were reluctant to be drawn into an industrial conflict at a time when unemployment was still high. They would only come out in support of the miners if they felt—as they had felt in July 1925—that their own interests were directly

---

[1] Citrine, at the Special Conference of Executives, 20th January 1927. Report of Proceedings, pp. 41–42. Hereafter referred to as *Report*, 1927.

affected by the threat to force down wages in all industries. Nobody could tell, however, until the Royal Commission reported and the issue between the miners and the owners came to a head, whether this would be the case again in 1926. Left-wing critics later fastened upon the inactivity of the General Council in the winter of 1925–6 as further proof of the 'betrayal' of the rank and file by their leaders, but there is little evidence to show that the rank and file of the trade-union movement were any more eager than the Industrial Committee to prepare for a fight and thereby run the risk of provoking it.

Although Bevin was not a member of the Industrial Committee, he was no more in favour of forcing the pace than they were. In February, he reported to the General Executive Council of his Union:

"There is undoubtedly a big change of opinion [since the Scarborough T.U.C.] and I am inclined to the view that the general feeling now is that nobody wants a row; this must not lull us into a sense of security.

"I have a feeling that there is not intimate contact between the Miners and the rest of the movement. . . . I should not be prepared to ask this Union to go in to fight on the nationalisation of the mines—that is a political question which must be settled by the community. I do not think for one moment that the community desires the miners to have less wages than they are at present receiving, or longer hours. In fact, I take the view that the miners have established their case. But it cannot stop there. I have vivid recollections of the 1921 Movement (Black Friday) and even last July I did not feel too happy about what the rest of the unions were expected to obtain for the Miners."[1]

In this mood of uncertainty, Bevin, like the rest of the trade-union movement, waited to see the report of the Royal Commission.

7

In the meantime, there was plenty to occupy him. Despite the anxiety he expressed after the election of 1924, 1925 proved to be a good year for the Union. The deficit left by the two big strikes of 1924 (£78,000) had been wiped out and a considerable sum placed in reserve: the surplus on the year's working amounted to £109,000, a figure not to be reached again for another ten years. Work had

1 General Secretary's Quarterly Report, February 1926.

begun on Transport House, the first trade-union headquarters to be
built in the vicinity of Parliament and a deliberate move by Bevin
to underline the national standing of the Transport and General
Workers. Agreement had been reached with the T.U.C. and the
Labour Party to bring their central offices into the same building.
At the February meeting of his Executive Bevin was given authority
to negotiate for the necessary extension of the site. Transport House
was an ambitious undertaking—the North Block alone cost £35,000
to build—and any General Secretary with such responsibilities on
his mind was likely to think carefully before committing his union in
advance to strike in support of the Miners.

On 10th March, after six months' work, the Royal Commission
on the Coal Industry published its report.[1] Baldwin had gone to a
lot of trouble over its membership and excluded anyone connected
with the industry on either side. Its chairman was Sir Herbert
Samuel, a former Liberal Home Secretary and recently High Commissioner in Palestine. His colleagues, only three in number, were
Sir William Beveridge, then director of the London School of
Economics; General Sir Herbert Lawrence, Haig's chief of staff,
now a banker; and Kenneth Lee, chairman of a successful
Manchester cotton firm. No representative of Labour was invited to
serve on the Commission, but this fact added the more weight to a
report which afforded little satisfaction to the colliery owners.

If it saw no merit in nationalising the mines, the Commission
turned down the Mining Association's suggestions for shifting the
burden of the industry's problems on to the backs of the miners.
Longer hours, it pointed out, would only produce more coal which
could not be sold; lower wages were only a temporary expedient for
an industry which stood in need of drastic reorganisation, and the
Commission declared itself to be "strongly of opinion that national
wage agreements should continue".

"We cannot agree," the Commissioners added, "with the view presented to
us by the mineowners that little can be done to improve the organisation of
the industry and that the only practicable course is to lengthen hours and
lower wages. In our view large changes are necessary in other directions
and large progress is possible."

There followed a series of detailed recommendations for the re-

1 Cmd. 2600 (1926).

organisation of the industry on a more efficient basis, including nationalisation of the mineral (though not of the mines); the amalgamation of many of the smaller pits; the application of scientific research to the use of coal and its by-products; improvements in methods of sale and transport, a national wages board and a series of reforms to improve the working conditions and welfare of the miners.

At the same time the Commission said plainly that, as an immediate measure, a reduction in the wages fixed in 1924, at a time of temporary prosperity, was inevitable. If the Government's subsidy was excluded, three quarters of the nation's coal was now being produced at a loss. The subsidy could not be continued indefinitely: it was not only costly (£23 million for nine months) but indefensible to single out one industry from all the others, many of which were equally depressed, for special treatment. But if the subsidy were withdrawn and nothing done to reduce costs, then many mines would have to close. The only way to save the situation temporarily and so give a chance for permanent improvement by reorganisation was to cut wages.

Neither of the parties to the dispute, however, nor the Government, as Bevin later pointed out,[1] really accepted the Commission's Report. The Government took a fortnight to decide its own attitude and then, on 24th March, issued the following statement:

"The conclusions reached by the Commission do not in all respects accord with the views held by the Government and some of the recommendations contain proposals to which, taken by themselves, the Government are known to be opposed. Nevertheless . . . for the sake of a general settlement, the Government for their part will be prepared to render all such measures as may be required of the State to give the recommendations effect, provided that those engaged in this industry—with whom the decision primarily rests—agree to accept the Report and to carry on the industry on the basis of its recommendations."

This sounded well, but in fact amounted to an abdication of responsibility. "Provided that those engaged in this industry agree to accept the Report"—but the whole history of the coalmining industry since the war plainly showed that there was no chance of agreement between the two sides if they were left to themselves.

If the Government had any doubt about this—and it is scarcely

[1] Article in *The Record*, May–July 1926, p. 240.

credible that they had—the course of the negotiations in March and April must have removed them. By making agreement a precondition of Government action, instead of taking action to provide a basis of agreement, the Government virtually invited one side or the other to exercise a veto. Both sides were only too ready to accept this tacit invitation.

The mineowners, scarcely bothering to pay lip-service to the recommendations for reorganisation, insisted on district agreements and lower wages. Without bothering about negotiations, they put their demands into the form of an ultimatum with a time limit. Notices were posted ending the existing terms of service after 30th April; the new terms offered, varying from district to district, involved drastic cuts. The Durham miner would lose 18/4 a week; a hewer in South Wales would see his earnings reduced from 78/- to 45/10 a week. The miners, profoundly sceptical about the prospects of any reorganisation being carried out by the owners, insisted that they would not agree to wage reductions even as a preliminary condition of reorganisation. This was to ask them to buy a pig in a poke without any guarantee that there would ever be any reorganisation once the owners had got their way. The miners reckoned that they knew the owners and they were equally determined not to give an inch. They adhered to the same three points as before (on the first two of which they now had the Commission's support): a national agreement; no longer hours; no reduction in wages.

8

On 9th April, a delegate conference of the Miners' Federation was due to meet in London. The night before, Herbert Smith and the other Miners' leaders asked the Industrial Committee of the General Council for a firm commitment to the three-point programme on which the Miners intended to make their stand. The Industrial Committee had endorsed this programme as recently as 19th February, but they declined to repeat that endorsement in the same unconditional terms now. "Matters have not yet reached the stage," Citrine wrote to the Miners' Federation, "when any final declaration of the General Council's policy can be made." The

Committee, of course, expressed their general support of the Miners' case, but they were no longer prepared to bind themselves to the Miners' programme in advance of negotiations.

"This Committee is of the opinion that negotiations between the Mining Association and the Miners' Federation should be continued without any delay in order to obtain a clear understanding with regard to the Report of the Royal Commission and to reduce points of difference to the smallest possible dimensions."[1]

What had happened to change their minds, a change of which much was made later by left-wing critics looking for the first signs of 'betrayal'? The answer is: the publication of the Samuel Report. Unlike the miners, the mineowners or the Government, the Industrial Committee—and the General Council—took the report seriously. Arthur Pugh, chairman of the Industrial Committee and of the General Council, later wrote:

"It appeared to me that sound tactics implied an acceptance by the miners of the Report in substance, subject to subsequent negotiations on any point of reasonable modification, thus throwing upon the mineowners the responsibility for the rejection of the report."[2]

Pugh believed that the Miners underestimated the importance of the Report's recommendations for the reorganisation of the industry and he laid stress on the Commission's proviso:

"Before any sacrifices are asked from those engaged in the industry, it shall be definitely agreed between them that all possible means for improving its organisation and increasing its efficiency should be adopted as speedily as the circumstances in each case allow."

Bevin agreed with this view. He wrote after the Strike:

"I must confess that the Report had a distinct fascination for me; I felt that if minds were applied with the right determination to give effect to it, what with reconstruction, regrouping and the introduction of a new element in the management of the industry, there would in the end be produced a *higher* wage standard. It may have meant some adjustments in varying forms, but this is nothing new; everyone of us has had to face these problems

1 T.U.C. General Council: Minutes of the Special Industrial Committee.
2 From an unpublished lecture by Arthur Pugh, "Coal, the Miners' Federation and 1926".

in other industries across the table and met and overcome similar conditions over and over again."[1]

To put it more plainly than anyone cared to at the time, the mining industry would never be able to pay a proper wage until it had been reorganised—and reorganisation meant closing uneconomic pits and drastically reducing the number of miners employed. To those outside the industry this was obvious, and if a thorough reorganisation could be secured, Bevin and other trade-union leaders felt that a temporary reduction in wages was a price worth paying for it.

The miners did not share this view. They were as reluctant as the owners to face reorganisation, which would mean thousands of men being forced out of the industry. Their stubborn adherence to their three points was in part due to fear of seeing the wider issue of the industry's future opened up. They had lost all faith in inquiries and reports, the recommendations of which were never carried out. Their distrust of the owners was absolute; they hated them with a bitter and accumulated hatred. The leadership of the Miners' Federation has been criticised, but not by the miners; whatever their shortcomings, Herbert Smith and Cook accurately reflected the mood of the districts. They thought only in terms of a 'fight'. The mineowners were in the same mood: it was a head-on conflict of power in which each side meant to make the other admit defeat. The General Council, on the other hand, thought in terms of negotiation, believing that the report of the Royal Commission offered a genuine chance to solve the problems of an inefficient industry incapable of paying a living wage until it had been reorganised.

This difference of purpose became disastrously clear in the course of the General Strike, but it was there from the beginning, at least from the time the Report was published, and the miners' leaders were certainly aware of it at the time. This accounts for the barely concealed suspicion with which Herbert Smith and Cook always regarded the action of the General Council. But they were equally well aware that they needed the T.U.C.'s support and so found it politic not to press the difference to the point where it might lose them that support—just as the Industrial Committee found it

1 *The Record*, article already quoted, May–July 1926.

politic to leave the ambiguity unresolved for fear of weakening the Miners.

9

By the middle of April, such negotiations as there had ever been between the miners and the mineowners had broken down. The owners' insistence on district in place of national agreements, and their refusal to discuss reorganisation until the miners accepted the wage cuts dictated under the time-limit of 30th April, brought the T.U.C. Industrial Committee and the Miners closer together. Whatever the differences of view about the Royal Commission's Report, trade-union opinion still supported the miners in regarding negotiations in which one side was expected to accept the other's demands in advance as no negotiations at all. Until the mineowners withdrew their notices with the time-limit of 30th April, genuine negotiations could not take place.

On 14th April, the T.U.C. Industrial Committee called on Baldwin and urged him to bring the two sides together again. He agreed to do this, but still refused to make any proposals on the Government's behalf, in particular any proposals for the reorganisation of the industry. Here was the strength of the Miners' case: neither the owners nor the Government showed any intention of taking seriously the long-term recommendations of the Report to which the Industrial Committee attached so much importance.

When the owners and the men met again, it was only to restate the terms of the deadlock. The owners still insisted that the miners must accept an immediate cut in wages and district in place of national negotiations. In such a situation, the Industrial Committee saw no alternative to supporting the miners in their refusal to agree. After waiting until a week before the lock-out, the T.U.C. on 23rd April summoned a conference of trade-union executives for Friday, the 29th, the day after the delegate conference of the Miners' Federation.

The full General Council of the T.U.C. did not meet between 24th March and 27th April. Bevin, who was not a member of the Industrial Committee, felt so ill-informed of the course of negotiations that on 21st April he got in touch with A. J. Cook and asked to be put in the picture. After reading through Cook's notes of the various meetings, he wrote to him on the 22nd and asked if it would not be possible for the Miners to state a figure for earnings in each district which they would be prepared to accept.

"At the moment, I must say, that as the talk is in quantums, minimums, percentages, etc. it is rather difficult for the ordinary man like myself to understand. . . . There seems to be danger of drifting into a fight on slogans rather than money."[1]

Bevin himself sat down on the 23rd and dictated the draft of a scheme for putting into effect the recommendations of the Royal Commission for reorganising the industry. He amended this and dictated a second draft on the 26th, the main features of which were the appointment of expert commissioners in each of the districts to decide on the steps necessary to secure the efficient and economical working of the pits (including the closing down of mines); the establishment of a national board composed of representatives of both sides of the industry and independent members, with power to fix national minimum grades of pay, and of district boards to settle the application of these grades locally; arrangements for the registration of miners, and for dealing with those displaced or transferred to other industries. Pending the reconstruction of the industry by these means, Bevin proposed that the Government should continue to pay a subsidy to make up losses and the miners should draw their present wages.[2]

In the meantime, he took steps to prepare for a widening of the dispute by discussing with his officers the conditions on which the Transport and General Workers would agree to take part. His mind turned back to the ideas he had embodied in the constitution of the Industrial Alliance. The unions involved should hand over full powers to a central body charged with settling the problem. Before pledging his own union, Bevin wanted to know the answer to three questions: What other unions were prepared to support the miners to the same extent? Were the miners prepared to hand over their problem to a central body, "to use their brains before applying brute force"? Would the miners allow a negotiating committee to reach a settlement on the basis of the Royal Commission's Report, subject to

1 Ernest Bevin to A. J. Cook, 22nd April 1926.
2 These various drafts are preserved in Bevin's papers.

consultation with them before anything was accepted? If these questions were satisfactorily answered, the central body, Bevin emphasised, must have the final authority in deciding whether to accept any settlement or not.[1]

None the less, before meeting the General Council on the 27th, neither Bevin nor any other member of the Council outside the Industrial Committee had any idea how near they were to a break-down.[2]. The impression left on the public by the continuation of talks and by the Press was optimistic: it was widely believed that a settlement would be reached before the lock-out became effective.

10

At this point it is convenient to introduce Bevin's own account of the General Strike which he gave a fortnight after its conclusion. It is a verbatim record, filling thirteen foolscap pages of typescript, of a report which he gave to a number of the officers of his own union on 27th May 1926.

Bevin begins by describing the meeting of the General Council on the 27th April:

"The General Council found, as I have already said, that the only steps that had been taken were of a mediatory character. No definite proposals on the part of the Council itself had been formed and put down. At the General Council there was a feeling that the Miners should be supported, but the form and nature of the support seemed to be in doubt in their minds.

"I consulted with my colleagues at Head Office and I took the line on behalf of this Union that what we did in the July previous (1925) we were not prepared to repeat. That just meant that we should endeavour to hold up coal —to boycott it—and anyone who knew the Government's plans knew very well that that would be absolutely ineffective and foolish. I found too, that, as usual, there was a lot of talk on the General Council by people who thought they were not going to be involved.

"When the Council decided it was necessary to support the Miners, I personally made up my mind that it had to be a much wider dispute than anything attempted before; that it would have to be practically every section represented on the General Council in it. I then made a speech to

1 Bevin's notes, headed 'Position of the T.G.W.U.', dated 26th April.

2 "It was not until 27th April that we or the full General Council were even asked to consider the position of a possible breakdown in negotiations". Bevin in *The Record*, May–July 1926, p. 242.

the Council in which I insisted that the dispute should pass into the hands of the General Council—the right to call out, the right to control absolutely and the right to come to a decision as to settlement, to be in the hands of the General Council."[1]

In every dispute, especially those involving the coal industry, it was always the transport unions which were expected to come out on strike if wider support was to be given. The reason for this was obvious: a transport strike was the quickest and easiest way in which to bring pressure to bear on the public and the Government. Bevin and the transport leaders, however, objected to their unions being expected to bear the brunt of common action on every occasion, while others never risked anything. They objected even more strongly to being told that they were cowards or lacking in solidarity when they hesitated. For the transport workers were, in any case, far more vulnerable to blacklegging and volunteer service than other occupations, a fact which had weighed heavily with Bevin at the time of the proposed Triple Alliance strike in 1921.

In 1925 it was again the transport unions that were called on to impose a boycott on the movement of coal; in 1926 Bevin was determined that the burden and the risk must be shared by all the unions.

The General Council now set about two urgent tasks. The first was to draw up proposals for action in support of the Miners. It is a striking fact that, despite Citrine's memorandum of 28th January and inconclusive talks between the Industrial Committee, the Miners and the Co-operative Societies, no scheme of action was prepared on the trade-union side until three days before the lock-out was expected to begin. The Government's plans to deal with such action, it is worth recalling, had been put into shape before the end of the previous year.

A small committee "to consider ways and means of co-ordinating action in the event of a strike taking place" was hurriedly appointed. Of its six members, Bevin was the most active and Purcell the chairman. This was the forerunner of the Strike Organisation Committee as the Special Industrial Committee was of the later Negotiating Committee.

Purcell's committee worked quickly enough to put its report

1 Bevin's statement to his officers, 27th May 1926. Hereafter referred to simply as *Bevin*.

before the General Council on 28th April, but its plans were kept in reserve. For the Council at the same time approved proposals for carrying out the reorganisation of the coal industry on the basis of which the Industrial Committee was to go on trying to secure a settlement. These proposals (accepted by the miners' leaders) had certain points in common with those Bevin had framed earlier in the week. They expressed the T.U.C.'s purpose throughout the dispute, to get the negotiations away from the immediate issue of wages and hours and to start on a reorganisation which would make it possible for the industry to pay a proper living-wage. With this brief to guide them, the Industrial Committee, led by Arthur Pugh and J. H. Thomas, returned to Downing Street, where the Prime Minister had taken charge of the negotiations between the owners and the Miners' Federation since the beginning of the week.

I I

On Thursday, 29th April the executive committees of 141 trade unions, numbering 828 in all, met in the Memorial Hall, Farringdon Street. The T.G.W.U. was represented by its full Executive Council and the national officers. Bevin took his place on the platform with the other members of the General Council and with Ramsay Mac-Donald and Arthur Henderson representing the Parliamentary Labour Party.

There was nothing revolutionary about this sober, working-class conference, as solid and representative a body of ordinary sensible middle-aged Englishmen, Welshmen and Scots as you could find, with a scattering of left-wing enthusiasts from the Communist Party and the Minority Movement.

Arthur Pugh, who presided, opened the proceedings by giving his audience a summary account of the negotiations up to date and reading to them the proposals for reorganisation agreed between the General Council and the Miners' Federation. A resolution was moved by Thomas endorsing the Council's efforts to find a settlement and instructing it to continue negotiations and secure the withdrawal of the owners' lock-out notices, now due to expire the next day. Thomas was less reassuring about the chances of a settlement than Pugh had been, but it was Bevin, seconding the resolution in the one powerful speech of the day, who roused the delegates to a sense of the emergency.

"You are moving to an extraordinary position. In twenty-four hours from now, you may have to cease being separate unions. For this purpose, you will have to become one union with no autonomy. (Cheers.) The miners will have to throw in their lot and come into the course of the general movement and the general movement will have to take the responsibility for seeing it through. But at the moment we feel that to begin wielding any sort of threat in connection with the negotiations, in the stage they are in now, would be to place a weapon in the hands of our opponents. We are asking you to stay in London. You are to be our Parliament, you are to be our constituent assembly, an assembly where we will place the facts and the figures and the proposals and the problems that have to be submitted for calm judgement and at the end take your instructions."[1]

After a brief discussion, the resolution was carried and the Industrial Committee went back to resume negotiations with the Miners and the Government.

The Conference met again the next day (30th April) but had to while away twelve hours until half-past eleven at night before the Negotiating Committee (as it now began to be called) returned to the Hall. The delegates passed the time in the smoke-filled hall by singing—everything from music-hall songs to 'Lead, Kindly Light' —while members of the General Council played nap or solo-whist.

After discussions with the Prime Minister which lasted until 1.30 in the morning of Friday the 30th, the Negotiating Committee and the Miners at last received the proposals which Baldwin had succeeded in extracting from the owners less than 24 hours before the lock-out came into effect. The owners consented, under pressure, to a national agreement, but insisted on a return to the 1921 rates (which meant a uniform reduction of 13 per cent in the miners' standard wages) and on an extension of the working day from seven to eight hours. Baldwin, in forwarding these terms to the Miners at midday on the 30th, reaffirmed the Government's willingness "to give effect to such of the proposals in the Report as we believe will be of benefit to the industry," adding, however, instead of definite proposals for reorganisation, the promise of yet another inquiry into the best method of following up the Commission's recommendations.

1 T.U.C.: *The Mining Situation. Report of Special Conference.* Hereafter referred to as *Report*, 1926. 29th April–1st May 1926, pp. 16–17.

Thus, instead of continuing negotiations on the reorganisation of the whole industry and securing the withdrawal of the time-limit set by the lock-out notices, as the T.U.C. wished, the most Baldwin offered was the immediate sacrifice from the miners demanded by the owners, with no withdrawal of the notices and no guarantee to do more than 'investigate' reorganisation in the future.

I 2

The miners, naturally enough, rejected the owners' terms but did not break off the discussions. Instead, they put forward the proposals for reorganisation drafted by the General Council on the 28th. Throughout the evening of the 30th the Negotiating Committee, reinforced by MacDonald and Henderson, tried to get the Prime Minister and other members of the Cabinet to accept these as a basis for settling the whole question of the industry's future. Herbert Smith declared that the Miners were prepared to sit down and deal with the report from page one to the end—including, as this clearly implied, a possible reduction in wages as part of the price of reorganisation. But he refused to commit the Miners to a reduction in advance of the negotiations or in isolation from the other proposals to be discussed for putting the mining industry's house into order. "I want to see the horse I am going to mount," was his reply when Baldwin pressed him.

On this point the discussions broke down, confirming the Miners' belief, firmly held from the beginning, that the Government had never been serious about putting into effect the long-range recommendations of the Samuel Report and accepted the owners' view that the way to deal with the problem was to cut the miners' wages. In face of the T.U.C.'s efforts to move the negotiations on to the wider ground of reorganising the industry in such a way as to end the recurrent mining crises, Baldwin's Cabinet refused to take the responsibility (which the Government alone was in a position to assume) for treating the future of the mining industry as a national issue.

When this point had been reached in 1925, the Government had given way and intervened, but the situation was no longer the same. Baldwin could not afford the appearance of submitting to the Miners' demands a second time without risking a revolt in his own Party and the Cabinet. This time, the Government was prepared and there was a party in the Cabinet which believed the time had come to finish once and for all with threats of a general strike by calling what they regarded as the unions' bluff and teaching them a lesson. Baldwin did not belong to this party, but he could not be indifferent to its views or to the support they commanded in the Conservative Party. His position is easy to understand, for his hold on the Party was by no means secure. But it is equally easy to understand why the representatives of the General Council, who were more anxious than any other party to find a solution and avoid a clash, felt that the Government was abandoning the role of arbiter in favour of forcing the owners' demands upon the miners.

Tired and dispirited, the Negotiating Committee made its way back to Farringdon Street half an hour before the time-limit imposed by the mineowners' notices. There was no chance left of avoiding a coal stoppage: the question now was how widely it would spread. Pugh and Thomas limited their speeches to an account of the last twenty-four hours' negotiations. Decisions were postponed until the next day, but as they left the hall, the general secretaries of the different unions were each given a copy of the plans for action drawn up by Purcell and Bevin. Before the conference reassembled at noon on Saturday 1st May they were asked to call their executives together separately and decide whether they were prepared to accept the General Council's recommendations. The Government did not wait to hear the result. On the evening of 30th April, while the Prime Minister was meeting the Negotiating Committee in the House of Commons, the King held a special meeting of the Privy Council at Buckingham Palace. A proclamation declaring a state of emergency under the Emergency Powers Act was drawn up and signed. As the delegates poured out of the Memorial Hall in search of their lodgings, instructions were already going out to put the Government's plans into effect. One side at any rate was ready.

13

Next morning, Saturday 1st May, while reports came in that every pit in the country was idle and close on a million colliery workers

Above. The General Strike: two of the miners' leaders, Herbert Smith (left) and W. P. Richardson. *Below*. T.U.C. leaders leaving Downing Street, November 1926. Left to right, J. H. Thomas, Alonzo Swales, Ben Turner, Arthur Pugh, Walter Citrine.

Sunday night
May 2/1926

Our Position is that we are prepared to take the report, as a whole and enter into conference of ~~adjusting~~ ~~consideration~~ clauses fully.

A National ~~Board~~ Board to be set up, upon ~~the~~ which the miners, shall be represented.

who shall examine the whole report And advise the Government. on each ~~matters of~~ reorganisation step necessary to give effect to the report

And they shall deal with the immediate Matters ~~of reorganisation.~~ or taken all steps necessary to avoid. depression of the working standards.

And. shall report on the steps necessary. to deal with ~~Larger~~ the Problems. ~~our~~ for which a larger Review is necessary.

~~And ~~ ~~taken~~ ~~as a complete~~ ~~review the~~ ~~early after~~

The top page of Bevin's notes made during the discussions on the night of May 2nd 1926 (*see page* 311).

out, the executive committees of the various unions met to discuss the proposals drawn up by Bevin and Purcell. The most important decision they had to take—based, as Bevin said, upon the constitution of the Industrial Alliance—was to hand over their powers to the General Council and carry out its instructions "both regarding the conduct of the dispute and financial assistance".

This was a bigger step than the trade unions had ever before been willing to take: it meant handing over to the General Council the power to bring out or send back their members, without consideration of agreements which had often taken years to win; it meant placing the jealously-guarded control of each union's funds in the hands of the T.U.C., and it meant taking both steps in the interests not of their own membership but of the miners. It says much for the solidarity of the trade-union movement that, when the roll of affiliated unions was read out at the resumed conference just after noon, only one society, numbering fifty thousand members (Havelock Wilson's Seamen) refused to accept these far-reaching proposals. A number of small unions, with only a single representative present, deferred a decision until they could consult their executives, but they numbered no more than 319,000 members. All the unions of any size representing a total membership of 3,650,000 voted the powers asked by the General Council without reservation.

But what did the trade-union representatives gathered in the Memorial Hall believe they were voting for? What meaning did they attach to that ambiguous phrase, "the conduct of the dispute"?

The document hastily drawn up by Purcell's Ways and Means Committee on which they made their decision began by listing the trades in which work was to cease "as and when required by the General Council". They included all forms of transport, printing, iron and steel, metals and heavy chemicals, building (except housing), electric and gas power. But no date was fixed and the rudimentary instructions left it uncertain whether a strike had already been decided upon or whether they were only to be put into effect in the event of such a decision being taken.

Bevin, who was put up by the General Council to explain their policy to the conference, was equally ambiguous. For the greater part of his speech he spoke as if a national strike were now certain and fixed the time for it to start at the end of the shift on Monday night, 3rd May. Defending the General Council's delay in making preparations on the grounds that they had wanted to avoid all provocation, he described the Government's proclamation of a state of emergency as a declaration of war and likened the Government's action "as equal in stupidity to the actions of the well-remembered Lord North and George III combined".[1] On the other hand, Bevin concluded: "The last announcement I have to make is that no person in the first grade must go to work on Tuesday morning, *that is to say, if a settlement has not been found.*"[2]

Did the mandate given to the General Council include the power to resume negotiations at once in advance of the strike or was it only a mandate to conduct the strike to a successful conclusion? This is a crucial point, for the charge later brought by the miners against the General Council was that, by opening negotiations with the Government, they acted in bad faith. At the conference of executives held in January 1927, for instance, A. J. Cook declared: ". . . . the decision of the 1st May was to stand against the miners having a reduction in wages. I repeat that we had nothing to negotiate on."[3]

Bevin, however, and the other members of the General Council strongly repudiated this claim. If that had been the case, Bevin told the later conference of executives, "you, in fact, handed over your powers to the Miners' Federation and not to the General Council at all. That is not what you did. We may have made all the mistakes in the world, but that does not affect the question of whether or not we had the power to do what we did do."[4]

Rejecting the Miners' version, Bevin as well as Citrine and Thomas argued that the use to which the General Council was authorised to put its powers was (1) to call out the men working in certain specified trades at midnight on Monday, 3rd May, *if a settlement had not been found;* (2) to offer to resume negotiations in the hope of finding such a settlement.

---

1 *Report* 1926, p. 34.
2 Author's italics.
3 *Report,* 1927, p. 35.
4 Ibid p. 45.

14

Before the conference of executives re-assembled at noon on 1st May, the General Council called in the miners' representatives (Herbert Smith, Cook and Richardson) and asked them if they agreed to place the conduct of the dispute from then on in the Council's hands. To this they agreed, subject to the right to be consulted during negotiations and particularly before any terms were accepted. No reservation was made which would exclude negotiations and limit the General Council's conduct of the dispute to the organisation of a sympathetic strike. The one reservation made by Smith (in which he was fully supported by the General Council) was a refusal to accept the Report, and, in particular, to accept its recommendations of a reduction in wages, in advance of negotiations.

In the confusion and excitement of the occasion, with feeling running high, what counted was the appeal for unity. With memories of Black Friday on both sides, neither the General Council nor the miners cared to risk that unity by pressing the other too hard. The miners' leaders believed that the T.U.C. was now committed to a strike in their support and, if they had any doubts, suppressed them. The original difference of view, latent from the publication of the Commission's Report, but overlaid in the course of the negotiations, was left unsettled. The Miners' Executive, convinced that it had to come to a fight and never seriously believing that negotiations would lead anywhere, set off home for their districts as soon as the conference of executives broke up. What mattered, as Herbert Smith had said in 1921, was "to get on t' field". So far as they were concerned, the decision had been taken. They could see no reason to remain in London and they were nowhere to be found when the Negotiating Committee wanted to refer to them later that night.

The General Council, on the other hand, faithful to its policy of negotiation and believing that the executives' vote empowered them to conduct the dispute as they saw fit, proceeded in equally good faith to draft two letters to the Prime Minister the same afternoon. The first offered, in the event of a strike, to co-operate in the distribution of essential food supplies; the second announced that negotiations would hereafter be conducted by the T.U.C. not by the

Miners, and expressed their readiness to resume talks "at any moment should the Government desire to discuss the matter further".[1] In sending these letters, the General Council saw nothing at all inconsistent with the course it had put in train earlier in the day. The request to the unions to call out their men on the Monday night still stood; arrangements to organise the strike continued to be made, but it was common sense to try and get a settlement without a strike if this were at all possible. The General Council certainly took no steps to conceal what it was doing. The text of the letters was read to the Miners' Federation office over the telephone and a copy sent round by hand. No protest was received from the miners, whose Executive had already left for home, unknown to the General Council. Instead, by 6 p.m. there came a reply from the Prime Minister, inviting the Negotiating Committee to meet him at once. By half-past eight, the Committee's members had been collected and sat down with the Prime Minister to see whether a formula could be devised which would allow negotiations to begin.

15

Bevin took no part in these negotiations which, at the Prime Minister's suggestion, were conducted by three from the trade-union side—Pugh (the Chairman of the General Council), J. H. Thomas and Alonzo Swales (of the Engineers)—and three members of the Cabinet, Baldwin himself, Birkenhead and Steel-Maitland (the Minister of Labour). Citrine and Sir Horace Wilson were present to keep a record of the discussion.

By the early hours of Sunday, 2nd May, the talks produced a draft formula which looked promising:

"The Prime Minister has satisfied himself . . . that if negotiations are continued (it being understood that the notices cease to operate), the representatives of the T.U.C. are confident that a settlement can be reached on the lines of the Report within a fortnight."

The T.U.C. representatives left Downing Street, promising to submit this draft to the General Council and the Miners' Federation

[1] Text of the letters in W. Milne-Bailey: *Trade Union Documents* (1929), pp. 244–5.

and to let Baldwin have their reply by lunchtime on the Sunday.

At this point the misunderstanding between the Miners and the General Council came into the open. Cook had not received the copy of the letter to the Prime Minister sent round to the Miners' offices the previous afternoon. He only learned that the General Council had sent representatives to Downing Street by chance when he ran into Mary Quaile, one of the T.G.W.U.'s women organisers, out for a walk on the Saturday evening. Citrine rang Cook up between 1 and 2 a.m. to tell him what had happened and asked him to meet the full General Council at their headquarters in Eccleston Square on the Sunday morning. It was then the turn of the General Council to learn with astonishment that the Miners' Executive had left London and were not available. Telegrams were at once sent off to recall them for consultation, but unfortunately no one thought to telephone Downing Street and tell the Prime Minister what had happened. As a result, the Cabinet, which had been summoned to meet at noon, was kept waiting and broke up impatiently without receiving any message from the T.U.C. It was not until 9 o'clock on the Sunday evening that the meeting between the representatives of the T.U.C. and the Prime Minister took place and the delay appears to have had a substantial effect in hardening opinion on the Government side.

The General Council itself took a considerable time to make up its mind on the proposed formula. Bevin, in the account already quoted, admitted his own belief that "underneath it all there was no doubt that the settlement provided for a reduction of wages or an increase in hours". Had there been any private understanding to this effect?

"I questioned Mr. Thomas very closely on this last point, and while they kept saying it might or might not involve that, at the same time, to act in a perfectly straight manner, I came to the conclusion that was really what it meant . . . and that the Prime Minister would be satisfied in advance so far as a reduction was concerned, irrespective of what might happen afterwards."[1]

Despite the doubts, the General Council eventually decided to recommend the Miners to accept the formula as the best they could hope to obtain and the Negotiating Committee arranged

1 *Bevin.*

to meet the Prime Minister, Birkenhead and Steel-Maitland at 9 p.m. on the Sunday evening to discuss its interpretation. It soon became evident, Pugh says, that during the hours of delay,

"the attitude of the Government representatives had changed. They appeared to think that the Council representatives had known at the previous meeting that the miners were away from London."[1]

Baldwin now pressed Pugh and his colleagues for a straight answer: Would the miners accept the formula? More than that—as a result, no doubt, of his own discussions with the Cabinet, in which there was a powerful section opposed to compromise or concessions, he was no longer willing to leave any doubt about the meaning of the formula. Lord Birkenhead presented a second draft (known as 'the Birkenhead formula') which brought out into the light the issue which the Negotiating Committee had been trying to avoid:

"We will urge the miners to authorise us to enter upon a discussion with the understanding that they and we accept the Report as a basis of settlement, and we approach it with the knowledge that it may involve some reduction in wages."

Could the General Council any longer accept the formula, if the implications Bevin had suspected were spelled out in so many words? Even if they were willing to do so, would the miners accept it?

16

While the three trade-union leaders and Citrine were still talking with the Prime Minister and his colleagues, a message was sent in that the Miners' representatives had at last arrived and Pugh and Thomas broke off the discussion to see them and the rest of the General Council.

The Miners' Executive was taken upstairs to the Chancellor's Room in No. 11 Downing Street. There they found the rest of the General Council, soon joined by the sub-committee which had conducted the negotiations. For some time, the discussion turned on the 'formula', not the so-called Birkenhead formula of which Pugh

1 Pugh's lecture, "Coal, the Miners' Federation and 1926".

and Thomas said nothing, and which was never shown to the General Council, but the original draft.

"But," Bevin says, "it became perfectly obvious that even amongst the General Council itself there was not a feeling of confidence in advising its acceptance because of what might be underlying it. I then suggested that we should get on rather different lines to discussing these wretched formulas —taking a word out here and putting one in there—and I proceeded to draft something. As a matter of fact it was then actually in course of preparation, but it had never seen the light of day. With the exception of one word, the Miners agreed to it."[1]

Amongst Bevin's papers are to be found eight sheets torn from a ruled pad and covered with successive drafts scrawled right across the page in his unmistakeable hand. At the top is written the date, "Sunday night, May 2, 1926" (See plate facing page 305).

Breaking away from the idea of a preliminary formula on which the discussion had hitherto been conducted without any agreement on what it meant, Bevin reverted to the suggestion he had made in his own draft proposals of 23rd and 26th April. He proposed the establishment of a National Mining Board composed of representatives of the Government, the miners and the mineowners with other members drawn from Labour and employers outside the coal industry. To this Board should be entrusted an examination of the whole of the Commission's report with the duty, first, of deciding the steps to be taken to reorganise the industry and then, after they had completed their proposals, of determining "what adjustments shall be made, if any, by all parties necessary to cover the interim period subject to the maintenance of a national minimum and the Seven Hours' Act". The Board was to be given wide powers to acquire all the information it needed, including the right to examine each company's books, and the Government, as well as both sides to the dispute, was to bind itself to accept its findings.

Bevin had got seven clauses down on paper and one o'clock had struck, when the Prime Minister's secretary came up and asked the Negotiating Committee to return. With agreement so near, the Committee were reluctant to go, but on a second request, Pugh, Thomas, Swales and Citrine went down.

While the trade-union leaders were at work on Bevin's draft

[1] *Bevin.*

311

upstairs in No. 11, the Cabinet had been meeting in No. 10. They had already spent a large part of the day waiting to hear from the General Council and they were kept waiting again while Baldwin and Birkenhead met Pugh and his sub-committee. L. S. Amery, who was a member of the Cabinet, writes:

"We kicked our heels for hours. Presently after 11 p.m. an exhausted Baldwin came in and collapsed in an arm-chair leaving it to Birkenhead to state the very inconclusive result. . . . Some of us would have been prepared to continue negotiations so long as there was the faintest chance of agreement. But opinion had hardened very much in view of the fact that notices ordering the General Strike to begin next day had been sent out, regardless of the negotiations, the night before. While we were still discussing, the news arrived that the *Daily Mail* had been suppressed by the printers who disliked the leading article. This tipped the scales. It was clear that the only issue that now mattered, for the Government and the public, was whether Government and Parliament were to surrender to coercion. A note previously drawn up by the Cabinet was now stiffened to make it quite clear to the trade union leaders that negotiations could not be continued unless the interference with the Press was repudiated and the General Strike called off. We dispersed about 12.30 leaving Baldwin to hand the note to the trade union leaders and go to bed."[1]

The note spoke of 'overt acts' which had already taken place, "including gross interference with the freedom of the Press" as "a challenge to the constitutional rights and freedom of the nation".[2] Before conducting any further negotiations, the Government demanded "both repudiation of the actions referred to . . . and an immediate and unconditional withdrawal of the instructions for a general strike".

17

When the four trade-union leaders came in, quite unprepared for the Government's abrupt change of tone, Baldwin was alone and ill at ease. He handed them the letter and briefly informed them that

1 L. S. Amery: *My Political Life*, Vol. II (1953), pp. 483–4.

2 There was only one 'overt act'. The printers at the *Daily Mail* refused to print the Monday issue of the paper unless the leading article, which denounced the threatened general strike as a revolutionary movement, was altered. This action was taken on their own initiative without reference to the General Council or to their own union.

the Cabinet took so serious a view of the *Mail* incident that it had decided to break off negotiations forthwith.

The first reaction of the General Council to the news was one of bewilderment. They knew nothing of the 'overt acts' to which the Cabinet referred and, when they learned what had happened at the *Daily Mail* offices, protested strongly that they could neither be held responsible nor believe that a Government would take such action over so trivial an incident.

Anger rapidly succeeded to bewilderment. After twenty-four hours of negotiation in which they had exerted all their influence to avoid a clash, the Government's decision to break off appeared a deliberate provocation, the pretext for which would not stand up to examinations. True, instructions had been sent out to prepare for a national strike, but in the General Council's view this was a precautionary measure. What were they negotiating for, if not to secure a settlement which would make these instructions unnecessary? In the General Council's eyes, it was the Government, not the trade unions, which was forcing the issue and raising the question of the constitution. This was an industrial dispute and it was not on the General Council's initiative that it was turned into a contest of power between the trade-union movement and the State. Their sole object, they repeated, was "to secure for the mineworkers the same right from the employers as is insisted upon by employers from workers—namely, that negotiations shall be conducted free from the atmosphere of strike or lock-out . . . a principle which Governments have held to be crucial in the conduct of negotiations".[1]

As soon as Pugh finished reading the Cabinet's communication, a confused clamour broke out, everyone trying to speak at once. It was Bevin's powerful voice which made itself heard.

"I propose that we depute someone to draft a reply and that in the meantime we continue our discussion where we left off when the message came, for a basis of settlement has to be found sooner or later, and as we have made good progress on the job we had better go straight on and finish it."[2]

Bevin's proposal found immediate support and for two hours the

1 General Council's reply to the Cabinet, 3rd May 1926.
2 The description is that of an eye-witness, W. Milne-Bailey, in *The Advance* (the paper of the Amalgamated Clothing Workers of America), 28th May 1926, p. 12.

General Council and the Miners' Executive continued their discussion in the Chancellor's room while the lights were put out in No. 10 and the Prime Minister went to bed. A reply to the Government's ultimatum, protesting at the sudden rupture of the negotiations was drawn up but, when Pugh and Citrine went downstairs to deliver it, they found the Cabinet Room and the rest of the house in darkness. There was nothing to do but return to Eccleston Square from which the General Council dispatched its reply dated 3.30 a.m. on Monday 3rd May.

Bevin was still anxious to get agreement on the terms of a settlement and, after a few hours' sleep, met Pugh, Citrine and the three miners' leaders in his own office at Central Buildings, Westminster. Only one point of substance remained to be settled. In his original draft Bevin wrote that, after the proposed National Mining Board had completed their proposals for the reorganisation of the coal industry, "they shall determine what adjustments shall be made, if any, by all parties, necessary to cover the interim period, *subject to the maintenance of a national minimum and the Seven Hours' Act*". A national minimum or *the* national minimum? It was the old issue in a new form. The miners' leaders wanted to rule out any reduction even if reorganisation was guaranteed: hence their insistence on *the* national minimum, i.e. the minimum accepted in the 1924 agreement. On that Monday morning, Smith, Cook and Richardson finally agreed to substitute 'a' for 'the'. But when they took the draft to their full Executive, meeting in a room in the House of Commons, the change was repudiated by 12 votes to 6.

Bevin had attended the meeting of the Miners' Federation. Defeated there, he brought the draft back to the General Council, arguing that the miners had handed over their powers and must accept the General Council's ruling as final. The draft was adopted by the General Council with the original wording of 'a national minimum'. Hurriedly stuffing the papers into his pocket, Bevin walked back to the House of Commons—it was then four in the afternoon—and saw the proposals delivered to MacDonald. Not content with this, Bevin got in touch with Frederick Leggett, of the Ministry of Labour. Handing Leggett a copy of his proposals, he urged him to get the Prime Minister to put them forward in the House that evening. If he did, Bevin assured Leggett, Henderson would be ready to accept them on behalf of the Labour Party.

Leggett went to Sir Horace Wilson, the Permanent Secretary of the Ministry of Labour. Wilson's only response was to ask if the T.U.C. were prepared to accept a reduction in wages. As they were not, the Government was not interested. Bevin still hoped and expected that MacDonald would produce his proposals in the House, but the Leader of the Labour Party made no reference to them. Possibly he hesitated to do so in view of the miners' objection to the change the General Council had made.

Whatever the reason, Bevin never changed his opinion that, if the draft had been made public in the debate that Monday evening, before the strike began, the course of events might been different. But the chance was lost and within a matter of hours the men came out.

As the evening shifts ceased work on the night of 3rd May, the whole transport system of the United Kingdom came to a standstill.

CHAPTER 12

The General Strike
1926

I

THE RESPONSE to the strike took both sides by surprise. The T.U.C.'s instructions by no means called for a universal stoppage of work. Members of many unions were instructed to remain at work: these included engineering and shipyard workers, textile and wood workers, the Post Office and the distributive trades. But in the occupations called out the response was remarkably high. The million mine-workers already out were joined by another million and a half men employed in transport, the docks, the railways, printing (including the Press), iron and steel, the metal and chemical industries, building and the power stations.

It is easy to underestimate what this meant. A trade union is not an army, in which orders are obeyed without question and the responsibility is taken by those who give the orders. There were many men who by their action that Monday night and Tuesday morning risked secure jobs and pensions for which they had been paying for years. They did so with their eyes open, knowing that if the strike failed, they would have great difficulty in getting their jobs back; might see themselves replaced by younger men; might be left, in the dockers' phrase, "on the stones" for months, reduced to the ranks of the unemployed. Working men do not go on strike lightly, least of all when unemployment is high, trade slack and there is no dispute in their own industry. Too much was at stake for them and the families dependent on them to indulge in gestures. The response to the call for a national strike was a remarkable demonstration of working-class unity and of unselfish support for the miners.

The company's own figures for the biggest of the four railway networks, the London, Midland and Scottish Railway, will serve to illustrate the solidarity of the railwaymen. Of 15,062 engine drivers employed by the L.M.S., 207 reported for work on the first day of the strike; of 14,143 firemen, only 62; of 9,979 guards, only 153. On this first day of the strike, the L.M.S. succeeded in running 3.8% of its normal passenger service. By the end of the strike, this percentage had been raised to 12.2%. But this was largely with the aid of volunteer crews. The continued solidarity of the men is more accurately reflected by the figures for goods trains which, on the last day of the strike, represented no more than 3% of the L.M.S.'s normal traffic.[1]

In London, not one of the General Omnibus Company's 3293 buses was moved on the first day of the strike; on 11th May despite the extensive use of volunteer drivers, the number still did not exceed 526. No more than a hundred of London's trams were ever got on the roads on any one of the nine days of strike. In the London docks, not a single cargo was touched for the first four days and the work of unloading was only then begun by volunteers with the aid of the navy and under the cover of fully-armed detachments of troops, equipped with machine-guns and armoured cars.

In all the principal industrial areas of the country there was a similar response. Public transport was brought to an abrupt halt, every steel-works and blast furnace as well as every pit was silent. Nor, contrary to Government reports at the time, is there any evidence of a substantial return to work by the time the strike was called off nine days later. The news of the General Council's decision to end the strike was greeted, not with relief, but with disbelief and anger. More than twenty-four hours after orders were sent out to return to work, the number of men on strike (on 13th May) had actually increased by 100,000.

Apart from the miners and the railwaymen, no other union was so deeply involved in the strike as the Transport and General Workers and none responded with greater loyalty. Bevin had few anxieties about the efficiency with which the Union's organisation would meet the demands made upon it. Orders calling out 90% of the members, 350,000 men, had already been sent over his name. He left the rest, with justifiable confidence, to his national and local officers. His own energy and organising ability were needed, not at Central

1 These figures are given in Julian Symons: *The General Strike*, pp. 95–96.

Buildings, but round in Eccleston Square, the headquarters of the T.U.C.

2

After the conference on the Saturday, the General Council set up a number of sub-committees to consider the problems which would have to be faced if the strike took place. After fifteen years' talk about a General Strike, Direct Action, and "wielding the power of labour", the plain fact was that no plans of any sort existed. An amplified version of their original instructions produced over the week-end by the Powers and Orders Committee—Purcell, Bevin and four others—did not carry matters much further forward. Within a broad general directive, the individual unions were left to call out their members, provide for strike pay and organise picketing. Local committees to be formed from the unions involved had to make their own decisions, with little to go on in the way of directions and every opportunity for the widest possible variation in their application.

Throughout Monday and Tuesday a mounting flood of inquiries, protests, reports, demands for clearer instructions, requests for rulings, problems no one had thought of, poured into Eccleston Square and soon threatened to engulf the General Council. The T.U.C. organisation, a handful of officials and office staff, was totally inadequate to cope with an operation which would have strained the resources of a fully-equipped army command. Committees could find nowhere to meet; the telephone line was jammed with calls; deputations, dispatch-riders, trade-union leaders, Labour M.P.s, journalists, cameramen tramped up and down stairs looking for someone to speak to, while in the midst of this bedlam, the General Council in full session attempted to discuss policy, listen to the reports of the committees, make decisions, answer questions and issue instructions.

By the end of the first day it was obvious to Bevin that this state of affairs could not continue. He persuaded the General Council to hand over the actual conduct of the strike to a small Strike Organisation Committee, the former Ways and Means, or Powers and Orders Committee renamed. The chairman of this committee was Purcell, but from the beginning he was overshadowed by Bevin. Although he had joined the General Council a few months before,

Bevin provided the driving force and direction behind the conduct of the strike for the remainder of the nine days which it lasted. This appreciation of the role he played is taken from an eye-witness account published shortly afterwards:

"The reputation of many of Britain's budding Lenins has been badly bruised by their conduct during the Strike. The fire-eaters were the first to feel the weight of the forces arrayed against them.
"The big man of the strike, if anyone was entitled to that epithet, was Ernest Bevin. It was his quick brain and natural genius for organisation that saved the strike from being a complete fiasco. . . . Fresh from his agile brain came the scheme for the organisation and administration of strike headquarters. All through the first week, cool and unflurried by anybody or anything, he kept the machine of his making smoothly at work. He could be called 'The Dictator of Eccleston Square', to whom all applied and sought advice. His word was absolute."[1]

Under Bevin's leadership, the Organisation Committee set about bringing order into the confusion of committees and departments with overlapping responsibilities.

The issue of transport and food permits was handed over to a Transport Committee representing the transport and railway unions and operating from the N.U.R. headquarters at Unity House. A Building Committee took over the question of which building operations should be allowed to continue and moved out to the Building Trade Workers' offices at Clapham. To deal with public services, Bevin brought in the workpeople's representatives on the Joint Industrial Council for Electricity and Gas. An Intelligence Committee set about collating reports from all parts of the country to form an up-to-date picture of what was happening and worked closely with the Publicity Committee, responsible for the production of the *British Worker*, the T.U.C.'s rival publication to the Government's *British Gazette*. An Interviewing Committee dealt with callers, telephone inquiries and deputations, while the Propaganda Department undertook a campaign of meetings and provided speakers to address them.

Communications were of the first importance. The Transport

1 From an interesting anonymous article by 'A Labour Correspondent' in the *Yorkshire Evening News*, 27th May 1926. The *Sunday Express* took the same view: "He was the only one (of the trade union leaders) whose reputation was enhanced by the general strike. He alone took a comprehensive view. He made up his mind while others drifted. He acted while others talked—not for the first time."

Department at Eccleston Square organised the use of cars and motor-cycles and a Dispatch Department was started to handle a courier service which by the end of the first week covered the greater part of the country and maintained a daily service. In setting up the different committees and departments, Bevin not only drew on the General Council and T.U.C. headquarters, but on the officers, staff and premises of the big unions and the Labour Party. Bevin's own secretary, Mae Forcey, acted as secretary of the Strike Organisation Committee.

The T.U.C. relied, even more heavily, on the initiative and resource of the local strike committees which rapidly organised themselves in every town of any size and, finding themselves forced to make their own arrangements, often showed a remarkable capacity for self-help and responsibility.

Bevin never pretended that they did not make mistakes. Amongst those mistakes were the decision to call out the printers (since the absence of newspapers hit the trade unions more than the Government which was able to rely on the B.B.C.); the failure to call out the post-office workers, and the delay in the issue of strike orders to the engineers and shipyard workers. From first to last, it was a feat of improvisation which left far too much to chance and local initiative. But it worked. Thanks to Bevin, the failure to make plans in advance did not prove fatal. Unlike those who had talked of Direct Action for years, but were unequal to events when the time for action came, there was at least one man on the General Council who grasped what had to be done and did it.

3

Much criticism was later directed at the General Council for calling a national strike without adequate preparations. But this does not go to the heart of the matter. At a pinch, as Bevin and the local strike committees showed, organisation could be improvised. The real criticism to be made of the trade-union leaders, including Bevin, is that they had not sufficiently thought out the consequences of the course on which they had embarked. The lack of preparation was only a part of a wider failure to grasp clearly where their policy was leading them.

Revolution
See page 274

The General Strike 1926

The General Council was indignant at the suggestion that it was launching a general strike. It took pains to avoid any use of the term, speaking of a national strike, sympathetic action on a large scale in an industrial dispute. It was the Government which talked of a general strike and a challenge to the constitution; both were indignantly repudiated by the T.U.C. It is equally clear from the history already related that the General Council was reluctant to engage in a national strike, that it preferred negotiation—even after the strike orders had been issued—and that it was 'astounded' (to use its own words) when the Government broke off negotiations on what appeared to be a trivial pretext. It was the Government's action which precipitated the strike; there was no party on the General Council which wanted a 'show-down' as there certainly was in the Cabinet.

But this hardly settled the matter. From the time Bevin joined the Dockers' Union, the trade-union movement had never shaken itself free of the syndicalist belief in Direct Action. Very different views were taken of its scope, some—especially in the period 1919–21—being prepared to use it for political aims, others limiting it to industrial objectives. By 1926, it is true, syndicalist slogans had lost much of their hold over trade unionists' imaginations, but the idea that in the last resort, if they were pushed too far, the unions had the right—and the power—to bring the economy of the nation to a standstill and secure what they demanded by direct action was still there at the back of their minds.

It was a muddled notion. None of the trade-union leaders, for instance, had thought out the contradiction between such a claim and their belief in Parliamentary institutions. Attempts by Mac-Donald and other members of the Labour Party to point this out were angrily rejected.

Nor had the issue of power been squarely faced. Bevin spent much time between 1918 and 1926 in the search for more effective means of organising and exerting trade-union strength. He tried a variety of approaches from federation and the Triple Alliance to amalgamation, from the establishment of the General Council as a 'general staff' for the trade-union movement to the Industrial Alliance. At conference after conference the T.U.C. had debated how best to create a concentration of power which would prove irresistible and habitually employed revolutionary phrases and military metaphors to describe its use. Yet no one seems to have considered the consequence of such schemes from a wider point of view than that of the trade-union movement. However much the unions might protest that they were only acting in defence of working-class interests and that they had no intention of raising a constitutional issue, no Government could fail to regard industrial action on a scale which brought the economy of the country to a standstill as a challenge and bring the full resources of the State into play. The T.U.C. could hardly complain if the Government took at least some of their slogans and threats seriously, after the speeches and resolutions at the Hull and Scarborough conferences, the experience of Red Friday and the jubilation of the Left at Baldwin's 'capitulation'.

The object of the strike was, after all, to force the Government to intervene. This was the way the threat of 'extended industrial action' had worked in 1925, and before that. But, now that the Government had made up its mind to take up the challenge, what did the unions expect to happen? If they thought about the matter at all, most trade unionists would probably have replied that, after a few days, the country and the economy would be in such a mess that the Government would *have* to act to promote a settlement. If necessary, they might have to stay out a little longer, but in the end (as the Miners were to argue) the stoppage of work, by itself, was bound to force the Government's and the employers' hands.

But was this true, even with two and a half million men on strike? As the first week of the conflict drew to an end, the answer appeared to be doubtful. The strike was successful, but it was not decisive. The Government's arrangements, thanks to the use of road transport, were working well and they still had considerable resources in hand. No attempt, for instance, had yet been made to arrest the strike leaders, and the armed forces had only been employed sparingly. The season of the year was favourable (the weather was fine and sunny for most of the nine days), there had been ample time to make preparations on the Government side, and public opinion, although sympathetic to the miners' original case, responded strongly to the Government's claim that the strike was a challenge to the constitution. With the aid of volunteers the civil authorities were able to prevent the breakdown at which the strikers aimed without calling on the military, who remained in reserve. There was a vast amount of inconvenience, but food and milk continued to be distributed, stocks of coal and oil were not exhausted, people got to work in one way or another and the B.B.C. kept open a channel of communication even in a land deprived of newspapers.

4

The General Council, then, had to face the question, whether they would go further and intensify the strike. It would not be difficult to call out more workers. On 7th May, the decision was actually taken to bring out the engineers and shipyard workers on the 11th. But where would this lead them? The unions' funds were far from inexhaustible and strike pay was already making heavy inroads on them. Every day the strike continued and—particularly if it were to be extended—increased the risk of a serious clash between strikers and the police. While no lives were lost, it is untrue that there was no violence during the General Strike. There were violent episodes with police charges in a number of towns, including London, Glasgow and Liverpool. If the strikers' mood became ugly and the authorities had to call on troops to keep order, the General Council would lose control and the Churchill party in the Cabinet would be given a free hand. If this happened, the result could not be in doubt. Without arms or military organisation, working men could not withstand armoured cars and machine-guns. In the process, the trade-union movement painfully built up by many years of hard effort would be destroyed, its funds exhausted or confiscated, its prospects of revival crippled by punitive legislation. These were the possible consequences which the trade-union leaders had now to confront if they pressed home the challenge to the State on which they found themselves reluctantly embarked.

If they were unwilling to go further and could not make the strike effective simply by sitting tight, what were they to do? Bevin had no doubt:

"About the Friday or Saturday morning, when the Strike had been on about a week, the Strike Organisation Committee indicated to the General Council quite clearly that it was time something was done to get negotiations going somewhere. You could not sit in the Strike Organisation room, with deputations and committees coming in all the time from all over the country, without sensing pretty clearly how long we could carry it. I felt and said that we would reach the maximum of strength about the following Tuesday—then it would be a case of 'holding out' and I thought approximately three weeks would be necessary after that to clean up."[1]

But how was the General Council to take up again the negotiations which had been broken off by the Government?

The Cabinet adhered to its ultimatum: before talks could be resumed, the T.U.C. must call off the strike. This faced the General Council with an equally hard decision the other way, for to capitulate openly, after the response to its orders had been so complete, was bound to create disillusionment, to lead to bitter recriminations and to set the trade-union movement back for a generation. The one way out of their dilemma appeared to be to find some third party to mediate between themselves and the Government. In the account already quoted, Bevin says:

"Purcell and I had been working together on the Organisation Committee to mobilise public opinion to force negotiations. Mr. C. P. Scott, of the *Manchester Guardian*, had succeeded in calling a splendid meeting of the whole of the Lancashire business people. We knew he was going to do it. The Archbishop of Canterbury was working, as also were several big interests in the City, and at that moment our object was to try and get such a powerful body of people—commercial, religious and otherwise—to appoint a committee which would have acted as a mediatory committee between us and the Government. I went to the General Council and reported what was in our minds; our idea was to despatch Purcell to Manchester the next day. He knows the place very well and the people in it. Our scheme never fructified because within a few hours negotiations were opened by the Negotiation Committee with Samuel, who had been brought back or came back from Italy.

"We decided on the Strike Organisation Committee that, as they were meeting Samuel and that, presumably, he was in touch with Baldwin, it would not serve any good purpose our trying to get some other form of mediation."[2]

5

After the publication of the Commission's report, Sir Herbert Samuel had gone back to Italy with the intention of settling there.

---

1 Bevin's oral report to a Union committee, 22nd July 1926.
2 *Bevin.*

His return to London and his offer to help were made entirely on his own initiative. The other members of the Royal Commission were unwilling to join him and, at his first meeting with Baldwin and members of the Cabinet, the Government's position was made perfectly plain. In a letter dated 8th May, Sir Arthur Steel-Maitland, the Minister of Labour, wrote to Samuel:

"It is therefore plain that [the Government] cannot enter upon any negotiations unless the strike is so unreservedly concluded that there is not even an implication of such a bargain upon their side as would embarrass them in any legislation which they may conceive to be proper in the light of recent events.

". . . While they are bound most carefully and most sympathetically to consider the terms of any arrangement which a public man of your responsibility and experience may propose, it is imperative to make it plain that any discussion which you think proper to initiate is not clothed in even a vestige of official character."

The Negotiating Committee of the General Council, however, with whom Sir Herbert got in touch through J. H. Thomas, was eager to accept his offer to help, notwithstanding his careful insistence upon the unofficial character of his initiative. Jimmy Thomas was quicker than any other member of the General Council to see the quandary in which they were now placed and he was determined to find a way out.

A series of secret meetings took place in the Bryanston Square house of Thomas's friend, Sir Abe Bailey, the South African mining magnate. With the advice of Thomas, Pugh and the other members of the Negotiating Committee, Samuel drew up proposals for implementing the Commission's recommendations, based upon the draft made by Bevin on the night of 2nd–3rd May and handed by him to Ramsay MacDonald. Samuel and the Negotiating Committee tried to meet the miners' objection that the promised reorganisation of the industry was only another trick to get them to agree to wage reductions. They met several times on Friday and Saturday, 7th and 8th May, and the first draft of Samuel's proposals was placed before the General Council on the morning of Sunday, the 9th.

Both the Miners' representatives on the General Council were absent throughout the dispute. Robert Smillie, the former president of the Miners' Federation, left London before the national strike began and for unexplained reasons never put in another appearance; Tom Richards, their other representative, was ill. This was unfortunate, for the miners' suspicions of the General Council had been re-awakened by the week-end negotiations before the strike began. They were strengthened when, in the Commons' debate on the Monday night, 3rd May, Thomas revealed that there had been a second formula, the Birkenhead formula, discussed between Baldwin and the three trade-union representatives, Pugh, Swales and himself, on the Sunday evening. Neither Bevin nor any other member of the General Council had known of this second formula which specifically mentioned a reduction of wages but had not in fact been adopted or placed before the Council. Thomas's unauthorised reference, however, which Baldwin answered by reading out the formula to the House, convinced Herbert Smith and the other miners' leaders that something was going on behind their backs and had a powerful effect on stiffening their opposition to any negotiations.

It was doubly unfortunate that the first discussions between the Negotiating Committee of the General Council and Sir Herbert Samuel—for which Thomas again was responsible—took place without the knowledge of the Miners' leaders. Not until the morning of Sunday, 9th May, when the proposals had begun to take shape, were Smith and Cook called in and asked for their opinion. Even if the Negotiating Committee was within its rights in starting negotiations, subject to consultation with the miners, the way in which it acted was certain to create trouble. "We were ignored," Herbert Smith later declared.

"If anything was happening at Eccleston Square, we were not in it. We knew nothing of a definite character until Sunday, 9th May. . . . It then came out that there had been meetings with Sir Herbert Samuel. . . . The Miners had had plenty of Sir Herbert Samuel, we knew him quite well and did not want any further dealings with him."[1]

The Miners' reply to the General Council's inquiry was an uncompromising 'No'.

1 *Report*, 1927, p. 17.

6

The following day, Monday the 10th, Pugh and Citrine took Herbert Smith, Cook and Richardson to meet Sir Herbert Samuel and see if any changes in the proposals would remove their objections. Three hours' discussion failed to make any impression on Smith's angry insistence that he would not consider any reduction in wages, whatever assurances were given about reorganisation. Stubbornly convinced that he was right, he stuck grimly to the question of wages and shut his mind to the larger issues which now preoccupied the General Council.

In the course of Monday, Sir Herbert Samuel reduced his proposals for a settlement to a brief memorandum. He proposed:

(1) that the present and future disputes in the coal industry should be referred to a National Mines Board, with representatives of the miners and the owners, other independent members and an independent Chairman;

(2) that there should be no revision of the previous wage rates *"unless there are sufficient assurances that the measures of reorganisation will be actually put into effect"* and that the new Board should have the responsibility of ensuring that the necessary steps were actually taken;

(3) that, after agreement had been reached on reorganisation, the Board should prepare a new wages agreement on simplified lines, with no reduction for the lower-paid men and an irreducible national minimum for all colliery workers;

(4) that negotiations in any case should not be resumed until the lock-out notices had been withdrawn.

In a joint meeting with the Miners' Executive that evening (Monday 10th May), the General Council told the miners that they regarded the Samuel memorandum as a satisfactory basis for re-opening negotiations. The miners did not. In the course of a heated argument, the strongest pressure to accept the proposals came from the railwaymen's leaders, Thomas and Bromley, who threatened to take their men back if the strike were not called off. "Take them back," was the only reply this threat elicited from Herbert Smith, who retorted by asking pointedly what guarantees the T.U.C. had received that the Government or the mineowners would accept Sir Herbert Samuel's proposals.

Withdrawing to the Labour Party's offices next door for discussion among themselves, the Miners' Executive returned after three hours to announce that they had deleted the clauses (summarised under [3] above) which provided for a new wage agreement. It was not the lack of guarantees to which they objected but any scheme which did not exclude reduction of wages. If the measures for re-organisation were actually put into effect, they added, there would be no need to revise the previous wage rates.

When this decision was communicated to the General Council in the early hours of Tuesday morning, the Council urged the miners to put forward constructive proposals of their own. None was offered. The gap between the miners and the General Council was rapidly growing wider. At the conference of executives on 1st May, Smith had been ready to negotiate on the Samuel Report, provided that the miners were not asked to commit themselves to a reduction in advance. The Samuel Memorandum in fact went further than the Report to meet the miners but, once his suspicions were aroused, Smith became wooden in his obstinacy and fell back on their original position: 'Not a minute on the day, not a penny off the pay'. In effect, this meant no negotiations at all. On the other side, Thomas and Bromley represented a growing opinion in the General Council that, unless a settlement could be reached soon, the whole trade-union movement was in danger of disaster, and that the need to get a settlement must override everything else.

7

On Tuesday, 11th May, the General Council tried again. The Negotiating Committee met Sir Herbert Samuel and returned with a revised version of his memorandum. This embodied a number of suggestions which Bevin had handed to Milne-Bailey, one of the T.U.C. secretaries, for Samuel's consideration. Three new proposals were added, all in the miners' interests. The subsidy was to be renewed for the period of negotiations; new workers over eighteen were not to be recruited if unemployed miners were available, and those thrown out of work by the closing of uneconomic pits were to be provided for (a) by transfer to other employment, with Government assistance and with the provision of new houses to accommodate them, and (b) by maintenance payments (at the expense of the State and in addition to unemployment pay) for those who could not be transferred and for whom alternative employment could not be found.

Later on the Tuesday afternoon, the Negotiating Committee reported back to the full Council. Bevin, preoccupied with the work of the Strike Organisation Committee, had so far taken no direct part in the negotiations. There was, in fact, no one on the Negotiating Committee who could stand up to Thomas, a master of negotiating tactics and a man who was bent upon getting a settlement, whether the miners liked it or not. Thomas had carried the Negotiating Committee along with him and he now convinced the rest of the General Council. Bevin's account of what followed is best given in his own words:

"I did not happen to be at the General Council, but I must not try to escape responsibility. I had been meeting other people on other matters and did not get back until 6.30. When I got there, I met the Negotiating Committee coming out. I said to George Hicks, 'What has happened?' He said, 'They have adopted the Samuel proposals.' I asked what that meant and his reply was that, if they were accepted, it meant the finish. I urged him to be very careful and pointed out that they had not yet seen the Miners. I also urged care with regard to demobilising our forces. I told him to hesitate a bit.

"That was all in the street. I went upstairs and waited with the others. The Negotiating Committee came back again at about 7.30 and reported several verbal alterations. Now this is the crucial point. The Miners were sent for.

"Pugh, tired, worn and a little bit sick of things, did tell the Miners they had to take it or leave it. Well, with a temperament like Smith's that was asking for a stubborn opposition, but it was due to an unfortunate tiredness.

"Smith immediately wanted to know why he had not been at the negotiations that afternoon when the final document was arrived at. He was there the previous day discussing it with Samuel and the Negotiating Committee. He wanted to know the reason for being left out.

"Then a hullabaloo took place on that point. I appealed to the Miners that, with all the strain and stress of running a strike on their behalf, they should not exaggerate every little incident that occurred but that they should take the document on its merits, examine it and see whether it offered a solution to their trouble.

"After a good deal of persuasion, the Miners retired, returned about 11 p.m. and rejected the document. I still think that, if . . the Samuel memorandum had been accepted by the Government, there have been no better proposals put forth as a solution to the mining trouble. I would stand up against any miner in the country on the merits of that document and the

Miners' M.P.s welcomed it when we went into the House that night.

"Well, after the Miners went, everyone on the General Council felt that there would be no solution in conjunction with the Miners' Executive, but that it had become necessary to reach a decision without them. We were responsible for four times as many people as they had in the field and therefore the question of whether the Miners accepted it or not was discarded altogether. We said that the Conference gave us the job and, just as when a Group in this Union puts a job in the hands of the Union, the Executive has the power to decide the issue, so the General Council for the purpose of this problem was the Executive for the Movement. We took the line that the Miners were no more in it than anyone else . . .

"With others I categorically questioned the Negotiating Committee. We asked, 'Does it mean, if we call the strike off, that the Samuel document is to be made public, that the Government is to accept it, and that lock-out notices are to be withdrawn simultaneously with our ordering resumption of work?' Categorically, these questions were asked three times and in each instance the answer was 'Yes'. Well, you have negotiated and I have negotiated, and you know you have to take the word of negotiators. We took their word. I have since heard things that made me uneasy.

"The Prime Minister rang us up at a quarter to one before the strike was called off. I concluded that what we had been told of the Prime Minister being in possession of the information was correct and that he was actually waiting in Downing Street to know whether we accepted the document or not. No suspicion entered my mind at all, but I did suggest that we ought not to see the Prime Minister that night.

"We were tired and had given no thought to demobilising. I felt, in view of the heated nature of the Miners that night, we should see them next morning and really try to get a united body. Nevertheless, I was under no qualms about calling the strike off on the assurance received on the Samuel document.

"I have heard since that the Prime Minister was told from our own side that we might be wanting him early in the evening, but still, when the Prime Minister's secretary rang up Citrine as to whether we would be wanting to see him that night, having listened to the report of the Negotiating Committee, I came to the conclusion that everything was as reported and I voted for the calling off like any other man would have done under similar circumstances."[1]

Other accounts do not add much to that given by Bevin. When Pugh told Herbert Smith that the General Council had agreed to accept Samuel's proposals as a basis for negotiations and to call off the strike, the Miners' President asked: "Is that the unanimous decision of your Committee?"

[1] *Bevin.*

Pugh: "Yes."

Smith: "Is it not possible for us to sit down and see how far we can get? Is it just crossing the t's and dotting the i's?"

Pugh: "That is it, Mr. Smith; that is the final decision, that is what you have to consider as far as you are concerned and accept it."

Smith: "Do you people realise the serious position you are putting yourselves in? Are you going back without any consideration for the men who are going to be victimised in this movenent? Are you not going to consider that at all?"

"I appealed to them," Smith added later, "as I never appealed to anybody in my life to consider it. I was told that each union could manage its own business if the miners would accept the Samuel memorandum."[1]

8

The strength of the Miners' position was its consistency. The wrangle about 'guarantees' was beside the point. As Herbert Smith made perfectly clear, with or without guarantees, the miners were not prepared to accept the Samuel memorandum or any settlement which did not rule out a reduction in wages. Nor did they offer any proposals of their own in place of Samuel's. They had never believed in negotiations; they believed the dispute could only be settled by a fight and they were prepared to see it through.

The weakness of the Miners' position was its impracticability. No one can doubt the integrity of Herbert Smith and Arthur Cook or fail to admire the courage of the men and their wives, but this does not alter the fact that hatred of the owners, an outraged sense of justice and a grim determination to die in the last ditch did not add up to a practical programme. As Harold Laski wrote to his friend Felix Frankfurter after the strike was called off:

"The miners were impossible. They never budged an inch throughout. They have no plans, and, if they had their way, the T.U.C. would be out until Domesday. Even now, they have nothing to say except that they won't budge. I have certainly never seen more hopeless (tho' more courageous) leadership than theirs . . ."[2]

1 Herbert Smith, *Report* 1927, p. 19.

2 Harold Laski to Felix Frankfurter, 24th May 1926, quoted in Kingsley Martin: *Harold Laski* (1953), p. 66.

The question Bevin and the other members of the General Council had to ask themselves was whether they were prepared to go on risking the future of their own unions and their own members in support of a position which virtually excluded any chance of negotiating a settlement.

The miners might be able to contemplate a strike of six, twelve, even more weeks, certain that, however long they stayed out, no volunteers would move in to work the pits. The transport unions, however, knew that long before six weeks had elapsed, the Government would be forced to take drastic action to get transport moving and that the brunt of such action—and of public resentment— would have to be borne by their members, not by the miners. They had already mortgaged their union funds and their members' jobs to support the miners, but if the miners were not prepared to accept a negotiated settlement at all they could not go on indefinitely.

Nor did the thirty members of the General Council, with a wide experience of negotiations between them, believe that prolonging the strike would get the miners any better terms. Pugh, the Chairman of the Council, told Herbert Smith that better terms could not be obtained if the strike went on for a week or ten years.

The railwaymen's leaders were ready to call off the strike then and there. It was Bevin who interposed the delay to allow one more attempt to preserve a united front. In voting for the Samuel proposals he had made up his mind on the strength of the assurances from Thomas and the other members of the Negotiating Committee that they could rely on the Government's accepting them as well. Thomas did not pretend that they had received any formal guarantee from the Government side, but the Negotiating Committee gave Bevin and the other members of the General Council the impression that the Cabinet would be willing to accept Samuel's proposals once the strike was called off. In a letter which he sent out to the branches of his union, Bevin wrote:

"You may take it from me that we, who were not on the Negotiating Committee, were assured that the Samuel document would be accepted, that the lock-out notices would be withdrawn and that methods of resumption would be discussed forthwith."

This statement, as we shall see, is consistent with Bevin's attitude when the General Council's representatives met the Prime Minister the following day. It is also borne out by a letter to the Press, published a few days after the strike, in which Bevin and two other members of the General Council accused Baldwin of bad faith and called on Samuel to speak out. "Will he deny that consultations took place between Mr. Baldwin and himself on the terms of the Memorandum?"[1] The answer was that no consultation had taken place, but Bevin continued to believe that Baldwin knew very well what was happening, even if he had not committed himself.

9

The final appeal to the Miners for which Bevin called was left in his hands. The miners refused to see Thomas, and Bevin was accompanied on the Wednesday morning (12th May) not by the Negotiating Committee, but by Purcell and the other members of the Strike Organisation Committee. The account which follows is taken from the Miners' Federation's notes and substantially agrees with Bevin's own briefer record.

"They came," said Bevin, "with a difficult message, but they would not lack courage in putting it. The General Council decided last night to terminate the general strike today at noon, and informed the Prime Minister accordingly.[2] He appealed to us [the Miners] to make common cause with them, even if we did not agree with them: if we did not, the terms offered might not be so good afterwards; not only so, but it would prevent a gesture of the same kind in the future if any other union was attacked and it would split the whole industrial and political movement in this country. He claimed that the decision of the General Council was arrived at because in many trades there was an uneasiness among the men who were entitled to pensions and superannuation. Although we had rejected the formula last night, he appealed to us to go back with them as we came out; that would show a spirit of solidarity unequalled in this or any other country and he believed the terms offered would help the miners ultimately if not immediately. His union paid out £360,000 last week."

Bevin's argument was supported by Purcell and by Ben Turner, of the Textile Workers, who expressed the view that the general strike

1 Quoted in Julian Symons, *op. cit.*, p. 222.
2 Bevin's account confirms this: "I also told them we had decided to go to the Prime Minister—it was just as well to tell them straight."

was on the 'slippery slope' and that an unauthorised return to work was already taking place.

Herbert Smith's reply was as unyielding as ever. He complained bitterly of unfair treatment and intrigues behind the Miners' backs:

"So far as he was concerned, he wanted to tell them frankly there was more enthusiasm for the general strike amongst the rank and file than there was amongst the General Council. They had been continually on the doormat of the Prime Minister since and before the strike began without our knowledge and so far as he was concerned he would have no more truck with politicians in an industrial war."[1]

Smith agreed to put Bevin's request to his Executive but the issue was not in doubt. When Cook brought down their refusal, it was a quarter to twelve. Bevin had just time to jump in a cab and get to Downing Street to join the Negotiating Committee who were due to meet the Prime Minister at noon.

Before Bevin went to the Miners' Federation offices, the question had been raised:

"If we go to Downing Street, what is to be the attitude? First, the Strike to be called off. Secondly, we had to discuss the resumption of work in an organised manner, and thirdly arrangements for negotiations on the basis of the Samuel Memorandum."[2]

The interview with the Prime Minister, however, followed a very different course.

"Before we got there, the decision of the Miners had been given to the Press. When we got to Downing Street, it was on the tapes . . . Baldwin knew that the movement was split.

"When we went in, Sir Horace Wilson[3] came to the door of the Cabinet Room. He said 'You want to see the Prime Minister?' Thomas said 'Yes.' Wilson then said, 'Well, Mr. Pugh and Mr. Thomas, what do you want to see the Prime Minister for?' They replied, 'We want to see him on the position.' The reply to this was 'You know the Prime Minister will not see you before the strike is called off.'

"I said at the back, 'For Christ's sake let's call it on again if this is the position.' Thomas then said 'We have come to call the strike off,' and we then went in and sat down."[4]

1 The Miners' notes of the interview were read out by A. J. Cook at the Conference of Executives in January 1927. *Report*, 1927, p. 21.

2 Bevin's account to the Union's Biennal Delegate Conference, July 1927.

3 Permanent Secretary at the Ministry of Labour.

4 *Bevin.*

Whether Bevin was right or not in attaching so much importance to Baldwin's knowledge of the Miners' decision, it at once became clear that the Government was not prepared to discuss terms. They were received by Baldwin and six of his colleagues in the Cabinet Room. To Bevin's surprise and anger, neither Thomas nor Pugh mentioned the Samuel memorandum or the withdrawal of the mine-owners' notices. Even more important, nothing was said about the way in which the strike was to be called off or of protection against victimisation when the men returned to work. The T.U.C. offered unconditional surrender.

All that Thomas did was to appeal to Baldwin to respond to the General Council's decision in a generous way:

"We trust your word as Prime Minister. We ask you to assist us in the way you only can assist us—by asking employers and all others to make the position as easy and smooth as possible, because the one thing we must not have is guerrilla warfare."

Baldwin found no difficulty in replying in equally vague terms without committing himself to anything at all.

10

No one else on the trade-union side offered to speak and there the interview would have ended, had it not been for Bevin. Astonished to hear no mention made of negotiations on the mining dispute or of guarantees against victimisation, he could not keep silent. His words were awkward and embarrassed, but alone of the General Council representatives he tried to press the Prime Minister.

"We have taken a great risk in calling the strike off. I want to urge it must not be regarded as an act of weakness but rather one of strength. . . . It took a little courage to take the line we have done. I want to stress Mr. Thomas's point and ask you if you could tell us whether you are prepared to make a general request, as head of the Government, that ready facilities for reinstatement and that kind of thing shall be given forthwith.
"I remember after the 1912 strike, when we were beaten, Sir Joseph Brood-bank went into it very carefully and the loss in output and transport was something like 25 per cent for some time until the war. We do not want that kind of thing. We have had a row, and it does upset things, but we are quite willing to co-operate with our men to repair the damage just as much as the

employers, but the employers are the people who can facilitate that kind of feeling. I am sure they would respond to you if you issued that as a statement. It would be very helpful to us if before we left the building we could have some indication in that direction.

"You said, sir, also you are going to call the parties together in order to effect a just settlement . . . I do not know whether I am overstepping the bounds, but I would like you to give me an idea of whether that means that there will be a resumption of the mining negotiations with us, or whether all the negotiations have to be carried on while the miners still remain out . . . "I really felt in the event of our taking the lead in assuring you we were going to play the game and put our people back that it was going to be free and unfettered negotiations[1] with the parties very speedily because thousands of our people cannot go back if the others are still out and if the colliers are still out it is going to make it extremely difficult to get a smooth running of the machine. Those are the two points I wish to put to you."[2]

Baldwin declined to be drawn:

"You know my record. You know the object of my policy and I think you may trust me to consider what has been said with a view to seeing how best we can get the country quickly back into the condition in which we all want to see it. You will want my co-operation and I shall want yours . . ."

With these generalities Baldwin brought the interview to an end:

"Now, Mr. Pugh, we have both of us got a great deal to do, and the sooner you get to your work and the sooner I get to mine the better."

Pugh was only too glad to agree and got up to go; it was Bevin again who introduced the discordant note:

"I am a little persistent. I do not want to take up your time, but shall we be meeting on these two points soon?"

All he got for his pains was a polite snub. "I cannot say that, Mr. Bevin," Baldwin replied. "I think it may be that, whatever decision I come to, the House of Commons may be the best place in which to say it." With that the T.U.C. representatives had to be content.

In a depressed silence they walked through the door of No. 10 out into the sunlight of Downing Street. Ben Turner (who had not opened his mouth) wrote in his diary:

1 i.e. a withdrawal of the owners' notices.
2 From the official report issued by Downing Street on the evening of 12th May.

Above, left. Harry Gosling. *Above, right.* A. J. Cook arriving for a miners' delegate conference, November 1926. *Below.* The General Strike: the Prime Minister, Stanley Baldwin, leaving the back entrance of No. 10 Downing Street.

The General Strike. *Above.* Lord Birkenhead, Neville Chamberlain and the Rt. Hon. W. E. Guinness arriving for the Cabinet meeting on the morning of Sunday, May 2nd 1926. *Below.* Ramsay MacDonald and Ben Tillett leaving Eccleston Square.

"G.C. flabbergasted at nothing being settled about miners' lockout notices. Retired and felt dismayed . . . left at 1.10 disappointed and disgusted. Papers out soon about T.U.C. surrender."[1]

Bevin was not so resigned:

"When we got outside, I said to Thomas and Pugh: 'There is something wrong here' . . . I felt we had been let down, that either the Government had let Samuel give assurances he ought not to have given, or Samuel had over-estimated what he could do, or we had placed too great an importance on the Samuel position. Certainly the proceedings were not in conformity with the arrangements of a quarter-to-one the night before.
"We came out and went back to Eccleston Square where I expressed myself quite freely. I said, 'Something has happened and the best way to describe today, if we are not quick, is that we have committed suicide. Thousands of members will be victimised as the result of this day's work.' "[2]

I I

The announcement that the strike had been called off without securing the withdrawal of the mineowners' notices or any settlement of the original dispute came as a profound shock to the local strike committees and the rank and file of the trade unions. However strong the reasons which convinced the General Council that this was the only course they could take, the way in which they carried out their decisions and the curt manner in which they announced it produced a disastrous impression.

At the beginning of the week, the *British Worker* had carried, under the heading "ALL'S WELL." a special message from the General Council:

"From every town and city in the country reports are pouring into headquarters stating that all ranks are solid, that the working men and women are resolute in their determination to resist the unjust attack upon the mining community . . .
"The General Council's message at the opening of the second week is:— Stand Firm. Be Loyal to Instructions and Trust your Leaders."

Only the day before (Tuesday) the engineers and shipyard workers had joined the strike on the instructions of the General

1 Ben Turner, *About Myself* (1930), p. 312.
2 *Bevin.*

M

Council. The pessimism expressed by Thomas, Bromley and other members of the General Council did not reflect local feeling in the country. Nine days after the strike began solidarity was still surprisingly strong and morale high. The General Council had given no indication that it did not share this confidence. On the contrary, up to the very last moment before ending the strike, it went on calling for uncompromising resistance, and gave no hint of the secret negotiations in which it was engaged, of the anxieties it felt or of the danger of a split with the Miners.

There was no preparation at all for the abrupt and arbitrary reversal which now followed, no consultation of union executives, no attempt to put the case for calling the strike off. Little wonder that to most trade unionists, angered and bewildered by the news, it appeared only too evident that they had been let down by their leaders and their loyalty betrayed. The fact that the miners, even when deserted by their allies, refused to give up their struggle added shame to the humiliation and anger at the General Council's surrender.

In the original instructions approved by the conference of executives on 1st May, one of the conditions to which the General Council attached the most importance was Clause 5:

"The General Council further direct that the Executives of the Unions concerned shall definitely declare that in the event of any action being taken and trade union agreements being placed in jeopardy, it be definitely agreed that there will be no general resumption of work until these agreements are fully recognised."

It now became clear that, in their anxiety to call off the strike, the General Council had taken no steps to implement their own instructions. No arrangements were made for an organised return to work; each union was left to scramble back and make the best arrangements it could with employers. Nothing so alarmed and aroused Bevin as the discovery that this had been left to chance. Men returning to work, especially on the railways, found themselves refused employment or forced to accept terms which might include reduction of wages, loss of seniority and, in some cases, a ban on trade-union membership. Many employers were eager to take advantage of the General Council's unconditional surrender to break the power of the unions and end collective bargaining.

As soon as he discovered what was happening, Bevin sent out instructions to his own members to stay on strike. In this situation, the trade unions were saved, not by their leaders, but by the local committees and the rank and file who, on their own initiative, decided to stand firm and refused to be panicked. On 13th May, in fact, the strike was more solid than ever and 100,000 more men were out.

The Prime Minister's statement to the House of Commons on the afternoon of the 12th failed to give the lead for which Bevin asked. That evening Bevin and other members of the General Council went to see the Prime Minister a second time and urge him to take a stand against victimisation.

"Worthington-Evans[1] said: 'You called the strike off at 12 o'clock, but now you have called it on again.' I replied, 'We have called off the strike against the constitution as you put it, but now we have called a constitutional strike to defend our wages and agreements.'
"We discussed the position with the Prime Minister and he indicated that he was broadcasting a message that night. I asked him whether I might read it. He permitted me to do so and I told him it was very sentimental but not very effective. I asked him to put in the phrase that trade unions and employers should meet forthwith to arrange a resumption."[2]

12

These and other representations had their effect. The next day, Thursday, the 13th, Baldwin went a good deal further. He told the House of Commons that he would not countenance any attempt by employers to use the situation to force down wages or launch an attack on trade unionism. Baldwin's attitude, the general relief that the country had weathered the crisis without disaster and the realisation that the trade unions were in no mood to submit to humiliation—all these combined to temper the demand for reprisals. The railway companies were the most unyielding. They insisted on suspending the guaranteed week except for men who had not gone on strike and as late as October, 45,000 railwaymen were still out of jobs, partly, of course, as a result of slack trade made

1 Secretary of State for War.
2 *Bevin.*

worse by the strike, but partly from a refusal to reinstate those who had been most active in the strike.

Bevin threw himself into the defence of his own members' agreements. Despite the efforts of his officers, there was still much to be done. His first concern was the London docks. At the price of admitting that the Union had broken its agreements, he secured a settlement which preserved the terms of the national agreement and put back all the permanent men employed in the Port who—especially in the supervisory grades—stood loyally by the dockers and might well have been penalised by the employers.

With London safe, he caught the train to the West and took in hand the situation in Bristol and Gloucester.

"In Bristol 670 blacklegs had signed on in the docks. I never saw such a thing in my life. The railwaymen were backing in and taking away from the blacklegs. Blacklegs four-deep were registering all day at the place where I was negotiating. Jim Garmston (the Area Secretary) and I stuck it for ten hours and now there is not one blackleg left. They are all cleared off the dock."[1]

Bevin's own efforts were matched by those of his officers. None of the precious national agreements was lost and by the end of May Bevin was able to report that, out of 353,000 members who had come out on strike, the Union had failed to get back less than 1,500.

13

By failing to stand by its own instruction for a concerted return to work—"one back, all back"—the General Council abandoned its responsibility for the strike, left every union to fend for itself, and devil take the hindmost. Its explanations—or lack of them—only added to the confusion.

First statements from the T.U.C. made it sound as if the Government had accepted the Samuel memorandum. An official message from the General Council, carried by the *British Worker* on 13th May, declared that they had "obtained assurances that a settlement of the mining problem can be secured which justifies them in bringing the general stoppage to an end". Another message sent out in a circular

1 *Bevin.*

letter to unions announced that the strike had been called off "in order that negotiations could be resumed to secure a settlement in the mining industry, free and unfettered from either strikes or lock-out". This may well have been due to a genuine misunderstanding on the part of the members of the General Council in which Bevin shared up to the meeting in Downing Street. It is indeed impossible to make out from the evidence what the members of the General Council believed. Whether they were deceived by Thomas, whether it was wishful thinking or not, some of them—including Bevin—certainly seem to have thought that the Government had agreed to resume negotiations, continue the subsidy and get the owners' notices withdrawn. But there is no excuse for the fact that no mention at all was made in the General Council's announcement that the miners refused to accept the Samuel memorandum and were remaining on strike.

When the truth became known and Baldwin denied categorically that the Government had agreed to any conditions, the impression was inevitably created, however one-sided, that in its desire to get a settlement at any price the General Council had panicked, "had sold the miners" and betrayed the rank and file.

The charge of betrayal was repeated again and again by the Left and the miners. Bevin, however, although in talking to his own members he never concealed his indignation at the way in which the strike was brought to an end, was equally emphatic in defending the General Council's decision to call it off.

Criticism of the General Council, in his view, was based upon one or other of two uncriticised assumptions: either that, if the strike had only been continued for a week or two more, the Government would have capitulated without the strikers doing more than blockade the nation; or that the General Council from the first should have prepared for a revolutionary movement designed to overthrow the capitalist system.

The General Council, however, rejected both assumptions as unreal and the evidence supports their view. The fact that morale was high and solidarity unbroken in many districts does not prove them to have been wrong. What the local strike committees did not see but the General Council was forced to realise was that, once the Government had made up its mind to use the full resources of the State to defeat the strike, something more than morale and solidarity were required. The general strike had not in fact proved to be the decisive weapon which Labour had long assumed it would be.

This created a new situation. No doubt, the General Council was to blame for not foreseeing the implications of the action for which they called and the dangers to the trade-union movement with which they were now confronted. But the illusions which had blinded them were common to the whole trade-union movement. Indeed, much of the criticism directed against the General Council sprang from the fact that the Left in particular and many of the keen trade unionists continued to nurse these illusions after the General Council had been forced to recognise the unpleasant facts which stared it in the face.

The General Council, therefore, in Bevin's view, was right to seek a way out by negotiation. It was impossible in the circumstances in which they found themselves to recall the conference of executives, lay the position before them and thrash out their course of action in debate. They had to act quickly and they had to act on their own responsibility.

14

It is easy to lose oneself in a maze of controversy about the powers which the Miners' Federation handed over to the T.U.C. or what was said at the conference of executives on 1st May. Bevin's position at least was clear. In the discussions on the Industrial Alliance he had foreseen that a situation of this sort might arise, calling for prompt decision without the chance to put into operation the slow-moving machinery for democratic consultation. To meet it he insisted that the unions must hand over their powers to the body directing the strike—in this case, the General Council—and accept its decisions without argument. He pressed the miners strongly on this point during the discussions of the Industrial Alliance constitution, repeated it in his speech to the conference of executives and would never have agreed to call his own union out in their support if he had not believed that his view had been accepted. This was the one guarantee against a repetition of Black Friday and when the miners once again insisted on their right to decide for themselves and their inability to depart from a decision of their national delegate conference, Black Friday was repeated.

Bevin was prepared to maintain that, even if the miners honestly believed the course proposed by the General Council to be wrong, they ought to have accepted it. But he was, in fact, convinced that the Samuel memorandum offered the best chance the miners ever had of a lasting settlement of the problems of their industry. Admittedly, the T.U.C. had no guarantee that the Government would accept Samuel's proposals and the discovery of this fact in the interview with the Prime Minister came as a shock to Bevin. None the less he continued to argue that, if the miners had maintained a united front with the T.U.C. and if Baldwin had not known before he met the General Council that there was an open split in the trade-union ranks, the Government would have found it impossible to refuse to negotiate on the basis of the Samuel memorandum.

This is a point on which there can be no certainty. Bevin may have been right. The Government was certainly aware that negotiations were going on and in a broadcast on the evening of 8th May, Baldwin had declared "no door is closed"—he was ready to parley with anyone and, once the General Strike had been called off, "to discuss the terms upon which the coal industry is to be carried on, to see that justice is done both to the miners and the owners." As chairman of the recent Royal Commission, Samuel was in a strong position and his recommendations, backed by the offer of a united trade-union movement to call off the general strike and accept his proposals, would undoubtedly have made a big impression on public opinion, against which the party of 'unconditional surrender' in the Cabinet would have found it difficult to hold out. Baldwin had to handle a difficult situation in his own Cabinet and with the skill which he could command as a politician when he exerted himself, he kept his hands free. No Prime Minister would have agreed to bind himself in advance, but the lack of 'guarantees' does not invalidate Bevin's argument, any more than the fact that, when Baldwin found he had to deal with a divided trade-union movement, he subsequently proposed different terms for a settlement.

On the other hand, Bevin may have been making the best of a bad case. He was certainly disgusted with the weak attitude which Thomas and Pugh displayed in the interview with the Prime Minister and furious at the way in which the General Council abandoned its responsibility for the strike without any guarantees on the reinstatement of the men who had followed its instructions. Even if they could do nothing more for the miners, they should, he felt, have held out in the defence of their own members before calling the strike off unconditionally.

15

After six months' further resistance, ended only by hunger and despair, the miners went back to work in December 1926 on terms which cut their wages, lengthened their hours, replaced the national with district agreements and left them worse off than ever. Export markets lost during the strike were never recovered; unemployment remained high. So bad were conditions in the coalfields that the Lord Mayor of London opened a Miners' Relief Fund.

The coal industry was neither nationalised nor re-organised. The opportunity offered by the Samuel memorandum and the Samuel Report did not recur and the Miners' Federation did not recover from the defeat of 1926 before the war. One may well ask whether, even if it meant accepting some reduction in wages, the miners would not have done better to have listened to Bevin's plea and accepted the General Council's advice.

CHAPTER 13

A Turning-Point
1926

I

On 4th May, the second day of the strike, Beatrice Webb wrote in her diary:

"For the British trade union movement I see a day of terrible disillusionment. The failure of the General Strike of 1926 will be one of the most significant landmarks in the history of the British working-class. Future historians will, I think, regard it as the death-gasp of that pernicious doctrine of 'workers' control' of public affairs through the trade unions and by the method of direct action."[1]

This was a bold forecast to make when the Strike had only just begun, but it proved to be fully justified. The General Strike is the watershed in the history of the trade-union movement between 1910 and 1940, the thirty years of Bevin's career as a trade unionist. On the far side of 1926, we enter a different climate of opinion from the turbulent years of the earlier 1920s.

Between the end of 1921 and May 1926 strike action had never again been on the scale of the years 1919–21, and the majority of industrial disputes had been settled by negotiation. But trade-union thinking—and, in a crisis, trade-union action—was still strongly coloured by Marxist and syndicalist beliefs in the class war, the inevitability of conflict between capital and labour, the imminent overthrow of capitalism and direct action to secure the trade unions' objectives by force. There had been a revival of militancy in 1924 and 1925, culminating in the episode of 'Red Friday'. By 1926, the aggressive mood was ebbing, but it was still strong enough to bring the unions out solidly in support of the summons to strike.

1 *Diaries*, 1924–32, p. 92.

Until the slogan of direct action had been put to the test and the trade-union leaders forced to recognise its revolutionary implications—even in an industrial dispute—the movement could not shake itself free from the arrested assumptions of the immediate post-war period. This was the sense in which Bevin spoke of the General Strike as 'inevitable' and Beatrice Webb described it as "a proletarian distemper which had to run its course".

The first assumption to go by the board was the belief that it was possible to create an instrument of power with which the unions could force the employers and the State to accept their demands, as they had in July 1925 by the threat of an embargo on the movement of coal. Schemes for an industrial alliance along the lines debated a hundred times in the previous ten years could not survive the repetition of Black Friday on a greater scale, the open split with the Miners' Federation and the collapse of a united front at the end of the General Strike.

History proved stronger than the argument for unity. The individual unions had come into existence independently, each acquiring its own characteristics and an ingrained feeling in favour of autonomy. Later attempts to impose unity or logic, although not without partial successes in amalgamation, have always broken down over the same issue, the surrender of autonomy. The arguments for unity were still as strong as ever, but the effort to realise it in practice by creating an organisation sufficiently cohesive and disciplined to stand the strain of national action was now abandoned.

The events of 1926 showed Bevin and the other union leaders that there were limits not only to their power but also to the use they could afford to make of it unless they were prepared to risk being carried much further than most of them meant to go. Industrial action on a national scale was bound to have political and constitutional implications whether intended or not. The unions did not abandon the use of the strike weapon, but henceforward they looked on it as a weapon to be used only in the last resort and strike action on the extended scale of the Triple Alliance or of May 1926 was never again attempted during Bevin's career as a trade-union leader.[1]

1 The average number of workers involved in strikes and lock-outs in each of the three years 1919–21, was 2,108,000; in 1926, 2,751,000. In each of the thirteen years, 1927–39, it was 308, 100.

2

In the pessimistic mood which followed the General Strike, there was a strong inclination to fall back on the view that the unions' only concern was to defend their members' interests as best they could and not concern themselves with anything else. Bevin regarded this as an admission of defeat, a relapse into the old sectionalism with each union fighting on its own narrow front. The trade-union movement still disposed of considerable power, as the solidarity of the men in the General Strike had demonstrated: it had to find a way to make that power felt without involving itself in a challenge to the State. 'Never Again' was not enough. There must be some middle way between the revolutionary aims of syndicalism and the unions' abandonment of any claim to interest themselves in more than wage negotiations.

It was largely thanks to Bevin and Citrine that the T.U.C., after the defeat of 1926, renewed the claim of organised labour to make its views heard in all major decisions, national as well as industrial, even if it now tacitly accepted limits to the means it could adopt to enforce those views.

At the 1927 Trades Union Congress, Bevin set out to give a lead on economic policy by putting up three linked resolutions on behalf of the T.G.W.U.[1] At the 1928 Congress, defending the decision of the General Council to engage in the Mond-Turner talks[2] he told the delegates:

"I look forward to the time when the General Council will be coming and laying before this great parliament of its own creation annual reports on the discussion of great economic problems, trying to direct your attention on lines of analysis, lines of investigation and not mere debating points blown by the wind. Thus and thus only will the movement be really intelligently dealing with the real economic problems of our times."[3]

The part Bevin played not only in the Mond-Turner talks but in setting up the Economic Committee of the General Council; his presentation of that Committee's controversial report to the 1930

1 See below, pp. 387–88.
2 See below, c. 15.
3 T.U.C. Report, 1928, p. 451.

T.U.C.; his readiness to serve on the Macmillan Committee on Finance and Industry and on the Economic Advisory Council set up by MacDonald—all these are stages in the logical development of the new line of policy which he was trying to work out.

Measured by immediate results, its effect was negligible. The hopes which Bevin at one time entertained of the Mond-Turner talks were disappointed; the T.U.C.'s views on economic policy or un-employment had little influence even with a Labour Government in power and in 1931 the General Council was unable to persuade MacDonald and Snowden to abandon a policy which Bevin and the other trade union leaders believed to be disastrously wrong. But if we look beyond 1931, it is evident that the policy followed by Bevin and Citrine in the years following the General Strike laid the foundation for the steady growth after 1938 in the practice of con-sulting the trade unions by Government and industry. By the 1940s, the T.U.C. had become accepted as a national institution with an authority which it was very far from enjoying on the morrow of the General Strike. The slow accumulation of that authority was the work of Bevin and Citrine who gave the General Council a sense of direction again at a time when its credit had sunk so low that there was a danger of its becoming moribund. In the process, its role changed from that of a general staff, Bevin's original conception in 1920, to that of a policy-making body, the Cabinet of organised labour, with the task of forming and expressing trade-union views on all important national and international issues.

3

The Webbs, like Ramsay MacDonald, hoped that in the long run the failure of independent action by the trade unions would lead to the rehabilitation of political methods and recognition of the need to work through the Labour Party and Parliamentary institutions to secure the changes which the working class sought.

This was a difficult conclusion for a man with Bevin's views on politics and politicians to accept. MacDonald's first attempt to draw the lessons of the strike, in an article published in *The Socialist Review* for June 1926, roused Bevin to angry protest.

The Labour Party's position during the General Strike had been unenviable. The Party leaders' efforts to help had been barely tolerated; it had been made perfectly clear that this was a trade-union show and that the politicians had better keep out. In private MacDonald was highly critical of the unions' tactics and leadership. In public he did his best to keep up the façade of unity, but, once the strike was over, he found it difficult to conceal his views completely.

"The General Strike," he wrote in *The Socialist Review*, "is a weapon that cannot be wielded for industrial purposes. It is clumsy and ineffectual. It has no goal which, when reached, can be regarded as victory. . . . Some critics, who have responsibility for nothing, blame the General Council; some blame the miners. The real blame is with the General Strike itself and those who preached it without considering it and induced the workers to blunder into it . . .
"I hope that the result will be a thorough reconsideration of trade-union tactics. If the wonderful unity in the strike . . . would be shown in politics, Labour could solve the mining and similar difficulties through the ballot box."[1]

This was an issue on which Bevin had crossed swords with MacDonald at the last Labour Party conference. Events since had proved MacDonald to be right and Bevin wrong. But Bevin was in no mood to admit this. He was still too angry and sore, too deeply involved in the effort to prevent the effects of the Strike destroying the work of years to appreciate such detached conclusions. He sat down and wrote a letter to Arthur Henderson into which he poured out all his pent-up irritation and his deep-rooted distrust of Mac-donald. He left nothing unsaid, harking back to the London tram strike during the Labour Government of 1924 and MacDonald's handling of the Zinoviev letter. Bevin accused MacDonald of "stabbing us in the back":

"I cannot see my way clear to support the Labour Party and to take part in its propaganda so long as Mr. J. R. MacDonald as its leader continues his present policy in relation to the industrial side . . .
"I claim we had courage in calling that strike, in running it and in facing our job when it had to be called off, and this is not the time for the leader of the political party to be going around challenging the policy of the in-dustrial side . . . and trying to weaken the morale of our people by casting doubt upon our judgment in calling the strike."[2]

1 *The Socialist Review*, June 1926, p. 8. Bevin kept a file of MacDonald's speeches and articles on the General Strike.
2 Ernest Bevin to Arthur Henderson, 4th June 1926.

Henderson, who understood Bevin far better than MacDonald ever could, handled his outburst with good sense. Instead of placing Bevin's letter before the National Executive of the Labour Party, as Bevin demanded, he brought the two men together, smoothed Bevin down and patched the quarrel up.

An invitation from Brailsford to put the General Council's point of view in *The New Leader* brought an equally vehement refusal. When Brailsford told Bevin that his attitude was impossible and that the trade unions were paying a heavy price for their neglect of the Press, Bevin replied:

"While you admit you were badly informed you wrote in a manner intended to cast reflections upon those who had to take responsibility on the General Council for the Movement.

"Even if all you said were true, it is sufficient for the other side to pull the movement to pieces without you indulging in it.

"Here was a great, a tremendous thing . . . yet epoch-making events do not appeal to you as much as the muddy side of casting doubt and suspicion. That is and always has been my complaint against the so-called 'intelligentsia' and their 'superior' attitude of mind.

"With regard to our refusal to talk to you and people in your category in the movement, believe me we have very good reasons. The 'superior class' attitude is always there in relation to the trade union leader who comes from the rank and file. We do not like your patronage and naturally withdraw from it.

"I take it there is no use in prolonging this correspondence; I do not feel at home outside my own circle of trade union work."[1]

Bevin's immediate reaction, however, did not last. There was a marked improvement in relations between the trade unions and the Labour Party between 1926 and 1929 which bore fruit in the election of the latter year. Without losing his distrust of politicians, Bevin abandoned the indifference to wider issues which he had paraded in 1924 and showed a more constructive, more committed attitude to the second Labour Government of 1929–31 than he had towards the first. The break-up of the Government in 1931 led him to intensify, not to relinquish, this interest in political action.

1 Ernest Bevin to H. N. Brailsford, June 1926. Bevin put no date on his letter which was in reply to Brailsford's of 8th June.

4

Immediately after the General Strike was called off, Baldwin took the initiative in putting forward terms for a settlement of the coal dispute. On 14th May he sent to the Miners' Federation and to the owners proposals which retained many, though not all, of Sir Herbert Samuel's suggestions: a national agreement and a National Wages Board, with an independent chairman, to draw up a new wage agreement and prevent future disputes. At the same time he offered a Government grant of £3,000,000 to soften the immediate reduction in wages pending negotiations through the Wages Board. Both sides rejected these proposals, the miners still refusing to consider any scheme which involved a reduction in wages.

Behind the scenes, Bevin was active in trying to frame a formula on reorganisation which would give the miners sufficient guarantees to persuade them to accept the Government's proposals. He was convinced that they still offered better terms than the miners could hope to secure by continuing their fight. Among his papers are to be found a number of drafts dating from the second half of May which he put up to the miners' leaders and to the Minister of Labour. He was wasting his time. The miners' only reply to a long and persuasive letter which he wrote on 1st June was a two-line note from Cook:

> "Dear Mr. Bevin,
>   Thanks for notes. I think you understand our position. Mr. Smith made it quite clear.
>   Yours,
>   A. J. Cook."

After that Bevin made no further efforts, nor did Baldwin. In June 1926, the Government introduced a bill to suspend the seven-hour day in the mines, a measure for which the owners had been pressing and which the Samuel Report had opposed. A second bill took up some of the more positive recommendations of the Report, including a levy on mining royalties for miners' welfare schemes. But the Government now reverted to its earlier attitude of leaving the industry to settle its own troubles.

Relations between the Miners' Federation and the General Council remained strained. Offers of mediation were curtly refused. Apart from such limited financial assistance as the other unions were able to afford, the Miners asked for only one thing from the rest of the trade-union movement, an embargo on the movement of the imported coal on which British industry now depended. Again the brunt would have fallen on transport and Bevin was as strongly opposed to this as the leaders of the railway unions. He told a meeting of the National Docks Group of his Union in July:

"I have the memory of Glasgow, Hull and Birkenhead before me—where men came out in 1921 and never got back. Unless a union can see its way clear to face a lock-out of the docks an embargo cannot be indulged in. . . . To pick out small sections of men and tell them to carry the weight of the embargo means leaving them on the stones or putting the docks out in support.
"I asked the Miners' Federation leaders to guarantee that their people would not go in and blackleg us—but some of the volunteers on the docks were the men we came out to support . . ."[1]

In face of this opposition on the part of the unions concerned, the proposal was dropped.

The General Council originally proposed to summon the adjourned conference of trade-union executives on 25th June 1926 in order to present its report on the General Strike and to justify the decision to call the strike off. At the last moment, the conference was postponed on strong representations from the miners' leaders, who urged that public discussion while the coal dispute continued could only harm the miners' cause. The miners' request roused considerable resentment on the General Council. Some of the miners' leaders had not hesitated to make bitter attacks on the Council, and Cook, the Federation secretary, published a pamphlet purporting to give the inner history of the strike and roundly accusing the General Council of treachery. To postpone the conference meant leaving those attacked without any chance of answering their critics, and the railway leaders, Thomas and Bromley, opposed the suggestion. Although the decision was inevitably used against them, it says much for the General Council's sense of responsibility that, after a sharp debate, they finally agreed to postpone the conference, which was

1 22nd July 1926.

352

not held until January 1927. Bevin, despite his anger at the attacks to which the Council continued to be subjected, took the miners' side and voted without hesitation for postponement.

5

In the long run, it might have been better to have had the matter out there and then. The delay left the impression that the General Council was afraid to face its critics and the self-denying ordinance observed by the leaders could not stop the discussion continuing throughout the movement, with an incomplete or distorted version of the facts to go on.

For, however stoutly Bevin and others might proclaim that the General Strike did not represent a defeat, the rank and file concluded that it did.

Total trade-union membership fell from five and a half million before the strike to well under five in 1927. The Miners' Federation itself, the core of British trade-union strength, was badly shaken and had to face a breakaway in the Midlands before the end of the year. Not until 1934 was the drop in trade-union membership finally arrested.

The accumulated funds of the unions, which stood at £12,500,000 when 1926 began, had been reduced to under £8,500,000 by the end of the year. Most of the remaining funds were held on account of friendly benefits; strike funds had been almost completely drained.

Worst of all was the decline in morale. The response to the initial call-out had been an impressive gesture of working-class solidarity. That mood was destroyed by the way in which the strike ended, by the bitter feeling that the rank and file had been let down by their leaders and the subsequent victimisation. The militant spirit which characterised the unions in the years after the war was finally burned out in 1926.

The Transport and General Workers shared in the general decline. 1926, 1927 and 1928 all marked a fall in membership, broken by the amalgamation with the Workers' Union in 1929, but resumed in 1930–32. With almost all the members drawing strike pay, the nine days' General Strike and its aftermath cost the Union close on £600,000, a financial set-back from which it took years to recover.

But for the support which they had given to the miners, Bevin reflected bitterly, the T.G.W.U. would have been the second wealthiest union in the country. Now he had to start again from the beginning in order slowly to build up its financial strength to the point it had reached in April 1926.

His immediate anxiety was to find sufficient ready money to meet the Union's obligations to its members and to complete the construction of Transport House. Dispute benefit paid out in the first week of the strike alone reached a total of £291,869; this exceeded the liquid assets of the Union. Bevin however advised his Executive not to take up their share of the £71,000 loan from the International Federation of Trade Unions which the T.U.C. secured at 5% interest. He had his own plans for raising a loan abroad, free of interest.

It would be tedious to set out the expedients Bevin and Hirst adopted—including a voluntary levy of 6d. a week on their members—in order to re-establish the Union's finances. It was uphill, unrewarding work in the prevailing mood of disillusionment, and for some years to come the Union was hardly in a position to face any major dispute which was likely to be prolonged. No doubt, realisation of these facts predisposed Bevin, like other union leaders, to follow a policy which would avoid the industrial conflicts of the past few years and give the movement time to recover.

6

While he pondered on the events of April and May, there was much to occupy him. In the course of the summer, the Union's central offices were moved from Central Buildings to Transport House, where work continued on the additional accommodation for the Labour Party and the T.U.C. in the South Block. Routine work—finance, organisation, looking after the members of the Union who had lost their jobs through victimisation—took on a fresh importance in the aftermath of the strike. A number of men, mostly colliery engineers and winders belonging to the Power Group of the Union, were out of work and cost the Union £8,000 a week as long as the coal dispute lasted. The time of the General Council, too, was taken up with appeals for help—financial, legal, advisory—from unions which had been hard hit by the strike, especially those with small membership.

The annual conference of the T.U.C. was held that year in Bournemouth. By agreement between the General Council and the Miners' Federation there was no full-dress discussion of the strike, despite angry attempts from the floor to evade the president's vigilance. In the course of a debate on the powers of the General Council, an amendment was moved, with the support of the miners, to confer greater powers on the Council forthwith without wasting time on any further inquiry.

Bevin was opposed to drawing premature conclusions from the events of May and he spoke with such authority that he carried the Congress with him:

"I want to see, not recrimination, but a real examination, a real clash of opinion as to the merits and demerits of the policy referred to in the General Council's report arising out of the recent national strike . . .
"Carrying a resolution like this is like reorganising an army immediately on the signing of an armistice. You have to wait."[1]

The last debate of the Congress was started by Arthur Horner, of the miners, who attacked the *Herald* for the line taken by its editor during the General Strike. Bevin made a forceful defence of editorial freedom.

"Is the *Daily Herald* to become purely a stereotyped paper and avoid criticism? Fail to provoke that and it fails to arouse interest and, what I should regret, fails to have a mind of its own on the great problems of the day . . .
"Unless the editor and the staff can express their thoughts and are prepared at times to face even your hostility if they believe they are right, then the paper is not worth its salt in developing thought and in moulding public opinion."[2]

7

A few days after the Trades Union Congress, Bevin crossed to France for the conference of the International Transport Workers'

1 T.U.C. Report, 1926, p. 383.
2 Ibid, pp. 454—5.

Federation in Paris (15th–21st September). Edo Fimmen gave a long and critical report on the General Strike to which, Bevin explained, the British delegation was not free to reply. Bevin and Tillett, however, put in some hard work in the trade conferences into which the delegates split up. Bevin made a powerful plea for securing international uniformity of practice in the loading and un-loading of ships' cargoes, a technical issue which led to a good many disputes between dockers, seamen and shipowners. He won over the conference to his view and an advisory committee representative of both dockers and seamen was set up to work out a joint agreement acceptable to both parties.

Bevin's greatest success at Paris, however, was in securing a loan for his own union from the Continental transport unions. The T.U.C. had raised £71,000 at 5% interest from the International Federation of Trade Unions for the whole of the British trade-union movement. Bevin raised no less than £27,667 (at 1926 values, a large sum) interest free, with three years in which to repay it. Nine nationalities and thirteen organisations contributed. The largest sums were offered by the Czech railwaymen (£5,000), the Swedish and German transport workers (£5,000 each), the German railway-men (£3,675) and the Dutch and Belgian transport workers (£2,000 each). The balance came from Swiss, Austrian, Polish and Danish trade unions. With this secured, Bevin was able to return to London in time to meet the Union's commitments to its members and the latest instalment due for the construction of Transport House.

Hardly had he returned than he was off again, this time to the United States.

The invitation to go had taken him by surprise. The Government proposed to send over a commission to study industrial conditions and industrial relations in the United States and Canada. Anxious to secure representation of the trade unions as well as of industry and the Ministry, Steel-Maitland, Baldwin's Minister of Labour, suggested Bevin who had made a big impression on him and whom he described to Baldwin as "the ablest leader in the Trade Union movement, with a combination of practical ability and imagination greater than that of any other".[1]

Bevin was in two minds about accepting the invitation. He was

1 G. M. Young: *Stanley Baldwin* (1952), p. 121.

both flattered and suspicious. What was the purpose of the visit; would he be placing himself in a false position, if he went? On the other hand, there was a great deal of attraction in another visit to the New World, especially after the events of the summer. His friends urged him to go and his Executive, when he consulted them, took the same view. Still not altogether sure that he was right, he sailed from Liverpool at the end of September.

8

Bevin's visit to the United States could hardly have come at a more opportune moment. At the time of the Bournemouth T.U.C. he had not yet made up his mind what policy the trade unions ought to follow. He was still turning over in his mind the lessons of May, depressed by the aftermath of the strike, the recriminations and the falling away of trade-union strength. To be lifted out of this, and to be flung into the brash, vigorous world of America in the booming 1920s acted as a powerful stimulus and set his mind teeming with new ideas.

In the ten years since he had first visited the United States, American industry had entered fully on its characteristic modern phase of development. Mass production and the conveyor belt; standardisation; hire-purchase sales; high wages; the separation of management from ownership and the rise of a managerial profession —all these were still unfamiliar outside the United States, and the report which the delegation produced is largely devoted to a description of what now appear as the commonplaces of American industrial development, but then amazed the traveller with their novelty.

Trade unions played nothing like the role in American industry that they did in Britain.[1] The strongest trade-union tradition in the U.S.A., powerfully represented in the American Federation of Labour, was that of the craft unions, more concerned with maintaining the privileged position of their members against the flood of

---

[1] Only 25 per cent of those employed in American manufacturing, mining, and transport industries were members of trade unions, compared with 44 per cent in Great Britain. *Report of the Delegation appointed to study industrial conditions in Canada and the U.S.A.*, Cmd. 2833 (1927), p. 25.

cheap immigrant and negro labour than with fighting the employers. There was nothing corresponding to the big general and industrial unions which had grown up in Britain and conditions were unfavourable to such a development, not only the size of the country and the variety of conditions, the mixture of races and the mobility of labour but the intense individualism of American society which was as strong among the working as among the propertied classes. The basis of working-class solidarity on which to build up a powerful trade-union movement did not exist in the United States.

The majority of American employers—and probably of American workmen—were openly hostile to the principles of trade unionism. They did not believe in collective bargaining and argued that the working man, with the high wages which an expanding industry could afford to pay, was better off than if he belonged to a union which acted as a drag on production and on the initiative of those who wanted to work harder and earn more money. This was an argument Bevin had to listen to many times.

It was all very well, he retorted, so long as industry and trade were booming; but what happened when a trade depression set in and men were fired in thousands? The State made no provision for unemployment, sickness or old age comparable with that provided in Britain. Out of a job, the American working man could starve. Once he was over the age of forty, industry had no interest in him. Even when he was in a job, he had to accept the wages and conditions offered; he lacked the organised power to drive a bargain with his employer on which alone Bevin believed he could rely. In 1926 no one was willing to pay attention to Bevin's question, What would happen when a depression came? Three years later it was the only question that mattered.

Nothing Bevin saw in the United States shook his belief that, in the conditions of the United Kingdom at any rate, strong trade-union organisation was indispensable for any improvement of working-class standards of life. Nor, like most Englishmen visiting the U.S.A. in the 1920s, was he much impressed by what he saw of American life. Although he found it easy to get on with Americans, even when he disagreed with them, he thought their civilisation crude, noisy, boastful and materialistic.

It would be a mistake, however, to suppose that Bevin went round the United States with a closed mind and learned nothing from his experience. If he was distrustful of much that he was told at chamber of commerce luncheons, he showed an inexhaustible interest in visiting factories, stopping to talk with the men on the floor, asking questions, collecting figures, penetrating into local trade-union headquarters. Determined to find out for himself what hours were worked and what wages paid, he was sufficiently open-minded to be impressed by the best of the plants he visited and to appreciate good relations between a company and its workmen even when these were conducted on principles in which he had little faith.

On the other side, even the most opinionated of American employers was surprised by meeting an Englishman so different from the etiolated caricature then current in the United States. Few of them had encountered an English trade unionist before, still less one whose personality and opinions expressed the confidence of Bevin's. When, on his second night in the United States, he was called upon to follow the chairman and speak at the dinner given by the National Chamber of Commerce, he showed no hesitation in standing up and challenging most of the sacred assumptions in the American business man's philosophy. Bevin's capacity for plain-speaking embarrassed his chairman, but won him the respect of many Americans who admired outspokenness as a virtue. As he remarked in a letter to his secretary, Miss Forcey, American industrialists were so used to delegations who received everything they were told with respectful credulity, that they were taken aback by a man who expressed scepticism and knew enough to find out the truth for himself.

9

The Commission spent the first ten days in the manufacturing cities of the east coast, where it was deluged with statistics and optimistic explanations of the superiority of American industrial and business methods. Bevin had to struggle to keep his feet and not be submerged by the flood of new impressions and confident assertions. His early letters home were scrappy and incoherent, but it did not take him long to recover from the first overpowering impression of American hustle and prosperity, and he began, in his own phrase, "to get a grip on the investigation".

From New York they travelled by way of the General Electric

works at Schenectady to Detroit, already the headquarters of the American automobile industry and the showpiece of modern mass-production methods in the Ford plant. Detroit made an unfavourable impression on Bevin. In his notebook he wrote:

"A hard cruel city. The Lancashire of the last century, excepting labour is more difficult to get and they have to pay higher wages. No culture. Blasé, gaudy, noisy. No one talks to you except in dollars and mass production and the way they boss labour. A very undesirable place."

Relations between Bevin and Sir William Mackenzie, the chairman of the delegation, had been strained from the start. Bevin suspected Mackenzie of being only too willing to accept the views of American business men on trade unions, the 'open shop' and the benefits of free enterprise. Mackenzie was equally irritated by Bevin's independence and his insistence on taking nothing he was told at face value. When the chairman proposed that they should leave Detroit and go on into Canada, Bevin refused to agree, and the delegation broke up into three separate groups.

Bevin made up a party with one of the employers, Michael Dewar, and F. W. Leggett of the Ministry of Labour. Devising their own itinerary, they worked their way through the industrial belt of Ohio to Pittsburgh and then on to Chicago. Leggett was amused by Bevin's unconcealed efforts to discover everything he could about American tinplate production, competition from which had badly hit the tinplate workers in South Wales who belonged to Bevin's union. At one steel plant in Youngstown, Ohio, Bevin was turned away by an indignant employer who declared that he wanted no agitators in his works, but he took the rebuff philosophically and did not allow it to disturb his good relations with his two companions.

Bevin was deeply impressed by the advantage American industry derived from the huge domestic market represented by a single political unit with a population of 120 million and no internal barriers to trade. At the end of his second day in the United States, after a day's talk with the Embassy officials, he wrote in the notebook he kept:

"I came to the conclusion that the road my mind has been travelling is a correct one:

a. That Britain must have a customs union within the Empire, and
b. With Europe as well, if possible.
c. Or, if Colonies will not join then with Europe without colonies.
d. That the associated manufacturers must meet Labour and review economic field with a view to raising consuming power of the population included in the geographical area mentioned above.
e. That we must then in the industrial *service* mentioned above, determine how to meet the demand at cost which will definitely raise the standard of living."

He returned more than once to the same idea of creating a larger economic unit comparable with the United States and at Milwaukee proclaimed his belief that there would be a United States of Europe within fifty years.[1]

10

In Chicago, Bevin left the other members of the delegation and set out alone for the west coast. It was a relief to be on his own and to have time to collect his thoughts, after more than a month's continuous talking and questioning. Sitting out on the observation platform he felt a keen enjoyment of the deserted landscape after the crowded life of cities and hotels. Would he not be happier, he asked himself, abandoning public life and following in the track of the pioneers? As the train began the long pull up into the Rockies, he wrote:

"Here and there we pass oil wells with just a tiny village all alone up here. I saw the men starting off to their work this morning. No hustle. They looked happy as they greeted each other. I think I prefer it to the towns. Would I be happy or would I get restless? Not, I think, if I had the life I want. Last night I was reading Hudson's *Green Mansions*—that story of the dissatisfied squirrel. I love it. I wondered whether I wanted to emigrate—but I did feel awfully like that squirrel."

He was back in Washington by 21st November in time to join the rest of the delegation for the last lap of their visit. The friction between Bevin and the chairman came to a head in Philadelphia.

---

1 Interview with The *Milwaukee Leader*, 6th November 1926. The *Milwaukee Leader* carried on its mast-head the slogan "Unawed by Influence, Unbribed by Gain".

While he was out in the West, Bevin found that the programme had been altered and a big lunch party arranged with the leading anti-trade-union employers and representatives of the company unions.

"I asked what the game was. There is no doubt the plan was to use us like the *Daily Mail* to boost U.S. efficiency and listen to the decadence of the Old Country. But I said if there were to be speeches, they had better let me talk publicly or else everybody shut up. I was going to defend our show and further I would not eat with a blackleg union although I would meet them and hear their views."[1]

The delegation spent a further fortnight visiting factories, meeting industrialists and business men. Bevin became more and more involved in political arguments and stoutly refused to be impressed by the superiority of American industry or the American way of life. This did not disturb him—"I have to be careful to be provocative," he wrote home, and he succeeded. He was genuinely convinced that the industrial boom in the United States could not last, that a slump was inevitable and that its effect on the American workman, with nothing to fall back on but private charity and the community chest, would be disastrous. He put these conclusions bluntly to a dinner party given by a number of industrialists and bankers in New York. They were so disturbed by his views that they gave a second dinner to the delegation to persuade him that he was wrong, but they had no more success the second time than the first and Bevin refused to withdraw a word he had said.

Despite his pessimism about a slump, what he saw of American industry opened Bevin's eyes. He was convinced that this was the pattern which British industry too must follow if it was to stand up to American competition. Nineteenth-century industry would have to adjust itself to the methods of the twentieth—large-scale organisation and mass production; the increased use of machinery; the application of scientific methods to production, management and marketing—and nineteenth-century trade unionism would have to make the same adjustment, if it was not to find itself at a hopeless disadvantage.

On the other hand, he was neither attracted nor impressed by the American practice of industrial relations. He told a conference of works managers at Oxford after his return:

1 Letter to Miss Forcey, 24th November 1926.

"All this talk about the workers in America sharing in the increased prosperity and control of industry is pure humbug . . . I found nothing miraculous in America. Nothing that has been brought into existence there has been the result of greater capacity than exists in this country."[1]

What he had seen of American capitalism left him more convinced than ever of the job the unions had to do. But it would have to be by different methods than those they had pursued since the end of the war. The real value of Bevin's visit to America was not in providing him with models for imitation, but in bombarding him with new impressions, in stimulating and crystallising his own ideas at a time when the trade-union movement in Great Britain had reached a dead end.

When he returned at the end of 1926, he had thrown off the mood of pessimism in which the General Strike had left him. He grasped very clearly the *impasse* in which the trade unions found themselves and in the next few years he was to show his resourcefulness in finding a way out of it. In the process his role changed and the difference between the period before and after 1926 is as clear in his own development as it is in the history of the trade-union movement. At this point, then, we may well pause to take stock of the man whose fortunes we have followed so far.

I I

No man became a trade-union leader at the time Bevin did without the instincts and temperament of a fighter. The docks were a rough world in which to come to the top and Bevin could never have held the dockers or mastered his rivals if he had not possessed the physical and verbal toughness, the big voice and force of personality which the dockers expected in any leader.

From the time that he joined the trade-union movement he lived in an atmosphere of conflict and rivalry, and the experience left its mark on him. There was nothing meek about Bevin in his fighting days. Conscious of his abilities, he showed little respect for his elders in the trade-union movement, made no effort to conceal his scorn for those who disagreed with him and cared little whom he offended by plain speaking. "His strength," said one of his more

1 *Daily Herald*, 1st October 1927.

perceptive critics, "lay in himself; his weakness in his relation with others." He did not suffer fools gladly and his positive personality made it hard for men of lesser gifts to work, and even more to disagree, with him.

His prejudices were strong and hard to overcome. Fiercely independent, he reacted strongly to any suggestion of patronage, especially from those who were better-educated than himself, and he was inclined to look on anyone from another class as an enemy. Politicians he despised and journalists he treated with hostility. The Press retaliated, especially during the 1924 strikes, with a caricature of the trade-union boss drawn from life.

For all his self-confidence, he was highly sensitive to criticism, quick to resent opposition and to take it as a personal attack. Many said of him that he took everything too personally and could not face opposition without losing his temper. One reason for this was the strength of his suspicions. He was a reserved as well as a suspicious man, hard to get to know, and once he suspected that someone was trying to "get at him" or down him, he could be brutal in the vehemence with which he hit back.

The same things continued to be said of him well into the 1930s—that he was rough and overbearing, opinionated and conceited, a dictator who shouted down his opponents and treated those who disagreed with him as if they were trying to start a breakaway union.

This was Bevin as his critics saw him. A man with his temperament and outspoken views was bound to make enemies. Nor had his rapid rise in the trade-union movement failed to provoke jealousy and arouse criticism. But if there had been no more than this to Bevin, it would be impossible to explain how he came to occupy the place that he did in the Labour movement.

Like other men of strong personality, Bevin had a far from easy temperament; his confidence and determination were not lightly purchased without their compensating black moods. Nor, like any other human being, was he without his share of mortal failings and contradictions. But to those who knew him and penetrated his reserve, these faults appeared small by comparison with the true proportions of the man.

Arthur Deakin once remarked that Bevin had displayed no more 'ego' than he needed to get where he did in face of the handicaps and opposition he had to overcome. He would never have succeeded, if he had not hardened his will and drawn upon all his resources of determination. The result was to throw into sharp relief the aggressive and assertive side of his character, especially during the early 1920s, when he was in and out of one industrial clash after another and fighting all the time for the amalgamation on the success of which he had staked everything.

But throughout the 1920s, Bevin was widening his interests and not only learning rapidly but growing in stature all the time. To compare the Bevin of 1930–31, at the time of the second Labour Government and the Macmillan Committee, with Bevin at the time of the first Labour Government, the strike leader of 1924, is to see at once the distance he had travelled and the gain in confidence which he had made. The same determination, all the old force and ability were there, but tempered by a maturing of powers, a deepening of character and experience.

It was not until the amalgamation was secure that the worst of Bevin's anxieties lifted and that he felt able slowly to relax his guard. In 1926 he was at the beginning of his full development, and the change in circumstances after the General Strike helped to bring the other sides of his personality into prominence. Up to 1926, he had given convincing proof of his outstanding ability as a man of action, as advocate, negotiator, and organiser. In the years that followed, he was to reveal other and rarer gifts as a leader and policy-maker which hitherto had not been brought fully into play.

12

He was not yet forty-five, a man of middle height, broad-shouldered and heavily-built, with a characteristic rolling gait. His massive head matched his build, the thick black hair brushed back from a wide forehead but falling forward in the heat of argument. His face was broad and full, with a fine skin and a dark, almost olive-coloured, complexion. It was a strong, expressive face, quick to show feeling, its two most prominent features the watchful brown eyes and the big mouth already firmly lined.

His physical appearance, powerful and emphatic, was an inseparable part of his personality. It expressed in his look, his stance and walk the qualities which attracted attention the moment he entered a room or climbed on to a platform: energy, force and determination.

He was a man of strong feelings, with a deep instinct of loyalty. No man ever attached more importance to keeping his word or observing obligations. The unforgivable crime, in Bevin's eyes, was treachery: once he suspected anyone of not playing straight, he could be implacable, and once his confidence was lost, it was almost impossible to recover.

Although an entertaining, and at times a fascinating, companion when he was in the right mood, with a great store of anecdotes on which to draw, he was not by nature a gregarious or sociable man. He did not easily admit those he met to his confidence or allow them to penetrate the warmth and humanity which lay behind his formidable defences.

His private tastes were simple and changed little throughout his life. During the 1920s, he lived at No. 130, The Vale, Golders Green, a house to which he had been attracted by the neighbouring open fields. As these were built over, he moved to Central London and during the 1930s made his home in a flat in South Moulton Street.

If he had a week-end free, nothing gave him more pleasure than to take his wife and his daughter, Queenie, for a drive into the country or down to the Sussex coast for a bathe. He liked driving, and had a succession of open tourers, delighting to be out in the open air however cold the weather. He was equally fond of walking, and never lost his love of country scenes. Constant travelling gave him a wide knowledge of Britain and its regional differences with a vast number of acquaintances whose faces and names he rarely forgot. There was a strong vein of sentiment in his character and a visit to Bristol, especially in later years for the annual Bristol festival of the Union, was always an occasion for meeting old friends (including Frank Sheppard) and talking over old times.

He retained from Bristol days a lifelong affection for the old-style music-halls and variety shows; a good bill at the Coliseum or the Holborn Empire delighted him. So did a good tune and a good voice. He had a gramophone from early days and amongst his favourites were Galli-Curci, Clara Butt, Melba and Caruso. He enjoyed singing himself, but had a poor ear and found it hard to keep in key.

His job made heavy inroads into Bevin's private life. He was away many week-ends, and even holidays were always in doubt until the last moment. He never lost his interest in the Workers' Travel Association, of which he became president in the 1930s, and more than once took his wife and daughter on a tour abroad or on one of the cruises in the *Esperance Bay* which the Association organised on his suggestion.

There was not a trace of social pretentiousness or snobbery about Bevin. The part which he began to play in public affairs did not affect his attitude to other people; he spoke with the same directness, whatever company he was in, and even after he became a Cabinet Minister remained as natural and unaffected in his tastes and pleasures as he had been while still a working man in Bristol.

But the passion and absorbing interest of his life was his job, the Union he had created and the working-class movement with which he had identified himself. Bevin was at one time accused of over-great ambition, but his career provides little evidence to support this, once he had established the Transport and General Workers' Union. He made no effort to employ his great abilities for personal advancement or gain. He declined any honours, did not seek a Parliamentary career and refused the offer of a seat in the House of Lords.[1] Up to within a year of the age when he expected to retire, he was content with the position of General Secretary of the T.G.W.U. with the presidency of the T.U.C. as the highest honour to which he looked.

He took immense pride in the organisation he had built up and enjoyed to the full the power which he exercised in the Union, the T.U.C. and the Labour movement. But the position which power brings with it meant little to him, any more than social position or wealth. From beginning to end of his career he saw himself as the representative of the class from which he sprang. He knew far better than their critics the human weaknesses and limitations of the men and women he represented, but his loyalty to them was never shaken. However awkward and difficult he might be as a colleague, he had an unfailing and imaginative sympathy with ordinary working men and women; to him, they were "my people" and he understood and felt their problems as his own. To attack these problems he brought

1 See below, p. 457.

not only intelligence and passion, but patience and persistence, refusing to give up even when, as in the case of the decasualisation of dock labour, he had to fight the opposition of his own members as well as that of the employers and to wait a quarter of a century to achieve his object.

What marked him out, however, even more than his persistence, was the breadth of mind with which he pursued his purposes. Much of his life was spent in negotiating on detailed questions of wages and hours, the routine business with which every trade-union leader has to deal and in which the majority of them became so absorbed that they found it difficult to look further afield, or when they did, fell back on the stock phrases of socialist propaganda. Bevin, however, especially after his return from the United States in 1926, never tired of telling the trade unions that, if they wanted permanently to improve the condition of the working class, they had to take a wider view, had to grasp the importance of industrial organisation and finance, of international trade and world politics, which, however remote they appeared in the slums of Salford and Swansea, directly affected the lives of every working man and his family. It was this grasp of what was happening outside the ordinary run of working-class and trade-union experience—without his ever losing his foothold in it—that was to make Bevin the outstanding trade-union leader in the years that now follow.

13

If the first impression of Bevin on most people was the impact of his personality, it did not take long to discover that behind it there was a powerful natural intelligence which came as a shock to those whose own intellectual confidence was derived from elaborate training at school and university and who looked upon Bevin as an uneducated man. On no point do those who worked with him or met him in negotiation, including the ablest industrialists and civil servants of his time, agree more closely than his swiftness in grasping an argument or seizing on the essentials of a problem. There was nothing ponderous or slow about Bevin's processes of thought. He had a remarkable gift for cutting through the complexities of a situation and reducing it to simple elements. He was equally resourceful in suggesting ways to meet a situation. "He swarmed with ideas," says one of his former officials.

Once he caught hold of a problem, he never dismissed it altogether from his mind, but went on thinking about it, sometimes for years, until he came up with a solution which satisfied him. An example of this is his interest in international economic development, dating from the first World War, constantly recurring in the years between 1929 and 1940[1] and finding expression after the second World War in the Organisation for European Economic Co-operation (O.E.E.C.) and the Colombo Plan. Nothing was more characteristic of Bevin than his intellectual tenacity, the refusal to let go of a problem until he could hit on a way of solving it.

He found it easier to do this by talking than by putting his ideas down on paper. An old injury to his hand left his fingers stiff: he found difficulty in using a pen, and his hand-writing was clumsy and ill-formed. Sometimes he would dictate a memorandum to clear his mind; more often, he would collect two or three of his officers and try out his ideas on them, letting his mind range as he talked, throwing out suggestions which months later he might pick up again and develop further.

Talk served another purpose. Bevin read comparatively little and never widely. He picked up ideas far more from conversation than from reading, using the people he met as other men use books. One trick which caused frequent irritation was his habit of appropriating other people's ideas and repeating them as his own, often to the original source, with considerable self-congratulation and no acknowledgement.

He was an excellent listener, absorbed and attentive, with an astonishing memory for anything he had once heard. One day, after his return from the United States, he was talking to Captain Green, the secretary of the Joint Industrial Council for the Milling Industry. Bevin was recounting some of the speeches he had made, one of which, given on the spur of the moment and dealing with the economic condition of Europe, particularly impressed Green. So much so, that he wrote down the gist of the subsequent conversation in his journal the same night:

1 Cf., for example, the reasons which led him to accept the Ministry of Labour in 1940, pp. 652-3 below.

N

" 'How the devil do you know all this, Bevin,' I asked, 'so that you can talk to experts on their own ground. Do you read?'

" 'No,' he said simply, 'I have no time for reading. I just meet everybody and keep my ears open. I must have a mind like a sponge: it just soaks up all it hears.'

" 'Yes,' I said, 'but besides this absorption, there's something else; there's *you* unconsciously assimilating what matters, picking out what your mind wants to remember and rejecting the debris.'

" 'Perhaps,' he replied, 'and there's also luck. I have most amazing luck.' And he went on to tell me how on a visit to Berlin he ran into a civil servant he had known in London who was on the Reparations Commission, how he dined with him and Bradbury and sat up talking till 2 a.m. and heard all about the work of the Commission at first hand; how once in Amsterdam an Italian had arrived, having escaped from Italy before Mussolini could arrest him and how he heard all about the Italian labour problem at first hand from him, and so on."[1]

Most of all he drew upon his own experience. Not only had he great powers of observation and a retentive memory: he continually reflected on what he saw and heard, and as he added to his experience, went on learning all his life. The cast of his mind was practical, not in the sense that he was hostile or indifferent to ideas, but in the sense that he continually tested ideas against experience instead of reaching them by a process of abstract thought, or, as more commonly is the case, by emotional association. What he distrusted most in the intellectuals was the gap between their ideas and experience, a gap which could lead highly intelligent men to make extraordinary errors of judgment.

His own judgment was intuitive rather than analytical. This applied to his judgment of people as well as of situations. "I can smell a wrong 'un," he declared with conviction, "as soon as I walk into a room." He would go on turning over a problem in his mind, trying it out this way and that, talking about it, asking and as frequently rejecting the opinion of others, until a conclusion suddenly crystallised. In an astonishing number of cases it was the right conclusion, but he could give no clear account of and was little interested in the processes by which he had reached it.

Unlike many practical men, however, Bevin's experience was never a closed book. He came back from every committee on which he served, every journey he made abroad, with his mind teeming with new impressions and new ideas. His journeys to America and

[1] I am indebted to Captain Green for this extract from his journal.

Central Europe, his visits to the I.L.O. conferences at Geneva, his membership of the Macmillan Committee, his voyage to Australia in 1938, each of these represents a stage in a continuing process of self-education, followed almost immediately by some fresh initiative which can be traced to the stimulus of new experience.

For the most surprising of this unusual man's gifts was imagination. "I am something of a dreamer," he told the 1927 Trades Union Congress and proceeded to set the conference by the ears with a proposal to establish a European Customs Union. Twelve years later he startled the Southport conference of the Labour Party by proposing an economic union between the Western democracies and the Commonwealth. Both proposals cut clean across accepted Labour ideas on international relations and irritated practical politicians and socialist intellectuals alike; a quarter of a century afterwards we see things differently and are left regretting that the man who seized upon and turned the Marshall plan into reality only reached the Foreign Office after the war. What other trade-union leader would have thought it worth while in the early months of 1940 to summon a meeting of his union officers to talk to them about the importance of Africa?

A score of other illustrations will come to light as this history progresses. Automation and the shortening of the working week; the impact of science on industry; a comprehensive State pensions scheme; industrial rehabilitation; the application of medical research to industrial health problems. Whatever he was engaged on, from drafting a convention on the prevention of dock accidents to the details of unemployment insurance, his imagination would open up its relation to a wider background. Behind any problem he saw people and possessed the gift of making ordinary men and women feel part of the movement of history. He enlarged the dimensions of everything he touched, endowing particular and local problems with the significance of general issues and those who had to manage them with a sense of purpose.

CHAPTER 14

Aftermath of the Strike
1926 – 1927

I

WHILE BEVIN was in America, trouble had blown up again in the London docks. The occasion was trivial: the suspension of one of the Union's dock officials, Fred Potter, pending investigation of complaints of a disciplinary nature against him. But the London docks had been a trouble centre from the beginning. Opposition to the amalgamation had never been wholly overcome: old feuds, disappointed ambitions and personal dislikes still smouldered beneath the surface and contributed to a suspicious, grumbling attitude of mind.

The focus of opposition had always been Fred Thompson. A born dockers' leader, a big man physically, strong, tough and courageous, Thompson had ambition and the capacity to make a good speech. He was not a clever man: the brains were supplied by Potter, and the combination of Potter and Thompson was dangerous.

After defeating Thompson in the ballot for the general secretaryship, Bevin had sought to placate him by keeping him as the Area Docks Group Secretary, a key post in view of the importance of the London docks. The only result was to increase Thompson's confidence in his own strength and his contempt for Bevin. As a member of the Communist Party and the Minority Movement, Thompson was a loud critic of the Union's 'bureaucracy' and Bevin's 'yellow streak' in refusing to adopt more militant tactics.

There was a strong opinion in the London docks that Bevin ought to have fought the issue out with Thompson in 1923 at the time of the unofficial dock strike. Bevin preferred to re-establish his leadership by the successful dock strike of 1924 and to avoid a split in the

Union if he possibly could. But in the aftermath of the General Strike, with Bevin out of the country, Thompson and Potter seized the opportunity of the latter's suspension to challenge the Union's authority openly. Cards were issued on behalf of a new union, the National Union of Transport and Allied Workers, of which Thompson was named as provisional secretary.

The issue did not take long to decide once it came to a head. Every officer the Union could spare was sent down to the docks, and the attempt to lead a breakaway collapsed ignominiously. After October, 1926, no more was heard of Thompson and Potter or of their National Union.

The surprise lay not in the attempt, but in the rapidity and completeness with which it collapsed. Bevin's absence made no difference. The critics who had called the amalgamation a one-man show were proved wrong. When it was put to the test, loyalty to the Union proved strong enough to hold it together, whether Bevin was there or not. Without the General Secretary to guide them, the Executive Council and the other officers—notably John Cliff, the Assistant Secretary—proved perfectly capable of mastering the crisis. Far from detracting from Bevin's achievement, this enhanced it: the organisation he had created had acquired an independent life and strength of its own.

2

The outcome of the affair in the London docks was satisfactory, but there were too many danger signals for Bevin to feel any complacency. He returned from America to find the trade-union movement at a low ebb. The miners had been forced to return to work on the owners' terms. The Government was reported to be preparing anti-trade-union legislation. Every union had lost members and in the prevalent mood could expect to lose more. The membership of the T.G.W.U. had dropped by a tenth since the General Strike and the voluntary levy had so far failed to produce anything like the sums required to pay back the money they had borrowed. Postponing everything else until he had pulled his own union together, Bevin flung himself into the task of restoring the members' and the officers' morale.

As a prelude to the national campaign which he proposed, he called a conference of Union officers from all over the country to meet at 'Shornells', a large house owned by the Royal Arsenal Co-operative Society at Bostall Heath, near Woolwich. The General Executive Council interrupted its quarterly meeting to attend in full strength, and over the week-end of 18th February 1927, the conference devoted five long sessions to a thorough discussion of the organisation and policy of the Union.

Bevin took great pains in preparing for the 'Shornells' conference. Those attending it were invited to write beforehand and set out the criticism and issues they wanted to hear discussed. Each of the sessions was introduced by a written paper and a shorthand record taken of the debate which followed.

He opened the first session by describing his impressions of industry in the United States and the changes likely to occur in this country. The Saturday evening was devoted to discussing a paper by Harold Clay on the lessons of the General Strike. In summing up the discussion, Bevin made no more attempt than Clay to disguise the mistakes that had been made, but the greatest weakness, he insisted, was the poor leadership of the miners.

"Cook, Richardson and others were trying to square an economic theory with industrial action, and that cannot be done. That is where I think the Minority Movement goes wrong. You can work and struggle for a theory, but you cannot square it with your immediate difficulty.

"Cook asked me if I hadn't an economic theory to guide me in my settlement. I said 'No, of course not.' I have got a theory for society in substitution for the present one, but we have to deal with our business on business lines and whilst working under a capitalist system we have to have regard to it accordingly."

The whole of the following day was spent in examining the weaknesses in union organisation and finance which five years' experience had brought to light, and the conference ended on the Monday afternoon after a further session devoted to the Union's political activities.

To read through the record of the 'Shornells' discussions is to get a far clearer insight into trade-union democracy than can be obtained from any formal constitution or voting statistics. For three days, the men who ran the Union, General Secretary, national and local officers, lay members of the Executive, altogether two hundred and fifty men, met on equal terms, free to argue, criticise and ask questions about every side of the Union's activities. No issue was avoided. The level of discussion was high, the questions and comments shrewd. There was no 'platform', no opposition. Every man there felt it to be as much 'his' union, shared the same sense of responsibility for it as Bevin. Bevin's leadership of the Union was put to the severe test of judgment by his officers, and vindicated, not by any assertion of authority or formal vote, but—something far more impressive—taken for granted without inhibiting the expression of independent opinions.

In calling the 'Shornells' conference, Bevin was concerned with more than the practical value, great though it was, of a thorough review of the Union's work. Well aware of the depressing effect of the events of 1926, he saw the importance of re-creating in the officers of the Union pride in the organisation to which they belonged, and confidence that the jobs they were doing were worth while. Alf Short put it in a sentence when he said, on the Monday morning: "I went away yesterday feeling that we were doing a magnificent work and that the General Secretary and the Executive should be congratulated on bringing us together."

3

Bevin did not intend to leave it at that, however. Throughout the spring of 1927 he spent every day he could spare away from his office travelling to one town after another, addressing the members of the Union not only in big rallies but joining in branch meetings, holding area and trade group conferences, putting fresh heart into local committees, listening to their problems, leaving behind some of his own superb energy and confidence. It was an exercise in that difficult art of 'communication' which is the key to union leadership. His encyclopædic knowledge of local conditions, his uncanny memory for faces and names made it work at which he excelled and work which he loved. However fatigued he might be by the constant travelling and speaking, he never failed to draw from contact with the ordinary members of the Union reinforcement of his own sense of purpose and fresh pride in the organisation he had created.

After London, he moved to Merseyside and Lancashire; then to the Midlands, Yorkshire, the Potteries, Scotland, the north-east coast, Southampton, the West Country, right into Cornwall and Wales. In between he returned to London for a round of committees or other urgent business, then set off again. He took with him two or three of the national officers, John Cliff, Harold Clay, Archie Henderson, and called in the services of the Executive members in their own localities. Each visit lasted two or three days.

Sometimes Bevin found himself speaking in a big public hall or theatre, often in a trade-union or Co-op. hall with the paint peeling off the walls, down the shabby, crowded back-streets of Salford, Walsall, Bootle or Bradford. Between them they addressed some two hundred meetings, at half of which Bevin himself was the chief speaker.

The results of such a campaign are impossible to determine, but it is reasonable to conclude that, if Bevin and the other national officers had not thrown themselves into it and had let things slide, there might well have been a much bigger slump in membership and morale in the mood of apathy which followed the General Strike. A general union was more vulnerable than a craft or even an industrial union to loss of membership. In 1926 the Union lost 40,000, 10.8% of its membership, double the proportion for the trade-union movement as a whole. In 1927 the further fall in membership was cut to 16,000, 4.8%, a lower proportion than the average fall in trade-union membership of 5.7%. Hardly less important was the financial recovery. The deficit of £396,000 in 1926 —a figure equal to three quarters of the total annual income—was converted into a surplus of £61,000 for 1927.

By the time the Biennial Delegate Conference met at Swansea in July, Bevin believed that they were through the worst and had turned the corner.

Much had happened since the delegates last gathered at Scarborough on the eve of Red Friday, but Bevin, fresh from his visits to the areas, felt himself better informed of the mood among the rank and file than any of his critics and approached the week's proceedings in the Patti Pavilion with confidence.

Inevitably the Executive's report on the General Strike was challenged from the floor, one delegate describing the trade unions as "an army of lions led by a few jackasses". Bevin and Tillett had little difficulty in replying to the attack and the report was carried by a sweeping majority. Bevin went on to move the reversal of the changes made in the rules two years before when hopes rode high of creating the Industrial Alliance. The mood now was very different:

"We are not averse to it in principle," Bevin told the delegates. "But what the Executive are not prepared to do, with the movement in its present state of development, is to hand their power to a central authority, until the movement itself is prepared to consolidate its forces. . . . My experience of 1926 has taught me that there is no half-way house on this matter."[1]

Ever since the General Strike, the Communist-led Minority Movement had been active in attacking the leaders of the General Council and the big unions as traitors to the working-class cause and in demanding a more militant policy—whatever that might mean in the circumstances of 1927. They had a number of supporters among the delegates to the Swansea conference and a hot debate took place on the Minority Movement's activities. Criticism of the Communist tactics came not so much from the platform as from the floor. Payne, secretary of the Dalston garage branch and later a leader of the Rank and File movement among the London busmen, attacked the Minority Movement for splitting the trade unions and accused them of trying to organise a breakaway among the London bus and tram branches after the General Strike. He was answered by a Communist delegate who told the conference: "You have either to keep sliding more and more to the right, towards the Liberal Party—and that is what is happening—or you must slide more and more to the left and the Communist Party." This display of Marxist logic did not appeal to the delegates who, after a long debate, turned down the Minority Movement by a sweeping majority.

4

The most important piece of public business before the Swansea conference was the Government's Trade Disputes and Trade Union Bill. Baldwin, despite his appeals for an industrial truce, had given way to the pressure from his party, and the Government's Bill introduced four major changes into the law affecting trade unions.

1 Verbatim typescript report of the Third Biennial Delegate Conference 1927.

It declared illegal any strike "other than or in addition to the furtherance of a trade dispute within the trade or industry in which the strikers are engaged", or designed to coerce the Government "either directly or by inflicting hardship upon the community". It limited the right of picketing and declared 'intimidation' to be illegal. It insisted that the political levy paid by most trade unions to the Labour Party should only be collected in cases where the members had given written notice of their wish to pay it ('contracting in' instead of the existing arrangements for 'contracting out'). Finally, it debarred established Civil Servants of any grade from becoming members of any union or association connected with the T.U.C.

The Bill was framed without consultation with the trade unions, whose leaders the Government treated as if they were engaged in a conspiracy against the State which put them outside the political pale. Nothing was more bitterly resented by Bevin, who regarded the Bill as an act of petty vindictiveness inspired by class and party spite. He swore that he would never rest content until it was removed from the Statute Book and twenty years later he had the satisfaction of helping to repeal the Act.

For the present, the trade unions could only protest. They set up a joint committee with the Labour Party which fought the bill clause by clause in the Commons and succeeded in introducing minor modifications in the text. Even then the terms of the Bill were so loosely drafted that it could be held to make any major strike illegal. How, for instance, would the courts interpret the 'trade or industry' within the limits of which strike action was to be confined, or define the point at which inconvenience to the public became coercion of the Government or hardship upon the community? The uncertainty of the legal position alone imposed restrictions on the trade unions for fear of a successful action for damages similar to that brought against the Railway Servants in the famous Taff Vale Case at the beginning of the century. No one could know that, in fact, the prohibition of 'illegal' strikes would never be invoked during the nineteen years for which the Act remained in force. Nor could any-one foresee that, despite the Labour Party's loss of a quarter of its total income from affiliation fees, resentment against the Goverment's pursuit of a party advantage would help to strengthen working-class support for the Labour Party sufficiently to turn

Baldwin out in two years' time and enable MacDonald to form his second Government.

Part, and an important part, of the reason for this unexpected result was the thoroughness with which the trade unions organised a national campaign against the Bill. Bevin played a major role in this, addressing meetings up and down the country and taking every step he could think of to get the highest possible percentage of his own members to continue paying the political levy. The Transport and General Workers' Union, engaged in organising a larger number of industries and appealing to the principle of sympathetic action by one section in support of another, was in an exposed position under the ban on strikes which crossed the ill-defined line between one 'industry' and another. Bevin advised his Executive to pay no heed to the risks they might run and to refuse to modify their rules and practice. At the Union's Swansea conference he attacked the vague legal generalisations contained in the Act and moved a strongly-worded resolution which condemned the penalising of sympathetic strikes "as a violation of the right of men to withhold their labour".

As a gesture of solidarity with the Labour Party which was fighting the Government's Trade Union Bill in the House of Commons, Bevin invited Ramsay MacDonald to make the closing speech at the end of the conference. He wasted no words in introducing Mac-Donald. It was the other way round: all his pride came out in the words with which he introduced the Union to the Party leader.

"This Union represents, I think, a great epoch in the development of the organisation of the working class in this country. It has been an attempt to unify not merely their power to fight, but to unify their intelligence, to pool their resources . . .

"We are imbued with the idea that we are the last great class to march onward, to rise to power and equity. We believe that we shall rise to the occasion.

"It is the credit side of the balance sheet of state expenditure on the spread of knowledge to have in this conference men drawn from all trades, from all parts of the country dealing with a mass of problems of national life in a manner which would be a credit to the British Parliament itself."

5

When the T.U.C. met at Edinburgh in the autumn, Bevin was selected by the General Council to move the resolution of protest on behalf of the whole trade-union movement, and did so in a speech which was all the more effective because of its moderation. The trade unions, Bevin argued, had done more than anyone to introduce conciliation, arbitration and other procedures of negotiation into industry, often in face of strong resistance from employers, and had tried more persistently than either the Government or the employers to find some basis for industrial relations other than that of conflict. If Baldwin was sincere in his repeated appeals for industrial peace, Bevin concluded, the best way he could advance it was to repeal an Act deliberately designed to hamper the peaceful functions of the trade unions.

To show that Bevin was not playing with words when he spoke like this, it will be helpful to turn for a moment to the affairs of a small but highly important trade, flour-milling, in which he saw—and helped to create—a working model of industrial relations rationally conducted by both sides.

The National Joint Industrial Council for the flour-milling industry, set up in May 1919, had now completed its eighth year. The original national agreement drawn up in 1919 remained intact and had been restored after the General Strike. Wages moved up and down—there had been a reduction of as much as 17/- a week in 1921-2—but always by agreement after negotiations between the two sides and always within the framework of the agreement.

Technical education was taken over by a joint committee (of which Bevin was a member) and organised in classes and correspondence courses throughout the country, the examinations being conducted by the City and Guilds of London Institute. In 1924, agreement was reached on a guaranteed week—a week's work or a week's pay—and on overtime rates for week-end work. In 1927, a joint Factories Committee was set up which produced a report on safety appliances in mills and remained in existence to see its recommendations put into effect. Another joint committee conducted an investigation into the extent of skin disease among workers in flour mills. The same year, faced with over-production of flour, the

T.G.W.U., now representing all but a small proportion of the men, negotiated a new agreement on wages for a 44-hour week and on the regulation of short-time.

Why the milling industry should have so successful a record in industrial relations would make an interesting study. Admittedly, it was a sheltered trade, subject to none of the fluctuations in demand which disturbed export industries; it also employed a much smaller number of men than the mines, engineering or textiles. The lessons to be drawn from it may well have been inapplicable to large-scale heavy industry. No doubt also much of its success was due to the men involved, A. E. (later Sir Albert) Humphries and his successor as chairman of the employers' side, Sir Norman Vernon; Captain L. H. Green, who held the unique position of secretary to both sides of the National Joint Industrial Council; P. C. Green, secretary of the milling section of the T.G.W.U., and Ernest Bevin. In the course of time, these men came to know each other well and to acquire confidence in each other. There were sharp disagreements and plain speaking at times. When the chairman introduced the new wage agreement in July 1927 with the remark that he abominated the notion of the class war, Bevin retorted:

"I desire to point out that whether we believe in the class war or not, the struggle the workers have is to emerge from it; and so long as there is such a marked contrast between the standard of living which the employers set for themselves, and so long as such differences exist, there will inevitably be a class struggle going on."[1]

But neither side pushed the differences to the point where they lost sight of their common interest in organising the industry in such a way as to keep it reasonably prosperous. The employers showed themselves willing to discuss the problems of the industry and its organisation with the unions—a point to which Bevin attached the greatest importance. As a result the change to concentrated large-scale production in the years that followed was carried through with a minimum of dislocation to management or labour.

1 National Joint Council for the Milling Industry, Report of Annual Meeting, July 1927.

6

The principal preoccupation of the General Council during 1927 was the joint campaign with the Labour Party against the Trade Disputes Bill. But there were other problems of longer standing which took up much of the time of the Council and its committees.

Three trade-union congresses in succession had discussed trade-union organisation and the General Council had been instructed as long ago as the Hull Congress of 1924 to produce a plan which would secure a drastic reduction in the number of trade unions by providing for the organisation of workers by industries, and which would establish "unity of action without the definite merging of existing unions by a scientific linking up of same to present a united front". After two interim reports at Scarborough and Bournemouth, a small committee of the General Council (the Organisation Committee) with Ernest Bevin as its most prominent member and Vincent Tewson as secretary, produced a final report for the 1927 T.U.C.

The General Council took its time, but it did the job thoroughly. A large amount of information was collected by the Research Department and by inquiries addressed direct to the unions. From this emerged a picture, still incomplete in some parts, of the extraordinarily complicated, overlapping pattern of industrial relations, incapable even of explanation except by unravelling the threads of historical development which had led to the organisation of workers in the same trade by as many as a dozen or a score of different unions in different parts of the country. There were difficulties in defining an industry[1]; even if agreement could have been reached on this, who was going to make the different unions, particularly the general unions like Bevin's which already accounted for a fifth of total trade union membership, hand over large blocs of membership to other organisations? Who was going to make the men concerned, many of whom had strong feelings of loyalty to their own organisations, transfer to another union?

1 At the Edinburgh T.U.C. Bevin remarked: "We all have different ideas of what industrial organisation means. I went into a conference once and an employer said to me: 'You are a docker; what are you doing here in our trade?' I said: 'In one town I organise the midwives, in another the grave-diggers and everything between is the Transport Workers.' That did not solve the problem".

The ambitious schemes of reform discussed at Hull and Scarborough were reduced to a questionnaire which the General Council prepared to send out to its affiliated unions, asking whether they were prepared to consider negotiations for amalgamation or working arrangements with other unions and, in the event of a favourable reply, offering the General Council's good offices in getting such negotiations started.

When the report was presented to the 1927 T.U.C. at Edinburgh, there were protests from the Left and accusations that the general unions were standing in the way of progress. But the General Council had history and the facts on its side:

"You cannot solve the problem of the Labour movement," Bevin told the Congress, "by sitting down and framing resolutions. The most conservative man in the world is the British trade unionist when you want to change him. You can make a great speech to him on unity, but when you have finished, he will say 'What about funeral benefits?' . . . You cannot make a man leave the union and the men he has been associated with all his life for some theory. He will not do it, and no scheme you can organise in the Congress can make men transfer against their will. You have to carry your membership with you in reorganising the movement."[1]

In the changed atmosphere of the post-General Strike period, not even the powerful block vote of the Miners, the Engineers and the N.U.R. could carry Congress. The motion to refer back the Report was defeated by two million votes to 1,800,000. Bevin was delighted. He regarded 'organisation by industry' not only as incompatible with the existence of the sort of union he had built up, but as another of those slogans which, by fostering illusions and ignoring hard facts, led the Labour movement into the pursuit of dogmatic fantasies and handicapped its development. Throughout his trade-union career he worked steadily for the improvement of trade-union organisation by promoting amalgamation and working arrangements with other unions, but it was a practical policy which started from the facts as they were, not from a blue-print of some ideal pattern.

1 T.U.C. Report, 1927, p. 298.

7

A second question which constantly figured on the agenda of the General Council was that of international unity or, more simply, relations with the Russian trade unions. The T.U.C.'s efforts to establish working arrangements with the Russians through the Anglo-Russian Joint Advisory Council ran into trouble on two opposite sides. The International Federation of Trade Unions, the Amsterdam International, to which the T.U.C. belonged, represented the point of view of the Continental trade unionists, men who had too much experience of fighting Communists in their own countries to view patiently the efforts to reach an accommodation with the rival Red trade union international made by the I.F.T.U.'s British President, Purcell, and other members of the General Council. At the same time, the General Council found itself violently attacked from Moscow for the part it had played in the General Strike and its members denounced by name as traitors to the working class.

Bevin was not a member of the General Council's International Committee which bore the brunt of this uncomfortable situation. He regarded the I.F.T.U. as too much concerned with politics and preferred the method of international co-operation on an industrial basis through the trade secretariats like the International Transport Workers Federation.[1] If there had to be a trade union international, he thought it common sense that it should include the Russians and he was inclined to be critical of the implacable attitude of the Continental trade unionists.

What convinced him was again a practical, not a doctrinal, test. Any international organisation, he believed, must respect the right of the national organisations affiliated to it to conduct their own affairs in their own way. The Russians, who fiercely resented any criticism of the methods they employed in the Soviet Union, had no right to criticise the way in which the T.U.C. conducted the General Strike and he laid down as a condition of admitting the Russian trade unions to the I.F.T.U. their renunciation of any interference in the internal affairs of other working-class movements, including the

---

1 At the meeting of the General Council on 22nd March 1927, he went so far as to suggest that trade unions affiliated to one of the international secretariats should be allowed to contract out of affiliation to the I.F.T.U.

abandonment of support for breakaway unions and such Communist organisations as the Minority Movement.[1]

Citrine put the issue precisely when he introduced this section of the General Council's report at the Edinburgh T.U.C. in the first of a long series of speeches on international affairs notable for the cogency of the argument and the speaker's mastery of the facts:

"The experience of the Russian trade unions," Citrine said, "has been entirely different from the experience of the unions in Europe as a whole. . . . They have felt that, unless the methods they have adopted and the principles they believe in are adopted by the other movements, the revolutionary movement they have built up will be menaced. . . . It is because of this that they approached the Anglo-Russian Council from the conception of the absolute right of the Russian movement to dictate its policy to the rest of the world. . . . The conception of the British trade union movement is radically different. Our movement has been built up on the principle of autonomy for its units nationally, and internationally on the authority of the British trade union movement to decide its own methods of progress."[2]

After four years of patient effort, even the admirers of Russia found it difficult to contest the justice of the General Council's decision to wind up the Anglo-Russian Joint Council. The most that A.J. Cook felt able to do was to beg Congress to defer a decision. Bevin at once rose to answer him. "If the General Council had not come to this Congress and submitted this recommendation, the people who pillory us all the time would have called us cowards and afraid to face it." Congress, he insisted, must decide one way or the other. Congress did—by a four to one majority in favour of the General Council's report.

Without any inconsistency the conference went on to pass a unanimous resolution condemning the Baldwin Government's decision to break off diplomatic and trading relations with the U.S.S.R. Neither Bevin nor Citrine shared the hatred of the Soviet Union which possessed many members of the Conservative Party. The T.U.C.'s quarrel was not with the Communist experiment in Russia but with Communist tactics in the trade unions in this

1 These views are to be found most clearly expressed in a memorandum which Bevin dictated on 31st January 1927, in an effort to clear his own mind on the issues involved.

2 T.U.C. Report, 1927, pp. 358–9.

country. Earlier in the Edinburgh conference the General Council's condemnation of the Minority Movement had been challenged by Harry Pollitt and other Communists. The Minority Movement, Citrine answered Pollitt, was set up by the British Bureau of the Red International of Trade Unions; resolutions drawn up by the Comintern were passed on by it to trade-union delegates and then presented as a spontaneous expression of rank-and-file opinion. "Our friends," Citrine added, "the paid members of the Minority Movement, dare not alter a line or a comma in the resolutions they received to be presented here. Talk about free expression of opinion!"[1] The majority against the Minority Movement was even more crushing than on the decision to end the Anglo-Russian Council; its supporters could muster no more than 148,000 to 3,746,000 on a card vote.

8

All in all, Bevin was highly satisfied with the Edinburgh T.U.C.

"Congress this year," he wrote, "was brought right up against the real problems and difficulties of the movement, and it could not evade the clash of forces within the movement; it had to discuss and vote upon them, and this meant that nearly every point that has been agitated for years was brought out—and it is good that it should be so. .... Attacked on the right by the Tories and on the left by the Communists (and we have as much confidence in one as the other) Congress determined to turn neither to the Right nor to the Left, but to go straight on with its work."[2]

After the left-wing enthusiasms of the Hull and Scarborough congresses and the confusion which followed the General Strike, the T.U.C. had swung back to a centre course and on all the major issues Bevin found himself sharing the views of the majority of delegates.

But he was rarely content to do no more than that. The Edinburgh T.U.C. is also noteworthy for Bevin's first attempt to give a lead to trade-union opinion on international economic policy. In his new mood Bevin felt that it was no longer sufficient for trade unionists to bargain for a fairer share of the national product; they

1 Ibid., p. 324.
2 *The Record*, September 1927, pp. 48–49.

must interest themselves in the economic conditions and policies which determined the size of the product. Nor was it enough to go on repeating socialist slogans; they must come to grips with the national and international problems of the present.

The Transport and General Workers' Union put up three resolutions which were meant to be taken together. The first two, moved by Archie Henderson and Ben Tillett, directed the General Council to investigate and report upon the effects of tariffs on trade and employment and on the international organisation of trusts and cartels. Both were carried without opposition. Bevin reserved for himself the controversial proposal to instruct the General Council to further "a policy having for its object the creation of a European public opinion in favour of Europe becoming an economic unity".

In words that were to become the commonplaces of the European movement twenty years later when he was Britain's Foreign Secretary, Bevin drew directly upon his American impressions:

"I did not find that the American capitalist was any more beneficent than the British capitalist. I did not find that there was any greater genius in America for organisation. . . . But what I did find was this—that I went there from a little island and I was asked to compare its possibilities with a continent. I found that there were 130,000,000 people within one economic entity, with no tariffs, with a mobility among the people to move about without the boundary handicaps that apply to Europe. . . . If we are to deal with the problems of Europe, we have got to try to teach the people of Europe that their economic interests, their economic development have to transcend merely national boundaries."

Bevin went on to link the economic difficulties of Europe with its political fragmentation after the war.

"I am a little bit of a dreamer; I think it is necessary. We have debated all week as if Britain had no industrial problem to solve, but Britain has got a problem and it is no use attacking unemployment unless we try at least to make a contribution towards its solution. One of the complications throughout Europe has been the creation of a greater number of national boundaries as a result of the Versailles Treaty breaking up the proper organic distribution of commodities, dividing the great Danubian area into several divisions, distributing and handing the ownership of raw material from one country to another."

The only solution, Bevin argued, was "to inculcate the spirit of a

United States of Europe—at least on an economic basis, even if we cannot on a totally political basis".

Twenty years before his great effort to translate the Marshall Plan into action, Bevin urged the Trades Union Congress:

"Cast your eye over Europe with its millions of underfed, with its millions of people with a wretchedly low standard of living. We can have mass production; we can have intensified production and we must direct the consuming power to absorb that mass production to the millions of people in Europe whose standards of living . . . are capable of being raised 1,000 per cent by bringing together their productive capacity in return for the craftsmanship of our own Western Europe."

As soon as he sat down, he was hotly assailed from the Left. Figgins, of the N.U.R., and Cook accused him of betraying the true cause of internationalism in favour of a European exclusiveness. Tomkins, of the Furnishing Trades Association, declared that the working class must not be diverted from its true objective, the overthrow of capitalism. Bevin retorted that the only way to fight capitalism effectively was to take a leaf out of the capitalists' book and look at economic problems from a wider standpoint than the purely national. None of their problems, whether under capitalism or socialism, could be solved by action restricted within the existing political frontiers.

"The only means to get rid of the provisions of the Versailles Treaty and the Danube plan is by our organising Europe on an economic basis instead of by political divisions. . . . Go to Vienna today, a great city trying to live upon a small agricultural area around it, when all her true economic forces ought to be in Hungary and other countries which were carved out by the Versailles Treaty. We want an indivisible united nation spreading from the borders of Russia right to the borders of France."[1]

It was a surprising speech at the end of a congress marked by the common sense and sobriety of its views. It illustrates very well that unexpected imaginative flair in Bevin which made him something more than the ablest trade-union organiser of his generation, that indefinable gift of leadership which enabled him time and again to lift a conference like this out of its preoccupation with routine business and remind it of the magnitude of the issues with which it was concerned.

1 T.U.C. Report, 1927, pp. 391–6.

9

At the Labour Party conference, which followed at Blackpool a month later, MacDonald asked for a mandate to draw up a programme of action on which to fight the next election.

Since the General Strike, the Independent Labour Party, under the leadership of James Maxton, had taken on the role of pacemaker on the Left which the Communists had tried unsuccessfully to fill. Affiliated to the Labour Party and with strong representation on the Labour benches in Parliament, the I.L.P.'s challenge to MacDonald's and Henderson's leadership was much more telling than the Communists'. Its programme of 'Socialism in Our Time' disdained compromise for the sake of winning votes and attracted many who had been disheartened by the achievement of the first Labour Government.

The I.L.P.'s most controversial proposal was a minimum Living Wage for every citizen, to be made a first charge on the national product and the immediate objective of a Labour Government. By committing the Labour movement to this policy in advance of an election, the I.L.P. hoped to pin MacDonald down if he should be returned to office.

Both before and after the General Strike, the I.L.P. tried hard to draw Bevin into their campaign. An invitation to take the chair at a delegate conference of London trade-union branches to discuss the 'living wage' policy roused all Bevin's suspicions. He had no intention, he replied, of attending any delegate conference called by an outside body.[1]

He wrote to Fenner Brockway, the secretary of the I.L.P., that he had had enough of minority movements calling conferences and dabbling in the wages question: "You will discover you cannot handle wages by attaching them to the tail of a particular slogan."[2] After the General Strike, when the I.L.P. took up the miners' cause and was highly critical of the General Council, Fenner Brockway tried again, but with no more success.

MacDonald's move at the 1927 Labour Party conference was

1 Letter of 13th April 1926, to Allen Skinner, industrial secretary of the I.L.P.'s London Divisional Council.
2 Letter of the same date to A. Fenner Brockway.

designed to take the wind out of the I.L.P.'s sails by empowering the
Labour Party's National Executive to draft the next election
programme. Bevin took occasion to warn the I.L.P. not to cut
across the unions' functions and drag wages into a political programme. The first Labour Government had not been able to
establish socialism and they had to face that fact.

"I agree with a bold programme, but a good many delegates talk as if all the
people in the country were class-conscious socialists. . . . There are many
more who are anxious to have their wage problems and their working conditions dealt with. The only thing I am afraid of in programmes is that they
may be over the heads of the people—something they cannot understand. I
do not know why you are so terribly desirous of being meticulous as to
phrases. Have we not the right to fight for power, and then to use our power
when we get it as much as the other political parties in the State?
"When some of our friends draw up programmes, they are something like
manifestos . . . I would rather see a short programme of immediate
objectives that Labour can really hope to accomplish and then we can go
back and say: 'At least we have done what we said we would; we have
delivered the goods.' "[1]

Bevin felt that the 1927 Blackpool conference of the Labour Party,
like the Edinburgh T.U.C., had carried out a necessary stock-taking,
rid the movement of illusions, refused to be led astray by the
Utopian slogans of the Left, whether Communist or I.L.P., and
faced up to the facts of the political and economic situation. The
Socialist millennium was not round the corner, and its approach
would not be hastened by elaborating programmes incapable of
realisation which might provide emotional satisfaction to a handful
of left-wing intellectuals but would do nothing to win working-class
votes or improve working-class conditions. The immediate need was
to draw up a short programme which stood some chance of putting a
Labour Government into office at the next election and which a
Labour Government, once in office, stood some chance of putting
into effect.

He approached the tasks of the trade unions in the same practical,
down-to-earth mood. He was a Socialist, but this did not excuse
him from the duty of trying to do something about unemployment,
wages and conditions of work under a capitalist system. A man
whose theories about the increasing misery of the working classes

[1] Labour Party Conference Report, 1927, pp. 185–6.

under capitalism and the futility of trying to alleviate it, stopped him from taking action was not, in Bevin's view, fit to take on a trade-union leader's responsibilities. His loyalty was to the class he came from, not to the abstract principles of Socialism; he thought himself none the worse a Socialist if, pending the establishment of a better order of society, he did what he could to improve working-class conditions under the existing system. The gulf between his attitude and that of the Left was shown by the very different reception they gave to the proposal that the T.U.C. should accept the invitation to engage in talks with a group of employers under the chairmanship of Sir Alfred Mond.

CHAPTER 15

The Mond-Turner Talks

1928 – 1929

I

FROM CORRESPONDENCE preserved among Bevin's papers, it is clear that proposals for such talks between employers and trade-union leaders had been in the air since the beginning of 1927. As early as January of that year, less than a month after Bevin's return from America, Lord Weir, head of one of the biggest contractors firms in the country, wrote to Bevin, whom he had met in New York. A meeting followed in March at which Arthur Pugh and George Hicks, the chairman of the General Council, were present as well as Bevin and further correspondence was exchanged until Bevin broke off on the grounds that the Government's Trade Union Bill made further discussion impossible.[1]

Weir returned to the attack after the Edinburgh T.U.C. at which George Hicks, in his presidential address, had recommended "a direct exchange of practical views" between those entitled to speak for the two sides of industry. Hicks added that this would be of far more value than a national conference under Government auspices. A few days later Weir wrote to Bevin and, referring to Hicks's speech, renewed his invitation to a meeting of trade unionists and employers.[2] Bevin agreed[3] and after further soundings a formal letter was dispatched to the General Council on 23rd November, signed by Sir Alfred Mond, Weir and eighteen other leading industrialists. They invited the T.U.C. to meet them and discuss the possibility of greater co-operation in meeting the difficulties of British industry.

1 Ernest Bevin to Lord Weir, 19th May 1927.
2 Lord Weir to Ernest Bevin, 19th September 1927.
3 Ernest Bevin to Lord Weir, 30th September 1927.

"We realise," Sir Alfred Mond wrote, "that industrial reconstruction can only be undertaken with the co-operation of those empowered to speak for organised labour. . . . We believe that the common interests which bind us are more powerful than the apparently divergent interests that separate."

The talks which followed offered Bevin the opportunity for which he had been looking to pursue a new policy in the vacuum (to use his own phrase) in which the trade-union movement found itself after the Strike. Bevin did not repudiate the old policy. Granted the attitude of the employers and the Government in the years since 1921, he believed the unions had no option but to fight, if they were not to be driven back to conditions worse than had existed before 1914. Nor did he believe that the fight, culminating in the General Strike, had been in vain. By their resistance the trade unions had forced the employers and Government alike to admit that the trade unions were too strong to be destroyed, and were there to stay. But the belief that resistance could do something more than this, that strikes or the threat of strikes, even a general strike, could be used as an instrument with which to carry out positive purposes and initiate, instead of merely preventing, change had been exploded. In a time of national emergency such as the war or in times of high employment such as the years immediately after the Armistice, these were tactics which might work for a time, but they were limited in effect. As soon as circumstances changed, the employers set about taking back the concessions they had been forced to make.

Since 1921, the high figure of unemployment had kept the balance tipped against organised labour. But even if it swung back the other way, Bevin asked himself, what permanent advantages were to be gained by this see-saw conflict? Was 'beggar-my-neighbour' the limit of practical wisdom in industrial relations? Was it impossible to find an alternative basis in the obvious fact that employers and workpeople had a common interest in the prosperity of the industry on which both were dependent for their living?

What stood in the way? There was no doubt of the answer in Bevin's mind, the same answer that he had given ten years before in the discussions of the Bristol Association for Industrial Reconstruction: the attitude of the employers. So long as the employers refused to treat their workmen as partners in industry, so long as they denied them any voice in management or a share in responsibility, relationships between them were bound to be unsatisfactory.

393

It was a one-sided answer, but Bevin was right in believing that the initiative had to come from the employers' side. Fortunately, as he was ready to admit, there were employers as well as trade unionists who had reached the same conclusion after the General Strike, that industry was paying too high a price for the conflict between management and labour. Circumstances too were favourable. 1927 and 1928 saw the high-water mark of prosperity between the wars. With profits rising, most employers were not eager to press any advantage to the point of industrial dislocation. The most far-sighted of them, out of enlightened self-interest, not philanthropy—a motive Bevin rightly distrusted—were prepared to make a new approach.

2

There were obvious reasons why the trade-union leaders should be more ready to listen to such an approach in the autumn of 1927 than they had been before. The fall in trade-union membership left them anxious. The mood of anger after the calling off of the General Strike was succeeded by one of apathy. Company unionism was on the increase and the humiliation inflicted by the Government's Trade Disputes Act had further reduced the authority of the T.U.C. Militant slogans had lost their attraction, as the 1927 Congress showed; despite the angry protest of A. J. Cook, even the Miners were glad enough to listen to suggestions that might end the tragic succession of strike and lock-out in their industry.[1]

There were other reasons, too, which strongly influenced Bevin. Big changes were taking place in industry. The word 'rationalisation' was beginning to be used; new processes, new methods of industrial organisation were being introduced; the concentration of ownership and control in industry was creating more powerful combines. If these developments took place without the unions having any voice in them, the men they represented would be reduced to a still greater degree of dependence upon their employers.

"I shall never forget my experience in America," Bevin told the 1928 T.U.C. "You talk of rationalisation and great changes in America, but the

1 Cf. Herbert Smith at the 1928 T.U.C.: Report, p. 437-9.

unions there are outside of it. When I saw the great changes that must come in this country, I never rested a moment . . . to try to create a position that would get us in on the inside instead of on the outside shouting at them."[1]

Collective bargaining on wages and hours was no longer enough. If the unions wanted to exercise some influence on the decisions which determined wages and hours, if they wanted to reduce unemployment and forestall the effects of rationalisation, they had to go further than meeting the employers' representatives to negotiate new wage agreements. They had to talk to the men at the top who took·the decisions, and talk to them about wider questions than rates of pay and the length of shifts.

3

Bevin's views at this time on the future of industry and the right strategy for the trade unions to pursue are well set out in a number of drafts which he dictated for an article in a special *Manchester Guardian* supplement at the end of November 1927.[2]

He found himself, he wrote, attacked on two sides. A Communist critic had recently said of him: "Bevin is a good negotiator in handling the wages and conditions of his people, but the trouble is, he stops there and does not use his own influence and his organisation for the purpose of overthrowing the capitalist system." An employer, on the other hand, had written to accuse him of being too political and only interested in the abolition of private enterprise.

"Both these activities," Bevin commented, "proceed from the assumption that Industry and Society are static. One says, 'Every endeavour must be directed towards preventing change' and the other says, 'Change is so imperceptible that it is necessary to turn the whole thing right over.' "

But industry and society were changing all the time. 'Rationalisation', the catch-phrase of the day, meant in practice the increasingly large-scale organisation of industry. Far from being opposed to it, Bevin said straight out that he welcomed it. He preferred to deal

1 Ibid., p. 448.
2 Citrine contributed an article "The Next Step in Industrial Relations" to the same supplement. This is reproduced by W. Milne-Bailey: *Trade Union Documents* (1929), pp. 431–8 and, when read in conjunction with Bevin's article, shows the common ground shared by the two men.

with one or two big companies which could afford to take long views than with a mass of small employers who survived only by pinchbeck economies.[1] But rationalisation was being pursued in a one-sided fashion. The employer interpreted it to mean the elimination of competition between one firm and another, but wanted to preserve competition in the labour market in order to keep down wages—organising industry to prevent competition, disorganising labour to perpetuate it.

This was a short-sighted policy. The unions were bound to fight rationalisation if their members were to be excluded from the benefits it could bring; if they were allowed to share in them—for example, by reducing the working week—both sides stood to gain.

Bevin had been quick to notice the growing divorce between ownership and management in the United States. In a revealing comment on the new managerial profession, he wrote:

"As Industry has passed out of industrial ownership to the large-scale organisation, this type is becoming of far greater importance. He is the man who has to get the job done and to be continually inspiring, organising, directing the affairs of his great undertaking. I frankly confess in my job, the large-scale organisation of labour, I feel more akin with this type than I do with the so-called director."

Such a man, Bevin felt, was likely to be concerned far more with the development of industry, with what he could keep in rather than take out of industry for the payment of higher dividends. This was the crux: the distribution of the proceeds of industry. With management, he argued, there could be a common interest that could never exist between organised labour and capital.

4

In 1919, when the last Industrial Conference met, the unions, after their experience during the war, had looked to the Government to bring the two sides of industry together and to take the initiative in pressing for reforms. Their attitude towards the Government now, after the experience of the General Strike, the miners' lock-out and the Trade Disputes Act, was very different. Baldwin's appeal for an

[1] Cf., his remarks to the same effect at the 1928 T.U.C. Report, pp. 445-451.

industrial truce did not square, in trade unionists' eyes, with his Government's record. The fact that Mond's invitation was the result of an independent initiative was its strongest recommendation.

The original plan on the employers' side had been for a meeting between either the Federation of British Industries or the National Confederation of Employers and the General Council of the T.U.C. Opposition in the two employers' organisations led to this being dropped in favour of an invitation from twenty (later twenty-four) individual employers who, between them, held directorships in 189 companies (in 98 cases the chairmanship) and included two past presidents, six vice-presidents and three other members of the Executive of the F.B.I. as well as the chairman and past chairman of the National Confederation.

Bevin was not interested in the representative or unrepresentative character of the group. To those who argued that none of the employers had any power to make or implement agreements, Bevin replied that he was thinking of something bigger than wage agreements. What he wanted was not formal negotiations but a frank exchange of views and information, the more informal the better, over the whole range of economic questions affecting industry. His aim was to establish a pattern of consultation, to persuade the employers to pay more attention to the point of view of labour and, if possible, to reach agreement on a joint policy in economic matters which they could press on the Government and on the other employers.

It was important, if only for the shaken prestige of the T.U.C., that the approach should be made to the General Council, and Bevin wisely refused to be drawn into private discussions. But he was indifferent to the question of representative status on the other side. Representing only themselves, the men who signed Mond's letter were still as powerful a group of employers as could be assembled in the Britain of 1927. Besides Mond himself and Lord Weir, they included Sir Harry MacGowan (I.C.I., chemicals); Lord Aberconway, David Davies and Lord Londonderry (coal); Sir David Milne-Watson (the Gas, Light and Coke Company), Sir Hugo Hirst (electricity), A. E. Humphries (flour-milling), Sir Josiah Stamp (L.M.S. Railway), Sir John Cadman (Anglo-Persian Oil Co.), Sir Charles Parsons (shipbuilding and engineering), Sir Herbert Austin, Sir Edward Manville (Daimler and B.S.A.), Sir

Arthur Dorman, Sir Robert Hadfield and Sir Frederick Mills (steel); Kenneth Lee (textiles); Samuel Courtauld, the pioneer of rayon, and Lord Ashfield, the head of London transport.

These were the men with whom Bevin wanted to get to grips, the men who had the power to shape industrial policy, not the subordinates sent to conduct wage negotiations.

The question Bevin asked was whether any subject would be excluded. Were they prepared to discuss finance, management and markets, as well as unemployment and the ordinary range of trade-union interests? "When Sir Alfred Mond ruled nothing out," Bevin told his Executive, "I at once decided that it would be well to go on and to consider everything."

The General Council proceeded with deliberation. Mond's letter, sent on 23rd November, was placed on the agenda for the Council's meeting on 20th December. After discussion, a motion to accept the invitation, moved by J. H. Thomas and Ben Tillett, was carried and a sub-committee of six, later re-named the Industrial Committee, was appointed to make the arrangements.[1] A similar committee was appointed by the employers' group[2] and a joint conference to be attended by the full General Council was fixed for 12th January 1928.

The announcement of the meeting at once filled the headlines and caught the nation's imagination. There was a widespread desire felt by many people for an ending of class bitterness, for what was vaguely called "industrial peace". New Year sermons and leading articles overflowed with goodwill, usually accompanied by the reading of patronising lessons to the misled workers. Bevin, down in Bristol to address the Rotary Club,[3] told his audience of business men that, if the conference got no further than sentimental platitudes, it would fail. What the workers wanted was industrial justice, not industrial peace, but he did not conceal his interest in the forthcoming talks.

1 Its members were Ben Turner, of the textile workers, the chairman of the General Council; the veteran Will Thorne and Bevin representing the two big general unions; Thomas of the N.U.R.; Tom Richards (Miners' Federation) and Arthur Pugh (Iron and Steel Trades) with George Hicks (Building Trade Workers) as substitute and Walter Citrine as secretary.

2 This consisted of Sir Alfred Mond (chairman), Lord Londonderry, Sir David Milne-Watson, Sir Hugo Hirst, Lord Ashfield, Lord Weir and the Hon. Vernon Willey.

3 9th January 1928, reported in the *Western Daily Press*.

5

The joint conference took place in the Royal Society's rooms at Burlington House, where the General Council and the employers were entertained to tea by the President and Council. Apart from an emotional outburst from A. J. Cook, the proceedings passed off stiffly but without event. The trade-union leaders were in earnest in insisting that they did not mean to compromise their principles and Thomas asked for a frank recognition from the employers that they could only solve the problems before them with the co-operation of the established trade-union movement. Bevin and Citrine, who supplied the driving force on the trade-union side from the beginning, pressed for assurances that no issue would be excluded, a point on which they were amply met by Mond's proposed agenda.

"For the first time in history," the General Council reported to the executives of its affiliated unions, "the representatives of organised Labour have been invited to meet a group of important industrialists to discuss the finance and management of industry; new developments in technology and organisation, the organisation of industry itself, nationally and internationally; means for assuring the status and security of workers and methods of achieving the highest possible standard of living for all. These are the things the Trade Union Movement has been claiming for years to have some voice in, and for years it has been denied that voice."[1]

Once the preliminaries were over, the conference left the main work to its two committees, which met frequently throughout the spring of 1928 and prepared a number of joint statements for the full conference when it re-assembled on 4th July.

The T.U.C. representatives, logically enough, made recognition of the trade unions the starting-point of the talks and secured two surprising statements from the employers' group. The first said unequivocally that it was "definitely in the interests of all concerned in industry" for workmen to belong to a union affiliated to the T.U.C. or some other bonafide union and that negotiations were facilitated by such membership. There were many employers in 1928 who did not agree with a word of this or with the repudiation of victimisation after the events of 1926 which followed in the second statement.

1 T.U.C. General Council, Industrial Committee: Report to the Executives, 17th February 1928, pp. 7–8.

The joint committee then drafted recommendations for the creation of a National Industrial Council representing both sides of industry and charged with the appointment of joint conciliation boards to deal with disputes which the normal machinery in any industry failed to settle. The final statement to be laid before the full joint conference dealt in brief and vague terms with the more rational organisation of industry—including the concentration of production and ownership in larger units—welcoming this development but insisting on better provision for the workers displaced in the process.

Some hard work had been put in by both sides and Bevin's papers include several drafts of each statement, with explanatory memoranda prepared by Milne-Bailey and the T.U.C.'s small but efficient research department. Like most documents produced by revision and compromise, the statements themselves lacked sharpness or originality, but the process of reaching agreement and the fact that trade unionists and employers could agree at all on such thorny questions as victimisation and rationalisation were more important than anything put down on paper. All the statements and recommendations were adopted by the full conference, when it met in July, and a resolution was passed to continue the discussions in the autumn.

6

This decision was unsuccessfully challenged by a minority on the General Council. George Hicks, whose presidential speech at the Edinburgh T.U.C. had been used as the peg on which to hang Mond's original invitation, joined Alonzo Swales and the A.E.U. in protesting against the unrepresentative character of the employers' group,[1] but the leader of the Left's opposition continued to be A. J. Cook.

Although elected to the General Council in 1927, Cook refused from the first to be bound by any doctrine of collective responsibility and held himself free not only to make public what took place at its

---

1 At its meeting on 26th June 1928, the General Council turned down a motion by Hicks calling for the abandonment of the Mond-Turner talks but declaring the T.U.C.'s willingness to engage in discussions with a *representative* body of employers.

meetings, but to attack its other members and its secretary, Walter Citrine, as 'traitors', 'collaborators' and worse. The situation was complicated by the fact that, while its Secretary was making these public attacks on the T.U.C., the Miners' Federation was asking for and receiving the full support of the General Council in fighting the breakaway miners' union in Nottinghamshire.

An agreement between the General Council and the Miners' Executive to put an end to personal attacks (2nd March) was broken by Cook's publication of the pamphlet *Mond Moonshine*, and Cook went on to join Maxton in a campaign against the 'betrayal' of the working-class cause by trade-union and Labour Party leaders.

Working-class audiences, however, if they bothered to come to meetings at all, listened with scepticism to Cook's and Maxton's over-wrought emotionalism. The campaign against 'Mondism' was a flop and at the 1928 T.U.C., held at Swansea early in September, the General Council defeated its critics by over three million to 566,000 on a card vote.

The opposition put up its strongest team—Brownlie and Swales, of the Engineers, George Hicks and Cook—but they could not shake the impression left by Citrine's lucid introduction or by the hammer blows of Bevin's common sense. It was a combination which was to carry many trade-union conferences, Citrine using his extra-ordinary command of facts to open the discussion, Bevin reserving his fire until the end. Bevin spoke for half an hour at the end of a day-long debate, but he held his audience to the last minute, not by appealing to sentiment, but by sheer force of argument.

"It is all very well," Bevin answered Cook, "for people to talk as if the working class of Great Britain are cracking their shins for a fight and a revolution, and we are holding them back. Are they? There are not many of them as fast as we are ourselves."

It was the job of the political party to bring about the changes that could not be effected across the negotiating table or in relations with employers at all. But the trade unions had to deal with facts as they were, had to face the problems of the moment, unemployment, for instance.

"Whom can you meet to discuss unemployment with? Government depart-ments who do nothing? No, I would rather sit down with some considered policy on a problem of that character facing the capitalists themselves across the table—not in alliance with them, for I am no more in alliance with them than I am in alliance with the dockowners or anybody else whom I have to fight every day. Is the strike the only way to fight? Cannot we fight by discussion as well as by starvation? Cannot we fight by intelligence?"[1]

7

Unemployment was the question to which the Mond-Turner group turned the whole of its attention once the meetings were renewed in the autumn.[2] Since the end of the post-war boom in 1920, there had seldom been fewer than a million and on occasion over two million workers, one-tenth to one-eighth of the insured industrial population, out of work. Unemployment was by far the biggest social problem of the inter-war years in Britain and every conceivable remedy was at one time or another suggested as a means of solving it.

The interim report drafted by the Mond-Turner group and presented to the full joint conference on 12th March 1929 refers to many of these suggestions in passing. Its main emphasis, however, is on two or three specific proposals which Bevin presented to the group in November.

Bevin had no doubt that the causes of unemployment were complex and deep-rooted: there was no simple panacea to remove them. But there were, he believed, certain immediate steps which could be taken to reduce the numbers of those unemployed at once. They could begin, he suggested, by eliminating the oldest and the youngest from industry. 340,000 men and women, he discovered, were still working after they had reached the age of sixty-five. If they could be induced to give up their jobs by the offer of an adequate pension, and if, at the same time, the school-leaving age could be raised from 14 to 15, thereby keeping half a million youngsters out of the labour market, the number of jobs available for those between the ages of 15 and 65 would be sharply increased. Bevin calculated that this would cut the current unemployment figure from one and a half million to 900,000.

---

1 T.U.C. Report, 1928, p. 450.
2 Under the joint chairmanship of Sir Alfred Mond (now elevated to the peerage as Lord Melchett) and Ben Tillett, the new chairman of the General Council.

Bevin proposed a weekly pension of £1 for a single person, 35/– for a married couple, on condition that they gave up work, and he spent considerable time on working out with the aid of an actuary the cost of such a pension. He also proposed the amalgamation of the unemployment and health insurance schemes, together with the old age pension fund, into a single consolidated insurance scheme financed by the same tripartite pattern of contributions from employer, worker and State. Far better, he argued, to spend money on retiring the older men whose efficiency was already failing than in paying unemployment benefit to younger and more active men; it would cost little more and it would be a much more intelligent way of spending the money.

In the long run, Bevin saw as clearly as anyone that British industry could only compete with American and German if it were modernised; hence his insistence to the Swansea T.U.C. on the rationalisation of industry as a development to be welcomed. But, in the short run, reorganisation and mechanisation were daily adding to the numbers of the unemployed by turning men out of jobs. He therefore urged upon the employers, and persuaded them to include in the joint report, a recommendation to take the trade unions into consultation on the problem of displacement created by technical advance.

The mining industry, with a quarter of a million miners unemployed, was the most striking case of an industry standing in need of rationalisation and incapable of absorbing again anything like that number in employment in the mines. Coal would have to be dealt with as a special case and the report recommended the Government to institute special relief measures in the mining areas, including organised schemes for resettlement in other parts of the country and other industries.

Of the report's three other recommendations—the provision of better credit facilities to enable firms to modernise their plant; the creation of a national development fund, and the organisation of proper facilities (including loans, if necessary) for overseas emigration —the first in particular attracted Bevin's support. He was convinced that the currency and banking policy of the Treasury and the Bank of England paid insufficient attention to the needs of industry, as, for instance, at the time of the decision to restore the gold standard. The joint report strongly recommended a full-dress inquiry into monetary policy, an inquiry which was put in hand before the year was out, with Ernest Bevin as a member of the Macmillan Committee appointed to conduct it.

8

This interim report by the Mond-Turner group was intended only to set down immediate proposals, leaving for further discussion the long-term policy problems which lay at the root of unemployment. To Bevin's regret, these discussions never took place. Following the conference in March 1929 at which the interim report was presented, the meetings were suspended while talks took place between the T.U.C., the F.B.I., and the National Confederation of Employers on the possibility of periodic consultations between the three bodies. After long-drawn-out negotiations agreement was reached in the course of 1930 and consultation on a number of questions took place before the fall of the second Labour Government.

The results, however, were meagre. Bevin was quite right in believing that, once the informal procedure of the Mond-Turner talks was abandoned for meetings between representative bodies, both sides would for ever be looking over their shoulders and all hope of real discussion would be lost. Under the impact of the slump and rising unemployment, the atmosphere in which the original meetings took place was rapidly changing. The gap between the two sides was beginning to widen again. The attendance of the employers at the group's later meetings began to fall off; the recommendations of the joint conference were accepted neither by the F.B.I. nor by the National Confederation; the National Industrial Council never met. By the time the second Labour Government fell in the summer of 1931, the T.U.C. was in revolt against the economic policy which the National Government was formed to implement with the full support of the City and the employers.

In practical terms, then, the Mond-Turner talks led nowhere, a verdict supported by the renewed bitterness which the 1931 crisis left on the Labour side. But there is more to be said than this.

Even on a short view, the talks helped to gain for the unions a valuable breathing-space after the setback of 1926 and checked the hostility on the part of the employers inspired by the Trade Disputes

Act of 1927. It helped the General Council in particular to recover some of the prestige it had lost after the General Strike and to avoid being reduced to the ineffectual position of the Parliamentary Committee it had replaced.

In the longer perspective which is possible today, the talks acquire added importance as another phase in the erratic development of improved industrial relations in this country between 1914 and 1945. As was the case with the original discussions leading up to the Whitley Report at the end of the first World War, each attempt to put relations between management and labour on to a more rational basis ended either inconclusively or in apparent failure, yet we can see now that, by the time Bevin ended his tenure of the Ministry of Labour in 1945, the situation was altogether different from that which had existed when he first joined the Dockers' Union in 1910. The Mond-Turner talks contributed to that change.

This is obviously true in Bevin's own case. After the years of conflict culminating in the General Strike, they marked a resumption of that interest in a new approach to industrial relations which, beginning in the Bristol Association for Industrial Reconstruction, had never been wholly submerged by the search for more effective methods of organising trade-union strength. Once revived, that interest never lapsed. Despite the setbacks of the intervening years, it continued to exercise a powerful influence on his conduct of trade-union affairs until, as Minister of Labour in the wartime coalition and the most powerful figure in the post-war Labour Government, he was at last able to give effect to the ideas which he had elaborated in the course of such discussions with employers over thirty years.

9

May 1928 saw the realisation of another of Bevin's dreams, the opening of Transport House. To the passer-by, cutting across Smith Square and turning a curious eye towards the bombed ruins of the eighteenth-century church of St. John, Transport House is a large, not very distinguished brick building at the corner of Dean Bradley Street. Bevin saw it with different eyes. He remembered the shabby terrace house in Princes Street, Bristol, where he had joined the Dockers' Union; to him it was nothing short of marvellous that a working men's organisation, with a subscription of 6d. a week, could rise from renting a house in a back street to building, at a cost of well over £50,000, an eight-storey office building of its own within a stone's throw of the House of Lords.

It was a triumph which even the most disgruntled of his critics would find it hard to grudge him, for if ever a building was due to the determination of one man, it was Transport House. Since his visit to America in 1915, Bevin had had in his mind a headquarters equal to the status which he claimed for the trade-union movement. No other union in the country up to that time had built offices of anything like the size or spaciousness of Transport House, which was designed to house the national offices not only of the Transport and General Workers' Union but of the Trades Union Congress and the Labour Party as well. He had the imagination to grasp the psychological as well as the practical advantage to the movement of an impressive building of its own with the political and trade-union sides brought together under the single roof. Here, for thirty years, were to meet the General Council of the T.U.C. and the National Executive of the Labour Party as well as the General Executive Council of the Transport and General Workers' Union. 'Transport House' became as closely identified in political phraseology with the Labour movement, as Downing Street with the Government and Fleet Street with the Press. Bevin, to use an American phrase, thought big and grasped the truth that, unless the Labour Party and the T.U.C. did the same, their claim to exercise power would fail to carry conviction.

The opening ceremony took place on 15th May. Harry Gosling presided, Ramsay MacDonald delivered a moving speech, astonishingly empty of any meaning, and was accompanied on the platform by the short, square, bearded figure of Ben Turner, chairman of the General Council, and by George Lansbury, chairman of the Labour Party's National Executive. There were tributes to Bevin, not unmixed with feelings of jealousy, the presentation of a golden key and the unveiling of memorial plaques, including one to the Executive Council which had taken the decision to build Transport House and another to the workmen who had erected it. Afterwards, the invited guests were taken to see the new Council Chamber, the Board Room and Transport Hall. In the evening there was a dinner at Maison Lyons in Shaftesbury Avenue, complete with musical items, a round of speeches and much sentiment about the past. It is doubtful if Bevin had many illusions about the feelings with which some of the guests—Ramsay MacDonald, for instance, Ben Tillett or some of the other trade-union leaders—regarded him, but he was undisturbed: let them carp and criticise behind his back, he had accomplished what he set out to do and he was secure in the loyalty and affection of the people whose opinions he most valued, the members of the Union, his own folk.

10

Twice that summer, Bevin went abroad, the first time towards the end of May when he attended the International Labour Organisation conference at Geneva as one of the T.U.C. representatives. It was his first visit to an I.L.O. conference and it made a deep impression on him, converting him into a firm supporter of the I.L.O. for the rest of his life. It is not difficult to see why.

The International Labour Organisation was the one effective contribution of the international Labour movement to the peace settlement at the end of the first World War. Its constitution was written into the Treaty of Versailles, and the first conference was held in Washington in October 1919. Each succeeding year there was an annual conference devoted to one or more specific questions —night work, hours of labour, the protection of young people, etc.— and attended by tripartite delegations from each country, representing separately the Government, the employers' and the workers' associations.

The secretariat under the guidance of the I.L.O.'s remarkable director, the former French Socialist Minister, Albert Thomas, built up for the first time a body of accurate information about labour conditions in all parts of the world and helped successive conferences to draft a series of international conventions and resolutions which, as they have been ratified or adopted by various countries, have gradually built up an international labour code and set new standards for labour conditions throughout the world.

All this was still in the making when Ernest Bevin went to Geneva in 1928. The principal subject for discussion at the conference, the prevention of industrial accidents, was a good test of the new organisation. Dockers came second only to miners in the high rate of accidents and Bevin had been protesting for years at the indifference of the port authorities and employers, as well as of the men, to the risks created by worn-out tackle, lack of proper fencing and the failure to enforce the most elementary safety precautions. It was part of the attitude towards casual labour in the docks which Bevin had set himself to root out on both the masters' and the mens' side.

With ships of all nations coming in and out of ports, only international agreement on the standardisation of equipment and safety regulations offered any chance of improving the position. The International Transport Workers' Federation had appointed a Dockers' Advisory Committee with Bevin as chairman and this had done valuable work in preparing a draft for the I.L.O. conference.

Neither the British Government nor the British employers, however, liked the proposal for a convention aimed at influencing legislation. The Government's representatives at the 1928 conference advocated propaganda in favour of 'Safety First' in preference to legal obligations. The employers' spokesman, Mr. Cuthbert Laws, an old opponent of Bevin's, demanded that any question connected with the docks should be referred to the Joint Maritime Commission of seamen and shipowners due to meet the following year.

Speaking for the first time in an I.L.O. conference, Bevin answered both suggestions as the spokesman of the workers' group and at once impressed this critical audience with his grasp of the subject and the force with which he presented his argument. Propaganda, he declared, was of no effect without support in legislation. He dismissed the other proposal, to refer dock accidents to the Joint Maritime Commission, as evasion on the part of the employers. With no governments represented on the Joint Maritime Commission, the shipowners would be in a strong position to block any action. Bevin not only pressed successfully for the question to be retained on the agenda at Geneva but secured the appointment of a separate committee to discuss the dockers' problems apart from industrial accidents in general.

Bevin again led the workers' group on this committee and acted as one of the two vice-chairmen. Its business was to draw up a questionnaire, on the answers to which a draft international convention could later be based. This questionnaire was to be sent out to all interested parties, including governments, and Bevin defeated every attempt by the employers to limit its scope. At one point, the employers walked out of the Committee, and the Secretary-General had to be brought in to effect a compromise. After three weeks' work Bevin had the satisfaction of seeing the committee and the full I.L.O. conference endorse an agreed draft. For the moment, this was as far as he could get, but he had no intention of leaving the matter unfinished.

II

A fortnight after his return from Geneva, Bevin set off again, this time for Stockholm where the International Transport Workers were due to hold their biennial conference. Accompanied by his wife, he sailed from Newcastle (with tickets booked by the Workers' Travel Association) and had the pleasure of renewing acquaintance with his old friend, Charles Lindley, the secretary of the Swedish Transport Workers, who acted as hosts to the conference.

With his immense capacity for learning from new experience, Bevin always enjoyed travelling abroad. He admired the Scandinavian countries for their common-sense democracy and their achievements in social and educational reform. The Swedish Social Democrats were already within sight of a clear majority in the *Riksdag* and the I.T.F. conference met in the Swedish Parliament House under the presidency of Charlie Cramp, of the N.U.R.

The main work of the conference was done in the separate trade commissions. Bevin presided over the dockers' and presented its report at the plenary session. He urged the affiliated organisations to do everything in their power to get their governments to adopt the I.T.F. draft convention as their reply to the questionnaire sent out by the I.L.O. A dock strike was in progress at Antwerp while the conference was sitting and a proposal for a loan of £21,000 to help the Belgian dockers was put to the delegates. So large a sum could only be raised if the T.G.W.U. agreed to repay the money it had borrowed in 1926 before the date on which it was due. Bevin agreed without a moment's hesitation and had the satisfaction of seeing the Antwerp dockers win a substantial increase in their wages.

The conference listened to a paper by its general secretary, Edo

Fimmen, in which he argued that, in keeping with the capitalists'
transfer of production to the colonies in order to exploit their cheap
labour, the trade unions would have to organise the working classes
of the non-European world. In support of his thesis, Fimmen
pointed to the fact that, apart from two delegates from the Argentine,
one from Canada and one from Palestine, all the 107 delegates
present came from European countries. Characteristically, Fimmen,
with his strong left-wing views, linked this with the fight against imperialism and militarism. Equally characteristically, Bevin got up
to challenge him. The resolution proposed, he argued, was too high-
flown and brought politics into what should be a matter of trade-
union organisation. What mattered was to build up transport unions
in the non-European countries. Bevin had no more success than at
earlier I.T.F. conferences in persuading the delegates to forego
rhetoric for practical considerations. All except the British voted
against his amendment, but they combined to elect him to the
General Council of the Federation the following day.[1]

Once the conference was over, the delegates made a long excursion
to the far North as guests of the Swedish railway union. Bevin
visited Narvik and Abisko, saw the Land of the Midnight Sun, met
some of its Lap inhabitants and inspected the iron mines of Kiruna,
before returning to London, tired but enthusiastic, a week after
leaving Stockholm.

It is worth while breaking the chronological sequence of events at
this point to take in the 1929 I.L.O. Conference and round off the
history of the international convention on the prevention of accidents
in the loading and unloading of ships. Bevin was again the leader of
the workers' group in the international committee which was set up
to work over the draft convention prepared by the I.L.O. secretariat
in the light of the replies received to the 1928 questionnaire. It was
dull, detailed work—the height of the coaming round a hatchway,
the width of gangways, the frequency with which chains and hoisting
tackle should be renewed, the handling of dangerous cargoes. Every
clause had to be argued out with employers reluctant to add to their
costs and Governments reluctant to add to their obligations. Bevin
stuck as closely as he could to his I.T.F. brief and after twenty-five
meetings the committee produced a final text which the conference

1 Proceedings of the I.T.F. Congress, held in Stockholm, 9th–13th July 1928,
pp. 153-4.

adopted by 84 votes to 22, with the British employers abstaining.

Bevin did not believe that the drafting of the convention by itself would alter the position at all; it would have to be followed up by steady pressure on governments to ratify it. But the issue had been raised, a standard had been set and the dockers' unions in all countries had now an objective towards which to work. Before the convention came into operation, it was revised in 1932, but its subsequent history does not belie Bevin's hopes. By the beginning of 1958 the revised version had been ratified and translated into national legislation in nineteen countries, including the United Kingdom—not a sensational result, assuredly, but a steady unspectacular contribution to the improvement of the dockers' working conditions on which the one-time Bristol carter had set his heart.

12

For years Bevin and the T.G.W.U. had been pressed to extend their interest in the dockers to seamen. The National Union of Seamen, under the despotic control of Havelock Wilson, had become a company union working hand in glove with the employers in the Shipping Federation. Membership was enforced by the employers and in return Wilson ruthlessly suppressed any demand—the eight-hour day, for instance—which might inconvenience the shipowners. Little was done for the seamen, whose conditions were amongst the worst of any industry. Yet so complete was the hold which Wilson and the shipowners together exercised over the engagement of seamen that it was difficult to remedy what had become an open scandal. Any protest, leave alone attempts to start a rival union, was certain to be followed by the dismissal and victimisation of the men involved.

Wilson had long been a scornful critic of the trade-union movement's politics and of the Labour Party. In 1926, his was the one union which refused to join the national strike and during 1927–8 he gave full support, including financial help from the Seamen's funds, to the breakaway 'non-political' miners' union started by George Spencer in the Nottinghamshire coalfield. So far the T.U.C. had treated Wilson with tolerance, if only because his position was so strong that any action against him was likely to prove ineffective.

This inactivity was loudly denounced by the Communists and the Minority Movement. Wilson's open support of Spencer's breakaway miners' union finally forced the General Council's hand. The Miners' Federation demanded the expulsion of the National Union of Seamen from the T.U.C.[1], and the T.G.W.U. agreed to organise a marine section for the enrolment of seamen.

Bevin proceeded with deliberation. He knew that Havelock Wilson was ill and that there were younger men in the Seamen's Union—including the general secretary, W. R. Spence—who were out of sympathy with the highly personal policy Wilson pursued. In April 1929, Wilson died and although Bevin went ahead and held the first delegate conference of the new marine section,[2] a truce was agreed between the two unions in July. Bevin was immensely relieved and in the course of the next few years went out of his way to establish close working relations with Spence and to give steady support to his union in pressing for improvements in the seamen's conditions. Thanks to his restraint a conflict was avoided which could only have done damage to the interests of the seamen and of trade unionism in general.

These years, 1927–29, were critical in the development of another industry in which Bevin and his union were deeply involved. Motor transport began rapidly to overtake all other forms of public transport in the 1920s with far-reaching social as well as economic consequences.[3] The advantages were obvious but were offset by the unregulated and wasteful competition between rival companies and between the different forms of transport, bus and tram, rail and road. Apart from the N.U.R., the Transport and General Workers' Union was the major union involved. Its members were bound to suffer from a situation in which companies tried to undercut their rivals by paying lower wages, demanding longer hours and frequently ignoring safety regulations.

Bevin believed that there was only one way in which to solve the problem, by treating it as a whole. It was no use trying to deal with it section by section, tramwaymen's wages, conditions of work in the road-haulage companies, or the hours of work on the buses. The

1 This was voted by the Swansea T.U.C. in September 1928.
2 7th May 1929.
3 There were 975,783 motor vehicles (including motor cycles) on the roads in 1922; 1,888,726 in 1927.

root of the trouble was the uncontrolled competition. This competition was not in the public interest. In London, for instance, while the central areas and the West End were over-provided with alternative services, other parts to the north and east of the city were left without any adequate means of public transport. A cheap and efficient transport system was a national need but it could only be provided, Bevin argued, if it was treated not as a source of private profit but as a public service. The State must intervene, if not to take over public ownership as he believed the logical course to be, then at least to establish public control.

The larger private interests were already taking steps to reduce competition by buying up controlling interests or coming to terms with their rivals. In London, for instance, Lord Ashfield had brought the Underground companies and the London General Omnibus Company under single control. As a union leader, Bevin preferred negotiating with one or two big companies, but this only simplified, it did not solve, the problem, since it did not provide the element of public control which Bevin believed essential.

In 1929, the Government at last agreed to appoint a Royal Commission on Transport, a step for which Bevin and the T.G.W.U. had long been pressing. The Union's proposals, presented to the Commission by John Cliff, argued for public control of all road services, both passenger and goods, by a system of licensing in the hands of traffic commissioners.

By the time the Commission produced its first report, a Labour Government was in power and Bevin was in a stronger position to make the Union's views effective. The Royal Commission's recommendations did not go as far as he would have liked, but the Road Traffic Act of 1930 and the Road and Rail Traffic Act of 1933, based on its report, provided the machinery of public control on the lines suggested by the T.G.W.U. This was the framework within which the road transport system of this country continued to operate until the nationalisation measures introduced by another Labour Government after 1945.

13

Despite all Bevin's efforts the Union's membership and income still remained substantially below the level they had reached before the General Strike. 1928 was a bad year for unemployment in many of the trades the Union organised—in the docks, for instance, and in the tinplate and galvanising industries. That year membership stood at 316,000, sixty thousand less than in 1925 and lower than the figure for 1927. There were plenty of new members, Bevin reported to his Executive; the difficulty was to keep them. The Union had repaid most of the money it had borrowed, built Transport House and begun to replace its reserves, but so long as the membership and the income failed to recover it was impossible to make effective economies in administration, on which the Union was still spending over three quarters of the money it received in contributions.

Bevin kept a sharp look-out for any chance to increase membership by amalgamation. For a time he had been hopeful of reaching agreement with the Electrical Trades Union, but these negotiations lapsed at the time of the General Strike. In November 1927, however, he reported to his Executive on informal talks with the Workers' Union, the third of the big general unions, founded by Tom Mann in 1898.

The Workers' Union was more truly a general workers' union than the T.G.W.U. It had nothing corresponding to the solid nucleus of dockers and road-transport workers which was the strength of Bevin's original amalgamation and this may have accounted for its declining fortunes. Its members consisted of unskilled and semi-skilled workers scattered through a variety of trades, particularly in engineering; it had a high turnover in membership and by 1927 it was in low waters financially. This did not deter Bevin. Experience taught him that no union was likely to consider amalgamation unless it was in financial difficulties and he believed that the membership of the Workers' Union, once transferred to his own organisation, could be turned into an asset.

The weakness of the Workers' Union's bargaining position allowed Bevin to incorporate their hundred thousand members without making any major alterations in the structure of his own union. For a year or two, the T.G.W.U. had to carry a swollen staff of officers and spend funds and energy on building up the branches it took over. But Bevin's gamble, taken at a time of rising unemployment, was justified within a few years. Membership rose by 107,000 immediately, fell back a little in 1930–32, then rose uninterruptedly from 1933 onwards. Coming at a time when the Union's recovery from the setback of 1926 was still making slow headway, the amalgamation gave the T.G.W.U. a fresh impetus which helped to carry it through the worst years of the Depression. It now secured a decisive lead in numbers over the rival general union, the General and Municipal Workers, and by 1937 became—and has remained—the largest of all British trade unions.

14

By the time the Biennial Delegate Conference of the Union met at Newcastle (July 1929), most of the questions with which he had been dealing—the new amalgamation, the marine section, the Royal Commission on Transport, the Mond-Turner talks—had reached a point where Bevin could give a satisfactory report to the delegates. On the Mond-Turner talks and every other issue that mattered Bevin and the Executive carried the conference with them and, to mark the achievement of the new amalgamation, Bevin was presented with the bust of himself by Whitney Smith which still presides over the Council Chamber of Transport House.

It was indeed a quiet conference—and for a very good reason. Two months before, a General Election had turned Baldwin out of office and put back Labour, still in a minority, but for the first time with the largest number of seats, 287, of any party in the House. At the beginning of a new period of office there were high hopes of effective reform and little disposition among the delegates at Newcastle to worry over-much about the past.

His participation in the Mond-Turner talks had not weakened Bevin's belief in the need for separate working-class representation in Parliament through the Labour Party. He turned the Union's organisation on to a campaign to secure the payment of the political levy, constantly speaking and writing in support of 'contracting-in' as the answer to the Trades Disputes Act of 1927.

"Employing interests—the railway interests, the docking interests—are powerfully represented in the House . . . the Trade Union *has* to come in, or the workers' interests go by the board."[1]

A Socialist himself, he was prepared to justify the political activity of the Union on purely trade-union grounds, in order to protect its members against the powerful political pressures exerted by the employers.

The Birmingham conference of the Labour Party in 1928 adopted as the Party's programme *Labour and the Nation*, largely written by R. H. Tawney. It was a general statement of Socialist aims which satisfied neither the I.L.P. (who wanted to commit the Party to sweeping Socialist measures immediately on coming into power) nor those, like Bevin, who wanted a short election programme. Majority opinion in the Party, however, was far closer to Bevin's than to Maxton's views. The election programme, when finally published, was cast in the practical terms for which Bevin had called in 1927 and gave pride of place, not to Socialism (which was not mentioned), but to conquering unemployment. It was in fact very largely borrowed from Lloyd George's programme for the Liberals, with its proposals for a big public works programme on Keynesian lines to put new life into the economic system.

Bevin worked hard during the 1929 election campaign, speaking up and down the country and marshalling all the resources of the T.G.W.U. in support of the Labour Party. The result was gratifying. Amongst the 287 Labour M.P.s were seven of the Union's candidates and six of the Workers' Union's. Eight more members of the T.G.W.U. and five of the Workers' Union found seats, although not included on the official list of candidates financed by the two unions. With road transport certain to be among the subjects of legislation, this guaranteed a useful representation of the Union's point of view.

But Bevin took a wider view than this. Like every other member of the Labour Party, he believed that at last there was a chance to take effective steps to cure the ills from which the country was suffering, especially unemployment, the major issue of the election. He neither expected nor was asked to take any part in the new Government, but he was ready, if called upon, to place his energy and experience at the Government's disposal and eager to give it all the support he could. In the summer of 1929, with the Union strengthened by the new amalgamation and Labour again in office, his hopes ran high.

1 *The Record*, November 1927, pp. 104–5.

CHAPTER 16

The Search for an Economic Policy

1930

I

THE AUTUMN of 1929 was the last unsuspected moment of calm before the disasters which began with the Wall Street crash at the end of October and steadily multiplied until the greater part of the Western world lay under an economic blight. When the T.U.C. met at Belfast in September and the Labour Party at Brighton in October, MacDonald's Government had been in office too short a time either to produce convincing evidence of achievement or to stimulate criticism from disappointed hopes. Both conferences, as a result, were dull.

At Belfast, where Ben Tillett delivered the presidential address to the T.U.C., the three big debates all followed familiar lines. The miners again called for a reorganisation of the trade-union movement on the principle of one union for each industry, were opposed by the General Council as well as the general unions and again defeated. The Mond-Turner talks came in for further criticism, were defended by the General Council and vindicated by a large majority. Bevin took a prominent part in both debates but said nothing—indeed, there was nothing to say—which he had not said before. Finally, the General Council presented a detailed report on the disruptive tactics of the Communist Party and the Minority Movement which was hotly contested by a handful of Communist delegates but carried by an overwhelming majority. The General Council left it to individual unions to deal with their own Communists and made no attempt to impose a general ban. Bevin, however, made no attempt to proscribe Communists in the Transport and General Workers' Union, a step that was not taken until 1949 after Arthur Deakin had succeeded him as General Secretary.

At Brighton, the new Ministers gave a confident account of their plans, amongst them J. H. Thomas who, as Lord Privy Seal, bore the responsibility of dealing with unemployment. Bevin intervened to press on Thomas the value of large-scale plans for building new arterial roads (including the Severn barrage, still not built in 1960) and for modernising the port facilities of the country under a National Dock Board. He intervened a second time to urge on Philip Snowden, the new Chancellor of the Exchequer, the importance of an investigation into the banking system and the effect of financial policy on wages and employment.

Bevin's insistence upon the importance of finance was instinctive rather than dogmatic. He had no Socialist blueprint in mind for remodelling the monetary system. What impressed him as a negotiator was the extent to which wages and the employer's capacity to pay were determined by factors beyond the control, and frequently beyond the understanding, of either side. A change in the Bank Rate for instance could affect the whole of industry and throw thousands out of work. Who decided the Bank Rate? To whom were they responsible? What influenced their decision? How far were they aware of the effect of their decision on industry and the lives of working-class families? These were the questions Bevin asked himself, and had done ever since he saw the effect of the decision to return to the gold standard in 1925 on wages and employment.

When Snowden set up a committee under the chairmanship of Lord Macmillan and invited Bevin to serve on it, he accepted with alacrity. Just as he insisted in the talks with Sir Alfred Mond and his group that the trade-union side must not be pinned down to discussing wages and conditions, but should have the right to ask questions about the major decisions of management, so now he wanted to know more about the financial decisions which touched the class he represented, because of its lack of any margin, more sharply than any other in the community. They were not an economist's questions, but, as Bevin was to show on the Macmillan Committee, they were questions which, when pressed, could sometimes reveal uncriticised assumptions at the heart of the most refined technical arguments.

2

Bevin's biggest contribution to the Labour movement in 1929–30 lay outside the sphere of government. Ten years after George Lansbury had revived the *Herald* as a daily paper, it was still losing money. In 1920, largely thanks to Bevin's efforts, £143,000 had been subscribed by the unions, but in little more than a year this sum was exhausted, and in 1922 the General Council and the National Executive of the Labour Party took over ownership of the *Daily Herald* and of the Victoria House Printing Company which printed and published it. Throughout the 'twenties, Bevin continued to take a special interest in the paper, but neither he nor anyone else was able to find a way to make the paper pay.[1]

When the Trade Disputes Act cut down the trade unions' affiliation fees, the Party had to discontinue its subsidy. Soon afterwards, the T.U.C. had to reduce its own financial support. Circulation fell steadily,[2] and with it advertisement revenue.

In the meantime, other popular papers—in particular the *Daily Express* and the *Daily Mail*—were shooting ahead, building up mass circulations and capturing the advertising market. The *Herald* could not compete in number of pages, in circulation or in the free insurance schemes which were used to build up and hold a steady readership for its wealthier rivals. Technically, too, it was being left behind, especially when other papers began to print a northern edition in Manchester which the *Herald* could not afford to do. Above all, it was dull, an unsuccessful compromise between a propaganda leaflet, news of the movement, and a popular daily.

Bevin may not, as Francis Williams says, have had much idea how to make the *Herald* into the paper he wanted, but he had grasped, perhaps more clearly than anyone else in the Labour movement, the importance of a Labour daily at a time when the rest of the national Press was uniformly hostile. If a Labour Government were returned at the next election, Bevin pointed out, there was some danger that it would be the first British Government without a paper on which it could rely to put its point of view. When Bevin got up and said this

---

1 The losses on the *Herald* were: £113,661 (1920); £48,177 (1921); £84,756 (1923); £2,269 (1924); £11,881 (1925); £24,268 (1926); £25,280 (1928).
2 By June 1927, it was down to 383,000 a day; by October 1928 to 301,000.

at a trade-union or party conference, everyone agreed, but no one did anything and the circulation went on falling.

In the autumn of 1928, with a General Election certain in the next few months, Bevin decided that the time had come to take a direct hand. He went first to the General Council and then to the T.U.C. at Swansea. What was needed, he told them, was a large amount of capital—half a million pounds, or perhaps a million—to put the *Herald* on equal terms with its rivals. It was useless to think of raising such a sum by affiliation fees or a levy; it would have to be borrowed on the credit of the trade-union movement.

He found it harder than he had expected to raise the money. At one time it looked as if the Prudential Assurance Company might provide a loan of £300,000 and a draft agreement was drawn up between the Prudential and the T.U.C. This fell through, however, as did other approaches which Bevin made. Then, quite unexpectedly, the possibility of a new solution turned up in the spring of 1929. Even if Bevin had been successful in raising the money, there was still the problem of finding men with the experience and the organisation capable of putting the *Herald* into a position to compete with the *Express* and the *Mail*. The new proposal promised to solve both problems at the same time.

J. S. Elias, the managing director of Odhams, was a man who combined a simple, unassuming character with great business ability. Beginning as an errand boy when Odhams was a firm of jobbing printers, he had built it up into a highly successful publishing business, the publishers of Bottomley's *John Bull* amongst a number of weeklies and now of *The People*, a Sunday newspaper which he had raised from a circulation of 250,000 to two million. Elias was looking for a daily paper with which to occupy the silent presses of *The People* during the week. He thought, first, of the *Morning Post*, the failing representative of right-wing Conservatism; then of the Liberal *Daily Chronicle* which Lloyd George had recently sold. Both papers passed into other hands and Elias was still looking for the paper he wanted when John Dunbar, his editorial director and a supporter of the Labour Party, put forward the suggestion that he should take over the *Herald*.

There were big difficulties in the way. The *Herald* was not for sale and Bevin was determined to keep control of its political views and editorial policy in trade-union hands. All that he was prepared to consider was a partnership. But from the moment Elias and Bevin met they liked and trusted each other. In the end the two of them, with John Dunbar, found a way round the difficulties and reached an agreement which is still unique in newspaper history.

3

The Labour Government had just been formed, a fact which made the *Herald* a much more attractive proposition and left Bevin to act as chairman of the directors of the Victoria House Printing Company while Ben Turner, the nominal chairman, went off to become Secretary for Mines. Bevin's first idea was to create a body of trustees to safeguard the character of the paper, but this proved impracticable. Finally, an agreement was signed on 30th August 1929, setting up a new company, The Daily Herald (1929), with a share capital of £100,000. £49,000 was issued free to the T.U.C. in return for the sale of the copyright and goodwill of the *Herald* by the Victoria House Printing Company and £51,000 subscribed in cash by Odhams. Nine directors were appointed, four 'A' directors representing the T.U.C. (Bevin, Citrine, Tillett and Pugh), five 'B' directors representing Odhams. Elias became Chairman, Bevin vice-chairman. On questions of political and industrial policy only the 'A' directors were entitled to vote.

Characteristically, Bevin placed the safeguards of the *Herald*'s policy as a Labour paper in the hands of four representatives of the T.U.C. No one was invited to join the Board from the National Executive of the Labour Party or from the Parliamentary Labour Party. The political policy of the paper was defined in the articles of association as that laid down from time to time by the Labour Party Conference; its industrial policy as that laid down by the T.U.C. If there was any dispute between the directors whether a particular question fell within the definition of political or industrial policy, the question was to be referred to an arbitrator. The agreement named Lord Sankey, Lord Chancellor in the Labour Government, as the first referee and Sir William Jowitt, the Attorney-General, as his deputy. The surprising thing is that this partnership between the T.U.C. and a commercial, profit-making firm of publishers worked, largely thanks to the mutual confidence between Elias and Bevin.

But their partnership went further than agreement not to interfere in each other's sphere. Both believed that the five and a half million trade unionists and eight million Labour voters in the country offered the *Herald* a unique opportunity. The problem was how to take advantage of it. On his side Elias was ready to provide the organisation, to raise capital, put in new machinery, print a northern edition and run a free insurance scheme, but the mobilisation of the scattered strength of the Labour movement behind the new *Herald* could only be done by Bevin, and even Bevin might have quailed at the task after a ten years' losing battle to get trade unionists to buy their own paper.

The year-long campaign into which he now threw himself was undertaken in addition to his normal duties as a general secretary and a member of the General Council. It brought him no personal advantage and precious little thanks, was about the hardest way of serving the Labour cause anyone could think of and demonstrates how much energy Bevin was prepared to devote to realising an idea in which he believed.

With the help of Vincent Tewson (later to become General Secretary of the T.U.C.) and Surrey Dane (later to become managing director of Odhams) Bevin set about making the fullest possible use of the local organisation of the Labour Party and the trade unions. Beginning at Cardiff and Bristol, conferences were organised in the fourteen principal cities of the country to which delegates from all Labour and trade-union organisations in each area were invited. Through these conferences, Bevin succeeded in enrolling 32,000 canvassers, thanks to whose efforts over 600,000 new readers were registered before the first edition was printed. With the backing of Odhams the preparation of the campaign was carefully worked out, from a payment to every helper (and to the local Labour Party) for every hundred readers enrolled, to free gifts, a free insurance scheme and even a special publication, *The Helper*, which kept the drive for new readers going.

Bevin devoted every week-end for thirty-five consecutive weeks to travelling up and down the country, addressing as many as five meetings on a Saturday and Sunday and driving home his argument of the importance to the Labour movement of a successful national newspaper. At one time or another, most of the leaders of the Party and the T.U.C. were drawn in to speak or send a special message in support, but the brunt of this crusading work was borne by Bevin who week after week went straight from his office to the train on a Friday evening and did not get back until Monday morning, hoarse and tired, but ready to put in another full week's work in Transport House before starting off again the following week-end.

On Saturday, 15th March, the old *Herald* published its final number and the next day the Prime Minister, Ramsay MacDonald, came to Long Acre to start the presses printing the first number of the new. Edited by William Mellor, with double the number of pages and a new serial by Edgar Wallace, the paper at once reached and held the circulation of a million which Bevin had undertaken to provide. So successful was it that within ten weeks the *Daily Chronicle*, launched as a new paper only a few days before the *Herald*, was driven to amalgamate with the *Daily News* and became the *News Chronicle*.

4

Bevin and Elias straightaway set about launching a northern edition to be printed in Manchester. A fresh series of conferences and week-end meetings was organised, the campaign culminating in a huge carnival representative of the whole Labour movement in the North of England, Scotland and Wales. On 28th June, a procession three and a half miles long, preceded by more than a hundred tableaux mounted on carts and accompanied by twenty-five bands, wound its way through the streets of Manchester to the Belle Vue Gardens. It was a real northern occasion, complete with all the delights of the fair from Blackpool and ending in a dazzling display of fireworks.

To Bevin's disgust, neither the Prime Minister nor any of the leading members of the Cabinet could find the time to come to Manchester, despite repeated pleas. MacDonald spent the day instead at the Farnborough air display. In his absence, Bevin harangued the huge gathering and urged them to support the North's own edition of the new *Herald*. Afterwards, never more at home than in a great working-class festival, he joined the crowds, greeting innumerable friends and showing that unaffected ease of contact with his own people which he never lost.

A week later the northern edition of the *Daily Herald* went to press and rapidly increased the paper's circulation. In the teeth of intense competition from the rival popular dailies, the *Herald* more than held its own and two years later, in June 1933, beat Beaverbrook's *Daily Express* to become the first daily paper, not only in Britain, but in the world, to reach a circulation of two million. Bevin was delighted and took an unashamedly personal pride in the success of "my paper". He had every right to, for if the achievement owed much to the skill of Elias and Dunbar and the resources of Odhams, the essential link between the new *Herald* and the Labour movement had been forged by Bevin alone. There were, of course, critics who complained that the new paper compared poorly with the old *Herald* which Lansbury had edited in the early 1920s. There is some truth in this, but it is an unrealistic comparison. The heroic days of left-wing journalism were over. Even in 1920, when the militant spirit in the Labour Party and the trade unions was still strong, Lansbury's *Herald* had lost over £100,000. In 1929–30, it would not have lasted three months. The popular papers were capturing working-class readers by the hundred thousand and the only choice open to the movement was to see this happen and do nothing about it or to set up a popular paper of its own which met the other dailies on their own ground but kept open a channel for the Labour point of view. At a time when few working-class homes possessed a wireless, when television was still in the experimental stage, and when advertising and the cinema were under the control of interests hostile to Labour, the popular Press was the one effective means of mass communication to which the Labour movement could secure access, but only along the lines which Bevin and Elias developed.

Bevin was in fact already playing with the idea of a new Labour weekly, a working-class version of the *New Statesman*, to supplement the *Herald*. With this in view, he took care to keep the Victoria House Printing Company outside the scope of the arrangements with Odhams, believing that a printing and publishing business owned by the trade-union movement might well be put to good use. The loss of the *Herald* however hit the printing company hard. It took time and patience to unravel the financial arrangements and reconstruct the capital, longer still in a time of depression to find sufficient work to pay the men employed. Bevin used all his contacts in the trade-union world and on the other side of industry to secure business for the printing firm or advertisements in the publications which the company continued to produce. It was another job that brought only kicks and no ha'pence, a job without interest or prestige, one more anxiety to add to the obligations he already carried, but once he had accepted responsibility as chairman, he hung on tenaciously, never missing an opportunity to push the Company's interests, never giving up hope that one day he would succeed—as he never did—in hitting on a better way of putting across the Labour point of view in the Press.

5

Whatever his other preoccupations, Bevin missed few of the discussions of the Committee on Finance and Industry, which met throughout the year 1930. He was the only trade-union member of the Committee which was presided over by a judge (Lord Macmillan) and included four bankers, a former Secretary of the Treasury (Lord Bradbury), two professional economists, the president of the F.B.I., the president of the Association of Chambers of Commerce and the Chairman of Beardmore's. The Left was very unequally represented for a Committee appointed by a Labour Chancellor of the Exchequer: Sir Thomas Allen, chairman of the Co-operative Insurance Society who had little to say; J. T. Walton Newbold, one time member of the I.L.P. and the Communist Party, who had only too much to say, fancied himself as a student of economics and turned out to be a crank—and Bevin.

One of the two economists was Keynes, who had just completed several years' work on his *Treatise on Money* and published it while the Committee was sitting. The Macmillan Committee gave Keynes the opportunity to expound his conclusions and to ask the Treasury and the Bank some very pointed questions. He was ably seconded by Reginald MacKenna, chairman of the Midland Bank, a former Liberal Chancellor of the Exchequer and a sharp critic of Bank of England policy. A natural sympathy soon developed between these two and Bevin. Lord Bradbury displayed an icy disapproval in face of Keynes' arguments, but R. H. (now Lord) Brand, managing director of Lazards as well as a Fellow of All Souls, and the other economist, Professor Gregory, were prepared to take issue with Keynes and subject his conclusions to cross-examination. Indeed, it is impossible to read through the verbatim typescript record of the Committee's private discussions (which Bevin carefully preserved) without feeling a mounting sense of intellectual excitement. For nine hours, at the request of the Committee, Keynes set out, with his unequalled lucidity, the workings of the classical financial system, the reasons why it had broken down and the seven alternative remedies which he thought the Committee should consider.

Bevin was fascinated. He said little in these early meetings, but followed the argument closely, listening intently and occasionally asking a question. Nor did he assert himself when the Committee turned to the examination of witnesses. Fifty-seven in all appeared before the Committee, including the Governor and Deputy Governor of the Bank of England, the chairmen of the Joint Stock Banks, and Sir Richard Hopkins, Secretary to the Treasury. Besides representatives of industry, of commerce and the T.U.C., the Committee also heard the views of a distinguished group of economists: D. H. Robertson; A. C. Pigou; R. G. Hawtrey and A. L. Bowley— not to mention Major Douglas, the founder of Social Credit, Frank Wise, of the I.L.P., and the Economic Freedom League. Altogether forty-nine days were spent in listening to evidence and another nineteen in private discussions.

The Committee's terms of reference were wide. They were directed "to inquire into banking, finance and credit, paying regard to the factors both internal and international which govern their operations", and to examine the effect of monetary policy on trade and employment. This was a subject on which there was sharp disagreement among the experts and the Committee was by no means unanimous in its recommendations. In the process of their inquiry, however, they put together a report on the working of the monetary system which, in Sir Roy Harrod's words "takes its place in the great historic line of British currency reports".[1]

Bevin always referred with pride to his membership of the Macmillan Committee. His experience as a trade-union leader, his visit to the U.S.A. and the part he took in the Mond-Turner discussions had taught him much about industry and trade. But the operations of the City remained a mystery of which he had no direct

1 R. F. (Sir Roy) Harrod: *Life of John Maynard Keynes* (1952), p. 423.

experience. The eighteen months which he spent on the Macmillan Committee were another and important chapter in his education and, if Bevin was apt to believe too easily that he "knew all about" banking and currency afterwards, there is no doubt that he acquired far more knowledge of them than most trade-union leaders or the majority of politicians.

It is easy to see that Bevin would learn something from membership of such a committee, but what had he to contribute?

As the investigation progressed, the economic situation worsened. The unemployed had numbered 1,250,000 in the early months of 1929; a year later the figure reached 1,750,000 and in the early months of 1931, 2,600,000. It did not fall again below two million until July 1935. Bevin never lost sight of what was happening outside the doors of the Treasury Conference Room and, whenever the inquiry showed a tendency to settle down within the limits of the monetary system, he would interpose to bring it back to the effects of monetary policy on trade and employment. He showed a familiarity with the organisation of industry and the course of trade which none of the other members could rival. Nor was this only on the labour side. He moved with ease from the pensions paid in the milling trade and the calculation of wages in coal and engineering to the comparative prices of tinplate in South Wales and the United States, the concentration of shipbuilding or the organisation of the chemical industry. More than once, he described himself as an 'industrialist', feeling a common interest with the manufacturer and employer of labour against those who, in his view, 'lived off' industry.

An outsider not involved in the game (as Keynes and McKenna were, for all their criticism of the way it was played), Bevin was able to cut through discussion of the intricacies of the monetary system which fascinated Keynes and ask the plain question, What purpose does it serve?

Bevin looked upon money as a means of exchange, a device to meet the needs of industry and trade, to enable men to manufacture, buy and sell their goods. He regarded the international money market, dealing in money independently of the productive use to which it could be put, as 'usury', a word he frequently used with the full Aristotelian flavour of disapproval. The test he applied to a monetary system was whether it assisted the expansion of trade and employment or artificially restricted it. This point of view, although it neglected the advantages in "invisible exports" which the country derived from the City's role as a centre of international banking and insurance, served as a much-needed corrective to the equally one-sided view of bankers who thought too much in terms of the money market and too little of how their decisions affected the chances of expansion and employment in the very different industrial world of the Midlands and the North.

6

Most of the Committee's witnesses and several of its members shared the belief that a self-regulating monetary system based upon the gold standard and requiring only the occasional alteration of the Bank Rate was part of the natural order of the universe. The trade depression and the high rate of unemployment were no doubt regrettable, but neither Montagu Norman, the Governor of the Bank of England, nor Lord Bradbury would admit that these invalidated the assumptions on which the monetary system rested. In Bevin's view this was to stand economics on its head. There was nothing sacrosanct about the gold standard. If a monetary system based upon it failed to work, as Keynes demonstrated, then it should be changed. The sole test was its utility.

Bevin believed that in 1925 the Treasury and the Bank had made a disastrous mistake in restoring the gold standard at the pre-war rate of parity:

"That was the direct cause of upsetting every agreement with every employer in the country. . . . You return to the gold standard in 1925 and you give to a miner and a mineowner the job of adjusting industry. They do not know what has hit them. They have got to handle all the problems of a million men. I think that is where our trouble starts. If we had gone on to the gold standard *at the then ratio*, I believe we should have been leading the world today. We were getting on very well . . . I believe the break in prices started then. That was the thing that pushed us over the cliff."[1]

Keynes agreed with him. Britain's return to the gold standard had been followed by other countries and had led to widespread deflation and a prolonged fall in prices.

1 Private session, 23rd October 1930. Verbatim typescript, p. 23.

PROFESSOR GREGORY: "When you say you think we are primarily responsible, on what do you base that opinion?

MR. KEYNES: "Because we led the way at the beginning of 1925. I think the world was running on more or less an even keel then and everything was set for better times, and then we started our return to the gold standard."[1]

How was it that men as intelligent as Montagu Norman and Lord Bradbury, Secretary of the Treasury at the time, could have taken a step which, by suddenly revaluing the pound, placed a crippling burden on Britain's export industries, forcing them to slash their prices and drive down wages or lose their overseas markets?

Bevin was convinced that the answer lay in the City's ignorance of industry and its preoccupation with the money market:

"I followed Sir Ernest Harvey's (the Deputy Governor's) evidence very closely and I gathered that until quite recently, the Bank of England was run purely on lines of tradition. What I would like to ascertain is whether the tradition of the Bank actually takes into account the industry of the country or purely the money market? Following Sir Ernest Harvey's evidence right through, and I read it again and again, it seemed to me that the international money market was the sole guiding principle up to quite recently . . ."[2]

McKenna took the same point of view:

CHAIRMAN: "Is the general position you are placing before us this, that the method by which the Bank of England and the Treasury work our monetary system is dictated more by international considerations than by domestic considerations?

MR. McKENNA: "I should say solely by money market considerations."[3]

In Bevin's view, instead of monetary policy being guided by the needs of industry and trade, the Bank and the Treasury attached far too much importance to the maintenance of the pound's exchange rate, to the prestige of London as the centre of the international money market and to the "sacred cow" of the gold standard, leaving industry to bear the consequences in the shape of falling prices, wage cuts and unemployment.

1 Private session, 20th February 1930, p. 20. A passage marked in ink on Bevin's copy.
2 Private session, 21st March, p. 15.
3 Ibid., p. 10.

He made the same point over the recent rise in the Bank rate. The need to restrict or expand credit was judged in terms of the weakness or strength of the pound in relation to other currencies, not of industry's need of a liberal supply of credit to finance expansion and of a stable Bank Rate to avoid sharp rises in costs.

In cross examination Bevin pressed Montagu Norman on the possibility of separating the provision of credit into two parts:

MR. BEVIN: "For instance, assuming your external trade is good, and credit flowed to your external market until you get to a point where gold began to go out, and then you had to restrict credit, and that produced unemployment, is it possible to have some direction through public bodies, municipalities, of the whole operation of credit and therefore while you restrict one form of credit you maintain the volume of home credit, to prevent the blow falling upon the workpeople.

THE RT. HON. MONTAGU NORMAN: "I should say it is impossible."[1]

Norman's bleak negative was typical of the cold self-satisfaction, as it seemed to Bevin, with which the Governor of the Bank rejected every suggestion for altering monetary policy in order to improve trade or reduce unemployment. The fact that the unemployment figures were mounting rapidly in every industrial country, including Great Britain, did not mitigate the complacency with which the Governor regarded the operation of the monetary system, the rules of which (Bevin suspected) had come to possess an intellectual validity in the minds of many bankers quite independent of their use or harmfulness to the economic processes by which ordinary men earned their living.

7

Listening to the evidence, Bevin became more and more firmly convinced that, so long as world prices continued to fall and Great Britain adhered to the gold standard at the existing rate of exchange, there was no alternative to the permanent unemployment of two million men.

It was an argument which the rest of the Committee were reluctant

1 *Minutes of Evidence taken before the Committee on Finance and Industry,* Vol. 1 (1931), p. 217.

to accept, without, however, being able to suggest ways of dealing with the problem which carried any conviction.

The Chairman made it plain from the beginning that the possibility of abandoning the gold standard was excluded by the Chancellor of the Exchequer. Philip Snowden had become a Socialist on ethical grounds. So far as economics went, his principles were of the purest Gladstonian orthodoxy: he refused categorically to consider tampering with the gold standard or compromising with Free Trade, a refusal which was to cost the Labour Government dear. Every time the gold standard came into the discussion, the Chairman showed signs of anxiety, but Bevin was not to be silenced.

"Does not all this," he asked the Committee, "bring us round to the fact that we cannot do anything while we remain on the gold standard? . . .

Mr. Keynes: "I should like to try these other remedies first. They seem to me much more promising. It is very doubtful how far going off the gold standard would help the situation. . . . You would agree that devaluation would be a way of reducing wages, but you would say you would not object to it because it would reduce all other money incomes similarly?

Mr. Bevin: "That is so . . . I have no objection to facing increasing the value of money by reducing money incomes over all, if we are going to deal with every class in the community. But I have a profound objection to picking out just one class to bear the burden . . . I stand absolutely inflexible on this question of wages and on this suggestion of singling out one class of the community only as the means of adjusting the equilibrium."[1]

There was a further reason why Bevin advocated devaluation. He was struck by the heavy burden of debt and the National Debt in particular, the interest on which had to come out of the earnings of industry, adding to costs and holding down wages. In 1911 industry had to find £16 million a year to service the National Debt; by 1930 the charge had grown to £277 million a year. Who profited by this? Neither the workman nor the employer, but the unproductive *rentier* class. The interests of the *rentier*, Bevin complained, were treated as sacred: you could cut wages or unemployment benefit, but on no account must the *rentier* class be touched. Devaluation would ensure that sacrifices were equally borne by all classes (hence the opposition to it) and at the same time reduce the burden of debt. But his colleagues—including Keynes—shyed away from such radical proposals.

1 Private Session, 7th November 1930, pp. 15–18.

"What troubles me," Bevin told them, "is this. We are all prepared, apparently, with a kind of fatalistic feeling to allow two or three millions of our people to go on suffering like this, but we must not do anything at all to shake or shock the confidence assumed to be associated with money. Really, I cannot accept that view. It may be you will go on until you are forced to do the thing; as I heard somebody say this morning, that is generally what happens with orthodox finance—it goes on until there is a revolution, or something of that kind, and then things are much worse. . . . Supposing you go on for a month or a year, you have simply to face the situation that your monetary system does not expand with the ability to produce.

"I think it is bound to be one of two things.

MR. LUBBOCK: "You mean tariffs or devaluation?"

MR. BEVIN: "Yes."[1]

8

During the course of the next winter, 1930—31, a drafting committee set to work on the report.[2] To orthodox opinion its recommendations were sufficiently shocking: for the first time, it was proposed that the currency should be *managed* and that it should be managed in the interests of price stability.

The central banks were urged to follow a policy which, both internationally and within their own domestic markets, would encourage enterprise by providing better and cheaper facilities for credit. An international fund to guarantee loans was proposed and, after detailed suggestions for reforming the organisation and functions of the Bank of England, there followed other proposals for closer co-operation between the City and the world of industry designed to help industry obtain the capital and financial advice it needed.

All this, no doubt, marked a big step forward in banking practice and made the Macmillan report (with its invaluable description of how the system worked) a text book of monetary policy. To Lord Bradbury even this was too much and he refused to sign the report.

1 Ibid., pp. 21 and 29.
2 The drafting committee consisted of J. M. Keynes, Cecil Lubbock, Professor Gregory, R. H. Brand and the chairman, Lord Macmillan. A great deal of the work was done by Keynes.

To Ernest Bevin it was altogether too little. He signed the report and went on with Keynes, McKenna and three others to sign an addendum which set out Keynes's proposals for the expansion of investment at home by schemes of capital development. But, in Bevin's opinion, neither the main recommendations of the report nor Keynes's proposals measured up to the needs of a situation in which more than 20 millions were unemployed in the leading industrial nations of the West. Unperturbed by the fact that none of his more expert colleagues on the Committee would join him, Bevin proceeded to state his own views in two separate reservations signed only by himself and his Co-operative colleague, Sir Thomas Allen.

Bevin criticised the report for failing to place sufficient emphasis on the crippling effect of dead-weight debt and for refusing to contemplate the possibility of abandoning the present form of the gold standard. "We take the view that the Treasury and the Bank of England should be considering an alternative basis in order to minimise disturbance if such a contingency should arise." This was the shrewdest recommendation in the whole report, written four months before the abandonment of the gold standard which the experts refused to consider.

"In fact," Bevin continued, "private enterprise having proved totally unable to lift the country out of the morass in which it is, there seems no alternative but for the State to grapple with the problem and for large measures of State planning to be adopted." As a beginning, Bevin suggested that the Bank of England should be transformed into a public corporation and that any machinery set up for financing industry should be under public, not private, control. He conceded that the return to pre-war parity in 1925 made it more difficult to devalue the pound now, but he was not to be shaken in his belief that devaluation would have to come. As for tariffs, which Keynes recommended without much enthusiasm, Bevin remarked: "In a general way we do not believe in tariffs," adding that none the less he would prefer them to an all-round reduction in wages. His strong preference was for vigorous measures of State planning and reorganisation in the basic industries (coal and steel), together with the provision of transport and power as State services and the whole-hearted adoption of Keynes's schemes of capital development.

It was only a sketch of a plan, yet looking back on the stagnation of Britain's economy between the wars one may well ask whether the

433   P

untrained layman did not show more understanding than all the experts who sat on or appeared before the Macmillan Committee. In setting out the technical problems involved, he could not compete with the trained mind of a Keynes, but even Keynes was curiously diffident when it came to remedies. He saw the complexities and drawbacks of every course too clearly to choose with confidence between them. Bevin's instinct was surer. He was wrong in believing that devaluation would solve Britain's economic difficulties, but he was right in insisting that the issue could not be evaded, that devaluation would have to come. More clearly than any other member of the Macmillan Committee, Bevin grasped the scale of the economic problems with which they had to deal and saw that reform of the monetary system could no longer produce an adquate answer to them. A managed currency was not enough, if the rest of economic activity was left unplanned. Bevin concluded some rough notes which he jotted down on reading the report with this reflection:

"Laissez-faire, as understood before the War, can never be re-created. If for no other reason, the Russian Five Year Plan cuts across the whole thing. Whilst it may be impossible to introduce a similar form in this country, to leave our industries languishing and our people to the tender mercies of a worn-out nineteenth century system is an insane policy."[1]

9

Committees played a big part in Bevin's life. There were few days in any week when he did not spend several hours sitting round a table, listening, arguing, throwing off ideas, helping to draft recommendations. It was work at which he excelled, as almost every committee he served on recognised, and from it he drew a great part of the first-hand knowledge and experience on which he relied. An illustration of this is his membership at this time of two committees dealing with widely separated subjects, the Standing Committee on Mineral Transport and the Advisory Committee on Colonial Development.

The first of these was set up in 1927 on the recommendation of the Samuel Report. Industry still depended for its power on coal supplies, and every day the railways ran hundreds of coal trains to

1 26th May 1931.

the industrial districts and to the docks for export. Congestion in the sidings, delay in the turn-around of wagons, out-of-date equipment for loading at the ports could add considerably to the costs of industry and retard its efficiency. The task of the committee was to find out what improvements could be made. It laboured spasmodically at this task until the end of 1934, and by the time he finished, Bevin had added a great deal to his knowledge of the internal transport system and coal industry of the country, knowledge which was to stand him in good stead when he took over a major share of the responsibility for the nation's industrial production during the war.

The second committee opened up an entirely new world. The Colonial Development Advisory Committee was appointed by the Labour Government to advise on applications from the colonies for assistance under the Colonial Development Fund Act, 1929, and met forty-one times between the summer of 1929 and the summer of 1931. Bevin, the one man without colonial experience on the small committee, attended twenty-eight of its meetings, saying little at first but following with keen interest a set of problems and administrative methods unlike anything he had encountered before.

Most of the schemes on which the Committee had to advise were limited in scope. The initial grant of which they disposed was not more than a million pounds and there were few projects of the size of the Zambesi Bridge. Many of the grants or loans were for surveys or for visits by public health and veterinary experts. Others were used to finance housing and drainage schemes: a market in Barbados, roads in St. Helena, railways in East Africa, an improved water supply in Fiji, landing facilities and communications for the Cape-to-Cairo air route. It was the first time Bevin came into contact with the struggling, impoverished world of the under-developed countries. It aroused an interest and a sympathy in him which he was never to lose and which bore fruit in the support he gave to Arthur Creech-Jones as Colonial Secretary of the post-war Labour Government and in the Colombo Plan, the last great project to which he put his hand at the very end of his life.

10

On paper, by far the most impressive committee on which Bevin sat was the Economic Advisory Council which Ramsay MacDonald set up in January 1930. MacDonald had in mind an economic equivalent of the Committee on Imperial Defence. He meant to collect the ablest men he could find to discuss the economic problems of the country freely, giving full rein to their ideas without the political anxieties which must inhibit such discussions in the Cabinet. Mac-Donald himself took the chair, usually accompanied by Philip Snowden as Chancellor of the Exchequer, J. H. Thomas and one or two other Ministers specially concerned with economic questions.

MacDonald went to a lot of trouble to get the right men for his Council. He chose Tom Jones for its secretary and, among economists, brought in J. M. Keynes, G. D. H. Cole, and R. H. Tawney, with Hubert Henderson as an Assistant Secretary. The industrialists' point of view was represented by Sir Arthur Balfour, a steelmaster from Sheffield who had been chairman of the Committee on Industry and Trade in 1924; Sir Andrew Duncan, chairman of the Central Electricity Board; Sir Josiah Stamp, chairman of the L.M.S. Railway; and Sir John Cadman, of the Anglo-Persian Oil Company. Citrine and Bevin were the representatives of the trade unions, and the fact that MacDonald and Snowden—between neither of whom and Bevin was there any love lost—should again have chosen him is evidence of the reputation which his ability now commanded. The experiment, however, was not a success. The full Advisory Council met once a month and spent an hour or two in discussion before lunching with the Prime Minister. Its committees, of course, met between times, but only thirteen meetings of the Council were held between January 1930 and the fall of the Labour Government in August 1931. This represented a total discussion time of less than twenty-four hours spread over eighteen months. Even this figure is less impressive than it sounds, for a number of existing committees set up by the Committee on Civil Research were promptly transferred to the Council which had to examine reports and advise on a variety of topics from the Channel Tunnel and locust control, to the ravages of the tsetse fly, the training of biologists and agricultural research.

At the suggestion of Keynes and Bevin, a small committee was set up at the first meeting (17th February 1930) to examine the underlying economic situation and report on plans for action should the situation grow worse. The result was not encouraging. Keynes wrote to Bevin on 1st May:

"Cadman, Balfour, Cole and myself were present. After about half an hour's discussion it appeared that Balfour and Cadman were opposed to recommending any inquiry into the question whether a programme of capital development could help unemployment so . . . we broke up into two groups to prepare two reports."[1]

The conflict between the two points of view was irreconcilable. Balfour, and Cadman believed "that it was to sound and not to revolutionary methods that the country should look for its economic recovery". By this they meant a restoration of the position before 1914 by nineteenth-century methods. Britain must recover her export trade by cutting costs, reducing wages and abolishing the restrictive practices of the trade unions. State expenditure (and taxation) must be drastically reduced, especially expenditure on the social services and unemployment benefit. Intervention by the State must be avoided at all costs, as this would be fatal to the recovery of business confidence.

To men with the views of Balfour and Cadman (which Snowden and the Treasury largely shared) the programme proposed by Keynes, Tawney, Cole and Bevin—increasing purchasing power to get people to consume more, and using the resources of the State to launch big schemes of capital development under a national plan for economic expansion—appeared to be the raving of wild and irresponsible extremists. There was nothing specifically Socialist about such a programme: Keynes, as MacDonald pointed out, had put forward much the same proposals in the *Liberal Yellow Book* of 1928. But to those brought up to believe that the highest economic virtue was thrift, the notion of spending money to get out of a depression was contrary to nature. It was inflation, nothing less a word which, as Keynes pointed out, ended further discussion.

This split of opinion remained open for the rest of the Council's meetings and stultified any recommendations which MacDonald may have hoped to elicit from the discussions. Equally sharp was

1 J. M. Keynes to Ernest Bevin, 1st May 1930.

the division of views on the issue of Free Trade and protection on which a committee of economists appointed by the Council reported in the autumn. Keynes, Henderson and Stamp recommended a revenue tariff and protection for the iron and steel trade. Piguo and Lionel Robbins opposed them, describing proposals for protection as "mean and despicable". The attempt to divorce the expert discussion of economic issues from politics—and for that matter, from morals, theology and plain emotion—proved to be a chimera.

In the course of the summer, complaints from the Labour members of the Council, voiced by Bevin, led to an improvement in procedure. Some of the more miscellaneous items were removed from the agenda, more time was found for discussion and attention was directed to the country's major economic problems.

There was no lack of informed opinion. At its meeting on 24th July 1930, the Council had before it the considered replies of twelve of its members to a series of questions posed by the Prime Minister. The committee of economists appointed at this same meeting produced a systematic survey of the country's ills and the possible remedies in time for October, and the Council devoted four of its remaining five meetings to its discussion. Every conceivable remedy was canvassed, from devaluation to the nationalisation of steel, from protection to the re-location of industry. But no agreement was to be found and, as the economic crisis grew more serious, the meetings of the Council became less frequent. It met three times in the early months of 1931 and thereafter faded away.

In the earlier meetings neither Bevin nor Citrine had much to say. Bevin's first important contribution was a well-argued paper on rationalisation (June 1930) in which he pointed out that a full-length report presented to the Council on the rationalisation of the steel industry contained no provision for the men who might be put out of work, nor any suggestion that either the steel industry or the Government should make such provision. Bevin proposed a statutory obligation on employers to report to the Ministry of Labour or the Board of Trade any schemes for the concentration of works together with proposals for dealing with the workpeople who might be displaced. He also made the suggestion, to which he was to recur later, of a State pension at sixty-five, on condition that the man receiving it gave up his job.

In the later meetings, Bevin took a bigger part in the general discussion, arguing (with the support of Keynes and Cole) that, since the iron and steel industry was either unable or unwilling to make itself efficient, it should be transferred to public ownership and a protective tariff granted while its reorganisation was carried out. At the last meeting in April 1931 he said plainly that he did not believe any solution to the problem of unemployment could be found so long as Britain adhered to the gold standard. Was it not possible, he asked, to find some alternative basis for the currency or to apply to it the principle of the sliding scale familiar in wage agreements? The country, he added, was paying too high a price for the maintenance of a single industry, the London international money market.

Long before the final meeting, Bevin had lost the hope he had originally entertained that the Economic Advisory Council might be able to influence the Government's policy. It was too large in its membership, too broad in its representation and too formal in its procedure to do more than reflect the divisions of opinion among those who claimed to know what was happening. A smaller, more coherent and informal group like Roosevelt's famous Brains Trust would have achieved more, but hardly with MacDonald, for MacDonald lacked Roosevelt's determination to find an answer whether the experts could agree or not.

I I

Apart from the Macmillan Committee and the Economic Advisory Council there was a third forum in which Bevin tried out his ideas and continued his search for an economic policy which would offer some prospect of breaking through the contracting circle of depression and deflation. This was the Economic Committee of the T.U.C., the creation of which marked a further step towards working out an economic policy for the trade-union movement.

In a memorandum dated 8th November 1928, Milne-Bailey, the ablest member of the T.U.C.'s small research staff, pointed out that although T.U.C. representatives frequently attended international conferences, "they cannot present an economic policy which has been deliberately adopted by the General Council, nor have they the machinery behind them such as is possessed by the Government and other representatives to enable them to enter into discussions on equal terms.''

The Industrial Committee which conducted the talks with the Mond group of employers offered an obvious nucleus. Milne-Bailey's suggestion was to strengthen this committee, re-name it the Economic Committee, and bring international as well as national economic problems within its scope. His proposal was adopted in 1929 and a committee of ten was established, including Bevin. Milne-Bailey acted as secretary. It is hardly surprising that the new committee rapidly became the most important of all the General Council's committees. The surprising thing is that the T.U.C. had managed for so long without such a committee, or, for that matter, without an economic policy of its own.

The Committee's first task was to prepare the memorandum which the T.U.C. submitted to the Macmillan Committee and then to consider what policy the T.U.C. should adopt towards the Imperial Conference due to meet in London in September 1930. Both subjects were discussed with the F.B.I. through arrangements for joint consultation agreed upon as the final product of the Mond-Turner talks.

The Economic Committee's proposals to the Macmillan Committee followed much the same lines of thought that Bevin developed in the latter's discussions. Their report in anticipation of the Imperial Conference, however, broke new ground and stirred up a cloud of controversy in the Press and at the Nottingham Congress in September.

In May 1930, Briand's Government in Paris published a memorandum setting out proposals for a European federal union which bear a marked resemblance to the French proposals Bevin encountered as Foreign Secretary after 1945. It might have been supposed, in view of his advocacy of a United States of Europe at the 1927 T.U.C., that Bevin would strongly support such a plan. So far as this country was concerned, however, he took part in drawing up a report which expressly repudiated closer economic links with Europe in favour of a Commonwealth bloc.

The report, again drafted by Milne-Bailey, started from the assumption that neither the traditional British policy of free trade, nor world economic unity in the form of international agreements, the traditional Labour objective, offered practical solutions to the country's problems. The alternative which the Committee examined was to join or create an economic group in which there would be a rough balance between supplies of raw materials and food stuffs on the one hand and manufactured goods on the other, a group of nations practising Free Trade between themselves but putting up tariffs, if necessary, against outsiders, a group as self-contained as possible but with sufficient bargaining power to exchange products with other nations on fair terms.

The question was, Which group? The report considered three possibilities, the same three possibilities that have been discussed again and again in the 1940s and the 1950s—a European bloc, the Commonwealth, and an Anglo-American bloc. It is odd to find in 1930 language so strongly reminiscent of the 1950s:

"The factors in favour of a European block are that the countries of Western Europe are closely allied geographically; that they share a common plight due to the War[1] and a common apprehension of America's economic power and that they would probably be powerful enough to ensure the peace of the world. Further, the experience of the League of Nations and other international bodies encourages the hope that, when once the bloc was formed, the creation of machinery for international adjudication and administration would inevitably follow, and that this would in time evolve into an organ of genuine international government."

But the arguments against carried greater weight with the Committee. Apart from differences of race and language, the European countries were or aspired to become manufacturers whose economic interests were in constant conflict, a tendency accentuated by the strong influence of nationalism on their economic policies.

There was, no doubt, a strong case for an Anglo-American bloc linking the United States and the British Commonwealth. The difficulty, apart from distance and economic rivalries, was that few Americans saw any attraction in such a proposal, believing that the U.S.A. could manage well enough without any allies.

This left the Commonwealth, a group already in existence with economic links in the form of preferences, as well as the ties of sentiment and language; with abundant supplies of raw materials to balance its manufacturing capacity and with plenty of opportunity for the movement of population within the group. Without advocat-

[1] The first, not the second, World War.

ing any policy designed to exclude agreement with other countries, the report concluded that at the Imperial Conference:

"it would be in the interests of our own people and of the Dominions to press for as full a development as possible of the economic relations between the constituent parts of the British Commonwealth."[1]

12

That these views were Bevin's own and not simply those of the Economic Committee is shown by the speech which he made to the Commonwealth Labour Conference in July 1930, closely following the lines of the report, and by the fact that he was chosen to present the report to the Trades Union Congress in September.

Political controversy, however, made it difficult to put forward these ideas without appearing to take up an out-and-out Protectionist stand. In July 1929, Lord Beaverbrook had flung himself into a crusade for Empire Free Trade and in 1930 set up the United Empire Party with the support of his fellow Press magnate, Lord Rothermere. This independent initiative convulsed the Conservative Party and made protection and imperial preference the most explosive issues in politics.

The Economic Committee presented its report to the General Council on 28th May 1930. Its reception was not made any easier by the fact that the General Council read in Beaverbrook's *Daily Express* on the morning of their meeting an accurate summary of a report which they had not yet seen, under the headlines:

Trade Union Bombshell

Premier on Horns of Dilemma

Mr. Snowden's Theories Demolished

Report that will Alter Contemporary Politics

Bevin saw his name (complete with photograph) listed under the heading "The T.U.C. Crusaders" and arrived at Transport House in a fury. A stormy and protracted meeting of the General Council

1 The report is printed in the General Council's report to the 1930 T.U.C. held at Nottingham, pp. 208–217.

followed, at the end of which the Economic Council was instructed to take the report back, amplify their arguments and re-submit it.

Before the next meeting of the General Council the members of the Economic Committee added an explanatory memorandum which angrily repudiated any influence by the Beaverbrook-Rothermere 'crusade' and argued that tariffs were only one method of drawing closer the economic ties between members of the Commonwealth, a method to be adopted or rejected on the merits of particular cases, not in principle. This did not satisfy the Free Traders on the General Council, but their amendments were defeated and the report was finally adopted on 25th June.

When Bevin came to put the report to the Nottingham T.U.C. he did not shirk the issue of protection:

"I have never accepted, as a Socialist," he told the Congress, "that an inflexible Free Trade attitude is synonymous with Socialism. I look upon the fiscal weapon as a means of defence when circumstances require, but I do not look upon it as the basis of a solution to any problem at all. I do not believe that tariffs can solve our problem of unemployment at the present moment. On the other hand, I cannot reconcile the real operation of Free Trade with the organisation of industry under public ownership."

Bevin made it clear that the Economic Committee did not recommend protection—they only refused to rule out tariffs in certain circumstances. In fact, Bevin claimed, they had begun from a quite different starting-point, access to raw materials, which Bevin consistently regarded as one of the major causes of war. The right course, he argued, was international agreement to secure easy and equal access to raw materials. Failing that, they had to see that the great resources of raw materials in the British Empire were properly developed.

The time Bevin had given to the Colonial Development Advisory Council had not been wasted. Here was another case like the I.L.O. and the Macmillan Committee in which new experience stirred his imagination and gave him an interest which he never allowed to lapse. Reading his speech of 1930, it is natural to cast forward to the Colombo Plan twenty years later, in the same way as his speech to the 1927 T.U.C. at Edinburgh conjures up the Marshall Plan.

The main object of the Committee's report, he insisted, was to put before the Labour Government in time for the Imperial Conference "a proposal for a definite economic organisation within what is called the British Empire". The conference was going to be held in any case. "Were we to take a purely laissez-faire attitude, saying nothing and criticising afterwards, or were we to approach the problem that would arise with some mind upon the matter? I am no imperialist, but an Empire exists."

The immediate proposal of the Committee was to set up "an investigating organisation":

"How many of us delegates have facts to guide us in relation to this problem at the present time? Are we not entitled through the Colonial Governments for which we are responsible to say that we will not leave the economic exploitation of raw materials to the tender mercies of company promoters? Are we not entitled to have a real economic survey, a mineralogical survey, a biological survey, a geological survey? Are we not entitled to stipulate that the development of these raw materials shall be in an ordered manner."

Letting his imagination range, Bevin invested his theme with a sweep which no other speaker approached:

"Then when we go to a World Economic Conference and we find that one country has oil, another nation cotton and another rubber, it is not a case of armies or navies settling the business: but we shall say to the others, here are these resources at our disposal, resources which will be open to you, there being no restriction of raw materials for your needs, but in return, there must be no restriction of supplies imposed upon us so that we too may have the raw materials that we need without the fighting and the financial struggle that has gone on hitherto.

"We urge upon the Government that in addition to the political organisation of the Empire, there should be an economic organisation. It is not a case of jumping to tariffs as being a solution to the problem. They are merely the kind of thing that lazy minds jump to. We have taken a different way. We have gone to the foundation. . . . Let us accept our responsibility and prevent the exploitation of illiterate races, utilising the great resources under our command not merely for our own benefit but for the advancement of humanity as a whole."[1]

13

In the debate that followed, the report was roughly handled. The Communists attacked it as a further development of the policy of

1 T.U.C. Report, 1930, pp. 257–261.

class collaboration which marked the Mond-Turner talks. The shrewdest criticism, however, came from another quarter. H. H. Elvin, a member of the General Council, rightly pointed out that the actual report of the Economic Committee went further than Bevin's disarming speech and that the Commonwealth bloc which it proposed would lead to retaliation and increased obstacles to world trade. The miners declared that any such policy would end British coal exports (only one-fiftieth of which went to any part of the Empire), while other speakers underlined the conflict of economic interests within the Commonwealth, Canadian and Australian tariffs against British manufactures and the incompatibility between any bloc and Labour's internationalism.

Bevin retorted that, whether Congress liked it or not, other countries—including Russia—were already taking steps to protect themselves by making exclusive agreements and building up tariffs.

"What is Free Trade? 2,000,000 unemployed is the Eldorado of Free Trade and what is called the open monetary system. You have a price level of X. That price level tends to rise, a boom follows, you get increased imports with rising purchasing power. When imports rise to a certain point gold begins to leave the country. When gold begins to leave the country, it makes the Bank Rate effective on the discount market in the City of London. When the Bank Rate is effective, you restrict credit. When you restrict credit, you increase unemployment. When you have increased unemployment, you reduce wages and start at a new price level . . .
"What is the complaint of the bankers, the Chamber of Commerce and everybody against you today? That the trade union movement is so inflexible. That natural resistance has been re-inforced by social services which make it doubly difficult for the Free Trade system to work. It is no longer resilient, it is jammed."

Bevin had certainly not become a Protectionist overnight. He was prepared to agree to a protective tariff, but only on condition of the thorough reorganisation of the industries to be protected, not as a substitute for reorganisation, behind which inefficient industries could find protection from the need to put their house in order.

Unlike the Protectionist, he regarded a tariff as an expedient, not a panacea, nor did he look upon the choice between Free Trade and tariffs as the fundamental issue to be decided. Bevin's view was more radical. He had no faith in the open self-regulating economic system which the majority of business men, bankers and politicians still looked upon as the model to which Britain must return. The nation, according to the orthodox view, lived by foreign trade and foreign lending: hence the importance of Free Trade and the gold standard, London as the centre of the international money market and a balanced budget to preserve confidence in sterling. Bevin neither admired this system, the burden of which, he suspected, had been largely borne by the working class, nor believed that it would any longer work. The question now was whether the country looked for a positive alternative and tried to find some means of controlling economic forces, or concluded that there was nothing to be done until things righted themselves.

Temperamentally, as well as intellectually, Bevin rebelled against the attitude of those who preached 'Do nothing' in the name of economic realism or out of respect for economic premises which, he believed, no longer applied. "Friends," he said at the end of his defence of the Economic Committee's report, "I believe in organising ourselves."

The direction of his ideas is clear enough from the preceding pages: the increase of consuming power ('reflation', Keynes called it) in place of the policy of deflation; the expansion of investment at home by schemes of capital development under a national investment board; State intervention to secure the reorganisation of the basic industries—coal, steel, transport and power—as public services; the employment of a variety of expedients to increase or maintain foreign trade, from bilateral agreements to bulk purchase, from export credits to tariffs, without worrying about the inviolability of Free Trade; the abandonment of the gold standard in favour of a managed currency; the development of Commonwealth trade and resources.

After the General Strike and his visit to the U.S.A., Bevin had approached economic problems in a practical, down-to-earth mood. Socialism was all very well as the long-term objective of the Labour movement, but it offered little guidance to trade-union leaders who had to deal with the facts as they were. Yet the more Bevin "dealt with the facts as they were" the more he found himself driven back to the conclusion that the economic premises to which business men, bankers and economists continually appealed were breaking down all the time. The result of his experience in these years of sitting down to consider economic problems with an open mind, was to leave him more convinced than ever that only a radical approach to the nation's problems offered any chance of improvement at all. It made little difference what the approach was called—Planning, the New Deal, Socialism. What convinced Bevin (like Roosevelt) was not arguments about the nature of human society, economic principles or the pattern of historical development, but hard, practical experience. What chance was there, however, of the Labour Government taking action along these lines?

CHAPTER 17

The Second Labour
Government
1929 — 1931

I

EVERY TIME there has been a Labour Government in power in Britain, the trade unions have had to face awkward and unexpected problems.

Naturally enough, with their own party in office, Bevin and the other members of the General Council expected that they would secure a readier hearing for reforms which they had long advocated, than from a Conservative Government. At the top of the list stood the repeal of the Trade Disputes Act of 1927, followed by ratification of the Washington Convention on hours of work and the reform of unemployment insurance. In the trade unions' view, the State should accept the principle of the "right to work"—work or maintenance—a principle for which Bevin had argued since the days of the Bristol Right to Work Committee. If the State was not prepared to take positive action to create more employment, then it must at least bear the cost of maintaining the unemployed, not out of insurance which amounted to a heavy tax on industry and the employed worker, but out of general taxation to which all classes of the community contributed.

After considerable preparatory work, the T.U.C. had also drawn up a new Factories Bill and a new Workman's Compensation Bill which it hoped to see passed into law. Bevin was chairman of the Committee which produced the first and an active member of the joint committee with the Labour Party which drafted the second, acting as spokesman when the Bill was presented to Clynes, the

Home Secretary, in June 1930. Through another joint committee set up on his initiative to examine the economic consequences of disarmament, Bevin pressed on Government departments a variety of proposals ranging from compensation for redundant workers in naval dockyards to Government subsidies for the shipbuilding industry, prohibition of the sale of old merchant tonnage to foreign shippers and better credit facilities for trade with Russia.

Despite discussions with Ministers and assurances of goodwill, however, the General Council could record little or no progress with any of these projects by the time of the 1930 Congress, more than a year after the Labour Government had been formed. As spokesman of the General Council, Bevin made it clear both at the T.U.C. and at the Labour Party conference in Llandudno that they would insist on the repeal of the Trade Disputes Act, but he went out of his way to explain the difficulties in which the Government found itself.

A minority Government could hardly be expected to carry out the sweeping Socialist measures which Maxton and the I.L.P. demanded, but unemployment was a different matter. At the 1929 election the Labour Party had given "an unqualified pledge to deal immediately and practically with this problem". That pledge it had patently failed to make good. In June 1929, when it took office, the number of unemployed registered at the Labour Exchanges was 1,163,000, just under ten per cent of the insured population; in October 1930, after fifteen months of a Labour Government, it stood at 2,319,000; by December at 2,500,000, just under 20 per cent.

The Government could hardly be blamed for this drastic rise, which reflected a world-wide depression of trade; but nothing cut so deep or put so heavy a strain on Labour and trade-union loyalty as the failure to grapple with unemployment. Not even the two great wars have left a more lasting impression on the working class of this country than the human waste, frustration and demoralisation represented by these figures.

Within the Government a revolt was led by Sir Oswald Mosley who had been given a special responsibility with Thomas and Lansbury to deal with unemployment. Mosley was hotly critical of Thomas and, early in 1930, put up a memorandum to the Cabinet which contained a series of positive proposals to increase employment.[1] In the Cabinet, Snowden strongly opposed Mosley's programme. It would cost more than the country could afford; it was inconsistent with the maintenance of the gold standard and it would mean the abandonment of Free Trade in favour of a controlled economy. Snowden's opposition was decisive and the Cabinet rejected the proposals. Thereupon Mosley resigned from the Government and made so forceful a defence of his position in the House that MacDonald moved Thomas to the Dominions Office and assumed general responsibility himself for the Government's employment policy.

This solved nothing and by the time the Labour Party conference met at Llandudno in October 1930, the Government had to face a restrained but deeply troubled mood of anxiety among the delegates. Maxton's open attack on the Government for its "timidity and vacillation in refusing to apply socialist remedies" was easily defeated, but a motion calling for a full report on Mosley's proposals received over a million votes and in the ballot for the Party Executive Thomas was defeated and Mosley elected.

Like Lansbury, who replied to the debate, Bevin found himself in an uncomfortable position. The proposals which Mosley advocated largely coincided with his own ideas; in private, he was highly critical of Snowden's negative attitude and MacDonald's vagueness. But he distrusted Mosley, had no patience with his campaign to build up a following in the Party and would not compromise with his belief in solidarity and the unity of the Party.

Bevin's one important speech at Llandudno suffered from this conflict, yet for this very reason—as Lansbury recognised in his reply—it reflected all the more accurately the mood of many in the movement. On the one hand, he dissociated himself from the censure which the I.L.P. spokesman had passed on the Government, condemned the discussion in public of divisions within the Parliamentary Party and took care to avoid polemics, mentioning neither Ministers nor their critics. On the other hand, for all his studied restraint, he could not conceal his dissatisfaction.

Bevin argued that there was nothing temporary or accidental about mass unemployment, particularly in the export trades like coal. It had been a permanent feature of the British economy since

1 These are summarised by G. D. H. Cole in his *History of the Labour Party from 1914*, p. 237.

the end of the post-war boom, but it had been masked by a number of factors, among them strikes which had heavily cut production. Only now had the full extent of the problem been revealed.

So far the State had dealt with unemployment by an extension of poor law relief in one form or another. But the dole was not a solution. In the same way as the State acted to wipe out illiteracy, so now, Bevin urged, it must act to wipe out unemployment. If private enterprise could not organise industry in such a way as to employ the working population, the State must step in and take the responsibility, mobilising the nation's resources as if the country were at war and not hesitating to take over the basic industries as public services.[1]

In a newspaper interview following his speech, Bevin seized on the paradox of a Labour Government appealing to business men to make the old free enterprise system work when the growth of trade-union organisation and social services prevented the reduction of wages upon which it depended. "And we who, by trade union conditions and social services, have helped to create this rigid, inelastic position, seem afraid to apply our only alternative—Socialism."

2

The Government's difficulties were real enough. On top of the chronic unemployment which had persisted throughout the 1920s it had to contend with a world depression of unprecedented severity which led in a number of countries to the suspension or eclipse of parliamentary government. No country was immune from its effects, but they were bound to be felt intensely by a nation so dependent on foreign trade as Britain.

In face of this situation the Government found itself in an intolerably weak Parliamentary position. It did not command a majority in either House of Parliament. To remain in office it had continually to manœuvre in such a way as never to unite Liberal and Tory votes against it. Even if it succeeded at the cost of compromise in passing a measure through the Commons, it had to face a hostile House of Lords ready to remove any feature remaining in a bill

1 Labour Party Conference Report, 1931, pp. 197–9.

which might be offensive to Conservative opinion. Most of the important legislation introduced by the second Labour Government was so mutilated as to be hardly recognisable. This was the fate of the Coal Mines Bill, the Education Bill and of other bills dealing with the trade unions, electoral reform, land utilisation and the ratification of the Washington 48-Hour Convention.

But this is not the whole of the story. When every allowance is made for its difficulties, the fact is that the second Labour Government never put forward any programme of action adequate to the scale of the emergency. It was not prevented from doing this by the lack of a Parliamentary majority. Mosley's memorandum was rejected by the Labour Cabinet, not by the Opposition, and at no time in the year that followed did MacDonald make any show of introducing a comprehensive plan which might have gone beyond the limits set by Snowden's bleak insistence on Free Trade, the gold standard and a balanced budget.

This is not a question of the financial crisis in the summer of 1931 —that is altogether too short a perspective—but of the whole of the preceding eighteen months during which Bevin among others urged upon MacDonald the danger of failing to give a clear lead on the country's economic problems. Nor is it a question of Socialism, for the proposals made by Keynes and Bevin's favourite remedy, devaluation, stopped far short of anything that could be called Socialism.

If the Government had produced a bolder programme, it might well have failed to carry it through the House. This need not, however, have been a fatal objection. Few people expected the Government to last long, and it is arguable that it would have been better to follow the course suggested by Bevin of going to the country for a mandate (as the National Government did not hesitate to do) and saying that no minority Government could carry through measures adequate to deal with the situation. Even if they had been defeated—and the chances are that they would have been—the Party would have gained in the long run by showing that it had the will to act. Better to run the risk of defeat in defence of a policy which was in line with the Party's principles than to hang on to office until events overtook them and brought division and disillusionment in their wake.

In the summer of 1931, in the middle of a financial crisis, it could be argued that this was to put party before nation and to shirk responsibility. But this is not an argument that could be used in the autumn of 1930 or in the spring of 1931. On the contrary, what advantage was there to the nation or to Parliamentary institutions, any more than to the Labour Party, in a Government which remained in office without the power to act?

Whatever the force of these arguments, they clearly had no weight with the Cabinet. By the beginning of 1931, Bevin had little doubt that the Labour Government would never carry out the sort of economic programme which he believed the situation demanded. His loyalty to the Party still held, but in private he was gloomy and exasperated. Unable to exercise any influence on events, all he could do was to urge his own union to prepare for trouble.

As early as August 1930 (twelve months before the crisis of 1931), he told his Executive Council:

"So serious do I regard the present position that I consider it warrants a state of national emergency. The best brains of the country should be mobilised for the purpose of really tackling the problem instead of 'footling about' in the manner we are at the moment. . . .

"The bankers and the industrialists are already manœuvring for an attack on money wages. . . . This Union must be organised. Every available penny must be put to reserve in order that we may be ready when the crisis comes."[1]

3

Bevin concluded his report to his Executive with the words: "One thing stands out quite clear and that is that the workpeople must more than ever rely upon the trade union weapon." However much he might concern himself with national, party or T.U.C. affairs, he never forgot that his base was still the Union, the General Secretary's office from which he watched over the fortunes of the organisation he had created.

Unemployment and short time hit the Union hard. 1930, 1931, and 1932 each marked a fall in the total number of members which was not restored until 1934. The Union's income fell proportionately and it says much for Stanley Hirst's and Bevin's careful administration

1 General Secretary's Quarterly Report, August 1930.

that there were no deficits in these years and that the reserve fund was slowly built up again.

It took several months to complete the absorption of the Workers' Union, with its 100,000 members. Bevin took the opportunity to reorganise the central office at the same time. J. J. Taylor, a young man in whom Bevin put great reliance and who eventually became secretary of the Workers' Travel Association, was appointed secretary of the Political Department which now had to support a Parliamentary group of twenty-four, three of them Ministers. A new Information and Statistical Department[1] was set up at the same time.

At the end of 1929, Bevin reluctantly gave up the national secretaryship of the National Docks Group which he had held since the amalgamation, and at the end of 1930, another national secretary had to be found for the Road (Commercial) Transport Group in place of Archie Henderson, another ex-tramwayman among the Union's leading officers[2] who left to become chairman of one of the Boards of Traffic Commissioners established by the Road Transport Act.[3]

1930 also brought a considerable number of retirements amongst the Union's older officials, including Ben Tillett and Harry Gosling. At the age of seventy, Tillett hated the idea of retirement and fought strenuously against it. Several times he addressed the Executive Council on his own behalf and was allowed an extension of a year. When this expired, he appealed to the Biennial Delegates' Conference. The years had not lessened the antagonism between Bevin and Tillett, but Bevin advised the Executive to allow Tillett to address the Delegate Conference and leave the matter open to vote.

Tillett put his case in a rambling and sentimental speech, claiming a pioneer's right to die in harness. The reply was made by H. J. Edwards, a member of the Executive, not by Bevin. Edwards pointed out that Tillett had been given an extra year, would receive

1 This was placed in the charge of Miss Forcey. Her place as Bevin's secretary was taken by Miss Ivy Saunders, without whose invaluable help this biography could never have been written.

2 Others were John Cliff, the Assistant General Secretary; Harold Clay, and Stanley Hirst, the financial secretary.

3 Out of the twenty-six candidates (including Arthur Deakin) the Executive finally chose Jack Corrin from Birmingham to take Henderson's place. This was the post from which Frank Cousins rose to be general secretary of the T.G.W.U.

a pension which he admitted to be adequate and would continue to be one of the Union's M.P.s. The delegates' speeches were against the old man: others, like Jimmy Sexton, had retired without fuss and he must do the same. The vote was conclusive: 225 to 21 in favour of accepting the Executive's report. But Tillett never forgave Bevin and spent the remaining years of his life embellishing and adding to the history of Bevin's ingratitude.

When the time came for Harry Gosling to retire from the presidency he was seriously ill and Bevin, with greater tact than he had shown in 1924, did not press the matter, telling Mrs. Gosling that the president's salary would in any case be paid until the end of the year. Before then Gosling was dead. With the fierce pride which he always felt over the status of the working class, Bevin insisted that the president's body should lie in state at Transport House and so great was the affection in which Harry Gosling was held that hundreds of people came to pay their last respects to the Lambeth boy who had been apprenticed as a Thames waterman, amongst them Lloyd George, Lord Devonport, the dockers' veteran opponent in the Port of London, and a crowd of London dockers led by one of the brothers wearing his full Union regalia.

Harry Gosling was the first and only president of the Transport and General Workers' Union. With a more ambitious man, there might be a clash of authority which Bevin was determined to avoid. There was room for only one chief official in the Union, the General Secretary, and the place of a full-time president was henceforward taken by an elected lay chairman of the Executive Council. The first holder of the new office was Herbert Kershaw, a tramwayman from Bradford.

4

Gosling's death left another vacancy, the seat in the House of Commons which he had held for Whitechapel. The Party was anxious to find a place in the House for Stafford Cripps, who had just been appointed to succeed Sir James Melville as Solicitor-General. The politics of Whitechapel, however, which would normally have appeared a safe constituency for a Labour candidate, were transformed by the publication of the Government's White

Paper on Palestine. The Zionists were up in arms at reservations which Lord Passfield,[1] the Colonial Secretary and author of the White Paper, expressed on Jewish immigration into Palestine. Only a few days before, the Labour Party Executive at Llandudno had accepted the resolution of the affiliated Jewish Socialist Labour Party re-affirming Labour support for the establishment of a Jewish National Home in Palestine. The Colonial Secretary found himself in the centre of a sharp political storm in which the Labour Government was angrily accused by the Zionists of betraying the Jewish people. With 7,000 Jewish votes in Whitechapel, the prospects of Labour carrying the by-election were greatly reduced and the Labour Party hurriedly withdrew the suggestion that Cripps, a member of the offending Government, should stand for election.

In view of the accusation subsequently made against Ernest Bevin that he had always been an anti-Semite, the later history of this incident is of considerable interest. The Whitechapel constituency, which included Wapping, had a close connection with the London docks and the T.G.W.U. was bound to be deeply involved. Anxious to reassure the Zionists and placate the local Jewish vote, the Labour Party invited Bevin to stand. Henderson pressed him hard. Bevin's reply was unhesitating: it was impossible for him to carry out both his industrial and Parliamentary duties.

But that did not end the affair. The Union accepted the responsibility of finding a candidate for Whitechapel and put up H. J. Hall, a member of the Executive and a native of Wapping who had spent thirty years in organising the clerical and supervisory staffs in the London docks. Bevin in the meantime set to work to win back the Jewish vote. He kept in touch with Dov Hos, of Poale-Zion (the Jewish Socialist Labour Party) and met representatives of the Jewish organisations in Whitechapel. Once he discovered more precisely what was worrying them, he sent a memorandum to the Party saying bluntly that he shared their uneasiness about the White Paper and that, unless the Government were prepared to give reassurances, he would not be a party to a Union candidate standing for election.

Bevin's intervention, combined with equally emphatic protests from other friends of the Zionist cause, proved effective. With the agreement of the Jewish trade-union representatives Bevin put three

1 Better known as Sidney Webb.

specific questions to the Government to which he secured categorical answers. On 4th November, he issued a statement passing on the explicit assurance of the Government that they had no intention of altering the terms of the Mandate; no intention of stopping Jewish immigration and no intention of setting limits to the expansion of the Jewish National Home within the terms of the Mandate.

Jewish suspicions of Lord Passfield remained active, but towards Bevin their feelings were cordial and, despite the efforts of his three opponents to make trouble on the Jewish issue, Hall was returned to Parliament, although with a majority reduced from nine to one thousand.[1]

It was at this time that MacDonald asked Bevin, if he was not free to stand for the House of Commons, whether he would accept a peerage and strengthen Labour's representation in the Lords.[2] Bevin did not take long to reply. The day after his conversation with the Prime Minister, he wrote a long and friendly letter declining the offer.[3] Much has been made of Bevin's vanity, but it did not extend to the commonest of all vanities in public life, a place in the honours list. Neither then nor later was he interested in any honours: he died as he was born, plain Ernest Bevin.

But if Bevin was not interested in honours for himself, he did his best to secure them for men he believed had performed services worth honouring. Amongst them were J. S. Elias, the managing director of Odham's, and A. E. Humphries, the President of the Flour Milling Employers' Federation.

Despite the success Elias had made of the *Herald*, MacDonald would not listen to Bevin's suggestion that he should be raised to the House of Lords. Years before, when Elias and Odhams were the printers of Horatio Bottomley's notorious *John Bull*, Bottomley had cruelly publicised the facts about MacDonald's illegitimate birth. MacDonald never forgave this and he declined either to consider Elias's name or to listen to Bevin's appeal that he should meet Elias and let him explain his own innocence of any responsibility for Bottomley's action. It was not until Baldwin succeeded MacDonald as Prime Minister that Elias was raised to the peerage as Viscount Southwood.

1 This account is based on correspondence preserved among Bevin's papers.
2 MacDonald made a similar proposal to Citrine at the same time.
3 Ernest Bevin to J. R. MacDonald, 26th November 1930.

Bevin had better success with his efforts on behalf of Humphries, who received a knighthood in the New Year's Honours List for 1931. The co-operation between Humphries, Bevin and Captain Green, the secretary of the Flour Milling Joint Industrial Council, stood up to the strain of the depression years. Over-production in the milling industry had reached the point at which the employers were forced to combine in order to buy up and close down redundant mills. True to the views he had expressed at the Mond-Turner talks—in which Humphries had also taken part—Bevin did not oppose rationalisation but argued that the men displaced ought to receive compensation from the industry and help in starting a new job. This view was accepted by the employers and a committee consisting of Bevin, Humphries and Green met the principal firms and worked out a scheme. Only a small number of men were involved, but £19,000 was spent between 1929 and 1931 on resettlement. In some cases a man was helped to stock a shop, to purchase carpenter's tools or a horse and cart; in other cases the money was spent on an annuity, a subsistence allowance while a man looked for work, on completing house purchases, or removal expenses. In the meantime, the Council pressed on with technical education for the younger men and, after three years' preparatory work, both sides accepted a contributory pensions scheme for the industry which came into operation on 1st September 1931.

During this period of extensive modernisation and corcentration, there was not a single dispute or stoppage of work, a fact which supported Bevin's view that there was no inherent reason why the problems created by rationalisation could not be settled by co-operation between the two sides. The flour-milling industry continued to provide on a small scale the model of a new pattern of industrial relations for which Bevin had argued at the Mond-Turner discussions.

5

The prospects of bringing some order into the confusion of road transport were materially improved by the return of a Labour Government. In London, Bevin and John Cliff were strongly in favour of unifying the capital's passenger services under a single authority. Before the 1929 election, a private member's Bill had been introduced to achieve this by extending the control of the London Traffic Combine. When the Labour Government was formed, Herbert Morrison set to work on a Government Bill to accomplish the same result under a public authority. The London Passenger Transport Bill was, in fact, the one attempt at nationalisation made by MacDonald's second Administration. In principle, the T.G.W.U., which represented almost the whole of the bus and tram workers in London, strongly supported Morrison's scheme. But on one point there was a conflict of views between the Minister and the Union. Morrison was opposed to the direct representation of labour or any other interest on the proposed London Passenger Transport Board. He wanted to see it constituted as a board of experts, appointed solely on the grounds of individual ability and experience. Bevin and Cliff were equally insistent that the Board should include representatives of labour chosen by the unions concerned, or at least statutory provision for consultation of the unions before the appointments were made.

Rebuffed by Morrison, Bevin appealed direct to the Prime Minister in June 1931. He secured a minor concession in an increase of labour representation on the Advisory Committee and some alteration in the qualifications for membership of the Board itself. But Morrison won on the major issue. The Bill, however, was not passed into law by the time the Labour Government fell, and the controversy between Morrison and the Union, extended to the large and vexed question of workers' control in nationalised industries, was carried on to the floor of the T.U.C. and the Labour Party conferences.

Morrison was also the Minister responsible for one of the most substantial achievements of the second Labour Government, the Road Traffic Act of 1930, based on the reports of the Royal Commission on Transport and incorporating many of the proposals placed before the Commission by the T.G.W.U.

The Act did not go as far as Bevin wished, but it laid the foundations of a national system of road transport by sweeping away the chaos of 1,300 separate licensing authorities and replacing them by twelve traffic commissions. Each commission, under a full-time chairman, was made responsible for the road passenger services in its area, with power to enforce the co-ordination for which the Union had called.

All public vehicles were to be inspected and licensed. Insurance was made compulsory and Section 19 of the Act imposed limits on the hours to be worked by lorry drivers. Another section (93) provided for fair wages to be paid by the passenger undertakings, with a right of appeal to the Industrial Court of which the Union made good use.

The Union had to wait for the licensing of goods vehicles until 1933 and there were stubborn problems which no legislation could solve, in particular, enforcing the limitation of drivers' hours on the men as much as on the employers. But the 1930 Act provided a framework for the rapidly growing road transport industry, a framework within which the Union could attack the task of organising the men with greater chances of success.

The Union had an obvious interest in the passage of the Act, which made direct improvements in the conditions under which many of its members worked. This was, rightly, the first concern of Bevin and the other officers. But the measures for which they pressed were at the same time of benefit to the community as a whole. This is a point worth underlining for those who look upon trade unions solely as obstructive or restrictive agencies, forgetting the contribution which they have made to the general welfare by their successful pressure for reforms in the past.

With 97,000 members in the road passenger transport service, Bevin and his Executive claimed the right to enrol all the bus workers in the country. The N.U.R. was equally emphatic that it had an incontestable right to organise the men employed by any bus company in which the railways acquired a controlling interest. This was an old quarrel which had occupied both Executives for several years. Recommendations for the recognition of each other's interests, drawn up by a joint committee, were rejected by the N.U.R. Executive in January 1930 and, after a series of spirited exchanges, Bevin began an open campaign to win over N.U.R. members employed in the road transport industry. Not until 1931 was a truce declared and a settlement reached.

With other unions Bevin was more successful in reaching working agreements on demarcation. He came increasingly to regard such agreements as a more practical way of improving trade-union unity than the cumbersome method of amalgamation. Following the important report on Organisation by Industry adopted by the 1927

T.U.C. at Edinburgh,[1] Bevin acted as chairman of the Organisation Committee of the General Council which was given the task of encouraging amalgamation and working arrangements between unions. After two years' effort the Committee could report little success with the former: the only amalgamation of any size was that between Bevin's own union and the Workers' Union. Working arrangements, on the other hand, were easier, if only because they did not raise the issue of autonomy, the trade-union equivalent of that national sovereignty with which Bevin was to be much concerned in foreign policy after 1945. In August 1931, for instance, the executive committees of the T.G.W.U. and the Amalgamated Engineering Union agreed on the organising of the engineering industries. The year before, Bevin reached agreement with the National Union of Distributive and Allied Workers on the organisation of the catering trades. A third example is the good relations established with the National Union of Agricultural Workers, after the amalgamation with the Workers' Union had given the T.G.W.U. an interest in this field. The number of trade unionists among agricultural workers was so low and the problem of organisation so great in a countryside where nineteenth-century attitudes to trade unionism were still widespread, that there was plenty of room for both organisations and every incentive for co-operation.

6

While the T.G.W.U. continued to add to the trades in which it was acquiring a foothold, Bevin took up his old fight for decasualisation of the dock industry.

Shortly after the second Labour Government came into office, he began to press for a new inquiry into the progress of registration. At the end of May 1930, the Minister of Labour, Margaret Bondfield, announced that such an inquiry would be undertaken by the Maclean Committee which was now revived with the addition of further members from both sides of the National Joint Council for Dock Labour. Bevin, Tillett and four other officers of the T.G.W.U. represented the workman's side; the chairman was again Sir Donald Maclean and his deputies two of the men who had crossed swords

1 See above, pp. 382–3.

in the Shaw Inquiry, Sir Alfred Booth, the Liverpool shipowner and chairman of the Cunard Line, and Ernest Bevin.

There was no need to waste time in preliminaries. Every man round the table knew the problem thoroughly. This was, after all, the fourth inquiry into the decasualisation of dock labour since the war and the Committee got down to business at once. Its terms of reference were wide, but in practice it concerned itself with two sets of questions:

(1) What progress had been made with schemes for the registration of dock workers, and what obstacles prevented the further development of such schemes?

(2) What anomalies were produced by the application of the unemployment insurance scheme to port work, and how could these be removed?

All the old intractable problems at once reappeared: the surprising variety in the circumstances and character of dock work between different ports; the unpredictable and irregular demands for labour; the seasonal character of many trades.

Dock work had still a highly personal element in it. A docker stayed with a particular firm or preferred to work for a particular foreman, often valued highly the freedom to work or not to work as he felt inclined and lived in a closed world in which son frequently succeeded father on both sides of the industry, the history of past disputes was handed down and an intricate set of customs governed every operation. Bevin's drive for decasualisation brought him into conflict with this closed world, of which casual labour was the inherited way of life. The argument that they would be better off under a different system did not convince, and to some extent has still not convinced many dockers who clung to the old ways.

Since the Maclean Committee's report of 1924 there had been steady progress with registration schemes which had been adopted in thirty ports[1] and covered 86,000 workers, roughly two-thirds of the total. With unemployment rising, the registration system protected the regular port workers against a flood of casual labour pouring into the docks as had happened so often in the past. Both sides of the industry were now agreed on its value in raising the status of dock

---

1 All the major ports were included except Glasgow, the north-east coast ports on the Tyne and Wear and the Hartlepools.

work, providing a more reliable labour force and improving industrial relations. As a result of the Maclean Committee's report, a Standing Advisory Committee was set up by the National Joint Council for Dock Labour, and in the course of the 1930s this did a useful job in strengthening and extending the system of registration.

At this point, however, agreement between the two sides broke down. The National Council of Port Employers argued that the industry must proceed along the lines already tried, that efforts should be made to get the other ports to adopt registration and to improve the administration of the schemes. The adoption of registration, however, they insisted, must depend upon voluntary agreement between the parties, it should not be enforced by law, as Bevin wanted it to be. The gap between the two points of view came out most clearly over the question of unemployment insurance on which the committee of inquiry was unable to present any agreed recommendations and could only publish the conflicting sets of proposals laid before it.

7

For years the Union had protested—and the employers agreed—that a system of unemployment insurance based on a black and white distinction between lack of work and regular employment in a weekly paid occupation could not be made to fit dock work. The common experience of the docker, even in good times, was to work hard for two or three days, then to be without work for two or three more while waiting for the next boat to come in. The unit of his employment was not the week, but the day or half day, and most men were paid daily. To describe the two or three days in a week without work as unemployment in the same sense as it would be for a factory worker was to ignore the special character of the intermittent system of employment which had always been followed in the docks. Successive Ministers of Labour, however, refused to provide a special scheme.

The docker was not at all loth to take advantage of the situation. He had to pay his unemployment insurance out of the wages he earned in 2–3 days, not a week; in return, many of them thought it fair enough to work three days and then draw unemployment benefit for three days. As a result, the State found itself obliged to pay out far more in benefits than it received in contributions, and there were periodic complaints in the Press about 'subsidised idleness' and rackets at the taxpayers' expense. Bevin did not deny the existence of such practices, but they were within the law and so long as the Ministry refused to listen to advice and change the law in favour of a special scheme for casual labour, the onus rested on the Government, not on the dockers or the Union.

The Committee of Inquiry spent much time in examining the anomalies created by the existing system of unemployment insurance, but the employers and the Union took radically different views of the best way to remove them. The employers argued that the scheme should be put back on to a sound actuarial footing, that benefits should match contributions and any resulting distress be dealt with by public assistance, the new euphemism for the old Poor Law.

Bevin and the Union, on the other hand, argued that the right remedy was to attack the problems created by casual employment at the root and decasualise dock labour. After a series of discussions in its National Dock Group, the Union put up to the Committee a comprehensive scheme the key to which was Bevin's old proposal of maintenance, a guaranteed minimum wage for every registered port worker in place of the practice of casual engagement by the day, supplemented by drawing unemployment benefit.

The registration of dockworkers would be made universal and compulsory and employers would be free to engage only those registered by the local joint committee, instead of trying to keep a private pool of unemployed men in reserve for their own needs.

Every registered docker would be required to report for work at the calling-on stands once or twice a day. If none was available he would still receive a guaranteed minimum wage of 50/- a week. This was not intended to be a dole, but a maintenance payment to the man as a member of the port's registered labour force.

Bevin proposed that the necessary sum of money should be provided by transferring the contributions of State, employers and workers for unemployment insurance to a fund to be administered by the National Joint Committee for Dock Labour. The deficiency would be met by a levy on all goods and passenger traffic passing through the ports. The fund would also provide a pension of 25s. a

Transport House and its creator.

Bevin addressing the T.U.C. in 1930.

week for all dockers who had completed fifteen years of consecutive service, on condition that they retired from the industry. This offered a method of removing from the registers the growing proportion of elderly men incapable of hard physical work whom the joint committees were reluctant to strike off but who formed a serious obstacle to the recruitment of more active men.

It was a bold and imaginative scheme, the cost of which Bevin calculated would be £5 million a year in the early years (when the cost of pensions would be high), less the two and a half million pounds which the State was already paying in unemployment benefit. After the first five years, the cost would fall. In any case, Bevin argued, the extra £2,500,000 to be raised by levy was not too high a price for a country which lived by maritime commerce to pay in order to provide an efficient labour force in its ports.

The port employers refused to look at the scheme on grounds of cost alone. But their opposition went deeper than this. If the scheme were adopted it would increase the power of the Union, through compulsory registration, and reduce the freedom of the employer to make his own arrangements. As so often in his trade-union career, Bevin was up against the insistence of the employer on the rights of management which again and again proved to be a far more serious stumbling-block to the improvement of industrial relations than profits. Few, if any, of the employers saw the problems of the dock industry from a wider angle than that of their own port or firm. Bevin, whose Union was involved in almost every port in the country, saw them from a national point of view and had already made an impressive case to the Royal Commission on Transport in support of the view that the nation needed a plan for the development of its dock facilities in place of the wasteful and at times nonsensical competition between different ports.

8

A major weakness of the Union's scheme was the difficulty of getting it adopted by an industry which showed a strong resistance to change especially when it involved more organisation and less freedom. An illustration of this is the attitude of the Glasgow dockers. So strong was their feeling against registration that they turned down proposals put forward by the employers for setting up a scheme even when these had been accepted by the Union. The Glasgow docks branch of the T.G.W.U. set up an Anti-Registration League, warning Bevin that they would break away if any attempt were made to force them into a scheme and passing a vehement resolution which they sent to the Maclean Committee of Inquiry.

After a scornful reference to "amateur social reformers", the Glasgow resolution declared that, where registration had been put into effect, it had increased rather than diminished general under-employment:

"It is our opinion that, from the employers' point of view, registration has long since resolved itself into a mere instrument of discipline and coercion, and that from the point of view of our trade union officials, who are its insidious promoters, registration provides a solution to their vexed problem of stabilising the Union amongst the Glasgow dockers and thereby providing themselves with the maximum security in the undisturbed enjoyment of their salaries and superannuations.
"The proposed maintenance scheme we regard as only a palpable bait to involve us in the toils of the slavery of registration."[1]

Two representatives of the Glasgow branch gave evidence before the Committee and the chairman had to assert all his authority to prevent a stand-up row between them and the Union officers sitting on the committee.

Behind this attitude on the part of Glasgow lay a long and contentious history, as is the case with every dispute in the dock industry. The Glasgow dockers had formed the most important branch of the Scottish Union of Dock Labourers. The general secretary of the Scottish Union, Houghton, was keen to bring his organisation into the original amalgamation, but failed to secure the necessary percentage in the first ballot, largely because of the refusal of the Glasgow dockers to vote. Subsequently, Houghton and Bevin brought the union in, but there were protests from Glasgow where the leading group in the branch never really accepted the change.

The Glasgow opposition was based upon the men's strong desire to run their own affairs locally and not to accept decisions which, inevitably, were taken out of their hands once they became part of a

1 Ministry of Labour. Minutes of Evidence taken before the Port Labour Committee, 14th October 1930, (not published).

larger, national organisation. A major point at issue was the position of the eight paid officials who worked full time on Union business in the Glasgow docks. The Glasgow branch claimed the right to elect these annually, but was overruled by the General Executive.

Thereupon, a number of Glasgow members, including a member of the Executive, McLean, the chairman of the Glasgow branch, went to law and got a judgment in their favour which was upheld on appeal. The quarrel with the Union undoubtedly coloured the Glasgow view of registration, but the branch committee, had established its own control over the supply of labour and the distribution of work in the Glasgow docks. They did not want to see these arrangements disturbed or their preferential position undermined in favour of a scheme which would have meant sharing control with a joint committee representative of the employers as well as themselves.

In the early 1930s the quarrel developed into a trial of strength between the Glasgow branch and the Union. The Glasgow committee carried their threat into effect and set up the Scottish Transport and General Workers' Union. Nothing Bevin could do shook their hold on the Glasgow docks and, after ten years' resistance by the T.G.W.U., they were finally admitted to the National Joint Council for Dock Labour in 1944, on which they continue to sit as the sole representatives of the Glasgow dockers.

It is easy to represent this episode as a defence of democratic self-government against the tyranny of a trade-union bureaucracy out of touch with the rank-and-file members of the organisation. But Bevin, the General Executive and the National Docks Group Committee saw the issue differently. Bevin never forgot the lesson he had learned in the old Transport Workers' Federation, that particularism was the curse of trade unionism and national action the only effective means of improving the dockers' position. The employers argued, just as the mineowners did, that local variations made a national agreement impracticable. Bevin fought this view at the time of the Shaw Inquiry and experience strengthened his conviction that the only way to get rid of the evils of casual labour was by a comprehensive scheme applied nationally. He knew perfectly well that he had to fight ignorance, prejudice and conservatism on his own side. The action of the Glasgow branch played into the employers' hands; if other ports claimed the same freedom to make local arrangements as they wished, the chance of a national scheme would be lost.

For the moment, he could get no further than the endorsement of registration and the establishment of the Standing Advisory Committee to push it on. This was a gain and he did not despair. It had taken time to convert opinion to registration; it would take longer still to convert it to accept maintenance. The one thing to do was to go on arguing the case and educating his own members. It took him fifteen more years to get the scheme he wanted, but he never lost sight of his objective or relaxed his efforts.

9

The Maclean Committee did not complete its inquiry until well into 1931. In the meantime, during the early months of the year, the Government lost further ground in face of its difficulties. Its Education Bill was thrown out by the Lords and the Minister of Education, Sir Charles Trevelyan, resigned making it clear that his disagreement with the Cabinet extended to economic policy as well as education. Mosley, after publishing a more elaborate version of his memorandum with the support of John Strachey, Aneurin Bevan and other Labour M.P.s, broke away to form a New Party. If he failed to win many supporters from the Labour Party, his defection did not add to the prestige of the Government. When the Government at long last introduced its Trade Union Bill to restore the position prior to the passing of the 1927 Act, the Liberals joined the Conservatives in opposition and the Bill was so mutilated in committee that, at the beginning of March, the Attorney General announced that it would be withdrawn.

In the meantime, unemployment rose to the figure of 2,600,000 for the first three months of 1931 and rose again in the summer, reaching 2,750,000 in July.

Bevin was a member of the small T.U.C. committee which followed closely the fortunes of the Trade Union Bill in the House. He saw the Government's Parliamentary weakness at first hand. But what depressed him most was his conviction that MacDonald had lost his grip of the situation and that Snowden was bent upon pursuing an economic policy the opposite of that which Bevin believed any Chancellor (and most of all a Labour Chancellor) should follow.

On 11th February, the Conservatives moved a vote of censure on the Government's wasteful expenditure, especially in borrowing to meet the needs of the unemployment insurance fund. A Liberal amendment called for a special committee to review expenditure and recommend economies. Snowden accepted this proposal and the composition of the committee which he appointed left no doubt that it would come down heavily in favour of retrenchment. Besides the chairman, Sir George May, a former secretary of the Prudential Assurance Company, the committee consisted of four representatives of business and industry and only two of Labour, neither of whom carried much weight.

Snowden in fact accepted the view of the Government's critics that the country was living beyond its means and that drastic economies must be enforced. He looked to the May Committee to provide him with a report with which he could overcome the resistance of his own party.

As a trade-union leader, Bevin was bound to oppose such a policy which meant lower wages and reduced social services. But this does less than justice to the grounds of his opposition. The attitude of the T.U.C. in 1931 has too often been treated as if the General Council acted only in defence of a sectional interest in resisting cuts in wages and unemployment benefit which they knew perfectly well to be necessary in the interests of the country.

On the contrary, Bevin for one had long been convinced that the policy of deflation which Snowden, the Treasury and the Bank regarded as axiomatic was based upon premises which no longer held good. His experience on the Macmillan Committee and the Economic Advisory Council confirmed him in this belief and it must be said that the subsequent course of events and the change in economic thinking since 1930 give far more support to Bevin's than to Snowden's views.

The full extent of the contradiction between the two views was not revealed until the financial crisis of August. The leaders of the Parliamentary Labour Party were later to be much embarrassed by the fact that up to August 1931 they remained members of a Cabinet which accepted Snowden's policy as its own. Bevin's, however, was no last-minute conversion. Although loyalty to the Labour Government restrained him from public criticism, the stand he took up in the August crisis was fully in keeping with the views he had expressed in the Macmillan Committee and elsewhere. Neither MacDonald nor Snowden had any doubts about his views long before August 1931.

Bevin and the General Council were equally consistent in their opposition to the cuts in provision for the unemployed which played a crucial part in the break-up of the Labour Government in August. The scale of mass unemployment had long since outstripped the capacity of the Unemployment Insurance Fund to meet the demands made on it. The Government had to borrow to keep the Fund solvent and had to find further large sums out of general revenue to pay transitional benefit, i.e. maintenance grants after the twenty-six weeks' insured benefit was exhausted. Apart from the anomalies in its administration, the system was cumbrous and cried out for reform. On this point everyone was agreed and the T.U.C. steadily advocated a clean sweep, anomalies and all, in favour of a new approach.

The trade-union view, which Bevin strongly maintained, was that prolonged mass unemployment represented something altogether different from the occasional unemployment for which the insurance scheme had been designed. Unemployment had grown into a major social evil which could no longer be dealt with on the basis of insurance. Increasing contributions would not meet the case. This would only place a still heavier burden on industry and the employed worker without providing an adequate fund. The State must assume direct responsibility and no longer seek to discharge this by a partial contribution to an insurance scheme. The right course, Bevin and the T.U.C. argued, was for the State to take positive action to organise employment by public works and, if necessary, by acquiring and running as public services industries in which private enterprise run for profit could no longer provide adequate employment. This would be a far better use of public funds than pouring out money in a dole to maintain men in unproductive idleness. Whatever provision had still to be made for unemployment, the pretence of a self-supporting insurance fund which had continually to be subsidised should be abandoned in favour of a straightforward maintenance grant by the State, and this should be paid for out of taxation levied on the whole community not simply on the employer and the employed worker.[1]

The T.U.C., therefore, was far from defending the existing system, but they preferred even the existing system to the alternative proposed by most Conservatives and Liberals who insisted that unemployment should be provided for by an insurance scheme placed on a self-supporting footing and that additional aid from the State should be stringently restricted.

In December 1930 the Labour Government appointed a Royal Commission to examine the problem. To the T.U.C.'s indignation, the Commission's terms of reference perpetuated the unsatisfactory division of responsibility under the existing scheme and ruled out in advance any new approach to the problem. It was only under protest that the General Council agreed to give evidence at all and the Commission's interim report (published at the beginning of June 1931) confirmed their fears. Accepting the existing system and the need to make the insurance fund self-supporting, the Commission inevitably recommended higher contributions from the employed worker, reduced benefits to the unemployed and the stricter application of conditions.

In view of feeling in the Party, the Government did not attempt to put the recommendations into force beyond passing a Bill to remove anomalies. None the less the Commission's report was put to good use by those (including Labour's Chancellor of the Exchequer) who demanded radical economies in expenditure on the social services.

10

Bevin had repeatedly warned his Executive that a logical consequence of a Government policy of deflation must be a reduction in wages. In March 1931, the Economic Committee of the T.U.C. put out a statement, reiterating its view that wage cuts would increase rather than alleviate the country's economic difficulties:

"The application of such a policy can only intensify the slump by reducing the purchasing power of the community, thereby leading to further un-

[1] See the T.U.C. evidence to the Royal Commission, T.U.C. Report, 1931, pp. 157 seq.

employment. Nor is there any evidence that this is followed by an expansion of markets overseas leading to the absorption of the unemployed. Is there any likelihood that a fall in British selling prices will not be folllowed by similar reductions in our competitors' prices, leaving the relative position no better than it was before? Everyone knows perfectly well that action of this kind on our part would be inevitably followed by similar action on the part of other countries . . ."[1]

Undeterred by the logic of the T.U.C.'s argument, the National Confederation of Employers continued its campaign for wage reductions and on 12th May the port employers tabled a demand for a cut of two shillings a day in dockers' wages coupled with alterations in working conditions. Bevin had been expecting this and was determined not to give way.[2] For the moment, he succeeded in fending off a reduction, but he had no illusions about the weakness of his position if the employers called his bluff. With close on three million unemployed and widespread short time in the docks, no union could risk a strike. All he could do was to husband the Union's resources and wait.

The Government was waiting too. Knowing the opposition he would encounter in his own party to the programme of retrenchment he had in mind, Snowden produced a makeshift budget in April and was relying on the effect of the May Committee's report to prepare opinion for a more drastic budget in the autumn. An acute financial crisis had already overtaken Central Europe where a Vienna Bank, the Credit Anstalt, was driven to close its doors in May. From Austria the crisis spread to Germany where foreign investors began to withdraw the short-term loans with which the German recovery had been financed. But the impact of these events on Britain was delayed until the latter half of July. During June and early July there was an ominous lull in London and few people had yet taken the measure of the storm which was gathering.

In the middle of this lull, Bevin went up north to attend the Union's Biennial Conference at Blackpool (29th June–3rd July). On a sunny week in Blackpool, the three hundred delegates did not have much difficulty in enjoying themselves; but there were full attendances for the principal debates in the Winter Gardens,

---

1 T.U.C. Short Statement on Economic Policy, 16th March 1931.
2 Bevin's reply in *The Record*, Vol. X (1930-1), pp. 336–8. Bevin sent a copy of his statement to the Prime Minister.

presided over for the first time by the new chairman, Herbert Kershaw.

Bevin made two big speeches, the first on unemployment, the second on the National Debt and investment. He showed his skill in bringing home to his audience in simple terms the burden of the National Debt on industry and the worker. Arguing that since the war, when many of the loans had been raised, the purchasing power of the pound had doubled in value, Bevin asked why wages had to fall in accordance with the cost of living but the rate of interest was always protected. He suggested a cut of $1\frac{1}{2}\%$ in the State's and other fixed interest debts to take account of the changed value of money. This would make a substantial contribution to reducing costs and balancing the budget.[1]

Apart from his share in the debates on public affairs, Bevin made an interesting defence of his conduct of the Union's affairs. The occasion was a motion from the clerical section of the London docks that "the powers, the inaccessibility and independence of the General Secretary have increased, are increasing and ought to be restricted and defined". The motion, with its echo of Dunning's famous resolution of 1780 directed against George III,[2] voiced the grievances of the London clerical section at Bevin's refusal to go over the head of his officers and take the section's affairs in hand himself.

In moving the resolution, however, the speaker robbed his argument of much of its effect. The burden of his complaint was that Bevin had undertaken so much public work outside the Union that he was neglecting its interests. This was a difficult case to sustain and met with little support.

In answering the charge, Bevin spoke more personally than was usual with him:

---

1 Beatrice Webb write in her diary, 4th February 1931: "Germany, France and Italy have already repudiated through inflation a large part of their internal debt. . . . Britain for the past ten years has been governed *exclusively* in the interest of the rentier, tempered by unconditional outdoor relief. That is why we and our like are so well off! Ramsay MacDonald and Snowden and many other Labour Front Bench men, in their heart of hearts, do not wish a *change in policy*. . . . In home affairs it (the Labour Party) has no policy—it has completely lost its bearings". *Diaries*, 1924–32, p. 265.

2 John Dunning, M.P. for Calne, moved in the House of Commons in April 1780 "that the influence of the Crown has increased, is increasing and ought to be diminished".

"I helped to build this Union in groups and I have religiously refused to attend Group meetings unless it is a crisis. I think I am right. If you appoint Clay and Corrin and Beard to run national groups, I think they ought to do their jobs. I don't think I should be at every meeting. I will tell you why.

"I recognised the danger, in the first inception, of this Union becoming a one-man show. I don't suppose it is egotistical for me to say I have a forceful personality. I should be no good to you if I hadn't, but I recognise the dangers of it as much as you do, and I have tried to avoid exploitation of it as much as I can. When the national secretaries have had a problem, I have said 'For your own sake, try to get through yourself in order to develop responsibility.'

"I will tell you another reason. I represent the Executive Council and in wage crises my shot is the last one. Now, if you start firing the last shots in the first round, your power is destroyed. The other side know your strength. They know where you are and know your policy. While for two or three years when the Union was shaping, I had to be in hundreds of negotiations, I have tried since to back up my colleagues in everything they are doing. There is scarcely an important conference takes place without my colleagues in Head Office discussing the line they are going to take, and there is a team spirit in dealing with employers.

"Brother Parry has suggested that some of my colleagues feel irksome under my control. If a trade union official has anything to say to the General Secretary, he should be man enough to say it; if not, he is not man enough to stand up to other people. I know I have tried to establish discipline—you have to in a big union—but while sometimes I write as I feel, no one can say I carry malice beyond the letter."

As for outside work, Bevin asked, who was going to define what was important to the Union? Was it a waste of time to put the trade-union point of view on the Macmillan Committee or to force the Colonial Development Committee to look at wages and labour conditions in the colonies? In the whole of the campaign for the *Daily Herald*, he had never failed to complete a full week's work for the Union:

"I took my own time. I went 35 Sundays in that year without rest and I hardly ever confined myself, at any time, to the *Daily Herald*. I did Labour Party meetings at night. In the last General Election I covered 2,600 miles; I did 94 meetings and never cost the local Labour Party a single penny.

"I do not look for these committees. They are hard work . . . I start at six o'clock in the morning with these papers. I take them home at night, I hardly give a minute of the office time to any commission or other work that I undertake outside."

474

Bevin hardly needed to defend himself. The members might grumble on occasion, the officers complain that he was a difficult man to work with, but few even of his critics, faced with his commanding presence on the platform or listening to the grasp and force of his arguments, failed to recognise the strength and stature of the man. Since the days of the General Strike, he had steadily taken the lead in the counsels of the trade-union movement. By 1931, he was unquestionably the ablest and most influential member of the General Council. The members of his own organisation were proud of him and of the prestige he brought to the Union. The stormy years of the amalgamation and afterwards were over: his authority in the Union, though challenged at times, was never seriously in question. Henceforward he was to play a greater, not a more limited, part in the Labour movement.

CHAPTER 18

The 1931 Crisis

I

WHILE THE DELEGATES crowded in and out of the Winter
Gardens at Blackpool, fear and uncertainty were spreading in
Central Europe. On 13th July (the day the Macmillan Report was
published) one of the leading German banks, the Danat, was forced
to suspend payments. There were further failures in Germany and
neighbouring countries later in the month, and the crisis began to
affect the position of sterling. Between 15th July and the end of the
month the Bank of England lost gold at the rate of two and a half
million pounds a day. The measures taken by the Bank—raising the
Bank rate twice, securing credits in New York and Paris, increasing
the Fiduciary Issue—failed to restore confidence. The run on gold
continued.

The publication of the May Committee's report at this moment
had the greatest possible impact. It came out on 31st July, the day
after Parliament had risen for the long summer recess, leaving the
Government free from party pressure until October. It was hardly
surprising that Bevin and others believed Snowden had timed
the publication of the report deliberately.[1]

Both the Labour members of the committee refused to sign it and
presented a minority report. No one, however, paid the least
attention to this and the Labour Chancellor accepted in full the
gloomy picture of Britain's financial future drawn by the five
representatives of the business world.

[1] Beatrice Webb, who liked Snowden, noted in her journal after a talk to him a
few days later: "Without being conscious of it, Philip Snowden has completely
changed his attitude—from being a fervent apostle of Utopian Socialism, thirty
years of parliamentary life and ten years of Front Bench politics, have made him
the upholder of the banker, the landed aristocrat and the Crown." *Diaries*, 1924–
32, p. 279.

The May Committee estimated a budget deficit of £120 millions by April 1932. It was essential, the majority of its members argued, to balance the budget in order to preserve financial confidence. They therefore recommended new taxation amounting to £24 million and a reduction in expenditure of £96 million. Two thirds of the cuts were to be provided by slashing the sums spent on maintaining the unemployed, including a twenty per cent reduction in benefits.

On reviewing the report, the Cabinet appointed an Economy Committee of five,[1] the first meeting of which was fixed for 25th August, and the Prime Minister went off on holiday to Lossiemouth. Early in the second week of August, however, the Bank of England warned Snowden that heavy withdrawals by foreign holders of sterling had been resumed and that the credits they had obtained abroad would be exhausted in less than a month. On 11th August the Prime Minister broke off his holiday and returned to London. After a day of consultations, he summoned the Cabinet Economy Committee to meet on 12th August.

It is important to establish the problem which MacDonald and Snowden believed they had to deal with. On 11th August Sir Ernest Harvey, the Deputy Governor of the Bank of England, and Mr. (later Sir) Edward Peacock, one of the Bank's directors, gave the Prime Minister and the Chancellor the Bank's view of the situation.[2] They repeated it (with the Prime Minister's agreement) to Neville Chamberlain and Sir Herbert Samuel, as representatives of the other parties, and it is from a contemporary letter of Chamberlain's that we derive our knowledge of what the Bank's advice was.

Reporting to Cunliffe-Lister what he had been told by the Deputy Governor, Chamberlain wrote:

"The May Report confirmed the most pessimistic views circulating abroad as to the insolvency of the Budget. . . . The credits had to be encroached upon. . . . Enquiries in Paris and New York showed that there was no chance of a loan in either quarter.

"In these circumstances, the Bankers, i.e. the Deputy Governor and Peacock went to R[amsay] M[acDonald] and told him plainly (1) that we were on the edge of the precipice and unless the situation changed rapidly,

1 The five members were Ramsay MacDonald, Philip Snowden, J. H. Thomas, Arthur Henderson and Willie Graham, President of the Board of Trade.

2 Montagu Norman was ill. He collapsed on 29th July and played no part in the events that followed.

we should be over it directly; (2) *that the cause of the trouble was not financial but political, and lay in the complete want of confidence in His Majesty's Government existing among foreigners*; (3) that the remedy was in the hands of the Government alone . . .

"As they (i.e. the Bankers) were still in serious doubt as to whether any action would be taken, they asked to be allowed to put the facts before the other parties, R.M. assented . . ."[1]

The second clause (which I have underlined) is illuminating. The view which MacDonald and Snowden accepted absolved the bankers from responsibility. Nothing was wrong with the financial system and no steps of a financial character (e.g. to control the exchanges, stop the export of gold and go off the gold standard) were required. "The cause of the trouble was not financial but political," the lack of confidence felt by foreign financial houses in the policy of the Labour Government especially after the report of the May Committee and the Royal Commission on Unemployment Insurance. The Labour Government, according to this view, had allowed provision for the maintenance of the unemployed and other social services to threaten the balancing of the budget. "The remedy was in the hands of the Government alone." In order to restore the confidence of the bankers in New York and Paris and so save the pound, the Government must show its determination to balance the budget by drastic cuts in expenditure along the lines set out in the May Report.

To accept this advice meant also to accept the orthodox conventions of a currency system which Bevin and others in the Labour Party believed to be incompatible with Socialist objectives and which in any case, without any regard to Socialism, they were convinced could no longer be made to work. It is impossible to do justice to the attitude which Bevin and the T.U.C. adopted unless it is realised that they rejected from the beginning the Bank's view of the problem and the advice given to the Government. In Bevin's view, maintained throughout the meetings of the Macmillan Committee and endorsed by the General Council, the existing currency system based on the gold standard was breaking down. This had nothing to do with Socialism. It was a question of fact. The financial crisis of 1931 was a symptom of this breakdown and the bankers' advice, which was aimed at restoring the free working of the system, offered no remedy at all. MacDonald and Snowden,

1 Quoted in Keith Feiling: *The Life of Neville Chamberlain* (1946), pp. 190–1.

however, accepted the Bank's view and although other proposals, such as a revenue tariff, were considered by the Cabinet, the principal issue which divided and eventually led to the break-up of the Government was the extent of the cuts to be made in expenditure, in order to comply with the advice they had received.

Between 11th August and Sunday, 23rd August, a series of meetings took place in Downing Street, which, dramatically reported by the Press, added to the impression of mounting tension and alarm. The details of these meetings need not concern us; their purpose is clear enough.[1] On the one hand, MacDonald and Snowden were in touch with the leaders of the two Opposition parties and with the Bank of England in order to discover the size of the cuts which must be made if the Government were to receive the support of the other two parties in the House of Commons and to secure further loans abroad. On the other hand, they continued the discussions in the Cabinet on the cuts to which members of the Government were prepared to agree. A persistent gap appeared between the figures produced by the two sets of negotiations. The Cabinet was ready to accept a figure of £56,250,000, but finally split on the proposal of MacDonald to advance this to £78 million (including a cut of 10% in unemployment benefits). This was the minimum acceptable to the Opposition parties or likely to overcome the bankers' doubts in New York.

At the crucial meeting on the evening of Sunday, 23rd August, MacDonald had a majority of the Cabinet with him, but the threat of eight or nine resignations (including those of Arthur Henderson from the Foreign Office and Graham from the Board of Trade) could not be ignored. After an inconclusive discussion, the Cabinet agreed that MacDonald should see the King at once and inform him that they placed their resignations in his hands. This was the end of the second Labour Government.

---

1 For a detailed narrative, see R. Bassett: *Nineteen Thirty One, Political Crisis* (1958). Mr. Bassett's careful documentation is unfortunately marred by the partisanship with which he sets out to defend MacDonald and the National Government.

2

What part did Bevin and the T.U.C. play in these transactions?

Like most other members of the General Council, Bevin was away on holiday when the final stage of the crisis opened. He was back in London, however, for the quarterly meeting of his Executive on 17th August. His report to the Executive is of interest for two reasons: it shows that Bevin had already made up his mind about the causes of the crisis and that he had no idea what the Government were proposing to do.

"The crisis has not arisen as the result of anything that the Labour Government has done, or of the social policy of the country or even of the cost of unemployment. It has arisen as the result of the manipulation of finance by the City, borrowing money from abroad on what is termed a 'short term' or 'ready cash' basis, and lending it on long term, causing several of the big financial houses in London to wobble almost to the verge of bankruptcy, due to the fact that they could not realise on the loans made and thus meet the calls from those from whom they had borrowed. As is usual, the financiers have rushed to the Government, but they have put up a very good smoke screen, attributing the blame for the trouble to the social policy of the country and to the fact that the budget is not balanced . . .

"I am not aware at the moment as to the actual line the Government proposes to take but our attitude to the problem must be perfectly clear. We must stand firm for the equitable distribution of the new burdens over the community as a whole, based upon the capacity to pay. The City must not be saved at the expense of the working class and the poorest of our people."

Bevin said not a word in criticism of MacDonald or the Government, but the concluding sentences of his report had a self-reliant ring.

"I feel quite certain that before the Executive Council rises or shortly after, the Labour Government will be no more. There is talk of a National Government and interviews and intrigues are going on with the aim of placing the Government in a position of humiliation or driving them out. Whatever happens, it is essential that the trade unions should take a very firm line: there is danger of a complete debacle unless this Movement of ours remains steady."[1]

Much was later to be made by the Conservatives and supporters of

1 General Secretary's Quarterly Report, August 1931.

MacDonald of the charge of trade-union dictation to the Government. The T.U.C., however, did not force its views upon the Cabinet: it was the Cabinet which called it into consultation. The initiative came from Henderson who was far more alive to the danger of a split within the movement than the Prime Minister. He insisted that, besides consulting the leaders of the Opposition parties and the Bank of England, the Government must also consult its own party. Accordingly, on 13th August, the National Executive of the Labour Party and the General Council of the T.U.C. were summoned to meet the Cabinet Economy Committee on the following Thursday (20th August).

The invitation to the General Council was a recognition of the special position of the trade unions in relation to the Labour Party. Not only were most trade unions directly affiliated to the Party, but without trade-union support it could not have maintained its organisation: out of its income of £45,000 for the year 1930, for instance, £35,000 came from the trade unions. The trade unions elected 12 of the 23 members of the National Executive and dominated the voting at the Party conference by the system of block votes. These facts were recognised in the Party's constitution which, amongst its declared objects, listed as second only to the organisation of a political Labour Party, co-operation with the General Council of the T.U.C. in joint political or other action.

This special position of the trade unions has always distinguished the Labour Party from the other two major parties in Great Britain, and has been the subject of much controversy. To those like Mac-Donald and Snowden who came into the Party independently of the trade-union movement it was a cause of permanent irritation, but to Arthur Henderson, by origin a trade unionist and the creator of the Labour Party organisation, it was a natural and essential relationship.

Neither Bevin nor any other trade unionist claimed that the Prime Minister and the Cabinet were in any way obliged to consult the T.U.C. On the other hand, there was no constitutional impropriety —and obvious political advantage—in sounding opinion on the General Council. As Bevin remarked later, if the General Council had supported the Prime Minister, they would have been hailed as 'statesmen'; when they disagreed, they were accused of dictation and invading the privileges of the Cabinet. They were soon to find themselves attacked for anti-patriotic as well as unconstitutional behaviour.

The meeting on the afternoon of 20th August took place in the Council Chamber of Transport House. The General Council met beforehand and discussed the procedure to be followed. On Ben Tillett's motion, they wisely agreed to leave the chairman and secretary to seek as much information as possible and postpone discussion until later. At three o'clock they were joined by the members of the Labour Party National Executive and the Cabinet's Economy Committee.

MacDonald opened the meeting with a general statement which, as Citrine tartly remarked, told them no more than the leading articles they had already read. Consultation, Citrine added, could only take place if they were given more detailed information; otherwise, the General Council would have nothing on which to make up their minds. Snowden then reluctantly agreed to fill out Mac-Donald's sketch.

He began by saying that the May Committee's estimate of a deficit of £120 million was far too low. The figure to be provided could not come out of new taxation alone and cuts would have to be made in expenditure. The Cabinet had not yet reached definite decisions but he mentioned the proposals which they were considering. These included raising unemployment insurance contributions and restricting benefits; reducing the pay of teachers, the police and armed forces; reducing expenditure on roads and public works. On one point there was a misunderstanding which was later to lead to recrimination. The T.U.C. minutes record Snowden as saying: "They had not made any proposals for a reduction with regard to benefit." The General Council took this to mean that any reduction in unemployment benefits was ruled out; Snowden insisted that he meant nothing so definite, only that the Cabinet had not yet decided to make such a reduction.[1] When Snowden was asked how he meant to apply the principle of equality of sacrifice, he refused to be drawn: no Chancellor could be expected to give advance notice of the taxes he proposed to introduce. The meeting broke up soon after 4 o'clock amid confused and angry argument, and the General Council resumed its session alone.

[1] The question is fully discussed by Bassett, *op. cit.*, pp. 88–94. The account here is based upon the unpublished T.U.C. minutes.

3

Bevin was not the only man angered by the Chancellor's statement, but the Council sat down to consider his proposals one by one. There was not a single one to which they felt they could agree. A fortnight later Citrine explained to the full T.U.C. the considerations which had influenced them most:[1]

"We were faced with the position either of accepting or rejecting the programme of cuts, and leaving to trust the operation of the principle of equality of sacrifice for other sections of the community.

"Well, we wanted to assist the Government. None of us wanted to embarrass them more than they were obviously embarrassed at the moment. . . . But when you are faced with a policy against which you have been fighting for years and which you know will be disastrous, no course is left open to you but unequivocally to say, as the General Council said, 'We cannot subscribe to this policy.' . . . For years we have been operating on the principle that the policy which has been followed since 1925 in this country, of contraction, contraction, contraction, deflation, deflation, deflation, must lead us all, if carried to its logical conclusion, to economic disaster, and acceptance of this policy in the judgment of the General Council would have tied us and anchored us to that principle, and logically we could not later resist it when it spread to other channels."

Having reached this conclusion, the General Council discussed four alternative proposals to recommend to the Government. These were:

(1) replacement of the unemployment insurance scheme by a graduated levy upon the whole community, based on the capacity to pay;[2]
(2) the suspension of the Sinking Fund for the National Debt, the annual contribution to which amounted to £50 million;
(3) new taxation upon all fixed-interest-bearing securities;
(4) a revenue tariff.

The first three proposals were agreed to; after long discussion, however, the fourth was left open.

The General Council meeting did not break up until 8 o'clock.

1 T.U.C. Report, 1931, pp. 81–82.
2 This proposal had formed part of the T.U.C.'s evidence to the Royal Commission.

Bevin had time to get a meal and then joined Hayday, the chairman, Citrine, Arthur Pugh and A. G. Walkden to convey the Council's views to the Cabinet Economy Committee in Downing Street. The proceedings soon turned into an argument between Snowden on the one side, Citrine and Bevin on the other. Henderson did not speak at all, but no man present was more impressed by what he heard.

Citrine began by reporting the conclusions to which the General Council had come after considering the Chancellor's proposals. Bevin went to the heart of the matter when, according to the T.U.C. minutes, he "emphasised the point that the General Council felt that the Government's proposals meant a continuance of the deflation policy, and to that the Council were opposed".

Snowden brushed this aside:

"Whatever the causes of the present trouble might be, they were actually faced with the position they were in. Mr. Snowden said that if sterling went, the whole international financial structure would collapse, and there would be no comparison between the present depression and the chaos and ruin that would face us in that event. There would be millions more unemployed, and complete industrial collapse.

"Mr. Bevin disputed this statement."

Well he might. Exactly a month later, Snowden piloted an emergency bill through Parliament to suspend the gold standard—and none of the catastrophic consequences with which he had sought to frighten the T.U.C. followed.

"But Mr. Snowden insisted that his own view was correct.

"He then said that the importance of the weight of debt had been exaggerated. Calculations showed that a very large part of the national debt had been diminished in real value and not increased. . . . Nevertheless, there were considerable possibilities in this connection. . . . He had already made three conversions very successfully and he was quite alive to the possibility of doing more in this direction.

"Incidentally, he said, as the argument had been applied to *rentiers*, why not apply the same argument to teachers and to unemployment benefit, namely, that as prices had fallen it was equitable to make a reduction.

"Mr. Bevin said there was no analogy. The value of the services of teachers, police etc. was very different from that of *rentiers*.

"As regards the Sinking Fund, Mr. Snowden said he did not wish to say anything except that there were certain statutory obligations regarding the

Sinking Fund which had to be borne in mind. As regards the Revenue Tariff, Mr. Snowden said he would not say anything at all.

"Mr. MacDonald, summing up, said that nothing the General Council representatives had put forward touched the actual problem that faced the Government.

"Mr. J. H. Thomas asked what the General Council would actually do in the desperate situation which confronted the Government at the present time.

"Mr. Citrine said that the Council were not convinced that the situation was quite so desperate as was alleged. There were enormous resources in the country."[1]

The anger which MacDonald and those members of the Cabinet who supported Snowden's programme felt with Bevin and Citrine is reflected in Sidney Webb's comment: "The General Council are pigs; they won't agree to any cuts of unemployment insurance benefits or salaries or wages."[2] The impressions of the T.U.C. deputation were recorded by Citrine: "Some of us thought, as a consequence of that meeting, that two members of the Cabinet at least had made up their minds that nothing we could represent would materially alter their point of view."[3]

On the following morning, 21st August, the T.U.C. representatives at the meeting with the Prime Minister reported to the full General Council. Their account of the meeting was adopted and, on Bevin's motion, a copy was sent to the Prime Minister. MacDonald's reply was friendly in tone, but he was not to be moved.

"If [the Cabinet] took another course," he wrote, "the situation would rapidly worsen and unemployment would rapidly increase—far more rapidly than we have known it even during this terrible time of depression. . . . Nothing gives me greater regret than to disagree with old industrial friends, but I really find it absolutely impossible to overlook dread realities, as I am afraid you are doing."[4]

4

What were the grounds on which the General Council differed from the Prime Minister and the Chancellor?

1 T.U.C. General Council: Minutes of the meeting held at 10 Downing Street, Thursday, 20th August 1931, at 9.30 p.m.

2 Beatrice Webb: *Diaries*, 1924–32, p. 281.

3 Citrine at the Bristol T.U.C., Report, 1931, p. 83.

4 Ibid., p. 515.

The answer to this question is to be found in the Report on the Financial Situation of August 1931 which Bevin played a leading part in drawing up and which the General Council presented to the Trade Union Congress at Bristol on 9th September.[1]

The Council started from a refusal to accept the analysis of the financial crisis presented to the Government by the Bank of England. The Bank took the view that the lack of confidence in sterling was due to the belief that the Labour Government was extravagant in expenditure on social services, especially on the unemployed; that, as a result, it was believed that the budget would not be balanced and that a budget deficit of the order forecast by the May Committee would finally destroy confidence in the pound.

The remedy advocated by the Bank of England and by the leaders of the Opposition parties followed logically from this analysis: the Labour Government must reassure 'opinion', i.e. the opinion of the small number of people abroad responsible for withdrawing their holdings in sterling or hesitating to make further credits available. And it must do this by cutting down expenditure on the social services, including specifically the money spent on unemployment maintenance, in order to balance the budget.

On the contrary, says the General Council's report, the cause of the run on sterling is neither the general economic condition of Britain (which had been less badly hit by the world depression than the U.S.A. and Germany), nor the fear of a budget deficit. The cause is the financial crisis in Germany.

"Financial houses in London . . . had made loans to Germany which could not now be repaid at short notice. The funds lent to Germany had been borrowed by the British houses mainly from France and America, and considerable nervousness was shown in those countries owing to the fear that British credit might be affected. It is understood that the policy of the British financial houses referred to [2] has for some time been criticised on the Continent and, when the trouble in Central Europe occurred towards the

1 Text in T.U.C. Report, 1931, Appendix C., pp. 512–19. This report was drafted by W. Milne-Bailey and worked over by the Economic Committee before going to the General Council. It has been neglected by historians of the 1931 crisis, although it presents a more detailed and sober case than any of the Labour Party manifestoes.

2 Generally known as borrowing short and lending long. It is worth noting that this explanation of the crisis is the same as that which Bevin put to his own Executive in mid-August.

end of July 1931, the withdrawal of foreign balances from London became serious.

"Simultaneously, the report of the May Committee was published. This report painted an alarmist picture of our budgetary position. . . . The wide publicity given to this report greatly intensified the fears existing on the Continent and elsewhere. The British Press took up the cry and alleged that the economic position was so alarming that foreign confidence must be restored by drastic economies. . . . The press campaign exaggerated the difficulties of this country. . . . The result was to increase still further the withdrawal of gold from London."

The T.U.C. did not agree with the remedy proposed any more than with the analysis. Cutting Government expenditure and balancing the budget was no answer to the problem created by the German collapse. This is supported, it is worth noting, by the fact that the cuts in expenditure made by the National Government and the emergency budget introduced by Snowden in September did not stop the flight from the pound. In fact, all the leading industrial countries were running budget deficits.

The T.U.C. argued that the budget deficit and the May Report were dragged in to support a policy which provided no answer to the immediate crisis but which the City and the employers' organisations had long been urging on other grounds—further deflation aimed at cutting social services, unemployment benefit and, of course, wages. The fact that the Bank, the Opposition parties and the New York financiers all agreed in calling for reduced expenditure on social services and in specifying cuts in the provision for the unemployed could not be ignored. On the pretext of the financial crisis the Labour Government was being jockeyed into abandoning a social policy to which those who gave the advice were inflexibly opposed. No doubt, the advice may have been sincerely given, but it was partisan, not disinterested nor expert advice. It represented a point of view against which the whole history of the Labour movement was a protest.

Granting for the moment that it was essential to balance the budget, the proposals made appeared to the General Council to require disproportionate sacrifices from the poorest classes, the unemployed and the working class, many of whom were on short time. Even if the Chancellor proposed at the same time to raise the income tax (as he did, from 4/– to 5/– in the £, in September) this still did not represent equality of sacrifice. If the budget had to be balanced, then the T.U.C. urged, let it be done by an all-round cut in the form of a graduated levy upon the profits, income and earnings of all classes of the community, plus new taxation on fixed-interest securities, the real value of which had been enhanced by the fall in prices.

But, the T.U.C. statement continues, "it is not only because of the specific injury that would be caused to the workers by these cuts that the Council oppose the Government, it is also because the Council are convinced that the Government is approaching the whole matter from the wrong angle."

Dividing the country's economic problems into three, the General Council put forward their own suggestions.

First, to meet the difficulties from which British industry had suffered since the war, they proposed ending the policy of deflation, modernising and reconstructing the basic industries as public utility services and setting out to lighten the burden of international debt and reparations.

Second, to end the slump of 1929–31, they urged international action to raise the world level of wholesale prices. If this was obvious, none the less little had been done to secure such action.

Third, to deal with the immediate problem of the weakness of the exchanges, the General Council, for reasons already familiar, opposed a policy of wage reductions as self-defeating. They raised the question whether the pound could be maintained at the old parity and came out for devaluation as "the most effective means within the power of this country, if we have to act alone".

Finally, they recorded the suggestion of a revenue tariff and advised the T.U.C. to make a full investigation of fiscal policy immediately.

In giving the T.U.C. view at this length, I do not wish to maintain that the alternative proposals made by the General Council offered a solution to the Government's problem of August 1931. It is arguable that subsequent experience has shown that the direction in which Bevin, Citrine and the other T.U.C. leaders were looking for a solution was more likely to produce results than that in which Snowden, the Treasury and the Bank wanted to move. But this must be, admittedly, speculation. What the evidence seems to me to prove is that the General Council, in disagreeing with MacDonald and Snowden, was neither acting irresponsibly, nor evading the issue nor putting class before nation—or whatever other cliché their critics chose to employ.

5

For the moment, the exchange of letters between Citrine and Mac-Donald on the 21st ended the matter so far as the T.U.C. was concerned. They learned from their newspapers, with the rest of the world, that the Labour Government had resigned on the evening of Sunday, 23rd August, and on the following day that MacDonald had accepted the King's commission to form a non-party National Government in which the Conservative and Liberal leaders agreed to serve under his leadership.

There is no ground in the evidence for accusations that the General Council 'dictated' to the Labour Government. They were asked by the Prime Minister to express their views and told him that they believed the proposals which he and the Chancellor put before them represented the wrong policy to follow and that they could not support them. They were fully entitled to hold this view and to express it to the Cabinet when called upon to do so. They made alternative suggestions, but neither on 20th August nor later did they attempt to exercise pressure on the Government to accept them. As for the events of 23rd–24th August, which led to the fall of the Labour Government and the formation of the National Government, the General Council was neither consulted nor informed.

But, if the General Council did not 'dictate' to the Cabinet, there is no doubt that the stand which it took on 25th August was a decisive factor in the development of events. The National Executive of the Labour Party, a number of whose members were also members of the Government, was not in a position to offer effective opposition. Some of its members at least supported the view taken by MacDonald and Snowden and it was perhaps from a desire to avoid a split that Henderson asked the Executive to leave matters in the hands of those who were members of the Cabinet. The plain 'No' of the General Council, coming in the middle of the confusion, compromise and conflict of loyalties which divided the Parliamentary Labour Party, stiffened the resistance of the opposition in the Cabinet, in particular that of Arthur Henderson.

489

Henderson was the key figure. If he had given way, the opposition in the Cabinet would either have collapsed or been overridden. He made no pretence to be an expert in financial questions; he had been absorbed in international affairs for the past two years and was not altogether sure of his ground. There was no one who felt more strongly the pull of loyalty after insisting for years, to his own disadvantage, that MacDonald was the one man who could lead the Party. Yet Henderson's political instinct told him that MacDonald was making a wrong decision; that the conversations with the other party leaders and the bankers were leading the Cabinet into a false position.[1] The discovery that the trade-union leaders felt the same doubts and were firm in their opposition had a greater effect on Henderson than on any other member of the Cabinet. An old trade unionist himself, he spoke their language and had a respect for their judgment that was far from being shared by other Labour politicians. Had the T.U.C. supported the Chancellor's proposals, Henderson's doubts might have been overcome and the Cabinet might have accepted Snowden's recommendations. For it must be remembered that, on the evening of Sunday, 23rd August, when MacDonald finally pressed for a decision, he had a majority of the Labour Cabinet on his side.

This is again speculation, but it is supported by events after the Labour Government resigned.

When the Labour Cabinet met for the last time at noon on Monday, 24th August, MacDonald told them that he had been asked and had agreed to head an emergency National Government. It was by no means clear at this stage what would be the attitude of the Party and of the Labour ex-Ministers. The confusion in the Labour Party was increased by the formation of the National Government and the strong appeal which MacDonald made for all-party backing. As the *Manchester Guardian* said on 25th August: "It is one thing to lead a revolt like that of the nine Ministers, it is another to develop that revolt into a challenge to a National Government."

In this situation, the attitude of Bevin and Citrine was once again

[1] Beatrice Webb, who was the wife of a Cabinet Minister, recorded in her diary on 23rd August: "Henderson blames the P.M. for spending so much time in negotiation: he thinks it would have been far better to have settled really what the Labour Cabinet would be prepared to do in economies and resign if it were rejected by the Opposition". *Diaries*, 1924–32, p. 282.

clear-cut. Dalton records in his diary a meeting on the afternoon of the 24th immediately after it was known what MacDonald proposed to do.

"Straight round to Transport House, where in Uncle's[1] room is a council of war. With him are G[eorge] L[ansbury], Bevin, Citrine, Stanley Hirst, Middleton.[2] The Trade Union leaders are full of fight. They speak of financial assistance. 'This is like the General Strike,' says Bevin. 'I'm prepared to put everything in.' They send for X of the *Herald* to settle the line of tomorrow's leader. X—still under the influence of J.R.M. and P.S. [Snowden] who had been working on him very hard—had proposed to begin by paying tribute to the courage of those who are staying in. 'And what about the courage of those who are coming out?' asks Uncle. So the whole emphasis is changed.

"The *Herald* in the days that followed, under Bevin's influence, gave a fine lead."[3]

6

Bevin's opposition to the National Government has sometimes been dismissed as the product of the dislike which he and MacDonald had long felt for each other. But this is only a partial explanation. Whatever their personal feelings, the two men had been able to work together during the two years of the Labour Government. MacDonald offered Bevin a peerage and selected him as one of the members of the Economic Advisory Council. On more than one occasion, Bevin wrote privately to the Prime Minister or went to see him. During the last six months, it is true, Bevin had been more and more disappointed with the Government's lack of policy and MacDonald's lack of leadership, but he held himself in and avoided public criticism of the Prime Minister or of the Chancellor, with whose ideas on economic policy he totally disagreed.

MacDonald's action, however, in forming a National Government to carry out a programme repudiated by the Party of which he was the Leader appeared to Bevin to be a plain act of political treachery and folly. Argument about MacDonald's sincerity is

1 Henderson was widely (and affectionately) known by the name of 'Uncle Arthur'. It is worth pointing out that he was now 68 and a generation older than Bevin, Citrine, Dalton and Attlee.

2 Jim Middleton was the assistant secretary of the Labour Party.

3 Hugh Dalton, *Call Back Yesterday* (1953), pp. 273-4.

beside the point. Let us allow that MacDonald was as sincere in 1931 as Peel in 1846 when he repealed the Corn Laws. This does not alter the fact that, to those who did not accept MacDonald's view of the situation or agree with the policy he proposed to put into effect, his action was as indefensible as that of Peel appeared to Disraeli and the Tories in 1846. If MacDonald and Peel were justified from their point of view, so were Bevin and Disraeli from theirs.

Bevin no more accepted MacDonald's claim to represent a national point of view above parties than he had Lloyd George's in 1918. As Bevin saw it, MacDonald had first let himself be drawn into accepting the view of the anti-Socialist parties, no doubt sincerely held but incompatible with the principles of the Labour Party, and was now allowing himself to be used as an instrument to push through their policy over the opposition of his own party.

For the Tories and the Liberals, however sincerely they may have believed that their policy was in the national interest, were certainly not unaware of the political advantage of encouraging MacDonald to take the responsibility of carrying it out. At one blow they had turned the Labour Government out of office, secured the reversal of its policies in favour of their own and split the Labour Party. In Bevin's eyes, this was no issue of nation v. party, but of the anti-Socialist parties exploiting a crisis which they had deliberately exaggerated for their own political advantage.

When the Labour Party and the trade unions were convinced that the nation was confronted with a real emergency, they were capable —as they showed in 1915 and in 1940—of rising to the occasion and putting national unity before anything else. In 1931 they believed that they were being called upon to sacrifice their political beliefs and the integrity of their Party in the interests, not of the nation, but of the preservation of an economic and financial system which they repudiated.

This is not to argue that they were right—that is a question of opinion which every reader will answer for himself—only that in opposing MacDonald, Bevin and those who shared his views acted from conviction and in their own opinion would have been false to the principles which brought them into the Labour movement if they had acted otherwise.

What mattered immediately was to hold the movement together and prevent the Party splitting. The uncompromising attitude of

Bevin, Citrine and the other trade-union leaders helped to steady a party shaken by the loss of three of its leaders and torn by conflicting loyalties. The support of the trade unions meant the funds with which to keep the Party going, while, thanks to the agreement which Bevin had made with Odhams, the General Council retained control over the *Herald* and so preserved one independent voice in the general chorus of approval which greeted MacDonald's action.

Bevin and Citrine pressed strongly for the Labour Party to go into active opposition from the start. This decision was taken on Tuesday, 26th August, at a joint meeting of the Party Executive, the General Council and the Consultative Committee of the Parliamentary Labour Party. There was some plain speaking by trade-union leaders, including Bevin, who took the ex-Ministers to task for having gone as far as they had done in accepting the proposed cuts and compromising the movement's position.

Bevin would have preferred the General Council to issue a separate statement of its own position, but agreed for the sake of unity to a joint manifesto signed by all three committees. This was published the following day, 27th August, and drew from the Labour correspondent of *The Times* the comment that, although three pairs of signatures appeared at the bottom of the document, "the dominant voice is that of the General Council slightly subdued out of deference to the feelings of the Parliamentary leaders who have, since they left the Cabinet, accepted the essentials of the General Council's policy."

7

On 7th September, the Trades Union Congress opened at Bristol. The principal statements on the events of the past few weeks were made by Hayday, as chairman, Citrine and Henderson, who was present as a fraternal delegate from the Labour Party. There was little disposition to question their account and the General Council's report was adopted unanimously.

Bevin intervened twice to defend himself against left-wing attacks for the part he had played in the Mond-Turner talks and on the Macmillan Committee:

"I am not going to argue for any Mond-Turner report today," he told the Congress, "but to justify it in the conditions that existed when I presented it to the Belfast Conference and I say that if there had been a vigorous application in grasping the idea of rationalisation as I appealed to the Movement to do then, we should not be whining about it now. The situation which the Movement has got to face today is entirely different from that which it had to face in 1926, 1927 and 1928 . . . but I am not going to be a party to rejecting the work that has been done."[1]

The only other speech Bevin made at the Bristol Congress was a plea for a long-term policy of economic planning which had attracted him in the first place to the establishment of the General Council's Economic Committee. He offered no blueprint, insisting that a doctrinaire approach would lead nowhere, that it needed long and careful study. But the old economic order characterised by *laissez-faire* and the automatic operation of the Bank rate had broken down; it could not be patched together again by the sort of measures the National Government was proposing. A new world was coming into existence, of which the Five Year Plan in Russia and the industrialisation of the East were signs. That new world would upset many existing conceptions and would call for new forms of economic organisation. It was time to begin thinking what those forms should be.[2]

It is still an interesting speech to read, in some ways confused and vague, lacking the precision or lucidity of Citrine, ill-arranged and yet with the prophetic touch of imagination, that sense of historical change which mark Bevin's speeches off from the pedestrian oratory of most trade-union conferences with their stock perorations and appeals to emotion.

Parliament had already met before the T.U.C. Congress broke up, and on 10th September Snowden introduced his emergency budget. The economies included a ten per cent cut in unemployment benefits, increased contributions, the limiting of the benefit period to 26 weeks a year and a means test for subsequent 'transitional' grants.

The National Government was widely hailed as the saviour of the nation, Labour and the T.U.C. denounced as unpatriotic. But forming the National Government and balancing the budget did not

1 T.U.C. Report 1931, pp. 363–4.
2 Ibid. pp. 464–5.

save the pound. A loan of £80 millions raised by the National Government in New York and Paris was rapidly exhausted by the continuing run on gold and foreign currency. On 19th September, the Bank of England suddenly reversed its view and advised the Government to suspend the Bank's obligation, under the Act of 1925, to sell gold at a fixed price. The Government accepted the advice and by a Bill hurriedly passed on 21st September, Britain went off the gold standard. Bevin may be excused for feeling that he had been vindicated in the teeth of the experts' advice, the more so when none of the disasters foretold by MacDonald and Snowden actually came to pass.

Even before the abandonment of the gold standard, the possibility of a general election and a continuation of the National Government was being widely canvassed. In anticipation of such a decision, Henderson sounded Bevin on the possibility of his standing against the Prime Minister in his Durham constituency of Seaham. On 2nd September, Bevin sent him an interim reply:

"Dear Uncle Arthur,
"You will think that I am very difficult in regard to this political business, but I am very anxious to do the right thing. I am being pressed from all quarters to place myself at the disposal of the Labour Party. As indicated to you, however, I must discuss the position with my Executive.
"With regard to Seaham I do not think it wise to interfere or to hold up negotiations. If I ran at all, I should endeavour to get a seat near London, to make things as easy as possible.
"In the circumstances, I think I should tell them at Seaham not to bother. I will look at the whole position when I am at Scarborough next week. There is such a divergence of opinions in my own Society, that it is extremely difficult."

The day the Labour Party Conference opened at Scarborough (5th October), the Cabinet reached agreement on fighting the election without breaking up the National Government. The contest, in fact, became a straight issue between the Labour Party and all the other political forces in the country rallying behind MacDonald as Prime Minister.

Bevin was still reluctant to stand himself, but strong pressure was brought to bear on him by Henderson and the other Party leaders. He finally agreed, provided the Union Executive would allow him to retain the office of general secretary, if elected; in return, he undertook to pay the balance of his Parliamentary salary into the Union's political fund. He was at once offered the nomination for Gateshead which had returned a Labour majority of 16,700 at the 1929 election.

8

The overwhelming need at the Scarborough conference was to re-establish unity. There was no debate on the events of the summer and Mrs. Webb's verdict on the conference was "dull, drab, disillusioned, but not disunited".[1] The Executive put forward a number of policy resolutions, two of which, on monetary and trade policy, produced the only substantial debates.

Bevin and Citrine had been consulted in the drafting of these resolutions and the first in particular closely followed Bevin's views. It stigmatised the policy of deflation and the return to the gold standard in 1925; called for the banking and credit system of the country to be brought under public ownership; recommended the formation of a national investment board with statutory powers to control home and overseas investment and declared the object of monetary policy to be the stabilisation of wholesale prices at a reasonable level.

Bevin seized the occasion to vindicate the consistency of his own attitude:

"I have been trying as a trade unionist to get our people—and I think several Labour conferences—to abandon the policy of hoping to achieve socialism by taxation, and trying to achieve socialism by socialising the sources and real tools of industry . . .
"In 1925 at Liverpool I appealed to this Party not to take office without a majority. I believed that when the crisis came, finance would wring its neck, and it has done it. In 1927 at Blackpool when you were dealing with the surtax—mere quibbling in comparison with the problem itself—I appealed to you to tackle the very basis of finance—the gold standard. In the Macmillan Committee I appealed to every member to face up to an alternative method of exchange. But the Chairman, even Mr. Keynes, refused to look at an alternative. To every witness I said: 'What can you do to make this system work?' And what was their answer? An international conference. But supposing the international conference does not come off—what then? And their hands were held up in horror.

1 *Diaries*, 1924–32, p. 291.

Gateshead, 1931: "Vote for Bevin".

Unemployment.

"On the Economic Council for two years continually some of us urged that an honest devaluation was better than waiting to be pushed off, that we were making too many of our people suffer week in week out waiting for the inevitable to happen."

There were few in the audience who did not catch the grim note of satisfaction in Bevin's voice. Who had been proven right, the politicians or the trade-union leader? In the end, the Party had come round to his way of thinking and he let them know it.

"You can talk about socialising your railways and other things," he concluded. "Socialise credit and the rest is comparatively easy. That is the basis of the operation."[1]

Before the Conference ended, the Government announced the dissolution of Parliament and fixed the date of the election. There was little time for Bevin to organise his campaign before polling day on 27th October. He travelled up to Gateshead on 12th October, sharing a compartment from Leeds to York with Hugh Dalton who recorded in his diary MacDonald's remark to some of the members of the Economic Advisory Council: "You must remember the low mental calibre of those I have to work with," to which Bevin replied: "Mr. Prime Minister, you shouldn't say that sort of thing in front of *me*."[2]

The election was fought with a good deal of bitterness and recrimination on both sides. By polling day Bevin had lost any optimism about the result. Even in a working-class area like Gateshead, badly hit by trade depression and unemployment, the tide of opinion swung decisively in the Government's favour. When the result was declared, the 1929 Labour majority of 16,700 had been turned into a majority of 12,938 in favour of Bevin's National Liberal opponent, Magnay.[3]

In fact, he had not made a bad showing. Over the country as a whole, the Labour Party's poll fell by two million votes. The 289 Labour M.P.s of 1929 were reduced to 46, plus five I.L.P. members and Josiah Wedgwood who stood as an Independent. MacDonald

1 Labour Party Conference Report 1931, pp. 191–2.
2 Dalton *op. cit.*, p. 294.
3 The figures were T. Magnay (Nat. Liberal) 34,764; E. Bevin, 21,826; J. S. Barr (Non-Party), 1,077; J. Fennell (Nat. Labour), 187. Majority: 12,938.

won a personal triumph at Seaham, Thomas another at Derby. In County Durham, a miners' stronghold, the Labour Party held only two out of nineteen seats. Henderson was defeated at Burnley, and the only Labour ex-Cabinet Minister to get back at all was Lansbury, accompanied by two other ex-Ministers outside the Cabinet, Attlee (by a majority of 551) in Limehouse and Cripps (by 429) in Bristol.

MacDonald was returned at the head of a Government bloc with 556 seats in the House of Commons and a majority of 500 over all opposition parties. Despite the support of the T.U.C., the Labour Party had been overwhelmed; its representation in the House of Commons was less than it had been after the 'khaki election' of 1918, only four more than in 1910. The one consolation Bevin could find was the unity of the movement which emerged unimpaired from the crisis and the election. The loss of support to MacDonald's National Labour Party was negligible; no wedge had been driven between the trade unions and the political wing of the movement; the party had neither split nor compromised its Socialist character. In the long run this unity which Bevin prized so highly and to which he had powerfully contributed was to count for more than the setback at the polls.

9

The political defeat of 1931 marks the end of a period in Bevin's career as sharply as the industrial defeat of 1926. Between 1926 and 1931, Bevin had emerged on to the stage of national affairs. In the Mond-Turner talks, in the invitation to serve on the Macmillan Committee and the Economic Advisory Council, he had been recognised as the outstanding leader in the trade-union movement. Between 1929 and 1931 he was close to the centre of power, even if he failed to persuade the Government to adopt the policies in which he believed.

The defeat of 1931 changed this abruptly. Henceforward until the eve of the war, he was 'out', in a position where his ability and energy could only find expression, politically, in opposition. He still found plenty of constructive opportunities in the trade-union movement and the industrial field, but for almost the whole of his fifties, when he was at the peak of his powers, he was excluded from any direct influence on the course of national affairs, a fate which he shared with his great contemporary, Churchill. Not until he was fifty-nine did he hold office, and throughout the 1930s he had to sit and watch less able men fumble with problems on which he itched to get his hands.

But this does not mean that Bevin took no part in the politics of the 1930s. On the contrary, his reaction to the fall of the second Labour Government was quite the opposite to that which followed the fall of the first. After the election of 1924 he had been disillusioned with politics and had turned back to industrial action as the only reliable means of improving working-class conditions. His experience in the intervening years, however, confirmed by the defeat of 1931, convinced him that the trade unions must commit themselves more, not less, to political action and draw closer to the Labour Party. In the period beginning with the crisis of 1931, Bevin played a part in Labour Party politics which, as Francis Williams has justly pointed out, entitles him to be regarded as one of the architects of the Labour Party as much as of the trade-union movement.

The scale of their defeat came as a shock to the Labour Party and trade-union leaders. Although they polled seven million votes in all, the experience of most candidates showed the Party to be out of touch with a large section of working-class opinion. A few days after his return to London, Bevin put his own reflections down on paper in replying to a letter in which Josiah Wedgwood expressed his regret at Bevin's defeat.

"Never," Wedgwood wrote, "have I heard a T.U. leader speak as you speak, or understand as you understand. You could be Prime Minister. Ever since I first knew you in the Council of Action long ago, I thought here is everything combined. Now you may be disheartened, and inclined to work outside for ever, and I know that only through Parliament can democracy pull through."[1]

Bevin replied:

"I think the *Herald* was right that we were completely out-generalled, and I feel that the Labour Movement has still got a touch of the University complex. It will not stand up to a problem. . . . What is needed now is good

1 Josiah Wedgwood to Ernest Bevin, 29th October 1931.

educational work. What I learned in my own constituency was that we had lost, almost completely, the better artisan class, the better type of railwayman and craftsman and most of those who used to finance the old Labour electoral associations. . . . In their place we had a great mass of poor people on whose behalf the Labour Agent had been acting more or less as a relieving officer, representing them at Public Assistance Committees, Courts of Referees[1] and things of that kind. That lot swept in, but there were at least 10,000 whose votes are not consistently Labour. If something turned up the other way, they would just as easily go against you.

"The tragedy of it all is that the I.L.P. became purely an emotional body, a sort of Plymouth Brethren, and the Labour Party has not taken over the early educational work of the I.L.P. and the old S.D.F. I am going to devote my attention to some educational work of a practical kind."[2]

10

Bevin's mind had already been moving in this direction. During the winter of 1930–31, G. D. H. Cole took the initiative in founding two new bodies, the New Fabian Research Bureau and the Society for Socialist Information and Propaganda, which he hoped to see revive the role the Fabians had played in earlier years. In Cole's mind the function of the S.S.I.P. was to diffuse the results of the Fabians' research and to carry on educational work in the Party through a network of branches, although in practice the two functions became blurred. In order to avoid the mistakes made by the I.L.P. Cole insisted that neither body should put up candidates or seek formal affiliation to the Labour Party. In this way, they would retain their freedom to discuss and advance ideas without coming into conflict with the Party organisation.

With their strong flavour of Hampstead, Bloomsbury, and the University Labour Clubs, neither was the sort of body with which anyone would expect Bevin to be connected. His experience on the Macmillan Committee and the Economic Advisory Council, however, had made a deep impression on him and brought him into contact with a number of the younger Socialist economists like Cole and Colin Clark. He shared their anxiety at the Government's lack of a policy and not only joined the S.S.I.P. but accepted Cole's invitation to become its chairman.

1 In connection with unemployment benefit.
2 Ernest Bevin to Josiah Wedgwood, 31st October 1931.

The Society's real purpose, he wrote to J. R. Bellerby[1] before the 1931 crisis,

"is that of projecting ideas. It is not a ginger group to the Party or anything of that kind; it is an attempt to work out problems and to give the new generation something to grip. A good many of us feel that the younger people are just drifting; there is a kind of apathy which is appalling. The Fabian Society was more or less moribund and there was no body in existence to project ideas and policy. . . . We despaired of getting much done in this Parliament and, owing to the present stalemate in thought, very little was being done for the possible coming of the next Socialist Government.

"We have kept clear of dogma and this is an attempt to study and project in order to fill the niche for the next decade, like the Fabians and early Socialists did for us."[2]

Among other members of the S.S.I.P. were Attlee, Arthur Pugh, the two lawyers, Stafford Cripps and D. N. Pritt, Dick Mitchison, Raymond Postgate and Frank Horrabin. Bevin's willingness to join such a group marked a big change of attitude on his part and, if the partnership had proved successful, it might have strengthened the Labour movement at one of its weakest points, the gap which separated the intellectuals from the trade unionists. Unfortunately, the later history of the S.S.I.P. only deepened in Bevin's mind "the conviction already implanted by the behaviour of Moseley and Mac-Donald, that intellectuals of the left were people who stabbed you in the back".[3]

This was no fault of Bevin's. He took the chair and spoke at the inaugural meeting held in Transport House on 15th June 1931, and he found the time to read through and add his comments to a number of draft reports prepared by Cole, Colin Clark and others on economic planning, the public control of nationalised industries, banking policy, reform of the Cabinet and the reorganisation of Government departments.[4]

1 A Cambridge economist who had taken the chair of economics at Liverpool.
2 Ernest Bevin to J. R. Bellerby, 23rd May 1931.
3 Margaret Cole: *Growing up into Revolution* (1949), p. 150.
4 Bevin produced a memorandum giving his own views on the last subject as early as February 1931. He was impressed by the weakness revealed by the Economic Advisory Council and argued for a Cabinet of no more than eight, relieved of all detailed administrative work. The Foreign Office was to be amalgamated with the Dominions and Colonial Offices into a Ministry of Overseas Affairs, with Under Secretaries, each enjoying a higher rank than existing Junior Ministers, for the three main departments. The Ministry of Labour was to disappear, its responsibility for the enforcement of laws and regulations being trans-

Bevin's first thought on getting back to London from Gateshead was to intensify the work which they had begun. He wrote to Cole on 31st October:

"I feel convinced that the S.S.I.P.'s great opportunity has come . . .
"There is no deception like self-deception, and in the mining constituencies we have certainly been deceiving ourselves. They are absolutely fed up . . . with the talk of nationalisation over so many years. In addition the young men who came out for the Tories were far in advance of ours; there is no doubt about it, we have been living in a fool's paradise."[1]

Bevin had co-operated with Cole in producing a pamphlet, *The Crisis*, drafted by Cole and setting out the views which the two men shared on the character of the financial crisis and the measures which could be taken to solve it. Written with that lucidity which made Cole one of the outstanding university teachers of his time, *The Crisis* cast into more systematic form many of the criticisms Bevin and he made of the Labour Government's policy and is still worth reading for its analysis of 1931 on the economic side. It was published by the *New Statesman* with Bevin's as well as Cole's name on the cover and sold well. The S.S.I.P. was encouraged to press on with the publication of other pamphlets. Its other activities were setting up branches to act as study and discussion groups and organising lectures. Bevin himself gave the second in a series of six Sunday-night lectures in Transport House, to which Lansbury, A. L. Rowse, Frank Wise and J. M. Keynes also contributed.

Bevin took as his subject "The Election and the Trade Union Movement". His argument showed how far he had travelled since the mid-1920s:

"Every trade unionist knows the best investments we have made have been in political effort; every social development following it has been more effective than that gained in individual wage troubles."

ferred to the Home Office and its industrial side to a new Ministry of Commerce and Industry, covering home and overseas trade as well as agriculture and fisheries. The three other members of the Cabinet, besides these three Ministers, the Prime Minister, and the Chancellor of the Exchequer would be responsible for (1) transport and power, including coal; (2) defence, with an Under Secretary for each of the three services, and (3) health, education and local government, a combined Ministry of Social Development. Bevin attached great importance to adequate statistics and wanted a Central Statistical Office to be set up, directly responsible, together with economic planning and research offices, to the Prime Minister.
1 Ernest Bevin to G. D. H. Cole, 31st October 1931.

He did not conceal his opinion that it was thanks to the solidarity of the trade unions that the Party had not split in the present crisis, and he gave an assurance that the unions, far from relaxing their political effort, would be more ready than they had been in the past few years to help the Labour Party, especially in the work of political education.[1]

He returned to the same theme in talking to his Executive Council:

"One important thing revealed in this election is the need for more intense educational work on the part of the Labour Party. . . . A vote based purely on discontent is a very unreliable thing. Therefore, we must consider the taking of steps by literature, by meetings and by the spread of knowledge in every possible way in order to get the principles of socialism more deeply rooted in the hearts of the people . . .

"It is unwise to rely upon a violent swing back of the pendulum, because that may only come as the result of discontent with the policy of the Government and it will just as surely swing back again so soon as we begin to introduce the socialist policy unless we educate the people in the manner I have indicated. There is nothing for it but grim, determined effort and intensive and continuous educational work."[2]

Bevin's instinct was sound, but it was to take longer than he or any of the other Labour leaders realised before they were able to overcome the defeat of 1931 and win a solid majority for a Socialist Administration.

1 From a verbatim report circulated by the Information Department of the T.G.W.U. A shortened version was reprinted in the *Labour Magazine* for December 1931.
2 General Secretary's Quarterly Report, November 1931.

CHAPTER 19

Intellectuals, Busmen – and Hitler

1932 – 1933

I

LABOUR'S DEFEAT at the 1931 election was at once followed by a series of demands from the employers for a reduction of wages. Strikes were out of the question, but by skilful negotiation Bevin succeeded in every case in scaling the reductions down below the figure presented by the employers.[1] Each negotiation represented a long-drawn-out engagement and was the first charge on Bevin's time that winter.

The Gateshead Labour Party was anxious to adopt him as its candidate for the next election but he refused. All his energies were needed to hold the Union together and to defend its members' interests. Unemployment remained high, just under three millions from August 1931 to January 1933, when it reached the peak figure of 2,955,000. This was reflected in falling income from the branches, a steady drain in membership and an insidious atmosphere of defeatism. In 1932-33, trade-union membership reached its lowest point between the wars, little more than half the strength it had mustered in 1920.

There seemed no end to the trade depression; many young men growing up in the depressed areas had never been employed at all and lived entirely on the dole; the will to fight against their conditions had been sapped; there was little faith left in either political or industrial action, indeed in any form of action at all. It was the

---

[1] For example, the dock employers demanded a reduction of 2/- per day: Bevin got them to accept a reduction of 10d.

recognition of this mood which led Bevin to lay so much stress on educational work.

The claims of the Union left him little time to spare for the S.S.I.P. in the first half of 1932. To his regret, he had to give up the place which Cole wanted him to take on a Fabian visit to Russia, but he kept in touch and presided at the annual meeting of the S.S.I.P. on 28th May. In his presidential address, he attacked the habit of adopting slogans. To say that Capitalism was breaking down might be a comforting thought, but it was not true: Capitalism was adjusting itself far more rapidly than many people in the Labour movement imagined. The view that its breakdown was inevitable was the product of intellectual inertia. They had to think about the problems with which they were confronted instead of repeating slogans.[1]

For a long time he had been looking for an opportunity to start a weekly paper, designed to put the case for Socialism to working-class readers. He wanted a paper which would have to accept none of the compromises with popular taste which the *Herald* had to make, a paper avowedly Socialist in character and political in purpose, but dealing with social and economic problems in language that would attract the serious-minded trade-unionist, a Plain Man's *New Statesman*.

The Clarion, which Robert Blatchford had once made a powerful vehicle of Socialist propaganda with great influence on young working men of Bevin's generation, was in low water, and Bevin persuaded the Victoria Printing House Company to purchase it. The General Council agreed to invest £2,000, a new company was formed, of which Bevin became chairman, and the first number of *The New Clarion* appeared on 11th June 1932 at the price of twopence.

Bevin was eager for the new weekly to fulfil the same role as Blatchford's *Clarion* in his own day. A recruiting campaign was started for the Clarion Fellowship and the Clarion Cycling Clubs, and he went to a lot of trouble to get the best-known of the Socialist intellectuals as well as trade-union and Party leaders to contribute to it.[2] Bevin took care to keep himself in the background. Most of his

1 28th May 1932, reported in *The Record*, June 1932, p. 329.
2 In the course of the twenty-one months for which the *New Clarion* maintained an independent existence, Harold Laski contributed twenty-seven articles, Cole, Brailsford and A. L. Rowse some twenty each. Cole's contributions included a

own contributions were anonymous, but he wrote innumerable letters to trade-union and Labour Party branches asking for their support, begged money to keep the paper going, pestered his friends to write for it, held regular editorial conferences in his offices, and did everything he could to make the paper a success. To his great disappointment he failed. Although *The New Clarion* reached a circulation of 35,000, it fell short of the 60,000 necessary to avoid a loss. Like so many Labour publications, it lacked liveliness, but it was also the worst possible time to start a new venture in the precarious field of weekly journalism and after two years' persistent efforts, Bevin admitted defeat, negotiating the sale of the paper to Odhams.

2

In April 1932, Bevin took part in the sixteenth session of the I.L.O., and helped to revise the technical provisions of the 1929 Convention on the prevention of accidents in docks.

He went back to Geneva in January 1933 for a preparatory conference called by the I.L.O. to discuss the possibility of a convention on the reduction of hours of work. This was a proposal which strongly appealed to Bevin. He believed that, in the long run, industrial development must depend upon the willingness of both management and labour to accept a shorter working week: this was the only way in which to absorb technological progress without unemployment. But he also took the view that a reduction in hours ought not to be accompanied by a reduction in wages: if that happened, the worker would lose any share in the benefits of mechanisation.

The 1933 conference could do no more than open up the question. There was determined opposition from the employers, and the workers' representatives from other countries were afraid that too strong an insistence on the question of wages might destroy any hope of securing a convention in favour of reducing hours. Led by

series of twelve on outlines of Socialist policy which was later reprinted as a pamphlet. Others who wrote regularly for the paper included Lansbury, Frank Wise, Stafford Cripps, Morrison, Citrine, H. E. Bates and Phyllis Bentley on books, and John Grierson on films.

Bevin, the T.U.C. delegation refused to retreat in advance and Bevin was chosen to speak on behalf of the whole Workers' Group at the conference.

"The crux of the question," he argued, "is this. If poverty or unemployment were bred from famine, I could understand the employers' speeches, but poverty is bred now from a plethora. The world is suffering from too much, not from too little . . .

"It is said that you cannot enforce [such a convention]. . . . But you can establish international cartels and if you can establish cartels why cannot the basis of agreement be labour conditions as well as finance or spheres of influence? . . .

"In fact it will not increase costs of production. History is against the employers on this point. I well remember when the minimum wage legislation was introduced into our country. Every employer said it would increase the cost of production and destroy the industries to which it was applied. I challenge them to deny that every industry which was brought under the minimum wage conditions and the regulation of hours was more prosperous afterwards than it was under the old laisser-faire conditions which existed before."

Refusing to weaken the provision that wages should be maintained while hours were reduced, Bevin roundly declared:

"The workers are as close to the bone as they can get. I am going to be no party to admitting that the working classes have anything further to spare to contribute to a solution of our present economic conditions. They have been driven down both on their social services and on their wages during the last two years. They have made their contribution in advance and therefore the standard of living as expressed by wages must be maintained.

"My last word is this. Mr. Forbes Watson[1] said in his speech: 'Hope deferred maketh the heart sick.' Yes, but the sickness may take a course that is bad for Western Civilisation. A negative attitude means that the workers are driven to despair because there is no response to their request to get them out of the morass which they now find themselves in through no fault of their own. I would answer the proverb of Mr. Forbes Watson by a couplet

" 'Ill fares the land, to hastening ills a prey,
Where wealth accumulates and men decay.' "[2]

Bevin failed to secure a majority for the T.U.C.'s specific resolution safeguarding wages, but it was agreed to start work on a draft convention, and by the time Bevin attended his next I.L.O.

1 The British employers' spokesman.
2 *The Record*, February 1933, pp. 208–10.

conference in the summer of 1935 this was ready for further discussion.[1]

3

During the summer of 1932, Bevin made another journey abroad which left a deep impression on him. The occasion was the biennial conference of the International Transport Workers' Federation held in Prague.

The main business of the congress, as usual, was concerned with the international regulation of working conditions. Bevin took a full part in these discussions as chairman of the dockers' and of the motor drivers' trade conferences. But the controversial topics were political. The Federation Council had rejected a Czech proposal that a delegation should be sent to the Soviet Union to study conditions and establish relations with Russian transport workers. Bevin, who had not been present at the Council meeting when this decision was taken, described it as reactionary and called for its reversal.

"Whatever our views may be regarding the admission of the Russians to the I.T.F., there can be no doubt that the Russians have an entirely new economic philosophy, a philosophy which is in direct conflict with the rest of the world. What the General Council proposes is an ostrich policy, a policy of self-delusion by not studying the situation in Russia.
"The map of the world is being re-drawn . . . I can quite understand the Russians fighting for the world revolution, I can understand their difficulties, for they believe it to be incumbent upon them to defend their new economic system. . . . We are here dealing with an actual living instance of superhuman effort to rebuild a state on socialistic lines. Whether this is being done in a satisfactory manner is a matter about which the international labour movement should be well-informed."[2]

Bevin's plea for an open mind about the Communist experiment in Russia made little impression on men who had to face the bitter Communist attacks in the working-class movements of Central Europe and his motion was heavily defeated.

What impressed Bevin most, however, was not the congress but its

1 See below, pp. 575–6.
2 Proceedings of the I.T.F. Congress, Prague, 7th–13th August 1931, pp. 292–3.

setting. Central Europe in the summer of 1932 was on the edge of disaster, and the events of the next few years in Germany, Austria and Czechoslovakia already cast their menacing shadow before them. On his return to London, he reported to his Executive Council:

"The position in Germany is rapidly approaching one of civil war. Outside the *Volkhaus* in one of the towns we saw armed Social Democrats acting as pickets with other members of the Party inside also fully armed protecting their property against the Hitlerites and the Communists. . . . What is even more alarming is the war fever which is developing in Middle Europe. I sat in a middle-class café, the kind which in this country would cater for the civil servant and the small shop keeper, and when the band played a military march, the way the people rose and cheered, one would have imagined that war was being declared that night. This indicates the development of a very dangerous spirit. . . . As far as I could see, the workers of the European countries have little opposition left in them."[1]

Towards the end of November 1932, Bevin presided over an I.T.F. conference in Antwerp, summoned to consider ways of helping the dockers and seamen in Continental countries, and particularly in Germany, where they were faced with drastic cuts in wages. For the first time, to Bevin's satisfaction, a delegation of the National Union of Seamen was present and the threat of international action by the I.T.F. helped to stave off the attack on wages. His meeting with the German transport workers' leaders gave Bevin some insight into the precariousness of the German trade unions' position between the Communists and Hitler. Their fate when Hitler came to power two months later impressed him all the more sharply and was a major influence in rousing him to the dangers of Nazism and dictatorship.

4

The Economic Committee had now become the most important of the T.U.C. General Council's committees and Bevin spent a good deal of time with Milne-Bailey, its secretary, working over the reports which the Committee submitted to the General Council and the annual congress.

[1] General Secretary's Quarterly Report, August 1932.

As declarations of policy these had little effect; the real value of the Committee's work was in educating its own members and at second remove the other members of the General Council in the discussion of economic problems. Amongst the reports which the Committee drew up in 1932, *Tariffs and World Trade*[1] carried out the instructions of the Bristol T.U.C. to make a thorough investigation of fiscal policy, a subject on which trade-union opinion and trade-union interests were much divided. The Committee reached the unexciting conclusion that no general principles could be laid down and each case must be judged on its merits.

The admirable objectivity of their report, however, roused little enthusiasm at the 1932 Trades Union Congress, and Bevin's well-reasoned speech in defence of it failed to convince the critics who demanded a slashing attack on the Government for its abandonment of Free Trade in the Ottawa Agreements.

Another subject to be investigated by the Economic Committee was the public control of industry and trade. In the most radical of its reports, the Committee spoke rather slightingly of 'old-fashioned' Socialist notions of industries run directly by the State and came out strongly in favour of public corporations such as the Labour Government had proposed in the London Passenger Transport Bill. More than that, the report pronounced firmly in favour of Morrison's view[2] on the composition of the boards of public corporations. Bevin alone entered a strong protest which was circulated to the other members of the Committee.[3] He withdrew none of the Union's criticism of Morrison's London Transport Bill. "It is in our view positively the worst form of public control. We desire municipal control." Bevin found himself, however, in a minority of one on the Committee and the General Council adopted the report over his opposition.

The 1932 Trades Union Congress at Newcastle was a depressing affair. Apart from his speech introducing the Economic Committee's report on tariffs, Bevin took the lead in launching the fund to support the Lancashire cotton workers in a strike against reductions in wages, but even he could only raise £59,000 in place of

1 Published as a separate pamphlet.
2 Herbert Morrison as well as Hugh Dalton attended the meetings of the Economic Committee in 1931–2 as representatives of the Labour Party.
3 Dated 21st December 1931.

the £500,000 for which he called. The one other item to bring him to his feet was a Communist-inspired motion drawing attention to the dangers in the Far East (where Japan had begun her attack on China) and calling on the workers

"to smash the war plans of world imperialists by stopping the production and transport of munitions."

The facile phrases were too much for Bevin's sense of reality: it was an impracticable proposal and the dockers would have nothing to do with it.

"Why lead the British public—who have the power to put an end to this business together with the democracies of other parts of the world—to believe that we are ready to accept the responsibility for their apathy, their indifference, their toryism, and their opposition to us when we are advocating disarmament and peace? I have heard the non-unionist say: 'Why don't the dockers hold up munitions?' while he is looking for a job to make them. I do not want to be cynical. I hate war and all that it represents. I will do everything I can to end it, but I am not going to be a party to accepting a responsibility that I cannot carry out. There has been too much of that in the trade union movement and too much said afterwards as to how we led them up the garden. This resolution will, if it is adopted, cause more deception than anything else."[1]

The resolution was not even put to the vote.

It was not until the following year, after Hitler's rise to power and suppression of the German trade-union movement, that foreign affairs began to play a major part in T.U.C. debates. The 1932 conference, however, heard a report from the General Council on the reorganisation of a body through which Bevin and the trade unions were to make their biggest contribution to shaping the foreign policy of the Labour movement. This was the National Joint Council, later known as the National Council of Labour.

One of the obvious lessons to be drawn from the events of 1931 was the need for much closer understanding between the Labour Party and the T.U.C. This was accepted by both sides. The Labour Party, for instance, was invited to nominate two members of its Executive to attend the meetings of the T.U.C. Economic Committee. In the winter of 1931–32 proposals for reconstituting the

1 T.U.C. Report 1932, p. 364.

National Joint Council were adopted and a T.U.C. memorandum on the revision of its functions largely accepted. The Parliamentary Labour Party, as well as the National Executive of the Labour Party, was brought in, each sending its chairman and two other members to meet the chairman and six members of the General Council at least once a month. The size of the trade-union representation is striking. The chairman of the National Executive and the chairman of the General Council took it in turns to preside.

Bevin was not at first a member, but he was strongly pressed by Arthur Henderson to serve and took his place as one of the General Council's representatives after the Newcastle T.U.C. During the course of the 1930s, the National Council became the most authoritative body in the Labour movement in formulating policy, especially on foreign affairs, and was the main vehicle—besides the annual party conference—through which Bevin was able to influence the Labour Party's policy on foreign affairs and defence.

5

Unlike the Newcastle Trades Union Congress, the Labour Party conference at Leicester (October 1932) was far from being dull. Leicester was not a popular choice of meeting-place and the delegates showed themselves to be in a critical and difficult mood.

The Leicester conference had been preceded by a special conference of the I.L.P. at Bradford where the decision was taken to disaffiliate from the Labour Party and turn the I.L.P. into a militant left-wing Socialist party, uncompromised by the gradualist policies of Transport House. Not all the I.L.P. members agreed with the decision to break away and a substantial minority, led by Frank Wise, left the I.L.P., preferring to criticise Labour policy from inside rather than outside the Party. Wise's group formed the nucleus of the Socialist League (which was founded at the Leicester Conference) and contributed forcefully to the opposition which the platform encountered from the floor throughout the proceedings.

The mood of the conference was set by a resolution moved from the floor by Sir Charles Trevelyan which instructed the next Labour Government, with or without a majority in the House of Commons, to promulgate definite Socialist legislation immediately on entering office and to stand or fall by its principles. The delegates refused to listen to Henderson's plea not to tie the next Labour Government's hands and carried Trevelyan's motion without even a demand for a card vote.

The main business of the conference was to receive the first four reports prepared by a Policy Committee of the Executive which had been given the job of working out Party policy in detail after the 1931 defeat. The first, on currency and finance, was introduced in a series of resolutions by Hugh Dalton. Its proposals followed the lines along which Bevin, among others, had been thinking for some time: price stabilisation as an alternative to the gold standard; public ownership and control of the Bank of England; a National Investment Board. It omitted, however, any mention of nationalising the joint stock banks, a project on which the Executive had not yet reached a conclusion. This omission was challenged by Frank Wise, lately of the I.L.P., who moved an amendment to take over other banks as well as the Bank of England.

Bevin at once opposed him: it was impracticable and unnecessary. The worst course was for the Party to be carried away by rhetoric and persuaded to undertake commitments which it could not carry out: this had happened with the capital levy, added to the Party programme by the enthusiasts, only to be dropped later with equal irresponsibility. Putting himself in the position of the man who had to take over the control of credit, Bevin declared:

"Give me control of the Bank of England and I will not want to tinker with the out-of-date Joint Stock system which has been devised on capitalist methods. . . . We have to evolve new men, new techniques right from the foundation. . . . When I get the source I can create an entirely new machine of my own making to give effect to your policy."[1]

But the power of slogans over the delegates' minds was not so easily broken. Bevin heard himself described by one delegate as steeped in financial orthodoxy and likened to Philip Snowden. Stafford Cripps, making his first appearance as the prophet of un-compromising revolutionary virtue, turned the issue into one of seizing power or temporising with the capitalists and swept off on an emotional appeal to principle. Once its suspicions of compromise on the part of the platform had been aroused, a majority of the con-

1 Labour Party Conference Report 1932, pp. 190–1.

ference refused to listen to reasoned argument, and, to Bevin's anger, carried Wise's amendment by a narrow majority.

It fell to Herbert Morrison to move the adoption of the next two reports, on the national planning of transport and electricity. This time Bevin was on the other side of the fence. He did not intervene himself until the end of the debate, leaving it to Harold Clay to voice the Union's opposition. Clay did not attack the proposal to set up a National Transport and a National Electricity Board; he fastened on the point which had been at issue between Morrison and the Transport and General Workers' ever since the introduction of the Labour Government's London Transport Bill, the composition of the Boards.

The Executive's report repeated Morrison's thesis, that the only criterion in appointment to any public board should be ability, without the direct representation of Labour or any other interest. In other words, Clay argued, the workers were to remain shut out from power and responsibility; control was to be vested in the hands of an efficient bureaucracy without effective public control, a paternal bureaucracy, no doubt, ready to 'consult' the workers, but not to treat them as anything other than workers whose interests were limited to wages and hours. "I believe in political democracy," Clay added, "but I don't believe that can become complete until you have industrial democracy."[1]

Clay's speech impressed the conference, so much so that Morrison did not attempt to reply to the debate but offered to withdraw the controversial part of the report for further discussion without putting it to a vote. Only, Bevin agreed, if the whole question of workers' control was taken up again and not simply the particular amendment moved by Clay—an amendment, he added, which the Union had felt forced to table "because in our view Mr. Morrison was determined to force his point of view through".

Bevin's antagonism towards Morrison was unconcealed. None the less, it is a mistake to treat this as simply a personal issue between the two men, although it had a lasting effect on the relations between them. Socialism to Bevin meant something more than planning and public ownership; it meant a change in the status of the worker, the end of that exclusion from responsibility, the stigma of inferiority, which he had always regarded as the key to im-

1 Ibid., pp. 214–5.

proving industrial relations.[1] In this he was expressing much more than a personal opinion or the views of his own union. As the later course of the dispute shows, even when Bevin was prepared to accept a compromise which conceded the substance of his claim, the opposition was strong enough to defeat it at the Labour Party conference of 1933 and to override Bevin as well as Morrison. To anyone who follows the subsequent history of nationalisation after the war it may well appear that 'workers' control' has remained the most intractable problem of all in the Socialist reorganisation of industry.

6

On the Sunday before the Labour Party conference opened, the Socialist League held its inaugural meeting in the Leicester Co-operative Hall. The initiative came from Frank Wise and the breakaway group from the I.L.P. and it placed Cole and the Executive of the S.S.I.P. in a dilemma. Should they merge with the new body or not? Bevin did not oppose amalgamation—he even suggested including the remnant of the old Social Democratic Federation—but he distrusted the ex-I.L.P. members and took no part in the negotiations. The S.S.I.P. representatives, in fact, were outmanœuvred from the beginning and had to accept the terms dictated by Wise or risk losing half their members to the new organisation.

Their efforts to retain Bevin as chairman of the new body failed completely. The ex-I.L.P. members were determined to have Frank Wise and refused to accept Bevin in any office at all. Rather than see the negotiations break down, the S.S.I.P. representatives agreed.

Cole later wrote: "I regarded it as indispensable to carry Bevin into the new body, as the outstanding trade union figure capable of rallying trade union opinion behind it. . . . On this personal issue the negotiations very nearly broke down and I heartily wish they had."[2] In fact, the old antagonism between trade-union leaders and the I.L.P. rapidly reproduced itself with the Socialist League. Cole himself soon admitted his mistake and resigned, but the effect of the episode on Bevin was more permanent. It confirmed all his old prejudices. His genuine attempt to work with the intellectuals of the

1 Cf., his remarks at the Penscot conference in 1917, c. 4 above.
2 G. D. H. Cole: *A History of the Labour Party from 1914*, p. 284.

Party had ended, through no fault of his (nor, it must be added, of Cole's), in a rebuff.

When Cole invited him to become a vice-chairman of the New Fabian Research Bureau, which remained outside the amalgamation, he replied:

"I have decided to take no office at all outside of those I already hold and those within the Union. I think it better I should stick to my last."[1]

7

In the early months of 1933 *The New Clarion* published a series of articles by Bevin which were later reprinted as a pamphlet under the title: *My Plan for 2,000,000 Workers*. In these he elaborated the proposals for dealing with unemployment which he had consistently advocated since the Mond-Turner talks.

He began from the premise that, even if trade recovered, technological progress and the concentration of industry would make it difficult, if not impossible, to absorb the 2–3 million men and women who had been unemployed since 1929. The only prospect which the Chancellor of the Exchequer (Neville Chamberlain) had held out in a recent speech was the gradual reduction of the figure over a period of ten years. Writing as a trade-union leader, not as a Socialist, and appealing to men of good will in all parties, Bevin argued that it was both wrong and unnecessary to accept the continuation of so grave a social evil in a fatalistic spirit without making as determined efforts to tackle it as those which had eliminated slavery and child labour. He made five concrete proposals, each of which would release jobs for the most vigorous age-groups in the population, those between 16 and 60.

The first was to pay a State pension of £1 a week (35s. for a married couple) at the age of 65 to everyone earning up to £1,000 p.a. on the sole condition that they retired from paid work.

The second was to offer an optional pension at the age of 60 on the same condition.

The third was to provide invalidity pensions of 30s. a week for those who, as a result of war wounds, sickness or some industrial

1 Ernest Bevin to G. D. H. Cole, 29th September 1932.

accident, were physically unfit to follow a trade or undergo training. Provision for these three categories, at a conservative estimate, would release 600,000 jobs for younger and fitter men. The raising of the school-leaving age to 16, Bevin calculated, would free another 560,000 jobs held by youngsters who were paid inadequate wages and were liable to be dismissed once they asked for an increase.

Finally, following the discussion at the I.L.O. conference, Bevin proposed a forty-hour week, which he calculated would bring the total reduction up to more than two million.

Bevin did not pretend that his figures were exact, although Colin Clark, at that time a lecturer in statistics at Cambridge, examined them in a separate appendix and underwrote them as a conservative estimate. Nor did he present his proposals as a cure for unemployment: that, he remained convinced, could only be secured by organising the economy on a Socialist basis. His argument was that by practical measures of this kind, capable of being put into effect quickly, it was possible to reduce the scale of the problem to manageable proportions leaving a much smaller number of men to be absorbed by the development of new industries and a programme of public works. Once the labour pool had been reduced by the measures he proposed and the unemployable largely removed from it, a National Employment Board should advise the Government on the proportion private industry could absorb and the proportion for which the State would have to find employment.

Bevin put the annual cost to the State of adopting a comprehensive pensions scheme and raising the school-leaving age at a round £80 million. Against this could be set the savings in reduced unemployment benefit and poor law assistance, estimated at £50 million a year. That was on the assumption that the entire cost of the pensions scheme was to be met, as Bevin believed it should be, out of taxation. If necessary, however, he agreed that the pensions could be financed by a contributory scheme which would reduce the extra burden on the Exchequer from £80 million to £44 million a year.

The cost seemed small by comparison with the gain of making a determined attack on the insidious demoralisation of unemployment. Bevin sent a copy of his pamphlet to every Member of Parliament and newspaper editor; comment was surprisingly favourable and questions were asked in the House of Commons, eliciting the hackneyed promise to 'look further' into the proposals. But nothing happened. As Bevin pointed out in his pamphlet, when it was a question of drastic cuts to save the pound, the May Committee found it possible to make up their minds with great promptitude, but when it came to making decisions of the sort Bevin proposed, every conceivable objection was raised. The truth was that a majority of people in the country had come to accept a high rate of unemployment as inevitable and shut their eyes or shrugged their shoulders at the human waste and economic burden it involved. In the long run, it would have cost less to finance positive measures to promote employment than to continue paying out millions in a dole which did nothing to create work but only increased demoralisation and apathy. It was not the money that was lacking, but the will. Bevin's proposals, like so many others, fell to the ground because they required an effort of imagination and will which was beyond the sluggish mood of the nation and its leadership in the 1930s.

Against this mood which preferred to evade clear-cut issues and postpone decisions both in domestic and foreign affairs, Bevin's energetic temperament—like Churchill's—beat in vain. It was not dispelled until the crisis of 1940 created a new mood in which the radical changes of the 1940s, a decade of decisions in home as well as in foreign affairs, became possible.

8

When Bevin spoke of unemployment and the price the nation was paying for it, he knew what he was talking about. No one had a greater first-hand knowledge of industrial Britain in the Depression: the empty dockside streets with the little knots of men drifting away from the calling-on stands; the silent pits, with the miners squatting on their heels against the walls of the labour exchange; the shabby industrial towns of the North and Midlands, the dirty, crowded tenements of working-class London, with the ragged, sallow-faced children playing in the courts. This was Bevin's England, and what he saw made him angry and sick at heart.

During 1932 and 1933 he travelled continually up and down the country. His object was to meet branch members, to put fresh heart into the Union's officials, taking up their grievances, throwing himself into local negotiations, trying by his personal exertions to stem the tide of falling membership and falling income.

At times even he despaired. He reported to his Executive Council in August 1932:

"With unemployment steadily rising in the summer months, when normally we would expect a decline, the outlook for the coming winter is extremely black . . .

"I shall be very much surprised if, in the Docks section, in shipping and possibly in engineering, another round of attacks is not launched early in the New Year. If this be the case, I feel that whatever happens, whether we are smashed or not, we must throw all into the fight and lead the upheaval. This is the deliberate conclusion I have come to."[1]

There was a small minority in the Union which attacked Bevin and the other national officers for not putting up more of a fight and who argued that a greater display of militancy, at least in industries where the Union had a high percentage of membership, would produce greater results. This dispute was fought out in the London bus section, which, in the 1930s, took the place of the Docks Group in earlier years as the storm centre of the Union.

Why the London busmen should be one of the most militant industrial groups in the country is not, at first sight, easily explained. They suffered little from unemployment or the effect of the Depression; their average earnings were comparatively high; the London General Omnibus Company and its successor, the London Passenger Transport Board, were good employers and their conditions of work were better than in many industries. They comprised, however, a compact body of 20,000 men, highly organised in garage branches, with a strong sense of group solidarity and an equally strong tradition of industrial democracy which brought them into frequent collision not only with the company but with the Union's leadership.

From the first, the London busmen had been one of the most difficult groups to fit into the amalgamation. They did not regard themselves as part of the national passenger transport industry and were not content with the normal machinery of the national trade group. They pressed for and were conceded[2] a greater measure of self-determination through an elected Central London Area Bus

1 General Secretary's Quarterly Report, August 1932.
2 By the Anderton's Hotel Agreement. See above, pp. 192-3.

Committee which enjoyed the functions of a national trade group committee with its own full-time secretary and the right of direct access to the General Executive Council. This special machinery was used to the full. More delegate conferences were called in the London bus section, and the Executive Council spent more time in dealing with the affairs of its 20,000 members, than was the case with any other section in the Union.

The first trial of strength between Bevin and his critics came in 1932. At the beginning of that year the London General Omnibus Company proposed reductions in the busmen's wages on the grounds of falling revenue. Bevin fought a delaying action until July but he was not able to persuade the company to abandon either the proposed cut in wages or the dismissal of 800 employees who were declared to be redundant.

When the new terms to be laid before the men became known, there were vigorous protests. The lead was taken by Bert Papworth, the fiery secretary of the Chelverton Road branch who had recently received the Union's silver medal for recruiting 170 new members. He invited branch delegates to an unofficial meeting at which there was much criticism of Bevin and the decision was taken to set up a Provisional Committee of Garage Delegates, soon known as the Rank and File Committee. The Committee organised a series of unofficial mass meetings and received enthusiastic support from the *Daily Worker* and the Communists. A ballot by the Central Bus Committee produced a vote of 16,000 to 4,000 against the new agreement proposed by the Company and an official delegate conference demanded that the General Executive should authorise strike action.

Faced with this revolt, Bevin set to work to cut the ground from under the unofficial committee's feet by re-opening the negotiations. He persuaded the Company to abandon its claim to wage reductions, to cut the maximum working time from 9 to 8 hours and to guarantee that there would be no dismissals on the introduction of the new and faster schedules. This agreement was approved by a delegate conference and signed on 23rd September.

Outmanœuvred by Bevin, the Rank and File Committee continued its attacks on him, claiming—with some justice—the credit for the improvement in the new agreement. The *Daily Worker* published an article accusing Bevin and the other Union officials of acting as the agents of the Company against the interests of the men.[1] On 5th October, another unofficial conference called by the Committee decided to put the Rank and File Movement on a permanent basis, setting up committees in 'affiliated' garages. The Committee took over *Busman's Punch*, a paper run by a Communist group at Holloway garage. Their policy was not to form a break-away union but to stay inside the T.G.W.U. in order to fight attacks on wages and conditions and to oppose any 'weakness' on the part of the Union's leadership.

The next clash was not long in coming. In January 1933, the Forest Gate garage went on strike in protest against a schedule change accepted by the Union. The Rank and File Committee took the lead and within three days had brought out 20 to 30 garages with a threat of sympathetic activity by the Underground railway workers at Morden. The Central Bus Committee refused to recognise the strike but received a deputation from the Rank and File Committee. Immediate negotiations were promised and on this understanding the men returned to work. The Rank and File leaders claimed another victory for militancy, came out for a 7-hour day and won ten out of thirteen places in the delegation elected to represent the busmen at the Biennial Delegate Conference due to be held at Cambridge in July.

9

From the moment the Conference opened, it was clear that the London bus delegates meant to force a show-down with Bevin. When Bevin put forward his plan for reducing unemployment at the first session, one of their leaders, Frank Snelling declared:

"There is no solution to unemployment and we should stop talking of these damn reforms which have no meaning . . . I suggest, Brothers, that you turn this scheme down as impracticable. . . . What the hell do the bosses' problems matter to us? We should be doing everything in our power to help the day when capitalism will be overthrown."[2]

1 Bevin brought a libel action against the *Daily Worker* for this article. He was awarded £7,000 damages, but, as he had expected, proved unable to collect a penny and was £500 out of pocket after he had met the expenses of the case.

2 Verbatim typescript record of the Biennial Delegate Conference, Cambridge, 10th–14th July 1933.

The old charge of 'Mondism' was revived and Bevin accused of not even paying lip-service to Socialism. The attack was continued in the debate on a united front against Fascism, in which Papworth defended a routine Communist resolution, and another London delegate attacked Bevin and the T.U.C. for failing to stand up to Fascism.

The big debate came on the second day. Much time was taken up in recriminations about the events of the past summer and the unofficial strike in January, but the real issue between Bevin, the Executive and the other officials on the one hand and the Rank and File Committee on the other went much further than Bevin's original failure to secure better terms from the bus company on this particular occasion.

Frank Snelling, the chairman of the Rank and File Committee, asked why they insisted on keeping their organisation in being after this particular dispute was over. Because, he answered, they distrusted the officials and disagreed with the reformist policy which they and the Executive were pressing. They felt it necessary to set up a vigilance committee. The Rank and File Movement, he claimed, was the spontaneous expression of discontent and of a demand for a more aggressive policy on the part of the men. "It is only by continued combat with the boss class that you can do any good."

It was not the Rank and File Committee's militancy to which Bevin took exception; as he pointed out, there was hardly a man in the conference who had not at one time or another taken part in an unofficial strike and attacked trade union leaders for their lack of courage. He welcomed a more militant and critical spirit as a sign of health far preferable to apathy. What he objected to was the artificial fostering of discontent by setting up a permanent 'counter-organisation' within the Union which deliberately worked to destroy confidence in the Union's leadership and policy.

Bevin was convinced that the Rank and File Committee was following the Communist line. The fact that only two members of the Committee at this time were open members of the Party—although others, including Bert Papworth, later joined it—does not prove him to have been wrong. At the beginning of 1932 the Communist Party had taken up the tactic of "the united front from below which in Britain meant attempting to win the local organisations of trade unionism for their policy, and so securing a base of operations against the existing union bureaucracy".[1] There is no doubt that the Rank and File Committee was in close touch with the Communist Party and received its enthusiastic support.

Bevin has been criticised for seeing Communists behind any expression of opposition to his leadership. The evidence does not bear this out. He did not, for instance, accuse the breakaway movement in the Glasgow docks of acting under Communist inspiration, and he refused to implement the General Council's advice to ùnions in 1934 to alter their rules in such a way as to prevent Communists from holding office. In the case of the London busmen, however, anyone who has read through the files of the *Daily Worker* and *Busman's Punch* and noted the identity of views and even of phraseology, not to speak of the prominent part played by Communists and Communist sympathisers in the Rank and File movement, will hardly be surprised that Bevin accused the Committee of acting in the interest of the Communist campaign to discredit the existing trade-union leadership.

But the charges and denials of Communist influence can easily obscure the real issue. For, even if the Communists had been in no way involved in the Rank and File movement, Bevin's attitude would still have been the same. If the London busmen wanted a more militant policy, he argued, the Union's constitution provided them with ample opportunity to put their demands forward and to control the action of the officials through the Central London Bus Committee, elected by the men, and through the frequent delegate conferences. There was no need for the unofficial, duplicate machinery of the Rank and File Committee, with its 'affiliated' garages, its self-appointed leaders and its own publications. Bevin drew a clear distinction between an unofficial strike committee set up in the heat of the moment, to be dissolved when the strike was over, and a permanent organisation, the only purpose of which could be, he contended, to promote an 'internal breakaway' of the London bus section, a secession which would enjoy all the advantages of remaining inside the organisation while repudiating either loyalty or obligations.

The only result of such an agitation, if it was not aimed, as Bevin believed, at the capture of power inside the Union by a Communist minority, must be to weaken the Union's power by undermining

1 Henry Pelling: *The British Communist Party* (1958), p. 71.

the authority of any leader to speak for the men. Bevin, however, did not press his advantage at the 1933 Conference where the Executive's report on the episode was adopted by 215 votes to 30 and where there was plain speaking by a number of delegates as well as by Bevin himself. The members of the Rank and File Committee were given a fair hearing and Bevin contented himself with carrying an amendment to the rules which committed any member taking office to accepting the constitution of the Union and working through its machinery. The Rank and File Committee continued its operations unabashed and Bevin showed marked patience in tolerating their activities, if only because he wanted to avoid a breakaway.

But, however reluctant he might be to run the risk of a split, he had no doubt that the principle he was defending was vital to the existence of the Union and of any form of organised trade-union power. After four years' further agitation he brought the issue to a head, broke up the dissident organisation inside the London bus section and at the cost of an unsuccessful attempt to organise a rival breakaway union, vindicated the authority and unity of the Union.

10

During the course of 1933, Bevin virtually completed the team of officers with which he conducted the affairs of the Union down to his appointment as Minister of Labour in 1940.

As national secretary of the General Workers' Group, the Executive appointed a man whose role in the history of the modern trade-union movement is second only to that of Ernest Bevin. Arthur Deakin, a steel-worker by trade, had joined the Dockers' Union in 1911, a year after Bevin. A full-time official from 1919, he showed great energy in building up the Union's membership in North Wales and attracted Bevin's attention. His appointment as a national secretary in his early forties was the turning-point of his career. Three years later, he became Assistant Secretary and in May 1940, took Bevin's place as Acting General Secretary. By 1955, when he died, he was incontestably the most powerful figure in the trade-union movement.

In the summer of 1933, John Cliff resigned the Assistant General

Secretaryship to join the newly constituted London Passenger Transport Board. Cliff had played a leading part in the organisation of the road passenger industry, but he and Bevin were temperamentally antipathetic to each other and relations between them had not been easy. Bevin made no move to fill Cliff's place for a couple of years, partly in order to cut down expenses. In the meantime, the list of national secretaries had been completed by the appointment (February 1932) of Andrew Dalgleish to a new Metal, Engineering and Chemical group. In the later 1930s this group expanded rapidly and gave the T.G.W.U. a powerful place in the engineering and motor-car industries, especially in the Midlands. By the outbreak of war it was larger than the docks group and by 1942 represented over one third of the total membership of the Union, 400,000, a larger membership than that of most individual unions.[1]

At the time of the Biennial Conference it was still too early to speak of expansion. The fall in membership, however, continuous since 1929, had been arrested. In 1932, Bevin had taken the drastic step of removing close on 40,000 names of lapsed members from the books of the Union, reducing its total numbers to 373,000. The gain in membership in 1933 itself was marginal, just under 6,000, and not until the following year was the drop in income checked. But thereafter numbers and income mounted rapidly in an unbroken curve.

The reason for choosing Cambridge as the meeting-place of the conference was the opportunity it gave of visiting the Union's Convalescent Home at Littleport, in the Isle of Ely. The Home had been one of the assets which Sam March's National Union of Vehicle Workers brought into the amalgamation and the Union was justifiably proud of it. In the eleven years since the amalgamation £50,000 had been raised by voluntary subscription among the Union members, 10,000 of whom had benefited by spending a period of convalescence there. The previous year, Bevin had opened a new wing and during the 1933 Conference, fourteen motor coaches conveyed the delegates and their wives from Cambridge to Littleport for a day's outing and inspection of the Home. Bevin was in his

---

1 The national group secretaries now were: Harold Clay (Road Passenger Transport); Jack Corrin (Road Commercial Transport); Arthur Deakin (General Workers); Andrew Dalgleish (Metal, Engineering and Chemical); Dan Milford (Docks and Waterways). In 1934, J. H. Pearmaine took Arthur Deakin's place when the latter became Assistant General Secretary.

element, delighting in the company of old friends and filled with pride at this visible proof of what the Union could do for its members.

I I

Events during 1933, however, had already taken a course which during the next few years was to overshadow Bevin's satisfaction with the Union he had created and to face him, in common with other members of the Labour movement, with difficult and unfamiliar problems.

Looking back, it is easy to see now that the winter of 1932–3 forms a watershed between the post-war period culminating in the Great Depression and the pre-war era of Hitler. Nobody at the time however, could guess that with the slight improvement of trade during the winter of 1932–3 the slow process of economic recovery had begun and that, from the advent to power of Hitler in January 1933 until his death in 1945, issues of foreign policy, defence and eventually of war would increasingly replace the economic and social questions which have played so large a part in the earlier chapters of this book.

Much of the politics of 1933–4 in this country was still concerned with the familiar issues—unemployment, economic policy, the illusory hopes placed on the World Economic Conference which met in July 1933 and the aftermath of the events of 1931. But alongside these there appeared for the first time problems which were to dominate the agenda of politics by the middle of the decade.

Hitler became Chancellor of Germany on 30th January 1933 and in the following months the full force of the Nazi revolution was unleashed with the authority of the State on its side. Bevin and the other trade-union leaders were among the first in this country to grasp and condemn the character of the new régime in Germany. The suppression of the German trade-union movement and the confiscation of its property and funds brought it home to them in a way that diplomatic moves or changes in the balance of power could never have done. The German trade-union movement was the most powerful in continental Europe, its leaders familiar acquaintances at every international trade-union conference. Overnight they were arrested, their offices occupied, their organisations dissolved, collective bargaining and the right to strike abolished. No trade unionist, Bevin wrote in an article for his own members,[1] could ask for a clearer illustration of what dictatorship meant and how it would affect him in his everyday life.

The Communists, whose bitter attacks on the Social Democrats in Germany had contributed materially to weaken the opposition to Hitler,[2] belatedly swung round and on instructions from Moscow began to call for a United Front against Fascism. Invitations to create a common organisation received from the British Communist Party and from the I.L.P. were rejected by both the T.U.C. and the National Executive of the Labour Party. Instead, the National Joint Council, on which Bevin now sat as a representative of the T.U.C. General Council, issued a blunt statement of its opposition to dictatorship, whether Nazi or Communist:[3]

"If the British working class hesitate now between majority and minority rule and toy with the idea of Dictatorship, Fascist or Communist, they will go down to servitude such as they have never suffered."

There was little the Labour movement could do at this time more than protest and draw attention to the brutalities of the Nazi régime. But this was important, for public opinion was slow to be aroused and remained sceptical that such things as were everyday occurrences in Hitler's Germany could happen in any civilised country. On the instruction of the General Council, its secretary, Walter Citrine, prepared a report on *Dictatorships and the Trade Union Movement* which examined the growth of dictatorships in post-war Europe with a grasp of detail and balanced judgment which are missing from many contemporary analyses. While recognising the differences between Nazism and Communism, the General Council held to its view that the principle of dictatorship was the same whether of the Right or of the Left and in either case inimical to freedom. The T.U.C. refused to let itself be panicked by Mosley's Fascists or confused by the sophistical arguments of the Left:

"There are some who deny that freedom can exist in a capitalist society. They regard it as a bourgeois institution of no real value to the people. It is

1 *The Record*, May 1933, pp. 304–6.
2 Cf., the present author's essay, in *The Third Reich* (London 1955): "The German Communists and the Rise of Hitler".
3 *Democracy and Dictatorship*, 24th March 1933.

not to disregard the disabilities of a wages system under capitalist control of industry, to point out that in Great Britain an individual normally possesses certain liberties that are worth preserving. The State has not yet the authority to shoot citizens without trial. Nor do people disappear at the hands of a secret police; nor is criticism of the Government a crime . . .
"Against the tyranny of Governments and a return to economic servitude the institutions of free citizenship and the organisations of democracy are our strongest safeguards. . . . The freedom and independence of the unions would not be worth a day's purchase if these safeguards were destroyed."[1]

In its opposition to dictatorship and its recognition of the danger represented by Hitler's and other Fascist movements, the T.U.C., under the leadership of men like Citrine and Bevin, was as solid as a rock. At this stage, however, the danger was still seen largely in terms of the repetition in other countries of what had happened in Germany and Italy, the overthrow of democracy by Fascist movements from within, not in terms of aggression and war. The Brighton T.U.C., for instance, saw nothing inconsistent in September 1933 in instructing the General Council to organise an intensive propaganda campaign against war preparations; at the same time as it censured Hitler's dictatorship; while at the Hastings Conference of the Labour Party which followed in October, Sir Charles Trevelyan moved, and Dalton on behalf of the National Executive accepted, a unanimous resolution to the same effect calling for a general strike if war were threatened. Few people, not only in the Labour movement, but in the country at large, had yet recognised the consequences in foreign policy and defence which were to follow from Hitler's rise to power.

12

During 1933, the Labour Party Executive pushed on with the re-drafting of the Party's programme and presented the result to the Hastings Conference at which a series of debates took place on the report, *Socialism and the Condition of the People*.

The issue of 'workers' control', or more precisely of trade-union representation on the boards of nationalised industries, had occupied both the T.U.C. Economic and the Labour Party Policy Committees during the early months of 1933. Bevin finally agreed to a com-

1 T.U.C. Report, 1933, Appendix C., p. 434.

Trade unionist and Socialist intellectual: Ernest Bevin and Stafford Cripps in the 1930s.

Above. Biennial Delegates' Conference of the T.G.W.U., Cambridge 1923. *Below.* The Labour Party Conference at Brighton 1935.

promise which gave the Transport and General Workers the sub-stance of their claim. This was passed by the T.U.C. at its Brighton Congress, but turned down by the Labour Party at Hastings a month later, in favour of an amendment moved by Charlie Dukes, of the General and Municipal Workers, which insisted on statutory guarantees of direct trade-union representation. Bevin spoke in favour of the compromise resolution (which he had drafted) but the conference preferred Dukes's more precise amendment and carried it on a card vote.

Apart from this particular question, Bevin took no part in re-drafting the Party programme and raised no objection in the Hastings debates, but he made an immediate and powerful inter-vention when Stafford Cripps attempted to commit the Party to seeking emergency powers if returned to power in order to overcome any opposition to the passage of fundamental Socialist legislation.

Cripps argued in favour of two steps as soon as a Labour Govern-ment was formed. The first was the abolition of the House of Lords; the second was the passage of an Emergency Powers Bill enabling the Government to act by decree subject to later confirmation by Parliament. This should be followed, he urged, by a reform of Parliamentary procedure, and by the carrying out of a legislative timetable for the introduction of Socialist measures agreed upon in advance.

For months before the Hastings Conference, Cripps had been arguing that the Labour Party could not expect to carry through-going Socialist measures, even with a majority in the House of Commons, without encountering determined opposition:

"We must face the fact that those who at present hold the economic power will refuse their support to any Labour Government.
"It will be necessary, therefore, for the people, if they desire to carry through drastic changes within a short period of time, to have at their disposal machinery of Government which is capable of rapid action."[1]

The Press leapt on Cripps' speeches and articles to represent the left wing of the Labour Party, led by the intellectuals of the Socialist League, as a revolutionary movement aiming at a Jacobin, if not a Communist, dictatorship with Cripps assuming the role of Robe-spierre. This might be a caricature, but however much Cripps

1 Cripps in the *Daily Herald*, 12th April 1933.

529   S

denied that he was advocating 'dictatorship', to Bevin and other trade-union leaders[1] it appeared certain that the logical conclusion of Cripps' campaign, if it succeeded, would be to create the political climate which Mussolini and Hitler had exploited to establish their own dictatorships. At the very least, his views were a heavy electoral handicap to a Labour Party struggling to regain support after the defeat of 1931.

Cripps' speech at Hastings was more moderate, but Bevin refused to take it at face value. He demanded to know what connection there was between Cripps' amendment and the much more sweeping articles which he and other members of the Socialist League had written.

"I do not think there ought to be a change between the platform here and the platform outside. . . . Do you mean that under certain circumstances the parliamentary machine is to go? . . .

"We are not going to jump out of the frying pan into the fire. We cannot forget the psychology and attitude of our own people. The British race is very peculiar: it will not go about threatening to 'thug' people, but it will defend itself when it is hit. And who is going to fire the first shot in this battle? Are we going forward with our measures and when our enemies attempt to sabotage them, *then* go out to our people with a rallying cry to see our measures through the House of Lords, or are we going to use the House of Lords as an excuse for not putting forward our measures? I do not believe that the British people will follow us if we put it around in the way that is suggested."[2]

Cripps received support, from Attlee and Lord Ponsonby as well as from Frank Wise, but Bevin's challenge was too powerful to be ignored. On the chairman's suggestion, Cripps' amendment was not pressed to a vote but remitted to the Executive for a further report in 1934.

13

This was the first of many encounters in which Bevin and Cripps were to find themselves on opposite sides during the next few years. The contrast between the two men could hardly have been more

1 Cf. for example Citrine in *The New Clarion*, 24th June 1933.
2 Labour Party Conference Report, 1933, pp. 161–2.

strongly marked, Cripps slender and ascetic, the passionate doctrinaire to whom ideas were more real than human beings, Bevin thickset and earthy with a critical power of judgment tempered by long experience of men.

On both sides of his family, Cripps belonged to that high-minded, energetic, self-confident professional class which has played so remarkable a part in the history of this country in the nineteenth and twentieth centuries. Educated at Winchester like his father and grandfather before him, Cripps was a successful barrister who did not join the Labour Party until 1929 when he was forty, and almost immediately entered the second Labour Government as Solicitor General, before he had won a seat in the House. When the 1931 split and the subsequent election robbed the Labour Party of its front-bench leaders, Cripps, who retained his seat, was thrust into the position of one of the Party's spokesmen in the House of Commons. For this he was ill-equipped. He had little experience of politics or men and none at all of working-class life. His aunt, Beatrice Webb, who liked him, described him as "oddly immature in intellect and unbalanced in judgment . . . ignorant and reckless in his statements and proposals".[1] To Bevin he appeared the embodiment of all that most exasperated him in middle-class intellectuals telling the trade unions and 'the workers' what they ought to do.

'Intellectual' was a word which Bevin employed in a comprehensive and idiosyncratic way. It had little to do with Left or Right or even with a university education. Amongst those whom he described as 'intellectuals' at one time or another were Ramsay MacDonald, Sir Oswald Mosley, James Maxton and the I.L.P., George Lansbury, Stafford Cripps, Aneurin Bevan and the Socialist League, as well as more obvious candidates like Harold Laski and G. D. H. Cole. All these (apart from the fact that they were not trade unionists) had one thing in common: they displayed those characteristics which in Bevin's mind were the hall-mark of the intellectual–unreliability and irresponsibility.

They were unreliable even as intellectual guides because they went haring off after new ideas and new enthusiasms. They were too volatile, too likely to be swept along by some twist of intellectual fashion and forget what they had said six months before. "How could anyone have followed you in the last ten years?" Bevin wrote

1 *Diaries,* 1924–32, p. 304.

to G. D.H. Cole. "Really, old man, look how you have boxed the compass."[1] Intellectuals used words differently from the way ordinary men did, as verbal or emotional counters, without regard to experience.[2] Experience was Bevin's touchstone and he had no faith in a political judgment not firmly rooted in it.

Not only were they unreliable as guides, they were even more unreliable as allies. In an earlier letter to Cole, with whom he remained on friendly terms, Bevin wrote:

"When we have tried to associate with the intellectuals, our experience has been that they do not stay the course very long; hence our difficulty. . . . It is the necessity to work out our own salvation which is the driving force; whether the intellectuals are with us or not, we must carry on."[3]

The intellectuals were for ever breaking away to form new groups —Bevin had not forgotten his experience with the S.S.I.P. and the Socialist League—and the history of the Labour Party was littered with their abandoned initiatives. They suffered from an opposition mentality and still thought of politics as an indefinite perpetuation of University Labour Clubs in which nothing more serious was at stake than a resolution. A trade-union leader, although he might be in opposition politically, was in office so far as his members were concerned, responsible to them and expected to produce concrete results.

"You see," Bevin continued in his letter to Cole, "the difference between the intellectuals and the trade unions is this: You have no responsibility, you can fly off at a tangent as the wind takes you. We, however, must be consistent and we have a great amount of responsibility. We cannot wake up in the morning and get a brain wave, when father says 'turn' and half a million people turn automatically. That does not work."[4]

Cripps and the Socialist League drew from the events of 1931 the conclusion that the one thing that mattered was to stick to Socialist

1 Ernest Bevin to G. D. H. Cole, 25th January 1937.
2 Cf. Beatrice Webb's comment on "the occupational disease common among high-strung men and women who come out of a conservative environment into proletarian politics". *Diaries*, 1924–32, p. 97.
3 Ernest Bevin to G. D.H. Cole, 31st December 1935. This and the letter of 25th January, 1937 were replies to letters of Cole's in which he expressed his alarm at the split between the trade unions and the intellectuals and urged Bevin to use his influence to reduce it.
4 Ibid.

principles and avoid the compromises into which the Labour Government had been drawn. Bevin drew the opposite conclusion: the Labour movement had been split by the individualism of its leaders, by MacDonald's and Snowden's refusal to respect or be bound by the views of the majority.

Twenty years as a trade-union leader had taught Bevin that the only way in which to get anything done was to subordinate individual points of view to collective decisions, and however much you might disagree with a decision, to accept it loyally provided it had been reached in a democratic way. Nothing so much roused his anger as the claim on grounds of individual conscience or principle, not to put a different point of view before a vote—that he both accepted and practised to the full—but to refuse to be bound by a majority decision once a vote had been taken.

If anybody accepted membership of an organisation, Bevin believed, he must respect the obligation of loyalty, doubly so if he accepted the responsibility of leadership. If a man disagreed with a decision, he could resign or seek to change it by democratic means, but so long as he remained a member and so long as the decision remained in force, he had no right either to repudiate it or attack it in public.

To Bevin this was as much a matter of principle as Cripps' and the Socialist League's claim to freedom of conscience and the right to criticise. This was what responsibility meant, and until the Labour Party accepted it, he believed, as the trade-union movement had already done, it would never win a majority of the electorate to vote for it or, indeed, be fit to govern.

14

Bevin's relations with the National Executive of the Party were disturbed in the winter of 1933–34 by a dispute over a by-election at Clay Cross, a safe Labour seat in Derbyshire, which was caused by the death of one of the Union's Members of Parliament, Charlie Duncan, the former secretary of the Workers' Union. The Transport and General Workers' Union had made substantial contributions to the constituency organisation and as a matter of course put forward another Union candidate, Ben Smith, who had lost his seat at

Rotherhithe in 1931. The local Labour Party, however, under strong pressure from headquarters, offered the candidature to Arthur Henderson, still Secretary of the Party and now President of the Disarmament Conference, but without a seat in Parliament since his own defeat in 1931. Bevin was not consulted, and in a towering rage, he demanded an inquiry into this slight to the Union and himself, withholding the Union's affiliation fees to the Party until he obtained satisfaction. The National Executive had to exercise a great deal of diplomacy—including a joint inquiry with the Union and formal apologies—before he was appeased. The Union's affiliation fees for 1933 were not paid until April 1934 and the episode rankled in Bevin's mind for months afterwards.

After 1931 Bevin himself was not a candidate for office either in Parliament or in the Party. This gave him a great advantage in the National Council and at the annual Party conference. He spoke with the frankness of one who did not care, and did not need to care, whether what he said was popular or not. His place in the Party's counsels depended not upon the number of votes he could secure in the annual election to the Executive nor on a seat in the House of Commons, but on the unassailable position he held in his union and the T.U.C. The place which he occupied at Party conferences, not on the platform, but sitting in the body of the hall surrounded by thirty or forty delegates of the T.G.W.U., visibly expressed an independence which none of the leaders on the political side enjoyed. Nor was he indifferent to the weight which the block vote of the Transport and General Workers' Union gave his opinions.

But there were other trade-union leaders who possessed the same advantages and disposed of equally powerful votes: none of these, however, enjoyed a shadow of the influence which Bevin acquired in the Labour movement during the 1930s.

It was certainly not won by playing to the gallery. At one Party conference after another, he assaulted some of the most cherished traditions and prejudices of his audience, making no effort to appease his critics, attacking them head-on, hurling reproaches at them and accusing them of every crime in the trade-union calendar from treachery to blacklegging.

In his early days, the *Herald* had once described him as combining the qualities of a prize fighter and a tragedian. If he had the aggressive instincts of the one, he had also the other's sense of timing. He liked to wait until the most dramatic moment for intervention, usually towards the end of a debate when interest was beginning to flag, and then to revive expectancy by taking his time to walk to the rostrum and survey his audience before plunging into his speech.

Bevin had the temperament to rise to a big theme and a big occasion, but he was often at his best when he spoke on the spur of the moment, letting his thoughts come straight from his mind. His use of words was his own, and his style of speaking lacked grace, but he knew instinctively what was in the minds of a working-class audience and the arguments that would tell. He neither flattered nor talked down to them but told them bluntly what he believed, employing few of the orator's devices, but driving his way through his sentences until he reached the heart of what his audience felt and wanted to hear said.

There were times when the Left hated him, yet there was one thing they could never deny and one thing which never ceased to fascinate the intellectuals: the authenticity with which he represented and embodied in his own person the character and convictions of the English working classes, prejudices and all.

Here was one source of his authority. A second was his uncontested position as the spokesman of the trade-union movement and the role which he assumed as trustee of the trade-union stake in the Labour Party and the guardian of its trade-union traditions.

Bevin, however, was always more than a representative figure. What was remarkable about him was the capacity to combine the role of the experienced, down-to-earth trade unionist with the ability to let his imagination range boldly and to throw out original suggestions. It was intellectuals not ideas that Bevin distrusted. On more than one occasion when the Party was in danger of becoming obsessed with opposing the National Government, he summoned it to renew its energies by speaking like a prophet. He would turn from one role to the other, from the practical to the visionary in the same speech without a hint of apology or embarrassment.

"He was a restless man," said one of his officers, "always looking for something to create." He used the same phrase himself at the Norwich T.U.C., "I like to create". There was no problem which he came across that did not catch his attention and start him wondering what could be done with it.

Nor was his interest limited to those social and economic problems with which he possessed a long familiarity. No leader of the Labour Party was quicker—and few in any party were as quick—to grasp the implications of the rise of the dictators and draw the unpalatable conclusions which followed. This is only one, although it is the most important, example of his interest in foreign affairs. To take another, he was continually looking for opportunities to strengthen international co-operation on the economic side, through the I.L.O., through the Commonwealth or through some link to be forged between the Commonwealth and Europe.

The quality and consistency of his judgment were remarkable. The proof is to be found in re-reading today what he said in the 1930s, a test that few politicians' reputations could survive as well. Not only did he remember what he heard, but he thought about it as well, reaching conclusions of his own which sometimes startled his colleagues but which, looked at again today, show the intellectual grasp and trueness of judgment which he brought to bear on political and international as well as social problems.

Bevin mellowed a great deal during the 1930s and began to reveal some of the Shakespearian richness of personality which flowered in the 1940s. The integrity and convictions were still there, but he was more tolerant, less suspicious and reserved than he had been in the 1920s. If he showed an unabashed satisfaction in his own abilities and power, it was the open vanity of a natural man, uncorrupted by "the aristocratic embrace" which had proved fatal to more than one Labour leader, and unmoved by wealth, honours or position. He was himself on all occasions, as unimpressed by his surroundings as he was uninhibited in his emotions.

Still fierce in argument and never an easy man to convince or disagree with, his ambitions were satisfied, his purposes disinterested. He hated injustice and inequality as strongly as he had ever done, hated the indifference to human waste which accepted two million unemployed with equanimity. His anger sprang not from any sense of personal grievance, but from a desire to see something done, because he cared what happened, not to himself, but to other human beings, because he rebelled passionately against the complacency of those who said, "Nothing you do will make any difference".

If the vigour with which he expressed himself offended some, there flowed from him a confidence that was all too rare in the Labour Party of the 1930s. All through the 1930s the Labour Party was suffering from the after-effects of the 1931 split, divided, bickering and frustrated, condemned, as it seemed, to permanent opposition. There were times when Bevin, too, nearly despaired of the Party, but he remained loyal, refused to be discouraged, refused to give up his belief that one day they would come to power, a steadying, reassuring, massive figure amid the quarrels, fears and conflicting loyalties of an anxious decade.

CHAPTER 20

Politicians, Lorry-Drivers
and Sanctions
1934 – 1935

I

AT THE END of January 1934, Bevin gave one of his rare broadcasts under the title "The Britain I want to see".[1] Hitler's suppression of free institutions in Germany had left an indelible impression on him. This was one of the reasons for his anger with the Socialist League's talk of emergency powers, and he took the opportunity to make an emphatic statement of his belief in the democratic practice of politics:

"I have no confidence in the superman; the limitations of supposedly great men are obvious. I have spent my life amongst ordinary working people; place the truth before them—the facts, whether they are good or bad—and they display an understanding ability and courage that confounds the wisdom of the so-called great."

But, if he was prepared to defend parliamentary institutions, Bevin did not disguise his scorn for the politics of the National Government. Parliament, he pointed out, had recently voted £375 million for an equalisation fund without anyone turning a hair. The moment however that it was proposed to spend more money on the distressed areas or the unemployed, on preserving the nation's most valuable asset, the craft and skill of its people, the country could not afford it.

"I want a Britain that places humanity first. . . . I want to see a Britain that is constantly considering the development of its own national resources.

[1] It was published by the Labour Party as a pamphlet.

538

Why should our land be flooded when we have idle labour? Why should thousands of our villages be without an adequate water supply? Why should we have slums when we possess all the essentials to house our people properly?"

Could the nation afford it? "When I am asked what the cost of a particular scheme will be, I always put to myself the alternative, What will be the cost of not dealing with it?" If the country was prepared to spend millions on defence against external dangers, why was so little done to prevent "the strength of the nation being sapped by the fact that there are 12 million souls out of 40 million in these islands whose existence is far below the poverty line".[1] The consequences of poverty and unemployment were such in loss of moral fibre and physical deterioration that the nation could ill afford not to take drastic action.

Far more than lack of means it was, to use Bevin's own words, "a conception", "the middle class attitude of mind" which blocked effective action. The climate of opinion was changing, as Bevin was quick to realise.[2] Ideas of State intervention and of economic planning were replacing the orthodox teaching of *laisser-faire* in the most unexpected places, and the discussion of economic and social problems in the middle thirties was conducted in very different terms from those of the 1920s. But the pace at which ideas were translated into action was desperately slow. When the National Government finally brought itself to admit that the problems of the worst-hit areas—South Wales, Tyneside, West Cumberland and Scotland— were on a different scale from those of the rest of the country and appointed commissioners for the Depressed Areas (renamed Special Areas by the House of Lords), the grant made available amounted to £2 million, a pitiful sum by comparison with the operations of the New Deal in America.

With one of the four areas, South Wales, Bevin's Union had a long standing connection, and he knew at first hand, as all too few Ministers and civil servants did, the physical desolation and the human degradation of industrial Wales. In London 8.6% of the population was unemployed,[3] in Oxford and Coventry, 5%, even

---

1 From an article which Bevin contributed to *The Liverpool Quarterly* in April 1934.
2 Cf. two articles in *The Record*, March and April, 1934, pp. 181 and 204.
3 1934 figures.

in Birmingham no more than 6.4%. In Abertillery the figure was 50% and in Merthyr Tydfil 61.9%, although many of the men had already left to seek work elsewhere. To cross the Severn from southern England and journey across Monmouthshire and Glamorgan was to enter another world, a world of derelict communities and hopeless, listless faces. Every time Bevin made the journey he came back seething with anger at the complacency with which the rest of the nation and the Government could allow such conditions to continue.

If unemployment was worst in the mining villages, it was not much better in the Welsh tinplate trade. For reasons of economy, works were being closed and production concentrated with no consideration of the effect on the communities which depended on the trade for their livelihood. Early in 1934 Bevin got wind of a scheme on the part of Richard Thomas and Company, who had bought up and closed a number of works in South Wales with a view to building a new strip mill at Redbourne in Lincolnshire. Richard Thomas was the biggest manufacturer of tinplate in the country and such a step, taken without any consultation with the unions or the local authorities involved, threatened to deal a major blow to employment among the tinplate workers in South Wales. Bevin made a vehement attack on the proposal at the Annual Tinplate Conference and after lengthy negotiations, in which he played a big part, had the satisfaction of seeing the Redbourne project abandoned. Richard Thomas bought instead the derelict property of the Ebbw Vale Company in order to set up the most modern strip mill in the country, opened in 1938.

At both the T.U.C. and Labour Party Conferences of 1934, the Transport Workers put down resolutions drawing attention to the effect which the closing down of a big works could have on a district and to the fact that no machinery existed for dealing with the problem. "An industry can be moved without any obligation at all and the community that is left derelict has to pay the cost."[1] If the Government would not act to control such changes, Bevin urged local authorities, especially in an area like South Wales where many of them had a Labour majority, to combine in their own defence and develop their own resources.

In November 1934 Bevin made a powerful appeal to South Wales

1 T.U.C. Report, 1934, pp. 374–6.

to help itself at the official luncheon following the inauguration of the new Lord Mayor of Cardiff, who happened to be the Union's area secretary. In January 1935 he came down again, this time to explain his ideas to the Swansea Town Council. Six months later he was the principal speaker at a conference of thirteen local authorities called by the Mayor of Swansea, urging them to set up a regional authority for the area and to start new developments on their own initiative.

2

That organised public protest by the Labour movement could still make an impression on the Government was shown by the success of the campaign to secure the withdrawal of the grant regulations issued by the new Unemployment Assistance Board in January 1935. These meant a sharp cut in the payments made to many of the unemployed, and a bitter protest came from the distressed areas, from town councils, churches, trade unions and members of all parties. Accompanied by Lansbury, Attlee, Bevin and Citrine, an angry deputation from South Wales went to see the Minister of Labour. The effect of the new scheme in South Wales was to cut relief payments by £1,000,000 and the case which the deputation put forward was so strong that, as they came down the steps of Montague House, Bevin declared that, if the Government could ignore it, "they must have the hearts of a Pharaoh."

The National Council of Labour issued an Appeal to the Public Conscience and demonstrations were held in every industrial area in the country. It was a week-end of wild weather, with a fierce gale driving rain up the Welsh valleys, but 30,000 people assembled at Pontypool and stood in the rain to hear Bevin denounce the Government's treatment of the unemployed, "the third nation" which had grown up in Britain alongside Disraeli's two nations of rich and poor.

The Government had already had to face rough handling in the House and on 5th February the Minister announced the withdrawal of the offending regulations and the issue of a standstill order. It was a notable success for Labour and Bevin was quick to point the moral to local leaders who had begun to lose heart in face of what appeared to be a permanent blight on industrial Wales.

In the meantime he did what he could from the other end, badgering and corresponding with Ministers, with Sir Robert Horne and Sir James Milne of the Great Western Railway and with P. M. (later Sir Malcolm) Stewart, the Commissioner for Special Areas. Among the projects he urged were the development of oil refining at Llandarcy (strongly opposed by the South Wales miners), the transfer of the Arsenal from Woolwich, the improvement of transport facilities, the opening up of the South Wales coast to holiday traffic and the construction of a road bridge over the Severn.[1]

His interest in development schemes for South Wales brought Bevin into close contact with P. M. Stewart, who had been appointed to administer the Government's programme of aid for the depressed areas. The Commissioner's first report was published in July 1935[2] and was the subject of a special report by the General Council which Bevin was asked to introduce at the 1935 T.U.C. in Margate.

Bevin showed sympathy with the proposals the Commissioner had made to revive industry in the depressed areas, but argued that the limited powers and funds he had been given condemned him to failure from the start. In a long and closely-reasoned speech Bevin put forward a number of practical suggestions, the most important of which were to free the Commissioner from the limitations with which his authority to offer grants was surrounded and to increase the funds on which he could draw. Why, Bevin asked, was it possible to apply the methods of the Colonial Development Act to overseas territories, but not to Wales?

"It was easy for the Colonial Development Committee to advance money to build the Zambesi Bridge to link Nyasaland with Portuguese East Africa . . . but we cannot get a bridge across the Severn and cannot get a road developed because of the regulations that have been laid down."[3]

Refusing to make a political issue of the Special Areas, Bevin

1 Among Bevin's papers are several files of correspondence with local authorities and others who sought his aid during the 1930s in forwarding schemes for three great road bridges, over the Severn, the Humber and the Tay. Twenty years later all three schemes are still 'under consideration' and none of the bridges has been built.
2 *First Report of the Commissioner for Special Areas (England and Wales)*, Cmd. 4957 (1935).
3 T.U.C. Report, 1935, pp. 295-9.

offered the full co-operation of the T.U.C., if the Government would promise a grant of £20 million and give the Commission the power to co-ordinate schemes between different departments. The offer was ignored.

As a member of a party out of office there was no more Bevin could do. He was convinced that, if only the problem of the depressed areas were attacked with energy and imagination, it could be very largely solved, but like everyone else who tried he failed to convince the Government. In 1937, despite the migration of thousands of the younger generation in search of work, the rate of unemployment in the Special Areas was still double that for Great Britain as a whole and in certain parts was much higher. Like many other members of the Labour Party and many of the younger generation who belonged to no party, Bevin could never forgive the National Government for its failure to do more. More than that: what he saw in South Wales and the other depressed areas remained for him irrefutable proof of the social and human inadequacy of the capitalist society it was so zealous to preserve.

3

This failure was thrown into sharp relief by the fact that, in the rest of the country, the economic recovery, the first signs of which appeared in 1933, continued with little interruption until by mid-1936 total unemployment (even including the Special Areas) had fallen from its peak of 2.9 million in January 1933 to 1.6.

The causes of this recovery were manifold: amongst them were the continued growth of the home market and consumer industries, the beginning of a housing boom, a recovery in world trade, with the terms of trade moving in Britain's favour and so reducing the cost of imports by as much as a third. The policies of the National Government appear to have played no great part in the swing back towards greater prosperity—a double-edged argument which may be used to demonstrate either the ineffectiveness of the policy or to confirm the truth of the *laisser-faire* principles to which the older generation of Conservatives and Liberals still held.

Bevin always paid careful attention to trade statistics and at the end of 1933 he set to work to regain the cuts in wages suffered by the

Union's members during the Depression. By the end of 1934 he reported to his Executive with satisfaction that virtually every reduction had been won back with the exception of the dockers', the full restoration of which was delayed by the resistance of the port employers for a further year.

The end of the Depression took a great load from Bevin's mind. He had no longer to spend his time in persuading his members to honour agreements which, even if they were the best the Union could secure in the circumstances, all too often roused resentment by failing to do more than limit the employers' demands for lower wages and longer hours. Henceforward he was in a position to demonstrate the positive advantages of belonging to the Union by negotiating for wage increases or an improvement in working conditions and to take up, with renewed energy, the campaign to expand the Union's membership in trades which were still imperfectly organised.

There was plenty of scope for such expansion. While total trade-union membership began to recover after 1933 and reached 5.3 million by 1936, this was not more than 40 per cent of the insured population and not more than a third of the wage-earners in the country.[1] The T.G.W.U. succeeded in getting a foothold in the expanding metal, engineering and chemical industries which it was to use to good effect during the war years. But there were other groups—amongst them agricultural, building and clerical workers—which the Union attempted to organise with little return for its efforts.

Bevin took a particular personal interest in the road-haulage industry. He had begun his trade-union career by organising the Bristol carters and road haulage remained, with the docks and milling, one of the industries in which he played a unique role extending far beyond the organisation of the trade-union side.

The Road Traffic Acts of 1930 and 1933, which the Union had helped to secure, imposed statutory limitations on the hours a driver might spend at the wheel, and established a system of licensing.[2] The problem of enforcement, however, remained. The industry was split up into a large number of firms, many of them small in size.

1 Even after the second World War, when trade-union membership reached its peak of nine and a half million members, this did not represent more than two-fifths of the working population.
2 See above, pp. 458–60.

The employers were individualistic in their attitude; competition between them was fierce, and undercutting, the payment of low wages and the systematic evasion of regulations common practice. The men, amongst whom trade-union membership and organisation were poor, connived at this either to retain their jobs, to earn a bribe for keeping their mouths shut or simply for their own convenience when, by driving excessive hours and breaking the speed limit, they could get home earlier. Long experience had taught Bevin every trick in the trade and he was well aware that he would have to meet opposition from many of the men as well as the employers in trying to get national standards for wages and working conditions accepted.

Bevin's policy was to set up a national joint council through which, with the co-operation of the better employers, the Union could establish a code for the industry and bring pressure to bear on those who refused to comply with it. Bevin, however, had no hope of persuading the employers, a strong section of whom especially in the north of England was opposed to any 'interference', to set up such machinery voluntarily. He therefore pressed the Minister of Labour to take the unusual step of creating for the industry with Government authority a national conciliation board on which representatives of both sides should be invited to serve. After some hesitation the Minister accepted this advice and set up such a board in March 1934, with Sir Richard Redmayne, formerly Chief Inspector of Mines, as an independent chairman and Bevin as one of the two vice-chairmen.

Bevin threw all his weight into making the board a success and devoted much time to drafting detailed regulations for wages and conditions. In alliance with the more far-sighted contractors, Bevin and the other unions' representatives succeeded in getting the report accepted by the board, despite stubborn opposition from many of the employers. He then went up to Manchester in December 1934 and addressed a conference of 500 delegates from his own and the three other unions which were involved, although on a much smaller scale than the T.G.W.U.

Seventeen years had passed since he had convened the first conference of carters' unions in Manchester and persuaded them to agree upon a national programme. Since that time the amalgamation which he had promoted had largely overcome the divisions on the trade-union side which had wrecked his earlier campaign, but he had no doubts of the resistance which the enforcement of the Act

545

would encounter from many of the men as well as from the employers. Undeterred, he insisted to the delegates that they had to make the scheme work even if a majority of the men could not yet be brought to see that it was in their own best interests to do so.

He had not won his fight yet, but he had established the national machinery for which he had campaigned so tenaciously and secured a position from which he was able, before the end of the 1930s, to go a stage further in forcing organisation and the observance of proper conditions of employment on one of the most individualistic of British industries.[1]

4

Bevin never tired of urging the trade unions to interest themselves in the major issues of national policy. In the 1930s he applied the argument with as much force to foreign affairs as he had before to economics, and the National Council of Labour between 1933 and 1937 took the place in his activities which had earlier been occupied by the T.U.C. Economic Committee.

During the autumn of 1933 the National Council was in close touch with the leaders of the Austrian Social Democrats and trade unions. They were left in no doubt of the Austrian view that the Dollfuss Government was preparing to suppress the organised working-class movement and of the Austrian workers' determination to resist by force if attacked. When the attack was launched in February 1934 the Austrian workers more than redeemed their promise and fought heroically against machine-guns, tanks and artillery. But they fought alone, as the Hungarians were to do in 1956, and all that their comrades abroad could do was to protest, in bitter shame at their own impotence.

February 1934 made an even deeper impression on Bevin than Hitler's rise to power the year before. The Austrian working-class organisations had long held a leading position in the international Socialist and trade-union movement; moreover, the Austrian workers had fought, the Germans had not. But it was the cumulative effect that counted. This was the second working-class movement to be suppressed by a dictatorship within a year and if any doubts were

1 See below, pp. 618–19.

left about the character of National Socialism, they were removed by Hitler's brutal elimination of Roehm, Gregor Strasser and the victims of the June 1934 purge, followed a month later by the murder of Dollfuss and the unsuccessful Nazi *putsch* in Austria.

The National Council of Labour took such immediate steps as were open to them. They raised £30,000 (£27,000 from the trade unions) as a relief fund, and joined in organising the legal defence of the thousands arrested by the Dollfuss Government. But these were only palliatives. The question Bevin and every other leader of the Labour movement had to face was how the spread of Fascism was to be halted and fought.

One obvious step was to redouble their efforts to rouse public opinion to the threat of Fascism, not only abroad but at home where the blackshirted British Union of Fascists, under the leadership of the one-time Socialist Minister, Sir Oswald Mosley, was attracting large crowds to its meetings. Through the *Daily Herald*, through union branches and journals, and the local organisations of the Labour Party, through pamphlets, speeches and demonstrations, the facts about Nazi Germany and about Mosley's Fascist movement were given the widest possible publicity. At a time when many people were still confused or ignorant, this was a contribution in forming opinion which can easily be underestimated. Most important of all, however, Bevin felt, was to decide, in the light of the changed situation in Europe, what foreign policy the Labour Party should urge on the existing Government and should itself adopt in preparing to win an election and form an alternative Government.

The challenge presented by Hitler's and Mussolini's gangster politics caught both the Conservative and Labour parties unprepared and threw them into a state of confusion from which neither shook itself completely free until the war. The character of this confusion differed widely between the parties. On the Labour side, it sprang from the conflict between Socialist preconceptions about the causes of international conflict and the conduct of international relations and the immediate necessities of an increasingly urgent situation. This is, of course, only another instance of the classical pattern of tension in every radical party, between a Utopian left wing admitting no compromise with principles and a realist right wing impressed by the need to deal with the world as it is. In the case of foreign affairs the confusion was deepened by the fact that the Labour Party had so little experience of the conduct of foreign policy or responsibility for defence—nothing comparable, for instance, to the trade unions' practical experience of industrial relations—and by the fact that it remained out of power throughout the period.

Labour views on foreign affairs were derived from many different sources, amongst them pacifism, Marxism and the persistent, if frequently conflicting, radical criticisms of British foreign policy from Charles James Fox, Cobden and Bright to the Union of Democratic Control. Allowing for the infinite variety of individual opinion which has always been characteristic of political as well as religious dissent, few members of the Labour Party in the 1920s (including Bevin) would have disagreed with the view that conflict between nations—whether it took the form of imperialist rivalries, balance-of-power politics, secret diplomacy, armament races or war —was the product of capitalism. The capitalist classes in Britain as in other countries profited from and perpetuated this international anarchy in their own interests. By false propaganda, the exploitation of fear and an appeal to patriotism, the working classes had been duped into taking part in the war of 1914–18 only to see the hopes of a better world and a just peace held out in Wilson's Fourteen Points betrayed by the peace settlement and the attempt to overthrow the Soviet régime in Russia. Never again must they let themselves be tricked by patriotic propaganda or the plea of defending 'national interests' into support of another war. In the last resort the workers of every country must unite to prevent their governments going to war by a general strike, a proposition to which a resolution of the Hastings Conference committed the Labour Party as late as October 1933.

A few held, with Marxist rigour, to the doctrine that the only war which concerned the workers was the class war. The majority of the Labour Party, however—pending the establishment of a world community of Socialist states from which war would be automatically banished by the elimination of capitalism—found an outlet for frustrated idealism in support of the League of Nations. The logic of this was open to objection: the League was in fact an alliance of capitalist governments bent upon preserving their national sovereignty. But in an imperfect world, Labour felt that the League, "the Geneva spirit", still stood for conscience v. force, the rule of law v. power politics, international obligations v. national interests, arbitration in place of war, disarmament in place of armaments. If this was difficult to reconcile with the politics practised at Geneva, the remedy, Labour argued, was to strengthen the League.

'Strengthening the League', however, did not mean providing it with a backing of force; it meant stiffening the obligations of its member states, binding them more strictly to submit their disputes to arbitration and to disband the armed forces which they maintained for self-defence. It was, indeed, far more against default by the Government of their own country than against aggression by a foreign power that Labour was on its guard. This was especially true after 1931: there lay the enemy, in the National Government. If an act of aggression occurred, it was assumed that, provided the British Government stood by its obligations to the League, moral sanctions, the solemn naming of the aggressor, or at most economic sanctions, would be sufficient to halt it. Support for the League, therefore, and the campaign for disarmament, collective security *and* resistance to war went hand in hand.

Under the cumulative effect of successive—and successful—acts of aggression, the Labour Party was driven, step by step, to examine and in part to modify, in part to discard these preconceptions. It was a difficult and painful adjustment. Nor was it completed by Bevin's defeat of Lansbury over sanctions in 1935: Spain, appeasement, rearmament, conscription, each revived the debate in different forms. Suspended during the war, it was renewed in 1945.

5

Bevin was in the thick of this controversy before as well as after the war. Taking the period as a whole, from 1933 to his death in 1951, no man played a greater part in pressing upon the Labour Party the need to face realities in foreign affairs. Obvious enough after 1945 when he held the position of Foreign Secretary, this is hardly less true of the 1930s when he spoke for the trade unions.

The influence of the trade unions in the development of Labour's views on foreign policy during the 1930s has been neglected. Yet nobody who follows that development at close quarters will be inclined to underestimate the pressure which the trade-union movement under the leadership of Bevin and Citrine exerted on the Party's decisions and pronouncements.

An illustration of this influence is to be found in the first serious attempt to define Labour's policy in the new situation created by Hitler's capture of power, Germany's withdrawal from the League and the failure of the Disarmament Conference. On 28th February 1934, the three main committees of the Labour movement[1] met at Transport House to discuss the resolutions moved from the floor at the Hastings conference the autumn before. The more important of these had instructed the National Executive to consult with the trade unions and the international labour movement on steps to organise opposition to war, including a general strike.

It was the trade-union leaders who killed this last suggestion once and for all. Discussing the proposal with the Executive Council of the T.G.W.U. immediately after the Hastings conference, Bevin asked:

"Who and what is there to strike? Trade unionism has been destroyed in Italy and Germany; practically speaking, it does not exist in France; it is extremely weak in the U.S.A. . . . while there is no possibility of a general . strike against the Russian government in the event of war. What is left? Great Britain, Sweden, Denmark and Holland; virtually, these are the only countries in which any strong trade union organisations exist. Ought we, in the light of these facts, to go on talking glibly, misleading the people and ourselves as to what we could do with the general strike weapon in the event of a world war?"[2]

On the very day the meeting took place in Transport House, the Austrian workers' movement was being battered into submission. If war was to be stopped, the responsibility could not be left to the trade unions; it had to be shared by the whole community. The T.U.C.'s Standing Orders already clearly committed it to call a special congress if there was danger of war and beyond this the General Council refused to go.

They made this perfectly plain in the report, *War and Peace*, which was drawn up after the discussion on 28th February and approved at

1 The General Council of the T.U.C., the National Executive of the Labour Party and the Executive Committee of the Parliamentary Labour Party. The National Joint Council was representative of all three bodies and on special occasions such as this was reinforced by the attendance of all their members.

2 General Secretary's Quarterly Report, November 1933.

a further meeting of the three committees in June.[1] Equally important was the recognition in *War and Peace*, for the first time, "that there might be circumstances under which the Government of Great Britain might have to use its military and naval forces in support of the League in restraining an aggressor nation." Under the heading of Sanctions, the report affirmed "the duty unflinchingly to support our Government in all the risks and consequences of fulfilling its duty to take part in collective action against a peace-breaker".

It is true that the rest of *War and Peace* repeated at length Labour's attachment to peace and disarmament and that Arthur Henderson, in introducing it at the Southport conference in the autumn, went out of his way to reassure the delegates that it represented no defection from Labour's previous policy. But the mood of the autumn conferences clearly marked a change. At Weymouth Bevin warned the T.U.C. of the danger of Hitler and Mussolini turning to war as a way out of their economic difficulties and both the T.U.C. and the Labour Party conferences endorsed the report by huge majorities. Neither Lord Ponsonby calling for unilateral disarmament, nor Cripps and the Socialist League rejecting the League of Nations as an organisation of capitalist states and reviving the call for a general strike against war, received any support. The Labour movement still pinned its hopes on the League, but the possibility that support for the League might involve war was no longer excluded. The following year was to see it explicitly accepted.

6

Weymouth had been chosen for the 1934 meeting of the T.U.C. to enable the Congress to honour the centenary of the six Dorsetshire labourers who were sentenced to transportation for the crime of administering illegal oaths in forming a branch of the Friendly Society of Agricultural Labourers.

The occasion stirred Bevin deeply, recalling his own childhood in a West Country village and the lot of the agricultural labouring class from which he sprang. Speaking at the mass demonstration held in Dorchester, he told his audience:

1 T.U.C. Report, 1934, pp. 156–161.

"Whenever I am asked about the dictatorship of the Proletariat, of the Nazis, or any other form of it, I reply that I was born in a village and held under a dictatorship until I was fourteen—and I will see you to the devil before I have any more.

"The landlord does not fight to retain his land merely because of the money it yields him, but because of the power it gives him. The capitalist is the same. He will give you sport, welfare and charity and everything but one thing, and that is Power. He will hold on to that, the power to give you the sack, to impose his will and withhold from you the means of sustenance. Such power is unwarrantable."[1]

The Labour Party conference which met at Southport a month later amply vindicated Bevin's stand against Cripps the year before. Not only did the conference adopt an Executive report on parliamentary procedure which ignored the Socialist League's wish to see the Party commit itself in advance to the use of emergency powers,[2] but the new statement of policy adopted at Southport, *For Socialism and Peace*, was a clear challenge to those who claimed that Socialism could not be achieved by established Parliamentary methods. Cripps and the League accepted the challenge, urging the conference to substitute a programme couched in vague but menacing terms and promising to take whatever powers were necessary to push through root and branch measures. Their proposal was rejected by a ten to one majority and their other amendments met the same fate.

The Left, in fact, which had seized the initiative at the Leicester conference of 1932, suffered one defeat after another at Southport in 1934—on foreign policy, the Party programme and on the United Front. The demand for a United Front was increasingly being used by the Communists to draw the Left into vituperative attacks on the leadership of the Labour Party and the trade unions. The National Executive retorted by repeating its refusal to have anything to do with the Communists, revising its list of banned 'front' organisations and asking for disciplinary powers to deal with members of the Labour Party who took part in United Front campaigns organised under their auspices.

The Executive's request was hotly challenged by Aneurin Bevan. The powers for which the Executive asked, he declared, were

1 *The Record*, September 1933.
2 Labour Party Conference Report, 1934: pp. 261–3 (text); pp. 148–51 (debate).

designed to cover up its own "inertia, lack of enterprise and in-sipidity" by launching a heresy hunt.

Bevin was not a member of the Executive but he could not sit silent when this sort of attack was made. Nothing annoyed him more than the freedom claimed by the Left to snipe and gibe at the Party leadership and to go on criticising decisions with which they dis-agreed. Bevan's attack was typical of the irresponsibility, the scorn for organisation and discipline which Bevin most disliked in the in-tellectual rebels of the Left. Nor had he forgiven Bevan for cutting across the lines of the trade-union case in the House of Commons debates on the Unemployment Bill and he mounted the platform determined to give him a hammering.

In forming the Labour Party, Bevin began—a point he never failed to rub in—the trade unions had accepted certain obligations and had observed them. In return they expected loyalty towards the Party from its other members. The freedom claimed by Bevan and the Socialist League confused great issues and threatened to split the Party.

"A previous speaker said that the Communist Party was an insignificant party. It would not have been if you gentlemen had had your way; we would have been split like Germany was split. And if you do not keep down the Communists, you cannot keep down the Fascists. . . . Our friends on the Continent failed at the critical moment to maintain discipline as we propose to do now. This is where they went wrong and they got eaten out and undermined; when they had to take action, half of their members were in one party, half in the other."

When Aneurin Bevan appealed for the protection of the chair against Bevin's criticism of his part in the Unemployment Bill debates, Bevin retorted:

"Apparently my namesake can get on this platform and denounce the Executive and he is so thin-skinned that he cannot take his own medicine. No, in this Conference, Aneurin Bevan, you are not going to get the flattery of the gossip columns that you get in London. You are going to get facts. I am stating the case—when the Trade Unions had fought their damnedest to deal with this unemployed problem, had carried more responsibility than any other body in the country, that was the moment when in the House of Commons this loyalty was displayed. I take this view: when people get on this platform and talk about liberty of association, remember the times we are living in. Years ago it was easy . . . but with the voice of dictatorship on every side, I hope that there is sufficient self-discipline in this Party . . . that everybody will stand four square against every attempt to divide us."[1]

Bevin spoke roughly, but Aneurin Bevan's own intervention had invited it and he received little sympathy from the conference. His motion to refer back the Executive's report was heavily defeated.

7

Despite the interest which he was now taking in politics, Bevin remained an active trade-union leader as resourceful as ever in creating and seizing opportunities. Some of the best examples of this lay right outside the limelight of politics.

In co-operation with the National Union of Seamen he set up a Trade Union Parliamentary Committee for the Shipping and Waterside Industries, secured a Board of Trade Inquiry into recent losses at sea and started a campaign for revising the legislation governing safety and working conditions in the shipping industry.

Taking advantage of a dispute with a firm at Avonmouth which had hitherto refused to meet him, he persuaded the employers to join in setting up a national joint industrial council for the provender milling industry with a national agreement modelled on that which he had negotiated for flour milling.

When the 'C' license holders (firms employing their own delivery vans) were exempted from many of the conditions which the Road Traffic Act applied to haulage contractors, he got some of the larger firms to establish a joint committee voluntarily and to accept better conditions and wages for their drivers.

When the fish porters at Billingsgate Market turned to the T.G.W.U. to secure a settled scale of charges for their work, he persuaded the fish merchants to create a joint committee with the porters which virtually put an end to the disputes which had plagued the market.[2]

1 Labour Party Conference Report, 1934, pp. 140–141.
2 This information was given to me in a letter from Mr. T. J. Dove, for twenty-two years chairman of the Committee, as Superintendent of Billingsgate Market. After describing the personal part Bevin took in the negotiations, his facility in mastering the details of the trade and his skill in overcoming the suspicions on both sides, Mr. Dove wrote:

Add these examples to his efforts on behalf of the dockers, the bus and tramway men, the Welsh tinplate workers, the millers, the lorry-drivers, and one begins to form some idea of the scope of Bevin's work as a trade-union secretary.

After the amalgamation with the Workers' Union in 1929, the Union added little to its strength by the smaller amalgamations of the 1930s.[1] Further discussions with the E.T.U. led to nothing and Bevin would not look at the proposal of the N.U.R. for a single transport union which would have meant splitting the T.G.W.U. in half and excluding its growing number of members outside the transport industries. He preferred, in fact, to conclude working agreements with other unions rather than to become involved in the cumbersome procedure of amalgamation, and the steady growth of the Union was due almost entirely to recruitment and expansion into poorly organised industries. By the time he came to report to the 1935 Biennial Conference, the Union was already in sight of half a million members, more than a tenth of the total trade-union membership in the country.

There were few months when members of the Union were not involved in disputes, but the strikes of the 1930s were almost all local; there were none of the dour trials of strength which had marked the period up to May 1926. This meant that improvements in wages and conditions depended more than ever on skill in negotiation, not on militancy which, if the case of the London busmen is any guide, brought no material advantages.

Bevin was a masterly negotiator. Lord Citrine said, after twenty years as General Secretary of the T.U.C., that he had never met his equal, had certainly never met his superior, in negotiation.[2] Not only had he immense experience on which to draw, but the temperament as well as the skill to take advantage of every point.

"With the exception of two or three minor incidents, there have been no real stoppages and I am certain it is the influence Mr. Bevin had when he said at one of our meetings 'My word is my bond'.

"Although I did not agree with his politics I have nothing but admiration for him as a man and would like to see more men in high places with his integrity."

1 Amongst the unions incorporated were the 'Altogether Builders' Labourers' Society' and the Scottish Busmen's Union (1934); the National Winding and General Engineers' Society (1935); the Port of London Deal Porters (1939), and several other small unions in Scotland and Northern Ireland.

2 In a B.B.C. programme on Ernest Bevin, broadcast on 23rd April 1957.

He could be subtle and patient as well as tough, relying much on his ability to read the other side's minds and possessing an almost infallible instinct for knowing when he had reached the limit of concessions and had better settle.

He was often at his best when he had poor cards and little room for manœuvre. He knew how to bluff, how to draw a red herring, how to provoke the other side, how to lose his own temper and walk out, above all how to wait and keep a point in reserve, not revealing his full hand for a long time. He took the delight of a chess-player in a keenly fought negotiation, but once he had given his word he was adamant in insisting that his own side must keep their agreements and never hesitated to fight it out with the men rather than allow them to break the obligations they had accepted.

The most substantial strike in which the Union was involved in the earlier 1930s was in Ireland where, surprisingly enough, the establishment of the Irish Free State had not driven the British unions out. This was a standing provocation to Irish nationalists, the more so as the stronghold of nationalism in the purely Irish trade unions was also a transport union which Jim Larkin had founded and led in the famous Dublin strike of 1913.

Such union and national rivalries had as much to do with the twelve-week strike of the Dublin tramway men at the beginning of 1935 as any economic causes. The dispute cost the Union £24,000 in strike pay, but Bevin was determined to see it through if only to show that the T.G.W.U. could be as militant as its Irish rival. His private advice to the Union's Area Secretary in Ireland on this occasion deserves to be quoted as a classic illustration of trade-union tactics:

"Dear Sam,
   "My opinion is that the more the Government and the Company run after the men, and the more we run after them, the less likely are we to get reason. If the Company think you an agitator and want a settlement, they will be stubborn. If the Irish Government think you are on the doorstep, they will put tremendous pressure on you and prevent direct meetings, because everyone wants to save their face. If the men find you keep running after them, they will keep you running.
   "I think your attitude should be this—So far as the Company are concerned, just sit tight for another few days and do not show any anxiety whatsoever. With regard to the men, you should say: Every proposal I have obtained you have turned down, I am not going back for any further pro-

posals. You just have to hold on tight until something fresh emerges. Everybody will then begin to wonder where they are and whether they can deliver the goods, and probably by next week the whole matter will be placed in your hands to settle. You should then take a very strong line—that you cannot go to the Company and come back any more, and they will have to trust you to make the settlement . . ."[1]

Despite the guerilla tactics employed against it, the T.G.W.U. held its own and to this day maintains a larger membership in the Irish Republic than any national union except the rival Irish Transport and General Workers.

8

Not since the amalgamation was formed had Bevin and his Executive been able to present so satisfactory a report as they laid before the Union's Biennial Delegate Conference at Douglas in the summer of 1935. It was a lively conference with well-sustained debates in both public and private session. The criticism came from the Left, from London and Scotland with the leaders of the Rank and File Committee keeping up a running fire of dispute with the platform. For the first time Arthur Deakin appeared as Assistant General Secretary, a post to which he had been appointed at the end of 1934, but inevitably it was to Bevin, sitting hunched up over the long table across the platform, that delegates turned when the debate grew heated and the opposition was rarely satisfied unless it succeeded in drawing him into the argument. He had little difficulty in finding a majority for the Executive's policy on almost every point—except an increase in members' contributions—but he was never guilty of 'steamrollering' the opposition or of denying their right to criticise.

Many of the issues raised in private session were familiar stalking horses: the invasion of democratic rights by the growing power of the officials, the demand for the election instead of the appointment of officers, objection to the rule which reserved the right to call a strike to the Executive Council. If the national trade groups were to have this right in their own hands, Bevin answered, they might as well disband the Union. Nothing would please the employers more than to see the different sections fighting each other for the use of the funds.

1 Ernest Bevin to Sam Kyle, 3rd April 1935.

On one point the delegates were impervious alike to Bevin's appeals and to his sarcasm: they stubbornly refused to pay a penny more in contributions. The Union had paid out £900,000 in strike pay over the past ten years, Bevin told them, and the reserves were all too small if even one big trade group ran into serious industrial trouble. The Union needed more money if it was to organise the road-haulage industry or to drive a wedge into the automobile industry. The delegates agreed, but remained unmoved. All Bevin could do was to insist that, if they would not put more in, they could not have more out in the shape of additional benefits.[1]

Bevin was just back from an I.L.O. conference at Geneva[2] at which he had led the campaign for an international convention to establish the principle of a forty-hour week. In private session he told the delegates bluntly, with much support from the floor, that as great an obstacle to shortening the working week as the employers was the trade unionist who insisted on working 50, 60 or even 70 hours for the sake of overtime pay and who refused to share the work. In the public session that followed he strongly defended the attempt to reach international agreement on economic questions, however slow the procedure and however strong the resistance of interested parties and of economic nationalism. There were three conditions, Bevin concluded, essential for world stability: an international currency and international agreement on access to raw materials, neither of which should be the object of speculation; finally, an international agreement on minimum standards for labour.

The debate on foreign policy produced a number of left-wing attacks on support for the League of Nations: Bevin's reply was far from being an uncritical defence of the League. He had hesitated a long time, he told the delegates, before signing the report on *War and Peace*; the argument that had convinced him was that support for the League, with all its imperfections, was the only alternative to a return to the old diplomacy. As for the obligation to go to war under the Covenant of the League, "it is like a man entering a Union."

"You cannot enter with reservations. You have got to be straight. I cannot help what the National Government is doing.[3] We did not write

---

1 In the course of the discussion on finances, Stanley Hirst gave the proportion of T.G.W.U. members paying the political levy: it amounted to 57 per cent.

2 See below p. 575.

3 A reference to the negotiations with Italy and France over Abyssinia.

this document for the National Government; we wrote it for the Labour Movement. If I joined a Union and I was called upon to go on strike, what would be thought of me if I said I would not, but exercised my own discretion at a critical moment?"[1]

Bevin's common-sense argument hit off exactly the mood of the conference.

There was little more support when the London Rank and File Committee tried to carry a resolution in favour of a United Front with the Communists. An attempt by a Bradford delegate to hold Bevin responsible for the T.U.C. letter recommending unions to debar Communists from office fell flat when Bevin told the conference that he had not even been present when the General Council approved it and that he agreed with the Executive's decision not to implement the T.U.C.'s recommendation.

But, if Bevin was opposed to penalising members of the Union for their political opinions, he left no doubt at all what he thought of those who, in the name of a united front, were splitting the Labour movement by their attacks on its leaders. The Communists, he declared, were incapable of sincere co-operation because on every issue they took their instructions from outside. The moment France signed an alliance with the U.S.S.R., the French Communists were ordered to execute a *volte-face* and withdraw their opposition to the French Government's arms credits in the Chamber. The French Communists, like the British and the German, had abandoned their independence in favour of following the tortuous instructions of the Comintern. No one had lost more by these dishonest tactics than the Russians:

"By God, I wish Russia could have seen that if she had never supported the Communist Party in England but allowed the British trade union movement to help Russia she would have been in a much better position than today. . . . The philosophy of the Red International cannot mix with our form of democracy. You had better accept that and try to do the best we can with the facts before us."[2]

1 Verbatim typescript record of the 1935 Biennial Delegate Conference, pp. 248–255.
2 Ibid.

9

Communist tactics and the United Front were again a subject for debate when the T.U.C. met at Margate in the first week of September, but by then everything else was overshadowed by Mussolini's threat to attack Abyssinia and the plain question, how far the Labour movement was prepared to go in support of the League now that the hypothesis of 1934 had been translated into fact and an undisguised act of aggression was about to take place.

Until the middle of the summer Hitler and German rearmament had diverted attention from the Abyssinian appeal to the League. In March Hitler announced the re-introduction of conscription and an end to the limits which the Treaty of Versailles had set on German rearmament. Taken by surprise at the strength of the German Air Force, Baldwin's Government proposed increased expenditure on the expansion of the R.A.F. If any criticism was to be made of this proposal it was Churchill's, that the Government had delayed too long in making it and still had not taken the measure of the dangers with which they were confronted. The Labour Party, however, was faced with a new version of its old dilemma.

Long accustomed to identify the League with disarmament and the renunciation of war, Labour had reluctantly brought itself to recognise that support for the League might involve the use of force. It still sought to draw a sharp distinction between force used in support of a system of collective security and force as an instrument of national policy. In the absence, however, of an international army and air force at the disposal of the League, the only forces available were those under the control of its member governments. But to vote for an increase in these meant trusting the National Government to use them to uphold the authority of the League and not, as Labour believed it would prefer, in order to abandon collective security and pursue a policy of looking after British national interests with sufficient backing in armed force to strike a good bargain with any potential aggressor.

On the other hand, to vote against the increase for which Baldwin asked meant running the risk of seeing the League reduced to impotence for lack of sufficient force to make its authority effective. From this dilemma there was no escape so long as the Labour Party

George Lansbury leaving the Foreign Office after an interview with Sir Samuel Hoare in 1935.

Above. Ernest Bevin and Sir Walter Citrine (centre) at the 1937 T.U.C. *Below.* C. R. Attlee and Hugh Dalton at the Labour Party Conference of 1937.

remained out of office and unable to control the foreign policy of the Government or the use which it might make of any increased armaments placed in its hands.

The Government's revised estimates for the Air Force were debated on 22nd May. The previous day the whole of the Parliamentary Labour Party met the General Council and the National Executive to discuss the attitude they should adopt. A decision was deferred until after the speech which Hitler was expected to deliver that evening and the conference was resumed the following day.

Citrine and Bevin were appointed to put forward the General Council's point of view and, in agreement with Dalton, argued that it was difficult to vote against an increase in the R.A.F. sufficient to give the country at least parity in air power with Germany.[1] The effect, however, of Hitler's well-timed speech promising to observe the obligations of the Locarno Pact was to revive illusions, and the Parliamentary Labour Party decided to vote against the Estimates. "Our policy," Attlee told the House, "is not one of seeking security through rearmament but through disarmament." Inevitably, however, the Labour Party laid itself open to the charge that, having called for strong support for the League, it was now running away from the logical consequences of its own policy.

10

The Government's diplomatic activities in the first half of 1935 lent a good deal of colour to Labour's suspicions. The Stresa conference, the evident reluctance to force an issue with Mussolini over Abyssinia and the conclusion of the Anglo-German Naval Treaty, all suggested that the Cabinet was more interested in reaching private settlements behind the scenes than in giving a strong lead at Geneva.

The Government, however, with an autumn election in view, was impressed by the results of the Peace Ballot which were published at the end of June and which showed a much greater measure of public support for the League of Nations than it had expected. Of the 11.6 million people who took the trouble to vote, over 11.1 million were in favour of Britain remaining a member of the League and 10 million ready to support economic and other non-military sanctions

[1] Cf. Hugh Dalton: *The Fateful Years* (1957), pp. 63–64.

against an aggressor. Even on the controversial question of military sanctions, nearly seven million were ready to enforce them as against 2.3 who voted 'No' and 2.4 million who were doubtful. The marked stiffening in the Government's support for the League, in public at least, between the summer and the general election of the autumn reflected the impression left by these figures.

It was, in any case, impossible to ignore much longer the obvious preparations for the invasion of Abyssinia which Mussolini was making all through the summer.

On 24th July the National Council of Labour called on the Government (in which Baldwin had now succeeded MacDonald as Prime Minister) to make its attitude clear, and Lansbury, as Leader of the Parliamentary Labour Party, gave assurances to the new Foreign Secretary, Sir Samuel Hoare, that the Opposition would support him in any stand he made at Geneva. The Assembly of the League was due to meet on 11th September and the T.U.C. assembled at Margate immediately before, conscious that its proceedings would be closely followed for their reflection of British public opinion.

Faced with the actual threat of aggression, no longer with an hypothesis, neither Bevin nor Citrine hesitated for a moment: they must carry through the policy of support for the League, whatever the consequences. When the three national committees of the Labour movement met at Margate on 2nd and 3rd September in preparation for the big debate on the 5th, the trade-union leaders pressed for explicit approval of the use of sanctions against Italy. Cripps opposed them, but did not put in an appearance on the second night when the committees voted on the draft resolution. Bevin stated explicitly that Lansbury neither opposed the resolution nor abstained, but voted for it.[1] After condemning the conduct of the Fascist Government, the resolution pledged the T.U.C. to "firm support of any action consistent with the principles and status of the League to restrain the Italian Government and to uphold the authority of the League."

When he put the resolution to Congress, Citrine made no attempt to evade the issue of sanctions:

"There is only one way of dealing with a bully and that is by the use of force. Moral resolutions are no good. . . . It may mean war, but that is the thing we have to face. There is no real alternative now left to us but the applying

[1] In a letter to C. H. Wilson, 8th October 1935: "That I swear to."

of sanctions involving, in all possibility, war. But I say this. If we fail now, if we go back now, war is absolutely certain. I ask you what will happen to Germany, if Italy can treat with contempt the nations of the world who have plighted their word to preserve peace?"[1]

In following Citrine, Bevin did not waste time in repeating what had already been said. His own views on sanctions were as clear as Citrine's but he had argued in the joint meetings of the three national committees that neither denunciation of Mussolini nor even the threat of sanctions was enough. It was thanks to Bevin that the resolution finally approved concluded with two paragraphs that struck an entirely different note. He began his speech by reading them out to Congress:

"While resolute in refusing to permit Italy to profit by any act of aggression, this Congress recognises the necessity of eradicating the evils and dangers arising from the economic exploitation of colonial territories and peoples for the profit of imperialist and capitalist Powers and groups."

The Government was urged to call a World Economic Conference and place on its agenda "the international control of the sources of raw materials with . . . . economic equality of opportunity for all nations in the undeveloped regions of the earth".

This was a theme which had long fascinated Bevin[2] and, treating the issue of sanctions as already settled so far as the T.U.C. was concerned, he made the outstanding speech of the Congress on the need to look further ahead than the immediate crisis and to deal with the causes of war.

There was no doubt in Bevin's mind where these were to be sought. Sanctions, if they were to be effective, would have to prohibit access to the twenty-five or so basic materials which supplied all the metals and power for both industry and war.

"If these materials were internationally controlled, produced according to world requirements, and could be obtained by every industrial nation by purchase and not by conquest, 90 per cent of the world causes of war would be entirely removed."

1 T.U.C. Report, 1935, p. 349.
2 In his broadcast of January 1934, he said: "I am convinced that the attempt to monopolise raw materials and their development by the concession method is one of the greatest causes of conflict between nations."

The League was primarily a political organisation. It must extend its interest to economic questions and discuss these in open conference just as the I.L.O. discussed labour problems. The old method which Mussolini was trying to imitate of grabbing a piece of territory in order to exploit its resources was out of date. "But immediately you settle the Abyssinian question and stop Mussolini, then tomorrow you have a quarrel with another nation over raw materials or over another sphere of influence." They had to find some other way in place of economic nationalism, "which puts nations in cages and expects them to remain at peace."

Britain had a unique opportunity to offer a lead.

"We say to the world, we recognise that from the day we trod the imperial path, there has been a great change in world requirements, world demands and the seeking of opportunities for all peoples of the world.
"We have been left the . . . responsibility of an Empire and we will not break it up, we will not destroy it. It is at least a third of the world linked together in various forms. Instead of breaking it up we will carry it a stage further forward by using an economic organisation that we can create through the League and from empire organisation we will pass into the stage of world organisation."[1]

The combination of Citrine's precise, lawyer-like mastery of the facts to present a case and Bevin's larger, sweeping strokes to sketch a policy proved, once again, its power to convince a trade-union audience. When Bevin sat down, there were cries of "Vote, Vote," and although the debate continued, its result was certain. By 2,962,000 to 177,000 Congress voted solidly in favour of sanctions with the clear understanding that sanctions might mean war.

I I

The T.U.C.'s vote was the reflection of a much larger body of opinion in the country as a whole which was more strongly in favour of resisting aggression than at any time again until after the occupation of Prague. Hoare's speech at Geneva in September had commanded widespread support—evidence of the response which might have been evoked by stronger leadership in foreign policy

[1] T.U.C. Report, 1935, pp. 354–7. It was the first rough statement of an idea Bevin was to develop more fully in 1938–9. Cf., below, c. 22.

during the 1930s. Never, perhaps, were the chances of successful resistance to the dictators higher.

At this moment, Bevin learned to his anger that three leading members of the Labour Party could no longer accept the policy confirmed by the three national committees as recently as 3rd September and endorsed by the T.U.C. on the 5th. On 20th September when public opinion was more firmly behind that policy than ever before, the *Daily Herald* announced that Ponsonby had resigned the leadership of the Labour Party in the House of Lords and that Cripps, the chairman of the Socialist League, had resigned from the National Executive. Even more serious, the Leader of the Party, George Lansbury, made public his disagreement with his Party's policy in the Sunday Press and while—as Dalton put it—"he wouldn't resign on his own initiative, was asking us (the National Executive) to settle the question for him [and] was rushing about the country speaking against the Party's international policy."[1] The impression of a divided leadership unfit to bear the responsibility of government could hardly have been more damning. It was against this background that Bevin went down to Brighton for the Labour Party Conference.

The debate which opened in the Dome on the morning of 1st October was the longest in the history of the Party; none has been more charged with emotion.[2] The vote at the end of the morning session on the 2nd was taken literally on the eve of war, for Italian troops began their advance into Abyssinia the following day and news of their long-prepared attack was expected hourly.

If a majority of the delegates crowding into the Dome that Tuesday had decided to vote for sanctions, it was a decision reached only after a struggle and involved for many the painful abandonment of long-held beliefs and a crisis of conscience.

The resolution which Hugh Dalton introduced on behalf of the Executive was identical with that which the T.U.C. had voted for at Margate a month before. It was, Dalton argued, the logical conclusion of the League policy which the Party had followed since the Great War. Reaffirmed by the Southport conference the year before and by the T.U.C. in 1934 and 1935, it had been stated by Lansbury himself in the House of Commons as recently as 1st

1 Dalton, *op. cit.*, pp. 66–67.
2 Labour Party Conference Report, 1935, pp. 153–193.

August. On that occasion, Dalton reminded the conference, the Leader of the Party had told the House:

"The Labour Party will support the Government by every means in its power so long as the Government stand quite firmly by their obligation under the Covenant of the League."

Now the time had come to ask, "Do we stand firm in this crisis for the policy to which we have so often pledged ourselves, or shall we turn tail and run away, repudiate our obligations under the covenant of the League and signal 'All Clear' to Mussolini?"

Dalton was answered by Cripps. So long as a capitalist government was in power, he declared, he was not prepared to trust them to use their military power for other than imperialist and capitalist aims. The League was "nothing but the tool of the imperialist powers". The only course open to the workers was to fight against capitalism, and he urged the conference to vote against the resolution.

The debate continued throughout the day and towards the end of the afternoon the chairman called on Lansbury to speak. He was greeted, says the official report, "with loud and prolonged applause," the whole conference—with the exception of a trade-union group seated round Bevin—rising to its feet to join in the ovation.

Now an old man of seventy-six, Lansbury enjoyed a respect and affection in the Labour movement which few have equalled. He had spent his life in a series of crusades against poverty, injustice and exploitation, and no one in trouble had ever gone to him in vain. For the last four years he had been the Leader of the Party, an office which he did not seek and for which his natural temperament as a rebel and a nonconformist little suited him. Pitchforked into the position by the defeat of the other senior members of the Party in 1931, he had forced himself to discharge duties he disliked, despite the deeply felt loss of his wife and a serious illness. He had now, however, reached a point where he felt that he could no longer remain silent in face of decisions which ran counter to his lifelong conviction, on the grounds of Christian pacifism, that the use of force in any circumstances was morally wrong.

At any time the speech of a leader offering to resign on an issue of conscience would make a strong appeal to the sentiments of a Labour Party conference. Its effect in this case was doubled by the affection in which Lansbury was held and by the fact that many of the delegates had been troubled by similar doubts, even if they had reluctantly come to a different conclusion.

Lansbury made no attempt to defend the inconsistency of his position:

> "I agree with those who think it is quite intolerable that you should have a man speaking as leader who disagrees fundamentally on an issue of this kind. . . . And I should not consider an expression of opinion hostile to my continuance as leader as anything more than natural and perfectly friendly."

Nonetheless, he continued, he had never been more convinced that the movement was making a terrible mistake:

> "It may be that I shall not meet you on this platform any more. (Cries of 'No'). . . . When I was sick and on my back, ideas came into my head, and one was that the only thing worth while for old men to do is at least to say the thing they believe and at least try to warn the young of the dangers of force and compulsion . . .
>
> "It is said that people like me are irresponsible. I am no more irresponsible a leader than the greatest trade union leader in the country. . . . If mine was the only voice in the conference, I would say in the name of the faith I hold, the belief I have that God intended us to live peaceably and quietly with one another—if some people do not allow us to do so, I am ready to stand as the early Christians did and say 'This is our faith, this is where we stand and if necessary, this is where we will die.' "

Lansbury had never spoken with greater sincerity and his statement of personal faith stirred his audience deeply. It was only as the applause died away and the wave of emotion subsided that Bevin was seen to rise to his feet and without hurrying make his way to the platform: the moment for which he had been waiting had come.

12

To follow such a speech was difficult enough: to fly in the face of the sentiment to which Lansbury had made so strong an appeal needed a determination which few men command. The obvious course was to pay a personal tribute to Lansbury and then, leaving his declaration on one side, to turn the debate back to the argument in favour of sanctions. But Bevin was in no mood to play the politician or to wrap up what he felt.

"Let me remind the delegates," he began, "that when George Lansbury says what he has said today, it is rather late to say it, and I hope this Conference will not be influenced by either sentiment or personal attachment. I hope you will carry no resolution of an emergency character telling a man with a conscience like Lansbury what he ought to do. If he finds that he ought to take a certain course, then his conscience should direct him as to the course he should take. It is placing the Executive and the Movement in an absolutely wrong position to be taking[1] your conscience round from body to body to be told what you ought to do with it."

At this there was an angry outcry from many parts of the hall. But Bevin, refusing to withdraw, shouted above the interruptions that Lansbury had been guilty of disloyalty and went on to prove it, detailing step by step the meetings of the National Council of Labour in which the policy Lansbury now repudiated had been discussed, adopted and confirmed, with Lansbury present as Leader and making no public protest, from February 1934 down to and including the meeting at Margate before the T.U.C. debate.

Lansbury protested later that on a number of occasions he had drawn the Executive's attention to his own pacifist views and had been begged to stay as Leader, but this does not invalidate Bevin's argument. By agreeing to remain, he placed both himself and the Party in a false position, accepting a responsibility which it was too late to disavow on grounds of private conscience.

As Bevin drove home his points, his argument began to tell, even with a hostile audience. When Lansbury tried to answer at the end of Bevin's speech, the conference would no longer listen to him and not a man rose in his defence.

But Bevin had not finished yet. For three years Sir Stafford Cripps, while a member of the National Executive and a leading spokesman of the Party in the House, had claimed the right to criticise and oppose the Party's programme from the platform of the Socialist League. Now he too stepped aside from responsibility, at the moment of decision, threw up his place on the Executive and urged the conference to reject its policy.

Bevin turned on him with bitterness:

"People have been on this platform today talking about the destruction of capitalism. The thing that is being wiped out is the trade union movement.

1 This is the version in the official report. According to others who were present, he spoke of 'trailing' or 'hawking' his conscience round.

. . . It is we who are being wiped out and who will be wiped out if Fascism comes here. . . . All the speeches that have been made against this resolution ought to have been made last year at Southport and the people who oppose this resolution ought to have had the courage of their convictions and tabled a resolution to the effect that we should withdraw from the League of Nations. You cannot be in and out at the same time, not if you are honest."

Cripps had been present at the Margate meeting of the three national committees but, after briefly expressing his opposition to the resolution, failed to put in an appearance when the vote was taken on the second evening.

"When you have been to a meeting of this character and have taken your decision, you have to stand to it and see it through . . . I feel bitter in my very soul about it, because if this Movement is going to win the country, when it is faced with a crisis, it has got to give confidence that it is capable of coming to a decision . . . I feel that we have been let down, every one of us in the General Council feels we have been let down."

Only at the very end of his speech did Bevin return to the question of sanctions and call on the conference to give as near a unanimous vote as possible, "leaving it to those who cannot accept the policy of this great conference to take their own course." Yet more than any other speaker he contributed to the final result, a vote of 2,168,000 to 102,000 in favour of full support for the League. By his intervention, deliberately reserved until after Cripps and Lansbury had spoken, he cut through the intellectual and emotional confusion they had created to set clearly before the conference "the choice (in the words of one of the delegates, Mrs. Hamilton) between the satisfaction of one's personal conscience and one's duty as a citizen."

"I recall (she adds) that, as I came away from the conference session with George Ridley, I found that he shared my sense of deep relief and agreed that E.B. had pulled the Party out of a sentimental morass into which it had been in real danger of sinking. He compelled a naturally sentimental body to see an issue in larger than personal terms. He had to attack Lansbury to make the issue clear. But it was not the personal attack, but the sense he conveyed of the responsibility of the issue itself that gave force to his speech and carried the conference."[1]

Others saw it in a different light, conceding the force of Bevin's argument but unable to forgive the bitterness of his attack on

1 In a letter to the author, 17th December 1956.

Lansbury or the retort he is reported to have made to those who reproached him afterwards: "Lansbury has been going about dressed in saint's clothes for years waiting for martyrdom: I set fire to the faggots."[1] Few who have described the episode since have failed to censure him for "an unnecessary brutality".

The timing of Bevin's speech was certainly deliberate: he waited until Lansbury had spoken and much of what he said was in his mind before he came to the conference. But the mood in which he addressed it was anything but one of cold calculation. On the contrary, he startled the delegates by the vehemence with which he spoke, his face dark with anger, his hands gripping the rail as if he would break it. The interruptions he met goaded his temper; feeling the hostility of his audience he shouted down their protests, refusing to take back a word he had said. This was the rough side of Bevin, the dockers' leader of the earlier years arguing with a noisy mob of strikers on the waterfront, his voice hoarse with the effort to make himself heard. It was as much a part of his nature as the patience he could show in negotiation or the power with which he could kindle the imagination of an audience.

But Bevin's anger sprang from something deeper than the opposition he met. His deepest instincts were loyalty and responsibility to the men he led. Both were outraged by the behaviour of Lansbury and Cripps, men who had accepted the responsibilities of leadership, had accepted decisions or at least let them pass without taking the proper course of resigning, and then backed down, on the grounds of conscientious or intellectual scruples, when they had to be implemented.

Even now Lansbury had not resigned the leadership of the Party but pushed the onus of asking for his resignation on to others and took full advantage of his moral dilemma to make a highly emotional appeal to the Party to revise its policy. Far from accepting the view of Lansbury as a political innocent, Bevin wrote: "Why, even on the night he was speaking at the conference, he was trying to manipulate the time so that nobody could reply to him that night. He is not a guileless old gentleman; I have known him for years and have worked with him."[2]

1 Francis Williams, *Ernest Bevin*, p. 196.
2 Ernest Bevin to C. H. Wilson, 9th October 1935. Wilson had written to express pain and regret at Bevin's treatment of Lansbury.

These may well have been exaggerated suspicions and unfair to Lansbury.[1] But there is no doubt that Bevin, always a suspicious man, believed them to be well-founded. For, as the letter already quoted makes clear, there was always at the back of his mind the fear that 1931 would be repeated. In 1931 the last leader of the Party, MacDonald, had set his individual judgment above a collective decision, splitting the Party and leaving it to suffer the worst electoral defeat in its history. With the next election imminent, Bevin was determined to prevent another split and not only to answer Lansbury's and Cripps' arguments but to destroy their credit as leaders. Lansbury had appealed in personal terms to the conference: Bevin answered him in the same terms:

"Who am I to let my personality protrude as compared with this great Movement? Who is any man on this platform? . . .
"The great crime of Ramsay MacDonald was that he never called in his party, and the crime of these people is that they have sown discord at the very moment when candidates want unity to face an election."

At the end of the conference Bevin remarked:

"If there was one debate in which I would have liked not to have spoken it was the one in which I did speak. I go away from conference after thirty-five years' labouring work with a sad heart. I have lived through three splits in the Movement and I do not want any more."[2]

But he offered no apology. He had done what he believed had to be done, regretting the necessity but not his own action. From this view he never departed.

13

Lansbury could scarcely retain the leadership of the Party after his defeat at Margate: he resigned on 8th October. Had his resignation been deferred until after the General Election, Morrison, out of the House since 1931 but playing a big part on the National Executive and the Policy Committee, would have had strong claims to succeed him, but the question of the leadership was brought to a

1 Cf. Raymond Postgate: *Life of George Lansbury* (1951), for a different view.
2 Labour Party Conference Report, 1935, p. 243.

head by the Brighton debate a few weeks too soon for Morrison. With its choice limited to existing members, the Parliamentary Labour Party elected Attlee, Lansbury's deputy, to take his place, and he remained to lead the Party for more than twenty years.

If the choice had fallen on someone else, in particular if Morrison had been elected to succeed Lansbury, Bevin's future career might well have followed a different course. Had Morrison been the leader of the Labour Party it is unlikely that he could ever have established a close understanding with Bevin or that Bevin would have served in a Government of which he was the head. With Attlee, on the other hand, Bevin established a mutual confidence which matured into a firm political friendship and was to prove a factor of great importance in the history of the Labour Government after the war.

Although, by precipitating the choice of the leadership at Brighton, Bevin contributed to these later developments and thereby unconsciously influenced his own future career, at the time he neither knew nor very much cared who might become leader in Lansbury's place. What mattered to the exclusion of everything else was to show that the Labour movement was united. The issues were too big to be played with. Only by speaking with a united voice could Labour hope to influence events by holding the Government to firm support of the League; only by overcoming its own divisions and doubts could the Party hope to persuade the electorate that it was fit to govern.

On 3rd October Italian troops invaded Abyssinia, and four days later the Council of the League condemned Italy for resorting to war in disregard of her obligations under the Covenant. Indignation at Mussolini's action ran high and the Government still spoke in the same resolute tone that Sir Samuel Hoare had adopted at Geneva in September.

Stealing the thunder of the Left, Baldwin presented his Government to the country as the champions of collective security and fixed a general election for mid-November. Making the most of the divisions amongst the Labour Party's leaders over sanctions and the earlier vote against rearmament, the Conservatives captured the initiative on foreign policy and convinced many who had replied to the Peace Ballot that they were more to be trusted than Labour to give firm support to the League.

Bevin, although not a candidate, was in the thick of the fight.

The Union had eleven official candidates in the field and contributed more than £8,000 to the Labour Party's funds. He himself undertook a heavy programme of electioneering, speaking in more than twenty constituencies as far apart as Rochdale and Rotherhithe, Shipley and the Forest of Dean. Outflanked by the Government on foreign affairs, he concentrated his attack on their domestic record, the treatment of the depressed areas, the means test and the widespread poverty still to be found in the industrial towns.

Labour recaptured many of the seats it had lost, winning 154 compared to 46 in the 1931 election. Its poll was within a few thousand of the 8.3 million of 1929, a million and six hundred thousand up on that of 1931. But Baldwin's majority was still secure, more than 240 over Labour and the Liberals combined. The Tories were back in office for another five years, Labour condemned to the continued frustration of opposition.

It may well be doubted whether in the year of the King's Jubilee, with economic recovery well under way and a strong lead from the Government on foreign policy, Labour could ever have won the 1935 election. But the impression left by the Brighton debate was not wiped out by the subsequent vote in favour of sanctions. A party whose Parliamentary leader and his chief lieutenant repudiated its policy at the moment when it had to be carried out was under a heavy handicap when it asked to be entrusted with the responsibilities of government. The result of the election in Bevin's eyes wholly justified his censure of Lansbury and Cripps. Meeting his own Executive in December, he remarked:

"If Labour is to win, it must demonstrate that it is capable of accepting responsibility; that it is not only eager to govern, but prepared to do so; and individualism such as that which has characterised certain persons in the past must be checked. Having passed through the 1931 trouble and knowing that we were on the eve of an election with our leadership in the state it was, I felt compelled to express my bitter resentment. . . . We had to spend one and a half days at Brighton on a debate demonstrating the division in the Party on a matter of foreign policy which, if its leaders had sunk their personalities in the interests of the greater Movement, need not have lasted two hours."[1]

When the National Government, once safely back in office, abandoned the promise of firmness with which it had won the

1 General Secretary's Quarterly Report, December 1935.

election and led the retreat from sanctions, Bevin felt more convinced than ever that he and those who thought like him must let neither sentiment nor tradition stand in the way of bringing the Labour Party to face the responsibilities of foreign policy.

CHAPTER 21

Chairman of the General
Council
1936 – 1937

I

BEVIN FOUND relief from the frustration of politics and a release for his energies in taking up his old battle for the improvement of working conditions. Immediately after the election he left for the second of three I.L.O. conferences which he attended between the summer of 1935 and the autumn of 1936.

At the first, held in June 1935, he had resumed his efforts to persuade the conference to adopt a convention on the forty-hour week. A little to his own surprise he succeeded, although the employers' group voted against it.

The British Government, however, skilfully evaded every effort by the T.U.C. to pin it down to the passage of legislation giving effect to the convention. Faced with strong opposition from the employers, unless a reduction in hours was accompanied by a reduction in wages, successive Ministers of Labour blandly informed the General Council that they could not consider introducing legislation to make the forty-hour week compulsory until the possibility of voluntary agreement by both sides, industry by industry, had been thoroughly explored. This, as Bevin admitted at the 1936 T.U.C., was an effective retort. There was much opposition in the trade-union movement to any reduction in hours which might interfere with the opportunity to earn overtime pay. Bevin had little hope of tackling the problem in individual industries unless the principle was first established in law. This he never succeeded in achieving. The steady reduction in unemployment reduced the force of his immediate argument, that of spreading the work. His second line of argument, the increasing mechanisation of industry (automation, in the version of the 1950s) was not affected but made little appeal to trade-union opinion. Although resolutions in favour of the forty-hour week continued to figure on the T.U.C. agenda, by the time a Labour Government came to power the demand was all for greater production and it was not until after his death that progress in automation forced the question of hours to the forefront again.

Bevin had better fortune with the second cause which he took up at Geneva, in October 1935, that of the seamen. For a nation as proud of its sea-borne trade as the British it is a surprising fact that two of the worst paid and most shabbily treated groups of workers in the country were the dockers and the merchant seamen. The National Union of Seamen had recovered its independence after the death of Havelock Wilson, but it still lacked either the membership or the resources to fight the shipowners on its own. Bevin not only helped to secure them the support of the T.U.C. and the Labour Party but took a lively part in the campaign to improve the low wages and the disgraceful conditions in which many seamen had to live while at sea.[1]

Co-operating closely with W. R. Spence of the Seamen's Union, Bevin tried three lines of approach. The first, organised by the trade-union Parliamentary committee in which the T.G.W.U. joined the N.U.S., was to secure a Board of Trade Inquiry into the loss of a number of British merchant ships at sea and then to present the evidence in such a way as to arouse public opinion to the scandalous neglect not only of the men's welfare and health but of ordinary safety through undermanning, worn-out equipment and the continual use of ships no longer fit to put to sea.

The second was to oppose the renewal of the Government's shipping subsidy unless specific assurances were given on improvements in the conditions of the men and some share in the benefits of the subsidy. This was a continuation of the fight which Samuel Plimsoll had waged in the House with his attack on 'coffin ships' in the 1870s.

The third was to work for the adoption of an international con-

---

1 According to figures quoted in the House of Commons (11th and 28th February 1936), seamen's wages were £2 17s. 6d. or less for an 84-hour week, with 10/- deducted for food and no allowance for the expenses of a home on shore.

vention by the I.L.O. This had direct relation to the other two lines of attack, since the argument always used by British shipowners in refusing improvements was foreign competition at cut rates although they themselves opposed any attempt to establish the international regulation of conditions or hours.

2

The conference in Geneva which Bevin attended at the end of 1935 was intended as a preparation for a later conference, eventually held in October 1936. Bevin, although nominally only one of the advisers to the British seamen's delegate (Spence), in fact led and spoke for the whole workers' group. He was anxious at this stage not to press the dispute with the owners beyond the point at which they might agree to a compromise. But both his major speeches left no doubt of his determination to secure a seamen's charter before he had finished.

If competition in the shipping industry had forced freight charges below an economic return, the remedy for this, he argued, was not to attempt to cut labour costs still more, but to regulate this ruinous competition by international agreement. The first step to this was agreement on conditions and hours. True, it was impossible as yet to reach any international agreement on wages. But, Bevin retorted, he suspected that the shipowners and the British Government only introduced the question of wages with an eye to discouraging the men's demand for the reduction of hours (a forty-eight hour week) and an adequate scale of manning, questions which *were* capable of being regulated internationally.

Such arrangements, the shipowners said, were not practicable.

"Why not? You have got the Baltic Conference, you have the North Atlantic Conference, you have the Australian Conference, and in these three conferences you have sat down and fixed what the public should pay: and yet you say you cannot sit down and fix an adjustment of rates in order to give the seamen anything like regularity of conditions.

"I do not believe you, if you will pardon me for saying so. Do not tell us that the brains of my countrymen have become so atrophied that we cannot organise a business to pay more than £2. 16. 0. a week of 84 hours for one of the most essential services that the country has. . . . Other maritime countries have introduced the eight-hour day and have not gone out of business as a consequence. . . . The greatest output per man in the world is found in the countries with the highest wages and the shortest hours, and this is true of every industry. While I know I am not going to change your mind, I am sorry. . . . It makes me as a Britisher feel sad when I come to international conferences time after time and hear my country taking a reactionary line, instead of leading, as it ought to do as the oldest modern industrial country in the world, in the advance of social progress not only for itself but for other countries."[1]

3

Bevin's wisdom in leaving time for public opinion to produce a change of attitude was soon confirmed. By August 1936 when the Seamen's Union held its annual conference (in Transport House), he was able to congratulate the delegates on substantial progress in negotiations with the shipowners and received the Union's Gold Badge in appreciation of his efforts. In October he was back at Geneva and had the satisfaction of seeing the I.L.O.'s Maritime Conference carry six conventions and two recommendations by large majorities. Taken together, these constituted the international charter for which the seamen's unions had campaigned, without success, since the first I.L.O. Maritime Conference of 1920.[2]

Bevin was the outstanding figure of the conference. One witness called him the "Minister Plenipotentiary" of the world's seamen. He spent three weeks wrestling in committee over the text of the most important convention—that on hours of work and the manning of ships—then delivered a powerful speech which helped to swing the votes of a number of governments and to secure the necessary majority. He ended with an unusual appeal to the employers:

"Shipping is one of the most vital methods of transcending the barriers which keep nations apart. The more those barriers can be broken down, the more

1 Proceedings of the Preparatory Maritime Conference, Geneva, November–December 1935. I.L.O. (Geneva) 1936: pp. 198–200; 229–32.

2 They covered the liability of the owner in the case of the sickness, injury or death of a member of the crew; the application of health insurance to seamen; the minimum professional requirements of masters and officers; annual holidays with pay; the limitation of the hours of work not only for seamen but for officers, stewards and catering staff; and a fixed scale of manning according to the tonnage of the vessel with minimum requirements of age and sea-going experience.

you can reconcile the difference between countries, and the more you can do away with barriers in the form of subsidies, quotas and so on, the more you will be able through shipping to make a big contribution to the ends in view. That being so, I should like to ask the Employers, who naturally wish to achieve this result, why they raise their hands to hold back even their own emancipation from the handicaps which have hindered them in the economic nationalism of the last ten years.

"Is it too late to ask you to try to rise above the mere payment of a little overtime in order to accomplish something by which in the end you will gain as much as the workmen who sail in your ships? I do wish that employers could have a little more imagination, and would not be so influenced in their calculations by mere monetary factors. After this Convention has been in operation for a year or two, if anyone comes to Geneva and seeks to do away with it, every one of you who votes against it today will resist its removal from the statute books of the world; yet now you are opposing your own progress. Is it not this timidity, this fear, this lack of imagination, which is holding the world back and holding it in thraldom today?"[1]

When he sat down and the vote was taken, the convention was carried by 62 votes to 17.

4

But politics could not be pushed aside for long. In October 1935 the Labour Party had reluctantly brought itself to accept the argument that support for the League meant sanctions and that sanctions might mean war. Between the Brighton conference and the Edinburgh conference of October 1936, however, the foundation of Labour's views on foreign affairs was knocked away by the demonstration that the League of Nations was unable to prevent the conquest of Abyssinia by Italy. A system of collective security remained the aim of Labour policy, but the chances of establishing such a system in the near future were hardly less remote than those of eliminating capitalism. Neither slogan offered a practical guide to action in face of the immediate threat of further aggression by Mussolini and Hitler. The painful question which had been settled for the moment by the vote at Brighton was thus reopened, this time with no easy way out of the difficulty by agreeing on strong support

1 Proceedings of the 21st and 22nd sessions of the I.L.O.: 4th Maritime Conference, 6th–24th October 1936. I.L.O. (Geneva) 1937, p. 88 and pp. 131–3.

for the League and leaving it to each individual member to decide for himself what that support involved.

The National Government's retreat from a policy of sanctions against Italy had begun before the election. The storm of anger which the Hoare-Laval Pact aroused in December forced Baldwin to make further gestures, to get rid of Hoare and replace him at the Foreign Office by Eden as a sop to supporters of the League. But, as Professor Mowat shrewdly points out, the Hoare-Laval deal "was as effective as if it had succeeded. It doomed the League and it doomed Abyssinia."[1] By May 1936 the Italians had won, thanks in part to the use of poison gas against the ill-equipped Abyssinian forces. The British Government announced that it would abandon sanctions on 18th June, less than nine months after the election, and in face of the stinging sarcasm of Lloyd George[2] and their other critics lost the debate but carried the vote in the House of Commons.

The Government's record on sanctions provided an admirable argument for those who were reluctant to abandon Labour's traditional programme of disarmament and the 'outlawry of war'. When the Government published the White Paper of 3rd March 1936 with a new programme for restoring the country's defences, three days' discussion in the three national committees of the Labour movement ended in a decision to oppose. Dalton, who worked closely with Bevin in an effort to persuade their colleagues of the gravity of the situation, wrote in his diary: "The Party won't face up to realities. There is still much more anti-armament sentiment and many are more agin' our own Government than agin' Hitler."[3] Indeed the amendment moved by Attlee in the Commons debate might well have been copied unchanged from any Labour Party manifesto of the past fifteen years.

Two days before the debate opened, on 7th March, Hitler moved his troops into the demilitarised zone of the Rhineland, defying the provisions of both the Versailles and the Locarno treaties. The Labour Party was caught as unprepared as—with far less excuse—were the British and French Governments. When the National Council of Labour met on the 12th, Bevin carried a motion to invite

1 C. L. Mowat: *Britain between the Wars*, p. 561.
2 "There is no evidence that the Government ever meant business over sanctions. . . . Now they are running away, brandishing their swords—still leading." Quoted, ibid., p. 562.
3 Hugh Dalton: *The Fateful Years* (1957), p. 88.

the Bureau of the Labour and Socialist International and the Executive of the International Federation of Trade Unions to meet them in London as soon as possible. The conference took place on 20th–21st March, and Bevin and Dalton were appointed to present the British point of view.

They found a readier hearing for their arguments from their Continental than from some of their British colleagues. The declaration approved by the conference condemned Hitler's action and accepted the lesson that "wanton aggression cannot be restrained by moral appeal. Any would-be aggressor must be confronted with an overwhelming superiority of force. . . . National armaments should now be regulated with this end in view."[1] But there was no response from British public opinion, either inside or outside the Labour Party, comparable with the anger roused by Mussolini's attack on Abyssinia. Lord Lothian's comment, "After all, the Germans are only going into their own back garden", was accepted by Churchill as a representative view, and Dalton told the House of Commons that public opinion would not tolerate military or even economic sanctions to turn the German troops out of the Rhineland.[2] The Government needed no holding back. Its object was to avoid war, to go on talking until the danger was past, and the second chance to halt the dictators before it was too late was allowed to go begging.

Nor was Baldwin's appointment of Bevin's old opponent at Bristol in 1918, Sir Thomas Inskip, as Minister for the Co-ordination of Defence calculated to impress would-be aggressors.[3] A group of Tories—Churchill, Amery, Lloyd, Edward Grigg—combined to warn the Prime Minister of the inadequacy of the country's defences, but they failed to spur the Government into greater activity. So far as Labour was concerned, an even wider gulf separated it from Churchill, the unrepentant imperialist and hammer of the trade unions in 1926, than from Baldwin. The fact that Churchill advocated a bigger arms programme only confirmed the Labour Party's opposition. It voted against all the Service Estimates in the House of Commons and when Dalton challenged this decision in the

1 The resolution is printed in the Labour Party Conference Report, 1936, pp. 302–3.
2 26th March 1936.
3 One unkind comment declared that there had been no such appointment since the Emperor Caligula made his horse a Roman consul.

Parliamentary Labour Party, he was defeated by 57 votes to 39.

Bevin felt as much distrust of the Government as any other member of the Party, but with a surer instinct than the politicians he cut through the web of sophistries and conflicting emotions in which the Labour Party had become entangled to reach the plain conclusion that, if the dictators were to be stopped, Britain must rearm. He refused to be diverted by the argument that this meant voting for the National Government. What did that matter by comparison with the issues now at stake? Loyal to the Party, he refused to claim for himself the public freedom to attack majority decisions which he had condemned in Cripps and Lansbury, but he threw all his weight in the Party's counsels against those who wanted to go on evading the question of how aggression was to be resisted.

His influence is clearly to be seen in a characteristic passage from the manifesto *Labour and the Defence of Peace* which the National Council, after much discussion, published in May 1936:

"Labour must be prepared to accept the consequences of its policy. A man who joins a trade union accepts the obligation of collective action in defence of its principles. A man who enjoys the collective security of a trade union must be prepared to take the risk of loyalty and his principles when a strike or lock out is threatened. Similarly, a Movement which supports the League system cannot desert it in a crisis."

But the Manifesto still talked in terms of a League system of collective security which was patently bankrupt, repeated many of the old shibboleths and shied away from the question, what was to be done now that the League had failed?

5

By the time the 1936 Party conference assembled at Edinburgh in October the question was still without an answer. For the first time for several years the National Council of Labour failed to produce an agreed resolution which could be debated first by the T.U.C. and then by the Party conference. At Plymouth, where the T.U.C. met the month before, there had been no general debate on the international situation. Explaining this omission in answer to a question, Bevin told the conference that the time had come to re-examine the movement's policy in the light of events since the Weymouth and Southport conferences of 1934:

"In this examination it will be necessary for this Movement to take new responsibilities. . . . The question of collective security is in danger of becoming a shibboleth rather than a practical operative fact. . . . We are not going to meet the Fascist menace by mass resolutions. We are not going to meet it by pure pacifism. . . . If in certain respects it means uprooting some of our cherished ideals and facing the issue fairly in the light of the development of Fascism, we must do it for the Movement and for the sake of posterity."[1]

Bevin's hint was plain enough and was accepted without challenge with that practical common sense which distinguished the discussion of foreign affairs in the T.U.C. from the debates at Labour Party conferences throughout the 1930s. But how far Bevin's opponents in the Party were from agreeing with him—and how remote from reality—was shown by a much publicised letter which Sir Stafford Cripps sent to the Glasgow *Forward* on the eve of the Labour Party conference.

Urging every effort to stop recruiting for the armed forces in order to force the Government to take the unpopular step of conscription, Cripps wrote:

"I think it is likely that, if Great Britain were conquered by Germany, Socialism would be suppressed, though that is not certain . . .
"But suppose you attained your object and Great Britain won another imperial victory, what then? British Fascism would be less brutal than German, but the world situation would be no better. Another Versailles peace, another period of acute suffering for the workers, and then the next war. That's all."[2]

Cripps was no longer a member of the Executive, but he was still the leading figure in the Socialist League and the prophet of the Left especially among the younger generation. In any case, as the debate at the conference soon showed, the Party's National Executive was itself deeply divided on the attitude to be taken in face of the danger of war.

The resolution which Dalton introduced on behalf of the Executive

1 T.U.C. Report, 1936, p. 358.
2 *Forward*, 3rd October 1936.

bore all the marks of compromise and ambiguity. In one paragraph it spoke of maintaining such defence forces as were required by obligations under the League and "the preservation of the people's rights and liberties". In the next, "the Labour Party declines to accept responsibility for a purely competitive armament policy . . . and reserves full liberty to criticise the rearmament programme of the present Government." Dalton, after making much of German rearmament, was prepared to say that in this situation Labour—if it came to power—would be compelled to provide an increase in British armaments, but he said nothing of Labour's policy in opposition. Morrison, also speaking for the Executive, declared categorically that the resolution meant voting against the Government on armaments. Attlee, trying to straddle the opposite positions, told the conference: "There is no suggestion here that we shall support the Government's rearmament policy." Then what did the resolution mean?

If the debate that followed had been deliberately designed to show the hesitations, evasions and divisions of the Party, it could hardly have been more effective. Once again it was left to Bevin to cut through the confusion and pin the conference down.

"I thought," he said, "when the Executive put down this motion, that this was a clear departure from the votes that have been given in the House on the Estimates during the last few months."

Now he was not sure and he asked for a plain answer. In the meantime he made his own position clear and alone among the Labour leaders put the case for rearming without hedging.

"I say this to Sir Stafford Cripps. If I am asked to face the question of arming this country, I am prepared to face it. . . . Which is the first institution that victorious Fascism wipes out? It is the trade union movement. . . . We saw our Movement go in Germany. . . . Our men shed their blood in Austria—and nearly everyone of them was a trade unionist.

"I regret that there appears to be this desire in every line of the resolution to put in something to make clear that we do not agree with the National Government. Does that not go without saying? Would not one paragraph have done it? Then it could have gone on with a very clear statement of what *we* intended to do."

This was no time for equivocation:

"If ever there was a time when, whether it is popular or unpopular, we have got to tell our own people the truth, it is now and we must do it fearlessly, whatever the consequences may be . . .

"The International Movement are wondering what we are going to do in Britain. Czechoslovakia, one of the most glorious little democratic countries, hedged in all round, is in danger of being sacrificed tomorrow.[1] They are our trade union brothers. They want to know what the British are going to do. You cannot save Czechoslovakia with speeches. We are not in office but I want to drive this Government to defend democracy against its will, if I can . . . I want to say to Mussolini and Hitler: 'If you are banking on being able to attack in the East or the West, and you are going to treat the British Socialist Movement as being weak and are going to rely on that at the critical moment, you are taking us too cheaply.'

"I look back to 1914—I am firmly convinced that it was the mentality of an Arnold[2] that led us into the war. The Liberals of that day never made themselves clear. They let this country drift on until we were in it and then they used propaganda to prove it was a righteous cause."

After all the muddle and equivocation, Bevin's speech marks him out, head and shoulders above the rest, as the one man in that assembly with the judgment and the courage to give the leadership of which not only the Labour Party but the whole country stood in such need. Although without that command of language which Churchill enjoyed, Bevin's speech at Edinburgh displayed the same firm grip of what was at stake, the same uncompromising response to the danger as his great contemporary.

"I believe," he told the conference, "that if this great Movement says to Hitler: 'If you are going to rely on force—while we fight for justice for everybody in the world—if you are going to rely on force and the forcing of your system, either through espionage, either through Mosley, either through your finance, we will stand up four-square to it.' It is the best thing that can be done for peace. I thought this resolution intended to ask us to face clearly up to that position.

"Reference has been made to the League of Nations. It has been proved weak. Do not let us get into that attitude of mind. We have had Empires that took centuries to build. The League of Nations is the first puny attempt at world organisation. Empires cannot last; that we are all agreed upon. Shall they break up and become the elements of scramble and warfare, or shall we try to build a League and a world organisation gradually to translate empire into world organisation instead? I believe the League of

1 The date of this remark is worth noting: it was made two years before Munich. Bevin, commonly regarded as an uneducated man, never made the mistake of referring, as Chamberlain did in 1938, to Czechoslovakia as "a far-away country" of whose people "we know nothing".

2 Lord Arnold had put the pacifist case in the debate.

Nations offers a great opportunity. Raw materials, markets and all the rest, depend upon maintaining this institution, and . . . while I would vote for armaments to defend democracy and our liberty, I would also say, strive with all our might . . . to build the great moral authority behind international law, that in the end law will triumph by consent instead of by force. "I am afraid, however, that we may have to go through force to liberty. With the philosophy of Fascism in the world, I feel that unless that is checked it will be inevitable. Therefore, I ask this conference to get a clear declaration from the platform as to what it means. Do not let us, as responsible men and women, bungle the issue."[1]

Attlee's reply, unfortunately, did not supply the answer for which Bevin asked. Although the resolution was carried by a big enough majority, it was anybody's guess what the vote meant and the Parliamentary Labour Party went on opposing the Government's rearmament.

6

The confusion in the Party over foreign policy was thrown into sharp relief by the Edinburgh debate on Spain. Franco's rebellion against the Republican Government in Madrid had begun in July 1936 and the Civil War which followed aroused in the British Left the same generous and ardent sympathies as the liberal revolts of the nineteenth century. The Spanish Civil War was the last of the volunteers' wars which had begun with the Greek War of Independence and the South American revolts of the 1820s, at once a test of conscience and a symbol of protest which stirred the emotions of the younger generation as no other event in the pre-war decade.

All Bevin's sympathies lay with the Republicans. He hated Fascism and saw in the grandeurs and miseries of the Spanish struggle a continuation of the same war which the Austrian Socialists had fought in the working-class districts of Vienna. But emotion was not a substitute for a policy. The Spanish Civil War was dominated from the beginning by the question of foreign intervention and Bevin and the other members of the National Council of Labour found themselves confronted with the same dilemma which, in one form or another, underlay every discussion of foreign policy in

1 Labour Party Conference Report, 1936, pp. 202-4.

the 1930s: How far were they prepared to go in aiding those who were attacked by the Fascist powers? Were they prepared to run the risk of a general war? If so, how could they go on voting against rearmament? As Bevin remarked at Edinburgh: "It is not rhetoric that is going to solve this problem; it is not eloquent speeches; it is sitting down in committees with bitter facts to face." Spain was not an issue apart, it could not be treated separately from those larger questions of foreign and defence policy on which, as the Edinburgh conference showed, the Labour movement was sorely divided and still inclined to vote against rearmament in one session and call angrily for resistance to Fascism in Spain in the next.

This dilemma was felt even more acutely by Léon Blum, the Socialist Prime Minister in Paris, who was trying to hold together a Popular Front Government and to avoid deepening the bitter divisions which already split France. Blum took the initiative in proposing a non-intervention pact among the Powers and with some misgivings the National Council of Labour, which had much stronger links with Paris than with Madrid, adopted the same policy. Had it been possible to enforce non-intervention strictly on both sides, there is no doubt that this would have been not only in the general interest—thereby reducing the danger of a European war—but also in the interests of the Spanish Government, since the rebels were assured of greater support from Mussolini and Hitler than the Republicans were likely to get from Britain and France or than they could afford to accept with impunity from Soviet Russia. It was on these grounds that Bevin defended non-intervention at the T.U.C. in September 1936 and secured the support of the Congress by the big majority of 3 million votes to 50,000.

By the time the Labour Party conference met a month later, however, evidence had begun to accumulate of the one-sided way in which non-intervention was working, and Greenwood and Bevin, attempting to defend the same policy, had to meet much stronger criticism from the floor. Two delegates were present from the Spanish Government, one of whom, the celebrated Communist La Pasionaria, had a Scots mother and spoke in eloquent English. Their appeal for aid stirred the conference deeply and the National Council, hurriedly summoned to meet under Bevin's chairmanship, began to beat a retreat from a policy which was so manifestly out of keeping with feeling in the Party.

Three weeks later (28th October), the National Council decided to withdraw Labour's support for non-intervention and to press for recognition of the Spanish Government's legal right to buy arms abroad. Bevin did not disagree: once he was convinced that Mussolini and Hitler were breaking the non-intervention pact, he shared the general indignation in the Labour movement at the farce to which it was reduced. But he did not deceive himself with the belief that to call for arms for Spain and to denounce the hypocrisy of non-intervention was a sufficient answer—any more than to demand sanctions against Italy had been in the case of Abyssinia.

There were many who rode off on the wave of emotion roused by Spain and evaded the question of rearmament. To Bevin, however, Spain reinforced rather than diminished the need for the Labour Party to face the issue of arms for Britain as well as Spain. He told the Executive Council of the T.G.W.U. at their December meeting:

"I am one of those who has a deep-rooted conviction that the challenge from the Fascist states is coming to the Democratic States at no distant date. That does not of necessity mean war, but in my opinion it will if the Democratic States fail to produce cohesion and unfortunately that does mean arms. . . . If we are to win the votes of the people they must be told quite frankly where we stand. They want to know whether we will in any crisis that develops do the job and face the consequences."[1]

Bevin came as near to despairing of the Labour Party after the Edinburgh conference as he ever did, and several times that winter he remarked to Francis Williams that the trade unions would have been in a stronger political position if they had not committed themselves so completely to one party.[2] But he was prepared to apply to himself the same strict standards of loyalty which he demanded from others. However impatient he felt with the irresponsibility which marked the Edinburgh debate on defence, he did not allow it to appear in public. Instead, he stuck grimly to the task of trying to bring the Party round to his point of view by force of argument, and before another year had passed he had reached more than half-way to success.

1 General Secretary's Quarterly Report, December 1936.
2 Francis Williams, *op. cit.*, p. 202.

7

The *Herald* was a constant target for the attacks of the Left through-out the controversies of the 1930s, and Bevin, the key figure among the trade-union directors of the paper as well as the bane of the Left, came in for a large share of the abuse. Odhams had adhered loyally to the agreement with the T.U.C. and, despite heavy losses, fought a spirited battle all through the thirties with Beaverbrook and the *Express*, first one, then the other, taking the lead in circulation. It was much more a popular than a party newspaper, but with a cir-culation of two million it was a big asset to the movement, however much it fell short of the militants' ideal of a propaganda broad-sheet.

Bevin was proud of the *Herald*, referring to it as "my paper" and giving all the support he could to Elias and Dunbar in their com-petition with Beaverbrook. He conducted a large correspondence with members of the Labour Party and trade unions[1] irritated by the omission or occasional misreporting of some item of local news. From time to time he himself protested at the treatment of some theme—the amount of space devoted to the royal family or the reporting of the Rhineland crisis. He read every issue with care and was frank in his criticism, but he rarely attempted to interfere with its day-to-day editorial direction and never used the paper as a plat-form for his personal views.[2] He looked on himself as the trustee of the movement and he was scrupulous in insisting that policy must be guided by the decisions of the Party and the T.U.C. and not by the views of individuals.

The value of Bevin's judgment was shown at the time of the Abdication. The *Daily Express*, the *Mail*, and the *Mirror* all came out in vigorous support of the King and many might have been tempted to use the crisis to whip up feeling against the National Government. As Bevin wrote to Attlee:

"We cannot forget that old Baldwin 'did' us over the Trades Union Act, over Abyssinia, over rearmament, and over Peace at the last general elec-

1 Several boxes, crammed with letters, are retained among his papers.
2 Francis Williams: op. cit. pp. 163–5. Mr. Williams was editor of the *Herald* in the later 1930s. This point is fully borne out by the correspondence between Bevin, Elias, Dunbar and the editor which I have read in full.

tion. . . . The risk of personal government is great: on the other hand so is the risk of backing the Government without the facts."[1]

Bevin took great care to keep in close touch with Attlee throughout the crisis, and, despite the temptation to make political capital, the *Herald* never wavered in support of the constitutional against the sentimental view. When the crisis was over, Attlee wrote:

"My dear Ernie,
"I think you would like to know . . . everyone says that it was among the two or three papers that kept its head and dealt with the matter in a statesmanlike, not merely a sensational, manner. I know this was largely due to you. Hence this letter.
"With all good wishes,
Yours,
Clem."[2]

8

In September 1936 Bevin was elected as chairman of the General Council of the T.U.C. No office he ever held gave him greater satisfaction and but for the war it would have been the peak of his career. He had now been a member of the General Council for eleven years; no other man in its history had, or has, exercised greater influence, and none represented it with more authority.

Bevin's membership of the General Council had coincided almost exactly with Walter (now Lord) Citrine's period of office as general secretary. On every big issue—the Mond-Turner talks; 1931; foreign policy; rearmament—they had been in agreement and their combination of talents in pushing a policy through the T.U.C. was invincible. Their gifts were unusually complementary: Citrine lucid and methodical, drawing upon his famous note-books for the facts, Bevin ranging and impressionistic, throwing out ideas; the one a master of exposition, the other of conviction and imagination. Citrine opening a T.U.C. debate on behalf of the General Council and setting out all the issues, Bevin getting up to close it and sweeping his audience along with him—this was perfect casting and rarely did they fail to carry the day.

1 Ernest Bevin to C. R. Attlee, 7th December 1936.
2 C. R. Attlee to Ernest Bevin, 16th December 1936.

Yet their agreement was largely coincidental, hardly ever the result of previous discussion together; they never met in private or socially and each was critical of the other. In part this was a matter of temperament. Each man was irritated by the methods and personality of the other, and each being a masterful man himself accused the other of trying to dominate the General Council. Citrine looked on his office as general secretary of the T.U.C. as giving him a unique claim to represent the views of the trade-union movement. Bevin, its most powerful personality, enjoying the independent status of general secretary of a big union, yielded first place to no man. It says much for both men that, in the interests of the movement, they suppressed their feelings sufficiently to agree so often on policy and to preserve a common front in public: it was one of the most successful involuntary partnerships in modern politics.

By a fortunate coincidence, a month after Bevin was elected chairman of the General Council, Hugh Dalton became chairman of the National Executive of the Labour Party. The contrast between the three leaders of the Labour movement during the year 1936–37 could hardly have been more pointed. Attlee, the leader of the Parliamentary Labour Party, as well as Dalton, came from an established middle-class family. The son of a City solicitor, the future Labour Prime Minister had been educated at Haileybury and Oxford; Dalton, the son of a Canon of Windsor and former tutor of King George V, at Eton and King's. Here were two men whom Bevin might well have regarded with suspicion as intellectuals and politicians, neither of whom belonged to the working class or to a trade union. Fortunately, to the great gain of the Labour movement, he got on well with both of them. Dalton stood nearer to Bevin in his views on foreign policy and defence than any other member of the National Executive and they collaborated closely, each determined to do all he could to remove misunderstanding between the industrial and political wings of the movement.

Bevin and Dalton were agreed that the most important job they had to do during their year of office was to bring the Party to take a more realistic view on defence. This was far from meaning that Bevin felt any confidence in the Government. When Mr. Basil Sanderson, the chairman of the Port Employers, sounded him out on the possibility of the T.U.C. supporting a recruiting drive, Bevin replied shortly that before he went on any platform to urge men to join the Forces, he would want to ask a lot of questions about the Government's foreign policy.

"I pointed out that the attitude of his confrères and class generally in relation to Spain had caused us grave disturbance. It was quite clear that because the Spanish Government was a government of radical outlook, the whole sympathy of their circle was with the Fascists, and that they regarded Franco as a patriot. Would they regard it as proper and patriotic for the military of this country, when they had a government of working people they did not like, to break their oaths and throw us over?

"Mr. Baldwin had the whole-hearted support of Labour over Abyssinia. Immediately he got that support he turned it to political account by springing an election and taking political advantage. . . . Another factor was the bitter treatment meted out to the unemployed by the Means Test and the treatment of the distressed areas. How could any Labour man, with the past ten years before him, appeal to men to join the Army?

"One last point I put strongly to him: in the old days of the Liberals and Tories, there was some consultation as to policy, but since 1931 Labour had been treated like a caste apart. It was not for us to appeal or be suppliants; it was for them to come to us and for the first time to recognise Labour as equals."[1]

Nonetheless, Bevin was convinced that the international situation made it essential for Britain to rearm and that it was politically disastrous for the Labour Party to continue to oppose the Government's arms programme. At its March meeting (1937) he told the Executive Council of his Union:

"From the day Hitler came to power, I have felt that the democratic countries would have to face war. I believe he was taken too cheap. We have been handicapped by the very sincere pacifists in our Party who believe that the danger can be met by resolutions and prayers and by turning the other cheek. While I appreciate the sincerity, I cannot understand anybody who refuses to face the facts in relation to the happenings in China, in Abyssinia, in Spain, all virtually disarmed countries. I cannot see any way of stopping Hitler and the other dictators except by force."[2]

In July 1937, Dalton again raised the question of voting against the Army, Navy and Air Force estimates in the Committee of Supply. This traditional Socialist method of opposing militarism

1 Notes of a discussion with Mr. Basil Sanderson, 3rd November 1936, dictated by Bevin on the 5th. Bevin also refused to meet Duff Cooper, then Secretary of State for War.

2 General Secretary's Quarterly Report, March 1937.

Bevin and Frank Snelling, one of the Rank and File leaders, at the London bus strike inquiry of 1937.

was still supported by many members of the Parliamentary Labour Party including Attlee, Morrison, Greenwood, Shinwell and Jim Griffiths; but with strong support from the trade-union members and from Bevin outside, Dalton carried the majority. When the Service votes came before Parliament (26th–27th July 1937), only six members of the Labour Party voted against them: after that date the Labour Party abandoned its Parliamentary opposition to rearmament.

9

The National Council of Labour, under Bevin's and Dalton's chairmanship, now produced the restatement of Labour's views on foreign policy and defence which Bevin had promised the T.U.C. in 1936. After a lengthy review of international relations since the war and an attempt to vindicate Labour's earlier policy, *International Policy and Defence* said bluntly: "In consequence of these events the League of Nations, for the time being, has been rendered ineffective . . . and commands little confidence, largely owing to lack of British leadership."

While proclaiming its determination "to strengthen and reinvigorate" the League, the National Council of Labour declared:

"A Labour Government will unhesitatingly maintain such armed forces as are necessary to defend our country and to fulfil our obligations as a member of the British Commonwealth and of the League of Nations."

This still left open the question of Labour's support for the existing Government's rearmament programme. The most that Bevin and Dalton could get the National Council and its constituent bodies to accept unanimously was the statement that a Labour Government "in the present state of the world must be strongly equipped to defend this country . . . and would therefore be unable to revise the present programme of Rearmament".

It was far from being an incisive document, but as so often in the Labour movement's discussions of foreign policy and defence, the debates at the two autumn conferences made clear what the resolution left unsaid, that acceptance of the report meant the abandonment of opposition to rearmament.

At the 1937 T.U.C. Bevin was in the chair and it was left to Citrine to draw "the conclusion that some increase of rearmament is indispensable, if this country is to face its obligations."[1] The result of the debate was a solid vote of 3,544,000 to 224,000 in favour of the report. There was more opposition at the Labour Party conference at Bournemouth, when Lansbury[2] and Ponsonby repeated the pacifist arguments against the use of force and Aneurin Bevan made a powerful speech against trusting the National Government to use the arms it asked for against the Fascist Powers.

This time Bevin was free to speak and with the support of two of the younger 'intellectuals', Philip Noel-Baker and Richard Crossman, he carried the burden of the argument. He went to the heart of the matter when he told the conference that they were too much obsessed by the National Government. They should look at the question from a less insular point of view and consider how Labour Party policy appeared to their friends on the Continent. In Czechoslovakia, for instance, they had begun to wonder, "not where the National Government but where the Labour Movement stood and whether in a crisis they could rely on us."

They must do all they could to overcome economic nationalism, to show friendship to the peoples of Central Europe, "but if you are going to reply to the hand of friendship with a bomb on our Movement, we are not going to leave ourselves defenceless for you to do it."[3] The attempt to move the reference back of the report was defeated by 2,169,000 votes to 262,000 and this time no one was left in any doubt, as they had been at Edinburgh the year before, what the vote meant.

10

More than anything else it was the Spanish Civil War which produced the swing in Labour opinion between 1936 and 1937. Spain had the same effect in rousing the Left to shed its pacifism and fight Fascism as the suppression of the German and Austrian trade unions had had on Bevin and the trade unionists. A curious reversal

1 T. U. C. Report, 1937, Citrine's speech, pp. 402–7.
2 Fresh from a personal peace mission to Hitler and Mussolini.
3 Labour Party Conference Report, 1937, pp. 207–8.

of parts took place. 'No war' and 'non-intervention' now became the slogans not of the Left but of the Right, and the Left began to attack the Government, no longer on pacifist grounds for its militarism, but on anti-Fascist grounds for its appeasement of the dictators.

The Labour Party had abandoned support for non-intervention at the end of October 1936, but it could find no satisfactory alternative policy towards Spain. To make an appeal for funds was straightforward: by the summer of 1937 the trade unions had contributed £40,000 to the International Solidarity Fund and 4,000 Basque children had been brought to England. Nor was there any hesitation in denouncing German and Italian intervention or the bombing of Guernica; in standing up for the Spanish Government against those sections of British opinion which supported Franco, and in pressing the British Government to allow the purchase of arms.

But when it came to action, what—short of direct intervention by the British and French Governments—had Labour to propose? The Left might convince itself that a determined stand on non-intervention would call Hitler's and Mussolini's bluff, or that freedom to purchase arms would allow the Spanish Government to match the supplies pouring in from Italy and Germany; but if Hitler and Mussolini proved not to be bluffing and increased their intervention on Franco's side, was the Labour Party prepared to run the risk of a general war? The plain answer was, No.

The question, of course, was largely academic, since there was not the least prospect that the British and French Governments would be willing to intervene. But frustration only added to the bitterness with which the Left assailed not only the Government but the official leadership of the Labour movement for its hesitations and lack of zeal.

It was in this mood that a new attempt to create a United Front "against Fascism, Reaction and War" was launched by Cripps and the Socialist League, the Communist Party and the I.L.P. in January 1937. They were supported by a new militant weekly *Tribune*, founded by Cripps, Bevan and G. R. Strauss the same month.

The only result of this fresh call for 'unity' was to reopen old divisions. The United Front began by attacking the political leadership of the Party; the National Executive retaliated by ex-

595

pelling the Socialist League (27th January) and when the League dissolved itself (in March) forbade individual members to join with the Communist Party and the I.L.P. in the Unity Campaign which Cripps and his friends continued.

Bevin was not a member of the National Executive and so not directly involved in these decisions, but they had his full support and the United Front made no attempt to conceal their hostility to him. Mindful of his position as chairman of the General Council, Bevin maintained silence in public, but an exchange of letters with G. D. H. Cole shows how much he felt that Cripps' and the Socialist League's behaviour justified the warnings he had given in 1933 and succeeding years.

"You talk about driving Cripps out," Bevin replied to a private appeal from Cole. "Cripps is driving himself out. The Annual Conference came to certain decisions. If I did not accept the decisions of the Conferences of my own Union I know jolly well what the members would do with me. That does not stop me from being loyal and at the same time advocating within our own circles any changes I may think desirable. But joining up with the Communists who are out to destroy the trade unions and then asking us, who have done nothing at all to warrant the attacks on us, to stand it for ever and never hit back, well, you are asking too much . . .
"However, we shall have the storm, the large meetings, the enthusiasm and the cheering, and then just as in the case of Abyssinia, Germany, Spain and all the other big problems, it will be the trade unions who will have to do the practical work."[1]

Bevin refused to accept Cole's warning that to drive out Cripps and the Socialist League would be to lose the younger generation and the best workers the Party had. "I do not think," Bevin replied, "that Cripps will have a very big following." The Bournemouth conference in October vindicated his judgment. There was little patience with Cripps when he challenged the Executive's action, and Morrison had small difficulty in convincing the conference that persistent attacks on other members of the Party were not the best way to promote the working-class unity for which the critics called. In a straight vote on the United Front, Cripps secured only 331,000 votes against 2,116,000.

Bevin did not speak in the debate. Instead of stirring up more bitterness, he exercised his influence in favour of a change in the

1 Ernest Bevin to G. D. H. Cole, 25th January 1937.

Party constitution which was much desired by the constituency parties and opposed by many of the trade unionists. The change increased the number of constituency party representatives on the National Executive from five to seven[1] and placed their election in the hands of the constituency delegates not of the whole conference with its preponderant trade-union vote, as had hitherto been the case. Bevin made a strong plea for tolerance between the trade unions and the constituency parties. His own delegation was divided and only at the last moment was he able to cast the Union's vote in favour of the changes proposed. Some of the biggest trade-union votes went the other way but the proposals were carried, and the constituency delegates promptly proceeded to elect Cripps and Laski to the Executive.

I I

After the Bournemouth conference Bevin gave up his membership of the National Council of Labour, but he could look back with some satisfaction on his year of office as joint chairman. In co-operation with Dalton he had steered the movement towards a more realistic attitude on foreign policy and defence. He had seen Cripps and his other opponents on the Left suffer yet another defeat and put themselves into a position where they had had to dissolve the Socialist League. Finally, the Party had adopted a new and shortened programme[2] which corresponded very closely with his ideas on policy and on the right way to approach the electorate.

His own particular contribution to the new programme was a detailed and comprehensive pensions plan[3] based on the proposals he had first set out in his *Plan for 2 Million Workless* in 1933, and more than one speaker at Bournemouth paid tribute to the persistence and skill with which he had pushed the whole scheme through.

The two other chief proposals of his 1933 plan—raising the school-leaving age to 15 and as soon as possible to 16, together with the reduction of the working week to forty hours—were also written into

1 The trade unions had thirteen representatives; the Fabian Society and the Royal Arsenal Co-operative Society one each and the women's section four.

2 *Labour's Immediate Programme*, published March 1937 and unanimously adopted at the Bournemouth conference in October of that year.

3 *Labour's Pension Plan for Old Age, Widows and Children*, 1937.

Labour's Immediate Programme, which bore evidence throughout of Bevin's influence. The nationalisation of the Bank of England, but not of the joint stock banks; the co-ordination of all forms of transport under a National Transport Board; the pledge not to return to the gold standard and to set up a National Industrial Board; the promise to implement the conventions adopted by the I.L.P. and to make holidays with pay a statutory obligation; immediate action to help the distressed areas; the plain statement that a Labour Government would "unhesitatingly maintain such armed forces as are necessary to defend our country and to fulfil our obligations as a member of the British Commonwealth and the League of Nations" —all these represented views which Bevin had steadily advocated in and out of season, all were now accepted by the Party as part of its official programme. They were not, of course, Bevin's views alone, but no one had played a greater part in defeating the doctrinaires in the struggle over the character and programme of the Labour Party following the split of 1931. At the Leicester conference of 1932, the Left, represented by Frank Wise and the Socialist League, had been in the ascendant; by the Bournemouth conference their defeat was conclusive. The Labour Party had been re-formed, not on the pattern of the Socialist League or the I.L.P., nor on that of Lansbury and the pacifists, but by the centre group to which Bevin as well as Attlee, Dalton and Morrison belonged.

Both in 1931 and afterwards the influence of the trade unions had steadied the Labour Party: in 1931, when there was a danger that MacDonald might carry a greater number with him; afterwards, when the reaction threatened to swing the Party over to the Left. Bevin was the most powerful member of the General Council and the line followed by the T.U.C. reflected his own equal distrust of the compromises of MacDonald or the *laissez-faire* liberalism of Snowden on the one hand and the shrill advocacy of emergency powers on the other. As the leading representative of the General Council on the National Council he had helped to frame the programme gradually accepted by the Party during the 1930s as an alternative to either Right or Left and secured for it the solid support of the trade-union movement. By the end of 1937 the Party had found its centre of gravity and Bevin could withdraw from the National Council with the satisfaction of having accomplished the task he had set himself.

12

His interest in politics and the sense of urgency with which he followed events abroad did not distract Bevin from the other purpose which he had formed after the General Strike, to secure from the State and from industry recognition of the trade unions' right to be consulted on every major decision of policy. The ground gained up to 1931 had been lost in the years which followed. But with recovery there had come a change, a greater willingness to consult the unions on the part of employers and of the Government.

Bevin put the position frankly to the Bournemouth conference:

"The temptation to the trade unions, as time goes on, from the other Party granting concessions is very real. The industrial policy of your opponents has changed. Do not be under any delusion. The old bitter hostility which made the trade unions fight on the basis of the Taff Vale Judgment and similar things has gone. It is a new technique which is being introduced."[1]

Bevin saw the danger clearly enough: he had no intention of putting himself in the position of a Jimmy Thomas or a Frank Hodges. Nor had he abandoned his Socialism. He told his Executive:

"Everyone of us who has had to examine problems affecting our industries has come to the conclusion that, under the capitalist system of ownership, there is a definite limit to our progress. What is the use of gaining power if you cannot do the things which in your very soul you believe are necessary? . . . For instance, under the present organisation of the coal industry, I do not believe it is possible either to give the miners a reasonable wage or to provide coal at proper prices. I believe the industry must be socialised in order to do these things. . . . Again, take transport. . . . We all know that transport must be brought under public control and organised on an entirely new basis. I cannot see any representatives of the capitalist classes agreeing to a fundamental change in the ownership of the means of life."[2]

But, pending that fundamental change which could only be achieved with a Labour Government in power, a trade-union leader could not confine himself to opposition: he had to take advantage of

1 Labour Party Conference Report, 1937, p. 146.
2 General Secretary's Quarterly Report, December 1936.

any opportunity that offered to improve the position of the working class. Bevin no more believed that it was impossible to do this under capitalism than he accepted the view that there were no political rights worth defending in a capitalist democracy and nothing to choose, from the workers' point of view, between capitalist Britain and Nazi Germany. The whole history of the working-class movement in Britain was there to show that by combination and protest it had been possible to make improvements. The Britain of the 1930s was not the Britain of the 1880s in which he had been born, nor even of the 1920s. True, there had been no radical transformation of society. Between 15 and 30 per cent of the population still lived in poverty or on the edge of it.[1] But the atmosphere had changed. Social services and taxation had begun the redistribution of wealth; opinion in the 'thirties was far more receptive to ideas of planning and the Welfare State than it had been in the 'twenties, and the attitude of most employers had altered since the bitter days after the war. The tide of change moved sluggishly, but it was moving in the right direction.

It was not simply a question of wages and hours, important as these were. Organised labour was slowly beginning to be accepted as part of the national community on terms of equality. When Bevin first joined the trade-union movement it was still struggling for recognition, even of the right to collective bargaining. By the time he became chairman of the General Council, the right of the T.U.C. to be consulted on any legislation or to be represented on any inquiry dealing with social and industrial matters was taken for granted.

Shortly after assuming office Bevin was turning over some old reports of the Trades Union Congress and comparing the debates of the 1920s with those of the mid-thirties. He was struck by the extension of the T.U.C.'s responsibilities, responsibilities of which their predecessors had hardly dreamed. "Most of these things," he remarked to his Executive Council, "were to them propaganda points. Those were the days of advocacy. Ours is the day of administration."[2] The Left might deplore the decline in militancy: to Bevin it seemed rather a measure of the trade unions' success in pressing for reforms and in raising the status of organised labour.

A good illustration of Bevin's point of view is provided by the

1 Cf., Mowat, *op cit.*, c. 9, for a summary of the evidence.
2 Quarterly Report, December 1936.

invitation which the T.U.C. received from Baldwin in 1937 to nominate representatives on a committee of inquiry into the claim for an annual holiday with pay. To the Left this was typical of the petty reforms on which the trade unions wasted their energies instead of calling for a militant United Front "to resist capitalism, Fascism and reaction". Bevin saw it differently, as a chance to press for a benefit of immediate practical value to the men and women he represented.

He not only accepted the invitation on behalf of the T.U.C. but agreed to serve personally on the committee under Lord Amulree and threw himself into its work. Under his influence, a mass of evidence on the practice in different industries and other countries was assembled by the research departments of the T.U.C. and his own union, while Bevin himself took a prominent part in cross-examining the witnesses who appeared before the committee. Inevitably the committee's report[1] fell short of the proposals tabled by the T.U.C., recommending only a week in place of the fortnight's holiday for which Bevin pressed, but its recommendations were accepted by the Government and passed into law before the end of 1938. As a result the three million wage-earners entitled to an annual holiday with pay in 1938 increased to over eleven million.

This minor social revolution appealed strongly to Bevin. One of the distinguishing badges of working-class inferiority had been the fact that its members could never afford to go away for a holiday. By 1938–39 this was no longer true to anything like the same extent. For six years now Bevin had served as President of the Workers' Travel Association and he took a keen interest in the early stages of the remarkable expansion of holiday travel both at home and abroad which, retarded by the war, came to full development in the 1950s. He found time to read a paper to the British Health Resorts Association conference at Skegness (April 1937), urging them to realise that in future they would have to cater for large numbers of working-class families and to abandon the idea that anything was good enough for working folk. With a sharper eye for social change than some of the health resorts, Mr. Butlin opened the first communal holiday camp in the country (also at Skegness) in September 1937.

1 Cmd. 5724 (1938).

13

The Amulree Committee had been set up in answer to trade-union pressure on the Government to adopt the I.L.O. convention on holidays with pay. Another investigation which the T.U.C. initiated during Bevin's year of office was into labour conditions in the colonies. As he pointed out to the 1937 Congress there were 60 million people in the colonies, most of them without votes or trade-union organisation, for whose welfare the British Government was responsible. Far too little was known about their conditions of work or earnings and what little was known was disturbing. Labour troubles in the West Indies underlined the urgency of an inquiry. The General Council not only set up an independent advisory committee and gave advice to the colonial trade unions which were beginning to spring up but established close relations with the Colonial Office, urging it to set up a special Native Labour Department.

Bevin was equally quick to see the importance of the Royal Commission which the Government appointed in 1937, under the chairmanship of Sir Montague Barlow, to inquire into the geographical distribution of industry in Great Britain. Here was a question which not only touched on the problem of the depressed areas but reflected the growing anxieties about defence against aerial attack. Bevin again accepted an invitation to serve as one of the trade-union representatives on the committee and he was deeply disappointed when ill-health and overwork forced him to resign shortly after it began its investigations.

Another interest which Bevin had acquired in the days when he began to lend his help to the Manor House Hospital was the development of the country's medical services and the contribution their effective organisation might make to the prevention and cure of industrial diseases and rehabilitation. In 1932 he became a member of the Industrial Health Research Board of the Medical Research Council. The Board's field of inquiry was wide, covering the psychological as well as the physical factors involved in industrial employment and Bevin not only read with interest the papers circulated but soon began to have ideas for further research, amongst them a proposal to carry out an inquiry into the incidence of gastritis amongst London bus drivers, in which the Union as well as the London Passenger Transport Board co-operated.

Through the Board Bevin was brought into touch with a number of doctors interested in industrial and social medicine and during 1937 he secured the establishment of a joint committee of the General Council and the British Medical Association. Among the subjects which the committee discussed were the rehabilitation of injured workers (a topic which greatly attracted Bevin and to which he was to make a big contribution as Minister of Labour), a national maternity service, as well as improvements in the new Factories Bill and the national health insurance scheme. The doctors were quick to recognise the value of Bevin's experience, the imagination and power of analysis which he brought to their discussions. In September 1937 he was invited to read a paper to the British Medical Association at its annual meeting in Belfast and made a powerful plea for the co-operation of the medical profession with the trade unions in developing an industrial medical service.[1]

Stimulated by his meetings with the doctors, Bevin made a striking appeal to the scientists in his presidential address to the T.U.C. at Norwich. In words which appear trite today but came unexpectedly from the president of the T.U.C. in 1937 he declared:

"Science has made amazing progress, but society has not kept pace with it in making fundamental re-adjustments and assimilating the results of research, discovery and invention. There is not only a time-lag but the inertia and rigidity of our social and economic structure to be overcome. The General Council believe that men of science can make a great contribution by assisting such a movement as ours with their counsel and knowledge . . and have decided to establish a Scientific Advisory Committee."

In November 1937 he brought together a number of scientists to meet representatives of the General Council at a dinner in London.[2] Bevin threw out any number of ideas, asking for information on malnutrition, health, new lines of research, their application in industry and above all the social consequences of scientific discovery. The scientists were sympathetic and as a result of his intervention,

1 *British Medical Journal*, 25th September, 1937, Vol. II, p. 610. "The Wider Issues of Health Legislation in Industry," by Ernest Bevin.
2 Among those present were Professors Blackett, Boswell, Haldane, Hogben, Dr. Bernal, Sir Richard Gregory and Sir John Boyd Orr.

the T.U.C. was able to set up an advisory committee in 1938 to which the British Association for the Advancement of Science agreed to nominate expert advisers.

Throughout his year of office Bevin seized every opportunity to put the trade-union point of view. In January 1937, for instance, he spoke at the dinner of the Works Management Association; in February to the Foreign Press Association, at the Savoy; in March to the business men of the British and North American Luncheon Club.

Few, perhaps, of those who listened to him on such occasions were convinced by his arguments, but they were impressed by Bevin as the representative of the trade-union movement, impressed not only by his personality and the frankness with which he spoke but by his obvious grasp of the problems he was discussing. Unperturbed by the display of wealth or power, he was as naturally himself talking at an industrialists' lunch at the Savoy as he was sitting down to supper with branch members in Whitechapel or enjoying an outing with delegates to a union conference at Blackpool. Sure of himself in any company, he talked as directly and with the same unaffected equality to the chairman of I.C.I. or of the London Transport Board as he did to the doorman or the conductor of the bus which took him back to Transport House.

14

Once the Depression had lifted, the Union no longer demanded Bevin's whole attention, as it had in the 1920s. It was thanks to this that he had time to give to the T.U.C. and to the National Council of Labour. By the end of his year of office the T.G.W.U. was the largest trade union in the country, larger than the Miners, the Engineers or the N.U.R. Its 600,000 members represented eleven per cent of the total trade-union membership in the United Kingdom and the administration of so large an organisation could only be conducted by considerable decentralisation.

But Bevin was still very much the general secretary. If he was more prepared to delegate powers than he had been in earlier years, he still kept a firm hold on the policy of the Union and took an active part in the industries with which he had been long connected. From 1934 to 1937 he was chairman of the Joint Industrial Council of the

Flour Milling Industry without a break; in the second year, when he would normally have stood down for an employers' representative, he was re-elected on the proposal of the employers. He failed to get the advance in wages for which the Union pressed but he secured instead a reduction in hours and a guaranteed week which added to the already impressive record of the industry in labour relations.

The milling employers accepted Bevin's argument that the benefits of rationalisation in the industry should be shared by those who worked in it. Hours of work were cut to a working week of forty-two hours for shift workers, without any corresponding cut in wages. To meet the problem of short-time working, the employers agreed to guarantee the fixed rate of wages even for the man on short time, by making up the difference between his unemployment benefit and the sum he would have received for a normal week's work. This was an innovation of which Bevin was proud and which he defended with vigour and success when the Ministry of Labour questioned the legality of the practice under the Unemployment Insurance Act.

He tried, without success as yet, to get the port employers to consider a pensions scheme for dockers and, to his anger, saw the superannuation scheme he had introduced for the tinplate industry turned down after it had been accepted by the employers. Part of the trouble was the dislike of other unions (in particular the Iron and Steel Trades' Confederation) for the scheme; part, the opposition of the Communists who broke up a number of meetings at which it was being explained. When he tried to overcome the difficulties by re-casting the scheme, Bevin found that not enough men to launch it were prepared to sign. He reported to his Executive Council at the end of 1937 that after several years of negotiation the proposal was dead:

"I think it is a tragedy for South Wales, but it appears that a large number of the men take the view that if they become party to a superannuation they are merely saving the Unemployment Assistance Board expenditure. When a large community develops a relief complex of this character it is not good for democracy. In my view, having such a scheme as their own and as a right would have been of immense value. . . . Still, we have to bow to these things. Disappointing as it may be after all the work put in, the situation must be accepted."[1]

1 General Secretary's Quarterly Report, November 1937.

Bevin had no intention at all, however, of accepting the situation in the road-haulage industry where the efforts of the National Joint Conciliation Board to enforce standard wages and conditions had broken down in many areas in face of the stubborn opposition of the employers and the connivance of the men. He took the lead on the Board in pressing the Minister of Labour to carry out a further inquiry and, when the Minister set up a committee under Sir James Baillie, drafted the memorandum prepared by the Board and presented its views in person.

The Baillie Committee's report (May 1937)[1] largely accepted these views and put forward proposals based on them for new legislation which was embodied in the Road Haulage Wages Act of 1938. Bevin was determined to master the problem of bringing order into the road-haulage industry and after years of battering away at it he was within sight of success.

1937 also saw a step forward in the long-drawn-out struggle which he and Harold Clay had fought for the organisation of the provincial bus industry. In May, the municipal bus services were brought into the scope of the old National Joint Industrial Council for the Tramway Industry.[2] But the private company undertakings still remained outside. Many of them had now come under the control of three large combines and the rationalisation of services and the tightening up of conditions which followed when small, easy-going companies were replaced, led to an outcrop of unofficial strikes during 1936 and 1937. These greatly hampered the Union's efforts to secure a national negotiating body for the provincial busmen in the private companies' employment.

15

The London Rank and File Committee and the Communist Party showed much interest in these unofficial strikes. *Busmen's Punch* produced a provincial edition; and a Communist document, analysing the mistakes made by Party members in the Scottish strike and the lessons to be learned for the intensification of Party activity in the

1 Cmd. 5440 (1937).
2 Henceforward known as the N.J.I.C. for the Road Passenger Transport Industry.

bus industry, fell into Bevin's hands. It was a shrewd analysis and made quite clear the importance the Communists attached to such work:

"All comrades should realise that the T.G.W.U. is now the spearhead in this country of the drive against working class unity. Bevin's power depends on his position in his own union. A decisive change in the T.G.W.U. would result in the establishment of the United Front in this country. The whole Party thus has a special responsibility for work amongst this section of workers."[1]

Although the Rank and File leaders had captured control of the Union's Central London Bus Committee and Bert Papworth had been elected to the General Executive Council, the movement had made little progress since 1932 and in February 1937 *Busmen's Punch* published a sharp essay in self-criticism under the title, "Are We Going Wrong?"

Bevin felt as much distrust as ever of the Rank and File leaders, but he had to work with them now that they controlled the Central Bus Committee. Papworth was on the Executive as well, where he and Bevin watched each other like hawks—a situation which did not prevent each expressing a wry regard for the other's qualities.[2]

The Rank and File Movement stuck to its demand for a seven-hour day for the Central London bus drivers and although Bevin thought this too big a reduction to ask for at once he came round to the view that the men had a strong case on grounds of health which, they were convinced, was adversely affected by their working conditions. This opened up the possibility of official action by the Union, and the leaders of the Rank and File Movement, who hesitated to call a large-scale unofficial strike in support of their demand, agreed on their side to work through the constitutional machinery. Six months' preliminary negotiation in 1936 finally produced a date by which a new agreement was to be completed—February 1937—but the Transport Board was adamant in refusing to consider a reduction in hours.

The Board had its own difficulties, in particular the high rate of

1 T.G.W.U.: Minutes of the General Executive Council, 1937, pp. 207–8.
2 On their way back from one negotiation, Bevin remarked to Papworth: "Bert, you wouldn't make a bad negotiator if you'd only count ten before you opened your mouth." "If I did," was Papworth's retort, "you'd see I never got my damned mouth open at all."

compensation which had been fixed when the different undertakings were taken over. It was opposed to making concessions which, it claimed, would cost over half a million pounds and, in any case, considered that the Central busmen, with their relatively high rates of pay, must wait until the claims of the less well paid tram and trolley bus drivers, as well as of the country bus services, had been met.

These arguments did not answer the men's case. They were not asking for increased pay, but for a relaxation of the conditions in which they were expected to work. The traffic in Central London streets was rapidly increasing and traffic jams were a frequent occurrence; the speed limit had been raised first to 20, then to 30 m.p.h.; bigger buses had been introduced; there were no fixed stops and a driver who failed to stop when hailed was guilty of an offence. Yet bus crews were expected to keep to the precise timing of a rail-way and to make up for lost time by turning their buses round at the end of a journey and driving straight back without a break. Owing to the varying demand for transport at different times, schedules were a complicated maze in which the hours of duty changed from day to day. This meant irregular meal-times which, added to the strain of driving in heavy traffic and trying to keep to a rigid time-table, were believed by the busmen to be the cause of the gastric complaints from which many of them suffered. The men accepted the fact that these conditions were to some extent unavoidable, but claimed that, as a relief, their working day should be shortened.[1]

Nor were the men convinced that the Board could not afford to pay. As Bevin pointed out at the Inquiry in May, the Central buses made a profit from which the Board could meet the cost of shorter hours. The difficulty was that the Board wanted to use their profits on one service to balance their losses on another and to meet the obligation to pay a high rate of interest imposed on them by Parliament. What most irritated Bevin and the men was the belief that the Board was not prepared to consider their case on its merits, but had decided in advance to refuse any claim for a reduction in hours and to put these troublesome London busmen in their place.

Negotiations dragged on for two months past the day appointed for the new agreement. The Board still refused to discuss hours and on 31st March 1937 the Union tendered a month's notice to ter-

[1] On Bevin's advice they reduced their claim from a seven to a seven-and-a-half-hour day in place of the eight hours which they had worked since 1919.

minate the existing agreement. After further negotiations and the failure of the Ministry of Labour to achieve a settlement the General Executive sanctioned strike action and every bus in London came off the streets from midnight on 30th April.

16

London was crowded in anticipation of King George VI's Coronation on 12th May and there was a loud outcry against the irresponsibility of the chairman of the T.U.C. in allowing his men to go on strike at such a time. Bevin hotly denied that the Union had deliberately timed the strike to cause the maximum inconvenience to the public. Negotiations had been going on for over a year and there was no advantage to the Union in a conjuncture which gave the Press every chance to whip up indignation against the men and their leader, the 'dictator' of Transport House. In fact, Bevin was not in favour of strike action: he told the busmen's leaders that they had to face four to six weeks out of work and that even then he doubted if they would win. He would have preferred to try further negotiations, at least for another week, but the Bus Committee would not hear of it and on 1st May every man of the 26,000 in the section came out on strike.

The Minister of Labour at once appointed a court of inquiry[1] to investigate the dispute and the court held its first hearing on 2nd May. Bevin appeared in person to put the men's case and even the Rank and File leaders could find no fault with the way in which he did it in a speech which lasted over four hours. He traced the history of the labour relations with the Board and the growing resentment of the men at the intensification of their work with too little regard to the difficulties of driving a bus in crowded streets. London bus services could not be run as if they were a railway or a factory with operating hours and costs worked out to the minute.

"If you are going to try to run this great human family by a mind that operates on the system of the slide-rule, then you will never get an appreciation of the men's difficulties and what they are complaining about."[2]

1 Under the Industrial Courts Acts of 1919.
2 Report of the Court of Inquiry, printed in *The Record*, (May 1937), pp. 266–276.

The court's report (6th May) went a long way to vindicate Bevin's statement of the men's case. Certain of the schedules, they concluded, operated 'somewhat onerously' on the men, and while the injury to health had not been proven, a *prima facie* case for investigation had been established.

The Board had hitherto refused to consider any reduction in hours. Now they agreed to set up a joint body with the Union to investigate the question of health and agreed further that, if the inquiry justified the case for a shorter working day, they would be willing to consider it, even if it involved them in additional costs. Once the Union Executive had secured specific assurances on this and the Board's agreement to negotiate at once on other points, they believed the strike had secured its object and advised the men to accept the Board's offer.

At this point the latent distrust between the busmen's leaders and Bevin flared up. The Central Bus Committee dissociated itself from the Executive's view and the Rank and File leaders appealed to all ranks of the bus section to reject it. The leaflet containing this appeal was prepared in consultation with Emil Burns, a Communist Party member describing himself as a 'translator', who had acted throughout as an adviser to the Rank and File Committee and had been given membership of the Union's Kilburn branch as a cover for his activities. Many thousands of copies were printed and distributed to branches in time to influence the vote which turned down the Executive's advice by a large majority.

The vote was clear enough and Bevin did not contest it. But how did the Rank and File leaders propose to win the strike? Their immediate demand was to bring out the tram and trolley bus men. Bevin opposed such a move, on the ground that it would mean imperilling gains which the Union had secured for the tramway men after lengthy negotiation. Attempts by Papworth and Snelling to get the tramway men to declare an unofficial strike were turned down at a delegate conference and the Executive (which had already spent over £100,000 on strike pay) rejected a request that it should order the tramway men to strike. Protests, resolutions, meetings, loud abuse of Bevin by the Rank and File members as a 'Fascist' and a dictator, even the picketing of Transport House continued, but they did not alter the situation or add up to a policy. Londoners got to work by other means—the Tube as well as the trams were still running—and the Rank and File Committee was left flailing the air.

In the fourth week of the strike, Bevin judged the time had come to act. On 26th May the General Executive revoked the grant of plenary powers to the Central Bus Committee, and secured the return to work (without victimisation) on the same terms which the busmen had refused a fortnight before. On the 28th the men went back and the strike was over.

17

Bevin had played his hand with patience and skill, giving the Rank and File leaders all the rope they wanted. His advocacy of the men's case for a reduction in hours had been perfectly genuine. He advised the Bus Committee against a strike but accepted the vote in favour of it and his conduct of their case at the inquiry secured the substance of the men's claim. If they had followed his advice then, they would have called the strike off. But this was not enough for the Bus Committee. Why did they continue the strike? Because they distrusted the Board and Bevin and really believed they could gain more for the men? Or because, as Harold Clay said, a display of militancy—whatever the consequences—was the way in which the Communists hoped to capture working-class support and discredit the Union's leadership—political not industrial tactics?

Whatever their objective, for the moment they had the men's support, and Bevin did not attempt to stop them. Let them try out the militant policy for which they were always clamouring. Strike pay continued to be paid. But Bevin refused to take any responsibility for extending a dispute with which he did not agree. He sat back and waited until the bankruptcy of the Rank and File leadership had been shown up. Then he stepped in to pull the men out of the mess, settling the strike in twenty-four hours on terms which left them no worse off than if they had followed his advice a fortnight before. The contrast in effective leadership could not have been more pointed, and the bitterness of the Rank and File Committee's comments sprang from realisation that they had been outmanœuvred and shown up.

But this time the quarrel had gone too far to be left at that. For five years Bevin had let the Committee play its game with impunity and there were critics in the Union who said he should have acted before. On 4th June the Executive Council suspended the special constitution of the Central Bus Section and ordered an inquiry into the conduct of its members. Bevin took no direct part in its proceedings. For ten days the committee—eight members of the Executive, with Arthur Deakin as secretary—examined the evidence and heard the witnesses on both sides. Their recommendations were unanimous and were submitted to the Biennial Delegate Conference meeting at Torquay in July.

The steady growth of the Union in the last two years provided solid ground for satisfaction on the part of Bevin and the Executive in meeting the delegates. But everything else at Torquay was overshadowed by the report on the Rank and File Movement. It was presented by Arthur Deakin who traced the history of the movement as an illustration of the policy which the Communist Party had deliberately followed from the beginning of 1932. To support his case he quoted at length from a speech which a British delegate to the Communist International, J. R. Campbell, made at the Seventh World Congress in Moscow in 1935.[1]

"From the beginning of 1932," Campbell reported, "we have in a number of unions developed rank and file movements and there are important differences between these and the old Minority Movements which we were trying to develop previously. The Minority Movement was constructed in such a way that it appeared as a body outside the trade unions, dictating to the unions what they should do. . . . This enabled the officials to raise the question of loyalty and discipline. . . . It is not so easy with the rank and file movements because they grew up from within the unions and cannot be open to the same charge and can defend themselves against expulsion tactics in a way that rallies a greater amount of support than the old form of opposition movement could do."

This policy, Campbell claimed, had proved much more successful:

"We have 3,200 members who work actively in the reformist trade unions . . . 600 are holding trade union office of some kind, either in the branches, the district committees and in one or two exceptional cases, in the executives of the reformist trade unions. Our total membership is only 7,700 . . . but [that] is altogether an inadequate expression of the influence we have already won in sections of the British working-class movement."

1 Campbell's speech was published in *The Communist International*, Vol. XII, No. 16, 20th August 1935.

Attempts were made at the time, and have been since, to dismiss Campbell's claims as exaggerated and Deakin's case as 'anti-Communist hysteria'. It will hardly appear so to those who have followed Communist tactics in the trade-union movement closely. *Busmen's Punch* had been prepared with the assistance of Communists in the black-listed Labour Research Department, and Deakin was able to quote from a number of Communist directives giving instructions for the exploitation of unofficial strikes in the passenger transport industry. After summarising the evidence in relation to the Rank and File Movement, he moved the adoption of the report, which recommended that the Movement should be declared a subversive organisation, membership of which was incompatible with membership of the Union; that three members (A. F. Papworth, W. Payne and J. W. Jones) should be expelled from the Union and that four others be debarred from holding office for varying periods.

The debate that followed lasted the rest of the day. All the old arguments were repeated—the spontaneity of the Rank and File Movement; the strength of the support it received from the London busmen; its innocence of any connection with the Communist Party; the failure of the Union to provide militant leadership; the subversion of democratic rights by the bureaucratic tyranny of the officials. There were more than a dozen speeches from the floor, showing a wide range of opinion. "Because we are members of the Union," Payne asked, "have we got to be stifled?" Why had the General Secretary not come down and addressed the men while the strike was on? Because, Bevin retorted, if I had, I should have attacked you for continuing the strike. Why did you let it go on so long? Because you were afraid to 'carry the can' and take the responsibility for calling it off. You left it to me to get you out of the mess and then attacked me for failing to lead.

The Committee's report was carried by 291 votes to 51 and the next day Bevin introduced an amendment of rule to strengthen the Union's right of expulsion. The later history of the dispute is interesting. A section of the Rank and File Movement carried out their threat to lead a break-away and established a National Passenger Workers' Union which survived the second World War but did not succeed in shaking the loyalty of the main body of London busmen to the T.G.W.U. A majority of the original Rank and File Committee, however, were opposed to any such move. The Communists in particular were against leaving the Union: they preferred to continue their activities from inside and when the Executive allowed Papworth and Jones—both of whom were now announced to have joined the Communist Party—to apply for re-admission to the Union, they accepted the offer and gave the assurances required that they would abide by the constitution of the Union. Both rapidly regained their position with the busmen and both were soon elected to the Executive Council of the T.G.W.U. of which the Communists very nearly captured control between 1945 and 1949. Papworth in fact became one of the Union's repre-sentatives on the General Council of the T.U.C., Jones chairman of the Central Bus Committee. This, it has been argued, shows the mistake Bevin made in driving militant trade unionists into the arms of the Communists. It may be so, but it is also possible to conclude that Bevin's belief that he had to deal with Communists, concealed or open, from the beginning is confirmed by the later history of these two leaders of the Rank and File Committee.

18

It had been an exacting year and for the first time Bevin found his constitution failing to meet all the demands he made upon it. He was fifty-six and his heart began to show symptoms of strain from which he was never again wholly free. The doctors warned him that he must reduce his commitments and take a long rest if he was not to kill himself. But he was determined to finish his year of office and he summoned up all his energies for the 1937 T.U.C. conference over which he presided.

As he stood looking down upon the six hundred delegates who filled the St. Andrew's Hall at Norwich, he felt a deep pride and affection for the class from which he sprang. The trade-union move-ment was its unique creation among British institutions, owing nothing to middle-class ideas or leadership. Here he was at home as in no other assembly. His loyalty to it was absolute. He spoke its language, understood instinctively its weakness and strength. Here he belonged, and never in that long, painful history of their struggle to achieve equality had the working classes of England produced a more representative leader than this West Countryman, steady as a rock, who had once organised a Right-to-Work Committee in the back streets of Bristol.

Much of his presidential address was devoted to a review of the year in industrial and international affairs. He drew particular attention to the labour problems of the colonial empire and singled out Palestine in order to express admiration for the achievements of the Jews in creating a national home.

The most characteristic passage came towards the end of his speech. Looking beyond rearmament to the danger of another slump, he asked if it was not possible for a nation which could organise a defence programme against war to show the same resolution in facing its other enemies, unemployment, poverty, malnutrition and disease.

"Have ready good schemes of public works, with all the necessary bills enacted and plans to start directly the present boom eases off.

"Create a great national development fund whilst you can afford it, which will avoid the necessity of increasing taxation, cutting unemployment pay and reducing social services during slump periods.

"Carry out a survey, first at home, then in conjunction with the Dominions, the Colonies and the World, and take note of the areas where the standard of living needs to be raised and be ready with credit facilities."[1]

Only once did he strike a personal note and allow his feelings to appear, in the final speech of the Congress when he expressed thanks for the silver bell which by tradition is always presented to the retiring president. When the tributes had been paid and the presentation made, Bevin turned to the delegates and said:

"There has been a kind of propaganda for many years to try to depict me as a kind of Dictator and an over-riding person. Well, it has been my lot since 1918 to bring together into one union 37 unions and anybody who has had experience of amalgamations knows that, unless those who are handling them can exercise tolerance, such a thing cannot be brought to a success.

"It has been a feature of certain sections of the Press to refer to 'This boss Bevin business' . . . It is not true. It is not true, as my colleagues on the General Council know; it is not true as our own union knows. What one tries to do is to collect and compose the differences of everybody in order to try to shape a policy for this great Movement.

"I have been very proud to be President of Congress . . . I like constructive work more than advocacy and more than platform work. I like to

1 T.U.C. Report, 1937, p. 76.

create things. The reason why I get into trouble with a good many people in the Labour Movement is this: I hold strongly the view that once a decision has been arrived at, nobody has the right to go outside and undermine what has been done. Never once have I challenged a decision of Congress; I might, if I thought it was wrong, try to alter it legitimately, but I have never challenged it.

"I am proud of this great Movement, proud of the work it has done nationally and internationally. The honour bestowed upon me I value more than any other honour. I would not change the loyalty of the 600,000 members of my union for all the pelf and place that society can give. It is the greatest pride of one's life to know that in the homes of thousands of one's mates there is belief in you; that they trust you and respect your integrity, and when you did me the honour of electing me to the chair of this Congress, I felt it very deeply because I believe, however controversial I have had to be at times, people have always given me credit for sincerity."[1]

It was the speech of a man looking back on a career which he believed to be drawing to its close. He was already talking of retirement when he reached the age of sixty and his words had a valedictory ring. It was in fact the last time that he addressed the Trades Union Congress as a member of the General Council or a delegate. In 1938 he was abroad and in 1939 the outbreak of war broke up the meeting of Congress. Far from this being the climax of his career. however, as he believed, it marked only the pause before he stepped on to the greater stage of war and world affairs. When next he spoke to the Trades Union Congress it was as their representative in a War Cabinet in which five men bore the responsibility of saving the nation and the free world from defeat.

CHAPTER 22

The Commonwealth,
War and Office
1938 – 1940

I

On 10th October 1937, immediately after the Bournemouth conference, the *Sunday Dispatch* confidently reported that Bevin would enter the House of Commons on retiring from the general secretaryship of his union and within a few months take over the leadership of the Labour Party from Attlee. Bevin angrily denied the report: "Your correspondent must have known he was lying when he wrote it." If he was drawn to any other job, it was the directorship of the I.L.O., from which Sir Harold Butler was retiring, but he held firmly to his resolution to retire from public life altogether when he was sixty and settle with his wife in the West Country. His daughter had married during the year and he felt that his frequent absences from home, especially during his year as chairman of the General Council, had made unfair demands on his wife.

His state of health reinforced these arguments. The change in his appearance between 1937 and 1938 was marked. If he went on at the pace of the past year, without a long rest, he would kill himself, and he was wise enough to recognise this. Various possibilities for a visit abroad were canvassed, but it was not until April that he finally accepted an invitation from Chatham House[1] to attend an unofficial Commonwealth conference in Australia during the autumn. He planned to leave England in July, travel out to Australia in leisurely style and complete the voyage round the world on his way home.

[1] The Royal Institute of International Affairs.

There was one task Bevin meant to see finished before he left for Australia: the passing of a new Road Haulage Bill. As soon as the Baillie Committee published its report, he began to urge the Ministry of Labour to give effect to its recommendations. He kept up a steady pressure—by telephone, interviews and correspondence—not only on the Ministry, but on the leading employers, many of whom he had come to know well, to prevent the sense of urgency slackening. The Ministry officials were sympathetic and the prospects of legislation in 1938 good, but Bevin was not prepared to rely on promises. He put in a claim for better wages and conditions in the London area at the end of October and, when it was referred to the National Conciliation Board, fought it as a test case. By March 1938 the dispute was still unsettled and one of the three employers' associations, the Associated Road Operators, walked out of the negotiations rather than bind themselves to carry out any settlement made by the Board.

This played straight into Bevin's hands. Knowing that legislation establishing the statutory regulation of wages was about to be introduced in Parliament and that many of the employers condemned the minority who had continuously refused to accept voluntary regulation, he called a nation-wide strike of all road-haulage workers in fourteen days' time. With a week to go the recalcitrant employers came to terms, all three associations recommending their members to accept the decisions of the National Conciliation Board and to pay an increase of three shillings.

Shortly afterwards the Road Haulage Wages Bill was brought in by the Government. Bevin followed every move intently, briefing the Labour Party spokesmen and the Union's own representatives in the House to fight the mass of amendments put forward by the employers. He wrote to F. W. Leggett at the Ministry of Labour with whom he had established close working relations: "I want to see this Bill on the Statute Book before I go away. I have worked so long to try to get this trade put right that I would not sacrifice it now for anything."[1] The Act, finally passed in July, retained the essential features for which Bevin had argued before the Baillie Committee.

The first was the replacement of the voluntary regulation of wages, hours and conditions of work by statutory regulation through a Central and Area Wages Boards. The second was the inclusion for

[1] Ernest Bevin to F. W. (now Sir Frederick) Leggett, 28th April 1938.

the first time of the 'C' licence holders, private carriers operating vans or lorries for transport of their own goods and comprising nearly three quarters of all operators and vehicles.

Effective enforcement of the law would largely depend upon the vigilance of the Union and Bevin launched a new campaign to raise the figure of 70,000 in the road transport group. But at last a legislative framework had been created for the industry, and even the most individualist of employers forced to accept the principle of regulation.

Bevin was appointed as one of the first members of the Central Wages Board. The Act was a personal triumph for his persistent advocacy and was recognised as such. He told the members of the Flour Milling N.J.I.C.:

> "I have always been encouraged by a remark I once heard Sidney Webb make in a lecture. He said if anybody in this country gets an idea which is good and which ought to be embodied in legislation, from the time it is promulgated to the time it is actually passed is usually twenty years."[1]

This was almost exactly true in the case of the road haulage industry. Bevin started bringing the unions together towards the end of the 1914–18 war. He made his first attempt to secure a national agreement and set up a joint industrial council in 1920. Disappointed by the Transport Acts of 1930 and 1933, he had accepted the voluntary machinery of the National Conciliation Board and made every effort to work it. Now at last he had won the Government and the majority of the employers over to his point of view and seen it translated into law.

2

He had less success as yet with the other stubborn problem to which he had devoted so much time, the decasualisation of dock labour. He took it up again in 1937, finding less opposition than before on the part of the employers but great practical difficulties. Without a guaranteed grant for ten years from the Government in place of assistance under the ordinary unemployment regulations, Bevin believed any scheme must fail and this he could not get. He had to

[1] Annual Report of the N.J.I.C. for the Flour Milling Industry, 1937-8.

be content with persuading the port employers to set up committees to consider pensions and holidays with pay for the regular dockers.

The Union was now growing rapidly. At the end of 1937 its members numbered 654,510 making it the largest trade union not only in Great Britain but in the world. In London and the South-east alone (Area No. 1) it had 183,000 members. The net rate of increase was nearly 2,000 a week: to keep this up and offset the turnover owing to death, retirement, and lapse of membership meant recruiting double that number. The year's income for 1937 was £931,091; the General Fund (despite the London bus strike) stood at £908,000 and the cash benefits paid to members since the amalgamation (1922) totalled more than £5 million—a considerable achievement on 6d. a week.

Six of the nine national trade groups were virtually major unions in themselves,[1] and Bevin's first task as general secretary was still to hold them together, to keep constantly in touch with their affairs and with their national officers. The constitution he had designed stood up well to the task and he used the general workers' group for the formation of new national groups—first, the metal, engineering and chemical trades; then the building trades group. Separate national sections already existed within the general workers' group for agriculture; for Government and local government services; and for flour milling. To these was now added a national section for fisher-men, following amalgamation with the Scottish Fishermen's Union and the Humber Trawlermen's Union, and the part taken by the T.G.W.U. in securing the passage of the Sea Fish Industry Act (1938).

Apart from the fishermen, amalgamation added little to the strength of the Union and Bevin preferred to extend the series of working arrangements which he had built up with other unions. At the end of 1937, he advised the Union to withdraw its claim to

[1] The strength of the National trade groups in 1938 was:

1. Docks	87,509	members
2. Waterways	8,000	,,
3. Road Passenger Transport	150,836	,,
4. Road Commercial Transport	79,991	,,
5. General Workers	171,000	,,
6. Building Trades	32,422	,,
7. Metal, Engineering and Chemical	96,037	,,
8. Administrative, Clerical and Supervisory	9,214	,,
9. Power Workers	28,709	,,

organise the nursing profession and the catering industry, in neither of which had it enjoyed much success, and to leave the field open to others. He broke new ground, however, and stirred up a colourful controversy when, to the indignation of an outraged Jockey Club, the Union took up the cause of the stable men after a crowded and enthusiastic meeting at Newmarket. Some of the members of the Jockey Club held early nineteenth-century views on trade union 'agitators' but Bevin was able to secure an immediate improvement in wages and conditions at Newmarket, while the Union gave full support to a long and bitter strike at the Lambourn racing stables in Berkshire.

This was the sort of incident which at once got into the headlines. Strikes were 'news', but as Bevin scornfully pointed out, hardly any paper thought it worth while to report the steady day-to-day conduct of industrial negotiations, often affecting many thousands of workers, which had become the real business of trade unions. There was hardly an industry in the country in which the T.G.W.U. did not represent at least a section of those employed, with its officers meeting the representatives of management on a hundred different committees and negotiating variations in the wage scales and working conditions of a thousand different factories and transport undertakings. The change in the role of the unions for which Bevin had argued at the time of the Mond-Turner talks ten years before had taken place almost unobserved: by 1938 they had become an essential part of the industrial structure of the country.

This change called for a different type of officer and organisation. The new generation of trade-union leaders had to undertake tasks of administration and negotiation very different from those of Tillett's and Sexton's generation, and, as Bevin had foreseen, they needed much fuller information with which to argue their case with managements, on a joint industrial council, before a tribunal or as delegates to an international conference. From the days of the Shaw Inquiry Bevin had realised the importance of an efficient Information and Statistics Department and at the end of 1937 he re-organised this by amalgamating it with the Political and International Department of the Union and bringing the whole under the direction of John Price, a young trade unionist who had spent two years at Ruskin College and later became a member of the staff of the I.L.O. One of Price's first duties was to prepare an education scheme which would train officers and lay members of the Union in the wide range of legal and economic as well as industrial questions with which they had now to be acquainted.

As part of the change in their position, the increase in social and industrial legislation during the later 1930s brought the trade unions more closely into touch with the Government departments. Bevin, for example, worked closely with the permanent officials of the Ministry of Labour in his campaign to secure regulation of the road-haulage industry and with other departments over such questions as industrial health, safety regulations and workmen's compensation.

Once again, as in 1914–18, it was war and the preparations for war in 1938–9 which accelerated the process, leading the Government to seek the co-operation of the trade unions over rearmament and defence more readily than they would ever have done on social and economic questions alone. The turning-point was Bevin's own appointment as Minister of Labour and National Service in 1940, but the first halting steps were taken in the spring of 1938 under the pressure of external dangers.

3

Bevin was still convinced that the root of the difficulty in international affairs lay in trying to solve economic problems, such as access to raw materials, by methods of diplomacy and war no longer appropriate to the changed situation of the twentieth century.

"This problem," he said at Bournemouth, "becomes a question of opportunity to live. . . . There is not a single state in Europe where a vast population can live by themselves. The old Austro-Hungarian Empire was economically perhaps the soundest thing that existed in Europe, even if politically wrong. . . . But even that with the teeming millions is not enough. The mere revision of the Versailles Treaty will not do. Is it too much to dream that we might yet change the name of the British Commonwealth to one of European Commonwealth and open up avenues without destroying the political institutions at all ?"[1]

Bevin returned to the same idea in an article for the January number of *The Record*:

1 Labour Party Conference Report, 1937, p. 207.

"The great colonial powers of Europe should pool their colonial territories and link them up with a European Commonwealth, instead of being limited British, French, Dutch or Belgian concessions as is now the case. Such a European Commonwealth, established on an economic foundation, would give us greater security than we get by trying to maintain the old balance of power. . . . It would make for a direct drive towards a United States of Europe which would give her a chance to live adequately."[1]

Part of the attraction of this idea to Bevin was his belief that it would offer scope for the energies of the German people and encourage them to look outwards. Writing to Emil Ludwig, the popular biographer, who had sent him his views on the German national character, Bevin advanced the view that the German character had been largely produced by the historical encirclement of the country which had produced a naturally introspective mood.

"If by some economic arrangement, Germany could be made part of a great Commonwealth of Nations, there would be a tendency for a more expansive mind developing over, say, the first or second generation."

He found it difficult to accept the view that there was "a German national character", arguing that regional and temperamental differences would assert themselves as soon as the weight of Hitler's dictatorship was lifted.

"I have ventured to advance the idea of linking up the British and French dominions with Europe, rather than with our own country, in the belief that if there was an economic opportunity over the wide areas of the World for raw materials and the raising of the standard of life generally, then this desire for conquest would recede. But if your assumption of the German character is correct, then nothing one could do economically would offer any hope. It seems to me if one is to accept your valuation as the final position, then the only hope for the world would be to crush Germany, and, as she rises, to crush her again, which gives one a very pessimistic outlook."[2]

Bevin had no patience with the proposal, widely canvassed at the time, to return Germany's former colonies. The right course, he argued, was to pool access to colonial resources among all the European nations and supersede national sovereignty over colonial territories in favour of a European, not a British, commonwealth. Nor had he any faith in the policy of appeasement on which

1 *The Record*, January 1938, p. 154.
2 Ernest Bevin to Emil Ludwig, then living in Switzerland, 2nd February 1938.

Chamberlain was now embarking with a new approach to Italy.

"Those who are building up their hopes upon some internal dissension breaking up régimes," he wrote in February 1938, "and those who are hoping that war will be avoided by some miraculous happening, are building upon sand. I have never believed from the first day when Hitler came to office but that he intended at the right moment and when he was strong enough, to wage war in the world. Neither do I believe, with that kind of philosophy, that there is any possibility to arrive at agreements with Hitler or Mussolini. But the time will come when it will be possible to do so with the German nation."[1]

It was to that time that Bevin was looking when he asked himself on what terms an offer could be made. In the meantime, "There seems to be no other way but to be strong in defence, it is the only language they understand and the only measure which can influence the régimes they control."[2] This belief was confirmed by Hitler's annexation of Austria a month later, and the General Council joined with the Labour Party in urging on Chamberlain the need for the other Powers in Europe, Britain, France and Russia to combine in resisting aggression.

Although Chamberlain rejected this advice as likely to divide Europe into two opposing camps and plunge the world into war,[3] the annexation of Austria at last brought a sense of urgency into the Government's plans for rearmament. In particular, the programme for the R.A.F. was increased, to provide 12,000 new planes in two years, and high priority given to equipping the army for anti-aircraft defence. The new plans required the diversion of a much greater part of the country's industrial resources to the manufacture of armaments and, for the first time since the original White Paper had been published two years before, an attempt was made to enlist the co-operation of the trade unions.

4

The Government's approach to the trade unions was not only belated but maladroit. When the Prime Minister invited the General

1 Draft of an article for *The Record*, dictated on 7th February, 1938.
2 Ibid.
3 In the House of Commons, 4th April 1938.

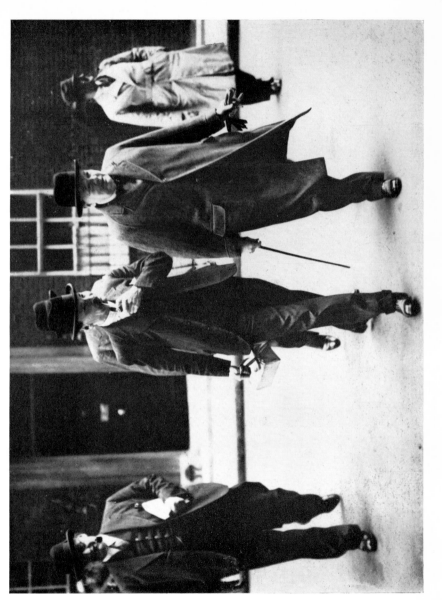

Bevin joins the War Cabinet, May 1940.

First day as Minister of Labour.

Council of the T.U.C. to meet him there were many in the Labour Movement who would have preferred to see the T.U.C. refuse as a protest against the Government's foreign policy. Bevin took a different view. However critical he felt of the Government's attitude in foreign affairs, he would not allow this to cloud his recognition of the country's need to rearm and he believed that, in their own interests no less than in that of the nation, the trade unions must not refuse to take their share of responsibility in carrying out the re-armament programme.

Citrine and the majority of the trade-union leaders shared Bevin's view and agreed to accept the Prime Minister's invitation. The meeting which took place on 23rd March was cool, but the General Council's reply to the Prime Minister's appeal for their goodwill left the door open for further negotiations:

"It places on record its conviction that in dealing with any government, the Council's conduct must be regulated by industrial and not political con-siderations, but at the same time it feels it necessary to draw the Prime Minister's attention to the grave concern which exists in the trade-union movement as to certain aspects of the Government's policy."

The General Council's reply was sent at the end of April. A month later, on 26th May, the Council, including Bevin, saw the Prime Minister a second time and put as forcibly as they could the objections they felt to the Government's policy: its attitude towards Spain, the signature of the Anglo-Italian agreement (on 16th April) and the fear that it would employ its increased arms to support rather than to oppose the dictators. To these they added criticism of the large profits which were being made out of rearmament and of the failure to consult the trade unions at an earlier date. Chamberlain, who was accompanied by Halifax, the new Foreign Minister, did his best to meet these criticisms, but the T.U.C.'s attitude had been stiffened by a meeting which had taken place the day before between the engineering employers and the Confederation of Shipbuilding and Engineering Unions.

Although the General Council strongly recommended that the Government should be represented in any negotiations with the trade unions, the engineering employers were left to meet the unions alone and they could do no better than come forward at once with proposals for the suspension of trade-union regulations and the 'dilution' of skilled labour by the employment of unskilled and women workers. The mention of dilution before the trade unions had been given any information about the Government's programme or needs was enough to revive bitter memories of the 1914–18 war. The suspicion was at once aroused that the employers were trying to rush the trade unionists and exploit the situation for their own advantage. Opposition to the Government on political grounds was thus strengthened by distrust on industrial grounds and negotiations came to a standstill.

Bevin was irritated with both sides. He thought the Government had handled the unions clumsily and failed to treat them frankly. In all probability, as had happened in the building trades, the Government's needs could be met without any suspension of trade-union regulations or dilution; in any case, the unions were in too suspicious a mood to agree to such proposals on the part of the employers unless they were taken into the Government's confidence and convinced by hard facts and figures that the urgency of the situation was such as to override all other considerations.

On the other hand, he suspected that much of the opposition, in the A.E.U. in particular, sprang from political motives.[1] He tried hard to get the Confederation of Shipbuilding and Engineering Unions to accept the view that they ought not to make co-operation in the rearmament programme dependent on agreement with the Government of the day's policies, but treat it as an industrial issue. Even on industrial grounds, although Bevin sympathised with the suspicions which the engineering unions felt towards the employers, he was clear-sighted enough to recognise that rearmament was going to go forward, whether the unions co-operated or not. The higher wages offered would attract labour to armament work and the unions would only weaken themselves by standing aside. His arguments, however—repeated by Deakin at the 1938 T.U.C.— failed to convert the engineering unions and when he returned from Australia in the autumn the co-operation of the trade unions in the Government's preparations for defence had still to be secured.

---

1 At the 1938 T. U.C. Jack Little, speaking on behalf of the A.E.U., said plainly: "If the Government would shift the embargo on the dispatch of munitions of war to Spain, that would throw the doors wide open for dilution." (Report, p. 302.)

5

During the spring of 1938 Bevin had been far from well, but he refused to leave until the Road Haulage Wages Act was safely passed. At last, in July, he was free to get away. He sailed from Southampton on the 9th in the company of Mrs. Bevin, bound for New York. There and at Washington he met and talked with American union leaders before going on to Canada by way of Chicago. They took the train through the Rockies to Vancouver, where they spent a week exploring Vancouver Island and the many small islands in the straits. It was the third time Bevin had crossed the North American continent and all his old joy in scenery and the open air was reawakened.

On 3rd August, joined by the rest of the British and the Canadian delegates to the conference, they sailed for New Zealand, a voyage which lasted three weeks and took them right across the Pacific by way of Hawaii and Fiji.

The Labour movement in New Zealand gave Bevin a great reception; Nothing he encountered on his travels put him in such good heart as the efforts of the one Labour Government in the British Commonwealth to carry through its programme of reforms and to win the next election, which was already imminent.

During the course of the voyage Bevin had become better acquainted with the other delegates from the United Kingdom and Canada. It was unusual company in which to find himself. Most of the delegates were either academics—Professor (later Sir Keith) Hancock, Miss Hadow, Sir Alfred Zimmern—or amateur politicians like the leader of the British delegation, Lord Lothian, and the most visionary among the prophets of the Commonwealth, Lionel Curtis, both of whom were identified with the high-minded imperialism of the *Round Table*. Few of them possessed Bevin's practical experience of men and politics and it was this, unfolded in a series of rich anecdotes and drawn upon at every turn in support of his arguments, which fascinated his fellow travellers.

The conference was held at the Lapstone Hotel in the Blue Mountains forty miles out of Sydney and lasted a fortnight. Altogether Chatham House and the Australian Institute of International Affairs had assembled ninety delegates from the four older

Dominions, India, Ireland and the United Kingdom. The meetings, of course, were unofficial in status, but representative of a wide section of political and national points of view. In the course of a fortnight's discussion most of the problems of the Commonwealth—constitutional, economic, strategic—and the characteristic attitudes of its different members towards them were laid bare. To Bevin it was a novel experience and, coming on top of the impressions left by his journey round the world, it had a powerful effect in crystallising his ideas.

He had always learned from experience and his Australian visit ranks as one of the formative episodes in the long process of his self-education. For years Bevin had been seeking a framework in which to carry out the proposals for international co-operation—access to raw materials, currency, trade, labour legislation, the raising of living standards—to which he attached so much importance. At times he looked for it in a United States of Europe; at other times, in the revival of the League of Nations with much more clearly defined economic functions. With the rise of the dictators in Europe, however, and the failure of the League, Bevin had been more and more attracted by the idea of the British Commonwealth as the nucleus of a group of nations which could work out common policies, with the great advantage that it was already in existence. Hitherto he had lacked the first-hand knowledge to give substance to the idea. His journey in 1938, taking him to three of the Dominions in turn, unfolding the potentialities of the Commonwealth before his eyes and introducing him in concentrated form at the conference to the clash of opinions which its problems aroused, provided the experience he needed to fire his imagination and opened a new world to him. He returned to England not only physically refreshed, but intellectually stimulated, full of ideas and with the energy to put them across.

Outside the conference, Bevin took the opportunity to see as much as he could of Australia and its cities, and to meet many of the Australian Labour leaders. Labour in New South Wales was divided into two factions, both of which tried to draw him into their quarrel. Bevin refused to take sides but soon found that private conversations were made the subject of public controversy in the Press and local Parliament. Apart from this experience, he was less attracted to the raucous and often corrupt politics of Australian Labour than by the Labour movement in New Zealand where the

Party was struggling with the responsibilities of office and making an effort, which won his immediate sympathy, to introduce many of the social reforms for which he had campaigned in Britain. Convinced that the Labour parties of the Commonwealth ought to meet and discuss their common problems, he suggested that the conference should be held in New Zealand in the Dominion's centenary year, 1940.

While Bevin was in Melbourne, the crisis over Czechoslovakia came to a head. Bevin at once cabled London that he was ready to fly back if the Union or the T.U.C. thought it necessary. At that distance it was difficult to make out what was happening, the more so as Chamberlain's first visit to Hitler at Berchtesgaden was followed by a stiffening of British and French resistance which gave no hint of the final capitulation at Munich. All he could do was to sit listening to the news bulletins, hoping that war would be avoided but absolutely convinced that to appease Hitler was to run straight into further trouble and that to desert the Czechs, a people he had long admired for their democratic spirit, would be a crime. It was still under the shadow of the crisis and with thoughts much preoccupied with Europe that Bevin said farewell to his friends and set out on the long voyage home across the Indian Ocean by way of Bombay, Aden and the Suez Canal.

6

Travelling overland from Marseilles, the Bevins reached London by the end of October. Four months away and a journey round the world had given Bevin a freshness of outlook very different from the depressed mood he found at home in the reaction from Munich. In the next few months more than one friend urged him to abandon thoughts of retiring and instead enter the House of Commons to give the Labour Party the leadership of which it badly stood in need. He was not to be moved. Had he been ten years younger, he told Francis Williams,[1] he might have felt differently, but within sight of sixty he was too old to start a new career. He even refused to accept the seat on the National Council of Labour to which the General Council had appointed him in his absence. But he did all he could to

[1] Francis Williams, *op. cit.*, p. 210.

give currency to the ideas he had brought back from his tour and to urge the Labour movement to think more seriously about the potentialities of the Commonwealth.

When Chatham House asked him to report on his impressions of the Conference, he told his audience that the greatest danger to the Commonwealth sprang from ignorance, lack of frankness in discussing conflicts of interest and distrust of the foreign policy pursued by the United Kingdom Government.[1] Imperial Conferences, attended only by government representatives and swathed in official secrecy, did nothing to dispel these misunderstandings. He proposed a 'League Assembly' of the Commonwealth countries with its proceedings conducted in public, all parties represented and the frankest possible statement of views.

Amongst the subjects which ought to be discussed the most urgent was defence. The United Kingdom was bound by the Eden declaration of April 1937 to go to war to defend any part of the British Commonwealth, but none of the Dominions had any reciprocal obligations. They insisted on being free to decide at the last moment whether they would come in or remain neutral. If Canada or South Africa was not prepared to accept any obligation, should the British people continue to be bound by so sweeping a commitment? The right solution, Bevin suggested, was for the different members of the Commonwealth to accept responsibility for the defence of particular areas, and to reach understanding on these in advance of a crisis.

The suspicion of Britain and the insistence on liberty of action was, in part, a reflection of constitutional uncertainties:

"The Balfourian dexterity which seems to be typified in the Statute of Westminster has outgrown itself. I am convinced that you will have to give the Dominions complete control over their own constitutions without interference from Westminster and allow them to modify those constitutions in whatever way they deem necessary."

Bevin's most interesting proposal, however, was his suggestion that the Ottawa Agreements between the Commonwealth countries (of the value of which in their existing form he was sceptical) should be extended to bring in other countries prepared to renounce

1 22nd November 1938. Text reprinted in International Affairs, Vol. XVIII (1939), No. 1.

aggression and to lower their tariffs. If the other colonial powers like Holland and Belgium could be brought in, so much the better; then their dependent territories and the British colonial empire could be thrown open to the other members to provide access to raw materials, markets and the opportunity for development which had been neglected in favour of treating colonies solely as strategic bases. In this way, the existing Commonwealth might be made the nucleus of a new League, with an economic basis in the expanded Ottawa Agreement which the old League had lacked.

Bevin installed a large globe on his desk in Transport House and talked to everyone he met about his Commonwealth trip and the conclusions he had drawn from it. He addressed an all-party meeting in the House of Commons urging them to set up a Select Committee on the administration of the Colonial Empire: "Our crime isn't exploitation, it's neglect."[1] He met the Overseas Settlement Board and gave it his views on emigration to Australia. He agreed to help 'Freeland', the League for Jewish Territorial Colonisation, and wrote several letters to Australian Labour leaders commending to them Jewish plans to establish settlements in Western Australia. He took up his plan for a Commonwealth Labour Conference and in the meantime did all he could to give practical help to the movement in New Zealand. When New Zealand stocks fell on the London Stock Exchange following Labour's victory in the elections, Bevin persuaded the Union to invest £110,000 and published the fact as evidence of his confidence in the Labour Government. Drawing on the experience of the *Daily Herald* he sent all the information he could that would help the New Zealand Labour movement to establish a daily newspaper and, with the agreement of the New Zealand Waterside Workers' Union, talked to shipping interests in London in an effort to remove difficulties over freight rates and port delays.

In February 1939 Bevin contributed an article on the Commonwealth to the *Spectator* and the same month took the chair for another discussion at Chatham House. On this occasion he linked his ideas about the Commonwealth with his earlier criticisms of the League of Nations and his unswerving devotion to the I.L.O.:

"I personally," he said, "have always approached problems from an

1 Francis Williams, *op. cit.*, p. 209.

economic point of view. The trouble with the League has been that it was given a political head, a Labour tail and no economic body. Had there been an economic conference similarly constituted to the I.L.O. and meeting every year to discuss the economic difficulties and raw material requirements of each state, the question of reparations, for example, would not have reached the magnitude it did and the present difficulties would, to a great extent, have been avoided . . .

"It is easier to induce nations," he added, "to discuss problems than to discuss politics. . . . For years it has been my job to promote unity amongst conflicting organisations and I would never have succeeded if I had put before them cut and dried constitutions. The only way to promote unity is to induce people to concentrate on problems with which they are economically confronted. In this way solutions to problems are sought rather than differences magnified."[1]

He had now found in the idea of an expanded Commonwealth the framework for which he had long been looking and he determined to make it the theme of a big speech to the Southport conference of the Labour Party at Whitsuntide.

7

Before the conference met Hitler occupied Prague, and Chamberlain, after an initial hesitation, at last abandoned the policy of appeasement. Bevin was far from convinced, despite the guarantees to Poland and Russia, that the Government could be relied on to stick to its new course and face the risk of war. But even if they could, this marked no great advance, only the end of a retreat. Bevin found it intolerable to sit still and watch war draw steadily nearer without searching for some way which would offer, not an alternative to confronting the dictators with force, but a more stable framework for security in the future. At Brighton in 1935 he had forced a reluctant Party to face unpleasant facts; now, at Southport in 1939, he showed his powers of leadership in a different way, by reviving faith, in a frustrated Party, that there was still scope for initiative in creating a new League of Nations.

The debate on foreign affairs, opened by Philip Noel-Baker, was a spiritless re-hash of every radical slogan ever coined in favour of peace and in lament at the wicked state of the world. Bevin alone

[1] From a verbatim note of the discussion sent to Bevin by Chatham House.

dispelled the lack of conviction in an unreal discussion and lifted his audience out of a routine condemnation of the sins of the Government by his conception of what could be made of the Commonwealth.

"I have come to this rostrum," he said, "to make a contribution to the practical side of this resolution. . . . Collective Security can never be effective as a final custodian of the peace if it is merely based on the policy of arms . . . I know that all our minds are influenced by the terrible dangers of war, but we have to carry our minds further than that."

There was need to work more closely with the United States. On this all were agreed.

"I suggest that possibly the quickest approach is for us to be willing to extend the great Commonwealth idea, in which the United States can be a partner, at least economically, even though it may involve a limitation of our sovereignty.

"I have already stated my views as to what the Ottawa Agreement has done in dividing the economy of Europe and other parts of the world, but it may now be turned in a new channel. . . . If you seek to end it, it might cause further disturbance. The proper method is to expand it. You are building up a system of collective security and guarantees and in addition you have a number of neutral countries who, whilst unable to come within that system, would be anxious to come within an economic Peace Bloc. May we not find that here is an instrument of tremendous economic attraction which can be used? If we invite countries like Scandinavia, Holland, Belgium, Russia, France and the U.S.A. who are willing to co-operate to come within our preference system, would not that for the first time result in a real pooling of the whole of the colonial empires and their resources? It would bring the 'Haves' together and they would in fact be controlling 90 per cent of the essential raw materials of the world. . . . If you can bring them together so far as military, naval and defence equipment is concerned, is it too much to suggest that an endeavour should be made to pool them economically and so equip ourselves with a far greater weapon than arms can give?"

But Bevin wanted to look further ahead.

"Having secured that, what should be our next step? Our appeal must be to the peoples of the aggressor countries. That appeal must be genuine, for many Germans have said to me, 'All you have offered us up to now are military pacts.' What have the democracies to offer out of their great abundance?

"The real trouble which is disturbing the world rests primarily in Europe and with Japan. Having pooled our arms, resources and economic power, cannot we then say, and mean it, to the people of these countries: 'Put away your weapons, discard them as a means of bettering your conditions of life and you can come in on the ground floor with the rest of us.' . . .

"In addition, here is a chance now to settle the problem of the colonies on a different basis. Transference of territory from one Great Power to another will not solve any economic problem. Neither is it any use to be hypocritical about our own position as a colonial power. . . . The right method of approach is to deal with the great resources of the world. Then we can say to the peoples I have referred to—'We have something better to offer than war can win.' Show to the peoples of the world that, whilst we are determined to resist aggression, the policy we are advocating gives them all a chance for 'a place in the sun' and a right to develop their standard of living. Show them that by the proper use of the instrument of peace they can achieve far more, both in standard of life and economic security, than war has ever been able to obtain."[1]

Bevin's speech not only roused the enthusiasm of his audience—it was the one speech that did—but attracted much attention outside the Labour movement. War came too soon to allow any chance of his ideas being carried further, but anyone who compares the declaration of Bevin's views on foreign policy in 1938 and 1939 with the ideas which became commonplace after the war—for example, the modification of national sovereignty and the functional approach to international relations—will be struck by the extent to which his mind was already moving in this direction.

The other big debate at Southport was on the Popular Front. Bevin had no more use for a Popular Front than he had for the United Front: if people wanted to oppose Chamberlain, let them join the Labour Party and help it to beat the Tories. But he did not take any public part in the discussion of the question, even when Cripps took up the cause and drove it so hard that he was expelled from the Party. Bevin shed no tears over Cripps' expulsion but he left it to others to put the case to the Southport conference where Cripps' attempt to get the Executive's decision reversed was defeated by a five-to-one majority.

8

It was defence which drew Bevin again into politics, if only because of the position which he held on the General Council, particularly during Citrine's absence in the West Indies on a royal commission.

1 Labour Party Conference Report, 1939, pp. 243-5.

The conversations between the Prime Minister and the T.U.C. in the spring of 1938 had gone no further. The Munich crisis, however, had revealed the gaps in British preparations for defence and in the months that followed urgent efforts were made not only to increase arms production and build up the Forces but to draw up plans for the organisation of the country's industry and communications in the event of war.

Bevin required no convincing of the need for such plans, but he was opposed to handing over the responsibility to government departments, even more to forming battalions of dock or demolition workers on military lines. As soon as he returned from Australia he flung himself into convincing, first the General Council, then the Government, that each industry understood its own problems better than anyone else and that the best course was for the employers and the unions to assume the joint responsibility for drawing up their own schemes.

During the winter of 1938–9 he took the leading part in preparing plans for wartime organisation in four key industries: docks, road haulage, demolition, milling and provender. In July 1939, for example, he persuaded the joint industrial councils for the flour-milling and provender industries to set up a Civilian Defence Committee. Through fifteen area committees this made provision for air-raid precautions, the pooling and transfer of labour and the continued production of flour and feeding stuffs in an emergency. The scheme was accepted by Sir John Anderson, who as Lord Privy Seal was now in charge of civil defence, and who went on to appoint Bevin as chairman of the Civil Defence Committee for the Constructional Industry with a brief to work out the industry's own proposals for demolition work.

Bevin was already a member of the Port and Transit Committee, virtually the same committee on which he had served his apprenticeship in the earlier war. With the backing of the dockers' delegate conference, he assumed responsibility on behalf of the Union for organising the transfer of dockers from east to west coast ports in the event of war and got the scheme accepted by the National Joint Council for Dock Labour. Finally, on the Road Transport Defence Committee he helped to draft the plans for mobilising the haulage industry, limiting requisitioning to the vehicles and keeping the men in civilian employment.

By upholding this principle of civilian employment in each case, Bevin kept the door open for the unions to maintain wages and conditions in wartime, and by making use of joint organisations with the employers allowed the unions to share fully in the decisions taken. But he was not only seeking to defend his members' and the unions' interests; he was convinced that a democratic society could only develop its full resources, if it drew on the capacity of its members for self-government and did not take the easier, but in his view less efficient, course of concentrating power in the hands of an over-worked civil service.

This same democratic philosophy coloured his opposition to conscription, the demand for which began to grow stronger after Munich. In December 1938, the T.U.C. agreed to join the National Service Committees which the Government set up throughout the country in an effort to stimulate voluntary recruitment for all forms of national service including civil defence. Doubts were expressed on the General Council but Bevin argued strongly that the trade unions should do everything they could to make a success of a voluntary system in preference to compulsion. He himself agreed to serve on the central National Service Committee and devoted much time to securing satisfactory conditions for civil-defence workers and to revising the schedule of reserved occupations. In February 1939 he led a T.U.C. deputation to ask the Prime Minister whether, in view of the responsibilities which the trade-union movement was now accepting, the time had not come to remove the stigma of the Trade Disputes Act of 1927.

In exerting his influence with the trade-union movement to secure support for the Government's preparations, Bevin had acted on explicit assurances from the Minister of Labour and Sir John Anderson that their scheme for voluntary recruitment was not intended to prepare the way for compulsion. Hitler's occupation of Prague in March, however, led to a complete reversal of the Government's policy. Strong pressure was now put on the Prime Minister by his own Party to silence doubts of the Government's change of heart by introducing compulsory military service. Several times in the weeks that followed Prague Bevin was approached privately with the suggestion that he should give a lead to the Labour movement by declaring in favour of such a step. He angrily refused.

The need to strengthen the country's defences was not in question. Whatever illusions may still have been entertained by other members of the Labour Party, Bevin had made up his mind long before Chamberlain that force was the only argument to use to Hitler. His opposition to conscription had nothing to do with pacifism, appeasement or the belief that war could somehow be avoided. No one on the Labour side had been more active in assisting preparations for defence. Why then did he denounce Chamberlain's action so emphatically?

Chamberlain argued that changed circumstances released him from his promise not to introduce conscription in peace-time. But Bevin, with his trade-union training, attached the greatest importance to keeping a pledge, whether it was convenient or not. The Government and the ruling class were doing just what they had done in 1915: after securing Labour's co-operation on a voluntary basis, they brought in conscription by the back door and tried to 'put it over' on the working class. The next step would be industrial conscription for which the employers had long been hankering. And just as in 1914–18, the conscription of men—despite all the fair promises—would not be accompanied by measures to conscript wealth, to check profiteering or control prices.

The reason given by the Government was the needs of a national emergency; but what difference was calling up 300,000 young men for six months' military training going to make, when there was not enough equipment for the men who had already volunteered to join the Territorial Army? It was a specious move, Bevin declared, to cover up the fact that the National Government had been fumbling with defence for years and had failed to provide adequate arms. It was typical of the Tory mind, he added, that the moment an emergency arose it turned at once to compulsion; the Tories had no faith in the ordinary man and woman.

"I have no hesitation in replying that our people will respond to defend their country, their houses and their families, if they are satisfied the cause is just and the defence of the country is the real issue at stake. It is not necessary to pass laws to take away their liberties."[1]

But how could they have confidence in the Government, Bevin

[1] *The Record*, May 1939, pp. 288–9. He had voiced the same views in a letter to John Rodgers, of I.C.I., at the end of March.

asked, when the same men—Chamberlain, Sir Samuel Hoare, Sir John Simon—were still in power who had been responsible for the record of retreat from Abyssinia to Prague? As late as January 1939, Chamberlain and Halifax had visited Rome, a visit followed by Mussolini's occupation of Albania and the completion of the Axis Pact of Steel. The guarantees to Poland and Rumania were all very well, but Chamberlain, who had been willing enough to visit Hitler and Mussolini, refused to fly to Moscow or to make a real effort to reach the understanding with Russia which was the obvious key to the defence of Eastern Europe. And these were the men, now lecturing the trade unions on their responsibilities, who had established the Means Test. Chamberlain, in Bevin's eyes, was the embodiment of the narrow-minded, self-righteous middle-class attitude towards the working class which had, at every stage, refused to take bold measures in attacking the problems of unemployment and the distressed areas.

If the Government now admitted that its foreign policy had been wrong, why did it not get out of office and give place to men who were not compromised by their own past actions? This, Bevin declared, would do far more than the introduction of conscription to establish confidence in the British Government and its tardy conversion to the need to stand up to Hitler's demands.

Nonetheless, once the Military Service Act had been passed, he exerted his influence against those who wanted the Labour movement to withdraw from all co-operation in defence preparations. Nor had he any patience with left-wing talk of industrial action to resist conscription. He continued to believe that the Government had made a mistake in abandoning voluntary action before it had been given a chance to prove itself, but the situation was too serious to stand aside or refuse to give all the practical help which he could.

9

In the midst of these anxieties, the Union held the last biennial delegate conference he was to attend as its general secretary, at Bridlington in July. Exactly fifty years after the London dock strike of 1889, out of which the Dockers' Union had been born, the T.G.W.U. numbered 700,000: the 'dock rats' of 1889 had become the nucleus of a union which outnumbered the total membership affiliated to the T.U.C. fifty years before. More striking than the growth in numbers was the change in functions: the Union of 1939 had achieved a measure of recognition from both State and industry hardly thought of at the time when the dockers struck for a wage of sixpence an hour.

In the process Bevin and the Union's other leaders had had to assume responsibilities and master problems of organisation and negotiation undreamed of even at the time of the amalgamation. Bevin was now on the eve of retirement, and with him would go the last of the generation of officers and committee-men which had carried through the amalgamation. Where were they to find the younger men who would take over responsibility, not only at the top but in the national, area and branch committees upon which, as Bevin well knew, the vitality of the Union and its power to recruit new leaders depended? With this in mind, he placed before the conference an education scheme designed to train members of the Union in the wide range of industrial negotiations and union organisation in which it was now involved.

The Executive's resolution on foreign policy pledged the Union's support for resistance to aggression, repudiated any attempt to reach agreement with the dictators, and urged the Government to complete an agreement with Russia. But Bevin was not content to leave it at that, going on to expound his plans for creating a more effective league of nations based upon economic co-operation. With Nazism,

"you can neither negotiate nor buy off; you cannot do anything of that character. All you can do is to stand up to it and prevent it from winning. But when you have prevented it from winning, do not make the mistake we made in 1919. We handled Central Europe in 1919 as if the Kaiser were still on the throne. We did the same with Russia. . . . In foreign policy you have got to look ahead."

As soon as the Bridlington conference was over, he sailed for New York. A three-day Congress on Education for Democracy had been organised at Teachers' College, Columbia University, under the chairmanship of President Nicholas Murray Butler and with the support of twenty-eight national organisations ranging from the American Bankers Association to the C.I.O. and the National

Association for the Advancement of Coloured People. Every step had been taken to give the Congress the widest possible coverage in the Press and on the radio, and among those from Britain invited to speak besides Bevin were Earl Baldwin, Lord Eustace Percy and John Murray.

Bevin took much trouble in preparing his address. Suiting himself to his American audience, he deliberately avoided any reference to Socialism. Instead he set himself to defend his own belief in democratic government (with which he tacitly identified Socialism as he knew it) in face of the challenge from the totalitarian systems. Unlike many essays in political philosophy it was an attempt not to argue from first principles, but to set down the beliefs on which he acted.

He defined democracy as "change by consent, upon the decision of the majority, without having to resort to force or the indulgence in tyranny".

"We must not confuse democracy with the maintenance of a particular form of economic or financial system; rather is it a condition which allows for change in the system itself and provides for such adaptation as the change in public need and opinion demands."

Until recently democracy had been limited to the political field: now that the need for collective action in the economic sphere as well had been accepted, the problem of democracy was how to solve its economic problems without destroying liberty.

Amongst the handicaps to democracy, Bevin singled out three for particular mention: lack of educational opportunity especially for the poor; fear, driving man to exercise his predatory instincts, and the opposition of vested interests to the enjoyment of political power by the masses.

"What were the vested interests which assisted in the destruction of democratic government? Big business; the great financial interests; the advocates of the theory of world revolution; political clericalism; military castes and the position of certain racial interests who thought they could procure their own safety by bribing the enemies of democracy. It would not have been possible for any of the Dictatorships which have come into existence since the end of the Great War to have done so without the aid of one or other or a combination of those four."

In a final section, Bevin went on to consider the steps necessary to safeguard democracy, especially its extension to international relations:

"I have no doubt that this will bring one into conflict with the idea of national sovereignty. National sovereignty has served a great purpose in the organisation of the world, but it must be accepted that the next stage in human development must be directed towards world order."[1]

10

All through the summer the news from Germany had grown more ominous and as Bevin was crossing the Atlantic on his way home, news came that Ribbentrop was flying to Moscow to sign the Nazi-Soviet Pact. War followed the first week-end of September.

If there had been time, Bevin might well have reflected bitterly on the lost opportunities of earlier years. But he had too much to do to waste energy on regrets and at least there was satisfaction in the fact that this time Britain and France had refused to connive at Hitler's act of aggression against Poland.

Although the Government had had long enough notice of the possibility of war, it was ill-prepared when it came. Plans to mobilise the country's economic strength had largely to be improvised in the last weeks of peace and early days of the war. New ministries and departments had to be set up; new committees; new controls and regulations, all adding to the anxious confusion in which the country awaited an aerial bombardment that did not come for another year.

Most Government departments were closely in touch with industry and many recruited temporary staffs from business men with first-hand knowledge of the commodities or industry they had now to control. No one, however, thought it important to consult the trade-union leaders, not as a deliberate slight, but simply because industry to the Chamberlain Government meant capital and management, not labour, at least not on anything like equal terms with the other two elements. Although this omission was soon corrected in face of vigorous protest from the trade-union leaders, it shed much light on the Government's attitude and meant that it

1 *Forward Democracy*, an address by Ernest Bevin (Victoria House Printing Co.), 1939.

started on the wrong foot with organised labour from the beginning.

The first tussle came over the Minister of Labour's Control of Employment Bill which was hurriedly introduced in the House of Commons on 5th September. Earlier in the summer, the T.U.C. had placed before the Minister its own scheme for the control of industry in wartime. This followed closely Bevin's idea of making each industry, through its own joint negotiating machinery, responsible for meeting the Government's needs, including increased production and the transfer of labour. There were obvious advantages to the trade unions in such a scheme which would oblige the Government to impose the machinery of collective bargaining on those industries in which trade-union organisation was still too weak to secure it. There were equally obvious disadvantages to the Government which was invited to put its powers into commission, although trade-union organisation and joint negotiations extended to only a third of the employed workers in the country.

The Ministry of Labour, however, after pointing out the objections to the General Council's scheme at a meeting on 19th July, thereafter let negotiations lapse, and introduced its own scheme for the control of employment without previously consulting the trade-union leaders. The result was an angry protest and hurried attempts by the Ministry of Labour officials to placate Citrine and Bevin by accepting a series of amendments which in effect robbed the scheme of most of its value. In fact, only one order was ever issued under the Control of Employment Act and by May 1940, when Bevin became Minister of Labour himself, little had been done to transfer manpower to the industries where it was most urgently needed.

The General Council was equally incensed to learn that, after repeated refusals, the Government was setting up a Ministry of Supply without consulting the trade unions or making provision for their representation on its committees. At an interview on 5th October, when the Prime Minister received the General Council in his room in the House of Commons, Citrine made it clear that the T.U.C. wanted something more than representation on the National Advisory Committee which the Ministry of Labour was setting up, they wanted direct access to all the departments whose activities might affect working-class interests. The trade-union movement, Citrine added, was wholeheartedly behind the Government in prosecuting the war, but the Ministry of Supply episode did not make co-operation easy: "It appears that the Ministry is either contemptuous of the Trade Union Movement or oblivious of its existence."

Chamberlain gave no immediate promise, but he also left no doubt that he wanted the full co-operation of the trade unions and as they walked back to Transport House, Bevin remarked that that day might well prove to be the turning-point in the long fight of the trade unions for 'recognition'. His forecast was soon proved right. On 16th October, the Prime Minister sent for the President of the T.U.C. and Citrine and read to them an instruction he had already sent out to all Government departments emphasising the need for "the most complete understanding and co-operation" with the trade-union movement. In the weeks that followed one department after another—the Ministry of Supply, the Ministry of Food, the Ministry of Shipping, the Board of Trade, as well as the Ministry of Labour—invited the T.U.C. to nominate representatives to serve on central and local advisory committees, some of which were specially constituted for this purpose.

The result of this was to make it easier for the trade unions to look after the interests of their members many of whom were immediately affected by the change to wartime conditions. Much of the negotiation over conditions which had hitherto been conducted with employers had now to be taken up with Government departments and Bevin was almost continuously employed in the first few months of the war in seeing Ministers or their officials about a variety of questions ranging from lighting on the docks and lodging allowances for building workers to the trade-union representation of A.R.P. workers.

That was all very well as far as it went and, after its initial failure to recognise the importance of consulting the trade-union leaders, the Government—and the Ministry of Labour in particular—leaned over backwards in their efforts to avoid labour troubles. But all this did not touch the real problem: how to mobilise the full economic resources of the nation for the struggle in which it was engaged.

I I

More than one of the Government's expert advisers urged it to impose control of labour and wages outright, whether the trade unions agreed or not. The Ministry of Labour, however, was strongly opposed to rushing the T.U.C., and Bevin, aware of the discussions that were going on in Whitehall, seized the opportunity of the Union's annual festival at Bristol in February to issue his own emphatic warning:

"If the Government is going to take the occasion of this war to invade the liberties of my people, I will lead the movement to resist this Government— or any other Government. This is not the only Government that can win the war: there is an alternative Government. The appetite for compulsion is growing and there is no ground for it."[1]

Despite the accession of Churchill and Anderson and the return of Eden, the Government of the country was still substantially in the hands of the men responsible for the policy of the 1930s. Among the nine members of the War Cabinet, besides Chamberlain himself, were Sir John Simon as Chancellor of the Exchequer, Lord Halifax as Foreign Secretary, Sir Samuel Hoare, Sir Kingsley Wood and Lord Hankey. Sir Horace Wilson, Secretary of the Ministry of Labour at the time of the General Strike and credited, rightly or wrongly, with much of the responsibility for the policy of appeasement, remained Permanent Secretary of the Treasury and high in the Cabinet's counsels.

Neither Bevin nor any other Labour leader could overcome his distrust of such a Government. The same distrust ruled out its reconstruction as an all-party coalition. The bitterness which had divided the parties during the 1930s on foreign as well as domestic affairs could not be wiped out overnight and so long as Neville Chamberlain remained Prime Minister neither Attlee nor anyone else could bring the Labour Party into a coalition, even if he had wanted to.

This lack of confidence was the root of the trouble. The trade unions were criticised at the time and have been since for their

1 *Western Daily Press,* 5th February 1940. Speech at the Bristol Festival of the T.G.W.U., 3rd February 1940.

refusal to forego wage increases and accept more drastic control of labour. Men like Bevin and Citrine saw perfectly well the argument in favour of both courses, but they lacked any confidence in the willingness or determination of the Chamberlain Government to impose equal sacrifices on all classes, and they were determined not to accept measures which would bear unequally on the working classes alone.

At the first meeting of the General Council with the Prime Minister after the outbreak of war, Bevin put forward the argument that it was the duty of the State in wartime to stabilise prices and meet the differences of cost out of direct taxation so that every member of the community should contribute. When the Government declined to take such action, and prices rose, Bevin claimed the same freedom as the business man or the industrialists to defend the interests of the men he represented and press for wage increases.

It needed little knowledge of economics to see that this was a situation which could not continue indefinitely. If the nation was ever to measure up to the demands of the war, there would have to be an end of "Business as Usual" for the trade unions as well as for the employers, drastic limitations on freedom of action, and sacrifices by all classes, including the working classes. But neither exhortations to the trade unions nor controls imposed over their opposition would meet the case. It was an economic problem to which there was only a political solution and it was fortunate that the crisis of May 1940 provided such a solution along the only lines that would work, by giving Labour not simply 'recognition' but power on equal terms and a full share of the responsibility for finding the answer.

12

The work of the Union had still to go on, and Bevin found himself and his officers faced with the heavy task of re-negotiating agreements to cover wartime conditions for almost all the 700,000 members of the Union, not one at a time as the existing agreements ran out, but all at once as soon as possible after the declaration of war. 37,000 members of the Union either volunteered or were called up; many thousands of others changed jobs or moved from one part of the country to another; in certain trades, fishing, for example, and dock work in the Port of London and other east-coast ports, there was a high figure of unemployment. Yet the Union maintained its membership, and soon began to add to it, bringing its total from just under 700,000 at the beginning of the war to over a million at the end.

Old problems still took up much of Bevin's time, chief amongst them the negotiations and drafting of the first Orders under the Road Haulage Wages Act, which were not ready for enforcement until 1940. One of the new problems with which he had to deal was the growing employment of women, with the Union trying to secure a "rate for the job", irrespective of sex, and a minimum wage for women of £2 a week. Another in which he played the biggest part himself was the reorganisation of the fishing industry. Hull, Grimsby and the other ports had been hard hit by the Admiralty's requisitioning of trawlers for mine-sweeping and other naval duties. Not only was there much unemployment in the ports but the most important supplement to the meat supplies of the country—not to mention fish and chips, one of the staple foods of the working classes in the North of England—was threatened.

Bevin took the initiative in persuading the five different Ministries concerned to attend a meeting at which Churchill, then First Lord of the Admiralty, agreed to take the chair (19th October 1939). The combination of Churchill and Bevin was formidable. In the course of a single meeting, they agreed on a number of suggestions which Bevin put forward and set up a Fisheries Advisory Committee which, in face of the increasing demands of the war at sea, enabled the fishing industry to adjust itself as well as circumstances would allow.

No less important was the fact that Churchill and Bevin, brought into co-operation for the first time in their lives, rapidly took the measure of each other. There could hardly have been a greater contrast: the patrician politician, master of the suspect arts of war and diplomacy, the working-class leader, immersed in the social and industrial problems of trade unionism.

On a number of occasions in the 1920s, Bevin had attacked Churchill as the most reckless and reactionary of Tory politicians— over intervention in Russia, the return to the gold standard, the General Strike, the Trade Disputes Act and Churchill's opposition to the grant of self-government to India. The Churchill of the 1930s, warning the nation against the threat of German power, was a different figure from the Churchill of the 1920s, but Bevin, fighting a parallel campaign to rouse the Labour movement to the same dangers, was still separated from him, not only by class and political barriers, but by past history.

Now, at a time when Britain was still ruled by a Government of half-measures, each recognised in the other the same quality of decision, the same capacity to rise to the height of great events. To his surprise, Bevin found in Churchill a politician capable of the prompt and bold action which he could never obtain from other Government departments: to his satisfaction, Churchill marked in Bevin a breadth of mind and a natural authority which he had never before met in a working-class leader.

This encounter was to bear fruit before many months had passed, but in the meantime Bevin remained on the outside, a powerful figure on trade-union deputations or advisory committees, a man whose views carried weight and whose experience was frequently called on to help solve particular problems, but excluded from any share in the responsibility for national policy or planning. It was a situation which left him restless and frustrated, conscious of his great abilities as an organiser and seeing the job that needed to be done, without the chance to take a hand in it.

Reports continually reached him through the Union of the muddle and inefficiency with which the Government's efforts to control industry were being pursued. One factory was on short time (but hanging on to its skilled labour force) while another could not meet its commitments for lack of men. One firm on war production was held up because it could not obtain supplies of a particular raw material or part, which another firm in the next town was happily continuing to use for peaceful household purposes. There were continual complaints of shortages and the failure to expand output, while factories stood idle for lack of work or because of a muddle over allocations. Not until April 1940 was the figure for unemployment brought below a million, despite the million and a half places left vacant by those joining the Services.[1]

Bevin poured out some of his criticisms in an address to the Institute of Transport in January. Several months after the war had begun, there was still no co-ordinated national transport system.

1 W. K. Hancock and M. M. Gowing: *British War Economy*, (1953) pp. 142–3.

The Government, Bevin declared, thought too much in terms of the railways which it had taken over for the duration of the war. The railway companies had always shown hostility to the use of other forms of transport, especially road haulage, and the Government was falling into the same trap. What was needed was a single authority responsible for all forms of transport—rail, road, shipping, canals—and capable of planning and using the nation's transport resources as a whole.

Why was more effort not being put into building new shipping? Was it because the shipbuilding interests were anxious not to see new yards opened and the Government accepted their view? Why had so little been done to create more inland storage away from the docks, which were bound to be the first target in air-raids? Why was more not being done to take advantage of the precious months free from air attack to meet these weaknesses in the country's transport system?

Bevin knew what he was talking about and his criticisms attracted sufficient attention for the Prime Minister to ask to see a copy of his address. Bevin sent it to him at once with an offer to help in any way that he could, but nothing further happened before the spring brought the real war thundering across the Channel.

13

More than once that winter, Bevin's mind turned to the plans for international development which he had sketched to the Southport conference of the Labour Party. "It is not enough," he told his Executive Council, "to mouth democracy. We have got to find a way to establish it for the world in the real and fullest sense, both politically and economically."

Towards the end of January 1940, he collected half a dozen of the Union's officers and M.P.s to talk to them about the future of the colonial empire and Africa in particular. "I believe," he told them, "that out of this war there should be a definite drive to end imperial positions as such." But how was this to be done? The mandatory system to which the Labour Party was committed did not attract him except in the special case of Palestine, nor would the single transfer of territory from one country to another solve anything.

What Bevin had in mind was a United Provinces of Africa to be created by pooling the African colonies of the five big empires, Britain, France, Italy, Belgium and Portugal. Some territories, of course, would have to be excluded—the Union of South Africa, for instance, French Morocco and Egypt—but the rest should be brought together under a common international administration, demilitarised and opened up for development in the interests of the peoples who lived there. India as well as Japan should be asked to share in the settlement and the United States to provide the chairman of the international body which would administer the Provinces pending the granting of self-government.

"I want you," he concluded, "to visualise this great territory united, with its land the property of the State, let out on lease, its communications directed by an international body, with great educational facilities and chances of development."

He took up the same theme in a speech to the Bristol Labour Party two days later with the suggestion that, as a first step, Britain and France should establish customs unions between their two empires.

"The new force created by the merged empires would mean that there was something of a definite character to offer the neutrals and an opportunity to ease the situation with the United States."

Nor did he exclude the possibility of bringing in Germany as well once she had been defeated and purged of Nazism.

The approach, he insisted, must be economic, but the results, if it were successful, would be political as well.

"If the five great empires could be brought together and pooled, the whole of that great area of Africa could be disarmed. The whole of it could be removed from the orbit of war and the conflicts of European states."[1]

It was only the germ of an idea and Bevin made no pretence that he had worked it out in detail, but of one thing he was certain: they could not afford to leave thinking about the future shape of the world until the war was over. "Do not wait, as we did in the last war, and let political passion dominate the making of a new world."

1 *Daily Herald*, 3rd February 1940.

There were many in the first winter of the war who, like Bevin, sought relief from the frustration of the 'phoney war' in the discussion of 'war aims'. Bevin's instinct told him plainly that this would not be a short war and was far from being won yet. But six months' experience had confirmed rather than overcome his distrust of the Government. Criticism, of course, was muffled by the need to preserve unity in time of war, but when the Norwegian campaign revealed the extent to which the country was still unprepared, Bevin could keep silence no longer. He burst out angrily in a May Day speech at Stoke-on-Trent.

"The time has come when there must be no mincing of words. It is no use disguising the fact that those who, like myself, have been constantly in touch with Government departments, are intensely dissatisfied with the kind of obstruction, lack of drive, absence of imagination and complacency which exists."

On the eve of battles which were only too clearly to justify his words, Bevin declared:

"I am afraid that the kind of middle class mind which actuates those responsible for strategy and government has little knowledge of the psychology and organising ability of the people in charge of the totalitarian states. . . . We cannot afford incompetence. We have no right to allow the lives of our soldiers and sailors to be played with."

The working people would give the country the production that was needed, if they knew what was wanted.

"But the damnable thing is they cannot put in the extra energy to give the soldier what he needs without also having to give bigger profits to the capitalists in control. The British working class want this war won. They know what is at stake. It is their liberty. But they want a Government that is going to please the nation before its friends and private interests."[1]

Bevin's speech reflected a mood of anger which was growing rapidly in the country and which found open expression in the vote of censure on the Government a week after Bevin spoke at Stoke-on-Trent. In the division on 8th May, more than thirty members of his own party voted against Chamberlain and another sixty abstained. Despite his formal majority, he could not continue in face of such a

1 *Daily Herald*, 2nd May 1940.

vote of no confidence and he sent at once for Attlee and Greenwood to see if the Labour Party would be willing to join a reconstructed Cabinet drawn from members of all parties.

The answer was plainly that Labour would never agree to come into a Government of which Chamberlain was the leading member. Somebody else must take his place as Prime Minister.

Before that question could be answered, on the night of 9th–10th May, the German Army at last struck in the West. Holland, Belgium, France were all invaded with a speed of advance and a concentration of force which swept aside the fixed defences like cardboard. Through the gaps poured the German tanks and dive-bombers. As Chamberlain, Churchill and Halifax met for the fateful meeting from which Churchill emerged as Prime Minister designate, members of the Dutch Cabinet arrived in London to seek aid for a country that was already half-overrun.

At 6 o'clock on the same evening (10th May) Churchill was received by the King and asked to form a new Government. An hour later, he met Attlee and Greenwood and offered the Labour Party a third of the places in a coalition government. The Labour Party was on the eve of its annual conference in Bournemouth and neither Attlee nor Greenwood was in a position to commit their party without consultation. Churchill did not demur, but before Attlee left he mentioned the names of four men "whose services in high office were immediately required".[1] The first name on the list was that of Ernest Bevin.

14

Bevin had taken no part in the events leading up to the fall of the Chamberlain Government or in the preliminary discussions between Attlee and Churchill. It was not until eleven o'clock on the Saturday morning, 11th May, when he came into Transport House to collect his papers before leaving for Bournemouth that the telephone rang and he heard Attlee at the other end of the line.

Attlee's first question was to ask him what he thought of the Labour Party joining a coalition. Bevin's reply was unhesitating:

1 W. S. Churchill: *The Second World War*, Vol. I, p. 526.

"In view of the fact that you helped to bring the other fellow down, if the Party did not take its share of responsibility, they would say we were great citizens but cowards."[1]

Only then did Attlee ask him if he would be willing to join the Government himself.

"I said, 'You have sprung it on me.' He said 'It is sprung on all of us, but we want someone from the industrial movement, from outside Parliament, to come in, not merely to run a department but to help the State in this critical hour.' "

Bevin asked for time to think and then walked over to the House to see Attlee at three o'clock. He was not easy about stepping into a Ministerial position from outside Parliament when there were many on the Labour side of the House who would be hoping for office. Quite apart from the approval of his own Executive, Bevin made it clear that he would only agree to serve if he was sure that his appointment had the support of the General Council and of the Party's National Executive. At this point, Bevin asked Attlee what office he would be expected to take. Minister of Labour, was the reply.

"I thought for a moment and I said to Attlee 'If the Ministry of Labour remains as it is now, purely a glorified conciliation board with the register for national service, unemployment and public assistance, it will be a waste of time.' "

The same point was made forcefully by Arthur Deakin and by the General Council when he consulted them at Bournemouth the following day. Why, he was asked, had he not held out for the Ministry of Supply (which went to Herbert Morrison) or the Ministry of Economic Warfare (which went to Dalton)? Something like Lloyd George's Ministry of Munitions in the first World War, Arthur Deakin argued, was the office which he should ask for. But a night's reflection had convinced Bevin not only that it would be wrong to bargain over office at such a time, but that the Ministry of Labour in his hands could be made into something very different from the minor office which it had hitherto been. His instinct did not mislead him.

1 The account that follows is that which Bevin gave to his own Executive Council two days later, on 13th May 1940.

A Ministry of Munitions would be reduced in stature the moment the fighting ended, but not the Ministry of Labour which, to take one instance alone, would be responsible for demobilisation and re-settlement. It was this more than anything else which influenced his decision, the belief, as he put it to Arthur Deakin that, at the end of the war, the Ministry of Labour would give him "the chance to lay down the conditions on which we shall start again", not only in industry, but in international relations as well. With his mind full of the possibilities opened up by the I.L.O. and his Commonwealth schemes, he told his Executive: "The Ministry of Labour can have the biggest say, next to the Foreign Office, in the Peace Treaties and the new economic arrangements that have got to be made."

That was for the future. For the present there was a job to be done that would tax even his energy and experience to the limit. It never occurred to him to doubt that he could do it: "I believe the men will respond to anything we want them to do if it is put to them in a proper manner." His one regret was the thought of leaving the Union.

"This is the most difficult part of all," he told his Executive, "I may never come back. Well, Brothers, if I do not,—you cannot tell how long the War will last—I really hate leaving the Union, but duty calls and I respond."

The General Council gave its approval on the 12th, the Union's Executive on the 13th, appointing Arthur Deakin as acting General Secretary in his absence.

On the afternoon of the 13th, he wrote to Churchill to accept his offer.

"I want, however, in accepting the Office to emphasise what I said on Saturday that I feel it is imperative that [the Ministry's] position and place should be strengthened in order to deal with the problem of labour organisation and supply, and that the Ministry must be in a position to make its contribution to the actual organisation of production so as to secure the right utilisation of Labour and not merely be regarded as an institution to supply the personnel."[1]

Behind the stiff phrases there was already the promise of Cabinet battles to come, but there was no time to bother about a precise definition of responsibilities in May 1940. On the 14th, as Bevin

1 Ernest Bevin to Winston Churchill, 13th May 1940.

came back to London, the midday papers announced the German thrust through the Ardennes. That afternoon he was already at work in his new office, at last in a position to show what energy and determination could do to mobilise the nation in its own defence.

Fourteen years before, in May 1926, almost to the day, he and the other members of the General Council had walked out of No. 10 Downing Street after calling off the General Strike. Now he was going back as a member of a Cabinet in which he bore, next only to Churchill, the responsibility of persuading the industrial workers of this country to work as they had never worked before, to put aside every regulation and agreement their trade unions had ever made and go on working until they dropped.

Grim but undeterred, he stepped through the door of No. 10 and out of sight. One career had ended; another was about to begin.

A Note on Sources

THE PRESENT VOLUME has been written almost entirely from original sources, although I have of course been much helped by other books dealing with this period and with the development of trade unionism.

I

The original sources fall into four categories:

A. A large mass of letters, memoranda, notes and papers relating to Bevin's career up to May 1940 which have been preserved thanks to the foresight of Miss Forcey and Miss Saunders and which were made available to me by Arthur Deakin. These I have referred to throughout as Bevin's papers.

B. Speeches and articles by Bevin, for which the most important single source is the T.G.W.U.'s journal, *The Record*.

C. The reports, minutes, and papers, both published and unpublished, of the different organisations with which Bevin was connected and the committees on which he sat. A great many of these, e.g. the Executive Council minutes of the Dockers' Union, and the papers relating to the amalgamation negotiations, have been kept with Bevin's papers. For others I am indebted to the kindness of those who allowed me to consult them.

As it would fill several pages to list these in full, I print below simply a list of the organisations and committees whose records I have used:

The Dock, Wharf, Riverside and General Workers' Union.
The Bristol Carters' and Warehousemen's Branch of the Dockers' Union.
The National Transport Workers' Federation.
The Triple Industrial Alliance.
The Transport and General Workers' Union.
The Trades Union Congress.
The T.U.C. General Council and its committees, especially the Economic Committee; the Organisation Committee; the Special Industrial Committee of 1925–1926; the Strike Organisation Committee, 1926; the Industrial Committee (Mond-Turner Talks) 1928–1929.
The International Transport Workers' Federation.

The International Labour Office.
The Labour Party Annual Conference.
The National Council of Labour.
The *Daily Herald*.
The Victoria Printing House Company.
The *New Clarion*.
The Society for Socialist Inquiry and Propaganda.
The N.J.I.C. for the Flour Milling Industry.
The National Joint Council for Dock Labour.
The Standing Advisory Committee for the Port Transport Industry, 1931–1940.
The National Joint Conciliation Committee for the Road Transport Industry.
The Road Haulage Central Wages Board 1939–1940.
The Industrial Health Research Board.

The Bristol 'Right to Work' Committee.
The Bristol Association for Industrial Reconstruction, 1917–1918.
The Port and Transit Executive Committee, 1917–1919.
Ministry of Reconstruction: Committee on Adult Education, 1917–1919.
Ministry of Reconstruction: Committee on Trusts, 1919.
Board of Trade: Central Committee under the Profiteering Acts, 1919–1920: Standing Committee on Trusts and sub-committees.
The Port of London Casual Labour Committee, 1919 (Roche Committee).
The T.U.C. Co-ordination Committee, 1919–1920.
Court of Inquiry into Wages, Rates and Conditions of Men employed in dock and waterside labour, 1920 (Shaw Inquiry).
The Council of Action, 1920.
Ministry of Transport: Committee on Inland Waterways, 1920–1921.
Court of Inquiry into the Tramway Dispute, 1921.
Court of Inquiry into the Stoppage of London Tram and Omnibus Services, 1924.
The Transport Workers (Registration and Guaranteed Week) Committee, 1924–1926 (Maclean Committee).
The Delegation to Study Industrial Conditions in Canada and the U.S.A., 1926.
The Standing Committee on Mineral Transport, 1927–1934.
The Conference on Industrial Reorganisation and Industrial Relations, 1928–1929 (Mond-Turner talks).
The Royal Commission on Transport, 1928–1930.
The Colonial Development Advisory Committee, 1929–1931.
The Committee on Finance and Industry, 1929–1931 (Macmillan Committee).
The Economic Advisory Council and its committees, 1930–1931.
Ministry of Labour: Port Labour Inquiry, 1930–1931.
The Baillie Committee on Road Transport (Goods) Wages, 1936–1937.

Board of Trade: Insurance of Hulls Committee, 1936–1937.
The Amulree Committee on Holidays with Pay, 1937.
Court of Inquiry into the London Bus Dispute, 1937.
Royal Institute of International Affairs: Commonwealth Relations Conference, 1938.

D. The personal recollections of those who knew Ernest Bevin, of whom I have interviewed over one hundred and twenty. They are of particular value for his early days and for impressions of character. I have not, however, relied upon such evidence for questions of fact or dates unless I could discover confirmation from documentary sources.

2

Amongst newspapers and periodicals I have made most use of the files of the following: *Dockers' Record, The Record* (the journal of the T.G.W.U.), *Busmen's Punch, Daily Herald, The Times, Morning Post, The Western Daily Press,* and *The Bristol Observer.*

3

I have read as widely as I could in the history of the period and the literature of trade unionism. The list which follows contains the titles of those books which have proved most valuable. I have excluded pamphlets and reports.

A. HISTORIES

C. L. MOWAT: *Britain between the Wars* (1955).
J. H. (SIR JOHN) CLAPHAM: *An Economic History of Modern Britain,* Vol. III (1938).
The History of the Times, Vol. IV., 2 parts (1952).
W. ARTHUR LEWIS: *Economic Survey 1919–1939* (1949).
G. D. H. COLE: *A Short History of the British Working Class Movement* (new edn. 1948).
G. D. H. COLE: *A History of the Labour Party from 1914* (1948).
G. D. H. COLE and RAYMOND POSTGATE: *The Common People, 1746–1946* (1948).
FRANCIS WILLIAMS: *Fifty Years' March, The Rise of the Labour Party* (1950).
FRANCIS WILLIAMS: *Magnificent Journey, The Rise of the Trade Unions* (1954).
S. and B. WEBB: *History of Trade Unionism* (rev. edn. 1920).
B. C. ROBERTS: *The Trades Union Congress, 1868–1921* (1958).

HENRY PELLING: *The Origins of the Labour Party, 1880–1900* (1954).
E. H. PHELPS BROWN: *The Growth of British Industrial Relations* (1959).
HENRY PELLING: *The British Communist Party* (1958).
A. HUTT: *The Post-War History of the British Working Class* (1937).
G. D. H. COLE: *British Working Class Politics, 1832–1914* (1944).
S. R. GRAUBARD: *British Labour and the Russian Revolution, 1917–1924* (1956).
ELAINE WINDRICH: *British Labour's Foreign Policy* (1952).
A. J. P. TAYLOR: *The Trouble Makers* (1957).
RICHARD A. LYMAN: *The First Labour Government, 1924* (1957).
W. K. HANCOCK and M. M. GOWING: *British War Economy* (2nd impr. 1953).
M. M. POSTAN: *British War Production* (1952).

B. AUTOBIOGRAPHIES

BEN TILLETT: *Memories and Reflections* (1931).
Sir James Sexton, Agitator.
J. R. CLYNES: *Memoirs*, 2 volumes (1937).
M. I. COLE (ed.): *Beatrice Webb's Diaries, 1912–1924* (1952).
M. I. COLE (ed.): *Beatrice Webb's Diaries, 1924–1932* (1956).
HARRY GOSLING: *Up and Down Stream* (1927).
PHILIP SNOWDEN: *An Autobiography*, 2 volumes (1934).
EMANUEL SHINWELL: *Conflict without Malice* (1955).
C. R. (LORD) ATTLEE: *As It Happened* (1954).
HUGH DALTON: *Call Back Yesterday; Memoirs 1887–1931* (1953).
HUGH DALTON: *The Fateful Years; Memoirs 1931–1945* (1957).
W. J. BROWN: *So Far . . .* (1943).
HARRY POLLITT: *Serving my Time* (1940).
THOMAS JONES: *A Diary with Letters, 1931–1950* (1954).
L. S. AMERY: *My Political Life*, Vol. II, *War and Peace* (1953).
(SIR) WINSTON S. CHURCHILL: *The Second World War*, Vol. I. *The Gathering Storm* (1948).
LORD TEMPLEWOOD: *Nine Troubled Years* (1954).
MARGARET COLE: *Growing Up into Revolution* (1949).
LORD SAMUEL: *Memoirs* (1945).

C. BIOGRAPHIES

FRANCIS WILLIAMS: *Ernest Bevin* (1952).
TREVOR EVANS: *Bevin* (1946).
M. A. HAMILTON: *Arthur Henderson* (1938).
G. M. YOUNG: *Stanley Baldwin* (1952).
(SIR) HAROLD NICOLSON: *King George V* (1952).
R. F. (SIR ROY) HARROD: *The Life of John Maynard Keynes* (1951).
SIR HENRY CLAY: *Lord Norman* (1957).
KEITH FEILING: *Life of Neville Chamberlain* (1946).
COLIN COOKE: *The Life of Richard Stafford Cripps* (1957).

658

A Note on Sources

R. J. MINNEY: *Viscount Southwood* (1954).
KINGSLEY MARTIN: *Harold Laski* (1953).
RAYMOND POSTGATE: *Life of George Lansbury* (1951).
G. McALLISTER: *James Maxton, Portrait of a Rebel* (1935).
JACK LAWSON: *The Man in the Cap; Herbert Smith* (1941).
JOHN McNAIR: *James Maxton, The Beloved Rebel* (1955).
VINCENT BROME: *Aneurin Bevan* (1953).

D. POLITICAL AND ECONOMIC STUDIES

R. T. McKENZIE: *British Political Parties* (1958).
R. BASSETT: *Nineteen Thirty One: Political Crisis* (1958).
HENRY PELLING: *America and the British Left: From Bright to Bevan* (1956)
C. F. BRAND: *British Labour's Rise to Power* (1941).
W. P. MADDOX: *Foreign Relations in British Labour Politics* (1934).
W. H. CROOK: *The General Strike* (1931).
JULIAN SYMONS: *The General Strike* (1957).
R. PAGE ARNOT: *The General Strike* (1926).
S. BRYHER (SAMUEL BALE): *An Account of the Labour and Socialist Movement in Bristol* (1929).
A. H. GLEASON: *What the Workers Want: a Study of British Labour* (1920).
W. MELLOR: *Direct Action* (1920).
W. A. ORTON: *Labour in Transition* (1921).
H. MORRISON: *Socialisation and Transport* (1933).
G. D. H. and M. I. COLE: *The Condition of Britain* (1937).
R. C. DAVISON: *British Unemployment Policy since 1930* (1938).
P.E.P.: *British Social Services* (1937).
P.E.P.: *Britain in Depression* (1935).
P.E.P.: *Britain in Recovery* (1938).
P.E.P.: *Men without Work* (1938).

E. INDUSTRIAL RELATIONS AND TRADE UNION STUDIES

LORD ASKWITH: *Industrial Problems and Disputes* (1920).
S. and B. WEBB: *Industrial Democracy* (1897; rev. edn. 1926).
J. B. SEYMOUR: *The Whitley Councils Scheme* (1932).
J. H. RICHARDSON: *Industrial Relations in Great Britain* (1938).
F. E. GANNETT and B. F. CATHERWOOD (ed.): *Industrial Relations in Great Britain* (1939).
A. FLANDERS and H. A. CLEGG (ed.): *The System of Industrial Relations in Great Britain* (1954).
G. D. H. COLE: *The World of Labour* (rev. edn. 1919).
G. D. H. COLE: *Organised Labour* (1924).
G. D. H. COLE: *British Trade Unionism Today* (1939).
G. D. H. COLE: *An Introduction to Trade Unionism* (1953).
N. BAROU: *British Trade Unions* (1949).
A. FLANDERS: *Trade Unions* (1952).
P.E.P.: *British Trade Unionism* (rev. edn. 1955).

B. C. ROBERTS: *Trade Union Government and Administration in Great Britain* (1956).

K. G. J. C. KNOWLES: *Strikes, A Study in Industrial Conflict* (1952).

H. A. CLEGG: *General Union, A study of the National Union of General and Municipal Workers* (1954).

JOSEPH GOLDSTEIN: *The Government of British Trade Unions* (1952).

R. PAGE ARNOT: *The Miners: Years of Struggle* (1953).

SIR A. PUGH: *Men of Steel* (1952).

E. C. P. LASCELLES and S. S. BULLOCK: *Dock Labour and Decasualisation* (1924).

H. A. CLEGG: *Labour Relations in London Transport* (1950).

V. L. ALLEN: *Trade Union Leadership* (1957).

V. L. ALLEN: *Power in Trade Unions* (1954).

W. MILNE-BAILEY: *Trade Union Documents* (1929).

W. MILNE-BAILEY: *Trade Unions and the State* (1934).

JOHN PRICE: *The International Labour Movement* (1950).

H. A. MARQUAND (ed.): *Organised Labour in Four Continents* (1939).

ERIC L. WIGHAM: *Trade Unions* (1956).

ALLEN HUTT: *British Trade Unionism* (rev. edn. 1952).

JOHN HILTON and others (ed.): *Are Trade Unions Obstructive?* (1935).

Index

Index

(character and gifts): 24, 37, 109,
143, 189-90, 196-7, 206, 224-7, 239,
243, 319, 363-71, 375, 388, 406, 409,
422-3, 425, 434, 455, 457, 473-5,
531-3, 534-7, 555-6, 567-71, 585,
588, 589, 590-1, 604, 614-16
Bevin, Dame Florence: 16, 93, 627
Bevin, Diana (Mercy): 2, 3, 4, 6
Billingsgate Market: 554
Birkenhead: 214, 352
Birkenhead, Earl of (F. E. Smith): 308,
310, 312
Birmingham: 187, 454, 540
Birrell, Augustine: 17, 18
Board of Trade: 63, 438, 643
Boer War: 11
Boilermakers, United Society of: 202
Bondfield, Margaret: 261, 283, 461
Boot and Shoe Operatives, National
Union of: 89
Booth, Sir Alfred: 127, 462
Bottomley, Horatio: 457
Bowley, Professor A. L.: 127, 128, 129,
426
'Black Friday': 143, 175, 179, 182, 183,
270, 271, 272, 275, 276, 307, 342,
343, 346
Blackshirts: 280
Blatchford, Robert: 505
Blum, Léon: 587
Bradbury, Lord: 71, 370, 425, 428, 432
Brailsford, H. N.: 258, 350, 505
Bramley, Fred: 283, 287
Brand, R. H. (Lord Brand): 425, 432
Bridgewater: 36, 37
Bristol: 3, 5, 6, 7, 10, 11, 12, 14, 16, 19,
29, 30, 31, 35, 49, 85, 93, 184, 187,
201, 249, 250, 340, 366, 422, 498, 544,
581
Bristol Association for Industrial Re-
construction: 71, 393, 405
Bristol Distress Committee (1908): 17.
Bristol Festival of the T.G.W.U. (1940):
644
Bristol Trades Council: 22
Bristol Labour Party: 57, 649
Bristol "Right to Work" Committee
(1910): 15, 17-19, 21-2, 448, 615
Bristol Rotary Club: 114, 398
Bristol Socialist Society: 14, 15, 30, 57
British Association for the Advance-

ment of Science: 604
British Commonwealth and Empire:
441, 442, 444, 445, 536, 598, 622,
627, 628, 630, 631, 633, 653
British Medical Association: 603
British and North American Luncheon
Club: 604
British Union of Fascists: 547
British Worker: 319, 337, 340
Brockway, Fenner: 389
Bromley, John: 105, 110, 327, 328, 338,
352
Brownlie, J. T.: 284, 401
Bukharin, N.: 231
Burns, Emil: 610
Burns, John: 27
Busman's Punch: 521, 607, 613
Busmen: 81, 143, 460, 606 (London
Busmen): 192-3, 219, 228, 239-42,
246, 377, 519-24, 607-14

CADMAN, SIR JOHN: 397, 436, 437
Canada: 97, 356, 360, 410, 627, 630
Canning Town: 134, 184
Campbell, J. R.: 247, 612, 613
Cardiff: 30, 35, 36, 39, 60, 157, 184,
187, 201, 214, 422, 451
Central Electricity Board: 436
Central Europe: 234, 371, 472, 476,
508, 509, 594
Chamberlain, Neville: 477, 478, 516,
624, 629, 632, 635, 636, 637, 638,
639, 642, 643, 644, 645
Chamberlain Government (1937-40):
209, 641, 642, 643, 644, 645, 650, 651
Chandler, A. J.: 205
Chatham House (Royal Institute of
International Affairs): 617, 627, 630.
631, 632
Chicago: 56, 361
Churchill, Winston (Sir Winston): 133,
149, 209, 265, 266, 267, 323, 499, 581,
585, 644, 646, 647, 653, 654
Churchill Government (1940): 651,
652, 653
Citrine, Sir Walter (Lord Citrine): 149,
283, 287, 288, 290, 294, 300, 306, 308,
309, 310, 311, 314, 327, 330, 347, 348,
385, 386, 395, 398, 399, 401, 421, 436,
438, 484, 485, 488, 489, 490, 491, 493,
494, 496, 506, 527, 528, 541, 550, 562,

662

Irish Transport Workers Union: 40,
556-7

JAPAN: 114, 266, 511, 633, 649
Jarrow: 163
Jewish immigration into Palestine:
456-7
Jockey Club: 621
John Bull: 457
Joint Industrial Councils: 83, 94-5
Joint Stock Banks, Nationalisation of:
513-4, 598
Jolly George: 133
Jones. J. W.: 613-4
Jowitt, Sir William (Lord Jowitt): 421
Joynson-Hicks, Sir Willian (Lord
Brentford): 279

KAY, H. W.: 186, 188, 195
Kean, W.: 288
Kerensky Government: 246
Kershaw, Herbert: 455, 473
Keynes, J. M. (Lord Keynes): 71, 265,
266, 267, 425, 427, 428, 429, 431,
432, 433, 434, 436, 437, 438, 439,
452, 496, 502
King, G. C.: 8, 16

LA PASIONARIA: 587
Labour Government (1924): 210, c. 9,
pp. 257-9, 264, 283, 349, 365
Labour Government (1929-31): 365,
417, 435, cc. 17-18
Labour Government (1945): 413
Labour and the Defence of Peace (1936):
582
Labour and the Nation (1928): 416
Labour and the New Social Order (1918):
77
Labour's Immediate Programme (1937):
598
Labour, Ministry of: 51-2, 120, 209,
239, 249, 251, 270, 314, 325, 351,
369, 405, 501, 545, 603, 605-6, 609,
618, 622, 642-4, 652-3
Labour Party: 42, 45-6, 73, 77-8, 89,
104, 164, 211, 230-1, 234-5, 243-7,
260, 285, 289, 292, 348-50, 378-9,
406, 416-7, 422, 424, 448-51,
468-71, 481, 489, 492-3, 494-500,
503, 511-2, 528-37, 541, 547-51,

553, 560-61, 565-74, 579-88, 595-9,
617, 632-4, 651-3
Labour Party Annual Conferences:
(Bristol 1916): 57 (Manchester 1917):
59, 73 (Nottingham, London, 1918):
77-8 (Southport, 1919): 104-5
(Brighton, 1921): 191 (Liverpool,
1925): 258-60, 285-6 (Blackpool,
1927): 389-91 (Birmingham, 1928):
416 (Brighton, 1929): 418 (Llandudno, 1930): 450-1 (Scarborough,
1931): 495-7 (Leicester, 1932) 512-4
(Hastings, 1933): 528-30, 548 (Southport, 1934): 551, 552-4 (Brighton,
1935): 565-71 (Edinburgh, 1936):
582-8 (Bournemouth, 1937): 594-7,
622 (Southport, 1939): 632-4
(Bournemouth, 1940): 651-2
Labour Party National Executive: 135,
143, 171, 230, 241, 350, 390, 406,
421, 450, 456, 482, 489, 512, 528,
532, 533, 550, 565, 571, 583, 591,
595, 596, 597, 622, 634
Lansbury, George: 15, 20, 36, 73, 92,
112, 149, 257, 271, 281, 286, 406,
419, 424, 449-50, 491, 498, 502, 530,
541, 562, 565-73, 594, 598
Larkin, Jim: 40, 556
Laski, Harold J.: 331, 505, 531, 597.
Law, Andrew Bonar: 103, 109, 123,
134, 136, 234
Leamington, Amalgamation conference
of transport unions at: 155, 188-91
League of Nations: 134, 441, 478-81,
488-9, 492, 510, 548, 550-1, 558,
560-2, 564, 566, 572, 579-80, 582,
584-5, 598, 631-2.
Lee, Kenneth, 398
Leeds Convention (1917): 73-76
Leggett, F. W. (Sir Frederick): 314-5,
360, 618
Lenin: 48, 100, 280
Liberal Party; 17, 244, 247, 259, 262,
377, 416, 492, 573, 592
Liberal Yellow Book (1928): 437
Lindley, Charles: 113, 180
Little, Jack: 626n.
Liverpool: 30, 119, 157, 204, 248, 260,
287, 323, 357, 496
Lloyd George, David (Earl Lloyd
George): 45-6, 48, 51, 62, 72-3, 76-7,